Handbook
of Organizational
Behavior

Handbook of Organizational Behavior

JAY W. LORSCH, editor
Graduate School of Business Administration
Harvard University

Prentice-Hall, Inc., *Englewood Cliffs, NJ 07632*

Library of Congress Cataloging-in-Publication Data
Handbook of organizational behavior.

    Includes bibliographies.
    1. Organizational behavior.   I. Lorsch, Jay William.
HD58.7.H355   1987   302.3′5   86-4866
ISBN 0-13-380650-2

HD
58
.7
H355
1987

Editorial/production supervision and
    interior design: Madelaine Cooke
Cover design: Lundgren Graphics, Ltd.
Manufacturing buyer: Carol Bystrom

Printed in the United States of America

10 9 8 7 6 5 4 3 2 1

ISBN 0-13-380650-2   01

Prentice-Hall International (UK) Limited, *London*
Prentice-Hall of Australia Pty. Limited, *Sydney*
Prentice-Hall Canada Inc., *Toronto*
Prentice-Hall Hispanoamericana, S.A., *Mexico*
Prentice-Hall of India Private Limited, *New Delhi*
Prentice-Hall of Japan, Inc., *Tokyo*
Prentice-Hall of Southeast Asia Pte. Ltd., *Singapore*
Editora Prentice-Hall do Brasil, Ltda., *Rio de Janeiro*

Contents

V   MANAGERIAL ISSUES

VI   ORGANIZATIONAL BEHAVIOR IN NONBUSINESS SETTINGS

Introduction

Whether they know it or not, managers at all levels in all types of organizations are constantly engaged with the issues addressed by the field of organizational behavior. A manufacturing-plant manager who attempts to improve work productivity is concerned with organizational behavior. So is a chief executive officer of a bank, who may be trying to reshape the bank's strategy to compete in a less regulated environment. So is a hospital administrator who is concerned with improving the working relationships and communication between medical and nursing staffs. Organizational behavior will be important to the head coach of a professional football franchise, who is interested in melding the offensive, defensive, and special teams into a cohesive whole, and also to the principal of a large urban high school involved in introducing changes in pedagogy and curriculum.

PURPOSE OF THE HANDBOOK

The purpose of this handbook is to provide a concise set of references about what is known in the field that can be useful to managers, students, and teachers of management. Its focus is on how people actually behave in organizations and why, not on how they "should" act. Managers who understand actual behavior are most likely to find ways of encouraging the behavior they feel is necessary to achieve the purposes of their organizations.

The first three sections of the book (General Overview, Organizational Behavior and the Underlying Disciplines, and Organizational Behavior and Methodologies) provide a perspective on the development of the field and its current state. This background should help managers understand the value and limits of the knowledge described in the following sections, which describe what is known about organizational behavior at different levels of organizations, in relation to specific applied issues, and in nonbusiness settings. For the practicing manager, these latter three sections are the essential core of the handbook, the storehouse of current knowledge that can be applied to specific management problems.

CURRENT STATE OF ORGANIZATIONAL BEHAVIOR

Organizational behavior is a young and dynamic field of inquiry. Although leaders have been grappling with the problems of building and managing organizations since at least the days of Julius Caesar, as Lawrence points out in his historical review (chapter 1), the field of organizational behavior is a twentieth-century phenomenon.

As Lawrence also points out, organizational behavior is an applied field. It has been developed by scholars who have one foot in theory and the other in the practical affairs of organization. Weick (chapter 2) expands on this point as he examines how action links the two worlds of organizational behavior—theory and practice.

The chapters by Levinson (chapter 4), Driver (chapter 5), Hall (chapter 6), and Hardy (chapter 7) demonstrate that the theoretical roots of organizational behavior are multidisciplinary. The contributors to the handbook themselves have backgrounds in a variety of disciplines, including psychology, sociology, social psychology, and political science, as well as multidisciplinary training in organizational behavior per se. Their colleagues in organizational behavior have a similar diversity in education and experience.

Because of this diversity and the youth of the field, no single comprehensive theory of organizational behavior has been developed. At the most general level the contributors to the handbook would probably agree that organizations and their parts can best be understood as complicated systems in which behavior is shaped by complex interacting forces. However, such general agreement would dissolve in any discussion of what forces are the critical ones for understanding specific issues or phenomena. What the field of organizational behavior has to offer practicing managers, then, is not a comprehensive overriding theory but a set of conceptual schemes that can be used for understanding specific issues. These conceptual schemes are like maps that can help the manager understand the complex organizational territory with which he or she must deal. But, the conceptual framework useful for one issue or at one level of organization may not be relevant in other contexts.

The practicing manager seeking to understand the field is confronted with another related problem. The knowledge base of the field has been built through a variety of research methods; zealous advocates of one methodology have often criticized the others. However, as Blanck and Turner (chapter 8), Blackburn (chapter 9), and Seashore (chapter 10) point out, each of the major methodologies—clinical, experimental, and survey—has its place historically and currently in the development of organizational behavior knowledge. These chapters should help managers assess not only the ideas presented in later chapters but also future studies in the field.

The manager who takes the time to explore these early chapters will come away with an understanding of the theoretical and methodological diversity of the field. This diversity, if sometimes confusing, is a reflection of the field's youth and dynamic nature. For the reader-manager who asks the right question— "What concepts can help me deal with a specific issue?" —the latter three sections of the handbook offer ample and rich answers. As Bennis points out in chapter 3, applying the knowledge of the field is neither a simple nor a well-understood matter. The theories are partial and incomplete, and our understanding of how to apply them is imperfect. Nevertheless, improvements in organizations have taken place as a direct result of applying knowledge from the field.

Historically, the field of organizational behavior has focused primarily on business institutions. Most of the pioneering research was done in business firms. Many of the prominent scholars in the field have been associated with schools of business administration. In fact twenty-one of the thirty-three contributors to this handbook have such affiliations currently, and such a proportion is reflective of the field as a whole. The natural consequence of this bias toward business organizations is a concern for issues and problems relevant to these institutions. This orientation is reflected in the chapters in sections IV and V. Managers of nonbusiness organizations will still find the handbook useful but will need to consider how to transfer what has been learned in business institutions to their own settings.

APPLIED ISSUES

The basic proposition underlying section IV is that the phenomena of interest in systems of different sizes can be understood by using concepts relevant to this particular category. Schein (chapter 11) develops concepts useful in understanding individuals and their careers, while Gabarro (chapter 12) describes a conceptual framework for understanding two-person relations. Similarly Alderfer (chapter 13) discusses what is known about the functioning of small groups and intergroup relations. Kimberly (chapter 14) outlines concepts for understanding whole organizations as a total system, while Whetten (chapter 15) outlines the knowledge developed about interorganizational relations.

This way of categorizing organizational phenomena has relevance to both business and nonbusiness managers. The various system levels exist in all types of organizations. The important question for the manager is to determine the system level at which the issues of concern exist.

The chapters in section IV focus on several specific managerial issues. Lawler (chapter 16) provides a framework for understanding reward systems, especially financial remuneration. Sutton and Kahn (chapter 17) explore ways to reduce the stress individuals feel as a result of their involvement in organizational life. Beer (chapter 18) examines the matter of achieving effective performance evaluations for employees. Friedlander (chapter 19) provides concepts for understanding work groups in the context of the larger organization in which they are embedded. Hackman (chapter 20) examines the issues of designing work teams. Galbraith (chapter 21) discusses concepts for understanding issues of organization design. Nadler (chapter 22) focuses his attention on questions related to the effective management of organizational change. Finally Schlesinger and Klein (chapter 23), Stewart (chapter 24), and Conger and Kotter (chapter 25) examine what is known about the issues facing first-level managers, middle managers, and general managers, respectively.

Again the issues addressed and the concepts employed have relevance for business and nonbusiness managers alike. Intelligent use of these chapters requires either kind of reader first to identify which issue or issues most resemble the problems he or she is trying to un-

derstand. Reading the relevant chapters will not provide automatic answers to a problem. Instead it should help the manager understand what concepts and ideas can be useful in diagnosing the forces creating the problem and what actions should be considered.

One final caution to the user of this volume: each chapter naturally reflects to some extent the interests and intellectual predilections of its author(s). In compiling a handbook of this sort, the editor can only assign broad topics to outstanding authorities in particular areas, leaving it to their judgment exactly what to include or omit. Because we have been fortunate in enlisting the help of a particularly outstanding group of contributors, the reader can have confidence that the salient issues in each area have been thoughtfully presented.

Handbook
of Organizational
Behavior

1

Historical development of organizational behavior

PAUL R. LAWRENCE

Organizational behavior is a young and rapidly growing area of systematic inquiry. It is therefore not surprising that professionals in the field are often preoccupied with its present and future, and seldom reflect on its past. Yet an understanding of that past and an awareness of how knowledge and expertise have gradually accumulated can enrich the field's identity and add meaning to current efforts.

Because work on organizational behavior has begun so recently, it is difficult to achieve an objective perspective on its history. As an involved participant over the past thirty-five years, I recognize that I bring a set of biases, unconscious as well as conscious, to the role of historian. Readers should be aware of this, even though my goal is to provide a detached overview of the field's development. To do this I will consider, in turn, the origins of the field, key events in its development, methodological issues, persistent theoretical disputes, and some general characteristics of the field.

Organizational behavior is a field of both research and practice. In terms of research, to paraphrase Pfeffer's definition, it encompasses the study of all aspects of behavior in and by formal organizations. As such it makes use of concepts from sociology, psychology, economics, political science, and anthropology. It treats as units of analysis everything from individuals acting, feeling, and thinking in an organizational context to groups, larger subunits such as departments or divisions, the organization as a whole, and even populations of organizations and the relationship of organizations to larger social structures such as the state and society.[1] As regards practice, organizational behavior is concerned with improving the performance of organizations in terms of the various criteria of different stakeholders. As a result, the practice of the field tends to focus on understanding the action alternatives available to decision makers inside organizations and predicting the consequences of their choices, on resolving conflicts about performance criteria and the distribution of outputs, and on the process of organizational change.

ORIGIN OF ORGANIZATIONAL BEHAVIOR AS A FIELD

Opinions differ as to when and how the field originated. Quite understandably, those who came from psychology into OB (as the field is often called) tend to trace the discipline back to the earliest contributions of trained

---

1. Jeffrey Pfeffer, "Organizations and Organization Theory," in *Handbook of Social Psychology*, 3d ed., ed. Garner Lindzey and Eliot Aronson (Westminster, Md.: Random House, 1985).

psychologists, usually anchored in the work on leadership and group behavior by Kurt Lewin and his colleagues in the mid-1940s. Those who entered the field from sociology tend to date the origins of OB around 1950, with the contributions of the "bureaucratic sociologists" such as Robert Merton, Philip Selznick, Alvin Gouldner, and Peter Blau. I argue that the field as we know it today was launched somewhat earlier with the closely related publication of Elton Mayo's *Human Problems of an Industrial Civilization* (1933), Chester Barnard's *Functions of the Executive* (1938), and Fritz Roethlisberger and William Dickson's *Management and the Worker* (1939). These three books created the most persistent paradigm of the field—the view of organizations as natural social systems—and established the multiple levels of analysis, the multidisciplinary approach, and the topical agenda that still characterize OB today.

These books drew upon various relevant kinds of knowledge without allowing any single discipline to dominate their argument. The sociology of Durkheim and Pareto, the psychology of Freud and Janet, and the anthropology of Malinowski were of primary importance. Under the influence of Lawrence Henderson, the noted blood researcher turned organization analyst, they all drew their model of science from the traditions of biology rather than physics. As a result, their models of organization reflected an awareness of the multiple causation, interdependencies, and feedback that also characterize biological systems. They followed biology in their emphasis on evolving a set of related concepts (not laws) that were useful in the context of action. Biology also led them to stress the methods of comparative observation and natural field experimentation without neglecting laboratory experimentation. The range of issues, both theoretical and applied, raised by these writers was amazingly wide. They touched on virtually all the topics explored in the current literature of organizational behavior.

Several other related events argue for dating the field's origin to the late 1930s or early 1940s. To the best of my knowledge, the first doctoral degree in organizational behavior was granted in 1941;[2] the first required M.B.A.-level course in the field was launched in 1942;[3] and the first textbook was published in 1945.[4]

Earlier works laid the foundation for OB. Henri Fayol and Frederick Taylor contributed greatly by addressing organizations as a technical problem, but their limited model of man prevented them from establishing the field. Max Weber might have launched the field had there been any direct follow-up to his writings before the 1947 English translation of his work.[5] Mary Parker Follet's writings anticipated the best of the applied tradition of the field. Elmer Southard and May Jarret's early work in "industrial mental hygiene" brought the psychiatric perspective to bear on problems of organization.[6] Other names could readily be added to this list of OB's ancestors.

KEY CONTRIBUTIONS IN OB'S DEVELOPMENT

A chronological review of key contributions to the field since its founding provides a useful perspective on the course of its development. My chief criterion in drawing up the following list was impact on the field. Arbitrarily limited to thirty contributions, the list will inevitably offend by omitting some favorites of every reader, but this price must be paid. Moreover, I have not included work published since 1978, finding it too difficult to judge the impact of more recent additions to the literature. The list is catholic, including works of considerable variety, the popular as well as the more scientifically rigorous. As indicated by the asterisks, some of the publications were selected as examples of institutional contributions. For brevity I comment here on only the most salient aspect of each work's impact on the field.

1. *1943**—Lewin's "group climate" experiments (with Lippit and White): distinguished autocratic, democratic, and laissez-faire leadership styles and contributed to the establishment of the Center for Group Dynamics. Related work by Lewin established the concepts of social force fields, life space, and stages of change.

2. *1947**—English translation of Weber's *The Theory of Social and Economic Organization*: defined the bureaucratic ideal type, sparked the study of the manifest and latent function of organizational practices, and contributed to the forming of the "bureaucratic sociologists" school.

3. *1947**—Bradford organized the first Bethel conference where T-groups were first started as a method

2. Awarded to George Lombard at the Harvard Business School.

3. "Management Controls," offered at the Harvard Business School.

4. Burleigh Gardner and David Moore, *Human Relations in Industry* (Homewood, Ill.: Irwin, 1945).

5. Max Weber, *The Theory of Social and Economic Organization* (New York: Free Press, 1947).

6. Charles D. Wrege, "Antecedents of Organizational Behavior—Dr. E. E. Southard and Mary C. Jarret, 'The Mental Hygiene of Industry': 1913–1920." Mimeo.

of learning about self and group process and the National Training Laboratory was launched.

4. *1950*—Bavelas's *Communication Patterns in Task-Oriented Groups:* described his and Leavitt's experiments on the impact of organization network designs on outcomes for high and low task complexity.

5. *1950*—Homans's *The Human Group:* established the prevailing paradigm for analyzing group behavior in organizations.

6. *1951*—The Ohio Leadership Studies associated with Shartle, Hemphill, Fleishman, and Stodgill: distinguished consideration and initiated structure dimensions of leadership.

7. *1958*—March and Simon's *Organizations:* established organization as a decision-making system satisficing with bounded rationality.

8. *1958*—Woodward's *Management and Technology:* established the contingent relationship between organization and technology.

9. *1958*—Fiedler's *Leadership Attitudes and Group Effectiveness:* established the contingent relationship between contextual factors and effective leadership styles.

10. *1959*—The Ford and Carnegie Foundation reports on business schools: persuaded deans to recruit considerable numbers of behavioral scientists to business-school faculties.

11. *1959*—Hertzberg, Mausner, and Snyderman's *The Motivation to Work:* distinguished between intrinsic motivators of work and extrinsic demotivators.

12. *1960*—MacGregor's *Human Side of Enterprise:* established Theory X and Y concepts by popularizing Maslow's theory of need hierarchy.

13. *1961**—Likkert's *New Patterns of Management:* consolidated the contributions of the University of Michigan Institute of Social Research in the "System IV" framework.

14. *1961*—Burns and Stalker's *Organization for Innovation:* distinguished organic and mechanistic organization forms.

15. *1962*—Chandler's *Strategy and Structure:* established the connection between organization form and business strategy.

16. *1963**—Trist, Higgin, Murray, and Pollock's *Organizational Choice:* consolidated Tavistock's contribution of the sociotechnical approach to organization design.

17. *1964*—Crozier's *Bureaucratic Phenomenon:* clarified the contingent relationship between organization form and culture.

18. *1964*—Blake and Mouton's *The Managerial Grid:* established grid theory of leadership and organization climate and gave impetus to the organization-development movement.

19. *1964*—Vroom's *Work and Motivation:* contributed significantly to the development of expectancy theory.

20. *1964*—Argyris's *Integrating the Individual and the Organization:* developed the possibility of achieving congruence between individual and organizational needs.

21. *1966*—Katz and Kahn's *The Social Psychology of Organizations:* consolidated systems thinking and the use of role theory.

22. *1967*—Thompson's *Organizations in Action:* accounted for organizational variations under the "norm of rationality."

23. *1967*—Lawrence and Lorsch's *Organization and Environment:* consolidated contingency theory and distinguished the differentiation and integration states and processes in organizations.

24. *1969*—Bennis, Benne, and Chin's *The Planning of Change:* provided a framework for understanding organizational change.

25. *1969*—Weick's *The Social Psychology of Organizing:* established the organizational enactment process and the loose coupling of organizations.

26. *1969*—Schein, Bennis, and Beckhard initiated the Addison-Wesley series on organization development.

27. *1972*—Walton's *How to Counter Alienation in the Plant:* described General Food's pet-food factory and established the potential of "high commitment" organizations.

28. *1973*—Mintzberg's *The Nature of Managerial Work:* focused attention on understanding what managers actually do.

29. *1978*—Miles and Snow's *Organizational Strategy, Structure, and Process:* consolidated the link between organization form and strategy.

30. *1978*—Pfeffer and Salancik's *The External Control of Organizations:* established the resource-dependency perspective.

This chronology reveals some rather conspicuous patterns. The 1950s and early 1960s were dominated by the contributions of psychologists primarily concerned with leadership and motivation, often from a normative perspective. For many organizational behavior professionals at the time, these two topics constituted the entire field. In the 1960s, more sociologically oriented contributions (starting in Europe) developed the "macro" topics of structure, technology, and task; and contingency theory became established as the dominant paradigm. The list also shows that the decade starting in 1958 was an unusually productive period. The 1970s, while less fruitful, gave evidence that OB was becoming a consistently multidisciplinary, multilevel field of research and practice. During these years we were discovering that organizational life is immensely diverse, that universal laws of organization will probably not be discovered, and that the field advances primarily by evolving more adequate concepts to order and account for organizational diversity.

METHODOLOGICAL ISSUES

Certain methodological issues have been perennial sources of discussion and controversy throughout the life of the field. I will comment briefly on six of the more salient issues. To give perspective, I have found it helpful to compare OB's methodological experience with that of the much older science of biology; Ernst Mayr's recent definitive history of biological thought proves useful.[7]

One of the first methodological issues that arises for any researcher is whether his or her work ought to be based on a formal hypothesis or on an open-ended exploratory question. Many OB professionals believe that new knowledge can be developed only by rigorously testing a hypothesis, but others have taken a less structured approach. The chronological review offers numerous examples of the fact that either starting point can be fruitful, but exploratory research has probably been the more productive. In biology a similar controversy has been waged. Mayr's comments from the perspective of a more mature science are instructive.

> The belief that a scientist had to supply absolute proof for all of his findings and theories prevailed until modern times. . . . In the majority of the conclusions of the biologists, it is impossible to supply proof of such certainty. . . . The new theory of science, based on a probabilistic interpretation of scientific conclusions, makes it inappropriate to speak of truth or proof as something absolute. . . . Scientists in their actual research often go back and forth between a phase in which they collect material or conduct purely descriptive or classificatory research and another phase of concept formation or testing of theories.[8]

A second methodological issue concerns the proper locus of research: should laboratories be favored over field sites or vice versa? Probably only a few purists in organizational behavior still argue that research that uses the controls a laboratory can offer is the only way to advance knowledge. Earlier this was a more widely held view borrowed from psychology. Of the contributors cited in the chronology, only Lewin, Bavelas, Fiedler, and Vroom drew their findings heavily from laboratory experiments. While laboratory work has clearly made important contributions, field-based studies tend to dominate the list.

The third issue involves the unit of analysis. Early disputes about the "proper" level of analysis—individual, organization, or some intermediate unit—have gradually given way to a recognition that work at several levels of analysis is not only appropriate but necessary. The organization as a whole cannot be understood simply by reducing it into component parts and studying only groups and individuals. Still, we cannot understand organizations without also developing useful concepts about individual and group behavior in organizations. Among the books listed as key contributions, most of those published after 1960 were multilevel studies. It is heartening to realize that, for the most part, OB now recognizes the value of the contributions from different levels of analysis—a perspective it took biology a longer time to achieve.

Organizational behavior shares with many other fields of study the controversy over the relative merits of quantitative and qualitative data. In general, this argument has been resolved in favor of the use of both kinds of evidence, but a lingering suspicion of "soft" data can be detected in some quarters. It is still possible to name schools that will not accept a nonquantitative doctoral dissertation. Here again, the lessons from biology are pertinent.

> The physical world is a world of quantification (Newton's movements and forces) and of mass actions. By contrast, the world of life can be designated as a world of qualities. Individual differences, communication systems, stored information, properties of the macromolecules, interactions in ecosystems, and many other aspects of living organisms are prevailingly qualitative in nature. One can translate these qualitative aspects into quantitative ones, but one loses thereby the real significance of the respective biological phenomena. . . . The qualitative aspects . . . are particularly important in relational phenomena, which are precisely the phenomena that dominate living nature.[9]

Similarly, qualitative observations are especially relevant to OB, which studies relations at multiple levels: interpersonal, group, intergroup, interdepartmental and -divisional, and interorganizational.

---

7. Ernst Mayr, *The Growth of Biological Thought* (Cambridge, Mass.: Harvard University Press, 1982), 23.

8. Mayr, *Biological Thought*, 25–28.

---

9. Mayr, *Biological Thought*, 54, 55.

A fifth methodological issue involves the choice between recording perceptions and attitudes and recording overt behavior. Should the researcher employ a questionnaire (or structured interview), or should a trained observer of behavior (or an audio- or videotape recorder) be used? To date, OB research has focused predominantly on perceptions rather than recording behavior directly or via archival records. Perhaps as recording instruments become more economical and unobtrusive this balance will shift. I find it hard to argue on any grounds other than practicality and economy against collecting both kinds of data in most studies of phenomena as complex as organizational behavior. Researchers in OB too often seem to use only the method with which they are most familiar and then seek grounds to justify its use. The use of the respondent's judgment in helping the researcher interpret behavioral data seems a step in the right direction.

The sixth and final methodological issue concerns the relative merits of cross-sectional and longitudinal research. This is one aspect of the larger debate between the advocates of action research, who believe that truth can be discovered only when the researcher becomes involved in an ongoing change process in the organization, and logical positivists, who favor the cross-sectional and arm's-length approach to objective knowledge. Once again, OB resembles biology rather than physics. As Max Delbruck put it,

> A mature physicist, acquainting himself for the first time with the problems of biology, is puzzled by the circumstance that there are no 'absolute phenomena' in biology. Everything is time-bound and space-bound. The animal or plant or micro-organism . . . is but a link in an evolutionary chain of changing forms, none of which has any permanent validity.[10]

Certainly the phenomena of organizational behavior are much more rapidly in flux. For this reason, dynamic, longitudinal research can be particularly valuable. At the same time, cross-sectional studies have contributed much to our understanding of organizational behavior. It seems important not to limit our methodological options unnecessarily, but to choose whatever approach seems most appropriate to the particular research circumstances. Perhaps this flexible approach is too much to expect; even in biology Mayr reports that "Even today some authors consider the experiment the exclusive method of science. Quite recently one of them remarked that 'an experimental approach to the origin of species is curiously absent from the works of Darwin.'"[11] The chronology, however,

provides some encouraging signs that the field of organizational behavior is returning, albeit in a more refined and sophisticated manner, to the eclectic, biology-oriented methodology practiced by its founders.[12]

THEORETICAL ISSUES

Eight theoretical issues seem to me to have been critical to the development of the field of organizational behavior. All have generated controversy; for some the controversy persists.

The first issue concerns values and is methodological as well as theoretical. It involves three dichotomies, all too intertwined to be treated separately: descriptive versus predictive research, basic versus applied research, detached versus normative research. Because the field is young and sensitive about its scientific respectability, OB professionals have been concerned particularly about this threefold issue concerning the proper role of scientific inquiry and its relation to practical affairs. Furthermore, OB's academic base has been primarily in business schools, which discipline-based departments have been inclined to stereotype and even denigrate. Their criticisms often pressured earlier workers in the field to undertake research that was detached, not normative; basic, not applied; and predictive, not "just a descriptive case study." This kind of research seemed the road to respectability, but there was a catch. If one actually did high-powered predictive research and produced strong causal statements, these statements inevitably carried normative implications whether they were made explicit or not. These normative implications, in turn, drew the field into the applied world, since knowledge about organizational behavior is relevant to practical affairs. The final irony was that the more basic and fundamental the new insights were, the more certain it was that they would have normative implications. So the drive to be predictive has forced the field to be normative and applied, with all the attendant discomforts.

Perhaps today we need to be reminded just how harshly OB professionals were criticized. They were accused of being merely servants of power and manipulators of the defenseless worker.[13] Today the field has, by and large, answered these charges. It now seems clear

---

10. Quoted in Mayr, *Biological Thought*, 69.

11. Mayr, *Biological Thought*, 855.

12. See especially Thomas and Tymon's recent paper, "Necessary Properties of Relevant Research: Lessons from Recent Criticisms of the Organizational Sciences," *Academy of Management Review* 7, no. 3 (July 1982): 345.

13. Such charges were especially directed toward the Western Electric studies. See A. Carey, "The Hawthorne Studies: A Radical Criticism," *American Sociological Review* 32 (1967): 403–16.

that good descriptive work and good predictive work go hand in hand in building knowledge. Solid predictions can, in fact, only be built upon careful observations and accurate description. To ask which contributes the most to science simply makes no sense. As a field we can also now unambivalently acknowledge the value of opportunities for normative and applied research. We are not ashamed to say that the generation of wealth through economic activity is generally useful; that enterprise has multiple outputs, intended and unintended; that people judge these outputs by multiple criteria; that the distribution of wealth among stakeholders inevitably generates some conflict; that many mechanisms exist to resolve these conflicts; and that all of the above can usefully be studied as part of the domain of OB. So this compound theoretical-methodological-value issue has largely been resolved as the field has matured. Reminding ourselves of this history may help to keep us from backsliding.

A second, more theoretical, issue that has attracted students over the years is the relation between productivity and worker satisfaction. Having moved through three stages, this issue too now seems largely resolved. The initial assumption was that high employee satisfaction increased productivity. This largely implicit assumption was based primarily on a simplistic interpretation of the relay-assembly-room experiments at the Hawthorne works.[14] Many subsequent studies found that this straightforward relationship did not always hold.[15] Either high or low satisfaction might be associated with either high or low productivity. So the second-stage conclusion was that productivity and satisfaction were not directly linked, since the relation seemed to depend upon other, largely unspecified, variables, such as worker predispositions, alternative jobs, contingent rewards, task characteristics, the parties' relative bargaining power, and styles of leadership.[16]

Finally, in the third stage, the concepts of both productivity and satisfaction were properly sorted out. It became clear that people seek satisfaction of many needs, some of which are not necessarily related to work and effort. At the same time, the kind of productivity required varies from job to job, ranging from simple repetitive work to highly challenging, changing work. With these distinctions has come the realization that a positive, mutually reinforcing association exists between challenging jobs and the satisfaction of a particular need for a sense of competence—an active need for many people. Other contextual variables, such as appropriate supervisory style, group relations, and rewards, are now seen as necessary supports for this primary association.[17] With these limited and contingent conclusions, the puzzling relation between satisfaction and productivity is gradually being sorted out.

Conflict versus collaboration is a third persistent theoretical issue. Again there has been a three-stage movement toward resolution. The initial, commonsense assumption was that collaboration reflected a state of health in an organization and that conflict indicated a waste of resources. This assumption was largely implicit in Mayo's work, but his emphasis on the importance of collaboration may have reinforced it. Gradually, this view was challenged. Conflict was obviously a widespread fact of organizational life and was sometimes associated with constructive change as well as with waste. A second-stage theoretical position was eventually established recognizing that if employees brought different skills and orientations to their work, there would inevitably be some conflict over the choice of appropriate ways to achieve organizational results.[18] Conflict of this sort was recognized as promoting innovation in an organization as long as each issue was resolved without great delay and cost. The third stage of theory development has addressed conflicts of interest or ends among the various stakeholders in organizational affairs. As mentioned above, we can now recognize the multiple outputs of organizations, the multiple preferences regarding outcomes, the inevitability of periodic conflict over the distribution of outputs, and the need for cost-effective conflict-resolution mechanisms. Even though a reasonable degree of collaboration among all contributors to an enterprise is a fundamental necessity, episodes of conflict are also essential for adaptation. But unless organizations develop effective conflict-resolution processes, one conflict can trigger another, leading to a continuing drain on resources.

A fourth theoretical issue that has concerned the field for many years is whether research should attempt to frame postulates describing universal organizational uniformities or contingent uniformities. Although progress has been made, this issue is still partly unresolved. Initially it was assumed that with careful sys-

14. F. J. Roethlisberger and W. J. Dickson, *Management and the Worker* (Cambridge, Mass.: Harvard University Press, 1939).

15. See, for example, W. F. Goode and Irwin Fowler, "Incentive Factors in a Low Morale Plant," *American Sociological Review* 14, no. 5 (1949).

16. For a review and synthesis of this literature see James V. Clark, "Motivation in Work Groups, A Tentative View," *Human Organization* 19, no. 4 (Winter 1960–61): 199–208.

17. See especially the treatment of this issue in Jay Lorsch and John Morse, *Organizations and Their Members* (New York: Harper & Row, 1974).

18. See Paul Lawrence and Jay Lorsch, *Organization and Environment* (Cambridge, Mass.: Harvard Business School, 1967).

tematic inquiry, general propositions would be found to describe all formal organizations; these propositions could in turn be used to guide practice in any organization.[19] As the great diversity of organizational life became apparent, the suggested universal propositions were found to have too many exceptions to be useful. It rather suddenly became apparent that organizations were pressed to come to terms with different environmental elements: different technologies, markets, governmental regulations, competitive innovations, cultural settings, and predispositions of available employees. That organizations evolved different internal arrangements to deal with these varying circumstances is not really surprising, but stating the problem in this form triggered a burst of research to discover these environmentally contingent uniformities.[20]

The enthusiasm sparked by the contingency approach has inevitably waned. Perhaps it will now be possible to develop a more balanced position on the issue. We are gradually learning that there can be great variability in the power and utility of contingent propositions; some are simply trivial. Trying to specify every possible contingency may distract us from the effort to find more powerful concepts that can guide practice. Each organization is unique, as is every biological specimen, but that fact should strengthen our search for patterns, not stop it. Perhaps we need to recognize that there is nothing intrinsically wrong with searching for universal properties of organizations. The diversity among organizations makes it unlikely that we shall find many such general truths, but slightly less universal propositions that cover broad classes of organizations and corresponding environments can be very useful. To let the idea of contingency slide into the exploration of an endless variety of minor, limited qualifications and thereby abandon the search for broadly powerful uniformities would be a great misfortune for practical managers as well as academics.

Another theoretical question has come into focus only in the past decade: is organizational behavior to be explored in terms of environmental determinism or organizational choice? The latent assumption for many years was that organizations largely control their own destinies—that is what management is all about. The study of organizational behavior was intended to help managers make fewer mistakes along the way. However, as attention turned to the environmental factors that condition and constrain organizational behavior, the door was opened for the students of organization populations to assert the more radical argument of environmental determinism.[21] Meanwhile we have also witnessed a more radical assertion of the theory of organizational choice.[22]

So far no synthesis has emerged, but possibilities can be anticipated. The world does not enforce an instant survival test of the fit between organization and environment, rather the two are "loosely coupled."[23] We might return to the analogy from biology: the fact that nature's coupling is so loose that it may take hundreds of thousands of years for a "misfit" species to die out does not falsify Darwin's theory of natural selection. It has also been argued persuasively that there is usually more than one way by which organizations can adapt successfully to a given environmental niche. Furthermore, even if the environment presses hard on an organization, choice is still relevant for organizational leaders facing alternatives that only hindsight can identify clearly as adaptive or maladaptive. In the last analysis, organizations are guided by human beings who potentially can move beyond trial-and-error procedures to learn from both experience and systematic research; such knowledge opens up additional areas of choice even as it illumines the nature of the constraints.

Closely related to the question of choice versus determinism is the still-unresolved conflict between the perspectives of information processing and resource dependency. The roots of the question go back to the early work at Hawthorne, when the implicit assumption was made that organizations are essentially production systems populated by individuals who form groups that need to be studied as social systems. This view was subtly shifted when the work at the Tavistock Institute gave equal treatment to the social and technical aspects of organizations.[24] Later March and Simon introduced the idea of viewing organizations as decision-making systems that process information. This approach has appealed particularly to those with an orientation toward cognitive psychology. The organization is seen as a decision-making system capable of reading its environment, en-

19. See, for example, the propositions developed by George Homans in *The Human Group* (New York: Harcourt Brace, 1950).

20. For examples see Robert B. Duncan, "Characteristics of Organizational Environments and Perceived Environmental Uncertainty," *Administrative Science Quarterly* 12 (June 1967): 1–47; P. N. Khandwalla, *The Design of Organizations* (New York: Harcourt Brace Jovanovich, 1976); and Jay Galbraith, *Designing Complex Organizations* (Reading, Mass.: Addison-Wesley, 1973).

21. See especially M. T. Hannan and J. H. Freeman "The Population Ecology of Organization," *American Journal of Sociology* 82 (1977): 929–64.

22. See John Child, "Organizational Structure, Environment and Performance: The Role of Strategic Choice," *Sociology*, no. 1 (1972): 1–22.

23. See Karl Weick, *The Social Psychology of Organizing*, 2d ed. (Reading, Mass.: Addison-Wesley, 1980).

24. See E. L. Trist, G. W. Higgin, H. Murray, and A. B. Pollock, *Organizational Choice* (London: Tavistock, 1963).

coding and evaluating the information, searching for relevant response programs, and finally basing action on a choice from a limited set of options.[25]

This emphasis has, in turn, been counteracted by a revival of the production model of organizations in the much more sophisticated form of resource-dependency theory.[26] The advocates of this theory see organizations as dependent upon the outside world for essential tangible resources and focus on the balance of resource control that is reflected in the relative power of organizational and environmental elements. How this polarity between the information and resource approaches can be resolved is not clear. One attempt at synthesis has been my own current work on the organizational implications of various combinations of resource scarcity and information complexity.[27]

A further unresolved theoretical problem is the tension between functional and historical analysis. The introduction of functional analysis to organizational study closely followed its widespread use in sociology and anthropology, with all the same strengths and weaknesses.[28] Functionalism has been attacked as tending to justify every current form of behavior without being able to explain change, especially radical change. The principal alternative approach is historical analysis.[29] A similar debate has been carried on in biology for many years, with physiologists, who study the functions of organs, cells, and so forth, in conflict with evolutionary biologists. Mayr reports that each camp now recognizes the essential contributions of the other to any complete explanation of biological phenomena: the functionalists continue to search for "proximate" causes, while the evolutionary people search for "ultimate" causes. Within the field of organizational behavior, there is now considerable interest in historical studies of developmental stages, which I hope will move the field in a similar direction and secure for OB the value of both approaches.[30]

25. See, for example, Walter Buckley, *Sociology and Modern Systems Theory*, (Englewood Cliffs, N.J.: Prentice-Hall, 1967).

26. See Jeffrey Pfeffer and Gerald Salancik, *The External Control of Organizations* (New York: Harper & Row, 1978).

27. Paul Lawrence, "Organization and Environment Perspective." In *Perspectives on Organization Design and Behavior*, ed. Andrew Van de Ven and William F. Joyce (New York: Wiley, 1981), 311–37; and Paul Lawrence and Davis Dy, *Renewing American Industry* (New York: Free Press, 1983).

28. Functionalism is associated in sociology with the work of Talcott Parsons and Robert Merton, and in anthropology with Bronislaw Malinowski.

29. See Alvin Gouldner, *The Coming Crisis of Western Sociology* (New York: Basic Books, 1970).

30. For examples of such current work, see Robert H. Miles, *Coffin Nails and Corporate Strategies* (Englewood Cliffs, N.J.: Prentice-Hall, 1982).

In commenting on this limited list of theoretical issues, I have clearly neglected the step-by-step development of theories explaining such phenomena as motivation, power, leadership, and group and intergroup processes. These developments will be carefully covered in other chapters of this volume. Knowledge is building in these basic areas of inquiry, though it often comes in waves, with periods of intense interest followed by times when the topic seems dry and worked out. After an arid period, the field swings back to these themes with fresh questions that can lead to new insights and better concepts. For example, recent renewed interest in leadership may be moving us out of such an extended dry spell.

GENERAL CHARACTERISTICS OF THE FIELD

Throughout its history, organizational behavior has displayed four characteristics worthy of some closing comments. First, I would note the field's rapid growth. It is difficult to document this growth in terms of numbers of professionals, because there is no single OB professional organization. Perhaps the best indicator is that enrollment in the OB division of the Academy of Management has now passed eighteen hundred. Since the field originated only some forty years ago, this represents rapid growth indeed.

A second characteristic of organizational behavior is its sustained capacity to bridge allied areas of study. Immediately after World War II, the field was dominated by psychologists interested primarily in motivation and leadership. In the years that followed, the field reached out to add the "macro" issues of the organization's linkage with its environment. In doing this, it drew extensively on the work of sociologists and built intellectual bridges to the work of business policy specialists and more recently to the economics of industrial organization. The field also extended its early interest in worker behavior and first-line supervision to undertake extensive studies of managerial behavior that drew upon the insights of students of psychodynamics and adult development. In the 1960s, some OB professionals began fresh work on goal setting and rewards, forming links to control specialists and behavioral psychologists. More recently, OB groups have joined forces with specialists in labor relations, labor economics, and personnel administration to develop more comprehensive perspectives on human resource management. Inevitably, as the field became increasingly involved in studying power dynamics, the work of political scientists has become relevant. Developing interest in organization culture has renewed the ties to anthropology. This long record of enrichment through working ties to other disciplines is probably unique in the development of an academic field. Later chapters will deal in detail with these disciplinary linkages. By drawing in ideas and methods from so many diverse allied areas, OB has kept alive the multidisciplinary tradition of its founders.

A third salient characteristic of the field is its tendency to recruit faculty from these related disciplines to work in organizational behavior in professional schools, usually business schools. There have been several waves of such recruitment, each followed by the gradual assimilation of these scholars into the field. The early wave of psychologists was followed by a wave of sociologists along with a healthy scattering of social psychologists, anthropologists, political scientists, historians, and economists. These recruits naturally brought the orientation of their particular discipline with them, as evidenced by texts with titles including phrases such as "organizational psychology" or "organizational sociology." When the recommendations of the Ford and Carnegie Foundation reports on American business schools stimulated especially heavy recruitment, the immigrants threatened to overwhelm the natives. The tension at times has been severe, but by and large, the accommodation process has been successful, and the field is stronger and richer for it. Also, this aspect of OB history may be unique in academic annals.

A final characteristic of the field has been its responsiveness to the important issues of the day. Organizational behavior has been accused of faddism. This charge, in my judgment, is half true, especially in the practice aspect of the field. The organization development (OD) movement has been dominated by a succession of techniques that provoke first enthusiasm and then disillusionment, driven by managers' desire for a quick fix for their people problems. On the positive side, however, OD provides the rough-and-ready testing ground for ideas; the willingness to risk trying an un-proven concept to improve the performance of organizations is not all bad. More importantly, however, the field has shown a marked capacity to respond to the broader issues of the times. It is not faddishness to focus on salient social issues: it is a highly appropriate goal. In the 1960s, when a general concern for social justice predominated, the response from our field was to study inner-city organizations, minority issues in traditional organizations, and human service organizations. More recently, public attention has turned to the broad issues of productivity and international competition, and the field is responding in its emphasis. Although some deplore this intimate involvement with contemporary value issues, I applaud it: OB is, after all, an applied field.

In fact, the strong bond between theory and practice is a crucial feature of organizational behavior. Theory has guided practice, and practice has provided crucial insights to research. Progress has been greatest when the two sides of the field move together. It is this hand-in-hand development of theory and practice that has made possible the ever-increasing application of OB to everyday organizational affairs. Today most large firms employ full-time specialists in organizational development and, even more importantly, judge their general managers to a considerable extent by their skill and competence in addressing the human side of the enterprise. Instead of diminishing these interests, the adverse economic conditions of the early 1980s seem to be intensifying them. Competence in the human aspects of management is no longer seen as a luxury but as an essential ingredient of business success. The theory and practice of organizational behavior have come a long way since its inception nearly fifty years ago, but there would probably be little argument that its work is barely started. Our theory ignorance and our practice mistakes are still great even as our phenomenon of study is rapidly changing. Examining our history can help to stimulate and focus our future efforts.

2

Perspectives on action in organizations

KARL E. WEICK

This chapter describes how action provides a link between the worlds of theory and practice. Four properties of action are salient in organized settings and determine much of what happens there.

1. Actions evoke justifications.
2. Actions displace thinking.
3. Actions create environments.
4. Actions require interaction.

When people act in organized settings they search for reasons that transform their actions into responses to some stimulus yet to be identified; they guide their actions by routines, direct perception, and situational demands rather than by prospective thought; they respond to environments of their own construction; and they act interdependently with others.

THE SETTING FOR ACTION

To ground organizational theory in the particulars of managerial action is also to say more about the settings within which those actions take place. Organizational settings only intermittently and locally cohere as if they were systems (Simon 1962; Katz 1974; Weick 1976). These settings are often tied together hypocritically by the rhetoric of rationality and goal attainment, a rhetoric that is usually mocked by the practices that actually work. Stated more compactly, organizations are mis-

named. To understand this inaccuracy is to understand the essence of managerial action and how managers might cope better.

The term *organization* implies more orderliness, coordination, and systematization than is commonly discovered when people look closely at joint action (Morgan 1981). The commonly used data collection procedures smooth over the irregularities, imperfections, and discontinuities that occur in daily organizational life (Kimberly 1980; Leach 1967), and so we researchers persist in using a term that exaggerates order. Researchers who study large organizations try to capture their size and apparent complexity by using surveys, averages, and synoptic measures in an attempt to say something about everything they observe. The costs of these strategic decisions are becoming clearer in the deepening irrelevance of organizational researchers for organizational participants (Perrow 1981; Thoenig 1982).

Managers work amidst a great deal of chaos. Order imposed upon conditions of divergent self-interest, career competition, turnover, shifting definitions of self, and uncertain resources is unstable and must continually be reestablished.

The real world of management is not orderly, well-defined, or clear as to its practices. It is a jungle of ideas, methods, techniques, and divergent philosophies that one might be tempted to call a mess. Textbook principles of organization, authority, command, and strategies for getting results comprise a logical and persuasive set of as-

10

sumptions. The real world of management, however, is loaded with confusion, stress, uncertainty, politics, trial and error, frustration, disappointment, and emotional disturbances, and in many cases is a maze of "the rat race of survivability." The real world of management contains upheavals, redirections, and realignments because of new threats, new vibrations, new conflicts, new concerns. (Mali 1981, 49)

Unpredictability is high in organizations, as in life. Managers who themselves are unpredictable must work continuously to make sense of unpredictable environments. Neither the managerial group, the organization, nor the environment is unitary. Failure is inevitable if we try to understand organizations by aggregating into higher units elements that themselves are not unitary (Mayhew 1980).

The managerial group is not unitary because concerns with career advancement keep people apart (Watson 1982, 271; Wilson 1982). The organization is not unitary because it is a field of interests (Borum 1980), a set of procedures for arguing, shifting alliances presided over by a dominant coalition, which spends its time maintaining dominance rather than seeking profit. The environment itself is not unitary (Zey-Ferrell 1981, 193) because it is defined relative to differing organizational interests and contains shifting amounts of resources managed by shifting interorganizational alliances (Robbins 1983, 154–56).

The combination of incentives, turnover, role ambiguity, and role overload threatens whatever order and equilibrium people are able to build on a short-run basis. Thus they need continual interaction, phoning, and meeting to reassure themselves and others that yesterday's routines are still in place and that the organization is unfolding today pretty much the way it unfolded yesterday.

Arrangements continually need to be renegotiated because of our inevitable uncertainty as to who will show up tomorrow, in what frame of mind, capable of doing what, and remembering which episodes from the past to use as precedents for and warnings about the future. Managers need to reassure themselves and their colleagues that things today are basically the way they were yesterday, that past agreements and understandings are still in force, and that it is okay to act as if it were "business as usual." In the flow of ongoing organizations, business as usual is a major accomplishment, not an automatic outcome. Business as usual reflects an over-determined state, most of whose determinants are neither known nor understood.

The disorder found in most organizations is held together by a combination of cognition and action. Action is energized, directed, and intensified by the labels that are attached to it, labels that originate in cognitive activity. But action leads and constrains cognition, and provides the raw material around which cognition is organized (Weick 1979). Because order in organizations is transient, managers need to make a strong and continuing effort to stabilize shifting events. Order is produced, contested, repaired, organized, and displayed in concrete situations by active people who are continually defining what that situation is about (Knorr-Cetina 1981, 6).

Action is a crucial source of order, not just because managers act, but because organizations themselves are action generators.

> Automatic, nonreflective action is built into organizations. They advertise not because they have identified a specified problem and have decided that advertising is the best solution, but because they have set up advertising departments and there are people whose sole responsibility is to advertise. Organizations create budgets because they possess forms and procedures and specialists for making budgets, not because they have explicitly decided that budgets will solve clearly identified problems that exist here and now. The action-generating mechanisms are copied from other organizations or learned in schools of management or carried forward by tradition, and claims that they solve problems are afterthoughts arising from the desires to appear rational and legitimate. (Starbuck 1982, 20–21)

The observation that organizations are successful generators of action often is lost on those who feel that a key issue in organizational theory is to explain what motivates people and why most people are not motivated (White and Locke 1981). The problem within organizations may be misdirected activity, fruitless activity, incorrect activity, or noncumulative activity, but the problem is not *in*activity.

Elapsed action becomes the stimulus for people in organizations to develop theories of what they have done and what will happen if they do it again (Dutton and Starbuck 1963; Meyer 1982). The assertion that organizations generate action thus becomes the start, not the end of an explanation of what is required to manage organizations. Left with unexplained action, managers need to explain its origins. Constructing consistent justifications that accommodate visible implications of the prior action is a prominent way managers explain what they have done.

ACTIONS EVOKE JUSTIFICATION

> Societal ideologies insist that actions ought to be responses—actions taken unreflectively without specific reasons are irrational and irrationality is bad . . . so organizations justify their actions with problems, threats, successes, or opportunities. Bureaucrats, for instance, attribute red tape to legal mandates or to sound practice. (Starbuck 1983, 94)

Organizations are action generators, but they also give and require reasons for doing things. Typically these reasons become salient after the action has occurred (retrospective rationality) rather than before (prospective rationality). Once action has been justified, subsequent explanations and options are restricted.

The most powerful set of ideas concerning the justification process originated in cognitive-dissonance theory (Festinger 1957; Wicklund and Brehm 1976). There is evidence that, during the period of time preceding a decision, people focus attention on the alternatives they eventually do not choose, whereas in the postdecisional state they concentrate on the chosen alternative (Jones and Gerard 1967). They are usually aware that in some respects the chosen alternative may be less attractive than the rejected one. To neutralize these jarring facts, once people make a decision they realign their cognitions and do such things as enhance the value of the chosen alternative, devalue the rejected alternative, deny that the decision was volitional ("I really had no choice"), minimize the importance of the outcome, enlarge the degree of overlap between the chosen and rejected alternatives, or persuade other people that the choice was a good one. Each of these resolutions has different implications for what the person will do next. More important, because these resolutions reduce tension, the person has some investment in preserving these altered views, especially in organizations where norms of rationality are pervasive.

People are disturbed by postdecision dissonance when they feel personally responsible for bringing about an aversive event—one that produces an undesirable outcome (Cooper, Zanna, and Taves 1978). To be responsible means that the person acted freely, cannot plead force, and could have foreseen what might happen (Goethals, Cooper, and Naficy 1979).

In addition to the combination of arousal, responsibility, and aversiveness, three other conditions can also create pressures to justify action. The first is inconsistencies between actions and one's self-concept (Aronson 1980; Bramel 1968). If people believe they are incompetent (e.g., qualitative overload), then discovering that they have been undercompensated or have made errors should not be disturbing. However, if people believe they are competent, then working for insufficient rewards,

using simple skills, and investing in failing enterprises all should be disturbing because they do not follow from the belief that one is a competent person who makes good decisions.

Dissonance effects can also be created by the frustration of motives such as (in an organizational context) the desire for power or achievement.

> When a person has the cognition that he has voluntarily chosen to commit himself to a behavior which has negative consequences for the satisfaction of some relevant, salient motive, a state of cognitive dissonance is created. The knowledge that the tension associated with a given motive is uncomfortable is inconsistent with the knowledge that one has agreed to accept it, continue to enter into more of it, and postpone behavior directed to available goals which could reduce their drive. (Zimbardo 1969, 15)

If I agree to postpone being reviewed for a promotion, this voluntary commitment to deprivation of achievement motives is dissonant *unless* I decrease the intensity of that motive. If I am able to do that, then even if someone suddenly presents an opportunity to achieve, I will reject it and act like someone for whom achievement is no longer an incentive (Weick and Prestholdt 1968; Zimbardo 1969).

Most managers confront inconsistent cognitions most of the time. Organizations are infused with the ideology that rational action is good and necessary and possible, but that ideology is very much at odds with what actually happens (Pfeffer 1981b, 194). The standards to which managers are held and the behavior that is held up to them as an example are impossible to attain and are seldom exhibited even by the people who enforce these standards. Hypocrisy is ubiquitous in organizations, and this necessitates continuous dissonance reduction. Because dissonance is so prevalent, one might hypothesize that managers would become accustomed to it, so that it would have little continuing effect on action. Dissonance probably retains its power to affect action, however, partly because self-concepts are involved, partly because Western ideologies treat inconsistency as error, and partly because self-concepts of managers are invested so heavily with themes of rationality and competence.

The third and most useful way to understand justification is by means of Salancik's (1977) extension of Kiesler's (1971) analysis of commitment. The starting point for Salancik's analysis is the assertion that beliefs align themselves with actions taken. It will be recalled that action *starts* the sequences we are interested in, it does not end them. The chronic error that economists make is to suggest that most relevant determinants occur before action takes place and that action flows automatically from correct analyses. However, action typically generates its own dynamics, constraints, and pressures for redefinition, most of which are missed by so-called rational models of decision making.

Salancik's assertion that beliefs align themselves with completed actions rests on three assumptions.

1. People like what they do.
2. People believe in the value of what they do.
3. People become what they do.

These three assumptions are usually invoked to explain choices: people choose things they like over things they dislike, things they value over things they reject, and things that flatter their self-concept over things that do not. Thus, a knowledge of preferences should enable us to predict choices. That is the way a rational analysis sets up the problem and that is precisely why we have such a poor understanding of managerial action.

When managers complete the actions encouraged by organizational conditions, they work backward (retrospectively) and use the *actions* to search for patterns of likes, values, and definitions of self that explain the outcome. Cognitions become defined *after* the action, not before it. The action becomes an excuse to reexamine the situation. But the action also serves as a constraint, because only certain likes, preferences, and self-definitions will justify the action (O'Reilly and Caldwell 1981).

Salancik argues that three conditions—visibility, irrevocability, volition—determine the degree to which a manager feels pressure to justify an action. When an action is visible, the person cannot deny that the behavior occurred. When an action is irrevocable, the behavior cannot be changed. The joint realities of visibility and irrevocability both signify that the action *has* taken place. When an action is also volitional, it becomes the responsibility of a specific person or group, who must then explain it.

Beliefs constructed in the service of justification tend to ride roughshod over evidence. Hence organizations are often described as collections of myths, stories, avoided tests, anecdotes, and beliefs that have only a modest fit with realities described by more detached observers (Boland 1982).

The implications of commitment are substantial. For example, commitment affects control systems. Accountability, a hallmark of rational organizations, can erode flexibility through the mechanism of commitment. Control systems make action visible, which increases commitment, which then decreases flexibility, experimentation, and early detection of failing courses of action. Control systems that emphasize visibility and ac-

countable discretion may encourage concealment of failure through increased investment in faltering enterprises—something control systems supposedly prevent (Staw and Ross 1978; Staw 1976).

If accountability is less visible because it is diffused rather than concentrated, if experimentation and incrementalism are institutionalized so that resources are invested in small quantities, and if individual choice is left slightly ambiguous, then organizations should remain flexible because commitments are softer.

So far we have argued that people's explanations of actions tend to be inaccurate and self-serving. That implication understates the complexity of cognition in organizations. When people search for justification, they often find real attractions as well as fictitious ones. People may trap themselves into unsatisfying jobs and failing projects when they justify earlier decisions, but they also may discover unexpected rewards.

At a time when promotion opportunities within firms have dwindled, people need to view career advancement as something other than simply ascending a hierarchy. Driver (1979), for example, urges people to cultivate spiral careers, in which they perform several different activities at a single organizational level, and forgo the idea of an upward linear career. As hierarchies become flatter and promotion less frequent, extra attractions discovered while justifying effort expenditure become more an important source of personal job enrichment tailored to the person's own unique interests.

Saying that an assignment "isn't so bad after all," can represent an effort to gloss over negative qualities, but it can also reflect discovery of subtle attractions that no one else noticed. The line between self-deception and genuine discovery is exceedingly thin, and there are no clear guidelines by which one can judge when one trails off into the other.

While some features of organizations seem highly committing (e.g., visibility and accountability of individual action), others suggest that commitment should be rare. For example, it is not clear how much choice managers actually have in their jobs (Marshall and Stewart 1981). Informal role prescriptions, formal job descriptions, and orders from the boss all imply that actions were forced rather than volitional, and therefore need no explanation. In many organizations managers speak the truth when they say, "I had no choice but to. . . ." To stress researchers, such statements signify occasions of low personal control and high stress (Miller 1980; Wortman and Brehm 1975); they are also significant to effectiveness researchers because they signify that organizations are not tied up by a set of commitments that will be defended at all costs. Ironically, some flexibility is preserved when people do things under duress because then they do not have to defend their actions personally.

Organizations may be more adaptable when commitments are harder to develop, because ambiguous events can be reversed with relative ease and because their consequences can be redefined in ways that favor revocation or adaptation. The very organizational chaos that people treat as evidence of poor management and lack of foresight can also favor adaptation, because people are less pressured to justify what they do. The fact that managers are tentative and seldom make irreversible decisions can be viewed as evidence of timidity, risk aversion, or confusion. At the same time, they may feel less pressure to develop myths that distort evidence. People who avoid irreversible action preserve adaptability.

In summary, organizations generate action in settings teeming with norms of rationality; organization members feel they must explain those actions as rational responses. Pressures to justify action intensify when there is evidence that attractive opportunities have been forgone, that outcomes are of questionable value, that incompetence may be perceived, or that what was chosen has no overlap with what was rejected (negative features of the chosen alternative and positive features of the rejected alternative can make this discomfort quite pronounced). Under these conditions, people search for exonerating explanations, reevaluate outcomes, and attempt to recoup losses by escalating commitment (Staw 1980).

Each of these resolutions squeezes some flexibility out of the organization's response repertoire (Bell 1967) and some accuracy out of the organization's perceptions of its environments and itself (Weick 1978). While justifications may uncover unsuspected skills, resources, and missions, they can also cause people to lose touch with themselves, what they are capable of doing, and what they want to do. As managers lose touch with their skills and their preferences and defend increasingly tenuous visions, they invite crises and collapse. The same explanations that prospectively may assist in planning, strategy making, and analysis often operate retrospectively to conceal assets and troubles. Managers who practice unselective justification can become estranged from themselves and the settings within which they operate (Lewicki 1981).

In disorderly organizational worlds, actions unfold in ways that are not predictable. Justification is an attempt to rationalize action and add predictability. When people attempt to live solely by norms of rationality, however, they too often try to recoup losses by escalating commitments and end up losing flexibility and judgment.

ACTIONS DISPLACE THINKING

Action can make thinking less necessary for several reasons, two of which are explored here. First, action can provide direct perceptual data that obviate the need for further thinking. Second, action can incorporate overlearned routines that do not require thoughtful monitoring.

Ecological action

Most managers are active, manage by walking about, thrive on face-to-face interaction, and are suspicious of any media that are less direct and less immediate (Mintzberg 1973, 1975). In contrast, our knowledge of perception, social knowing, and analysis is based primarily on studies of people who are *not* mobile (e.g., they rest their head on a chin rest while observing a static display).

To make sense of these drastically restricted stimuli, the experimental subject must use complicated cognitive operations (e.g., inference) that require considerable time and effort. Observing people under these conditions, researchers have concluded that human beings in general have to think about their world a great deal to cope with it (Huber 1980). This conclusion, however, is an artifact of the ecologically invalid displays with which they have been presented. Social knowing may require less cognitive inference than anyone has realized.

The possibility that action can substitute for cognitive inference has been discussed recently by Baron (1981), Neisser (1977), and Knowles and Smith (1982). In the following discussion, "perception" refers to the pickup of environmental information and "cognition" refers to the encoding, storage, and recall of this environmental information. Perception is usually viewed as a process that follows cognitive activities such as analysis, synthesis, inference, extrapolation, active construction, and the like ("Oh, now I see what's out there"). Direct perception, however, occurs before cognition and often renders cognition unnecessary. Orderly information is available to guide perception, especially when the person is allowed to move about. When movement is permitted, perception becomes more accurate, occurs more quickly, and involves less cognitive work.

If this line of analysis is plausible, it explains why detailed analyses of cognition and thinking explain so little of how managers act and what they know (Nugent 1981). Barnard, in his famous essay "Mind in Everyday Affairs" (1938, 308–309), observed that most managerial thought was so rapid that it was simply not possible to explain it by conventional processes of reflection and contemplation—processes perhaps used by most academics, and erroneously attributed to everyone else as well.

The importance of mobility for perception cannot be overemphasized.

> There is little danger of overload when information is obtained through exploration. Indeed, the more information that is available, the less confused the Gibsonian perceiver [person using direct perception] becomes. For example, the more perspectives one has on an object, the easier it is to know its essential identity; the more complete the rotation or the more contexts in which one sees an entity, the easier it is to establish what is invariant from what is changing. . . . Thus, the existence of overload may be more of a commentary on the lack of opportunity for adequate observation than any limitations of the perceiver. (Baron 1981, 66)

Multiple perspectives should facilitate the discovery of invariants, which reduces overload and increases accuracy. From an information-processing view, however, multiple perspectives should strain channel capacity more than a redundant viewing done from the same perspective (Axelrod 1973). Of particular importance for the exploration argument is the finding that when perceivers are not constrained and the context surrounding objects is not eliminated, visual illusions do *not* occur (Knowles and Smith 1982, 58). It is only when people have to use inferential processes in a fabricated environment that their senses play tricks on them and generate conclusions they would never make in the world outside the laboratory.

Managers seldom report being overloaded, perhaps because they observe events from several perspectives, see what is common, and base their actions on that core. None of this requires detailed analysis. The person who may be forced to analyze is the one who is confined to an office, a work station, a terminal, a printout, summarized data, or written words, all of which are incomplete fragments that require effort to synthesize. Conclusions drawn from these less-direct modes of knowing are more subject to error because they require more processing, with more fallible cognitive operations.

This line of reasoning predicts that the people who report the most stress from qualitative or quantitative overload should be those whose situation most closely resembles that of a subject in a classical perception experiment—those who are in a stationary position, given incomplete cues, and forced to make complex judgments in a contextless setting.

Managers are less active in the head, more active in the world. This difference used to be a source of ridicule because it was presumed that being highly active

in the head was the only way to cope with the world. That view is slowly being replaced by perspectives that are more sensitive to the ecology that surrounds perception and more awareness of the considerable amount of information that is out there and available with a minimum of inference. The important question for managers is how far they can get with unelaborated information before they have to resort to higher-order cognitive processes.

Daft and Lengel (1984) postulate that rich informational media are needed to register rich, complex environments. They argue that face-to-face contact has the most richness, followed by phone conversations, letters, and memos, with computer printout having the least richness because there is no feedback, it is dated, and it appeals to only one sensory modality. As we move back up the hierarchy, there is an increase in immediacy and accuracy of feedback, the number of sensory modalities being used, and the extent to which the data are acquired in real time. The rank ordering proposed by Daft and Lengel also corresponds with variations in observer mobility, which should mean that richness correlates negatively with the necessity to resort to higher-order cognitive processes and positively with the accuracy of judgments.

Mindless action

A second major explanation for the mindless quality of managerial action is that it consists of overlearned routines triggered by simple categories and coarse attributions of causality. All of these tactics insure that relatively little thought occurs unless situations are novel, difficult to typify, or have little precedent (e.g., an employee brings an infant to work to care for it).

The relative importance of nonthinking in interaction has been discussed from time to time, but it is only recently that investigators such as Langer (1978) and Thorngate (1976) have begun to pull these ideas together and extend them.

Langer quotes Alfred N. Whitehead to illustrate the major themes associated with investigation of mindless action.

> By relieving the brain of all necessary work, a good rotation sets it free to concentrate on more advanced problems, and in effect increases the mental powers of the race. . . . It is a profoundly erroneous truism, repeated by all copy-books and by eminent people making speeches, that we should cultivate the habit of thinking what we are doing. The precise opposite is the case. Civilization advances by extending the number of oper-

ations which we can perform without thinking about them. Operations of thought are like cavalry charges in battle—they are strictly limited in number, they require fresh horses, and must only be made at decisive moments. (Langer 1978, 40)

Action changes as it shifts from being consciously organized to more automatic. Over time, as an action is repeated, the number of cues that guide it is steadily reduced. In the early consciously monitored stages, numerous cues are noticed and influence the form of the action. As the same situation recurs, the person over-learns only that information that is seen to be available repeatedly. Thus, each time the event is repeated, less information is processed and actions gradually become guided by less information. The person eventually needs only enough information to trigger the complete action. Everything beyond this minimum is ignored, including cues suggesting that the old responses are no longer appropriate. When responses become overlearned, people become more confident, earlier in the unfolding of a situation, that they know what is occurring (Dailey 1971). As a result, they activate a full response more quickly and with less revision to fit particulars of the situation.

This is one reason why managers' judgments and decisions often do not improve as time passes. When they act on the basis of fewer cues with more confidence, they ignore more data, much of which implies the necessity to change the action. In most organizations, the combination of impression management, ambiguity, and multiple meanings reduces temporarily the trouble that can occur when nonroutine situations are treated as if they were routine.

Langer (1978) raises the interesting question of why we have come to feel that so much action is mediated by thought. It is relevant to consider her explanation, because so much description in organizational behavior assumes that managers think, analyze, and plan most of the time.

> When we think about people, since we ourselves are *thinking*, we are not likely to assume their behavior to be automatic. If that behavior is not correspondent with the information the situation presents to us, we may be led to erroneous conclusions about why they behaved the way they behaved. It is probably because of this—that people think they, or others were thinking; that we when behaving as people, think we are thinking; and when, we behaving as psychologists studying people, may actually *be* thinking—that we have overlooked all the non-thinking that takes place. (p. 39)

It is clear that people do think and do become aware of the fine grain of their ongoing action when situations are unfamiliar. Because most observers study relatively unfamiliar situations in order to learn more about them, they are flooded with unexpected events that require conscious effort to understand, and they are likely to assume that participants have to make the same effort.

This is why sustained direct observation is one of the few research techniques that can be relied upon to approximate the understanding that practitioners eventually have of their own situation (Bogdan 1972; Schwartz and Jacobs 1979). This is also why participant observers are so crucial to improve our understanding of managerial behavior. Managers take more for granted than researchers do, and thereby free their attention for more novel issues. We need to understand the routines of management so we can discover what kinds of cognitive and attentional resources are left for managers to direct at issues that no one has encountered before.

The final importance of understanding mindless action derives from the supposition that when people think about their behavior as they enact it, they destroy the spontaneous continuity of the action, produce a less-skilled performance, and become more dissatisfied with the outcomes. People who become self-conscious while delivering a speech find that this consciousness disrupts the flow of speech. Langer (1978, 41) hypothesized that "the positivity of postactivity evaluation varies inversely with the degree of conscious awareness of the activity. That is, the more one is involved in the event, the more one enjoys the event; and increased levels of involvement are achieved by not paying attention to the particulars of the situation [by not thinking]."

In summary, much interaction in organizations is rehearsed rather than spontaneous. People know in advance that the district manager is going to visit; they rehearse what they will say, tours are planned, people are coached on the answers to questions most likely to be asked—all of which restricts spontaneity and information exchange. People take turns saying their lines, suggesting the relevance of a dramaturgical model (Overington and Mangham 1982; Mangham and Overington 1982) concerned with rehearsing, backstage, frontstage, scripts, cues, muffed lines, and so on.

If organizations are heavily dramaturgical and if people play parts carefully worked out in advance, interest then focuses on the extent to which managers become what they have acted. When people believe they had some choice in performing their script, they may come to believe it.

Mindless routines are more likely to occur in mechanistic organizations operating in stable environments than in organic organizations operating in dynamic environments (Carroll and Tosi 1977). In organic organizations, processes are negotiated and assembled in different ways, depending on the problem (Argote 1982). If organizations are loosely coupled, it is more difficult to use routines unless they concern fundamentals of interaction. The only routines that work are simple rules: when in doubt, do something; if you're confused, ask someone; search in the vicinity of the problem.

ACTIONS CREATE ENVIRONMENTS

Environments, like organizations, may be either loosely or tightly coupled. Some organizational theorists assume that environments are coupled more tightly than organizations are, so that to survive, organizations must accommodate to the rate of change in those tight environments (e.g., Brittain and Freeman 1980; Hannan and Freeman 1977). Loosely coupled organizations survive in tightly coupled environments to the extent that their managers are skilled at sensing and diagnosing themselves and their environment (Hambrick 1981), that they can establish organizational structures that exploit attractive environmental niches, and that they can produce large-scale change swiftly when the attractive niches change. The valued manager is perceptive, with strong skills in organizational design and organizational development. In a tightly coupled environment, the organization most likely to survive is one with skilled people in boundary role positions who can distinguish between transient and permanent environmental changes (Aldrich and Herker 1977; Miles 1980) and flexible people in the technical core who are willing to do things differently with little forewarning in response to intelligence picked up at the boundary.

Other organizational theorists assume that organizations, or parts of them, are coupled more tightly than environments are (e.g., Schreyogg 1980; Colignon and Cray 1980). Specific coalitions or even forceful individuals can create environments when they modify regulations, build interorganizational alliances (Stern 1979, 1981), create demand (Ewen 1976), alter perceptions of the organization (Dunkerley, Spybey, and Thrasher 1981), and deter competitors.

A significant portion of the organization's environment consists of nothing more than talk, symbols, promises, lies, interest, attention, threats, agreements, expectations, memories, rumors, economic indicators, supporters, detractors, good faith, suspicion, trust, appearances, loyalties, and commitments—all of which are more intangible and more influenceable than material goods (Peters 1980; Gronn 1968; Weick 1980). Focused action within these less tangible environments attracts attention, induces avoidance, pulls concessions, forestalls competition, induces monitoring, and alters resource flows (Pfeffer 1981a). Whenever action is focused within largely symbolic environments, unrelated events become more closely associated with one another and their covariation increases. As managerial action varies, events cohere in different ways, which means that the environments that confront the organization also change. In this sense, the organization creates its environment.

When organizations exist in more pliant environments, the crucial managerial skill becomes the ability to focus action (Hirsch 1975) so as to rearrange loosely coupled environmental elements. Characteristics such as persistence, confidence, assertiveness, and visibility now become more crucial. In tightly coupled environments, forcefulness is wasted and may even be detrimental because it can preclude accurate sensing (Suedfeld, Tetlock, and Ramirez 1977). But in loosely coupled environments, assertion should be more predictive of organizational success. Important managerial characteristics are persistence, visibility, durability, consistency (Moscovici 1976, 1980), and interpersonal skills associated with gaining and holding attention (e.g., ingratiation, inducing obligations, physical attractiveness).

Finally, some organizational theorists argue that organizations and environments are both either tightly coupled or loosely coupled (e.g., Cherns 1980; Leifer and Delbecq 1978). Many people argue for reciprocal effects, but they fail to state whether they assume that tight or loose entities are affecting one another. That is not a trivial assumption, because when loose entities affect one another, environment-organization fit should be higher than when tight entities interact.

If reciprocal relationships are postulated, the theorist has to begin the sequence somewhere. The identity of that starting point makes a great deal of difference (Harrison 1981).

If, in the beginning, the environment determined structure, then the structure from which the next response is generated does not contain all the resources, capabilities, and options that it did before the environment imposed the initial constraint. Instead, a partially biased structure exerts an effect back on the environment—an effect that is always slightly weaker, slightly less forceful, slightly less deterministic, because the organization operates with a slightly less complete response repertoire. Since environments consist of other organizations and other people, it is not stretching the point to say that when the environment is the first mover, it exerts some influence over what the organization will demand and forgo in the next period by virtue of its initial effect on structure.

If the first mover is the organization, then the environment feeds back to it a more coherent and predictable set of demands than was likely before the organization took the first action. Again, there is reciprocity, but the reciprocity favors the organization in the sense that it shapes the environmental demands toward its own strengths.

The mechanism associated with a first mover resembles a self-fulfilling prophecy. The initial response, whether by the environment or the organization, pulls a second response that *preserves* the original definition of the situation implied by the original action. The second response is constructed to be a sensible act within that original framework. That serves to unbalance the control over reciprocal relationships. Each entity partially determines the response of the other entity, but the second response is generated on a field controlled by the initial responder and therefore accommodates to that initial response.

If the reciprocal relationship between organization and environment begins with an environmental influence on structure, then the reciprocity has a stronger thread of environmental determinism than of organizational determination, and the effective managerial actions will be those associated with sensing and internal design. If, however, the reciprocal influence starts in the organization, then the reciprocity favors organizational determination, and forcefulness and visibility become more crucial managerial qualities.

External environments

Both organizations and environments are loosely coupled. Managerial actions are a crucial input that organizes these fragmented settings. Thus, it is important to look more closely at what happens when managers confront external situations of modest orderliness. In many loosely coupled settings, the gaps that exist among events must be filled in at least by thought, if not by action. One way to do so is by presuming that there is a logic by which events cohere. These presumptions of logic are evident in the inferences about cause and effect that are assembled into cause maps (e.g., Ashton 1976; Bougon, Weick, and Binkhorst 1977; Goodman 1968; Axelrod 1977; Roos and Hall 1980; Porac 1981).

When managers act as if loosely coupled events were tied together as they are in a cause map, events often *become* more tightly coupled, more orderly, or less variable.

Thus the administrator of an extended-care unit in a hospital (Roos and Hall 1980) may presume that increased public relations activities directed at influential outsiders will stave off mounting internal pressures to follow the rules. Having presumed that the world hangs together like this, the pressured administrator spends more time away from the hospital, which makes him more visible to outsiders. The outsiders think about the hospital more than they did before they saw the administrator, which makes the outsiders' actions more predictable and focused. Their actions previously had been under the control of multiple agendas, which have now been edited down to a smaller set of items, with the hospital being more salient on all those lists. Through the simple act of becoming visible, the administrator makes more homogeneous the "environment" with which the hospital must deal. The administrator also makes the diverse outsiders more mutually relevant to one another, because each now needs some of the information that the others have. Furthermore, the administrator is in an advantageous position to resolve whatever uncertainties his contacts create, which means that he has acquired more power (Hinings et al. 1974).

This entire sequence draws together diverse forces into a more focused scenario that now has more effect on significant actors. The hospital becomes constrained by an environment that did not exist until the administrator changed the salience of events for outsiders. Demands on the hospital became more orderly under the influence of administrative action that itself was launched on the basis of presumptions that just such orderliness would and did exist. At the time the administrator first acted, none of the orderliness was in place nor was there any guarantee that this particular order, or any order for that matter, would be "there" to validate the initial presumption.

In the beginning, presumptions cognitively bridged the gaps among events outside the hospital. Confident action addressed to this presumptively logical world then gave it a tangible form that resembled the presumptive forms stored in the *a priori* maps in the administrator's head.

It is crucial to see that the issue here is *not* one of accuracy. Cause maps could be wrong and still be an important part of managerial action. The important feature of a cause map is that it leads people to anticipate some order "out there." It matters less what particular order is portrayed than that an order of some kind is portrayed. The crucial dynamic is that the prospect of order lures the manager into ill-formed situations that then accommodate to forceful actions and come to resemble relations contained in the cause map. The map animates managers, and the fact of animation, not the map itself, imposes order on situations.

Thus, trappings of rationality, such as strategic plans, are important largely as binding mechanisms. They hold events together long enough and tight enough in people's heads so that they do something in the belief that their action will be influential. To a significant extent, the order they find is an order created by the very actions thought to be *reactions* to demands that were there before action was even contemplated.

This enactment mechanism works precisely because environments are loosely coupled. Looseness by itself is often difficult to understand because causes produce effects only suddenly (rather than continuously), occasionally (rather than constantly), negligibly (rather than significantly), indirectly (rather than directly), and eventually (rather than immediately) (Weick 1982, 380). Such an unpredictable world cannot be relied upon or controlled. Presumptions, expectations, justifications, and commitments span the breaks in a loosely coupled system and encourage confident actions that tighten settings. The conditions of order and tightness in organizations exist as much in the mind as they do in the field of action. The field of action becomes transformed into something that resembles the mind's image whenever action takes place. But the order that is "discovered" is usually misattributed to external conditions rather than to the *a priori* mental images that triggered the actions of consolidation in the first place.

Such mundane properties of managerial action as confidence, assertion, and optimism now can be recognized as crucial resources by which organizational events are made orderly (March 1975; Zaleznik 1977). Confidence becomes more important the more pliant the setting, the greater the amount of uncertainty, the younger the organization, the higher the turnover, the more intensive the technology. All of these variables weaken the ties among events, which then increases the extent to which presumptions of order and consistent actions impose whatever structure exists among those events.

Consider the activity of divestment (Nees 1981). The presumption that it is possible to sell a firm, when put into action ("Do you want to buy my firm?"), may coalesce the fragments of the environment into homogeneous suspicion, which generates a uniform and forceful no. No then becomes the environment to which the divestor must accommodate. Top management's obsession with secrecy attests to the ease with which the act of inquiring shapes the environment with which they then must deal.

Problems often turn out to be environmental residues of managers' inquiring styles (Mitroff and Kilmann 1978). Changes in those styles of inquiring change the ways in which environments cohere, which in turn changes the problems that are "discovered."

Work on cognitive styles (e.g., McKenney and Keen 1974), for example, may be important because different styles of action flow from these inquiring styles and have differential effects on the environments being examined.

For example, consider the Myers-Briggs Type Indicator (Myers 1980). An extroverted sensing type who takes in data by direct inspection, processes these data by thinking, and orients to the world through the dominant perceptual process of sensing (ESTP), will be more active and more conspicuous than will an introverted intuitive type who processes data by feeling and reserves the dominant process of intuition for his or her own thoughts while orienting to the world through personal feelings (INFJ). If the ESTP is more successful in top management than the INFJ, the critical factor may not be analytical style but rather the greater ease with which the ESTP dominates and creates the environments through which he or she moves.

The environment is less crucial to the functioning of an intuitive type than it is to the functioning of a sensing type who relies on direct sensory data. Intuitives, in contrast, often imagine environments that have only a modest fit with what the sensing type would observe. Intuitives are interested in possibilities, not in sensed objects, because the sensed objects are interesting only in terms of what they might become. If sensing types are more attuned to environment, then theories that postulate environmental determinism might be supported when they are tested with CEOs (chief executive officers) who are sensing types but not when they are tested with CEOs who are intuitive types.

Internal environments

Top management in complex organizations does not design operating structures; it designs decision structures. It essentially divides the organization into subunits that then design the operating structures (Boschken 1982). Instead of managing the organization, management manages the process that then manages the organization; Kuhn and Beam (1982, 325–26) refer to this as "metamanagement."

To design a decision structure is not a simple matter. Top management selects the people who will be in the decision-making group. Thus personnel selection is a key means by which top management creates the environments that will constrain it in the future. This is a tricky issue, however. Just as top management does not know enough to make certain decisions, and hence forms the decision structure, it does not necessarily know enough to dictate who the members of the decision-making group might need for advice. Accordingly, top management must give up some of its control over the list of people who will be its agents. There is a big difference between the statements "I am in control" and

"Things are under control" (Antonovsky 1979). To manage complex systems is to know the difference and to relinquish individual control to gain system stability.

While top management is accustomed to saying, "Do what I tell you and I will reward you in proportion as you do it to my satisfaction," it adopts a different philosophy to manage dynamic complexity. The manager who sacrifices personal control by pushing decision making downward to subgroups says essentially,

> Do what you collectively think best in light of the objectives I have stated. I will try to reward you collectively as I will have no real way of knowing which persons had what effect in your decisions. In fact, you are probably better judges than I of whether your methods were the most effective available and which of your members are most effective. All I can do is to tell you whether your accomplishment as a group strikes me as reasonably satisfactory relative to my purposes.[1]

Abandoning unity of command (VanFleet and Bedeian 1977), the manager essentially says, "See what you can do and do your best." The manager does retain some control over the purse strings and over decisions to hire, fire, and promote people. However, since individual contributions are concealed within the group product, even personnel decisions will be difficult to make under this arrangement.

The manager still exerts some influence by seeing that wider organizational considerations are kept in mind when decisions are made between units, keeping decision makers informed of relevant constraints, replacing agents, and handling situations that exceed the range for which the group was designed.

This model of delegated control under conditions of dynamic complexity very much resembles the control structure found in universities (Bess 1982; Wilson 1981). The president of a university is unable to evaluate the intellectual products of the faculty. The best research goes the way the researcher wants it to go, not the way the administrator wants it to go. It is not possible for administrators to manage hunches or the pursuit of hunches, so they say essentially, "Keep busy and do research." Subsystems within the university decide most of the key issues, such as teaching and admissions requirements, and the only control presidents have over these subgroups is money and final approval of personnel decisions.

Questions of authority, legitimacy, and insubordination are greatly attenuated in universities, but the

same attenuation occurs in other organizations where the ties among subsystems are loose and responsibility is delegated to groups rather than to individuals (Blau and Alba 1982). It is sometimes objected that much organizational theory has limited generality because it is based on universities. But in fact the loosely coupled university structure is a prototype for complex organizations in general, where lower levels make top-management decisions.

Top management creates its own environment when it designs the internal structure that will generate recommendations and monitor the external environment. The degrees of freedom in this creation are limited, but they are not zero. To cope with complexity, top management does not have to give up completely nor does it have to settle for mere tactics. It does have to attend closely to structural and personnel matters and then walk away from them (Padget 1980, 602).

ACTIONS REQUIRE INTERACTION

People generate actions. And people are needed by one another when they generate these actions (Leavitt and Lipman-Blumen 1980). Whether imagined or actually present, people surround all managerial action.

To manage action amidst other people is to (1) identify the basic form in which this interaction operates, the "double interact"; (2) use others more intentionally in the process of self-definition; (3) provide conditions for constructing a sufficiently stable social reality, so that people can do what they are expected to do; and (4) offset the tendency for social cohesion to distort perceptions of external environments.

The double interact

The basic form of action when two or more people are involved is the double interact (Allport 1962). Person A does something in the presence of person B (B can be either physically present or imagined, as when one tries to anticipate top-management reaction to a presentation); B then responds to this action; and finally, on the basis of what B did, A either modifies or retains the initial act. What A's act meant initially is *not* known fully by A until he or she sees what B does. The act by itself means nothing apart from B's response. When B does respond, A knows what he or she has done and then can either reaffirm or modify that action to bring it closer

---

1. From A. Kuhn and R. D. Beam, *The Logic of Organization* (San Francisco: Jossey-Bass, 1982), 327, by permission.

Table 2.1

Act	Interact	Double interact	Type of influence
Affirm A	Affirm A	Affirm A	Uniformity
		Affirm B	Anticonformity
Affirm A	Affirm B	Affirm A	Independence
		Affirm B	Conformity

From R. H. Willis and E. P. Hollander, "An Experimental Study of Three Response Modes in Social Influence Situations," *Journal of Abnormal and Social Psychology* 69 (1964): 150–56. Copyright 1964 by the American Psychological Association. Adapted by permission of the authors.

to the initial intentions, which themselves are now clearer. Because the first action serves as an anchor and the second action is designed relative to the first, the double interact concludes with the second act by A. Additional acts merely trigger different processes that are less basic (e.g., when the sequence is extended to a fourth, fifth, or sixth act, the situation now becomes a debate).

The double-interact concept allows analysts to distinguish four basic ways in which action is coordinated. Consider table 2.1, which has been adapted from Willis and Hollander.

When a manager gives an order, the subordinate's reaction indicates what the original action meant, what is likely to happen, and what revisions are needed. Thus, if the manager says, "I think we need to cut costs," and the associate says, "I think we need to increase market share," the manager can then say either, "You're right" (conforming to the colleague's view) or "You're wrong; cost is the issue" (demonstrating independence). If the associate had said, "I agree with you; the problem is cost," then the manager might have kept this diagnosis, believing that the colleague was credible (uniformity), or might have changed his or her view, saying, "He's never agreed with me before so there must be something wrong"—an example of anticonformity.

The value of the double interact to explain managerial action is that managers often assume that their influence is unilateral and fail to realize the power of subordinates to withhold compliance and jeopardize joint outcomes (Knights and Roberts 1982; Dubois 1981; Butler and Snizek 1976).

Self-definition through self-fulfilling prophecies

Double interacts often unfold in face-to-face interaction, making action more complex.

[A] great deal of the work of organization—decision making, the transmission of information, the close coordination of physical tasks—is done face to face, requires being done in this way, and is vulnerable to face-to-face effects. Differently put, insofar as agents of social organizations of any scale from states to households, can be persuaded, cajoled, flattered, intimidated, or otherwise influenced by effects only achievable in face-to-face dealings, then here, too, the interaction order bluntly impinges on macroscopic entities. (Goffman 1983, 8)

Goffman (p. 8) suggests that many interactions in organizations can be viewed as people-processing encounters during which the impressions that are conveyed affect life chances. As a metaphor for interaction in organizations, he suggests the placement interview, a situation in which there is a quiet sorting that reproduces the social structures associated with statuses such as gender, race, physical attractiveness, class, and age. He argues that people processing such as is done institutionally by school counselors, personnel departments, psychiatric diagnosticians, or courtroom officials is ubiquitous. "Everyone is a gatekeeper in regard to something. Thus, friendship relationships and marital bonds (at least in our society) can be traced back to an occasion in which something more was made of an incidental contact than need have been" (p. 8).

Face-to-face interaction has a promissory, evidential quality in which people read indicators to guide subsequent interactions. Organizations are heavily evaluative contexts in which accountability, responsibility, blame, and credit are accorded freely and consequentially (Perry and Barney 1981). In that sense, it is relevant to assume that every day at work is like a placement interview during which a mixture of fact and fantasy influences how people read one another for indications of status and character.

A significant portion of what people know about themselves originates in how they are treated and labeled by others (Maines 1977). This process is especially complicated because the definitions other people send back to the original actor, who incorporates them as parts of the self, often are implanted in those others by the original actions of the original actor. People do create environments, and that means they often create the other people who then create them. Thus we begin to see the profound sense in which social behavior has a solitary core (Bateson 1975).

Self-fulfilling prophecies control much interaction with others (e.g., King 1974; Jones 1977; Snyder, Tanke, and Berscheid 1977). We interact with expectations of how events will unfold based on rumors, reputations, and nonverbal signals that are immediately visible. These expectations often control what we get back. For example, anticipating hostility, we walk guardedly into a situation and give off signals that *stimulate* the hostility we predicted would be there (Schwartz and Lever 1976).

Thus people create themselves by biasing the interactions in which they participate. Personal character does not exist until other people begin to define it for us by their actions and labels. But those actions and labels (e.g., "*He* is hostile, we are not") are often implanted by the person in search of character. Thus, I become the prophecies I project on others, which they redirect back to me. Since expectations are so prominent in organizations, conditions there seem ripe to encourage self-validating definitions of character that are essentially closed to the discovery of new data.

Social comparison and social reality

Because loosely coupled organizations generate uncertainty (Downey and Slocum 1975; Duncan 1972), people must rely more heavily on one another to define a workable reality (Pfeffer, Salancik, and Leblebici 1976). Social-comparison processes should be especially salient in loosely coupled systems where people find it difficult to assess their abilities and beliefs (Festinger 1954). If social comparison is crucial, then we would expect to find that people are especially sensitive to issues of similarity and dissimilarity, because these are the fundamental judgments that determine the appropriateness of comparison with others (Salancik and Pfeffer 1978).

When people are uncertain about an opinion or an ability, they select for comparison someone judged to be in rough agreement with what they believe or roughly at their level of competence. To fine-tune the comparison and validate the belief, they then communicate with the comparison person to move his or her position even closer or they change their own position so that it agrees even more with that of the comparison person. If neither of these mechanisms works, they reject the comparison and try again.

Out of these interactions people build a social reality with which they can cope. If comparable others are not available, or if similarities occur on marginal issues, then beliefs become unstable, actions become erratic, prediction and control decrease, and stress increases. Under conditions of high uncertainty managers should be sensitive to the necessity to build a social reality and the fact that people can do this more readily when there are salient bases for similarity. Highlighting existing similarities, providing conditions where people can disclose more information safely, making it more likely that they will discover similarities, or manufacturing similarities by putting people through intense socializations (Van

Maanen and Schein 1979), all can facilitate comparison, which facilitates reality construction, which increases predictability, control, and satisfaction.

Uncertainty directly creates one form of role stress—role ambiguity—and is indirectly involved in at least two other forms—quantitative and qualitative role overload (VanSell, Brief, and Schuler 1981). Often when people complain that they do not have sufficient skills to do their job (qualitative overload) or that they are asked to do too much (quantitative overload), it is not clear to them what is to be done, what skills are relevant, or what is important.

When social realities are built through the process of social comparison, ambiguities get resolved long enough for forceful action to be taken, which then consolidates a more certain environment. The extent of similarity determines the speed with which social reality is built, its stability, and its resistance to competing realities advanced by dissimilar people.

All of these social-comparison processes become less important when there is a physical reality to which questions of belief and ability can be referred. To the extent that organizations rely on tangible indicators that require a minimum of judgment, and to the extent that environments are stable and structures are predictable, then social comparison is less crucial and the organization should be able to tolerate a more diverse set of actors over longer periods of time with fewer negative effects on productivity. Diversity should be less troublesome in mechanistic systems than in organic systems because there is less need to construct reality. Similar others in a mechanistic system are redundant. Diverse others in an organic system amplify uncertainty and may encourage cliques among those people who are similar on at least some dimensions (e.g., all graduates of Seattle University), even if those dimensions are not central to task accomplishment.

A recent concept that highlights the necessity for social comparison is the suggestion that organizations are like paradigms (Pfeffer 1982, Chapter 7; Brown 1978; Lodahl and Gordon 1972). "A paradigm is a technology, including the beliefs about cause-effect relations and standards of practice and behavior, as well as specific examples of these, that constitute how an organization goes about doing things" (Pfeffer 1982, 227–28). The importance of a paradigm is that it infuses day-to-day activity with meaning and purpose. Paradigms control the interpretations people impose on new information and often determine whether they will even gather any new information. When paradigms are well developed, there is consensus on preferences and on definitions of the situation, which means that people within a subunit can speak with one voice and pursue a consistent course of action. This consolidated position can have substantial advantages in political struggles. When paradigms are less well developed and when uncertainty is higher, social comparison becomes more crucial, conflict is more likely, and forcefulness is compromised.

Thus social comparison and the social influence processes that accompany it are crucial means to develop the paradigms that solidify organizations.

Cohesion and accuracy

The complexities of interaction can be summarized in the form of a dilemma that confronts most managers, a dilemma we will call the "cohesion-accuracy trade-off." Emphasizing social cohesion risks establishing a biased, unreliable, misleading perception of the world. But to maintain perceptual accuracy is to run the risk of alienation and turnover when social cohesion is kept at a minimum.

The social systems in most groups in organizations are vulnerable to fragmentation and dissolution (Campbell 1972). To prevent this fragmentation members strive for at least four things.

1. Some degree of uniformity of belief
2. Some degree of acceptance of leadership and traditional authority
3. Willingness to learn vicariously from the reports of others (trust)
4. Willingness to participate in collective action

Honesty, dissent, innovation, and variation can threaten these four requirements. People who see things differently from other group members pose a threat to uniformity of belief, reject leadership and authority, imply a distrust for the reports of others, and resist collective action. Under these conditions, honesty has the potential to splinter the group or to invite rejection.

If a cohesive system tries to test reality it may fail, because the preference and beliefs that hold the system together bias how people test reality and interpret what they find. People see what validates the group's view, not what others outside the group might verify independently (Janis 1972; Tetlock 1979).

This bias can be reduced by designing a social system so that outcomes in the external world—those things people want to learn more about—occur *independently* of the preferences of individuals. The way to do this is to use norms and procedures in which no one—whether boss or colleague—can affect the answers. Obviously this is an ideal.

Organizations rely heavily on authority of position, precedent, prestige, and the majority view to influence

decisions. It makes little difference who produces the evidence: it is the evidence itself that counts. If the value of evidence is defined by who found it, then accuracy is sacrificed to cohesion. The only way to break free of ideas that preserve cohesion, continuity, and consensus is to make them vulnerable to experimental probes (e.g., Staw 1977). Then empirical evidence will be taken seriously whether presented by a very young person, a disliked person, or a minority group member.

The chronic danger in organizations is that the constructed social reality may be nothing but a wishful construction. It all depends on the degree to which the manager either imposes norms that neutralize the more severe effects of cohesion on accuracy or reduces cohesion to the minimum level necessary to sustain a group.

Accuracy can be promoted by following a series of norms in management (adapted from Campbell 1979, 192–96).

1. Tradition is a source of error rather than truth; be suspicious of received wisdom.
2. Stubborn, insubordinate, young geniuses are to be listened to even if their ideas go against the prevailing views of older, more established people.
3. Competence rather than likableness should be rewarded.
4. Contribution to effectiveness is the only legitimate basis on which to bestow status.
5. Dishonesty should be punished with ruthlessness and finality.

Many of these norms run contrary to the political nature of organizations in which information is "bent" to individual advantage. The very fact that these norms seem so unrealistic makes the point that accuracy will be in short supply unless interpersonal ties are overlaid with a set of restrictions that favor accuracy, are monitored continuously, and are firmly enforced.

A different approach is to weaken social ties. Compromises that favor accuracy over cohesion occur when there is less group to preserve. There are several ways to weaken social ties: recruit loners, tolerate high turn-over, design tasks so that people can perform them with relatively little instruction and relatively short apprenticeships, recruit people who have been similarly socialized and who therefore can coordinate and mesh their activities without much face-to-face supervision, assign individual projects that are basically self-contained, reward disagreement and conflict, develop a culture favoring individualism, use diverse reference groups as comparisons, and review performance at infrequent intervals (allow long spans of time within which people can exercise discretion).

These tactics minimize the necessity for close attention to the social system by reducing its scope and what is required to maintain it. Norms are not needed to offset social threats to validity, because the social threats themselves are minimal. In a thinned system, a combination of culture, group composition, division of labor, delegation of authority, and a broad definition of mission create a sensing mechanism with multiple sensors but fewer internal constraints that distort what is registered. The danger is that the manager will go too far and create disoriented, alienated employees who adopt every suggestion they hear.

CONCLUSIONS

The purpose of this chapter has been to lay the groundwork for a more general understanding of managerial action in organizations. We now know a good deal about what managers actually do (Metcalfe 1982; Kotter 1982; Davis and Luthans 1980), but we know less about the adequacy with which they do it, what they might be doing instead, how these actions address the dimly sensed problems associated with coordination and control in joint action, why these particular forms and not other ones persist, and what the lingering and larger effects are of repeated activation of these limited forms.

Answers to some of these puzzles may lie in illuminating the mechanisms by which theories such as population ecology, institutionalization, interorganizational relations, resource dependence, systems theory, loose coupling, or organized anarchies flow through, give form to, and constrain daily managerial actions. The relationship between theory and reality is seldom clearcut. Consider the "mushy ice problem" described by Kuhn and Beam:

> The law of levers states that weight times distance on one side of a fulcrum will equal weight times distance on the other side. If a restless polar bear walks toward one end of a slab of mushy ice that rests roughly centered on top of a mound of snow while a seal rests on the other end, any one or a combination of a number

of things may happen. The bear's end of the slab may go down and the seal's end go up, like a true lever, or the slab of ice may break in one or more places so that the bear goes down but the seal does not go up. The snow may compress so that both go down, or the snow fulcrum may be so broad and the ice so strong that the slab does not move at all. . . . If the slab of ice does not always behave as the law of levers prescribes, that fact does not invalidate the law. It merely means that the situation does not closely resemble the theoretical model of a lever. . . .[2]

When the facts are mushy, no theoretical model provides precise analysis and no seasoned investigator would try to find one that does. But one should not throw out perfectly good principles when the problems of application lie in the setting rather than the theory.

Principles of action bear on actual organizations just as principles of mechanics bear on mushy ice. Organization theory often discards useful ideas like dissonance in the face of unclear facts and then replaces the ideas with other flawed ideas. When the substitutes do not work either, the field is then left with nothing. It simply shuffles among formulations, all of which fare poorly because they are applied to disorderly events.

To ground an understanding of organizations in justified, interdependent action between two or more persons is to start with basics that do not evaporate whenever facts become less clear. To start with action is not to make reductionistic assertions that psychology is sufficient to understand organizational behavior. Action is no more psychological than it is sociological or economic. Action cuts across all disciplines and is fully understood by none of them.

Ultimately, organizational theories must be tested against what managers do and the consequences of their actions. The theories most likely to prove valid will be those that focus explicitly on what managers do when they construct, maintain, and use constantly shifting arrangements to acquire constantly shifting scarce resources.

---

2. From A. Kuhn and R. D. Beam, *The Logic of Organization*. 287–88, by permission.

REFERENCES
AND ADDITIONAL READINGS

Aldrich, H., and D. Herker. 1977. "Boundary Spanning Roles and Organization Structure." *The Academy of Management Review* 2:217–30.

Allport, F. H. 1962. "A Structuronomic Conception of Behavior: Individual and Collective." *Journal of Abnormal and Social Psychology* 64:3–30.

Antonovsky, A. 1979. *Health, Stress and Coping*. San Francisco: Jossey-Bass.

Argote, L. 1982. "Input Uncertainty and Organizational Coordination in Hospital Emergency Units." *Administrative Science Quarterly* 27:420–34.

Aronson, E. 1980. "Persuasion via Self-Justification: Large

Commitments for Small Rewards." In *Retrospections on Social Psychology*, ed. L. Festinger, 3–21. New York: Oxford University Press.

Ashton, R. H. 1976. "Deviation-Amplifying Feedback and Unintended Consequences of Management Accounting Systems." *Accounting, Organizations and Society* 1:289–300.

Axelrod, R. 1973. "Schema Theory: An Informative Processing Model of Perception and Cognition." *American Political Science Review* 67:1248–66.

———. 1977. "Argumentation in Foreign Policy Settings." *Journal of Conflict Resolution* 21:727–56.

Barnard, C. I. 1938. "Mind in Everyday Affairs." In *The Functions of the Executive*, 301–22. Cambridge, Mass.: Harvard University Press.

Baron, R. M. 1981. "Social Knowing from an Ecological-Event Perspective: A Consideration of the Relative Domains of Power for Cognitive and Perceptual Modes of Knowing." In *Cognition, Social Behavior, and the Environment*, ed. J. H. Harvey, 61–89. Hillsdale, N.J.: Erlbaum.

Bateson, G. 1975. "Counsel for a Suicide's Friend." *CoEvolution Quarterly* (Spring): 135.

Bell, G. D. 1967. "Formality versus Flexibility in Complex Organizations." In *Organizations and Human Behavior*, ed. G. D. Bell, 97–106. Englewood Cliffs, N.J.: Prentice-Hall.

Benson, J. K. 1977. "Innovation and Crisis in Organizational Analysis." In *Organization Analysts: Critique and Innovation*, ed. J. K. Benson, 5–18. Beverly Hills, Calif.: Sage.

Berg, P. O. 1979. *Emotional Structures in Organizations*. Farnborough, England: Teakfield.

Bess, J. L. 1982. *University Organization*. New York: Human Sciences Press.

Blau, J. R., and R. D. Alba. 1982. "Empowering Nets of Participation." *Administrative Science Quarterly* 27:363–79.

Bogdan R. 1972. *Participant Observation in Organizational Settings*. Syracuse, N.Y.: Syracuse University Press.

Boland, R. J., Jr. 1982. "Myth and Technology in the American Accounting Profession." *Journal of Management Studies* 19:109–27.

Borum, F. 1980. "A Power-Strategy Alternative to Organization Development." *Organization Studies* 1:123–46.

Boschken, H. L. 1982. "Organization Theory and Federalism: Interorganizational Networks and the Political Economy of the Federalist." *Organization Studies* 3:355–73.

Bougon, M., K. E. Weick, and D. Binkhorst. 1977. "Cognition in Organizations: An Analysis of the Utrecht Jazz Orchestra." *Administrative Science Quarterly* 22:606–39.

Bramel, D. 1968. "Dissonance, Expectation, and the Self." In *Theories of Cognitive Consistency: A Sourcebook*, ed. R. P. Abelson, E. Aronson, W. J. McGuire, T. M. Newcomb, M. J. Rosenberg, and P. H. Tannenbaum, 355–65. Chicago: Rand McNally.

Brittain, J. W., and J. H. Freeman. 1980. "Organizational Proliferation and Density Dependent Selection: Organizational Evolution in the Semiconductor Industry." In *The Organizational Life Cycle*, ed. J. R. Kimberly and R. H. Miles, 291–338. San Francisco: Jossey-Bass

Brown, R. H. 1978. "Bureaucracy as Praxis: Toward a Political Phenomenology of Formal Organizations." *Administrative Science Quarterly* 23:365–82.

Brunesson, N. 1982. "The Irrationality of Action and Action Rationality: Decisions, Ideologies, and Organizational Actions." *Journal of Management Studies* 19:29–44.

Butler, S. R., and W. E. Snizek. 1976. "The Waitress-Diner Relationship: A Multimethod Approach to the Study of Subordinate Influence." *Sociology of Work and Occupations* 3:209–22.

Campbell, D. T. 1972. "Objectivity and the Social Locus of Scientific Knowledge." In *Studies in the Philosophy of Science*, vol. 10, ed. R. S. Cohen and M. N. W Wartofsky. Dordrecht, Netherlands: Redi Reidel.

———. 1979. "A Tribal Model of the Social System Vehicle Carrying Scientific Knowledge." *Knowledge: Creation, Diffusion, Utilization* 1:181–201.

Carroll, S. J., and H. L. Tosi. 1977. *Organizational Behavior*. Chicago: St. Clair.

Cherns, A. 1980. "Organizations as Instruments of Social Change in Postindustrial Societies." *Organization Studies* 1:109–22.

Cohen, M. D., and J. G. March. 1974. *Leadership and Ambiguity*. New York: McGraw-Hill.

Cohen, M. D., J. G. March, and J. P. Olsen. 1972. "A Garbage Can Model of Organizational Choice." *Administrative Science Quarterly* 17:1–25.

Colignon, R., and D. Cray. 1980. "Critical Organizations." *Organization Studies* 1:349–65.

Cooper, J., M. P. Zanna, and P. A. Taves. 1978. "Arousal as a Necessary Condition for Attitude Change Following Induced Compliance." *Journal of Personality and Social Psychology* 36:1101–6.

Daft, R. L., and R. H. Lengel. 1984. "Information Richness: A New Approach to Manager Behavior and Organization Design." In *Research in Organizational Behavior*, ed. B. Staw and L. L. Cummings, vol. 6. Greenwich, Conn.: Jai Press.

Dailey, C. A. 1971. *Assessment of Lives*. San Francisco: Jossey-Bass.

Davis, T. R. B., and F. Luthans. 1980. "Managers in Action: A New Look at Their Behavior and Operating Modes." *Organizational Dynamics* 9, no. 1:64–80.

Downey, H. K., and J. W. Slocum. 1975. "Uncertainty: Measures, Research, and Sources of Variation." *Academy of Management Journal* 18:562–78.

Driver, M. J. 1979. "Career Concepts and Career Management in Organizations." In *Behavioral Problems in Organizations*, ed. C. L. Cooper, 79–139. Englewood Cliffs, N.J.: Prentice-Hall.

Dubois, P. 1981. "Workers' Control Over the Organization of Work: French and English Maintenance Workers in Mass Production Industry." *Organization Studies* 2:347–60.

Duncan, R. 1972. "Characteristics of Organizational Environments and Perceived Environmental Uncertainty." *Administrative Science Quarterly* 17:313–27.

Dunkerly, D., T. Spybey, and M. Thrasher. 1981. "Interorganizational Networks: A Case Study of Industrial Location." *Organizational Studies* 2:229–47.

Dutton, J. M., and W. H. Starbuck. 1963. "On Managers and Theories." *Management International* 6:1–11.

Ewen S. 1976. *Captains of Consciousness.* New York: McGraw-Hill.

Feldman, M. S., and J. G. March. 1981. "Information in Organizations as Signal and Symbol." *Administrative Science Quarterly* 26:171–86.

Festinger, L. 1954. "A Theory of Social Comparison Processes." *Human Relations* 7:117–40.

———. 1957. *A Theory of Cognitive Dissonance.* Evanston, Ill.: Row, Peterson.

Fisch, R., J. H. Weakland, and L. Segal. 1982. *The Tactics of Change.* San Francisco: Jossey-Bass.

Glassman, R. B. 1973. "Persistence and Loose Coupling in Living Systems." *Behavorial Science* 18:83–98.

Goethals, G. R., J. Cooper, and A. Naficy. 1979. "Role of Foreseen, Foreseeable, and Unforeseeable Behavior Consequences in the Arousal of Cognitive Dissonance." *Journal of Personality and Social Psychology* 37:1179–85.

Goffman, E. 1983. "The Interaction Order." *American Sociological Review* 48:1–17.

Goodman, P. S. 1968. "The Measurement of an Individual's Organization Map." *Administrative Science Quarterly* 13:246–65.

Gronn, P. S. 1968. "Talk as the Work: The Accomplishment of School Administration." *Administrative Science Quarterly* 13:246–65.

Hage, J. 1980. *Theories of Organizations.* New York: Wiley.

Hall, P. M. 1972. "A Symbolic Interactionist Analysis of Politics." *Sociological Inquiry* 42, nos. 3–4:35–75.

Hambrick, D. C. 1981. "Specialization of Environmental Scanning Activities Among Upper Level Executives." *Journal of Management Studies* 18:299–320.

Hannan, M. T., and J. Freeman. 1977. "The Population Ecology of Organizations." *American Journal of Sociology* 82:929–64.

Harrison, R. 1981. "Startup: The Care and Feeding of Infant Systems." *Organizational Dynamics* 10, no. 1:5–29.

Herr, J. J., and J. H. Weakland. 1977. *Counseling Elders and Their Families.* New York: Springer.

Hinings, C. R., D. J. Hickson, J. M. Pennings, and R. E. Schneck. 1974. "Structural Conditions of Intraorganizational Power." *Administrative Science Quarterly* 19:22–44.

Hirsch, P. M. 1975. "Organizational Effectiveness and the Institutional Environment." *Administrative Science Quarterly* 20:327–44.

Huber, G. P. 1980. *Managerial Decision Making.* Glenview, Ill.: Scott, Foresman.

Janis, I. R. 1972. *Victims of Groupthink.* Boston: Houghton Mifflin.

Jones, E. E., and H. B. Gerard. 1967. *Foundations of Social Psychology.* New York: Wiley.

Jones, R. A. 1977. *Self-Fulfilling Prophecies.* Hillsdale, N.J.: Erlbaum.

Katz, F. E. 1974. "Interdeterminancy in the Structure of Systems." *Behavorial Science* 19:394–403.

Kiesler, C. A. 1971. *The Psychology of Commitment.* New York: Academic.

Kimberly, J. R. 1980. "Data Aggregation in Organizational Research: The Temporal Dimension." *Organization Studies* 1:367–77.

King, A. S. 1974. "Expectation Effects in Organizational Change." *Administrative Science Quarterly* 19:221–30.

Knights, D., and J. Roberts. 1982. "The Power of Organization or the Organization of Power?" *Organization Studies* 3:47–63.

Knorr-Cetina, K. D. 1981. "Introduction: The Micro-Sociological Challenge of Macro-Sociology: Toward a Reconstruction of Social Theory and Methodology." In *Advances in Social Theory and Methodology*, ed. K. Knorr-Cetina and A. V. Cicourel, 1–47. Boston: Routledge & Kegan Paul.

Knowles, P. L., and D. L. Smith. 1982. "The Ecological Perspective Applied to Social Perception: Revision of a Working Paper." *Journal for the Theory of Social Behavior* 12:53–78.

Kotter, J. 1982. *The General Managers.* New York: Free Press.

Kuhn, A., and R. D. Beam. 1982. *The Logic of Organization.* San Francisco: Jossey-Bass.

Langer, E. J. 1978. "Rethinking the Role of Thought in Social Interaction." In *New Directions in Attribution Research*, ed. J. H. Harvey, W. J. Ickes, and R. F. Kidd, vol. 2: 35–58. Potomac, Md.: Erlbaum.

Leach, E. R. 1967. "An Anthropologist's Reflections in a Social Survey." In *Anthropologists in the Field*, ed. D. G. Jongmans and P. C. Gutking , 75–88. Atlantic Highlands, N.J.: Humanities Press.

Leavitt, H. J., and J. Lipman-Blumen. 1980. "A Case for the Relational Manager," *Organizational Dynamics* 9, no. 1:27–41.

Leifer, R., and A. Delbecq. 1978. "Organizational/Environmental Interchange: A Model of Boundary Spanning Activity." *Academy of Management Review* 3:40–50.

Lewicki, R. J. 1981. "Organizational Seduction: Building Commitment to Organizations." *Organizational Dynamics* 10, no. 2:5–21.

Lodahl, J. B., and G. Gordon. 1972. "The Structure of Scientific Fields and the Functioning of University Graduate Departments." *American Sociological Review* 37:57–73.

Maines, D. R. 1977. "Social Organization and Social Structure in Symbolic Interactionist Thought." *Annual Review of Sociology* 3:235–59.

Mali, P., ed. 1981. *Management Handbook.* New York: Wiley.

Mangham, I. L., and M. A. Overington. 1982. "Performance and Rehearsal: Social Order and Organizational Life." *Symbolic Interaction* 5:205–23.

March, J. G. 1975. "Education and the Pursuit of Optimism." *Texas Tech Journal of Education* 2:5–17.

Marshall, J., and R. Stewart. 1981. "Managers' Job Perceptions. Part I: Their Overall Frameworks and Working Strategies." *Journal of Management Studies* 18:177–90.

Mayhew, B. H. 1981. "Structuralism versus Individualism: Part I, Shadowboxing in the Dark." *Social Forces* 59:335–75.

McKenney, J. L., and P. G. W. Keen. 1974. "How Managers' Minds Work." *Harvard Business Review* (May–June) pp. 79–90.

Metcalfe, B. M. A. 1982. "Leadership: Extrapolating from Theory and Research to Practical Skills Training." *Journal of Management Studies* 19:295–305.

Meyer, A. D. 1982. "Adapting to Environmental Jolts." *Administrative Science Quarterly* 27:515–37.

Meyer, J. W., and B. Rowan. 1977. "Institutionalized Organizations: Formal Structure as Myth and Ceremony." *American Journal of Sociology* 83:340–63.

Meyer, M. W. 1979. "Organizational Structure as Signaling." *Pacific Sociological Review* 22:481–500.

Miles, R. H. 1980. "Organization Boundary Roles." In *Current Concerns in Occupational Stress*, ed. C. L. Cooper and R. Payne, 61–96. New York: Wiley.

Miller, S. M. 1980. "Why Having Control Reduces Stress: If I Can't Stop the Roller Coaster I Don't Want to Get Off." In *Human Helplessness*, ed. J. Garber and M. E. P. Seligman, 71–95. New York: Academic.

Mintzberg, H. 1973. *The Nature of Managerial Work*. New York: Harper & Row.

———. 1985. "The Manager's Job: Folklore and Fact." *Harvard Business Review* 53, no. 4:49–61.

Mitroff, I. I., and R. H. Kilmann. 1978. *Methodological Approaches to Social Science*. San Francisco: Jossey-Bass.

Morgan, G. 1981. "The Schismatic Metaphor and Its Implications for Organizational Analysis." *Organization Studies* 2:23–44.

Moscovici, S. 1976. *Social Influence and Social Change*. New York: Academic.

———. 1980. "Toward a Theory of Conversion Behavior." In *Advances in Experimental Social Psychology*, ed. L. Berkowitz, vol. 13: 209–39. New York: Academic.

Myers, I. B. 1980. *Introduction to Type*. Palo Alto, Calif.: Consulting Psychologists Press.

Nees, D. 1981. "Increase Your Divestment Effectiveness." *Strategic Management Journal* 2:119–30.

Neisser, U. 1972. "Gibson's Ecological Optics: Consequences of a Different Stimulus Description." *Journal for the Theory of Social Behavior* 7:17–28.

Neruda, P. 1968. *We Are Many*. Trans. Alistair Reid. London: Grossman.

Nugent, P. S. 1981. "Management and Modes of Thought." *Organizational Dynamics* 9, no. 4:45–59

O'Reilly, C. A., and D. F. Caldwell. 1981. "The Commitment and Job Tenure of New Employees: Some Evidence of Postdecisional Justification." *Administrative Science Quarterly* 26:597–616.

Overington, M. A., and I. L. Mangham. 1982. "The Theatrical Perspective in Organizational Analysis." *Symbolic Interaction* 5:173–85.

Padget, J. F. 1980. "Managing Garbage Can Hierarchies." *Administrative Science Quarterly* 25:583–604.

Perrow, C. 1981. "Disintegrating Social Sciences." *New York University Educational Quarterly* 12 no. 2:2–9.

Perry, L. T., and J. B. Barney. 1981. "Performance Lies Are Hazardous to Organizational Health." *Organizational Dynamics* 9, no. 3:68–80.

Peters, T. J. 1980. "Management Systems: The Language of Organizational Character and Competence." *Organizational Dynamics* 9, no. 1:3–26.

Pfeffer, J. 1981a. "Management as Symbolic Action: The Creation and Maintenance of Organizational Paradigms." In *Research in Organizational Behavior*, vol. 3, ed. L. L. Cummings and B. Staw, 1–52. Greenwich, Conn.: Jai Press.

———. 1981b. *Power in Organizations*. Marshfield, Mass.: Pitman.

———. 1982. *Organizations and Organization Theory*. Marshfield, Mass.: Pitman.

Pfeffer, J., G. R. Salancik, and H. Leblebici. 1976. "The Effect of Uncertainty on the Use of Social Influence in Organizational Decision Making." *Administrative Science Quarterly* 21:227–45.

Porac, J. F. 1981. "Causal Loops and Other Intercausal Perceptions in Attributions for Exam Performance." *Journal of Educational Psychology* 73:587–601.

Rados, D. L. 1972. "Selection and Evaluation of Alternatives in Repetitive Decision Making." *Administrative Science Quarterly* 17:196–206.

Reynolds, D. K. 1976. *Morita Psychotherapy*. Berkeley, Calif.: University of California Press.

———. 1981. "Morita Psychotherapy." In *Handbook of Innovative Psychotherapies*, ed. R. J. Corsini, 489–501. New York: Wiley.

Robbins, S. P. 1983. *Organization Theory: The Structure and Design of Organizations*. Englewood Cliffs, N.J.: Prentice-Hall.

Roos, L. L., and R. I. Hall. 1980. "Influence Diagrams and Organizational Power." *Administrative Science Quarterly* 25:57–71.

Ross, J., and K. R. Ferris. 1981. "Interpersonal Attraction and Organizational Outcomes: A Field Examination." *Administrative Science Quarterly* 26:617–32.

Salancik, G. R. 1977. "Commitment and the Control of Organizational Behavior and Belief." In *New Directions in Organizational Behavior*, ed. B. M. Staw and G. R. Salancik, 1–54. Chicago: St. Clair.

Salancik, G. R., and J. Pfeffer. 1978. "Uncertainty, Secrecy, and the Choice of Similar Others." *Social Psychology* 41, no. 3:246–55.

Schreyogg, G. 1980. "Contingency and Choice in Organization Theory." *Organization Studies*: 305–26.

Schwartz, H., and J. Jacobs. 1979. *Qualitative Sociology: A Method to the Madness*. New York: Free Press.

Schwartz, P., and J. Lever. 1976. "Fear and Loathing at a College Mixer." *Urban Life* 4:413–31.

Scott, W. R. 1981. *Organizations: Rational, Natural, and Open Systems*. Englewood Cliffs, N.J.: Prentice-Hall.

Simmel, G. 1971. "How Is Society Possible?" In *George Simmel on Individuality and Social Forms*, ed. D. N. Levine, 6–22. Chicago: University of Chicago Press.

Simon, H. A. 1962. "The Architecture of Complexity." *Proceedings of the American Philosophical Society* 106, no. 6: 467–82.

Snyder, M., E. D. Tanke, and E. Berscheid. 1977. "Social Perception and Interpersonal Behavior: On the Self-Fulfilling

Nature of Social Stereotypes." *Journal of Personality and Social Psychology* 35:656–66.

Starbuck, W. H. 1982. "Congealing Oil: Inventing Ideologies to Justify Acting Ideologies Out." *Journal of Management Studies* 19:3–27.

———. 1983. "Organizations as Active Generators." *American Sociological Review* 48:91–102.

Staw, B. M. 1976. "Knee Deep in the Big Muddy: A Study of Escalating Commitment to a Chosen Course of Action." *Organizational Behavior and Human Performance* 16:27–44.

———. 1977. "The Experimenting Organization." *Organizational Dynamics* 6, no. 1:3–18.

———. 1980. "Rationality and Justification in Organizational Life." In *Research in Organizational Behavior*, vol. 2, ed. B. M. Staw and L. L. Cummings, 45–80. Greenwich, Conn.: Jai Press.

Staw, B. M., and J. Ross. 1978. "Commitment to a Policy Decision: A Multitheoretical Decision." *Administrative Science Quarterly* 23:40–64.

Stern, R. N. 1979. "The Development of an Interorganizational Control Network: The Case of Intercollegiate Athletics." *Administrative Science Quarterly* 24:242–66.

———. 1981. "Competitive Influences on the Interorganizational Regulation of College Athletics." *Administrative Science Quarterly*, 26:15–32.

Suedfeld, P., P. E. Tetlock, and C. Ramirez. 1977. "War, Peace, and Integrative Complexity." *Journal of Conflict Resolution* 21:427–42.

Tetlock, P. E. 1979. "Identifying Victims of Groupthink from Public Statements of Decision Makers." *Journal of Personality and Social Psychology* 37:1314–24.

Thoenig, J. C. 1982. "Discussion Note: Research Management and Management Research." *Organization Studies* 3:269–75.

Thoits, P. A. 1982. "Conceptual, Methodological, and Theoretical Problems in Studying Social Support as a Buffer Against Life Stress," *Journal of Health and Social Behavior* 23:145–59

Thorngate, W. 1976. "Must We Always Think Before We Act?" *Personality and Psychology Bulletin* 2:31–35.

Van Fleet, D. D., and A. G. Bedeian. 1977. "A History of the Span of Management." *Academy of Management Review* 2:356–72.

Van Maanen, J., and E. H. Schein. 1979. "Toward a Theory of Organizational Socialization." In *Research in Organizational Behavior*, ed. B. M. Staw, vol. 1: 209–64. Greenwich, Conn.: Jai Press.

Van Sell, M., A. P. Brief, and R. S. Schuler. 1981. "Role Conflict and Role Ambiguity: Integration of the Literature and Directions for Future Research." *Human Relations* 34:43–71.

Watson, T. J. 1982. "Group Ideologies and Organizational Change." *Journal of Management Studies* 19:259–75.

Weick, K. E. 1976. "Educational Organizations as Loosely Coupled Systems." *Administrative Science Quarterly* 21:1–19.

———. 1978. "The Spines of Leaders." In *Leadership: Where Else Can We Go?* ed. M. W. McCall, Jr., and M. M. Lombardo, 37–61. Durham: Duke University Press.

———. 1979. *The Social Psychology of Organizing*. 2d ed. Reading, Mass.: Addison-Wesley.

———. 1980. "The Management of Eloquence." *Executive* 6, no. 3:18–21.

———. 1982. "Management of Organizational Change Among Loosely Coupled Elements." In *Change in Organizations*, ed. P. Goodman, 375–408. San Francisco: Jossey-Bass.

Weick, K. E., and P. Prestholdt. 1968. "Realignment of Discrepant Reinforcement Value." *Journal of Personality and Social Psychology* 8:180–87.

Weiss, C. H. 1980. "Knowledge Creep and Decision Accretion." *Knowledge: Creation, Diffusion, Utilization* 1:381–404.

White, F. M., and E. A. Locke. 1981. "Perceived Determinants of High and Low Productivity in Three Occupational Groups: A Critical Incident Study." *Journal of Management Studies* 18:375–87.

Wicklund, R. A., and J. W. Brehm, 1976. *Perspectives on Cognitive Dissonance*. Hillsdale, N.J.: Erlbaum.

Willis, R. H., and E. P. Hollander. 1964. "An Experimental Study of Three Response Modes in Social Influence Situations." *Journal of Abnormal and Social Psychology* 69:150–156.

Wilson, D. C. 1982. "Electricity and Resistance: A Case Study of Innovation and Politics." *Organization Studies* 3:119–40.

Wilson, J. A., ed., 1981. *Management Science Applications to Academic Administration*. San Francisco: Jossey-Bass.

Wortman, C. B., and J. W. Brehm. 1975. "Responses to Uncontrollable Outcomes: An Integration of Reactance Theory and the Learned Helplessness Model." In *Advances in Experimental Social Psychology*, ed. L. Berkowitz, vol. 8:277–336. 1977. New York: Academic.

Zaleznik, A. 1977. "Managers and Leaders: Are They Different?" *Harvard Business Review* (May-June).

Zey-Ferrell, M. 1981. "Criticisms of the Dominant Perspective on Organizations." *Sociological Quarterly* 22:18–205.

Zimbardo, P. G. 1969. *The Cognitive Control of Motivation*. Glenview, Ill.: Scott, Foresman.

3

Using our knowledge of organizational behavior: the improbable task

WARREN BENNIS

Not one rummy has been taken off of Baltimore streets by this research. Not one drunken husband has been dissuaded from beating his wife or one drunken mother from beating her child. These research projects are like exotic, expensively mounted butterfly collections, hidden away in vaults and only exhumed from time to time to display to other collectors of the rare and unusual in mutual reaffirmation of their elite status.
—Rep. Barbara Mikulski (D-Md.) (Fishman and Neigher 1982)

The basic question, then, is, What must we as researchers do in order to respond more usefully to the pragmatic questions that now face the field. . . . We cannot . . . remain in the aloof stance caricatured in the familiar picture of the basic scientist who prefers to seek after truth untrammeled by the yammerings of the secular world. The fact is that in the practical world in which we must find support for our research, we can only hope to settle for half-aloof.
—Morris Parloff (1979)

We are living in the most satisfying and unsettling period of human history—satisfying because we enjoy and profit from discoveries that enable us to live healthier, longer, more fulfilling lives; unsettling because we can no longer be certain that what we know today will be valid tomorrow. Should we move against this current? Or do we navigate it, utilize it, and allow it to lead us into a new era, with an air of enthusiasm and audacity? It is not, as Brecht said, "a night of disaster when a man sees the truth." On the contrary: it is a night of hope; it is disastrous only when the "truth" is neglected or misused.

Although they are not new phenomena, the nonutilization of knowledge and the lack of communication among different social groups become less tolerable as society finds itself unable to rely on tradition and more dependent on adaptability and knowledge that facilitates adaptation. We have produced many individuals with highly specialized knowledge greatly useful for society as a whole; we cannot afford to neglect them or their contributions. Equally important, they must be aware of the ways in which they can make their contributions most effective and appreciated.

Like C. P. Snow, I sense a growing separation between two isolated cultures. But the cleavage that troubles me is not the gap between scientist and humanist but that between men and women of knowledge who lack power, and men and women of power who lack knowledge.

Nowhere is this "implementation gap" more glaring than in the social sciences. Our literature demonstrates reliable and significant applications for social policy. Yet while theory and science proliferate, translation into practice lags behind. This was true over twenty years ago when *The Planning of Change* was first pub-

29

lished (Bennis, Benne, and Chin, 1961), and it remains true today.

Whenever the topic of a usable knowledge is raised—whether it arrogates too much or claims too little, whether it's the naïve technocrats selling the latest "instrument" or the naïve existentialist who feels you just have to get yourself in a good Zen mood and emote, whether it's the parlous situation described by Mikulski or the despair voiced by Freud or the "half-aloofness" advocated by Parloff, whether it's the discouraged OD (organizational development) practitioner, the hopeful theorist challenged by a theory of practice, or the skeptical CEO (chief executive officer)—I sense an obbligato of hope for a usable body of knowledge that will enhance the quality and character of our workaday lives.

This was, after all, the center of Kurt Lewin's contribution, his preoccupation with the relationship between theory and practice, between the abstract and the concrete. He once compared this task to the building of a bridge across the gorge separating theory from what he called "the full reality." He wrote, "The research worker can achieve this only if, as a result of a constant intense tension, he can keep both theory and reality fully within his field of vision" (Lewin 1948). Alfred North Whitehead (1947) commented pungently on the difficulty of braiding theory with practice. "In this modern world," he wrote, "the celibacy of the medieval learned class has been replaced by a celibacy of the intellect which is divorced from the concrete contemplation of complete facts."

This problem—How do we translate knowledge into action?—is both complex and deep, as well as chronically elusive. Perhaps this is why the question is either studiously avoided or, worse, written about in such a boring, monotonously shallow manner, uniformly ending up with bromides about "dire straits," dilemmas, and resistances of all kinds. The literature is so studded with a litany of restraints and resistances that one would wonder whether there is even a distant hope of an applied behavioral science. Whether this pessimism is due to the obvious difficulties inherent in translating knowledge into action, the unruliness of the field, or the numbing masochism of those of us employed in this pursuit, one can only speculate. What I'm impressed with is not the reality of obstacles (which is self-evident) but the challenge, excitement, and promise of a theory of practice.

Between the blur produced by saying too much at once and the banality that comes from dismissing mysteries, there remains the possibility of articulating just what it is that usable knowledge is all about. This chapter will be organized around three questions that may illuminate some of the darkness around this topic. Under question 1—"What's So?"—I will examine the present

context of applying knowledge to organizations. Question 2 is the flip side of question 1—"So What?" Here I will ask the readers to examine two short, state-of-the-art cases on the uses of knowledge to improve organizational behavior. Finally, with question 3—"Now What?"—I will attempt to bring the field somewhat closer to a theory of practice.

"WHAT'S SO?"

Lester F. Ward was one of the earliest social scientists in America to proclaim that "modern men" must extend scientific approaches into the planning of changes in their behaviors and relationships. He was well aware that we were already using our accumulating collective scientific intelligence deliberately to induce changes in the nonhuman environment. And he saw a major role for the emerging social sciences in extending a similar planning approach into the management of human affairs.

> Man's destiny is in his own hands. Any law that he can comprehend he can control. He cannot increase or diminish the powers of nature, but he can direct them. . . . His power over nature is unlimited. He can make it his servant and appropriate to his own use all the mighty forces of the universe. . . . *Human institutions are not exempt from this all-pervading spirit of improvement.* They, too, are artificial, conceived in the ingenious brain and wrought with mental skill born of inventive genius. The passion for their improvement is of a piece with the impulse to improve the plow or the steam engine. . . . Intelligence, heretofore a growth, is destined to become a manufacture. . . . The origination and distribution of knowledge can no longer be left to chance or to nature. They are to be systematized and erected into true arts. (Commager 1950, 208, 210, 213–14)

Ward's proclamation seemed foolish boasting, if not downright sacrilege, to many contemporary sociologists. William Graham Sumner wrote,

> If we can acquire a science of society based on observation of phenomena and study of forces, we may hope to gain some ground slowly toward the elimination of old errors and the reestablishment of a sound and natural social order. Whatever we gain that way will be by growth, never in the world by any reconstruction of society on the plan of some enthusiastic social architect. The latter is only repeating the old error again, and postponing all our chances of real improvement. *Society needs first of all to be free from these meddlers—that is, to be let alone* [emphasis added]. Here we are, then, once more back at the old doctrine, *laissez-faire.* Let us translate it into blunt English, and it will read: Mind

your own business. It is nothing but the doctrine of liberty. Let every man be happy in his own way. (Commager 1950, 201–2)

Current American controversies over the direction and management of social change seldom take the form of sweeping societal prescriptions and counterprescriptions or ideological debates—a form that Ward, Sumner, and their contemporaries gave to them. In large measure subsequent events have foreclosed the factual basis for Sumner's argument. *Laissez-faire* has been widely abandoned in practice, even by wide-eyed supply siders, as a principle of social management, whatever ghostly existence it yet enjoys in political platforms and pronunciamentos. Human interventions designed to shape and modify the institutionalized behaviors of people are now familiar features of our social landscape. "Helping professions" have proliferated since the era of Ward and Sumner. Professions of industrial and public management have taken shape. "Organization development" is as firmly established as social work.

All these activities aim to induce and coach changes in the behaviors and relationships of their various client populations. This focus is most apparent in new professions such as psychiatry, social work, nursing, counseling, management, and consultation in its manifold forms. But older professions, too, such as medicine, law, teaching, and the clergy, have been pressed increasingly to become agencies of social change rather than conservation. Resistances to the new role have developed, of course, along with the situational pressures that advance it.

Behavioral scientists, neo-Sumnerians among others, have been drawn, with varying degrees of eagerness and resistance, into activities of "changing," such as consultation, training, and applied research. Helping professionals, managers, and policy makers in various fields of practice increasingly employ the services of behavioral scientists to anticipate more accurately the consequences of prospective social changes and to plan for controlling these consequences. Sumner's ideological advice has been widely rejected in practice.

But it is equally true that Ward's hopes seem very far from realization today. Attempts to apply knowledge in planning and controlling organizational changes tend to be fragmented by the division of contemporary agents of change into specialized and largely noncommunicating professions. These attempts are thwarted too by noncommunication and noncollaboration among policy makers and action planners in the various institutional settings where planning has become familiar practice—industry, government, welfare, health, and education. Advocates and students of planned change have become

more cautious in their claims, less millennial in their hopes than Ward was.

Nowadays, ironically, the most exaggerated claims and counterclaims come from those who view the social sciences as some sort of aberrant techno-barbarism or as impotent nonsense. In his famous review of *The American Soldier*, Arthur Schlesinger, Jr., (1949) referred to sociologists as "fanatical in their zeal and shameless in their claims." From the radical-humanist perspective, Richard Sennett (1979) argues that "organizational scientists" have trained a generation of industrial leaders to become "therapeutic managers," benign parent substitutes who co-opt employees by controlling and creating "versions of reality" that can shift an employee's attention to "his own feelings instead of dollars and benefits he might receive." By engaging in a "lot of hocus pocus, these so-called change agents make workers feel helpless and vulnerable through the exposure of their feelings."

Among applied behavioral scientists, one can observe a parallel split between those who view OD as pernicious coercion and those who see it as meaningless stardust. David Bakan (1982), for example, argues that relations between the social sciences and the military have encouraged a "positivistic science, on the one hand, and a hierarchy-obedience-force military orientation, on the other. . . . The positivistic handicap in the social sciences keeps them from properly serving in the solution of political, social, and economic problems, thus exacerbating the world crisis and increasing the likelihood of war." Faucheux, Amado, and Laurent (1982) complain that OD engages in "fine-tuning and tinkering with the system" and inevitably gets stuck on a "human processual approach," which excludes fundamental change and simply maintains the status quo. (Here, they not only parallel Sennett's concerns, but echo them.)

On the other hand, McKelvey and Aldrich (1983) downplay the effectiveness of organizational science, which they believe fails to meet "the three criteria of the scientific method—classifiability, generalizability, and predictability."

Organizational science (or, alternatively, macro organizational behavior or organization studies) is much less visible on the applied front. The National Academy of Sciences, a body formed to offer advice to the Federal government, does not include organizational scientists. No President's council of organizational scientists exists, and organizational scientists do not frequent the halls of Congress. At UCLA, 100 teams of MBA students act as consultants to Los Angeles organizations each year and find numerous opportunities to apply their knowledge of their accounting and finance, marketing, industrial and labor relations, and operations research, but almost never find ways to apply ideas or findings from organizational science. In the 25 years since the founding of the *Administrative Science Quarterly*, Ouchi's (1981) *Theory Z* is the only book about organizational structure or form to reach the best-seller lists.[1] (McKelvey and Aldrich 1983)

Robert K. Merton observed a long time ago that popular acceptance of widely divergent views can be a sign of deep prejudice ("Jews are clannish . . . notice how they spread into Gentile communities!"). The radical difference between the McKelvey-Aldrich perspective and that of Bakan may be a case in point. One sees our science leading us to war, while the other argues that we have no science capable of leading us anywhere.

This ambivalence was well described by Kurt Lewin in 1944.

> The relation between scientific psychology and life shows a particular ambivalence. In its first steps as an experimental science, psychology was dominated by the desire of exactness. . . . Experimentation was devoted mainly to problems of sensory perception and memory, partly because they could be investigated through setups where the experimental control and precision could be secured with the accepted tools of the physical laboratory. . . .
>
> The term "applied psychology" became—correctly or incorrectly—identified with a procedure that was scientifically blind even if it happened to be of practical value. As the result, "scientific" psychology that was interested in theory tried increasingly to stay away from a too close relation to life. . . .
>
> It would be most unfortunate if the trend toward theoretical psychology were weakened by the necessity of dealing with natural groups when studying certain problems of social psychology. . . . Close cooperation between theoretical and applied psychology . . . can be accomplished . . . if the theorist does not look toward applied problems with the high brow aversion or with a fear of social problems. (Lewin 1951)

Kenneth D. Benne (1976) clarifies and elaborates this ambivalence in role terms which I find particularly useful. He draws a distinction between the cognitive worlds of behavioral scientists and of social practitioners and action leaders, arguing that effective collaboration requires recognition of epistemological differences on both sides of the social divide (see table 3.1).

Over the past two decades a substantial literature on organizational-behavior knowledge has been developing.[2] While the literature is abundant, the net findings are inconclusive. Beyer and Trice (1982) argue that one of the problems is a lack of convincing empirical data. "In the hundreds of sources we pursued, we did not find a single thorough review of the empirical literature on utilization." In their wide-ranging article, they point out that the literature on knowledge utilization has generally focused on the deficiencies of research, whereas they believe that utilization lags primarily because of the characteristics of organizations. It might be useful to reproduce a diagram that depicts their conceptualization.

By focusing on the organizational processes that facilitate or impede the utilization of organizational knowledge, Beyer and Trice manage to embrace most of the variables connected with effective utilization. But they largely overlook two other fundamentals: the quality and characteristics of the research and the nature of the relationship between researcher and client system.

Several scholars have proposed a more complete listing of factors affecting the application of promising new knowledge. H. R. Davis (1971) has argued that eight factors are necessary and sufficient to account for organizational behavior related to the use of such knowledge. They are conveniently captured in the acronym A VICTORY.

A = Ability,	The resources and capabilities of the organization to implement and subsequently evaluate the innovation; sanctions of decision-makers to adopt the innovation.
V = Values,	The degree of accord with the organization's philosophy and operating style.
I = Idea,	The adequacy of knowledge about the innovative procedure and the proposed action steps.
C = Circumstances,	Features of the organization environment relevant to successful adoption or adaptation of the innovation.

---

1. Later I will examine in some depth the effectiveness of "science" as an instrument for using knowledge; for now, I merely want to correct some errors in the McKelvey-Aldrich quote above. To begin with, the National Academy of Sciences does include a number of organizational scientists in its roster: Herbert A. Simon and James G. March are only two out of a total of ten or more (depending on how narrowly the term *organizational scientist* is defined). And there have been organizational best sellers before *Theory Z*. Peter Drucker's *Management* and Robert Townsend's *Up the Organization* are two dated examples, but on the very day this page is being written, there are at least three others: John Naisbitt's *Mega-Trends*, Peter and Waterman's *In Search of Excellence*, and Blanchard and Johnson's *The One-Minute Manager*—all with that dubious distinction.

2. Virtually the entire empirical base for all the generalizations contained in this chapter can be found in five sources: Lorsch 1979, 171–80; *Administrative Science Quarterly* 1982, 1983; Bennis, Benne, and Chin 1984; Glaser and Davis 1976; Havelock 1972; Weiss and Bucuvalas 1980.

T = Timing,

Readiness to consider the innovation; the particular combination of events at a given time that might affect the likelihood of implementation.

O = Obligation,

The felt need to change from existing modus operandi—or at least to try the proposed change.

R = Resistances,

Inhibiting factors—the organizational or individual disinclination to change, for whatever reasons.

Y = Yield,

The benefits or payoff from the innovation as perceived by potential adopters and by those who would be involved with implementation at the operating level.

Table 3.1 Cognitive worlds: behavioral scientists v. social practitioners and action leaders

The cognitive worlds of behavioral scientists	The cognitive worlds of social practitioners and action leaders
1. People and human systems which they study are not of interest as particular cases but as instances to confirm or disconfirm generalizations about people and human systems. Knowledge is organized around verbally (and/or mathematically) articulated generalizations.	1. People and human systems are clients or constituents. The social practitioner and action leader are concerned with particular cases, situations and practical difficulties in order to help, improve or change these. Knowledge is organized around kinds of cases, situations, and difficulties and takes the form of effective ways of diagnosing and handling them.
2. The occasion for inquiry is some gap or discrepancy in a theory or conceptual scheme. "Success" in inquiry is measured by attainment of more warrantable statements of variable relationships which fill the gap and/or obviate the discrepancy.	2. The occasion for inquiry is some difficulty in practice, some discrepancy between intended results and the observed consequences of actions or excessive psychic and/or financial costs of established ways of working. "Success" in inquiry is measured by attainment of ways of making and/or doing which are more effective in fitting means to ends and/or in reducing costs of operation.
3. Scientists try in the course of their researches to reduce or to eliminate the influence of extraneous values (values other than "truth" value) from the processes of collecting data and determining and stating the meaning of the data within the research context. Their knowledge is relatively independent of the uses to which it may be put.	3. Practitioners and action leaders try to find and interpret data which enable them to serve the values which they are committed to serve—"productivity," "health," "learning (growth)," and, in more political contexts, the "power," "freedom," and "welfare" of their "clients" or "constituents." Their knowledge is consciously related to use for some purpose or set of purposes.
4. Scientist set up their researches to reduce the number of variables at work in the situations they study, by controlling the effect of other variables. Experimental results take the form of statements about the relationships of abstracted and quantified variables.	4. Practitioners and action leaders (like historians and anthropologists) work in field settings where multiple and interacting variables are at work. Their understanding of situations tends to be holistic and qualitative, though they may of course use quantitative methods in arriving at their "estimate of the situation." Unlike historians and anthropologists, they do not attend to all the variables involved in the full understanding of a situation but rather to variables which are thought to be influential and accessible to their manipulation in handling the situation in the service of their chosen values.
5. Time, in the form of pressing decisions, does not influence their judgments and choices so directly as it does those of practitioners. They can reserve judgment, waiting for the accumulating weight of evidence. A longer time perspective operates in their judgments of what needs to be done now and later. Their statements of what they know are more qualified, less impregnated with their own hunches and insights as to what incomplete evidence means for purposes of action.	5. Time presses the practitioner to decide and act—judgments cannot wait. He or she must judge in order to meet deadlines, whether the evidential basis for judgment is "complete" or not. They must depend on their own hunches and insights in attributing meaning to incomplete or contradictory evidence. Their knowledge is impregnated with their own hunches and values. It is more personal, more dependent on their own ability to read a situation than the more impersonal knowledge which the scientist professes and communicates.

Table 3.2 Correspondence between components of behavior, organizational processes, specific behaviors involved in utilization processes in user systems

Components of behavior phase	Organizational processes	Specific behaviors involved in utilization processes	
		Adoption phase	Implementation
Cognitions	Information processes	Sensing, search	Diffusion
Feelings	Affective bonding	Affective reactions	Receptivity, commitment
Choice	Strategy formulation & control	Selections	Evaluation
Feedback			
Actions	Action generation	Adoption	Use, institutionalization

Note: Reprinted from "The Utilization of Process: A Conceptual Framework and Synthesis of Empirical Findings" by Janice M. Beyer and Harrison M. Trice published in *Administrative Science Quarterly* 27, no. 4 (December, 1982), by permission of *The Administrative Science Quarterly*, © by Cornell University 001-8392/2704.

Another acronymic list, CORRECT, has been proposed by Glaser and Taylor (1973). They cite seven attributes that determine how readily a research finding will be adapted. Some of these were previously identified by E. Rogers (1962).

1. *Credibility*—stemming from the soundness of evidence or from its espousal by highly respected sources.
2. *Observability*—the opportunity for potential users to actually see demonstrable evidence of the knowledge's effectiveness.
3. *Relevance*—to coping with persistent problems of major concern to influential people.
4. *Relative advantage*—least cost/high benefit compared to other options.
5. *Ease* in understanding/installation.
6. *Compatibility*—with user's values, norms, facilities, policies.
7. *Trialability*, divisibility, or reversibility—which permits less costly experiments and pilots.

Zaltman, Duncan, and Holbek (1973) offer the following list of attributes that are relevant to describing, explaining, and predicting responses to knowledge.

1. Cost.
2. Return on investment.
3. Risk and uncertainty—primarily on the part of early adopters, less on later adopters.
4. Efficiency.
5. Compatibility [same as Glaser's].

6. Communicability—ease of dissemination and clarity of results.
7. Complexity—of ideas and in actual implementation.
8. Scientific status—reliability, validity, generalizability, etc.
9. Perceived relative advantage—its visibility and demonstrability.
10. Point of origin—whether from within or without the organization.
11. Terminality—point beyond which adoption becomes less rewarding, useless, or even impossible.
12. *Status quo ante*—reversibility and divisibility.
13. Commitment—prior attitudinal or behavioral acceptance.
14. Interpersonal relationships—integrative or disruptive.
15. Publicness versus privateness—availability to all members of the system.
16. Gatekeepers—number of approval channels.
17. Susceptibility to successive modification—ability to refine, elaborate, or modify knowledge.
18. Gateway capacity—opening of avenues to other knowledge uses.
19. Gateway innovations—instrumental setting of state for large-scale innovations.

Other useful lists have also been prepared. Havelock and Lingwood (1973) proposed a ten-factor scheme, "with the acronymic name HELP SCORES, for diagnosing problems in the communication of new knowledge." Glaser prepared a table that conveniently summarizes four of the most widely used models.

Three other elements important to knowledge utili-

Table 3.3 Factors influencing the likelihood of adoption or adaptation of a seemingly promising innovation by an organization: integrated findings

H. Davis (8 factors)	E. M. Glaser (20 factors)	G. Zaltman et al. (condensation of 19 factors)	R. Havelock et al. (10 factors)
Ability to carry out the change	Capability and resources	Financial and social costs	Structuring capacity
Values or self-expectancy	Compatibility	Compatibility Publicness vs. privateness Impact on interpersonal relations	Homophily empathy
Idea of information about the qualities of the innovation	Credibility Ease in understanding and installation Observability Trialability Divisibility Reversibility	Communicability Divisibility Reversibility Complexity of concept or implementation Susceptibility to successive modifications Scientific status Point of origin Terminality	Openness
Circumstances which prevail at the time	Willingness to entertain challenge A climate of trust Structural reorganization		Proximity
Timing or readiness for consideration of the idea	Sensitivity to context factors Early involvement of potential users Suitable timing		Linkage Synergy
Obligation, or felt need to deal with a particular problem	Relevance Widespread felt need to correct undesirable conditions Shared interest in solving recognized problems	Degree of commitment	Energy
Resistance of inhibiting factors	Skill in working through resistances	Risk or uncertainty of various kinds Number of gatekeepers or approval channels	
Yield, or perceived prospect of payoff for adoption	Relative advantage An incentive system	Efficiency of innovation Perceived relative advantage Gateway to other innovations	Reward

Note: Adapted from E. M. Glaser, *Productivity Gains Through Worklife Improvement* (New York: Harcourt Brace Jovanovich, 1976), by permission.

zation deserve some discussion here: researcher/practitioner (or change-agent/client)[3] relationships; resistances to change; and stages/phases of organizational knowledge-utilization.[4]

---

3. These terms will be used interchangeably throughout this chapter.

4. Organizational change strategies would normally be included in any "thick description" of knowledge utilization, but will only be peripheral in this chapter. See Nadler elsewhere in this volume.

Research-practitioner relationships

In their recent paper, Mohrman, Cummings, and Lawler (1982), argue that "useful information cannot be produced *for* organizations, but must be generated *with* them. . . . Researchers and organizational members must become partners in the research effort. Such research should be action-oriented, jointly controlled, and involve relevant stakeholders from both researcher and user committees. Attention must be directed at the transactional contexts of the research."

Five rules of thumb suggest the kind of cooperative relationship most likely to lead to useful applications of knowledge.

1. The research focus must reflect the interests and concerns of the client system.
2. The practitioners should be involved in all phases of research.
3. The research team should include members of the client system, the more influential (within the client system), the better.
4. Frequent and honest communication between researchers and practitioners reduces the likelihood of resistance.
5. Early and continuous clarification of expectations between researcher and practitioner is essential.

Beckhard (1971), one of the most prominent organizational consultants, identifies seven key elements in the process of consultation:

1. It is necessary to establish a relationship with the several parts of the system before any effective problem solving can get under way.
2. It is important to establish a climate and procedures for feedback, both between the helper and the client system and among the parts of the client system.
3. The readiness and capacity of the client system to change need to be assessed by the consultant.
4. Since the change situation is primarily one of learning, the consultant should create conditions that favor learning.
5. Help offered should be in terms of client, not consultant, need.
6. The consultant should be able to withdraw from the relationship, if necessary, to permit independence.
7. Provision should be made for evaluation.

The crux of the researcher/practitioner (or change-agent/client) relationship is to establish a deliberate, collaborative process. Over twenty years ago in *The Planning of Change* (Bennis 1961), I wrote:

> A number of features distinguish the "deliberate and collaborative relationship": (a) a joint effort that involves mutual determination of goals; (b) a "spirit of inquiry"—a reliance on determinations based on data publicly shared; (c) an existential relationship growing out of the "here-and-now" situation; (and) a voluntary relationship between change-agent and client with either party free to terminate the relationship after joint consultation; (d) a power distribution in which the client and change-agent have equal or almost equal op-

portunities to influence the other; and (e) an emphasis on methodological rather than content learnings.

This stress on collaboration reflects important ethical considerations and even more important pragmatic considerations. The client can adopt new knowledge—knowledge at an angle to the organizational culture—only if the opposing forces in the client's situation can be reequilibrated on a new and desirable level. The change-agent needs to provide positive support and to facilitate the client's communication with itself—or, in more general terms, to make the client aware of the data necessary to diagnose the situation. Much of this information is available within the client system itself, if only the client can make it publicly available. Without *trust*, generated in and by collaboration, the change agent and client must work with limited and occasionally distorted data.

Field researchers studying natural organizations and cultures have long acknowledged their reliance on trust to counter their subject's strong resistances to yielding important data. Methodology textbooks offer rules and techniques for establishing rapport. Clients are no different from research subjects in this respect. Though in most cases they sincerely and seriously want help (want to change, want to use the knowledge constructively), powerful forces exist that tend to work against that change.[5]

The process of developing a collaborative relationship between client and change-agent may in itself provide a crucible for understanding the problems the client faces in his or her ordinary work and life environments. Many consultants, change-agents, and researchers cite problems in their evolving relationships with their clients as examples of the other relationship problems the client must deal with. To this extent, the collaborative relationship represents a microcosm of all other relationships.

In reality, it is difficult to find a purely collaborative relationship; the best to be hoped for is a commitment on the part of both the knowledge provider and the seeker to work toward building such a relationship. Although ambiguities and irregularities almost always exist, collaboration is a necessary condition for the successful use of organizational behavior knowledge, not only because it generates the necessary trust and facilitates the collection and interpretation of data, but also because the positive aspects of the relationship itself help

---

5. Like organizational researchers and change-agents, psychoanalysts have a difficult time with clients when they are eager and change-desiring; enthusiasm for the "secondary gains" may provide strong forces against fundamental change. Freud also warned against "resistance via partial incorporation," a defense so real and inviting that it often eludes well-intentioned change-agents.

overcome some of the resistance to change in the client system.

Resistance to change

In an overall analysis of factors accounting for resistance to change, Watson (1973) distinguishes between "resistance in personality" and "resistance in social structure." Personality factors include homeostasis, habit, primacy, selective perception and retention, dependence, illusion of impotence, super-ego, self-distrust, insecurity and regression, deprivation, and anxiety. Factors in social systems that contribute to the resistance of change are listed as conformity to norms, systemic and cultural coherence, the sacrosanct, rejection of "outsiders," hierarchy, affluence and leeway, restricted communication, and the nature of innovation.

Sometimes the behavior the change-agent construes as resistance may be a realistic preservation of the system's values, and not "defensive" at all. Klein (1966) reminds us that the change-agent may often define change in such ways that those who do not agree are seen as blind resisters of change. The change-agent appears to say, "We have values; the clients have psychological mechanisms." A more effective approach would be to view the occasion as an opportunity to work with the internal roles of the system, including those who defend (not "resist") the status quo, to foster mutually desirable change.

It may be useful to review some of the fundamental generalizations scholars have proposed in discussing resistance to accepting new knowledge.[6]

1. Resistance occurs when those affected by the change perceive it as threatening. It functions to protect the individual against fears and anxieties aroused by the implications of the proposed change. Almost all of the following conditions of resistance stem from this overarching factor.

2. Fear of loss of status or prestige or power—or just about any loss that will lower self-esteem—may prompt resistance. People who have benefited from an existing order or norm are unlikely to welcome a major change if they perceive that they will lose something.

3. Because any novelty may either threaten devaluation of the knowledge and skills presently required or require new knowledge seen as difficult to acquire, new knowledge may be perceived as threatening job security.

4. Resistance is aroused when proposed change challenges currently held beliefs and values. Some people cannot seem to give a fair hearing to proposals that appear to run counter to long and firmly held beliefs. Berlin (1969) points out, for example, that "learning new methods of working and especially using new models like public health concepts, are threatening to our established and already learned theoretical frameworks and practices." Since the practitioners' framework is essentially their professional value system, they are likely to protect all components with some fervor. Moreover, innovations backed by research findings may be especially threatening to professionals—especially when the theory has not itself been tested empirically (Glaser 1976).

5. Fear of loss of self-esteem or sense of competency and/or fear of exposure of weak points can arouse very strong resistance. One study in a mental-health setting, for example, reports that resistance emerged because of the researchers' failure to acknowledge directly the currently successful efforts of the client system (Poser, Dunn, and Smith 1964).

6. People resist changes they do not understand. Many investigators have found a high correlation between the unknown and high resistance. LaPier (1965) points out there is a pervasive fear of the unfamiliar among humans. "Fear of the unknown," he states, "can even override the uncertainty of acute physical pain." Repeatedly, it has been found that rejections occurred because of lack of adequate information. Sometimes it was because the knowledge (or innovation) was itself too complex.

7. In some enterprises one encounters a kind of resistance often waggishly referred to as NIH, or "Not Invented Here." Fox and Lippitt (1964), among others, found that teachers felt it would be beneath their status to borrow from others.

Perhaps the best summary of factors that affect resistance was compiled by Zaltman, Duncan, and Holbek (1973).

1. Among the possible determinants of resistance are: (a) the need for stability; (b) the use of foreign jargon; (c) impact on existing social relationships [and] personal threat; (d) local pride; (e) felt needs; and (f) economic factors.
2. Structural factors affecting resistance include: (a) stratification; (b) division of labor; and (c) hierarchical and status differentials.
3. Individual resistance factors include: (a) perception; (b) motivation; (c) attitude; (d) legitimization; (e) accompaniments of trial; (f) results of evaluation; (g) actual adoption or rejection; and (h) manner of dissonance resolution.

---

6. These generalizations are drawn primarily from the sources listed in note 2.

In attempting to reduce resistance to change, it is important to remember that most persons and client systems are in a quasi-stationary equilibrium, with some forces driving them toward change, others resisting. To reduce the resistance creates forward movement with less tension than if the change-agent tries only to override the obstacles. Advocates of new knowledge should be sensitive to the importance of the social role of the defenders who try to preserve the valuable elements of the old amid a tumult of change (Klein 1966).

Watson (1973) outlines the life cycle of resistance to an innovation and the psychological factors of individuals and groups that affect resistance.

1. Undifferentiated resistance.
2. Differentiated resistance.
3. Mobilized resistance, resulting in a "show-down."
4. Sufficient success so that only conspicuous error could remobilize the resistance, with supporters of change taking power.
5. One-time advocates of change becoming resisters of emerging change.

In her new book, *The Change Masters* Kantner (1983) remarks that "organizational theorists have produced much more work, and work of greater depth and intellectual sophistication, on the recalcitrance of organizations and their people—how and why they resist change—than on the change process." The inherent difficulty in measuring the elusive concept of change may be one important reason for this emphasis. Nevertheless, several behavioral scientists *have* attempted to outline the phases of change processes within organizational settings.

Stages in the process of knowledge utilization

Virtually all of the writing on stages and phases of organizational adoption of knowledge is fragmentary, speculative, and based on single cases. Thus the following generalizations should be regarded with a measure of skepticism.

Glaser (1976) has provided the most complete and thoughtful summary of the writings on the subject, ranging from Dewey's classic five-stage analysis of problem solving to Zaltman, Duncan, and Holbek's more recent two-stage process. Table 3.4, adapted from Glaser, summarizes the most commonly cited writings on the topic.

Despite differences in terminology, the parallels are substantial. All accounts of the change process begin with

Table 3.4   Stages of successful organizational change

Author	Date	Concern: awareness	Diagnosis: knowledge search	Consideration of alternatives	Action: implementation	Follow-through: evaluation
Lippitt et al.	1958	Need for change Get consultant	Clarification	Examination of alternatives	Actual change	Stabilize
Jenkins	1962		Analyze	Determine	Make the change	Stabilize
Jung, Lippitt	1966	Identify concern	Diagnosis	Retrieve relevant knowledge Formulate alternatives Determine feasibility (tests)	Adopt the innovation	Diffusion
Watson	1967	Sensing problem	Diagnosing	Inventing possible solutions Comparing Weighing Deciding	Implementing	Evaluating Revising
Greiner	1967	Pressures Arousal Intervention Reorientation	Diagnosis	Specific problems Invention Commitment	Experiment	Search for results Reinforcement Acceptance
Rubin	1968		Diagnosis	Alternative Selection	Strategy situation Initiate Install	Support transition link to permanent system

Note: Adapted from E. M. Glaser, *Productivity Gains Through Worklife Improvement,* by permission.

a drive or a need—a concern or a problem or some discrepancy between an ideal and reality. From there, each moves to some form of diagnosis or analysis. All theorists recognize a need for acquiring valid knowledge on the basis of the earlier diagnosis and move to an implementation state, succeeded by a "follow-up" or evaluation stage.

"SO WHAT?"

Some of the issues dividing the thinker from the doer may be illuminated by brief descriptions and appraisals of two applied social science projects. Both had multimillion-dollar budgets and commanded a great deal of attention. Aside from their monumental proportions, these projects were ambitious in design, intended to influence the policies of a large multinational firm and, in the less successful case, national and international policy.

To begin with, the national-level effort Project Camelot was an "action-research study" of "methods for predicting social change and internal war potential." Camelot was to take three to four years and to cost roughly $6 million. The research areas were regions believed to have a high potential for internal revolution; the starting point was Latin America, and future research was expected to cover several countries in Europe, Asia, and Africa. In the first of four phases it was proposed to examine existing data on internal war, and it was during this period that the project was interrupted.

The beginning of the end occurred when an invitation to many American and foreign social scientists to a four-week planning conference stated the objectives of the study and the identity of its sponsor, the U.S. Army. One scholar invited was John Galtung, a Norwegian sociologist teaching in Chile at UNESCO's Latin American Faculty of Social Science. His area of research is conflict and conflict resolution in underdeveloped countries. According to a fellow social scientist, Irving Louis Horowitz, Galtung gave the following reasons for refusing the invitation:

> He could not accept the role of the U.S. Army as a sponsoring agent in a study of counterinsurgency. He could not accept the notion of the Army as an agency of national development; he saw the Army as not managing conflict but even promoting conflict. Finally, he could not accept the asymmetry of the project—he found it difficult to understand why there would be studies of counterinsurgency in Latin American, but no studies of "counterintervention" [conditions under which Latin America nations might intervene in the affairs of the United States]. (Bennis 1970, 2)

In April 1965, shortly after the invitations were issued, Hugo Nutini, an assistant professor of anthropology at the University of Pittsburgh, made a trip to Chile on other academic business. Nutini offered to speak to his friends in the Chilean academic community about Camelot, and the Camelot authorities accepted his offer. Although it was not intended that research would be done in Chile, it was hoped that Chilean social scientists would participate. According to Chilean reports, Nutini met with Alvaro Bunster, vice chancellor of the University of Chile, and discussed the study without identifying the U.S. Army as the sponsor or making it clear which social scientists were involved in the study. At a second meeting, Nutini was confronted with a copy of the invitation that Galtung had received. He claimed that he knew nothing of the sponsorship, that he had been misinformed and would protest to Washington. At the same time, the letter was turned over to the Chilean press and to members of the Chilean Senate. The time was dramatically inopportune—shortly after the United States's intervention in the Dominican Republic.

Some American sources report a different course of events. Nutini was not given the opportunity to explain who the sponsor was nor to discuss the study. According to Camelot authorities, the "brouhaha" was Communist inspired, and Communist-dominated organizations and individuals were making a mountain out of a molehill. But while leftist newspapers played up the incident, people of all political opinions in Chile and throughout Latin America were disturbed by it.

Latin Americans were not the only ones concerned about the Pentagon's role in foreign affairs. Congress questioned the disparity in allocations that gave the Defense Department a much greater ability to fund research than the State Department had. State expressed concern that this kind of research was being done by the Defense Department and that such sponsorship might have a damaging effect on foreign affairs. And the State Department was accused in some governmental and academic circles of deliberately leaking the crisis to the press to emphasize the questions of appropriate sponsorship. Both senators and representatives who expressed themselves on the subject—and there were many—questioned the role of the military in the area of foreign affairs and social science research abroad.

For their part, academicians were concerned about the image of social science research and its future. They protested censorship and questioned the ability of the State Department to evaluate research.

Few parties were satisfied with the situation as it stood after Camelot.

In contrast, an apparent OD success story began in the mid-1950s at the Baton Rouge refinery of Exxon Corporation (then Esso), when some key members of management became favorably disposed toward sensitivity training. They felt that this experience-based learning could help to open up communication and develop trust within the organization (Rush 1973).

The company first asked behavioral scientists about the action-research method of using sensitivity training for managers. Sensitivity training (*T-groups* or *lab training* or *encounter groups* were terms used interchangeably) was then a relatively new development in the business community. A highly placed and influential corporate executive had been "through a lab" and was receptive to the idea of this activity for management development. At the same time, he specified that each operating plant's management should be free to choose whether to participate in this type of training, in keeping with Exxon's decentralization policy. After some other key executives had gone through the basic two-week sensitivity sessions—so-called "stranger groups" offered by the National Training Laboratories at Arden House in Harriman, N.Y.—they returned to their plants enthusiastic about the potential of this kind of "laboratory training" for what Exxon then called "organizational improvement."

At the Baton Rouge refinery, local management decided that sensitivity training was just what was needed to help the organization cope with changes then taking place in the operation of the refinery. Automation, union-management problems, staffing practices, and personnel reductions were causing some major problems at Baton Rouge, then the flagship refinery for the entire company. Underlying these problems was a fundamental problem of all the refineries—how to maintain a competitive-cost position. If the refinery was to retain its profitability, management believed, it would have to make changes with as little upheaval in the organization as possible.

Beginning in 1957 and continuing into the early 1960s, the refinery asked more than seven hundred supervisors, managers, and scientists to participate in what became known as a "classic, 14-day sensitivity training lab," conducted by outside, typically university-based "trainers" at a deluxe resort hotel. The alternative of sending all these managers to attend "stranger labs" would have been far more expensive, not as company-relevant, and too time-consuming, Exxon decided. To the best of my knowledge, these training sessions for teams of managers represent the first example of in-house laboratory training for management.

The company was more than satisfied with the results. It accomplished its goals: it was able to reduce its work force with no disruption (or at least fewer upsets with the union), carried out job enlargement and

enrichment programs, and cut costs, and its independent unions maintained their strength (Rush 1973, 60).

Despite that apparent success, the popularity of sensitivity training at Exxon began to fade in the early 1960s. Management believed that while it was extremely effective and had high value for the individual manager, it was not designed to accomplish work-related objectives.

The "Managerial Grid" then became Exxon's main source of organizational improvement. The Grid was first introduced at the Baytown, Texas, refinery, to improve its effectiveness and "to validate the concepts and the hypotheses of quantifiable changes in the culture of a functioning organization with multiple internal and external influences [as contrasted with a pure laboratory environment]" (Rush 1973, 61). As an action-research project with normative values, the project was followed and measured throughout (Blake et al. 1964). All told, about eight hundred managers at all levels of the management hierarchy participated in the Grid experiment. An evaluation study indicated that the organization changed in the direction posited by Grid theory. Exxon continued to use the Managerial Grid, and the program was extended to six hundred unionized workers, one of the first times that this kind of training was offered below the middle-management level.

Since the mid-1960s, no formal OD activities, such as the Grid or lab training, have been employed at Exxon, although Rush (1973), the historian of this event, reports that group process training is still used "on a selective basis . . . or in special circumstances."

Nor did Exxon extend Grid or lab training to additional facilities. A staff specialist, then an internal change-agent at Exxon, told Rush,

> "We were convinced that Grid was appropriate for the Baytown culture at that time, but since we have found we are able effectively to use other techniques of organization improvement, such as rational methods of problem solving and goal setting in a modified managing-by-objectives program" (Rush 1973, 61).

Why did Project Camelot fail while Exxon's organizational-development efforts were relatively successful? The critical factors appear to have been sponsorship, clearance, communication, and collaboration.

The Camelot project was launched by the American government, suggesting an acutely one-sided, pragmatic purpose. Almost all Latin American countries mentioned *sponsorship* as a reason for doubting the credibility of Camelot's approach. In the Exxon case, on the other hand, the decision to pursue OD was made at local plants—not in Houston or New York—with local option. At Baytown, the union too was consulted and maintained "joint ownership of the program with management."

The proposed host countries of Camelot apparently did not understand the project and its intent. Although it was claimed that these parties had been adequately informed, official assurances more often stressed that *henceforth* no such research would be done in a foreign country without its prior knowledge and consent. As Senator William Fulbright put it,

> The reason for its [Camelot's] offensiveness is obvious to anyone with an iota of common sense and it seems to me it should also have been obvious to the highly trained "scientists" at American University, as well as to the Army. At a time when U.S.–Latin American relations are complicated by our intervention in the Dominican Republic, it is not surprising that a project like Camelot should be interpreted as having some pertinence to a possible U.S. military intervention in Chile in the event of a revolution. (Bennis 1970, 3)

The failure to go to the top for *commitment*, as well as to gain the *cooperation, clearance, opinion*, and *advice* of all relevant parties to the research effort, both subjects and clients, betrays a disturbing naïveté. This naïveté cannot be explained solely by the fact that social scientists have had very little experience in applying their knowledge. The behavioral scientists working for Exxon were no better prepared and certainly no better trained than the Camelot social scientists.

In the Camelot project, foreign colleagues and field representatives were not taken into a *collaborative relationship*; they were not included in the sharing of ideas and opinions at all stages of research. In many countries, stability and dictatorship go hand in hand with oppression of the people and the absence of progressive government. Senator Fulbright and others felt that Project Camelot denied the possibility that "internal revolution" could be a change for the better, something to be promoted rather than squashed.

Lack of collaboration is always a disadvantage in a scientific undertaking; it can be fatal in one that explores sensitive areas and areas in which the researchers hope to influence their subjects. Giving help is always easier than receiving help, for the former role implies some expertise or superiority while the latter smacks of weakness or inadequacy. The psychology of giving and receiving help is beyond the scope of this chapter but clearly must be understood if U. S. foreign policy is to work or, at a less exalted level, if our knowledge is to be useful to policy makers.

The behavioral scientists working with Exxon seemed to understand the delicacy of their task and managed to use *sponsorship* (top management), *clearance, communication*, and *collaboration* in such a manner that in ten years the client system internalized (institutionalized) the capacity to make deliberate choices of its own about future training needs and developed the internal staff to implement them.

The normative goal of organizational development is to "humanize" bureaucracy.[7] Almost no one would argue against that goal, and certainly some improvements have been made, if not always in practice, then at least in theory. Such terms as *participative management, quality of work life*, and *socio-technical systems* reflect this tendency. These terms also reflect democratic values held by most social scientists with respect to their clients. But values (or normative goals) are only one consideration and perhaps not the most important. There is a pragmatic issue at stake as well. As organizations grow and diversify, they become more complex, and the problems of leadership, coordination, collaboration, and communication force themselves on our attention. Most knowledge utilization efforts have to do with maintaining the virtues of bureaucracy—its speed, precision, predictability, and efficiency—while trying to preserve an adaptability to change and a climate of creativity, personal growth, and satisfaction for the work force.

More specifically, OD efforts usually have all of the following general objectives:

1. To create an open, problem-solving climate throughout the organization.
2. To supplement the authority associated with the role or status with the authority of knowledge and competence.
3. To locate decision-making and problem-solving responsibilities as close to the information sources as possible.
4. To build trust among individuals and groups throughout the organization.
5. To make competition more relevant to work goals and to maximize collaborative efforts.
6. To develop a reward system that recognizes both the achievement of the organization's mission (profits or service) and organizational development (growth of people).
7. To increase the sense of "ownership" of organization objectives throughout the work force.
8. To help managers to manage according to relevant objectives rather than according to "past

---

7. I am using OD as an umbrella term to describe all those efforts whose general purpose is to enhance organizational functioning through the application of knowledge.

practices" or objectives that do not make sense for one's area of responsibility.

9. To increase self-control and self-direction for people within the organization.[8]

These normative goals of applied behavioral scientists can be linked to certain major concepts against which the work of OD is evaluated. The major concepts in use are organizational characteristics; culture, role, and climate; performance/effectiveness; motivation; communication; leadership/decision-making; work/health; conflict/adaptation/change; and managing the environment. As Katz, Kahn, and Adams (1982) remark,

> The study of organizations has many residences, but no single home. Its problems cut across a number of disciplines, both basic and applied, and make difficulty for the traditional separations between psychology, sociology, administrative science, public administration, social work, educational administration, and business management. . . .
> Some fields can afford the luxury of long separations between science and practice. Organizational study cannot. . . . We need models that, while less general, include relationships between variables that are identifiable and measurable in ongoing human organizations and *that specify conditions under which such organizations must operate* [emphasis added].

Paradoxically, while OD has grown phenomenally as a field of study, it has become less relevant to the specific conditions under which organizations must operate.

Spier et al. (1980) speak of an "exponential rise in the quantity of research and writing on OD," reporting a "nearly sevenfold increase in citations observed during the sixties over that observed during the fifties. . . . During the seventies there was a fourfold increase in relevant references over the number that appeared in the sixties." The authors then go on to mention "several surprises." They note that historians of OD have emphasized three roots of the field: laboratory training, action research, and survey feedback. A review of the literature discovered a spurt of OD-related laboratory-training articles in the 1960s, almost no OD-related action research articles, and, surprisingly, virtually no survey feedback articles. Spier et al. also reported a "surprisingly small" number of theoretical articles. Even in the 1970s, theory articles were ranked seventh, the lowest category. The authors were also surprised not

to find more references to sociotechnical systems and articles on the subject of conflict.

Their survey revealed that the articles of the past ten years were characterized by an emphasis on the consultation process and attempts to capitalize on the popularity of OD by relating it to many types of training, a focus on management's role in the change process, and the widespread diffusion of OD into nonbusiness organizations. I would add that the creative energies of the OD professional have been concentrated on the development of instruments and techniques that have found a profitable market, while theory development and research have been relatively neglected.

Equally ominous are the other trends reflected by the Delphi respondents in the Spier study. Their modal responses indicated a general lack of interest in "macrosystem interventions," in the development of "OD technology for dealing with economic turbulence, for the development of OD applications on non-rational ways of knowing, for further integration of OD with traditional management training, human resource developments and personnel functions, in OD as a line manager's function" (Spier et al. 1980, 18–37). There was also a good deal of disagreement as to whether OD would be responsive to problems of productivity and profits.

Increasingly, it appears, the practice of OD has become more remote from the basic institutional dilemmas that confront organizations. The major issues of the past several years have been virtually ignored by OD. Consider mergers and acquisitions as an example. In the three years from 1977 to 1979, over $100 billion went into acquisitions. I suspect that the following three years easily doubled that amount. But OD has done little to address the specific problems organizations face in implementing such new arrangements. Other hot issues would include union-management relations (note the interest in and preoccupation with the air controllers' strike, the professional football and baseball players' strike), multinational organizations and their relation to their host countries, plant closings, the growth of techno-information organizations, and the need to redesign their organizational structures. While theoretical and research papers have been written on these topics, there has been no discernible shift of OD practice to involve itself with the operational concerns.

Moreover, OD has tended to overlook some very important changes in the environment of organizations. So much has happened and so much of what we took for granted has been challenged. Since the Kennedy assassination in 1963, we have been swept down a slalom—through ghetto fires, the revolution of women and minorities, Vietnam, Watergate, corporate crimes, and all the rest. We began to learn in the late 1960s that the

---

8. I have found the work of Burke (1977, 1978), Burke and Goodstein (1980), and Mirvis and Berg (1977) especially useful in writing this section.

nation cannot solve its social problems simply by "throwing money" at them. And we realized as well that space-age technology is not a magic wand to wave away our worries. During the 1970s, we learned that there are no quick fixes, instant cures, or simple solutions to our most troubling problems: debilitating inflation, spiraling energy costs, persistent environmental hazards, political instability abroad, deep-seated social ills at home, famine, and threat of nuclear war.

H. L. Mencken once observed that "there's an easy solution to every human problem—neat, plausible, and . . . wrong." Recent years have borne out that observation, especially with respect to OD.

To be more specific, there have been dramatic changes in the context within which organizational behavior has evolved over the past two decades—the period during which OD has grown. Those responsible for governing the enterprise are spending more and more of their time managing external relations.[9] All organizations are surrounded by an increasingly active environment—one that is becoming more compelling and dominant in all kinds of decisions that affect the institution.

Leadership and decision-making have become increasingly intricate processes of multilateral brokerage, including constituencies both within and without the organization. More and more of the decisions made are public decisions; that is, they affect people who insist on being heard. Organizations will have to reckon with the growing role of media as a "fourth arm" of government available for use by the people who oppose or support a particular decision. No longer do things get done by a relatively small group of "movers and shakers." Increasing numbers of citizens and stakeholders, some only indirectly involved, are interesting themselves in every issue, and when the decision goes the wrong way, very noisily so. One colleague has described the contemporary organization as "a jungle of close decisions, openly arrived at" (Cleveland 1979).

The bigger the problem to be tackled, the more power is diffused and the more people have to be involved. Thus decisions become more and more complex, more and more specialized, affecting more and more different (sometimes conflicting) constituencies.

As more and more people have to be consulted before a decision is reached, frustration is inevitable, not only among leaders but among followers who ask, "Who's in charge here?" Leaders in turn ask, "How do you get everybody in the act and still get some action?"

The name of the game nowadays is ambiguity and surprise, and organizations have to operate under uncertain, ill-defined, and risky conditions. New competencies are needed to cope with the politicization of our institutions, by which I mean that our institutions are becoming the focus for a new kind of politics: mobilizing public opinion; working more closely with external—especially state, local, and federal agencies and legislatures—shifting constituencies and demographics; and tracking the changing character of their stakeholders.

No longer can the management of external relations be left exclusively to the public-affairs department. Top leadership and OD practitioners must be involved directly. In short, the political role of organizations must be reconceived. These trends in the organizational environment will become even more pronounced in the years ahead.

Now none of the above is new; the analysis of our society by pop sociologists and others, revved up by the ubiquitous living-room TV sets, has made the lay public all too aware of mega- and mini-trends. And, most certainly, OD practitioners are not insensitive to these sources. Indeed, a number of perceptive authors, including many of those responsible for chapters in this handbook, have made significant contributions to the interactions between the organizations and their turbulent environments. Fewer have tackled some of the issues mentioned earlier. And virtually all of the major organizational interventions stay with the mild and gentle interpersonal and human processual techniques.

Current OD practice, unfortunately, seems locked into a 1960s model, which continues to sell and, partly because of that receptive market, departs each day, more and more, from the vital functions of organizational existence. The paradox raised earlier is easily resolved: the popularity of the goods is inversely related to their significance.

"NOW WHAT?"

I have come across men of letters, who have written history without taking part in public affairs, and politicans, who have only concerned themselves with producing events without thinking of describing them. I have observed that the first are always inclined to find general causes where the others, living in the midst of disconnected daily facts, are prone to imagine that everything is attributable to particular incidents, and that the wires they pull are the same that move the world. It is to be presumed that they are both equally deceived.

—Alexis de Tocqueville[10]

9. CEOs I have interviewed reported that the biggest change in their role has been "managing external relations" (Bennis and Nanus 1985).

10. From *Democracy in America* (1835), quoted in Bennis (1973).

Knowledge n. Things you believe.

Theory n. System of ideas meant to explain something, chosen with a view to originality, controversialism, incomprehensibility, and how good it will look in print.
— From "A Fairly Concise Science Dictionary"[11]

Individuals are often pulled in psychologically opposed directions, such as love and hate for the same person, or acceptance and rejection. This ambivalence leads directly to distinctive problems: How is it that these opposed pressures persist? Why doesn't one or the other prevail? What psychic mechanisms are triggered by ambivalence? In contrast to this sort of psychological ambivalence, Tocqueville's comments on the differences between those who seek truth and those who engage in action focus on sociological ambivalence; incompatible normative expectations are incorporated in a single role of a single social status. This ambivalence is located in the social definition of roles and statuses, not in the feeling-state of one or another type of personality. Anyone who attempts to make practical application of knowledge will be afflicted by a sociological ambivalence, insofar as he or she occupies two domains—that of seeker of truth and that of applier.

Ambivalence is particularly great when we attempt to use knowledge on organizations. Unlike engineers or surgeons, who can dispense their knowledge without much human contact, those who practice OD must be deeply involved with our clients. Neutrality is impossible when profound human changes are at stake. The classical realm of science, the underpinnings of which are best expressed by the Hemholtz School of science and its robust heir, logical positivism, is at odds with the messy, unwieldy, deeply human findings of the social sciences. Natural scientists can "do" science on their subjects, but an applied behavioral science cannot subject its subjects to very much of anything. Its subjects must become co-investigators if the research is to have any meaning.

A second factor exacerbating ambivalence in applying organizational knowledge springs from the strong idealism most change agents bring to their task. Which is not to say that there aren't somewhere in the ranks a number of calloused, jaded types who ply their wares mechanistically; even those who do are not safely divided from their "other half," which clings steadfastly to Higher Ideals. George Orwell aptly described the tension between idealism and humanistic values. Malcolm (1980, 80) quotes him, saying,

> The essence of being human "is that one does not seek perfection, that one *is* willing to commit sins for

the sake of loyalty, that one does not push asceticism to the point where it makes friendly intercourse impossible, and that one is prepared in the end to be defeated and broken up by life, which is the inevitable price of fastening one's love upon other human individuals." I suspect that those of us engaged in applying knowledge to organizations are all failed saints in that our practice and ideals are all too frequently out of sync.

Finally, the change-agent's role ambivalence is deepened because there are essentially two strategies for truth gathering: in an "exoteric" mode one may generate knowledge for the public interest; "esoteric" knowledge, in contrast, is produced for one's learned colleagues. The exoteric mode springs from the direct experience of immediate, intimate relationship to the sources of data; the esoteric mode is consciously more detached, socially disengaged, and remote. Most change-agents and OD practitioners were trained esoterically but must practice exoterically. That is the major source of the ambivalence we must reckon with.

In the remainder of this chapter, I shall set forth some recommendations, first on knowledge/research and then on policy, which will not quiet the stirrings of the role ambivalence of which I speak, but may, at least mediate it.

Knowledge/research recommendations

Our society cannot delay dealing with its major social problems. We cannot consume our resources and pollute our environment and then hope to replenish and restore them. We cannot permit international relations to deteriorate to the point of resorting to nuclear weapons. Social unrest, a result of rising expectations and frustrated hopes, will eventually reach a point of no return. The social sciences will provide no easy solutions in the near future, but they are our best hope, in the long run, for understanding our problems in depth and for providing new means of lessening tensions and improving our common life.
— National Academy of Sciences (1969, 17)

There is a fable, carefully nurtured over the centuries by the basic scientists, particularly those who see basic as pure, about the relation between the scientist who acquires information and the problem solver who applies that information. The fable is that scientists acquire the knowledge, that this knowledge goes into the public domain, and that when a problem solver needs some knowledge to solve his problem, he extracts it from the public domain, uttering words of gratitude as he does so, and solves his problem. The actuality that the scientist has provided knowledge needed by the problem solver occurs in some mysterious fashion. Mysterious though the process is, it is so effective that no tampering must be allowed and, in fact, the less contact the scientist has with the problems of the problem solver, the more apt he will be to fill the public domain with knowledge of ultimately greatest import to the problem solver. This is the fable, but like all fables, it is a myth. It does not work that way at all.
— W. Garner (1972, 942)

11. Quoted by G. Storr (1983).

Western tradition going back to the Enlightenment has encouraged us to believe that the natural sciences lead to technology, which will make us all healthier and wealthier, so the social sciences, if applied, can solve our social problems. Underlying pronouncements about the need to draw on the social sciences to solve the ills of the world is usually a subtext that, as paraphrased by Weiss and Bucuvalas (1980), goes something like this:

1. Social science research produces knowledge about human institutional behavior. Knowledge has connotations of fact, truth, and replicability.
2. Action based upon knowledge is more rational than action based on experience, judgment, or intuition. Rational connotes the apt fit of means to ends, an efficient use of resources, and an increase in the predictability of outcomes.
3. Rational action by institutions will lead to good outcomes. Good means that the consequences are beneficial to society.
4. The good effects of rational action by institutions will be shared uniformly and equitably by all groups in the society.

But as Garner points out, it doesn't happen that way. We social scientists have not yet come up with eternal truths that are universally applicable. And since each advance we do make seems to uncover unsuspected complexities and new sources of variability, the quest for elegant and parsimonious laws of social behavior, on the model of the laws of physical sciences, may never be successful. Most of our speculations about knowledge utilization are based on biased hopes or hopeful biases—and the following recommendations on research are no exception.

Behavioral scientists and social practitioners are only beginning to accept the intellectual task of developing a valid framework for an applied social (or behavioral) science, but we can at least sketch out the desiderata of what can be called *valid* knowledge.

1. Seek an interdisciplinary applied social science that can take into consideration the behavior (including attitudes, feelings, etc.) of persons operating within their specific institutional environments.
2. Account for the interrelated levels (person or self, role, group, and macrosystem) within the social-change context.
3. Select those variables most appropriate to a specific local situation in terms of its values, ethics, and moralities.
4. Accept the premise that groups and organizations as units are as amenable to empirical and analytical treatment as the individual.

5. Take into account external social processes of change as well as the interpersonal aspects of the collaborative process.
6. Include propositions susceptible to empirical test, focusing on the dynamics of change.

To understand more specifically how we can move toward such a vigorous and viable applied social science, it may be helpful to consider some of the strategies of truth gathering. The following values (biases) should be taken into account in all action-research undertakings.

1. Research is a collaborative undertaking and can be enhanced by including members of the client system in the team effort.
2. The image of *organization* stems from a preference for observing process and change rather than order and continuity. Thus, it should not be disconcerting to confront contradiction and conflict.
3. The researcher's most productive stance is curiosity and dissatisfaction with current paradigms for understanding organizational life.
4. Findings should be important—not just interesting—and have demonstrable social relevance.
5. Research reports should contain a vivid description of the experience of researching. "Values" should be squarely faced in these reports. Research should report not only the findings but also the questions raised by the research.

The following list, adapted from Shulamit (1979, 11–12), contrasts the traditional methodological model of the social sciences with an applied methodology:

Traditional social science research model	An applied social science model
Rational, with emphasis on classifiability, generalizability, and predictability	A mix of rational, serendipitous, and intuitive phenomena in research and analysis
Scientific	Accurate, also artistic
Oriented to carefully defined structures	Oriented to process
Impersonal, detached, remote from phenomena	Relational, interactive
Oriented to prediction/control	Oriented to understanding
Validity/replicability	Interested in relevance of findings to users and scholarly communities
Objective	Objective and personal knowledge

Traditional social science research model	*An applied social science model*
Capable of producing laws and generalizations	Capable of producing specific explanations
Emphasis on replicable events and procedures	Emphasis on the unique, though frequently recurring, events
Capable of complete analyses	Capable of producing partial discoveries of ongoing events
Interested in addressing problems with predefined concepts, hypotheses	Interested in developing constructs stemming from direct field experience

The list is, itself, an exaggeration, but it should serve to underline a point alluded to earlier in connection with the McKelvey-Aldrich paper that, mistakenly, proposes that usable knowledge stems directly from the brow of the paradigm of the natural sciences.

Policy recommendations

With so many valid ideas missing their mark, with social science articles (written in the foreign language of the professional social scientist) mildewing in inaccessible journals, and with policy makers ignorant of or indifferent to pivotal facts, it is foolish to focus on the possible perils of closer cooperation between the realms of science and action. The ally of power is not necessarily the servant of power. For example, recently the California legislators responsible for drafting new legislation on the control and rehabilitation of drug addicts acknowledged that their opinions were largely formed by their friends, druggists, family doctors, and lobbyists. They reported being unaware of or antagonistic to the findings of the specialists who have produced a prodigious literature on this issue.

I offer six specific recommendations regarding policy issues.[12]

1. Deepen and broaden mutual understanding between scientists and policy makers. If the increasing alienation of the two cultures is to be diminished and finally obliterated, each must have an understanding of the other's system of values.

2. Develop the science of utilization. I believe that the social sciences must focus immediately on the research area of knowledge utilization; without such re-

search, all data loses some of its potential effectiveness at the pace we are acquiring new knowledge. It is a horrifying waste of human and material resources not to incorporate what is being learned into our way of life.

3. The yield of social science must be visible and useful. To exercise influence and effect, social scientists must communicate and reify their achievements in a form that the public can support. Worth is often measured by tangible product.

4. The public must vigorously support social science efforts. Before social science can yield substantial benefits on a regular basis, the public must invest in its future on a scale larger than anything we know today. Research serves many purposes beyond adding to the store of certified truth. It creates a bold, risk-taking culture. The hum of active research attracts brighter young people; it develops confidence in its various publics. The federal government is in the position to grant greater research funds than a private or public foundation or university. Yet a government that, with very little soul-searching, grants billions of dollars for work on weapons systems gives precarious millions to the social sciences—haltingly and on a year-to-year basis.

It is important to acknowledge that a good deal of progress has been made over the years with respect to federal attention to the financial needs of the social sciences, especially the applied social sciences. Starting with the National Academy of Sciences Advisory Committee on Government Programs in the Behavioral Sciences in 1969, a stream of encouraging reports has emerged from various governmental and professional association commissions.[13]

5. Social scientists must be social as well as scientific. The practice and vision of social science are predominantly Victorian, having been nourished in the great European universities of the latter half of the nineteenth century. Too often we see social scientists put their subjects through tricks, games, deceptions, tortures, to say nothing of psychological mayhem, with authoritarian detachment—as if subjects did not have intelligence, feelings, hypotheses, and expectations as well as some urges to subvert the whole experiment (Argyris 1980). There must always be understanding of the people with whom the social scientist works—especially given the methodological slant proposed above—whether they are

---

12. While the following is aimed especially at applied social scientists, the recommendations hold equal significance for other scientists who have a stake in the dissemination and use of their findings.

13. Implementation still remains wanting. Ironically, the task force and commission reports get better as the problems get worse. In any case, for the interested reader, note National Academy of Sciences report (1969), the National Science Foundation Board report (Special Commission on the Social Studies 1969), the President's Task Force on Science Policy (on which I served) (1970), and the following more recent articles: Lawler (1982), Fishman and Neigher (1982), and Tornatzky et al. (1982).

subjects or clients. There must be a strong commitment and responsibility to the idea of collaboration and mutual benefit. Without trust and commitment to the research task, the data generated are often stilted and incomplete, if not downright misleading.

The solution to this problem is not completely within the grasp of the individual social scientist. Rather, it must be the responsibility of institutions that educate Ph.D.s in the social sciences. It is astonishing that apprentice social scientists never receive any formal instruction in one of their primary tasks, teaching. It is equally shocking that they receive no systematic practice or supervision in the human side of the research enterprise. Understanding these matters is not a flash of lightning or a divine gift. It is learned the hard way, through guided experiences.

6. Social scientists must reexamine and modify their own values. They must aim for complete honesty in their research. They must not attempt to conceal the motives or the sponsor of the research, because the eventual denouement is inevitable (as we noted in Project Camelot) and can destroy the research beyond repair. Similarly, the sponsor must respect the social scientists and honestly, thoroughly, and thoughtfully consider any objections they may have, altering the plan of action if those criticisms are merited.

We tend to think of applied social scientists as experts, analysts, advisors, specialists, consultants, theoreticians (at times), designers, and sometimes merely temporary help. For the most part, the term is used to cover a myriad of relationships, many of which obscure and confuse the value that an applied social science exists to provide. At its most effective and professional level, an applied social science is profoundly important to what is occurring in the world today and is essential to fully realizing the potential that organizations represent for our lives. The context for that aspiration can be derived from the following two propositions:

1. Because they are self-referencing systems, organizations inherently lack vision with respect to themselves. The role of applied social science is essentially to provide the *possibility* that an organization can know itself.

2. Applied science can be a very important force because the management of our human institutions is one of the most significant problems facing the world today and because, at its most professional and powerful level, an applied social science exists not as a "thing to do" or as a set of tools or techniques, but as a relationship between an organization and a body of knowledge.

As we develop more advanced theoretical and methodological skills, we may become better able to empower our client organizations. The social sciences have in fact made a difference. Change does take place through the appropriate application of the social sciences and the efforts of OD. Organizations have enhanced the quality of work lives. Success stories outnumber disasters like Camelot. We do not fully understand the conditions under which changes take place, but clearly many gains have been made in applying knowledge to organizations.

Having started with the melancholy of Freud, it may be fitting to end with a quote from one of his heirs, a practicing psychoanalyst who describes the divine mysteries of patients' positive changes:

> At the end of *A Midsummer Night's Dream*, the human characters wake up and rub their eyes and aren't sure what has happened to them. They have the feeling that a great deal has occurred—that things have somehow changed for the better, but they don't know what caused the change. Analysis is like that for many patients. (Malcolm 1980, 162)

Like Puck and Oberon, applied social scientists have made things happen, even if the mechanisms are not well understood. An important goal for the future is to understand, far better than we do now, how and why these remarkable things actually happen to human beings in organizations.

REFERENCES

Administrative Science Quarterly 27, no. 4 (special issue, pt. 1, 1982).

Administrative Science Quarterly 28, no. 1 (special issue, pt. 2, 1983).

Argyris, C. 1980. *Inner Contradictions of Rigorous Research.* New York: Academic Press.

Bakan, D. 1982. "The Interface Between War and the Social Sciences," *Journal of Humanistic Psychology* 22, no. 1 (Winter): 5–18.

Beckhard, R. 1971. "Helping a Group with Planned Change." In *Social Intervention: A Behavioral Science Approach*, ed. H. A. Hornstein et al. New York: Free Press.

Benne, K. D. 1976. "Educational Field Experience as the Negotiation of Different Cognitive Worlds." In *The Planning of Change*, 3d ed., ed. W. Bennis, K. D. Benne, and R. Chin. New York: Holt, Rinehart and Winston.

Bennis, W. 1970. "The Failure and Promise of the Social Sciences." *Technology Review*. (September).

———. 1973. *The Leaning Ivory Tower*. San Francisco: Jossey-Bass, 10.

Bennis, W., K. D. Benne, and R. Chin. 1961. *The Planning of Change*. New York: Holt, Rinehart and Winston.

Bennis, W., K. D. Benne, R. Chin, and Kenneth E. Corey, eds. 1984. *The Planning of Change*. 3d ed. New York: Holt, Rinehart and Winston.

Bennis, W., and B. Nanus. 1985. *Leaders: Strategies of Taking Charge*. New York: Harper & Row.

Berlin, I. N. 1969. "Resistance to Change in Mental Health Professionals." *American Journal of Orthopsychiatry* 39:109–15.

Beyer, J. M., and H. M. Trice. 1982. "The Utilization of Process: A Conceptual Framework and Synthesis of Empirical Findings." *Administrative Science Quarterly* 27:591–622.

Blake, R. R., J. S. Mouton, L. B. Barnes, and L. E. Greiner. 1964. "Breakthrough in Organization Development." *Harvard Business Review* (December).

Burke, W. W. 1977. *Current Issues and Strategies in Organization Development*. New York: Human Sciences Press.

———. 1978. *The Cutting Edge: Current Theory and Practice in Organization Development*. San Diego, Calif.: University Associates.

Burke, W. W., and L. D. Goodstein, eds. 1980. *Trends and Issues in OD: Current Theory and Practice*. San Diego, Calif.: University Associates.

Cleveland, H. 1979. personal communication.

Commager, H. S. 1950. *The American Mind*. New Haven, Conn.: Yale University Press.

Davis, H. R. 1971. "A Checklist for Change." In *A Manual for Research Utilization*. Washington, D.C.: National Institutes for Mental Health.

Faucheux, C., G. Amado, and A. Laurent. 1982. "Organizational Development and Change." *Annual Review of Psychology* 33:343–70.

Fishman, D. B., and W. D. Neigher. 1982. "American Psychology in the Eighties." *American Psychologist* (May):533.

Fox, R. S., and R. Lippitt. 1964. "The Innovation of Classroom Mental Health Practices." In *Innovation in Education*, ed. M. B. Miles. New York: Bureau of Publications, Teachers College, Columbia University.

Freud, S. 1937. "Analysis Terminable and Interminable." Vol. 23 of *The Standard Edition of the Complete Psychological Works of S. Freud*. London: Hogarth Press.

Garner, W. 1972. "The Acquisition and Application of Knowledge." *American Psychologist* 27, no. 10:941–46.

Glaser, E. M. 1976. *Productivity Gains Through Worklife Improvement*. New York: Harcourt Brace Jovanovich.

Glaser, E. M., and H. R. Davis, eds. 1976. *Putting Knowledge to Use*. Washington, D.C.: Human Interaction Research Institute and National Institute of Mental Health.

Glaser, E. M., and S. H. Taylor. 1973. "Factors Influencing the Success of Applied Research." *American Psychologist* 28, no. 2 (February): 144.

Greiner, L. E. 1967. "Patterns of Organization Change." *Harvard Business Review* 45:119–30.

Havelock, R. G. 1972. *Knowledge Utilization and Dissemination: A Bibliography*. Ann Arbor, Mich.: University of Michigan Press.

Havelock, R. C., and D. A. Lingwood, 1973. *R & D Utilization Strategies and Functions*. Ann Arbor, Mich.: University of Michigan Press.

Jenkins, D. H. 1961. "Force Field Analysis Applied to a School Situation." In *The Planning of Change*. 1st ed., ed. W. Bennis, K. D. Benne, and R. Chin. New York: Holt, Rinehart and Winston.

Jung, C. C., and R. Lippitt. 1966. "An Orientation and Strategy for Working on Problems of Change in School Systems." Paper prepared for Cooperative Project for Educational Development, Center for Research on Utilization of Scientific Knowledge, Ann Arbor, Mich.

Kanter, R. M. 1983. *The Change Masters*. New York: Simon & Schuster.

Katz, D., R. L. Kahn, and J. S. Adams. 1982. *The Study of Organizations*. San Francisco: Jossey-Bass.

Klein, D. C. 1966. "Some Notes on the Dynamics of Resistance to Change," In *The Planning of Change*. 2d ed., ed. W. Bennis, K. D. Benne, and R. Chin. New York: Holt, Rinehart and Winston.

LaPier, R. T. 1965. "Adoption and the Adopter." In *Social Change*, ed. R. T. LaPier. New York: McGraw-Hill.

Lawler, E. E., III. 1982. "Strategies for Improving the Qualtiy of Work Life." *American Psychologist* 37, no. 5:486–93.

Lewin, K. 1948. *Resolving Social Conflicts*. New York: Harper and Bros. (Remark attributed to Lewin by his wife, Gertrud, in introduction to book.)

———. 1951. *Field Theory in Social Science*. New York: Harper, 168–69.

Lippitt, R., J. Watson, and B. Westley. 1951. *The Dynamics of Planned Change*. New York: Harcourt & Brace.

Lorsch, Jay W. 1979. "Making Behavioral Science More Useful." *Harvard Business Review* 57, no. 2:171–180.

Malcolm, J. 1982. *Psychoanalysis: The Impossible Profession*. New York: First Vintage Books.

McKelvey, B., and H. Aldrich. 1983. "Population, Natural Selection, and Applied Organizational Science." *Administrative Science Quarterly* 28, no. 1 (March): 101–28

Mirvis, P. H., and D. N. Berg, eds. 1977. *Failures in Organization Development and Change*. New York: Wiley.

Mohrman, S. A., T. G. Cummings, and E. E. Lawler. 1982. "Creating Useful Research with Organizations: Relationship and Process Issues." Paper delivered at conference held at the University of Pittsburgh, School of Business Administration, Fall.

National Academy of Sciences. 1969. *The Behavorial Science and the Federal Government*. Washington, D.C.: National Academy of Sciences.

Parloff, M. B. 1979. "Can Psychotherapy Research Guide the Policymaker?" *American Psychologist* 34:303.

Poser, E. G., I. Dunn, and R. M. Smith. 1964. "Resolving Conflicts between Clinical and Research Teams." *Mental Hospitals* 15, no. 5:278–82.

President's Task Force on Science Policy. 1970. *The Social Sciences.* Washington, D.C.: GPO.

Reinharz, S. 1979. *On Becoming a Social Scientist.* San Francisco: Jossey-Bass.

Rogers, E. R. 1962. *Diffusion of Innovations.* New York: Free Press.

Rubin, I., et al. "Initiating." In *Educational Change*, ed. R. R. Goulet. New York: Scholastic, Citation Press.

Rubin, L. J. 1968. "Installing and Innovation." In *Educational Change*, ed. R. R. Goulet. New York: Scholastic, Citation Press.

Rush, H. M. F. 1973. *Organization Development.* New York: Conference Board.

Schlesinger, A. J., Jr. 1949. "The Statistical Soldier," *Partisan Review* 16:856.

Sennett R. 1979. "The Boss's New Clothes." *The New York Review of Books* (September): 15–18.

Special Commission on the Social Sciences of the National Science Board. 1969. *Knowledge Into Action: Improving the Use of the Social Sciences.* National Science Foundation Report NSB 69-3. Washington, D.C.: GPO.

Spier, M. S., M. Sashkin, J. E. Jones, and L. K. Goodstein. "Predictions and Projections for the Decade." In *Trends and Issues in Organization Development*, ed. W. W. Burke and L. D. Goodstein, 12–37.

Storr, G. 1983. Reprinted in *World Press Review* (February): 36. (First published in *New Scientist*, 1982.)

Tornatzky, L. G., et al. 1982. "Contributions of Social Science to Innovation and Productivity." *American Psychologist* 37, no. 7:737–46.

Watson. G. 1967. "Concepts for Social Change." Washington, D.C. Cooperative Project for Educational Development by National Training Laboratories. Washington, D.C.: National Education Association.

———. 1973. "Resistance to Change." In *Innovations and Organizations*, ed. G. Zaltman, R. Duncan, and J. Holbek. New York: Wiley.

Weiss, C. H., and M. J. Bucuvalas. 1980. *Social Science and Decision-Making.* New York: Columbia University Press.

Whitehead, A. N. 1947. *Science and the Modern World.* New York: New American Library, Mentor Books.

Zaltman, G., R. Duncan, and J. Holbek. 1973. *Innovations and Organizations.* New York: Wiley.

4

Psychoanalytic theory in organizational behavior

HARRY LEVINSON

Organizational behavior encompasses the behavior of individuals, groups, and larger entities as they are interrelated in the functioning of organizations. It includes, too, the characteristic pattern of organizational actions over time, which is a reflection of the organization's knowledge, values, and goals; the kinds of people, the tactical system, and the control methods it employs; as well as the sociopolitical and economic context in which those actions occur.

People interested in organizational behavior are typically guided by one of four orientations. First, practicing managers have always dealt with organizational behavior by ad hoc, trial-and-error manipulation, or change of one or another variable. Following a more refined method, some observers describe the formation of norms, group practices, ethnic differences, and similar features and their relationship to productivity, power, and environmental circumstances. The classical Hawthorne studies exemplify this sort of descriptive sociology. A third, and perhaps the most widely practiced, orientation is the empirical-correlation: certain variables are defined and statistical measures representing them are then correlated with other measures of dependent variables and classes of behavioral outcome. Finally, there are those who believe that interpersonal, group, and organizational behavior can best be understood on the basis of a comprehensive conception of the individual person—in short, personality theory. The assumption be-

hind this last point of view is that because all behavior is that of persons, one cannot have an adequate macro theory that purports to deal with behavior unless one has an adequate micro theory.

If this assumption is valid, the motivation of individuals is crucial. It is individuals who are selected, assigned, inspired, appraised, compensated, and guided. It is among individuals that interpersonal conflicts occur and are resolved, differences are mediated, and tensions are ameliorated. Even when attempting to understand the differentiation and integration of a group, one of the important variables is its personality orientation (Lawrence and Lorsch 1967). And certainly if one is to deal with stress, an increasingly widely recognized organizational phenomenon, then one has to understand what precipitates stress for individuals (Levinson 1981a).

An understanding of individuals is crucial to the understanding of groups, although this interconnection is not always recognized in the group literature. Individuals in groups are still individuals, and though a group may demonstrate phenomena beyond those of individual persons, nevertheless that behavior is the result of the behavior of individual members of the group. What occurs in groups is not a negation of individual behavior but an addition to it, or an epiphenomenon, a product of individual behavior taken collectively. Much of the fundamental theory of groups and group functioning is drawn from individual psychology (Bion 1959; Rice 1969;

Bales 1970). Fundamental processes as described by these writers relate to recapitulations of filial and power struggles, as well as defensive, affiliative, and security maneuvers.

An understanding of the individual is crucial to understanding his or her relationship to the organization, whether it be a school, church, hospital, government agency, or business. Both individually and collectively, people unconsciously bring to organizations attitudes and expectations that are akin to those they developed toward their parents as reflected in the conception of the psychological contract (Levinson et al. 1962). Individuals unconsciously and symbolically treat organizations as recapitulations of the family structure in a given culture, and organizations in turn treat their members as if the individual were in some way bound to the group by familial ties (Levinson 1981b). Indeed, organizations encourage such affiliation, as contrasted with hiring individual contractors on a day rate. There is much talk of the organizational family; much effort to obtain commitment to organizational purpose, norms, goals, and achievement; much effort to create identification with organization leadership and its success; and indeed much gratification and pride on the part of individual employees in both the product or service and the organization's reputation and achievement.

There is indeed such a phenomenon as organizational personality. Organizations are created by dominating entrepreneurs who select people who serve their psychological needs and purposes. Those people in turn select others who "fit." As a result, organizations develop certain characteristic ways of behaving and relating both to their environments and to those who are within their fold. That there are model behaviors characteristic of organizations is evident to anyone who works with them. A group of managers from IBM is likely to behave significantly differently from a group of managers from Exxon or Sears, Roebuck. In terms of structure and tasks, organizations differ widely enough that they require different kinds of managers.

Organizations are concerned with understanding and meeting the needs of individuals as they seek to gratify those needs in their work. Needs may be conceptualized in many different ways, ranging from the simple classifications of Herzberg (1976), Maslow (1954), and McClelland (1975) to the much more elaborate conceptualizations of personality theorists.

Much of the managerial literature, particularly that having to do with leadership, is concerned with the manner in which managers and executives behave. There is widespread effort to develop effective managers and executives, and a large literature has developed on managerial styles and their effects on productivity, cohesion, morale, job satisfaction, stress, and the competitive position of the organization.

Individual behavior is also a key consideration in industrial and labor relations, where major goals include maintaining a sense of equity (Locke 1968), avoiding conflict and strikes, and understanding and coping with the defense mechanisms of people who are engaged in adversary relationships. A large part of the concern with organizational climate and morale has to do with determining which aspects of the work situation most affect people's feelings about themselves and their organization.

All of the policies and practices of any organization are intended to have a behavioral outcome. A building is designed so as to encourage people to behave in certain ways. An accounting method is intended to control people's behavior and to provide them with certain kinds of information, which in turn presumably will lead them to behave in certain ways. The manner in which an organization is financed will determine whether there are certain calendar points of intensified effort to meet financial obligations or whether people can behave in other ways because of different types of obligations to those who hold organizational debt.

All of these organizational phenomena imply the need to have a comprehensive understanding of the complexity of the individual.

MODES OF CONCEPTUALIZING BEHAVIOR

Medial psychology

One possibility is to assume that the observed behavior of the individual is determined by external forces. This sort of medial psychology (Eissler 1965) would include everything from assumptions about astrology to contemporary versions of conditioning and role theory. A key assumption is that the individual is responsive to external manipulations. In organizational behavior, this would mean rewards and punishments.

Research using a medial psychology as a base, referred to above as the correlation of measurable variables, has been the dominant mode of industrial and organizational psychology. Its major drawback is that the categories of data so manipulated have been at such a gross level that the variances within groups are larger than the variances between groups. Since the beginning of this kind of study, correlations have been small and limited. In addition, it is difficult to account for individual differences with such a frame of reference. It is even more difficult to integrate the large number of wide-ranging studies into a systematic mode of application.

Normative theories

The second set of assumptions has to do with what might be called *normative theories*. These are generalizations that apply to all populations. The work of Maslow, Herzberg, and McClelland falls into this category. Researchers following the same methods tend to get the same results. Others do not. Furthermore, it is difficult to predict individual behavior from normative conceptions: conceptualizations that fit everybody in general tend not to fit anyone in particular.

Usually, the broad, normative conception requires translation into a measurable variable—for example, from the concept of self-actualization to the inferred attribute of autonomy. The effort to extrapolate from a normative conception runs afoul of criterion problems and construct validity. Is autonomy the same as self-actualization, or even a good index of it? And what about the fact that, despite what they may say, not all people think autonomy is desirable? If self-actualization means fulfilling one's potential, then how do we deal with the fact that there are no adequate measures of potential? One cannot therefore define self-actualization by a device that has face validity or obviously represents that variable.

System theories

System theories represent a third kind of outlook. The previous two sets of assumptions are part theories because they deal with only a part of the person. All other empirical theories that presume to explain the motivation of individuals are also part theories. System theories, in contrast, are interactional theories. They seek to explain the behavior of the whole person, interacting with his or her environment, over a lifetime. System theories recognize the need for the arousal of the individual, but would include stimuli from within the person, as well as those outside the person. Moreover, between stimulus and response they would posit some mode through which the individual apperceives the stimulus, and, by doing so, gives it idiosyncratic meaning. Thus the person does not respond to the stimulus itself, but rather to his or her own interpretation of the stimulus. A system theory assumes, therefore, that the individual not only interacts with the environment, but also gives it

meaning and takes initiative with respect to it. Individuals, as self-motivating actors, adopt certain postures toward their environments and simultaneously enact the dominant themes of their own personalities, for which environments become media.

A system theory that assumes the initiative of the individual must be integrated with the rest of psychology. It requires an understanding of the levels of consciousness or awareness, of developmental psychology, and of the data of physiological and experimental psychology. It seeks to understand the whole person as the device for giving meaning and acting on that meaning. It therefore requires a comprehensive theory of personality.

The most comprehensive system theory of personality is psychoanalytic theory. Like any scientific theory, it has its strengths and limits, its holes and inconsistencies, and its supporters and detractors. Though many assert it is not amenable to empirical tests, it is supported by a large body of experimental evidence (Silverman 1976).

PSYCHOANALYTIC THEORY

Psychoanalytic theory originated with Sigmund Freud in Vienna in the 1890s. Freud was heavily influenced by Darwin, by his work with Charcot in Paris on hypnosis, and by his background in philosophy. As a neuroanatomist, he was knowledgeable about the development of the nervous system. He studied the cells of the nervous system and made original contributions to the understanding of the effects of cocaine. He was necessarily familiar with the anabolic and catabolic processes—the continuous growth and destruction that goes on in all cells and therefore in all agglomerations of cells. Physiologically, life is a matter of simultaneous growth and destruction. This perception led him to what is called the dual-drive theory.

Dual-drive

In all living organisms, if continuous physiological processes of growth and destruction goes on, dual-drive theory holds that they must have some effect on the way people feel, think, and act. There must be a parallel set of psychological processes—primitive, fundamental, sexual, and aggressive drives—which are assumed to be derived from and analogous to those physiological forces. As a Darwinian, Freud saw the sexual drive as necessary for species continuity and assumed that feelings of love and affection, sources of the constructive forces of the personality, are derived from it. The aggressive drive is the attacking component of the personality, which is necessary for mastering the environment in the interest of survival. The theory assumes that ideally the two drives are fused, with the sexual or constructive forces dominant, and channeled into everyday problem-solving activities. These include reproduction, pursuit of a career, acquisition of skills, rearing children, and, in general, the adaptive efforts of the individual. When, for various reasons, the drives do not work together, then there are difficulties. People may become inordinately self-centered or self-preoccupied, as contrasted with investing themselves in other people. The aggressive drive, untampered by the sexual drive, might be expressed in naked aggression, as in attack on other people. A surgeon cuts to save lives, a butcher cuts to sustain life, but a hoodlum waving a knife on the street threatens life. A major task of the personality is to manage these sexual and aggressive drives.

Indeed, many of the problems of living together are related to that management. Most of our laws govern the expression of sex and aggression. Most mores, folkways, and taboos deal with the same issues. The development of conscience is significantly related to the internal management of the expression of these drives.

These drives are assumed to be basic feelings, which in turn give rise to thoughts, and thence actions. Psychoanalytic theory always infers backward, from behavior to thoughts to feelings. To understand any given behavior, one poses the questions "What must a person have thought to act that way?" and behind that, "What must a person have felt to have thought that?" Psychoanalytic theory therefore gives a great deal of attention to feelings and thought processes, particularly those of which the person is not aware.

The theory assumes that the drives are the energy system of the personality. Both drives constantly press for expression. They operate without our awareness, just as we are unaware of the functioning of our lives. Psychoanalytic theory divides the personality into three components: id, super ego, and ego. The id encompasses the unconscious aspects of personality functioning— those memories, feelings, and thoughts of which we are not aware and cannot spontaneously nor voluntarily become aware. The super ego encompasses internalized values, controls, and rules of behavior—that which we ordinarily refer to as conscience. It also includes a person's idealized expectations of himself at his future best, designated as the ego ideal.

The ego ideal is an only partly conscious target toward which each of us strives. There is always a gap between the ego ideal and the self-image, the picture of oneself in the present. This gap makes for a constant internal tension as a person strives to move his or her self-image closer to the ego ideal. When a person feels he or she is approaching the ego ideal, or at least moving toward it, then there is a sense of gratification. With closer approximation there is elation. When a person feels he or she is not moving toward the ego ideal or is moving away from it, the resulting anger with self becomes depression. Depression, or anger with self, is the core of stress. Thus, the individual's greatest asset, his wish to like himself, which results in his effort to push his self-image closer to his ego ideal and therefore is the most powerful of all motivating forces, is simultaneously his greatest source of vulnerability. The higher the level of aspiration, the greater the sense of drivenness and the sense of stress. Simultaneously, stress is necessarily increased by any forces that lower the self-image or make the ego ideal unapproachably lofty. Unless either of these two conditions is present, there is no stress.

The third aspect of the personality is the ego. This concept includes the input, processing, and output aspects of the personality: the gathering of data by the five senses; the processing of those data in the form of concepts, memories, judgments, combined with previous feelings and thoughts; and the actions based on that processing. Feelings and thoughts give meaning to the information obtained. People react not to information alone, but to the meaning that they attribute to that information. Psychoanalysis, therefore, is significantly a psychology of meaning.

A major task of the ego is to channel the drives, governed by the requirements of the superego, into adaptive and problem-solving activities. Those activities that become repetitive for the person—characteristic ways of maintaining an equilibrium among the id, super ego, and ego, and of the whole personality vis-à-vis the outside world—become the dominant features of personality and are described as characterological.

Topographic

Psychoanalytic theory also conceptualizes levels of awareness or consciousness. It notes that there are aspects of ourselves of which we are not aware and cannot spontaneously become aware. These are referred to as unconscious. There are other aspects of the personality of which we can spontaneously become aware, as in remembering, recall, or in dreaming. These are referred to as preconscious. In addition then, of course, there is a conscious part of the personality: those activities of which we are aware. These three levels of awareness taken together are referred to as the topographic aspect of personality.

Developmental

Neurological development influences personality. As the brain grows, thought processes and feelings will change with the increasing capacity to think more conceptually and rationally. Dominant feelings will vary at different stages in neurological development, as evidenced by the interactions of children with others around them, especially parents or other caring figures. Given different kinds of thoughts and feelings at different points in time, children will experience the world around them, and particularly the parental figures, in different, sometimes significantly distorted, ways. Their patterns of relating to authority figures based on these early feelings will tend to become repetitive and to be apparent in their relationships with significant others. Developmental theory also conceptualizes phases in adult development and the particular adaptive efforts that characterize each phase.

Adaptive

Psychoanalytic theory also conceptualizes modes of psychological adaptation, which have to do with the formation of the personality and with maintaining its equilibrium. For example, personality is significantly formed out of the child's drive-motivated, conceptually formed feelings and thoughts leading to interaction with caring adult figures. The child, at first, emulates those figures or identifies with them. When those identifications become integrated within and are therefore a continuous component of the child, this is referred to as introjection. Another kind of adaptation is the characteristic manner of handling the sexual and aggressive drives in the form of work and play. Repression refers to the automatic process of making aspects of experience unconscious so that presumably they will be less disturbing. People also use mechanisms such as rationalization, idealization, reaction formation, and projection to cope with thoughts and feelings that might otherwise be stressful for them. To rationalize is to make up reasons for one's wish to act in certain ways. To idealize is to put a halo around others. Reaction formation refers to doing the opposite of what one feels (for example, a highly dependent person might deny those feelings by becoming counterdependent). Projection is the mechanism through

which we attribute to others our own negative feelings that we are unwilling to recognize and accept.

These six aspects of personality taken together constitute a system within which all aspects of personality can be conceptualized. The system also provides a mode for conceptualizing their interactions. Psychoanalytic theory can encompass almost all of the part theories that have attempted to explain various aspects of behavior; the reverse is not true.

CONTRIBUTIONS OF THE THEORY

The most significant contribution of psychoanalytic theory has been its elaboration of unconscious thought processes. There is a realm of feeling and thinking that is not readily examined either by the individual in whom those processes occur or by ordinary modes of inquiry. Over the last century, however, work has shown that this realm of thinking and feeling is governed by its own laws, and its regularities are understandable. That they are complex and difficult to verify is a given. But that should not deter us from trying to understand what goes on in people's heads any more than the analogous methodological problems should keep us from studying distant galaxies. Psychoanalysis as a science tries to evolve hypotheses related to those unconscious processes. Psychoanalytic theory traces the impact of earliest life experiences on the developing processes of thinking and feeling, and on characteristic modes of adaptation that human beings evolve to cope with the interaction between the individual—in a given physiological, neurological, and conceptual state—and the external environment, particularly other persons who have powerful emotional significance for the dependent child. Psychoanalytic theory seeks to understand the manner in which a person evolves his character or consistent patterns of behavior that uniquely identify the individual to himself and to others. It asserts that those patterns enable the individual to maintain psychological equilibrium in the face of conflicting demands of psychological needs, pressures from the external environment, and the requirements of his or her own system of internal governance. Psychoanalysis seeks to understand how children identify with and incorporate the models that surround them and how that attachment process, together with the processes of infantile thinking, affects the development of conscience, aspiration, values, and internal direction.

Psychoanalysis is a conflict psychology. It views the interactive process within the individual as one in which basic needs and wishes come into conflict with the governing and controlling agencies of the personality, and in turn with the external world—a process that needs to be managed and whose results are likely to be adaptive compromise. It seeks to understand the symbolic meaning given to persons, groups, organizations, and events by individuals and groups of individuals as a product of the child's earliest thought processes and relationships. It views the adult world and its activities not only in terms of their conscious manifest content, but also as a stage or social platform upon which the individual plays out unresolved unconscious conflicts from the past as he or she seeks to resolve them or obtain closure on the needs or demands represented by those conflicts. Psychoanalysis is simultaneously a treatment method, a theory of personality, and a method of research. It is with psychoanalysis as a theory of personality that I am concerned here.

DIFFERENTIATING THE THEORY

How does psychoanalysis differ from other modes of conceptualizing human motivation?

Cognitive psychology

A dominant area of contemporary psychology, cognitive psychology has to do with how one knows. Considerable research has been done on how people acquire information, how they remember it, how they organize it conceptually, how they make judgments, and what one or another perception may mean to the perceiver. However, cognitive psychology has little to say about how the perceiver *gives meaning* to his perceptions or how he determines which perceptions will be remembered and which will become unconscious. Cognitive psychology refers to goals and values, and even evolves modes of sampling those goals and values, but it rarely deals with the *origins* of those goals and values or their possible symbolic meaning.

For example, a widely quoted discussion of leadership is that of Vroom (1973). His thesis is essentially that people will seek paths to goals that are significant for them, and that career paths—paths to leadership and leadership styles—can be ascertained by questioning individuals. Clearly people do perceive manifest goals, but those manifest goals may well be in the service of unconscious goals that cannot be uncovered by questionnaire. Indeed, as has been demonstrated, when people attain certain goals, they often find themselves unsatisfying. When that occurs, obviously there have been hidden agenda. The psychoanalytic conception of ego ideal

would include the unconscious aspirations as well as those that are manifest, given greater depth and body to the concept of personal goal.

Something of the same sort might be said about the work of Deci (1971) on intrinsic motivation. Responses to questionnaires may enable us to identify needs, wishes, aspirations, and hopes but will do little to help us understand the motivations underlying those responses.

Social psychology

Social psychology focuses on group processes, the establishment and development of norms, people's wishes to be accepted into groups, group decision making, and social learning. Much contemporary work in social psychology has been devoted to participative management. Studies on quality circles and other adaptations of group decision making generally cannot explain why norms arise and why such activities fail (when they do). Barring successful trial and error, failures cannot be remedied without an adequate theory to help understand why they occur. Frequently it is because groups cannot maintain cohesion and effectiveness without leaders. Nor can group decision making be a continuously successful mode of practice in all organizations simply for reasons of time. There is a history of failure of participative management in certain cultures. And organizations with group ownership, such as plywood factories in the U.S. Northwest, have often had difficulty retaining managers. Much of social psychology is a fraternal psychology, preoccupied with peer interaction, whereas psychoanalytic psychology would put greater emphasis on understanding the meaning of the leader to the followers and the capacity of the followers to identify with that leader and thereby to establish ties to each other (Freud 1959).

Survey research is another popular area of psychology. It follows the same process of asking questions and summarizing the manifest answers. These are reported as if the manifest content in and of itself were singularly important. Sometimes, as in repetitive comparisons, it is. However, there is no way to understand the degree to which people answer in certain ways about certain problems when they are actually concerned about something else. Nor, without a theory of unconscious motivation, is there any way of reading between the lines of such responses symbolic meanings of significance to the individual or group.

Behavioristic psychology

Behavioristic orientations place a heavy emphasis on rewarding people for appropriate responses. Experience in industry indicates, however, that while the use of behavior modification incentives in plant operations may achieve initial success, it usually fails in the end. Apparently the rewards lose their significance and people no longer respond to them. Furthermore, a reward-punishment orientation of this kind assumes that somebody is manipulating the rewards, and people soon learn to manipulate back—a phenomenon I have called "The Great Jackass Fallacy" (Levinson 1973). Behavioristic orientations, applied to organizations, do not differentiate among conditions or individuals in significant ways and run the risk of quickly becoming rote. One incentive method is to ask people to set their own goals or objectives. After they have attained them, they are asked to set increasingly incremental goals. That kind of goal setting may have incentive relevance for limited periods of time. After a while it loses its motivating power, particularly when the goals themselves become superordinate goals requiring greater intensity of effort than the people are either willing or able to put out.

The principle of reinforcement is both old and fundamental. Yet it is a limited conception. What is reinforcing to one person may not be so to another. Today's reinforcement may not be effective tomorrow. And reinforcement will always occur in some kind of context. The significance of an organizational reward includes the person doing the rewarding and the conditions under which the reward is attained. Those issues of meaning are almost untouched in behavioristic theory.

PSYCHOANALYTIC CONTRIBUTIONS

What does psychoanalysis have to contribute to organizational behavior?

Selection

Psychoanalytic understanding is the basis for much of what goes on in contemporary managerial and leadership selection. An important contribution in recent years has been the work of assessment centers (Bray 1982). This method of selecting managers was developed from the early efforts of the Office of Strategic Services in World War II. The selection processes of that agency, in turn, were based on the work of Henry Murray in the Harvard Psychological Clinic (Murray 1938), significantly based on psychoanalytic theory. Murray evolved the Thematic Apperception Test, in which people made up stories about a series of pictures. These stories were scored according to how they reflected the twenty-six needs that Murray formulated from theory. The work of McClelland (1975), using three of the needs Murray formulated,

thus also derives basically from psychoanalytic theory. Because these methods have been divorced from their conceptual foundations and narrowed to measurable dimensions, their predictive ability is limited. Nevertheless, they demonstrate the power of psychoanalytic theory to serve as a base from which researchers of orientations begin. Neither Bray nor McClelland is psychoanalytically oriented, but are closer to a medial psychology, and since their work is limited in its scope, it may be said to be based on part theories.

The fundamental issues that differentiate leadership from management are exemplified in the work of Zaleznik (1975) and Maccoby (1976), and in my own work (Levinson 1981b). A crucial aspect of the differentiation has to do with the symbolic role, as well as the creative role, of the person in the leadership position. Psychoanalytic conceptions underlie the more dynamic aspects of the leadership role, namely the psychological meaning of the leader to the followers, the manner in which identification is evolved, and the significance of identification to maintaining organization cohesion, direction, and momentum.

To aid in the selection of chief executives, I have outlined the characteristics of successful leaders (Levinson 1980). These are basically drawn from psychoanalytic theory. Two diagnostic questions are derived from the dual-drive aspect of the theory: "How does this person handle aggression, the mastery component of the personality?" and "How does this person handle affection, the need for closeness or love and being loved?" It is also important to ask how a prospective CEO (chief executive officer) handles dependency, a fundamental developmental issue with which all human beings must struggle from birth to death. And finally, from the self-governing aspect of the personality, the superego, one must consider its purposive direction: "What is the nature of this person's ego ideal?" These questions serve as the basis for a comprehensive description of the candidate's characteristic behavior in multiple arenas.

For example, one may attack a marketplace vigorously, as in a marketing campaign, but be less straightforward in interpersonal contacts and perhaps even inhibited in relation to one's own children. The management of aggression is then a configuration and needs to be understood as such. And so it is with the other dimensions. When these configurations are combined into an overall pattern of behavior, then one has a sense of the multifaceted behavior of the individual.

Similarly, a job role might be described in terms of the requirements for handling aggression, affection, and dependency, and the gratification provided if the job is done well. One might then construct a behavioral job description whose complex configuration could provide a basis for fitting candidate to role. Such a system would represent a significant advance over cruder current methods.

Psychoanalytic theory also helps us understand the consistency of behavior and, therefore, the kinds of assignments to which a person may be best adapted. It underscores the problems of assigning new roles to people who must operate with their enduring patterns of individual behavior. It calls attention to the significance of stages of adult development for occupational roles and activities, and the stresses of transition.

Because of its richness, psychoanalytic theory makes it possible to take a more comprehensive approach to career guidance and career planning. The life cycle serves as the basis for thinking about not only the stages through which a person may live and the dominant psychological tasks of each stage, but also the preferred mode of behavior in each stage. By asking themselves the questions outlined in the previous section and by putting the answers together with the life-stage conception, individuals are better able to assess themselves and their own changing needs. For example, at later stages managers may become less individually competitive, more interested in developing their subordinates, more willing to seek the cooperation of colleagues and to temper the expectations of themselves they held earlier in their careers.

Managing change

Change represents a significant problem in organizations. To manage change successfully requires an understanding of object attachments, a fundamental contribution of psychoanalytic theory. Attachment and separation have received a great deal of attention in recent years from such people as Mahler (1968) and Jacobson (1971) in the United States and a range of theorists in Great Britain (Bowlby 1969, 1973, 1980; Winnicott 1958; Klein 1957). The process through which children become attached to adults and other objects and the significance of the loss of those attachments is fundamental to understanding the meaning of change as loss. Properly understood, change can be managed in a way that allows mourning to take place, thereby facilitating adaptation to new objects.

Performance appraisal

A key element in the transmission of organization culture is performance appraisal. Most performance-appraisal systems do not function adequately, as reflected in the rapidity with which those systems are changed. Dissatisfied with the system's output, management repeatedly tries to deal with its frustration by changing the forms. The major cause of failure in performance appraisal is the absence of raw data, specifically examples of behavior. I have suggested a critical-incident method of noting exceptional behavior, both positive and negative, when it occurs and providing immediate feedback (Levinson 1976). Managers are often reluctant to do this, however, because of their underlying unconscious guilt, which equates giving negative feedback with destroying the individual. These feelings of guilt are derived from unconscious fantasies, which are part of the primitive thought processes of the small child. Not understanding these feelings, people may formulate elaborate devices to try to cope with the resulting evasive behavior. These repeatedly fail. Understanding that, one can create methods for relieving the guilt, which will free performance appraisal of the psychological drag that presently makes it an exercise in futility.

Creativity

Much of the work on creativity, because it deals largely with unconscious thought processes, is enriched by psychoanalytic thinking. Picasso was heavily influenced by Freud, and a large part of the contemporary literary scene is significantly shaped by psychoanalytic thinking. With the development of psychohistory, we are learning more about the manner in which the intrapsychic conflicts of individuals are translated into their particular kinds of creativity and even leadership of religious movements and nations. Efforts to increase creativity among work groups by the use of such devices as brainstorming and synectics are based on the understanding of the need to evade one's own self-judgment and conscious control in order to allow unconscious thought processes to arise to preconscious levels and thereby to contribute to organizational innovation.

Structure and compensation

With respect to the structure of the organizations and modes of compensation, the work of Jaques (1976) is an example of the manner in which one can go from underlying assumptions of unconscious motivation to a psychologically logical organization structure with a conceptual differentiation between levels, and a compensation system that parallels that structure (all capable of empirical test). Jaques's conception of the time span of responsibility provides a stable and uniform basis of measure which is empirically verifiable (Jaques 1982). Almost all other theories of organization structure and compensation are ad hoc empirical efforts that do not systematically relate one to the other. Jaques's major simple theory is to advance.

Organizational diagnosis

Just as a physician must identify the disease before prescribing the treatment, organizational diagnosis provides a sound basis for action (Levinson 1972). This conception takes as its model the psychoanalytic conception of evolution from birth, and the multiple influences on that evolution that in turn manifest themselves in contemporary behavior. It is a framework for taking into account organizational history; organizational crises; organizational adaptive methods; organizational values; modes of transmitting, interpreting, and action on information; modes of coping with threats to the organism; and the evaluation of the organization's mastery patterns. A comprehensive diagnostic case study becomes the basis for selecting organizational interventions and for undertaking change efforts. Without a comprehensive view, such efforts are generally made either on an ad hoc basis or in response to some part diagnosis.

Questionnaire studies are frequently part of a diagnostic effort. As indicated earlier, however, most are too limited. One of the important contributions psychoanalytic theory can make to questionnaire interpretation and studies of climate, morale and attitude, is an understanding of the needs, concerns, and wishes of individuals and groups derived from inference and interpretations that consultants may make from answers to those questions.

Stress

Contemporary concern with stress has led to the evolution of many palliative efforts. Most of those elementary recipes for dealing with the manifest behavioral results of stress are a form of self-hypnosis. Understanding stress requires an understanding of what goes on within individuals and why one situation may be challenging to one person and stressful to another (Levinson 1981). None of the contemporary explanations of stress, except psychoanalytic theory, deals adequately with this problem. Most merely assert without explanation the fact of individual differences. Such conceptions do not reveal any relationship between specific organizational variables and specific individuals or groups that would prescribe managerial actions for preventing, alleviating, or ameliorating stress.

One important source of stress is the voluntary efforts of people to make mid-career changes, to separate themselves from their historical psychological anchors, and to assume new directions and new attachments. These efforts are merely described by other theories, but are significantly illuminated by psychoanalytic theory.

Theoretical base

Numerous part theories have been developed from psychoanalytic theory, as indicated above with respect to selection. In addition to those that undergird empirical studies, many part theories provide a basis for therapeutic and growth activities. These include Gestalt therapy, transactional analysis, and various other ways of trying to understand people and be helpful to them. The group-dynamics movement and its growth-group successor, the encounter movement, are based on earliest conceptions of psychoanalytic practice, namely the need to make conscious that which is unconscious by being able to speak about it. In encounter groups, confrontation with other group members compels the individual to overcome the barriers to communicating thoughts and feelings and brings to awareness psychological issues that presumably have inhibited his or her growth and development.

WHITHER THE THEORY?

Psychoanalytic theory is likely to become increasingly important in the field of organizational behavior. Managers and executives are becoming more sophisticated. The higher their level of abstraction and the greater the complexity they have to deal with in the form of economics, finance, marketing, control, and other aspects of management, the more sophisticated information they will demand about human behavior. They will not be satisfied with simple answers to complicated problems or with elementary practices like "group decision making," which do not adequately differentiate among people and groups or enable managers to deal with intragroup conflicts or to manage their own increasingly sensitive interactions. The more complex their interpersonal and organizational tasks, the more sophisticated a theory they will need.

A more complex theory of personality will also enable organizations to refine their selection processes, in turn permitting them to reassign personnel more rapidly and effectively to meet the changing needs of the environment.

Present performance appraisal and compensation systems are of little real use, as reflected in the proliferation of forms and the continuous effort people make to increase their status by manipulating points or weights assigned to aspects of their jobs. Moreover, contemporary performance-appraisal practices, especially for managers, cannot be defended in discrimination suits. As a result, organizations are under great pressure to develop more sophisticated performance-appraisal systems. The absence of behavioral information needed for coaching and counseling, for promotability, for selection, for translations into consistent patterns of behavior, for fitting individual to role—all indicate a need for a level of sophistication that can come only out of psychoanalytic theory or something even more refined.

If organizations are to facilitate individual development and provide career paths, there will be a greater need for counseling people and also for recognizing their limits. Organizations cannot choose wisely and people cannot evaluate themselves accurately without sophisticated criteria for making such choices.

Today we are increasingly aware of stress, of individual differences related to stress, of the importance of specific stress sources, and of the significance of psychophysiological or psychosomatic symptoms. At present, however, students of organizational behavior are engaged only in elementary discussion of these issues; we need to advance to a level more in keeping with the complexity of the phenomena under consideration.

The future will bring a need for more flexible adaptation and more rapid change; as a result, organizations will be less able to hold themselves together by compulsion or by money. The importance of leadership will become more and more apparent. Leaders must engage with their followers, and thus must understand their followers and understand the psychology of leadership. In addition, they need to understand themselves, their own leadership behavior, and the adaptation of that behavior to specific kinds of organizations, to specific times when certain kinds of leadership styles are appropriate, and to many specific kinds of followers with whom they are engaged.

Economic theorists have great difficulty predicting the direction of the economy and response to various kinds of economic adjustments. Their failures raise questions about the underlying assumptions economics makes about human behavior. These questions will demand more and more specific psychological answers, and because such answers hinge on human motivation, there will be a greater demand for answers that include unconscious considerations. We can expect more psychoanalytic research in this direction.

What are the limitations of psychoanalytic theory? Are there types of problems to which it does not apply?

Like any comprehensive deductive system, psychoanalytic theory has many limitations. Some of these have to do with concepts that are inexact and inferences that are difficult to test empirically. We are a long way from fathoming the human mind. Some of the theory's weaknesses have to do with the nature of the scientific model itself, built on the paradigm of late-19th- and early 20th-century science. However, contemporary developments in sociobiology have provided considerable support for the theory (Leak and Christopher 1982).

As a theory, psychoanalysis includes both concepts and content. The concepts will endure as a frame of reference for organizing content, which may well change over time. For example, some of Freud's conclusions about the psychology of women are less valid today than they were in his era. The content of thought processes and values will vary from culture to culture. Rivalry between father and son, for example, will have a different meaning in a culture like ours, which permits that rivalry to be in the open, than in a culture in which such rivalry must be tightly controlled because authority relationships within the family are highly structured. The degree to which that rivalry is open or suppressed, in turn, will have significance for how rivalry with more powerful others is handled in an organization structure.

To many practical problems of organization, psychoanalytic theory has little relevance. It will not have much to contribute to industrial engineering or engineering psychology. While psychoanalytic thinking may give substance to variables that are then included in computer models, it probably will have little influence on the mathematics of computer modeling. When managerial compensation must be manipulated to take advantage of changing tax laws, such empirical considerations are not likely to be aided by psychoanalytic thought.

Psychoanalysis has no theory of substantive learning, and thus cannot contribute significantly to formal education and training activities in organizations. That realm of employee and management development requires a different kind of psychology.

Like evolutionary biology, much of what is considered in psychoanalytic thinking is not yet amenable to empirical testing. Probably much of it never will be. Nevertheless, psychoanalytic thinking provides a conceptual framework for integrating the vast array of empirical findings in organizational behavior. Without such a framework, indeed, the application of empirical findings to organizational problems is a haphazard business. Too often "solutions" are tacked on to problems without taking into consideration the whole context, and because there are vast gaps in the empirical work done to date, the practitioner must rely heavily on intuition. While any profession will always require the application of intuition and experience, the more scientifically based that application, the better the practitioner can state his diagnosis as hypothesis and the more logically he can derive his applications, which are always then a test of that hypothesis. Psychoanalytic theory, with its potential for systematic integration of empirical findings and its comprehensive understanding of the individual, offers an opportunity both to enrich empirical research by providing new and testable hypotheses, and to bridge the work of organizational behavior researchers and theorists and organizational consultants.

REFERENCES

Bales, R. F. 1970. *Personality and Interpersonal Behavior.* New York: Holt, Rinehart and Winston.

Bion, W. R. 1959. *Experience in Groups.* New York: Basic Books.

Bowlby, J. 1969, 1973, 1980. *Attachment and Loss.* 3 vols. (1, *Attachment*; 2, *Separation*; 3, *Loss.*) New York: Basic Books.

Bray, D. W. 1982. "The Assessment Center and the Study of Lives." *American Psychologist* 37, no. 1:180–89.

Deci, E. L. 1971. "Effects of Externally Mediated Rewards on Intrinsic Motivation." *Journal of Personality and Social Psychology* 18:105–15.

Eissler, K. R. 1965. *Medical Orthodoxy and the Future of Psychoanalysis.* New York: International Universities Press.

Freud, S. 1959. "Group Psychology and the Analysis of the Ego." In *Complete Psychological Works of Sigmund Freud*, vol. 18. London: Hogarth.

Herzberg, F. 1976. *The Managerial Choice.* Homewood, Ill.: Dow Jones-Irwin.

Jacobson, E. 1971. *Depression.* New York: International Universities Press.

Jaques, E. 1976. *A General Theory of Bureaucracy.* New York: Halsted Press.

———. 1982. *The Form of Time.* New York: Crane, Russak.

Klein, M. 1957. *Envy and Gratitude.* London: Tavistock.

Lawrence, P. R., and J. W. Lorsch. 1967. *Organization and Environment: Managing Differentiation and Integration.* Boston: Division of Research, Harvard Business School.

Leak, G. A., and S. B. Christopher. 1982. "Freudian Psychoanalysis and Sociobiology." *American Psychologist* 37, no. 3.

Levinson, H. 1972. *Organizational Diagnosis.* Cambridge, Mass.: Harvard University Press.

———. 1973. *The Great Jackass Fallacy.* Cambridge, Mass.: Harvard University Press.

———. 1976. "Appraisal of *What* Performance?" *Harvard Business Review* 54, no. 4:30–48.

———. 1980. "Criteria for Choosing Chief Executives." *Harvard Business Review* 58, no. 4:113–20.

———. 1981a. "Power, Leadership, and the Management of Stress." In *Making Organizations Humane and Productive*, ed. H. Meltzer and W. R. Nord. New York: Wiley.

———. 1981b. *Executive.* Cambridge, Mass.: Harvard University Press.

Levinson, H., C. R. Price, K. J. Munden, H. J. Mandl, and C. M. Solley. 1962. *Men, Management, and Mental Health.* Cambridge, Mass.: Harvard University Press.

Locke, E. A. 1968. "Toward a Theory of Task Motivation and Incentives." *Organizational Behavior and Human Performance* 3:157–89.

Maccoby, M. 1976. *The Gamesman.* New York: Simon & Schuster.

Mahler, M. 1968. *On Human Symbiosis and the Vicissitudes of Individuation.* New York: International Universities Press.

Maslow, A. H. 1954. *Motivation and Personality.* New York: Harper & Row.

McClelland, D. C. 1975. *Power: The Inner Experience.* New York: Irvington.

Murray, H. A. 1938. *Explorations in Personality.* New York: Oxford University Press.

Rice, A. K. 1969. "Individual, Group and Intergroup Processes." *Human Relations* 22:562–84.

Silverman, L. H. 1976. "The Reports of My Death are Greatly Exaggerated: Psychoanalytic Theory." *American Psychologist* 31, no. 9:631–37.

Vroom, V. H., and P. W. Yetton. 1973. *Leadership and Decision-Making.* Pittsburgh, Pa.: University of Pittsburgh Press.

Winnicott, D. W. 1958. "Transitional Objects and Transitional Phenomena." In *Collected Papers: Through Pediatrics to Psychoanalysis*, ed. D. W. Winnicott. New York: Basic Books.

———. 1975. "Objects and Transitional Phenomena." In *Collected Papers: Through Pediatrics to Psychoanalysis*, ed. D. W. Winnicott. London: Hogarth.

Zaleznik, A., and M. F. R. Kets de Vries. 1975. *Power and the Corporate Mind.* Boston: Houghton Mifflin.

5

Cognitive psychology: an interactionist view

MICHAEL J. DRIVER

> "To think is to live."
> —Cicero

Thinking is at the core of all human endeavor, the source and bane of all activity. It is also the prime subject matter of cognitive psychology. Orginally, in the days of Wundt in Germany, all psychology was cognitive. All data were derived from introspection into thought processes. This approach reached a high peak in 1890 with the work of William James (1950).

However, a reaction set in to cognitive psychology with the rise of behaviorism. Thinking was reduced to either "motor behavior"—a sort of inner mumbling—or a purely useless epiphenomenon. What mattered was observable action, the chattering of the homunculus in the mind was of little real scientific value. This view persists to some extent in neobehavioral schools of thought, such as the behavior-modification approach, which emphasize the effect of environment on observable behavior.

Cognitive psychology never really died out however. It received major attention in the work of Freud, Jung, and the psychoanalytic school. And it has shown a remarkable revival in the United States in the last twenty years.

In experimental psychology there has been a renaissance of interest in the inner workings of the mind. Simon's ground-breaking efforts to program the thought processes of chess players and problem solvers has led to an explosion of interest in artificial intelligence. Programs

exist now that can offer psychotherapy and even medical diagnoses, based on prior analysis of the thought processes involved.

In the realm of physiological psychology we have made rapid progress in the understanding of brain function. The flow of information over sensory networks has been carefully mapped. The pursuit of the chemistry of memory is in high gear. Even the intricacies of central thought processes in the cortex are beginning to be penetrated. Electrical recording of brain potentials is proving helpful in enhancing our insight into cognitive processes.

In the area of personality, the emergence of theory and research on cognitive styles and cognitive motives is having a major impact. Cognitive styles refer to learned habits in information processing. Style models are being developed for every aspect of cognition: perception, memory, problem solving, learning, and decision making.

Cognitive motives refer to a relatively new class of motives that energize and direct thinking. They reflect a primal need of the human nervous system for patterns of varied stimulation. Their impact on thought process is so intimate that they must be included in any discussion of cognitive psychology.

The cognitive renaissance has impacted other more remote fields as well. Social psychology has abandoned its extreme behaviorist bias. We now see an emphasis on how people cognitively construct social reality. Cognitive processes such as social perception and attribution of causality are now ranked with cognitive motives, such as reducing dissonance, as central features of social psychology.

The field of organizational behavior is also beginning to connect with cognitive psychology models. In a recent discussion of organizational behavior in the 1980s, Cummings (1981) sees a strong emphasis on "internal processes of the individual" (e.g., information processing, problem defining, cognitive structuring). He then suggests that areas such as job perception, organizational structure, decision making, leadership, and performance evaluation will all show the impact of cognitive formulations in the future. Indeed a review of the literature already shows an increase in the number of articles on cognitive processes, cognitive styles and cognitive motives. This trend will not, I hope, swing too far. Clearly, human behavior is strongly influenced by powerful noncognitive forces such as basic drives. Social and physical phenomena beyond the cognitive constructs of any of us are affecting behavior whether we know it or not.

My goal here is to review the state of cognitive theory and to draw some of the implications for the future of the organizational behavior field.

ON THE FRAGMENTATION OF COGNITIVE PSYCHOLOGY

Perhaps in part because it has developed so rapidly, cognitive psychology has fragmented into a bewildering array of largely disconnected subfields. The major division seems to be into experimental, physiological and personality/style schools, which rarely, if ever, communicate. In 1967, for instance, a book called *Human Information Processing* by Schroder, Driver, and Streufert was published. Ten years later, Lindsay and Norman published a book with the same title. The first book took a style approach, the second a generalist, experimental view. It is safe to say that almost no cross-referencing between these books is possible. The situation today is hardly any better.

One reason for this fragmentation is the deep-rooted, perhaps stylistic, difference between the "two disciplines" of psychology (Cronbach 1975). The experimental group has always viewed individual difference as noise or at best as a minor source of variance. In contrast, the traditional individual difference or testing oriented psychology has tended to favor stable invariant person traits (e.g., IQ) that treat environmental forces as noise.

A trend called interactionism, which argues that behavior is a function of both environmental forces and personality factors, is slowly being recognized. Concep-

tually, this view traces back to Lewin (1935), but it has not played a central role in research. Owens and Schoenfeldt (1979) have offered one general route to a program of research integrating both factors. Some theorists (e.g., Atkinson 1981) have begun to examine both factors. But it is safe to say that psychology still remains largely divided. It is hoped that organizational behavior can avoid this counterproductive fragmentation. To assume that individual differences are trivial ignores the evidence of countless failures to replicate experimental findings when personality factors varied. Equally dangerous is the tendency to ignore powerful environmental forces in an excessive reliance on typologies.

At present organizational behavior seems more prone to the generalist experimental bias. Individual differences are often ignored or given secondary emphasis. Some assaults on the value of the individual-difference models are surfacing (White 1978). A journal reviewer of one of my more recent works (Driver 1979) queried the value of this chapter's "endless string" of individual differences in cognitive processes.

The present chapter will seek to show in some detail that both experimental and differential approaches are critical in understanding cognition and that both are vital in any application to organizations.

A third stream in cognitive psychology emerges from physiology and has some attractions for both the generalist and the difference-oriented schools. Although there is some resistance to reductionism, both camps appear to relish excursions into brain-wave analysis or the chemistry of memory. Somewhat less frequently the movement runs in the reverse direction, as physiological psychologists attempt to relate to the other camps (e.g., Boddy 1978). So far, however, the physiological approach has had very little influence on the organizational behavior literature. Hopefully, in the future, behavorial research will increasingly employ this rich mine of relevant data.

SYSTEMS THEORY: A SUBSTRATE FOR COGNITIVE THEORY

One of the factors leading to fragmentation in cognitive psychology has been the absence of a generally accepted theoretical framework. In my own work I have found general systems theory to be particularly useful. It has led to a truly interactionist view of cognition. The following summarizes my integration of systems theory.

Systems can be viewed as sets of interacting parts. A critical concern is how the parts are connected. Two extreme patterns are hierarchic and lateral systems. In

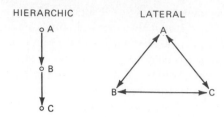

Figure 5.1 Two types of system linkage

a hierarchic system, parts are linked primarily in a one-way connection (see figure 5.1), whereas lateral systems have two-way connections. In cognitive systems, this distinction leads to very important insights into both cognitive processes (e.g, perception) and cognitive styles.

A second important issue is the system's structure: its complexity, flexibility, and permeability. Complexity has two aspects: differentiation (the number of parts in a system) and integration (the amount of connection among these parts). System complexity is a major factor in understanding cognitive structure, motives, and styles.

The second structural variable—fluidity or flexibility in connections—is linked to the type of connection in a system: hierarchic systems are less likely to be fluid than lateral systems.

Boundary permeability, the third structural variable, describes the system's interface with the environment. A permeable boundary permits easy access into the system, whereas an impermeable boundary tends to isolate the system.

From a functional perspective, systems can be said to maintain equilibrium between key inner states and external forces. They can also be seen to grow or increase in size as a result of interactions with the outside. This growth involves increases in differentiation and sometimes integration. Some believe permeability decreases with growth (e.g., Lewin 1935). As size increases, lateral systems seem to give way to hierarchic and less fluid systems.

Ashby (1964) notes a critical factor in growth: as the system's environment grows in complexity and fluidity so does the system. However, some system theorists, e.g., Simmel (Wolff 1950), see the opposite effect: as the larger system gets more complex, its parts get simpler. I believe that the apparent contradiction can be resolved as follows: when a system gets more complex in a hierarchic mode, its subsystems become simpler; a growing lateral system however must include increasing complexity and fluidity in its parts.

The systems approach can be used to posit a general personality system, as shown schematically in figure 5.2.

Each circle represents a subsystem within the total personality system. Note that subsystems overlap only partially, because only some aspects of each system are interconnected. In particular, the conscious ego is seen as affecting only parts of each of the unconscious subsystems, while unconscious thinking also only partially connects with other subsystems. This personality structure is not a purely hierarchic system; it is seen as lateral with permeable boundaries. Over time, each personality system can evolve various levels of complexity, fluidity, and permeability within and between subsystems. One extreme is a personality with apparent ego control (hierarchic) over all subsystems with no awareness of excluded areas because of an impermeable boundary around the ego. This issue will be seen again shortly when we discuss the nature of perception.

Many systems theorists (Bertalanffy 1951) believe that systems develop toward greater permeability, complexity, and fluidity. But this view also represents a generalist bias. In keeping with the interactionist position, I will suggest that *some* cognitive systems evolve as Bertalanffy and Lewin believe, whereas others develop in opposite directions reflecting both outer and inner forces.

The personality system presented here can play a vital role in any analysis of cognition as a system. Cognition is deeply affected by intake of new data. Perception is the intersection of sensory input and thinking. The memory system is the repository of all prior inputs and schemas for processing new data as well as for action on the environment. The ego is the site of reasoning and problem solving. The motor system is involved in action-related plans or "scripts," and as such is deeply involved in planning and decision making. Finally, motivation

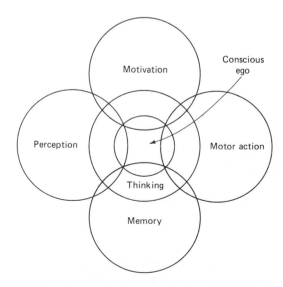

Figure 5.2 A personality-system model

plays a key role in directing and sustaining cognition, although it is clearly not a cognitive process per se.

In this chapter, I would first like to focus attention on perceptual processes, key aspects of consciousness. The most relevant personality subsystems will be the perceptual subsystem and the ego, although memory is also vital. An examination of the area of perception can, in miniature relief, shed light on how cognition is shaped by both general environmental and differential or personality forces. Then, I would like to review briefly the complex cognitive processes such as imaging, verbal thinking, problem solving, and decision making.

PERCEPTUAL PROCESSES: STIMULUS IDENTIFICATION

The perceptual subsystem identifies, evaluates, and filters stimuli coming in through the sensory nerves. The first and third of these functions can serve to illustrate cognitive processes from an interactionist perspective.

Consider the process of identification. How do we recognize a stimulus? We know that information coding in the sensory organs is highly discrete. Information is coded into the amplitude and frequency of electric currents and place location of neurons. The brain thus receives an electrical barrage bearing data on discrete features of the outside world— for example, the presence of an edge in the visual field.

As information ascends through a series of neuronal junctions, two things happen. Irrelevant noise is eliminated, and features are integrated into increasingly complex composites. For instance, at one point in the brain a complete three-dimensional replica of the body's sensory patterns—touch, heat, and so forth—is assembled (Boddy 1978). As one penetrates the sensory cortex one finds cells keyed to increasingly complex phenomena (Hubel and Wiesel 1962, 1968).

The implication might be that we have a built-in detection system capable of completely mapping the complexity of the outside world—with no editing. This model would accord with John Locke's concept of the mind as a *tabula rasa* in which almost all ideas enter from the outside.

Much current thought completely opposes this view however. For instance, the detailed features of a stimulus are not perceived first; it seems that we see global patterns first, then assign meaning to smaller detail features (Spoehr and Lehmkuhle 1982). Neisser (1963) believes that we create perceptions out of sense data and stored concepts; that before sensory data ever reach consciousness they are organized or interpreted by schema or concepts from our memory system.

Pribram (1975) suggests that this identification occurs in the subcortex. He sees a site of consciousness in a subcortical area called the geniculate nucleus, whose input is in turn edited in a second subcortical site, the visual colliculus. The visual colliculus may actually use memory templates to "feed forward" commands to the lower sensory junctions shaping incoming input to fit templates. It also receives feedback from lower systems on incoming input to determine whether the changed input now meets expectations. It is therefore a truly lateral system. Thus, preconscious expectations built by early global scanning of input can edit input to fit expectations before the input reaches central awareness. This process even fills in input not present in the sensory field at all—for example, completing a broken circle (Boddy 1978).

In sum, the weight of evidence is in favor of a *top-down* model of perception, in which central processes control input, a rather hierarchic system. Pribram's view suggests a more two-way lateral system in which input and expectations shape each other. The real question seems to be how hierarchic or lateral this process can be. We all, at times, see things that are not there. For example we may perceive a familiar, expected word and only later realize it was actually a different word. Some of the early perceptual studies of the Ames group at Princeton (Cantril 1950) showed that people could resist seeing a room distorted by a special lense. The lense made the walls of the room appear to lean back, yet people expected a normal room and that is what they saw—for a while. There were clear individual differences in how long the top-down process would prevail against "reality." Some held for a few seconds; others for very long periods. The extreme of this top-down pattern is the schizophrenic hallucination that persists on and off for years.

Clearly, the schizophrenic extreme is fatal to survival; but on the other hand, a pure bottom-up pattern is highly inefficient. Identification of input would become a very tedious, time-consuming business if no expectations were involved. Most people operate somewhere between these extremes.

The causes of this variation are both external and internal. For example, external stress increases a hierarchic top-down process. In the Ames room-perception study, students who were anticipating an exam or who had their feet in a bucket of ice water saw the "expected" room for much longer than did nonstressed persons. Enduring styles in perception also affect this process. One model suggests that people tend to learn either to repress unexpected input or to become sensitized to new input (the repressor-sensitizer style). Research has shown that repressors as measured on a test actually do block input (Carpenter, Weiner, and Carpenter 1956).

Long-term motivation may also be critical in this process. One central cognitive motive is the need for balance (i.e., certainty, structure). The stronger this need, the more we would expect top-down perception. Top-down perception may also be associated with impermeability of the boundary around the ego. An impermeable ego seeks conscious control over all phenomena and denies or blocks deviant events. An extreme of this pattern is seen in certain executives under high pressure who refuse to see reality.

The top-down issue is vitally connected to the understanding of perception and decision making in organizations. For example, strong top-down perception could play havoc with environmental scanning in strategic planning. Deviant trends in the environment would be lost. Conversely, a strongly top-down set of assumptions about a product's value can help motivate a marketing team. In practical terms, matching the degree of top-down process to tasks through selection of appropriate styles or through appropriate control over environmental forces would seem useful.

CONSCIOUSNESS, SLEEP, AND THE UNCONSCIOUS

We have noted that stimulus identification occurs in a preconscious brain site. That is, unconscious information processing goes on in the cognitive system, even when our conscious ego is in operation. Physiological research supports this idea through the analysis of specific electrical responses to given sensory inputs into the brain—called evoked potentials (EPs). The EP electrical signal comes in a series of waves. The first wave is connected with the early identification of the input. It is tied to sensory qualities. This process is called feature analysis. The early component of EP occurs whether a person is conscious or unconscious (Goff 1969).

Conscious processing takes two forms: normal and dream state. Normal consciousness is represented by a later secondary EP wave (often called the P300 wave). Its amplitude reflects the complexity of analysis of a stimulus. This wave declines as conscious awareness declines. The normal conscious perception process seems to connect an identified stimulus to a wider pool of logically related memories. It adds "context" to the bare stimulus (Boddy 1978).

The dream state represents a different mode of consciousness. It is associated with a stage of sleep known as rapid eye movement or REM. Dreams occur mainly during this REM stage, which is very much like normal consciousness (Williams, Holloway, and Griffiths 1973). During REM sleep there is intense activity in the brain and associated emotional systems. One major distinction between waking and REM consciousness is that the individual's muscle tone is very low in REM consciousness. A site in the subcortex has been found that usually blocks movement during REM sleep. From records of dreams we also know that the elaboration of stimuli in dream consciousness follows rules very different from those governing normal consciousness, as Freud noted in 1900 (1953).

This dream consciousness seems to be needed by human beings (Dement 1968). Deprivation of REM sleep causes compensatory increases in later sleep and even can increase dreamlike intrusions in normal conscious process (Boddy 1978). The exact nature of this need is controversial. One view sees evidence of basic motive (e.g., drive) satisfaction, as Freud originally argued (Dement 1968), while others see dreams as a way of organizing and analyzing particularly uncertain or frustrating inputs during the preceding day (Evans 1968). The connection of dream consciousness and creativity will be examined subsequently.

In sum, it appears that input is analyzed on three levels: a simple unconscious mode providing primary identification; a normal conscious level adding more complex detail from associations, especially in ambiguous cases; and a very different elaboration in dream consciousness. The relevance of dreaming to effective information processing in the conscious state remains a largely untapped issue. For instance, the effect of little sleep could seriously impair logic, yet enhance creativity.

ATTENTION AND COGNITIVE COMPLEXITY

A central aspect of the conscious process is attention—the focusing activity. Early models of attention posited a narrow focus, single-channel selective filter (Broadbent 1957). Stimuli would be dealt with one at a time; important ones would go into long-term memory, the others would be discarded. A separate short-term memory was suggested to hold inputs temporarily during analysis. Only some inputs then would pass the filter into long-term memory.

The existence of short-term and long-term memory systems has indeed been verified, but other aspects of the narrow focus model have been challenged. Inputs not on the "attended" channel do get complex evaluation (Treisman and Gelade 1980). Current thinking is moving toward a multichannel model of attention.

For instance, Kahneman (1973) has suggested that inputs are identified through an unconscious feature-analysis process using memory. All inputs are categorized into recognized categories. The identified inputs are then fed forward to an "allocator mechanism," which classifies input as to importance by cross-checking with the motivation system. The allocator assigns a percentage of conscious processing capacity to each input based on importance. This assumes that conscious processing is multichannel. The more channel capacity given an input, the more conscious it is. Some behavioral data does support this model; for example, people do seem to be able to do two cognitive tasks at the same time (Allport, Antonis, and Reynolds 1972) and multiple hypotheses can be employed simultaneously in concept learning (Vinacke 1974). Yet research also shows evidence for single-channel focus (Spoehr and Lehmkuhle 1982). Here again individual differences surface.

What determines channel capacity? A heuristic device for examining channel capacity in attention is to consider channel capacity an aspect of the complexity of the attention system. The more channels or information per channel, the higher the system complexity. System complexity in information processing systems has been extensively researched. There are two classes of determinant of system complexity: environment and personality.

Environmental load

One approach to the complexity of attention or channel-capacity issue centers on the idea of environmental load (Schroder, Driver, and Streufert 1967; Driver and Streufert 1965; Driver and Mock 1975). Load is defined as the rough summation of four factors.

1. Input complexity
2. Noxity—negative input
3. Eucity—positive input
4. Uncertainty

Briefly, the model suggests that the complexity of a conscious information-processing system shows a curvilinear relation to load. In line with system thinking it was suggested that as environmental complexity and fluidity (uncertainty) increased, cognitive system complexity and fluidity would also increase—up to a point. That point is where the genetic or learned limits of processing capacity are exceeded. In this condition, called overload, the cognitive system decreases in complexity as load increases. Much research supports the general pattern (see Driver 1979).

The mechanism that most likely integrates the effects of all load factors on information processing is the reticular-activation system (RAS), a subcortical mechanism that regulates the total activation of the cortical and subcortical information-processing sites. The RAS responds to emotional input (noxity, eucity) as well as to purely cognitive aspects of input, such as uncertainty or complexity (Boddy 1978). Increasing load results in higher RAS activation. The level of RAS activation seems to be closely tied to the complexity of thought processes—hence it is reasonable to assume that when load activates moderate RAS response-cognitive-system complexity, in this case attention channel capacity is at maximum; when load is more extreme, attention becomes more unidimensional. It should be noted that the connection between input load and RAS activation is clear in low to moderate input load ranges. The exact relationship between overload, RAS activation, and cognitive-system simplification is not yet clear.

While I know of no studies directly linking load to attention, other measures of cognition dependent on attention-channel capacity do reflect the predicted curvilinear pattern. Representative research on each load factor is briefly reviewed below.

INFORMATION COMPLEXITY
Information complexity can be defined in two ways.

External: the number of parts and connections in a stimulus (Solley and Snyder 1958; Vinacke 1974)

Internal: the number of cognitive-system parts (e.g., attention channels) involved in processing the stimuli (see Driver and Streufert, 1965)

Many separate research studies have shown an inverted-U-shaped relationship between information use and information complexity. Complex integration of input at first increases with input complexity then declines in overload. Simple responses to data show a different pattern of rising to a maximum asymptote and then leveling off with no overload decline (Streufert, Suedfeld, and Driver 1965; Streufert, Driver and Haun, 1967).

The above research is not explicitly tied to attention-channel capacity, but is quite suggestive. One could see a close relation between simple, undifferentiated responses to input and unichannel processing, and between complex, multidimensionally integrated responses and multichannel attention. Overload and very low load would be expected to induce simple, one-channel attention.

This effect is found by other researchers as well. For instance, very high (i.e., overload) levels of input complexity have been connected to

- error increase (Denny 1966, 1969);
- memory loss (Denny 1966, 1969);
- reducing relevancy estimates (Streufert 1973);
- chunking or grouping of stimuli (Posner 1965).

Moderate complexity has been linked to

- better learning (Noble 1952; Deese, 1965);
- increased amplitude of evoked potential and some additional EP waves (i.e., more complex processing) (Kahneman 1973);
- greater share of processing capacity in the attention mechanism (Lehman and Fender 1968).

This last finding is possibly the best evidence for the effect of input complexity on attention capacity per se.

Low input complexity has been tied to impaired thinking and motivation (Suedfeld, Glucksberg, and Vernon 1967; Suedfeld 1978). Constant repetition (very low complexity) can lead to the total loss of meaning in a stimulus (Vinacke 1974).

NOXITY, EUCITY, AND AFFECT

Noxity is defined as any input that generally induces negative affect (e.g., fear or anger). Eucity is any input that can produce positive affect (e.g., joy or excitement). Although individual differences as to what produces noxity or eucity undoubtedly exist, certain basic phenomena regularly induce noxity or eucity in most human beings (Tomkins 1962). For instance, the linkage of frustration and anger is well documented (Dollard et al. 1939).

The existence of at least two emotional systems (positive and negative) has good support, although a "general affect" model also has its backers. Of considerable importance here was the finding of specific sites for positive feelings and negative feelings in the subcortex of the brain (Olds and Milner 1954; Heath 1963). It is also possible that within positive and negative emotion domains there are specific sites for particular feelings, for example, rage, fear, elation. However, research to date suggests that all positive feelings have similar effects on cognitive-system complexity. Similarly, the varied negative emotions are quite similar in their impact on cognitive complexity.

Both emotional systems impact cognition indirectly via the RAS activation process and also directly via the emotional or somatic-arousal process. The somatic-arousal system involves the autonomic nervous system controlling heart rate, skin conductivity (GSR), breathing, and other body functions. The system also involves hormone secretion from the pituitary gland (Boddy 1978).

The effects of positive and negative emotion on thought are similar though not identical. Neither one is destructive to thought, as some cognitive theorists have believed. The research suggests an inverted-U–shaped pattern for both types of emotion in relation to cognitive complexity.

Perhaps the most relevant research on the attention-channel-capacity issue is my study of perception and noxity (Driver 1962). Noxity was measured as threat, while perception was measured via multidimensional scaling. The number of dimensions simultaneously used in perception (i.e., attention-channel capacity) first increased then decreased as threat increased.

Using a more general measure of cognitive complexity—information use—Streufert (1969); Streufert, Streufert, and Castore 1969) found that another noxity factor, namely, failure, also produced a curvilinear relation to cognitive complexity. Finally, the secondary EP wave in conscious attention shows gain in amplitude, with noxity increase similar to the gain shown for complexity increase (Kahneman 1973), suggesting increased complexity of processing.

This curvilinear model of noxity and cognitive process has found its way into other cognitive theories. For instance, Janis and Mann (1977) see high noxity as inducing such simplistic postures as avoiding negative input and decreasing information search. Conversely, moderate noxity leads to "vigilance," which is a complex mode of decision making.

The evidence on eucity is not as complete. While Streufert (1972) did find that a eucity factor—success—showed a curvilinear relationship with information use, other studies are less clear. For instance, Kahneman finds that positive input seems to decrease the secondary EP patterns (i.e., processing complexity), which is increased by all other load factors. A conclusion that eucity reduces complexity is not warranted, however, because this pattern may simply be due to the amount of eucity involved. Perhaps Kahneman studied information complexity and noxity in the range from low to moderate load, whereas eucity was in the moderate-to-high range. Moreover, other work has shown that complexity in information processing increases with the importance (i.e., positive meaning/eucity) of the situation (Glixman 1965; Glixman and Wolfe 1967).

In sum, the effect of noxity and eucity on cognitive complexity resembles that of input complexity, but eucity and noxity may differ in their curve pattern (see Schroder, Driver, and Streufert et al. 1967).

UNCERTAINTY

First, it is useful to distinguish uncertainty from complexity. Uncertainty has to do with unpredictability regardless of complexity. Logically, a very simple input can be unpredictable, while a complex input can be predictable. Research also shows that complexity and uncertainty are psychologically distinct phenomena. For instance, when a person scans a picture, areas identified with high uncertainty are quite different from areas of high complexity (Mackworth and Morandi 1967).

The effect of uncertainty on cognitive complexity is postulated to be curvilinear. High uncertainty can

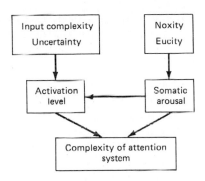

Figure 5.3 Situational forces in the complexity of the attention system

clearly simplify functions. For instance, Feldman (1981) finds that increased uncertainty can narrow one's focus. On the other side, physiological research shows that uncertainty increases the amplitude of the secondary EP, implying increased processing complexity just like complexity (Sutton et al. 1967). Thus, uncertainty increases and decreases complexity, with the direction of influence probably tied to the level of uncertainty involved. The curvilinear inference must remain conjectural, however, until research has examined the effects of a full range of uncertainty (low to high) on complexity.

Figure 5.3 summarizes the model explaining complexity in attention as developed to this point. It is a purely situational model of the experimental-school type, with no recognition of personality determinants. A more interactionist model would posit both cognitive motives and certain cognitive styles as vitally connected to the complexity of cognitive systems such as the attention process.

Personality influences on cognitive-system complexity

COGNITIVE MOTIVES

It was once believed that cognition was motivated solely by basic drives such as hunger or by emotions such as fear. It is now clear that cognition is motivated by itself. The brain appears to have powerful, unique, inborn motivation systems keyed directly to maintaining cognition.

The most general cognitive motive is termed optimal-arousal theory (Lindsley 1951; Hebb 1955). The notion is that the cognitive system using the RAS activation mechanism is set to maintain some optimal level of activation. When input falls too low to maintain optimal arousal, we seek stimulation. When the activation level is too high, we seek peace and quiet.

Other theorists (Berlyne 1960; Fiske and Maddi 1961) quickly built up a whole portfolio of specific cog-

nitive motives, such as needs for exploration, manipulation novelty, and the like. Two of these specific motives seem relevant to the attention problem. Environmental load, clearly related to cognitive complexity, includes input complexity and uncertainty. People's needs regarding these two dimensions will therefore be tied directly to cognitive structures.

The need for certainty, or balance between a person's expectations and reality, has been recognized in social psychology for some time (Heider 1946). Its best-known expression is Festinger's (1957) dissonance theory, which argued for a general tendency to seek balance between words and deeds. The organizational behavior literature abounds with assumptions that people seek certainty.

Yet researchers began to notice that some people did not avoid uncertainty. At first it was thought that uncertainty might be sought only when it would be useful (Cannon 1964). But even this rationale faded out as research confirmed the predictions by a number of theorists of a need for *uncertainty* (Fiske and Maddi 1961).

Driver and Streufert's (1965) general incongruity adaptation level (GIAL) model takes an intermediate position. This model builds on Helson's (1959) idea that concepts in the mind include adaptation levels or expectations about classes of phenomena in the environment. Thus, a concept of *apple* contains an expectation of what the average apple looks like. If input deviates from this expectation (e.g., purple apples) we are motivated to move the world and our expectations into conformity.

The general incongruity adaptation level assumes that each person builds an expectation of how much incongruity he or she will encounter. General incongruity includes uncertainty, novelty, frustration, conflict, ambiguity, and all forms of imbalance. This expectation is based on past experience. Thus, people will have high expectation of imbalance if they grow up with the uncertainty, while people growing up in placid environments will have low general incongruity adaptation levels.

For a low GIAL person, all uncertainty is unexpected and to be avoided, while a high GIAL person is motivated to avoid predictable settings and seek uncertainty, because this matches their general expectation. This model has received empirical support (Driver, Streufert, and Nataupsky 1969; Hunsaker 1975).

The variable patterns implied by the GIAL model might explain why people differ in their risk preferences (Coombs 1975). It also might suggest that high-GIAL types will seek high uncertainty, thus encountering high loads. Moderate and low GIALs will actively seek appropriate uncertainty levels, and hence loads commensurate with their expectations. All else equal, we might expect moderate-GIAL persons to seek moderate loads that would produce maximum attention channel capacity.

The second cognitive motive of interest here is complexity seeking. The dominant view is that people seek increasing complexity. As people adapt to one level of complexity they are motivated to seek a higher level. Such phenomena are found among animals (Dember, Earl, and Paradise 1957) and also seems to occur for humans (Berlyne 1957). However, this view has been challenged in several ways.

First, it seems that there is a limit to increasing preference. At the very least, the capacity of the brain limits preference. Second, it seems that too much complexity increase can overload circuits and produce a decrease in complexity preference (Hebb 1955). Moreover, it has been observed that some people have always disliked complexity (Barron 1953). Using the Helson adaptation-level model we might hypothesize that they grew up in simple settings and would resist any complexity.

Finally, it can be argued that the complexity being sought is an inner state of the brain—not just in the environment. The level of cortical activation may reflect directly the amount of system complexity inside the brain. It is this inner complexity state which is sought. External stimuli are only one source of cortical activation. The RAS also reacts to internal stimuli from memory as well as to emotional/somatic arousal. Thus, an inner state can be complex with very little apparent external environmental complexity evident.

At this point the personality variable of introversion/extroversion becomes critical. Jung (1971) developed these terms to describe the direction of energy flow in a personality. Extroverts aim energy externally; introverts focus it inward.

This model has been elaborated by Eysenck (1967) to suggest that extroverts have lower arousal levels than introverts. Therefore, extroverts need more complex external stimulation to maintain a moderate or optimal arousal. Introverts, in contrast, are very excitable, showing higher RAS levels. Therefore, they need less-complex external stimulation to maintain a moderate arousal level. Gray (1972) has further elaborated the model to suggest that introverts are more sensitive to negative emotion, while extroverts respond more to positive emotion.

Given the above, one might expect introverts to avoid complexity while extroverts seek it. Yet even this line of reasoning is not quite accurate. A final variable is needed: style in information use.

INFORMATION-USE STYLE

We have already seen earlier in the chapter an example of a cognitive style in the perceptual "repressor-sensitizer" variable. A more centrally cognitive style concerns the *amount of information used* in cognitive activities, such as concept elaboration, problem solving, or decision making.

In our initial formulation of this model (Schroder, Driver, and Streufert 1967), individuals were assumed to have learned different levels of complexity, which permit different amounts of information use. Physiological data strongly support this view. The work of Krech, Rosenzweig, and Bennett (1962) and Rosenzweig, Bennett, and Diamond (1972) paints an impressive picture of the structural effects of environmental complexity on the brain. Complex or enriched environments are found to produce more complex neuron cells, more growth inducing cells, and even more of the transmitter chemical involved in neural impulses. Not surprisingly, this enrichment leads to improved performance.

Conversely, low complexity or deprivation leads to impoverished physiological structures and performance. These environmental effects can be strongest early in life but may be continued in adulthood (Rosenzweig 1966).

Most of the work cited is based on animal studies, but data on human beings seem quite parallel. Low-input levels lead to brain atrophy in humans (Donaldson 1890); and to retarded performance (Rutter 1972). Conversely, studies of enrichment with human children show developmental gains (Brossard and Decarie 1971). These effects can be reversed in time (Kagan and Klein 1973), suggesting that structure and style can alter over a lifetime.

Thus, it is amply demonstrated that experience affects the complexity of cognitive structures and therefore the amount of information that is habitually processed.

The complexity model is not, however, a pure trait

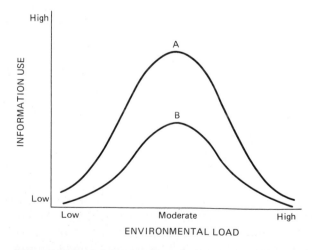

Figure 5.4 Information-use patterns as a function of environmental load

theory. We have already seen that information use varies in a curvilinear manner with environmental load. How does one reconcile this pattern with different levels of complexity in people? The answer developed by Schroder, Driver, and Streufert (1967) was to posit sets of curves of varied elevations—one for each level of complexity (see figure 5.4). Thus, a complex-style person would show a curve like A in figure 5.4, while a simple-style person would occupy curve B. Both style types show the pattern of increasing then decreasing information use as load increases. However, the complex person (A) maintains a higher information use than B in all load levels except extremes. While behavior changes with load, the pattern of behavior (or curve) is rather stable for a person. Only long-term exposure to an environment of different complexity could shift a person from one curve to another.

Extensive research has verified the existence of these curves in both laboratory settings (e.g., Driver 1962; Streufert, Suedfeld, and Driver 1965; Carlisle 1974; Driver and Mock 1975) and in field settings in organizations (e.g., Alawi 1973). The "metastability" of the curves has also been carefully analyzed (Driver 1982).

In general, the complex style might be expected to prefer more complexity than the simple style. Yet a simple linear relationship between style and preference for complexity does not exist. One must employ both style and extroversion/introversion to accurately predict complexity preference. Bryson and Driver (1972) studied complexity preference for four types of people: complex-style introverts, simple-style introverts, complex-style extroverts, and simple-style extroverts. The expectation was that complex-style introverts would not like complexity because when a simple stimulus comes in they elaborately analyze it and thereby satisfy their needs for complexity. A complex stimulus would overload them.

Simple-style introverts in contrast might seek external stimulation of moderate complexity because this could overload their circuits, producing the desired simplicity. The extrovert pattern was predicted to be simply a function of style, that is complex-style extroverts would like complexity and simple-style extroverts would not. The data clearly supported these predictions.

This analysis suggests that for extroverts moderate complexity preference would relate to maximum channel capacity. For extroverts, a moderately complex style would predict maximum channel capacity. Very complex-style extroverts might unwittingly overload themselves while simple extroverts would underload their systems. For introverts, the picture is more complicated. Complex introverts are likely to avoid moderate complexity because it could produce overload. For these people low-complexity preference relates to maximum channel

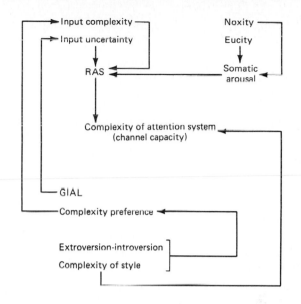

Figure 5.5 Interactionist model of attention channel complexity

capacity. For simple-style introverts, complex channel capacity seems impossible because they prefer overload.

We are now in a position to show a more complete interactionist model of attention channel capacity. In figure 5.5, note that style complexity impacts channel complexity in two ways: directly, in that complex-style people are likely to have more available channels and use them; and indirectly, by its effect on complexity preference. Other personality factors such as emotional tendencies can also affect channel capacities via noxity or eucity—but an exploration of these effects lies outside the boundaries of cognitive psychology.

The implications of this model for organizational behavior are perhaps most obvious in the area of coping with executive decision-making overload. The more we can understand what environmental and personality variables will predict multi-channel attention, the more we can help prevent excessive simplification in overloaded executive decision making. It may be a key to future success in senior management decision makers to sustain a multi-channel capacity to track multiple issues, even under stress.

LONGER-TERM COGNITIVE PROCESSES

Other cognitive processes, such as reasoning, concept learning, problem solving, and decision making could be analyzed in as much detail as the attention process. However, due to limitations of space, only a sketch of the more complex processes and some related issues will be offered.

Two modes of processing

An examination of cognitive processes must take into account the fact that the brain has two hemispheres that process data differently. Sperry (1964) found that the left side of the brain typically uses language to process information in a linear, analytic fashion. The right side, however, deals in iconic visual images. It is more holistic and nonlinear, seeing totalities.

When information is elaborated in conscious attention it is coded into two memories: visual and verbal (Boddy 1978). The two systems work parallel to one another during thought and can be traced by brain-wave patterns and even blood-flow movements to the brain. Problems requiring visual holistic processing reflect more electrical activity and blood flow to the right brain, while more analytic verbal tasks show this pattern in the left brain (see Doktor 1978; Doktor and Bloom 1977; Spydell and Sheer 1982; and Dabbs 1980).

These left-right patterns are not merely transient. People seem to have a more permanent stylistic orientation to the use of one hemisphere, which is correlated with occupation. Doktor (1978) finds that operations researchers tended to show left-brain patterns, while managers showed more right-brain tendencies. In a similar vein, Dabbs (1980) finds more left-hemisphere blood flow in engineers and more right-brain blood flow in architects.

This dichotomy based on hemispheres shows close affinities to a fairly simple cognitive-style model contrasting analytic with holistic thinking (Robey and Taggart 1981). Werner (1948) noticed that as children develop they move away from a loose syncretistic mode of thought and become more differentiated, more analytic. Kagan et al. (1964) also note increasing analytic tendencies with age.

Witkin et al. (1962) tried to connect the analytic style with independence from external (field) cues. He linked the holistic style with dependence on external cues. Measures using Witkin's techniques also show that analytic (field independent) patterns increase with age (Witkin, Goodenough, and Karp 1967). Other research generally supports the existence of a consistent style in the Witkin model. Typically, analytic-type people use more data, take more time, use computers more, like aggregated data, and even finish more tasks; whereas holistic types are more rigid in strategies, work faster, dislike computers and prefer raw data (see Lusk 1973; Doktor and Hamilton 1973; Barriff and Lusk 1977; Benbaset and

Dexter 1979; Benbaset, Dexter, and Masulis 1981; Vasarhelyi 1977).

In caution it must be said that the Witkin measures can be confounded by intelligence effects, and some research results are contradictory. On balance however, the distinction between the analytic left-brain and the holistic right-brain styles seems a powerful variable, particularly in such applications as matching people to jobs, designing information systems, and the design of work.

I would now like to look more closely at the operation of each hemisphere.

ICONIC PROCESSES

Iconic information processing involves manipulation of images. Images are mental reconstruction of actual perceptions. They have the same evoked-potential (EP) pattern as the initial stimulus (Weinberg, Walters, and Croro 1970). Subjectively, images seem fuzzier and smaller than the perceptions (Kosslyn 1980). They behave like perceptions in obeying the laws of psychophysics (Mayer and Boyer 1976).

People use images to map space up to a point, after which verbal schemas take over. For example, most people can image the United States but not North America. Therefore, Americans use a verbal schema that posits that all of Canada is north of the United States, which happens to be false (Stevens and Coupe 1978). Interestingly, some cognitive psychologists prefer to think that verbal schemas can accommodate all phenomena covered by iconic processes (Anderson 1978).

Clearly, some people do use images and are good at it. Good imagers are also good perceivers (Kosslyn 1980). They are holistic and quick rather than slow and analytic or linear in scanning visual data. The relevance of imaging processes seems particularly clear in the future design of organizational-communications systems.

VERBAL PROCESSES

Verbal or linguistic thinking is clearly not "silent motor responses" or subverbal talking (Lashley 1923). Like images, verbal concepts seem to be patterns of neuron firing, which are stored in many widely distributed sites in the cortex (Boddy 1978).

At a bare minimum, concepts are connections between two elementary words (i.e., x is y). Even the simplest word has meaning only through association with some action (see Boddy 1978). Thus we know what a concept means when we can tie it to some behavior using that concept. More elaborate associations are built up around concepts. Osgood (1957) found that concepts are typically connected to at least three basic dimensions: good-bad, strong-weak, and active-passive. Thus, most concepts have a basic word tied to some defining action and embedded in Osgood's semantic space. In addition, each person adds unique associations to each concept yielding idiosyncratic association patterns for the concept.

At a higher order, concepts are related into sets or classes by logical operation. Research is revealing interesting differences in how logic operates. For instance, propositions of inclusion (x is y) are easier to develop than comparisons (x > y) (Clarke 1969). Logical propositions also differ in their underlying complexity, that is, rules needed to process information. Hence, we can predict speed of thinking on the basis of rule complexity. For instance, a true positive proposition (x = y, true) is least complex and fastest, whereas a true negative proposition (x ≠ y, true) requires the most logical transformation and is slowest (Carpenter and Just 1975). A system-structure analysis of verbal and logical systems would seem highly promising but has yet to be assayed. As with iconic processes, better understanding of verbal/logical processes could greatly aid organizational communication. For instance, elimination of excessively complex propositions could increase communication speed.

Verbal systems of a still higher order called schemas may evolve (Anderson 1980). Schemas contain multiple dimensions, unclear boundaries, and varying weights for dimensions. Social schemas can be termed stereotypes. We also evolve scripts, which are action plans based on prior probabilities.

The highest order concepts might be concepts concerning learning or learning styles. Bateson (1975) and Argyris and Schoen (1978) note that we can evolve learning strategies that go beyond mere reaction to feedback and address changes in our mode of learning. Kolb (1976) has developed a learning-style model that suggests four possible modes:

1. *Assimilators* adapt the environment to themselves by abstract conceptualizing and reflective observation.
2. *Accommodators*, more shaped by the environment, use active experimentation and concrete experience.
3. *Convergers* use abstract conceptualizing but actively experiment in the environment.
4. *Divergers* take in concrete experience but then reflect.

Kolb finds accommodators to be linear or verbal in style, while assimilators are more holistic. Ching (1980) found the converger to be a low-information-use style. Even at the highest level of verbal concepts, styles seem to provide useful insights into processes. Hopefully, future research can explore the value of cognitive-style models at all levels of thinking.

Verbal systems usually work in conjunction with the iconic system. When they do, cognitive function is more effective. For instance, verbal learning is aided by providing visual images (Paivio 1965). An implication here is that a balanced iconic-verbal style may be more generally effective than over-emphasis on either process.

Intelligence, rationality, and higher-order cognitive process

One might expect rationality and intelligence to play a large part in higher-order cognitive processes, especially problem solving and decision making. Neither does.

Rationality is constantly violated. For instance, irrational hypotheses are often used repeatedly in concept learning (Vinacke 1974). Irrelevant data are used in decision making and logical aids to decision making are ignored (Bass 1983). Similarly, intelligence does not correlate with complex processes such as concept learning (Vinacke 1974) or problem solving (Forster, Vinacke, and Digman 1955). Its poor showing may be due to measurement problems, that is, intelligence tests are culturally biased; but a deeper issue may be more critical.

If intelligence means anything, it is the innate capacity to store and process information. Yet in day-to-day settings it seems that habitual cognitive styles predict behavior better than intelligence (Driver 1977). Absolute capacity may not often be a determining factor, while operating style is always relevant. One caveat here is that when intelligence is very low, capacity issues *are* relevant and intelligence is a useful individual difference to consider.

Generally, cognitive styles predict better than intelligence. Analysis based on style has two additional advantages:

1. Styles are learned, while aptitude is innate. Therefore, a style approach can lead to learning or development, not pigeonholing of people.
2. Styles are descriptive, while intelligence is normative. That is, low intelligence is clearly bad, whereas the value of styles is contingent. For example, an analytic style is desirable only if time is not short and data are orderly.

The implication here is that organizations relying on rationality or intelligence in managerial thinking may not be tracking the most powerful approach to human information processing.

Problem solving

Durkin (1937) outlined three common approaches to problem solving: trial and error, insight, and hypothesis testing. These strategies seem to approach being preferred styles in some people. They also show an evolution with age. Children first use trial and error, then shift to hypothesis testing only; finally they use hypothesis testing with trial and error employed when needed (Weir 1964).

Strategies in problem solving even seem to reflect national cultures. As Bertrand Russell remarked, "animals studied by Americans rush about frantically with an incredible display of bustle and pep and at last achieve the desired result by chance. Animals observed by Germans sit still and think, and at last evolve the solution out of their inner consciousness" (Hampden-Turner 1981).

One of the most elaborate studies of problem solving was developed by Bruner, Goodnow, and Austin (1956). They found four strategies:

1. Hypothesis testing—one at a time
2. Hypothesis testing—many at once
3. Focusing—incremental, one clue at a time
4. Focusing—multiple clues

Focusing seems to be an inductive mode somewhat akin to intuition. Its use increases as problems get more complex. Multiple focusing is connected with low dogmatism (or high fluidity) in cognition (Torcivia and Laughlin 1968).

In sum, it seems that the use of problem-solving strategies is determined by both situation and style. The Bruner, Goodnow, and Austin strategies are closely linked to decision style, to which I now turn.

Decision style

Decision style refers to learned habits in decision making. We have already seen one such decision-style dimension: information use. High-complexity use was contrasted with low-information-complexity use. In looking at people of complex style, Driver and Streufert (1965) noticed two patterns: one very structured; the other more fluid. This fluidity difference led to a second style dimension termed focus. High focus systems are rigid and hierarchic, with all elements ultimately tying into a controlling value, goal, solution, or decision. Conversely, low focus systems have fluid lateral connections, which means relativistic values, plural goals, multiple solutions, and multioption decisions.

Considering both focus and information use, one can define four basic decision styles, as seen in figure 5.6.

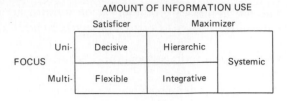

Figure 5.6 Basic decision styles

Each style has a characteristic information processing pattern easily seen in problem solving or decision making.

For instance, the decisive style uses relatively little data to reach a firm conclusion. In the Bruner, Goodnow, and Austin typology, a decisive person might use one-at-a-time hypothesis testing and give up only very reluctantly. The flexible style uses little data to arrive at a tentative solution which can change as the environment changes. In the Bruner, Goodnow, and Austin scheme this pattern could relate to the focusing or inductive pattern—one clue at a time. The hierarchic style uses large amounts of data and rigorously derives a complex, multiple-contingency plan. People of this type clearly fit the multiple-hypothesis-testing mode. Finally, the integrative style uses a great deal of data to simultaneously follow multiple options, which are open to constant change. The affinity of the integrative style to the multiple focusing strategy should be clear.

The decision-style model includes one additional style—systemic—which begins as an integrative style generating multiple options, but then shifts to a hierarchic process of ordering the options using a higher-order-priority schema.

In keeping with the interactionist philosophy, decision styles are not seen as traits. Instead, people seem to change styles systematically as environmental load changes. Thus, a person might show a systemic style under moderate load and shift to a decisive style under extreme loads. Whichever style occurs most frequently is called dominant; the other is termed the back-up style.

Measures of individual differences in style using this model have proven quite predictive of a wide variety of information-processing behavior (Driver and Mock 1975; Boulgarides 1973; Alawi 1973; Testerman 1976; Athey 1976; Hager 1977; Meshkati 1983). This is particularly clear in looking at decision making.

In sum, a useful trend in problem-solving research and application might be to identify critical problem-solving styles rather than to continue to try to isolate *the* way to solve problems. Even if a "best" approach existed, getting managers to adopt it may not be cost effective given the existence of contrary styles.

Decision-making processes

One view of the elements of the decision process is presented in figure 5.7. This is a fairly elaborate model which assumes a complex decision maker (see Driver 1979). Nevertheless, many decision theorists might regard it as a *minimal* set of steps for a good decision. For instance, Janis and Mann (1977) suggest that an optimal decision is one that will attain the decision maker's objectives and gain acceptance by others. To do this they set out seven criteria, which can be paraphrased in relation to the eight decision-process steps outlined in figure 5.7 as follows:

1. *Goal setting:* look at all objectives and values involved in one's choice.
2. *Problem detection:* there is no specific statement on this phase by Janis and Mann, but one could suggest providing mechanisms for ensuring that critical problems are not ignored.
3. *Problem importance:* again there is no specific statement by Janis and Mann. One could recommend developing priority lists with appropriate allocation of time and resources.
4. *Information search:* search intensively for new information and assimilate information or expert opinion that may disagree with preferred courses of action.
5. *Information evaluation:* canvass all possible alternatives; weigh all possible risks, costs, and benefits.
6. *Choice:* reexamine all alternatives including those rejected before making final choice.
7. *Implementation:* provide detailed contingency plan for execution of decision.
8. *Process evaluation:* no specific statement by Janis and Mann, but one could suggest a review of all steps in the light of results to improve the process in the future.

This set of criteria is by no means unusual. Katz and Kahn (1966), Elbing (1970), Feldman (1981), and other experts on decision process all basically support this emphasis on complex, elaborate decisions as leading to the "best" outcomes.

However, this evaluation is usually offered in the context of people's failure to use such elaborate processes. Simon (1957) was an early observer of the failure of many decision makers to maximize objectives through rational analytic processes. He termed this tendency satisficing. Janis and Mann (1977) note that under conditions of low or high threat (noxity) people tend to satisfice. They maximize only under moderate threat—as would be expected in view of the environmental load-cognitive complexity model discussed above.

In the literature on managerial decision making, the failure to adhere to complex criteria is particularly well documented. Researchers have noticed that the management-decision process is not linear but may be cyclic or even totally chaotic (Lindblom 1959; Soelberg 1967). Elaborate cost-benefit analysis is rare (Stagner 1969); simple procedures are preferred over complex techniques, such as PERT or linear programming (Bing 1971). In particular, econometric or mathematical models receive scant attention and even less use (Zeleny 1981; Cyert Dill, and March 1958; Crum, Klingman, and Tavis 1979).

Bass (1983) sums it up by suggesting that managers operate more by seat-of-the-pants intuition, experience, and pragmatic values. One could argue that this tendency reflects the manager's environment. High uncertainty often makes elaborate analysis ineffective (Alexander 1972). Time and resources are often limited (Bass et al. 1979). Political considerations often urge the use of "safe," experience-based, traditional approaches.

In such a world, either a decisive or flexible style would be appropriate. In contrast, the "ideal" decision processes advocated by theorists are clearly more in tune with a hierarchic or systemic style. This apparent gap is less extreme than it might seem, however. In the first place, not all managers operate with decisive or flexible styles. Contrary to experts' complaints about satisficing, some managers do use complex styles. Our data suggest that while satisficing styles are much more common at first-level supervision (Boulgarides 1973), hierarchic, integrative and systemic styles predominate in middle management (Alawi 1973). However, if an organization has a predominantly decisive culture, it favors that style. Even the complex middle manager may have to satis-

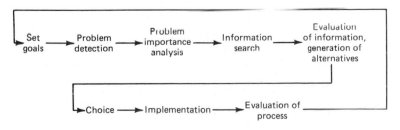

Figure 5.7 A model of steps in the decision process

fice unless buffered from load pressures and given support from the top on the use of nondecisive styles.

Secondly, not all situations really call for the complex decision processes favored by experts. In situations of low complexity and high time pressure, satisficing may be the best approach.

Some theorists would attempt to improve decisions by training managers to operate more complexly, for example, to think in a more analytic linear fashion or to use devil's-advocate procedures. But it is important to ask whether the situation warrants such complexity. Moreover, if the style of the trainee conflicts with training objectives, a more profound type of training in style change may be in order (Athey 1976).

Ideal models have been offered for each stage of decision making as well as for the overall process. Here again, lack of compliance with such ideals is deplored. And again, the solution may be to examine situational and personality factors that determine what is "best." In goal setting, for example, authors have differed as to the level at which goals should be set (Bass 1983). The best choice in goal setting might be related to the achievement needs of the individuals involved (Driver 1979) and to prior success or failure patterns in the situation (Filley, House, and Kerr 1976).

With respect to information search, recommendations for adventurous exploration of untried areas and for greater creativity (Bass 1983) would make sense if the decision styles of those involved were integrative and the situation were novel. The process of alternative evaluation might be conducted more effectively if it were done more openly and consciously, but only if the political culture, values, and styles of the participants permitted an open process as opposed to covert gaming (Argyris 1971).

In sum, an interactionist approach might go a long way toward resolving the disparity of ideal prescriptions and actual decision making in organizations.

Creativity

Figure 5.8 shows schematically the steps generally thought to be involved in the creative process. Note that a conscious logical solution will destroy the creative process. If our mulling on data gets a logical answer there is no creativity. The conscious process must fail and be interrupted. Why? Because creativity is unconscious. We "get" an idea from our unconscious.

It is not clear what cognitive processes are involved in creativity. Two lively candidates are the right-brain iconic system and the "dream consciousness." An involvement of the iconic system is suggested by the finding that daydreamers are more creative (Singer and Schonbar

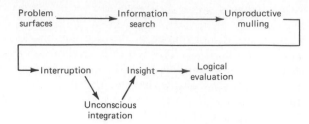

Figure 5.8 The creative process

1961). But, this result could also link creativity to a waking dream state. Moreover, it has been shown that REM sleep deprivation leads to increased waking fantasy (Cartwright and Monroe 1968). Although a definitive conclusion would be premature, it seems that creativity is more akin to dream consciousness than to iconic processing.

Like other cognitive processes, creativity is influenced by both personality and situational factors. In cognitive-system terms creativity is clearly related to flexibility or fluidity (Vinacke 1974; Eiduson 1959). It is also related to openness, that is, permeable boundaries (Vinacke 1974); divergent thinking (Getzels and Jackson 1962), liking for complexity (Eisenman and Robinson 1967); complex-information-search style (Karlins 1967) and integrative-decision style (Driver, Reynolds, and Boulgarides 1971; Sundby and Driver 1974). It is *not* strongly tied to an interest in people (MacKinnon 1963).

Situational factors linked to creativity include low fear, avoidance of the use of expert opinion, encouragement of cross pollination of functions or fields, use of groups, conscious use of overload and unproductive mulling, followed by interruption and the absence of deadlines, routine, and power differentials (see Gordon 1961). Creative environments and training can help foster creativity, but some of the personality factors listed above are also essential (Driver, Reynolds, and Boulgarides 1971). Finally, creativity is clearly not always desirable. In some settings, logic or tradition is far more effective than creativity.

ISSUES OF GENERAL COGNITIVE STYLE

Our discussion of cognitive styles has left a number of basic issues untouched. One issue concerns style consistency. Are styles enduring personality phenomena or do people simply use styles temporarily as needed, like strategies? Scott (1963) would argue that an individual may shift styles with content areas. Yet much of the style literature points to considerable generalizability of style to varied behavior areas (Goldstein and Blackman 1978). Where style scores are averaged over many cases, generalizability and stability of styles seem very high. For instance, the behavior of the average or typical decisive-style person is very reliably generalized over many content areas. A given individual may show variability in adherence to style, but some of this variability itself can be viewed as predictable, as seen in the decision-style model in figure 5.4. As load changes, style should change in a consistent manner. Patterns of style shift do seem to be "metastable." Nevertheless, measurement error and purely random factors will undoubtedly continue to underlie style variability.

It may also be helpful to distinguish the difference between memory and conscious processes in style. In dealing with new problems where memory is of low relevance, a person may use one consistent style pattern; however, when an old problem is worked based purely on past experience (memory), a different style may be seen, which was used and locked in at the time when the memory was laid down.

A second general issue concerns the issue of operating styles and self-image. People growing up in certain cultures are encouraged to use certain styles. For instance, the Latin culture values speed in decision making (Heller 1969). Similarly, certain organizations value a particular style, for example, the U.S. Air Force seems to value decisiveness (Hager 1977). Hence, a person often adopts a particular style in his or her self-image that fits his or her culture, organization, role, or self-ideal. The problem is that this style may not be the same as the operating style used when a person is not self-conscious.

Our research on decision styles has shown that there is no correlation between measures of decision style on a self-image questionnaire and measures of operating style (how one actually uses data). For instance, air-force officers generally identify consciously with a decisive style. On the other hand, they operationally use a style related to the demands of their work. Air-force flight instructors use a decisive operating style; physicists in the air force use an integrative operating style (Hager 1977). Therefore, it is crucial in style analysis to be on the alert for such discrepancies within a person and their effect on overt behavior. One might expect the self-image to control behavior in critical social interactions where one is very self-conscious and tries to play the right role; whereas the operating style might govern behavior in more everyday nonsocial settings.

A third style issue concerns the valuation placed on styles. Some style models adopt an evaluative posture that one style is "best." This posture is reminiscent of the intelligence field with its value-laden categories (e.g., genius, dull, normal). This evaluative approach can place extreme pressure on people to adopt "good" styles. However, our data suggest that no style is perfect in all settings. It also suggests that as people age, they find shifting styles (e.g., to an ideal) to be uncongenial, difficult, and sometimes impossible. A more practical approach might be to see the value of style as contingent on situations.

Finally, an intriguing issue remains to be solved. What are the essential and unique style dimensions that account for most cognitive behavior? There is a tendency to want to collapse all variables into a single dimension, such as the left brain—right brain dichotomy. However, a review of intercorrelation suggests that such mergers may be premature at this time. I would like to suggest the following as a possible minimal set of essential cognitive-style dimensions:

1. Open / closed boundary
2. High information use / low information use
3. Iconic bias / verbal bias
4. Linear process / holistic process
5. Creative / analytic
6. Empirical, inductive / deductive
7. Focused / multichannel
8. Thinking / feeling
9. People centered / idea or thinking centered
10. Top-down orientation / bottom-up orientation

Further research is needed to refine this set.

IMPLICATIONS FOR APPLICATION OF COGNITIVE PSYCHOLOGY

There is a wide range of application of the cognitive-psychology domain to both theory and practice in organizational behavior. Only a brief sketch can occur here. The generalist work alone suggests some possibilities already being realized.

1. Cognitive-process analysis has made it possible to write computer programs to perform an enormous variety of particular tasks. These tasks range from managing accounts to medical diagnosis. The computer can offer consistency and speed, which can be of great help in complex tasks. Current limitations on computers (e.g., creative thought) may someday be bypassed. One wonders, however, if computers can ever show the dynamic adaptability of human beings in cognitive tasks. The complex interplay of unconscious creativity, multiple unstable motive systems, and conscious systems of variable complexity may evade any computer.

2. Models of "optimal" cognitive process can be used to design training programs, as has been done by Kepner and Tregoe (1965). Such training would be even more valuable if accompanied by diagnostic skills in diagnosing when to use "optimal" processes and when not. A limitation in this approach, of course, is that deeply learned styles or motives may oppose the training direction.

3. Perhaps most valuable are insights into how to manage environments to produce optimal processes. Appropriate buffering of load factors, such as uncertainty or complexity, could greatly aid cognitive processes. For instance, secretaries trained to recognize optimal loads could act as critical filters for executives.

Even more powerful applications can come from an interactionist approach that recognizes both environmental and personality factors.

1. Knowing both cognitive styles of users and information load levels involved in tasks, one can design information systems optimally tailored to users and tasks (Driver and Mock 1975; Mock and Driver 1975). For example, we found that complex data helped people with complex styles, whereas simpler data helped those with simpler styles—a finding replicated by Carlisle (1974). This approach could go a long way toward reconciling data systems and users.

2. A most vital application at present is in the area of person-job fit. If the cognitive demands of a job are analyzed, a profile of the type of person needed to meet these demands can be specified. For instance, we might determine how many different inputs a person must attend to at once in a job. Executive jobs may require multiple-channel-attention patterns to permit rapid tracking of a great deal of information. The job profile for this job would specify a person with a moderately complex style (if extrovert), moderate uncertainty preference, and moderate complexity preference (see figure 5.4).

Once the job is profiled, people's relevant characteristics can be measured to determine how well they fit the job profile. If the fit is poor, job redesign or development of the person may be helpful. This approach is being tried in several firms with considerable success and acceptance.

3. Effective performance appraisal (Prince and Driver 1985) may require careful attention to load and style factors. For instance, an overloaded person may be unreceptive to even constructive input. Style factors can be critical in designing evaluation procedures; for example, a decisive person might respond well to short-term Management by Objectives (MBO) approach while an integrative type might prefer to be measured on longer term development of certain operating qualities.

4. Cognitive styles and environmental load are also critical to leadership. Certain styles gravitate toward particular leadership patterns. For instance, a person of flexible style seems to use social-emotional leadership, whereas the decisive style is more task oriented. Further, certain leadership patterns work best under particular load conditions. Cognitive theory can go a long way towards clarifying muddled issues in this area.

5. Even such macro issues as organization design or structure can benefit from cognitive theory. It is becoming clear that cognitive motives and styles may be key factors in determining organization structure (Bobbitt and Ford 1980; Mealiea and Lee 1979; Driver 1983). Similarly, cognitive styles may be important determinants of an individual's compatibility with existing structures. For instance, there is growing evidence that the people with a decisive style are uncomfortable with the matrix structure while those with the Integrative style are not (Alawi 1973).

Environmental load factors (e.g., uncertainty) already play an important role in organization-design literature (Lawrence and Lorsch 1969). The addition of style variables and their interaction with load may further progress in this field. For example, what organization design might we want for integrative executives in an overload environment?

6. A final application area is in strategic planning. First, style can be critical in determining planning roles in an organization. For example, the hierarchic style is well attuned to complex, elaborate, long-range planning, while the flexible style prefers to avoid planning, as it impairs ability to keep options open.

Second, knowledge of the styles prevailing in an organization can be important in selecting a strategy. For example, a strong flexible-style concentration in an organization would favor short-term entrepreneurial strategies, while the hierarchic style might favor long-term growth.

Clearly, strategy must consider environmental factors involved in load (e.g., environmental fluidity), but information about cognitive styles and motives of employees can be a vital addition to the planning process.

CONCLUSION: COGNITIVE PSYCHOLOGY AND ORGANIZATIONAL BEHAVIOR THEORY

A major part of this chapter has been devoted to demonstrating how both environmental and personality factors contribute to the attention process. This interactionist view is undoubtedly more complex than either a pure environmental analysis or a trait approach.

The acceptability of this approach will depend at least in part on the cognitive styles and preferences of those active in the organizational behavior field. In the past, both applied and theoretical organizational behavior has been rather simple in orientation. Simple panaceas (e.g., the sixty-minute manager) sweep through organizations in a seemingly endless parade. Theories in the field are few, and those that do exist are usually modest microtheories, despite occasional calls for broad integrating theory.

Simplicity, per se, is not an evil. In fact, science has been built using Occam's razor, favoring the simpler model where possible. "Where possible" is the rub. Simple models for simple phenomena are preferable without a doubt. Human behavior, however, seems to be a very complex phenomenon, and organizational behavior is perhaps even more complex. Hence, complex models may be essential, despite our preferences or styles.

Clearly, models can attain levels of complexity beyond anyone's capacity of understanding. This level may have been met by Guilford's (1967) model of intellect. He suggests that intellect consists of the interaction of 5 operations (e.g., cognitive) with 6 products (e.g., classes) and 4 content areas (e.g., symbols). Even Guilford did not seem able to operate with all of the resulting 120 cells.

The great challenge is to find models that adequately map the complexity of the phenomenal world and yet are simple enough to use. In the organizational behavior area we may have to accept more complex models than those of the past to get a closer mapping of organizational realities. To do so we have to become conscious of our own styles and complexity motives and adjust these to fit empirical demands.

It is hoped that cognitive psychology can provide models of appropriate complexity for the organizational behavior field, as well as offering insight into how we can adjust our thinking to meet the challenge of greater complexity.

REFERENCES

Alawi, H. 1973. "Cognitive, Task and Organizational Complexities in Relation to Information Processing Behavior in Business Managers." D.B.A diss., University of Southern California.

Alexander, F. 1972. "Choice in a Changing World." *Policy Sciences* 3:325–37.

Allport, D., B. Antonis, and P. Reynolds. 1972. "On the Division of Attention: A Disproof of the Single Channel Hypothesis." *Quarterly Journal of Experimental Psychology* 24:225–35.

Anderson, J. 1980. *Cognitive Psychology*. San Francisco: Freeman.

———. 1978. "Arguments Concerning Representations for Mental Imagery." *Psychological Review* 85:249–77.

Argyris, C., and D. Schoen. 1978. *Organizational Learning: A Theory of Action Perspective*. Reading, Mass.: Addison-Wesley.

Argyris, C. 1971. "Management Information Systems: The Challenge to Rationality and Emotionality." *Management Science* 17:275–92.

Ashby, W. R. 1964. *An Introduction to Cybernetics*. London: Methuen.

Athey, T. 1976. "The Development and Testing of a Seminar for Increasing the Cognitive Complexity of Individuals." D.B.A. diss., University of Southern California.

Atkinson, J. 1981. "Studying Personality in the Light of Advanced Motivation Psychology." *American Psychologist* 36:117–27.

Barriff, M., and E. Lusk. 1977. "Cognitive and Personality Tests for the Design of Management Information Systems." *Management Science* (April): 820–29.

Barron, F. 1953. "Complexity-Simplicity as a Personality Dimension." *Journal of Abnormal and Social Psychology* 48:163–72.

Bass, B. 1983. *Organizational Decision Making*. Homewood, Ill.: Irwin.

Bass, B., P. Burger et al. 1979. *Assessment of Managers: An International Comparison*. New York: Free Press.

Bateson, C. 1975. *Steps to an Ecology of the Mind*. New York: Ballantine Books.

Benbaset, I., and A. Dexter. 1979. "Value and Events Approaches to Accounting: An Experimental Evaluation." *The Accounting Review* 4:735–49.

Benbaset, I., A. Dexter, and P. Masulis. "An Experimental Analysis of the Human/Computer Interface." *Human Aspects of Computing: Communications of the Association for Computing Machinery* 24.752–02.

Berlyne, D. 1957. "Conflict and Information Theory Variables as Determinants of Human Perceptual Curiosity." *Journal of Experimental Psychology* 53:399–404.

———. 1960. *Conflict, Arousal, Curiosity*. New York: McGraw-Hill.

Bertalanffy, L. 1951. *Problems of Life*. New York: Harper & Row.

Bing, R. 1971. "Surveying of Practitioners' Stock Evaluation Methods." *Financial Analysts Journal* (May–June): 55–60.

Bobbitt, H., and J. Ford. 1980. "Decision Maker Choice as a Determinant of Organizational Structure." *Academy of Management Review* 5:13–24.

Boddy, J. 1978. *Brain Systems and Psychological Concepts*. New York: Wiley.

Boulgarides, J. 1973. "Decision Style, Values, and Biographi-

cal Factors in Relation to Satisfaction and Performance."
D.B.A. diss., University of Southern California.

Broadbent, D. 1957. "A Mechanical Model for Human Attention and Immediate Memory." *Psychological Review* 64:205–15.

Brossard, M., and J. Decarie. 1971. "The Effects of Three Types of Perceptual-Social Stimulation on the Development of Institutional Infants." *Early Child Development and Care* 1:211–31.

Bruner, J., J. Goodnow, and G. Austin. 1956. *A Study of Thinking.* New York: Wiley.

Bryson, J., and M. Driver. 1972. "Cognitive Complexity, Introversion and Preference for Complexity." *Journal of Personality and Social Psychology* 23:320–27.

Cannon, L. 1964. "Self Confidence and Selective Exposure to Information." In *Conflict, Decision and Dissonance,* ed. L. Festinger. Stanford, Calif.: Stanford University Press.

Cantril, H. 1950. *The "Why" of Man's Experience.* New York: Macmillan.

Carlisle, J. 1974. "Man-Computer Interactive Problem Solving: Relationships Between User Characterisitcs and Interface Complexity." Ph.D diss., Yale University.

Carpenter, B., M. Weiner, and J. Carpenter. 1956. "Predictability of Perceptual Defense Behavior." *Journal of Abnormal and Social Psychology* 52:380–83.

Carpenter, P., and A. Just. 1975. "Sentence Comprehension: A Psycholinguistic Processing Model of Verification." *Psychological Review* 82:45–73

Cartwright, R., and L. Monroe. 1968. "Relation of Dreaming and REM Sleep: The Effects of REM Deprivation under Two Conditions." *Journal of Personality and Social Psychology* 10:69–74.

Ching, L. 1980. "Learning Style and Information Usuage." Unpublished ms, School of Business, California State University at Sacramento.

Clarke, H. 1969. "Linguistic Processes in Deductive Reasoning." *Psychological Review* 76:387–404.

Coombs, C. H. 1975. "Portfolio Theory and the Management of Risk." In *Human Judgment and Decision Processes,* ed. M. Kaplan and S. Schwartz. New York: Academic Press.

Cronbach, L. 1975. "Beyond the Two Disciplines of Scientific Psychology." *American Psychologist* 30:116–27.

Crum, R. L., D. Klingman, and L. Tavis. 1979. "Implementation of Large Scale Financial Planning Models: Solution Efficient Transformations." *Journal of Financial and Quantitive Analysis* 14:137–52.

Cummings, L. 1981. "Organizational Behavior in the 1980s." *Decision Sciences* 12:365–77.

Cyert, R., W. Dill, and J. March. 1958. "The Role of Expectations in Business Decision Making." *Administrative Science Quarterly* 3:307–40.

Dabbs, J. 1980. "Left-Right Differences in Cerebral Blood Flow and Cognition." *Psychophysiology* 17:548–51.

Deese, J. 1965. *The Structure of Associations in Language and Thought.* Baltimore, Md.: Johns Hopkins University Press.

Dember, W., R. Earl, and N. Paradise, 1957. "Response by Rats to Differential Stimulus Complexity." *Journal of Comparative and Physiological Psychology* 58:514–18.

Dement, W., 1968. "The Biological Role of REM Sleep." In *Sleep: Physiology and Pathology,* ed. A. Kales. Philadelphia: Lippincott.

Denny, J. 1966. "Effects of Anxiety and Intelligence on Concept Formation." *Journal of Experimental Psychology* 72:596–602.

———. 1969. "Memory and Transformation in Concept Learning." *Journal of Experimental Psychology* 79:63–68.

Doktor, R. 1978. "Problem-Solving Styles of Executives and Management Scientists." *TIMS Studies in the Management Sciences* 8:123–34.

Doktor, R., and D. Bloom. 1977. "Selective Lateralizations of Cognitive Style Related to Occupation as Determined by EEG Alpha Asymmetry." *Psychophysiology* 14:385–87.

Doktor, R., and W. Hamilton. 1973. "Cognitive Style and the Acceptance of Management Science Recommendations." *Management Science* 19:884–94.

Dollard, J., L. Doob, V. Miller, O. Mowrer, and R. Sears. 1939. *Frustration and Aggression.* New Haven, Conn.: Yale University Press.

Donaldson, H. 1890. "Anatomical Observations on the Brain and Several Sense Organs of the Blind, Deaf Mute, Laura Dewey Bridgeman." *American Journal of Psychology* 3:393–442; 4:248–94.

Driver, M. 1962. "Conceptual Structure and Group Processes in an Inter-nation Simulation. Part One: The Perception of Simulated Nations." *Educational Testing Service Research Bulletin,* RB6245. Princeton, N.J.

———. 1977. *A Study of Education and Work.* Technical Report, Department of Management and Organization, University of Southern California.

———. 1979. "Individual Decision Making and Creativity." In *Organizational Behavior,* ed. S. Kerr. New York: Wiley.

———. 1983. "A Human Resource Data-Base Approach to Organizational Design." *Journal of Human Resource Planning* 6:169–82.

Driver, M., and T. Mock. 1975. "Information Processing, Decision Style Theory, and Accounting Information Systems." *Accounting Review* 50:490–508.

Driver, M., P. Reynolds, and J. Boulgarides. 1971. "Effects of Decision Style and Creativity Training on Creative Performance." Paper read at American Psychological Association Meeting.

Driver, M., and A. J. Rowe. 1979. "Decision-Making Styles: A New Approach to Management Decision Making." In *Behavioral Problems in Organizations,* ed. C. L. Cooper. Englewood Cliffs, N.J.: Prentice-Hall.

Driver, M., and S. Streufert. 1965. *The General Incongruity Adaptation Level (GIAL) Hypothesis: An Analysis and Integration of Cognitive Approaches to Motivation.* Institute paper 114, Institute for Research in the Behavioral, Economic, and Management Sciences, Purdue University.

———. 1969. "Integrative Complexity." *American Management Science Quarterly* 14:272–85.

Driver, M., S. Streufert, M. Nataupsky. 1969. "Effects of Immediate and Remote Incongruity on Response to Dissonant Information." *Proceedings of the Seventy-seventh American Psychological Association Meeting.*

Durkin, H. 1937. "Trial and Error, Gradual Analyses, and Sudden Reorganization: An Experimental Study of Problem Solving." *Archives of Psychology*, no. 210.

Eiduson, B. 1959. "Structural Analysis of Dreams: Clues to Perceptual Style." *Journal of Abnormal Social and Psychology* 58:335–39.

Eisenman, R., and N. Robinson. 1967. "Complexity-Simplicity, Creativity, Intelligence, and Other Correlates." *Journal of Psychology* 67:331–34.

Elbing, A. 1970. *Behavioral Decisions in Organizations*. Glenview, Ill.:Scott, Foresman.

Evans, C. 1968. "Dreams: A Functional Theory." *Electronics and Power* 14:323–25.

Eysenck, H. 1967. *The Biological Basis of Personality*. Springfield, Ill.: Thomas.

Feldman, J. 1981. "Beyond Attribution Theory: Cognitive Processes in Performance Appraisal." *Journal of Applied Psychology* 66:127–48.

Festinger, L. 1957. *A Theory of Cognitive Dissonance*. New York: Harper & Row.

Filley, A., R. House, and S. Kerr. 1976. *Managerial Process and Organizational Behavior*. Glenview, Ill.: Scott, Foresman.

Fiske, D., and S. Maddi. 1961. *Functions of Varied Experience*. Homewood, Ill.: Dorsey Press.

Forster, N., W. Vinacke, and J. Digman. 1955. "Flexibility and Rigidity in a Variety of Problem Situations." *Journal of Abnormal and Social Psychology* 50:211–18.

Freud, S. 1953. *The Interpretation of Dreams*. London: Hogarth Press.

Getzels, J., and P. Jackson. 1962. *Creativity and Intelligence: Explorations with Gifted Students*. New York: Wiley.

Glixman, A. 1965. "Categorizing Behavior as a Function of Meaning Domain." *Journal of Personality and Social Psychology* 2:370–77.

Glixman, A., and J. Wolfe. 1967. "Category Membership and Interitem Semantic-Space Distances." *Journal of Personality* 35:134–44.

Goff, W. 1969. "Evoked Potential Correlates of Perceptual Organization in Man." In *Attention in Neurophysiology*, ed. C. R. Evans and T. Mulholland. London: Butterworths.

Goldstein, J., and S. Blackman. 1978. *Cognitive Style*. New York: Wiley.

Gordon, W. 1961. *Synectics*. New York: Macmillan.

Gray, J. 1972. "The Psychophysiological Nature of Introversion-Extroversion: A Modification of Eysenck's Theory." In *Biological Bases of Individual Behavior*, ed. V. Nebylitsyn and J. Gray. New York: Academic Press.

Guilford, J. 1967. *The Nature of Human Intelligence*. New York: McGraw-Hill.

Hager, J. 1977. "The Feasibility of Using Decision Making Style as a Criterion for Career Assignment in the U.S. Air Force." D.B.A diss., University of Southern California.

Hampden-Turner, C. 1981. *Maps of the Mind*. New York: Macmillan, Collier Books.

Heath, R. 1963. "Electrical Self Stimulation of the Brain in Man." *American Journal of Psychiatry* 120:571–77.

Hebb, D. 1955. "Drives and the CNS (Conceptual Nervous System)." *Psychological Review* 62:243–54.

Heider, F. 1946. "Attitude and Cognitive Organizations." *Journal of Psychology* 21:107–12.

Heller, F. 1969. "The Role of Business Management in Relation to Economic Development." *International Journal of Comparative Sociology* 10:292–98.

Helson, H. 1959. "Adaptation Level Theory." In *Psychology: A Study of a Science*, ed. S. Koch. Vol. 1. New York: McGraw-Hill.

Hubel, D., and T. Wiesel. 1962. "Receptive Fields, Binocular Interaction and Functional Cytoarchitecture in the Cat's Visual Cortex." *Journal of Physiology* 160:106–54.

———. 1968. "Receptive Fields and Functional Architecture of Monkey Striate Cortex." *Journal of Physiology* 195:215–43.

Hunsaker, P. 1975. "Incongruity Adaptation Capability and Risk Preferences in Turbulent Decision Making Environments." *Organizational Behavior and Human Performance* 14:173–85.

James, W. 1950. *The Principles of Psychology*. Mineola, N.Y.: Dover.

Janis, I., and L. Mann. 1977. *Decision Making*. New York: Free Press.

Jung, C. 1971. *Psychological Types*. Princeton, N.J.: Princeton University Press.

Kagan, J., and R. Klein. 1973. "Transcultural Perspectives on Early Development." *American Psychologist* 28:947–61.

Kagan, J., B. Rosman, D. Day, L. Albert, W. Phillips. 1964. "Information Processing in the Child: Significance of Analytic and Reflective Attitudes." *Psychological Monographs* 78 (1, Whole No. 578).

Kahneman, D. 1973. *Attention and Effort*. Englewood Cliffs, N.J.: Prentice-Hall.

Karlins, M. 1967. "Conceptual Complexity and Remote Associative Proficiency as Creativity Variables in a Complex Problem-Solving Task." *Journal of Personality and Social Psychology* 6:264–78.

Katz, D., and R. Kahn. 1966. *The Social Psychology of Organizations*. New York: Wiley.

Kepner, D., and B. Tregoe. 1965. *The Rational Manager*. New York, McGraw-Hill.

Kolb, D. 1976. *Learning Style Inventory: Technical Manual*. Boston: McBer.

Kosslyn, S. 1980. *Image and Mind*. Cambridge, Mass.: Harvard University Press.

Krech, D., M. Rosenzweig, and E. Bennett. 1962. "Relations Between Brain Chemistry and Problem Solving Among Rats Raised in Enriched and Impoverished Environments." *Journal of Comparative and Physiological Psychology* 53:801–07.

Lashley, K. 1923. "The Behavioristic Conception of Consciousness." *Psychological Review* 30:237–72.

Lawrence, P., and J. Lorsch. 1969. *Organization and Environment*. Homewood, Ill.: Irwin.

Lehman, D., and D. Fender. 1968. "Component Analysis of Human Averaged Evoked Potentials: Dichoptic Stimuli Using Different Target Structures." *Electroencephalography and Clinical Neurophysiology* 24:542–53.

Lewin, K. 1935. *A Dynamic Theory of Personality*. New York: McGraw-Hill

Lindblom, C. 1959. "The Science of 'Muddling Through.'" *Public Administration Review* 19:79-99.

Lindsay, P., and D. Norman. 1977. *Human Information Processing*. New York: Academic Press.

Lindsley, D. 1951. "Emotion." In *Handbook of Experimental Psychology*, ed. S. S. Stevens. New York: Wiley.

Lusk, E. 1973. "Cognitive Aspects of Annual Reports. Field Independence/Dependence." *Empirical Research in Accounting: Selected Studies*. Chicago: University of Chicago Press.

MacKinnon, D. 1963. "Creativity and Images of the Self." In *The Study of Lives*, ed. R. W. White. New York: Atherton.

Mackworth, N., and A. Morandi. 1967. "The Gaze Selects Informative Details within Pictures." *Perception and Psychophysics* 2:547-51.

Mayer, R., and R. Boyer. 1976. "Mental Comparison and the Symbolic Distance Effect." *Cognitive Psychology* 8:228-46.

Mealiea, L., and D. Lee. 1979. "An Alternative to Macro-Micro Contingency Models: An Integrative Model." *Academy of Management Review* 4:333-46.

Meshkati, N. 1983. "A Conceptual Model for the Assignment of Mental Workload and Its Utilization in Enhancing Industrial Productivity." Ph.D diss., University of Southern California.

Mock, T., and M. Driver. 1975. "An Experimental Study of Alternate Accounting Feedback Systems and Differences in Cognitive Style of Information Processing." Proceedings of the American Accounting Association Meeting, Tucson, Arizona.

Neisser, U. 1963. "Decision Time without Reaction Time: Experiments in Visual Scanning." *American Journal of Psychology* 79:376-85.

Noble, C. 1952. "The Role of Stimulus Meaning (m) in Serial Verbal Learning." *Journal of Experimental Psychology* 43:437-46; 44:465.

Olds, J., and P. Milner. 1954. "Positive Reinforcement Produced by Electrical Stimulation of Septal Area and Other Regions of Cat Brain." *Journal of Comparative and Physiological Psychology* 47:419-27.

Osgood, C., G. O. Suci, and P. Tannenbaum, 1957. *The Measurement of Meaning*. Urbana, Ill.: University of Illinois Press.

Owens, W., and L. Schoenfeldt. 1979. "Toward a Classification of Persons." *Journal of Applied Psychology* 64:569-607.

Paivio, A. 1965. "Abstractness, Images and Meaningfulness in Paired Associates Learning." *Journal of Verbal Learning and Verbal Behavior* 4:32-38.

Posner, M. 1965. "Memory and Thought in Human Intellectual Performance." *British Journal of Psychology* 56:197-215.

Pribram, K. 1975. "The Neurophysiology of Remembering." In *Physiological Psychology: Readings from Scientific American*. San Francisco: Freeman.

Prince, J. B., and M. Driver. 1985. "Designing Career Sensitive Performance Appraisal Systems." In *The Design of Management Performance Appraisal Systems*, ed. S. Resnick and A. Mohrman. American Society of Personnel Administration Foundation monograph, Berea, Ohio.

Robey, T., and W. Taggart. 1981. "Minds and Managers. On the Dual Nature of Human Information Processing and Management." *Academy of Management Review* 6:187-96.

Rosenzweig, M. 1966. "Environmental Complexity, Cerebral Change and Behavior." *American Psychologist* 21:321-32.

Rosenzweig, M., E. Bennett, and M. Diamond. 1972. "Brain Changes in Response to Experience." *Scientific American* 226, no. 2:22-29

Rutter, M. 1972. *Maternal Deprivation Re-assessed*. Harmondsworth, England: Penguin Education.

Schroder, H., M. Driver, and S. Streufert. 1967. *Human Information Processing*. New York: Holt, Rinehart and Winston.

Scott, W. 1963. "Conceptualizing and Measuring Structural Properties of Cognition." In *Motivation and Social Interaction: Cognitive Determinants*, ed. O. J. Harvey. New York: Ronald Press.

Simon, H. 1957. *Administrative Behavior*. New York: Macmillan.

Simmel, G. 1950. *The Sociology of George Simmel*. ed. K. H. Wolff. New York: Free Press.

Singer, J., and R. Schonbar. 1961. "Correlates of Day Dreaming. A Dimension of Self-Awareness." *Journal of Consulting Psychology* 25:1-6.

Soelberg, P. 1967. "Unprogrammed Decision Making." *Industrial Management Review* 8:19-29.

Solley, C. M., and F. Snyder. 1958. "Information Processing and Problem Solving." *Journal of Experimental Psychology* 55:384-87.

Sperry, R. 1964. "The Great Cerebral Commissure." *Scientific American*, 42-52.

Spoehr, K., and S. Lehmkuhle. 1982. *Visual Information Processing*. San Francisco: Freeman.

Spydell, J., and D. Sheer. 1982. "Effect of Problem Solving on Right and Left Hemispheres 40 Hertz EEG Activity." *Psychophysiology* 19:420-25.

Stagner, R. 1969. "Corporate Decision Making, An Empirical Study." *Journal of Applied Psychology* 53:1-13.

Stevens, A., and P. Coupe. 1978. "Distortions in Judged Spatial Relations." *Cognitive Psychology* 10:427-37.

Streufert, S. 1969. "Increasing Failure and Response Rate in Complex Decision Making." *Journal of Experimental Social Psychology* 5:310-23.

———. 1972. "Success and Response Rate in Complex Decision Making." *Journal of Experimental Social Psychology* 8:389-403.

———. 1973. "Effects of Information Relevance on Decision Making in Complex Environments." *Memory and Cognition* 1:224-28.

Streufert, S., M. Driver, and K. Haun. 1967. "Components of Response Rate in Complex Decision Making." *Journal of Experimental Social Psychology* 3:286-95.

Streufert, S., S. Streufert, and C. Castore. 1969. "Complexity, Increasing Failure and Decision Making." *Journal of Experimental Research in Personality* 3:293–300.

Streufert, S., P. Suedfeld, and M. Driver. 1967. "Conceptual Structure, Information Search and Information Utilization." *Journal of Personality and Social Psychology* 2:736–40.

Suedfeld, P. 1978. "Characteristics of Decision Making as a Function of the Environment." In *Managerial Control and Organizational Democracy*, ed. B. King, S. Streufert, and F. Fiedler. Washington, D.C.: Winston.

Suedfield, P., S. Glucksberg, and J. Vernon. 1967. "Sensory Deprivation as a Drive Operation: Effects upon Problem Solving." *Journal of Experimental Psychology* 75:166–69.

Sundby, D., and M. Driver. 1974. "The Development of a New Procedure for Assessing Creativity in Counselors." Unpublished ms, Department of Management and Organization, University of Southern California.

Sutton, S., P. Tueting, J. Zubin, and E. John. 1967. "Information Delivery and Sensory Evoked Potentials." *Science* 155:143a–43d.

Testerman, W. 1976. "Decision Style and Job Selection in the Computer Industry." D.B.A diss., University of Southern California.

Tomkins, S. 1962. *Affect, Imagery, Consciousness.* Vol. 1, The Positive Affects. New York: Springer.

Torcivia, J., and P. Laughlin. 1968. "Dogmatism and Concept Attainment Strategies." *Journal of Personality and Social Psychology* 8:397–400.

Treisman, A., and G. Gelade. 1980. "A Feature-Integration Theory of Attention." *Cognitive Psychology* 12:97–136.

Vasarhelyi, M. 1977. "Man-Machine Planning Systems: A Cognitive Style Examination of Interactive Decision Making." *Journal of Accounting Research* (Spring):138–53.

Vinacke, W. 1974. *The Psychology of Thinking.* New York: McGraw-Hill.

Weir, M. 1964. "Developmental Changes in Problem-Solving Strategies." *Psychological Review* 71:473–90.

Weinberg, H., W. Walters, and H. Croro. 1970. "Intracerebral Events in Humans Related to Real and Imaginary Stimuli." *Electroencephalography and Clinical Neurophysiology* 29:1–9.

Werner, H. 1948. *Comparative Psychology of Mental Development.* New York: International Universities Press.

White, J. K. 1978. "Individual Differences and Job Quality— Worker Response Relationship: Review Integration and Comments." *Academy of Management Review* 3:267–80.

Williams, H., F. Holloway, and W. Griffiths. 1973. "Physiological Psychology: Sleep." *Annual Review of Psychology* 24:279–316.

Witkin, H., R. Dyk, H. Batterson, D. Goodenough, and S. Karp. 1962. *Psychological Differentiation.* New York: Wiley.

Witkin, H., D. Goodenough, and S. Karp. 1967. "Stability of Cognitive Style from Childhood to Young Adulthood." *Journal of Personality and Social Psychology* 7:291–300.

Zeleny, M. 1981. "Descriptive Decision Making and Its Applications." *Applications of Management Science* 1:327–88.

6

Organizational behavior: a sociological perspective

RICHARD H. HALL

This chapter focuses on the behavior of organizations as such. That is, instead of considering the individuals who make up the organization, we will assume that the aggregated whole functions as a distinct entity. As a practical matter, we often take this perspective in everyday life. For example, in each of the following excerpts from the *New York Times* of February 5, 1982, the organization is treated as the actor in the event being recorded:

> Even as interest rates have declined for big corporations and financial institutions over the past half year, rates have been rising for consumers. Just last week, for example, the Manufacturers Hanover Trust Company announced that the interest rate on its credit card loans would rise to 19.8 percent from 18 percent.

> The Koch administration, which successfully used a public-relations effort last year to persuade New Yorkers to use less water, is preparing similar campaigns designed to reduce litter and graffiti in New York City.

> Courts in Gdansk have sentenced 101 youths to jail from one to three months for participating in clashes with security forces there Saturday.

> The Navy today denied a Libyan accusation that F-14 fighters from the aircraft carrier John F. Kennedy buzzed a Libyan jetliner Sunday.

> The development of a retaliatory capacity in chemical warfare in order to deter the Soviet Union has become an essential element in the Defense Department's efforts to catch up with Soviet military expansion over the past decade.

> The Mets and the Reds reached agreement "in principle" yesterday on a trade that would bring George Foster, Cincinnati's leader in home runs and runs batted in for each of the last six seasons, to New York.

The focus on organizations as the unit of analysis falls squarely within the sociological tradition. As Scott (1981; 809) notes,

> Within sociology, the emergence of the field of organizations may be roughly dated from the translation into English of Weber's (1946 trans., 1947 trans.) and, to a lesser extent, Michels's (1949) analyses of bureaucracy. Shortly after these classic statements became accessible to American sociologists, Robert K. Merton and his students at Columbia University attempted to outline the boundaries of this new field of inquiry by compiling theoretical and empirical materials dealing with various aspects of organizations (Merton et al. 1957). Equally important, a series of path-breaking and influential case studies of diverse types of organizations was launched under Merton's influence, including

an examination of the Tennessee Valley Authority (Selznick 1949), a gypsum mine and factory (Gouldner 1954) a government employment and regulatory agency (Blau 1955), and a union (Lipset, Trow, and Coleman, 1965). For the first time, sociologists were engaged in the development and empirical testing of generalizations dealing with the structuring and functioning of organizations viewed as organizations.

To develop this sociological perspective, this chapter will examine four issues:

1. Organizations as realities
2. Organizations as actors
3. Some types and consequences of organizational actions
4. Organizations as responders

Before beginning the analysis, it should be noted that not all sociologists, let alone organizational theorists, would share the perspective taken here. Nonetheless, I believe that this approach makes an indispensable contribution to our understanding of organizational behavior.

ORGANIZATIONS AS REALITIES

A fundamental issue is whether to view the organization as a "real" entity. Understanding the reality of organizations requires some philosophical assumptions that must be made explicit. Following Burrell and Morgan (1979, 4–7), these are as follows:

1. In terms of ontology, a realist as opposed to a nominalist position is assumed. The nominalist position is that reality is constructed through the cognition of individuals. The External world is composed of artificial creations of peoples' minds. The realist position, on the other hand, is that the world external to individual cognition is a real one. It is made up of tangible and relatively immutable structures. Trees are real and so are organizations.

2. In terms of epistemology, a positivist position is assumed. Antipositivists believe that the world is relative and can only be understood from the perspectives of human actors in particular situations. Positivists assume that it is possible to search for and find regularities and causal relationships among organizational elements.

3. In terms of assumptions about human nature, a determinist position is assumed. People are seen as controlled by the situation or environment in which they are acting. The voluntarist position, in contrast, sees human actors as autonomous and free willed.

4. In terms of methodology, a nomothetic position is assumed. The nomothetic approach is based on hypothesis testing, with scientific rigor and systematic research protocols. The alternative approach is the ideographic position, which emphasizes detailed analyses of the meanings that people attach to situations.

These assumptions serve as guides for the analysis of organizational behavior. Organizational behavior is here viewed as the behavior of organizations.

This position is obviously not shared by many organizational theorists. Simon (1964) has argued strongly against rectifying the concept of organization. He views the organization as a system of interacting individuals. In his exchange theory, Blau (1964) emphasizes interactions between individuals as the heart of the organization. My own view is that the individualistic approach is too narrow and leads one to ignore critical aspects of organizations.

We view organizations as real first because they persist over time, beyond the tenures of their members. Individuals come and go, but the organization continues. The organization itself, of course, can be viewed as having a life cycle of its own, with a birth, maturation, and death (Kimberly and Miles 1980). But most of the organizations cited in the opening quotations have persisted through many generations of members.

To use a personal example, I will eventually leave the sociology department at the State University of New York (SUNY) at Albany through resignation, retirement, or death. Someone will be found to replace me, and my courses, committee assignments, and administrative responsibilities will be covered. Of course I hope that I will have made an impact on programs and people, but the main point is that the organization will persist through successive generations of students, faculty, and administrators.

Persistence over time is one of the key defining characteristics of organizations. In this classic analysis of forms of authority, Weber (1946) noted that charismatic authority had to be routinized if authority were to outlast the lifetime of the charismatic founder of an organization. The history of social movements is filled with the debris of organizations that did not endure. When a social movement or any organization does persist, it then has a reality of its own.

A second reason for accepting the fact of organizations' reality is that they develop and maintain *procedures*. Indeed, this is one of the reasons why organizations persist. Later we will consider some of the outcomes of organizational procedures. For the moment, the important point is that organizational procedures are designed to be implemented regardless of the specific personnel doing the implementing. Procedures can vary widely in terms of their focus and explicitness. They can define the techniques by which raw materials are handled, or specify the manner in which interpersonal relationships, both within and outside the organization, are to be carried out.

While the focus here is on organizational reality, the role of individuals must be considered. Procedures are creations of individuals, singly or collectively. Procedures are modified by individuals. Individuals also conform to or deviate from procedures. The procedures themselves are part of the organization.

The third aspect of organizational reality is organizational *goals.* (Perrow 1961; Simon 1964; Mohr 1973; Hannan and Freeman 1977a). Much of the controversy surrounding the issue of goals has to do with the analysis of organizational effectiveness. I strongly believe (Hall 1982) that goals remain crucial components of any consideration of organizational effectiveness, but that is not the issue here. For our purposes, the key aspect of goals is that they are critical components of the decision-making process, above and beyond the inputs of individuals and the external environment, and hence part of what makes the organization a reality.

Many activities carried on in organizations are unrelated to goals. Some are purely administrative, such as filling out forms that demonstrate compliance with a governmental regulation. Others are entirely social, such as gathering around the coffeepot or machine. Still other activities are responses to external pressures, such as designing automotive equipment that meets governmental standards. But when important decisions are to be made, organizational goals often play an important part in determining the outcome.

> SUNY-Albany, like the rest of the SUNY system and many other colleges and universities in the United States was faced with a budget cut. The university was informed that it would have to trim a specified number of positions from its personnel roster. It was up to each campus to determine where these cuts were to be made. Each vice president prepared a list of positions that could be cut. Each vice president also argued vehemently about the merits of cutting positions in the *other* vice-presidential areas, in order to protect the positions in his own area.
>
> This situation is one in which power might be assumed to be the critical variable. Indeed, earlier research (Pfeffer and Salancik, 1974) suggests that this is exactly the case. Hills and Mahoney (1978) report a similar finding, with the modification that in times of affluence, decisions are more likely to be made by workload or bureaucratic criteria, while in times of adversity, decisions would be made on the basis of power coalitions. The SUNY situation was certainly one of adversity.

> At the same time, goals did not just disappear from the situation. Issues such as the emphasis on research in the university, needs for the continued recruitment and retention of highly qualified faculty and students to achieve the goal of being a first-rate university, and reiterations of the importance of having a safe and attractive campus environment were voiced and served as much more than rhetoric. In the end, the cuts made were based on decisions that involved power coalitions and *goals.* In this particular university, a great deal of time and effort goes into the annual review of goals and priorities, so that the example may not be typical, but it would appear that such situations are not all that unique.
>
> The actual outcome of the cuts was that some faculty lines, some administrative lines, and some support lines (custodial, security, bus drivers, and so on) were cut. The cuts were not made on the basis of a simple formula, such as seniority or an across the board formula. Rather, each cut was analyzed from the standpoint of the impact it would have on the campus.[1]

In other words, organizational goals can transcend individual decision makers. This conclusion does not depend on an overly rational view of organizations. Rather, it emerges from an acceptance of goals as a component of the reality of organizations.

The fourth argument for organizational reality is the fact that purely organizational characteristics can be and are *measured.* When we consider corporate profit or loss, we actually are making an organizational measurement. Financial, scholarly, and popular measures of organizational effectiveness treat data such as profits as evidence of a truly organizational phenomenon.

Researchers have developed diverse means by which other important organizational properties can be measured. Lazarsfeld and Menzel (1961) and Lincoln and Zeitz (1980) have shown how data collected from individuals can be aggregated to the organizational level with strong explanatory power. Data about organizational properties can also be obtained from official records and other such "hard" sources. While the utility of measuring and interrelating organizational structural characteristics is under debate, much sound research has been based on the measurement of organizational properties. There is also a more limited set of studies dealing with relational phenomena in organizations, such as power relationships and innovation processes. It is fair to conclude that organizational researchers have been largely unable to capture the dynamics of organizational behavior, except in case studies. At the same time,

---

1. R. H. Hall, *Organizations: Structure and Process,* 3d ed. (Englewood Cliffs, N.J.: Prentice-Hall, 1982), 298–99. Copyright 1982. Reprinted by permission of Prentice-Hall, Inc.

from a positivistic point of view, the success in measuring organizational properties is indicative of their inherent reality.

Finally, we should consider the *individual*. People experience organizational reality. Approaching organizations from the perspective of symbolic interaction, Denzin (1977, 905–906) notes,

> Rather than focusing on formal structural attributes, the interactionist focuses on organizations as *negotiated* productions that differentially constrain their members; they are seen as moving patterns of accommodative adjustment among organized parties. Although organizations create formal structures, every organization in its day-to-day activities is produced and created by individuals, individuals who are subject to and constrained by the vagaries and inconsistencies of the human form. Organizations . . . are best conceptualized as complex, shifting networks of social relationships. The sum total of these relationships—whether real or only symbolized, whether assumed or taken for granted or problematic and troublesome—constitute the organization as it is sensed, experienced, and acted upon by the individual member. Power, control, coercion, and deception become central commodities of negotiation in those arenas that make up the organization.

While Denzin's approach is more individualistic and social-psychological than that taken here, his point illustrates well the thrust of this argument. Those who interact with organizations, from within or without, experience them as real.

Moreover, organizational properties directly influence the behavior of their individual members. Whenever a person follows organizational procedures, such as calling a specified telephone number to get approval for a credit-card purchase, it is the organization that is determining the behavior and not the individual. I am not arguing that all behavior in organizations is organizationally determined, but a good part of it is. It is probably fair to say that the more important the action is to the organization, the greater the individual input will be. Individual discretion increases at higher levels of the hierarchy, but even at the very top, organizational factors impinge upon individual behavior.

A useful approach is to view individual behavior as role behavior. Kahn et al. (1964, 31) note,

> To a considerable extent, the role expectations held by the members of a role set—the prescriptions and proscriptions associated with a particular position—are determined by the broader organizational context. The organizational structure, the functional specialization and division of labor, and the formal reward system dictate the major content of a given office. What the occu-

pant of that office is supposed to do, with and for whom, is given by these and other properties of the organization itself. Although other human beings are doing the "supposing" and rewarding, *the structural properties of organization are sufficiently stable so that they can be treated as independent of the particular persons in the role set* [emphasis added]. For such properties as size, number of echelons, and rate of growth, the justifiable abstraction of organizational properties from individual behavior is even more obvious.

Organizational properties are thus a determinant of individual behavior. In some instances they would be the dominant influence, while in others they would be less important.

Our final consideration of the individual comes from a tradition concerned with the nature and extent of the power that organizations have over individuals and classes of individuals. To the extent that members are oriented to it, an organization exerts power over their lives and actions (Clegg and Dunkerly 1980, 209–10). We will examine some other considerations from this power perspective in the next section. The basic point here is that economic and political control are seen as consequences of individuals' positions in organizations.

ORGANIZATIONS AS ACTORS

If the reality of organizations is controversial, the argument that they are capable of action may be even more difficult to accept. The position to be taken here is that human actors do in fact carry out organizational activities. On the basis of the arguments in the previous section, however, I will suggest that the actions carried out on behalf of the organization contain strong organizational inputs that can transcend the individual. I will also suggest that the outcomes of organizational actions can have broader ramifications than the actions themselves.

Some rather benign examples provide evidence for the manner in which organizations act. Cashing a personal check is an activity familiar to most adults. If I wish to cash a check at a branch of my own bank, the teller, after a rather perfunctory greeting, which is itself usually programmed by the organization through training, checks on the status of my account through the computer terminal at his or her station. These are not individual discretionary actions, but rather the result of bank policies. If I seek to cash a check at a bank where I do not have an account, I am refused. This again is that bank's policy. Policies and procedures are designed specifically to minimize human discretion in many situations.

Crozier's (1964) analysis of two French organizations provides additional documentation of organizational actions. He found that "impersonal rules delimit, in great detail, all the functions of every individual within the organization. They prescribe the behavior to be followed in all possible events. Equally impersonal rules determine who shall be chosen for each job and the career patterns that can be followed" (pp. 187–88). Crozier then went on to demonstrate that this creates a vicious circle in which the workers follow the rules for their own sake, ignoring the goals that the rules were originally designed to support.

Robert Merton's (1957) analysis of the "bureaucratic personality" emphasized the personal consequences of overadherence to rules and procedures. The bureaucratic personality becomes one of trained incapacity, because new conditions may arise for which the organizationally based responses are inappropriate.

Even interpersonal intimacy does not escape the long arm of the organization. Quinn (1977) found that organizations attempt to control romance through dismissals, transfers, reprimands, or other efforts to cool developing ardor.

These examples of the control of individual behavior are quite straightforward. The interpretation of organizational actions becomes more complex when their consequences for classes of people and the overall social structure are considered. Stolzenberg (1978) and Baron and Bielby (1980) have demonstrated that employers (organizations) are the primary mechanisms by which people are assigned to occupations and by which earnings are distributed among individuals. Braverman (1974) and his followers have suggested that this process represents an attempt by capitalists to extend organizational hegemony over workers by reducing skill requirements and the power of workers.

As an example of this point of view, Edwards (1979, 131) notes,

> Bureaucratic control establishes the impersonal force of "company rules" or "company policy" as the basis for control. . . . Capitalists were to retain overall control of the enterprise's operations through their power to establish the rules and procedures. But once the goals and structure were set, the management process was to proceed without need of, and (except in exceptional circumstances) without benefit of, the conscious intervention of the personal power of foremen, supervisors, or capitalists.

Writers such as Marglin (1974), Stone (1974), and Clawson (1980) have argued that this process is a conscious political attempt by capitalists to control the working class through skill degradation. Form (1981), on the other hand, presents evidence that indicates that skills have actually been upgraded since 1870. He also suggests that the current division of labor is based on efficiency, rather than power, considerations. Although both Clawson (1980) and Stone (1974) have presented limited evidence on the motivations of business owners in the early 1900s, we do not have convincing indications of whether the changes that took place during that era were based on a desire to control or a desire to be more efficient. Like Form, I believe that there is not enough evidence to validate the Marxist position that the motivation was control.

Regardless of the motivation, organizations do have policies in regard to the placement of different kinds of personnel. Miles, Snow, and Pfeffer (1974) and Kanter (1977) have documented the manner in which organizations discriminate against women. Discrimination against minority-group members is still greater. Through their hiring practices, promotional procedures, and opportunity structures, contemporary organizations persist in maintaining secondary labor markets for workers who are viewed as marginal. Policy can work the other way, of course, as in an organization that has a policy of affirmative action in hiring and promotion.

A very different analysis of organizations as actors can be found in Denzin's (1977) analysis of the liquor industry. He begins with the assumption that "an industry is like an individual . . . it has a character, a structure, a system of habits of its own. Its pattern is out of accord with a normative design; its activities conform very imperfectly with a charted course of industrial events" (Hamilton et al. 1938, 4).

Denzin then analyzes the criminogenic tendencies in the liquor industry, involving both intended and unintended violations of the legal code. He suggests that this tendency exists at all levels of the liquor industry and that it can be traced to the historical context of the industry's development and to relationships within the industry. According to Denzin, there are five "tiers" in the industry—distillers, distributors, retailers, drinkers, and state and local liquor-code enforcement agencies. Relations among these tiers and among organizations within tiers contribute to bribery of officials, shakedown of retailers, protection of licenses, and alterations of zoning codes. Such violations of law become the normal means of operation within the industry.

Here again it is individuals who carry out the actual illegal activity, but their actions are determined by organizational expectations. To balance the picture, we should point out that legal, moral, and societally beneficial actions also are the result of organizational expectations.

One final point should be considered in viewing organizations as actors. The modern organization is a *legal* entity, just like an individual person. Coleman (1974) notes that this legality is granted by the state, itself a legal entity. The state gives individuals rights and responsibilities. It does the same for organizations. The size of the modern organization, coupled with its legal rights, gives it tremendous power in contemporary society. Coleman also points out that the state or government is apparently more comfortable dealing with organizations than with individuals. There is a tendency to give organizations preferential treatment in areas as diverse as taxation and rights to privacy.

The recognition of organizations as legal entities and actors can be seen in civil and criminal court actions. Hall notes,

> Organizations, rather than individuals, can be held responsible for certain actions. Air New Zealand, for example, was held responsible for a crash that killed 257 people. (*New York Times* 1981). A new flight plan was put into effect which led to a collision course with a volcano. The crew had not been informed. The judge in the case also accused airline officials of attempting to conceal their mistakes. Swigert and Farrell (1980 81) analyzed the case of the Ford Motor Company which was charged with homicide. They found that the mass media shifted its orientation from the recognition of harm based on mechanical defects to an attribution of nonrepentance on the part of the offender. Swigert and Farrell concluded that a shift in public attitudes had occurred in which an organization was believed to have engaged in criminality in a form previously reserved for individuals. The fact that Ford was found not guilty does not alter the importance in the shift in public attitude.[2]

Given their policies and procedures, their structures, and their legal status, it is reasonable to treat organizations as actors in the social arena.

SOME TYPES AND CONSEQUENCES OF ORGANIZATIONAL ACTIONS

This section will consider the relationship of organizational characteristics to individual behavior, to other organizational characteristics, and to the important process of communications. My hope is that these illustrative examples will indicate the value of a sociological approach to understanding organizational behavior.

As discussed earlier, organizations can be considered as mechanisms of control. The exact degree to which an individual is controlled by the organization, and under what circumstances, remains a topic for serious research. It is well documented that organizations expect their members to exercise varying degrees of discretion. Some positions have job descriptions and procedural manuals that literally define every action and behavior that the incumbents are to perform. In some situations, technology exercises control over the worker, as on the assembly line or telephone switchboard. At the other extreme, a great deal of individual discretion is desired and anticipated in certain cases. The differences in the degree of individual discretion are related to hierarchical position and the occupational specialization or professionalization involved in the position. Even when high levels of discretion are anticipated and exercised, however, the organization is not removed from the equation. Blau and Schoenherr (1971) have demonstrated that when discretion is emphasized, the organization typically has exercised strong initial control in selecting the individuals involved. By hiring only personnel with specified credentials, the organization indirectly retains control over individual behavior. Through the process of socialization and selection, it also controls the behavior of personnel promoted through the system into higher-level positions (Kanter 1977). Organizations want predictable responses from their members and hence exercise direct or indirect control.

Organizational control is exerted through both formal and informal means. A *Wall Street Journal* article by Susan Chace (1982) about IBM's successful control of its workers' dress and social behavior, documents the case of a woman executive who was dismissed because she was dating a male executive of a competing firm. She subsequently sued IBM and won the case on the grounds that the dismissal was based on unwritten and thus unenforceable norms. But the culture of IBM was so pervasive that most employees could not distinguish between what was officially and unofficially mandated.

Organizations can never achieve perfect control over their members. The whole "natural system" approach to organizations (Scott 1981) is an attempt to demonstrate the importance of individual inputs and social interaction patterns for organizations. The point here is that, while imperfect in its outcome, control is attempted, and the behavior of individuals is influenced by organizational-control mechanisms.

Organizational characteristics influence the reactions of individuals to their work in the organization. Herman, Dunham, and Hulin (1975) report that a per-

2. R. H. Hall, *Organizations: Structure and Process*, 3d ed. (Englewood Cliffs, N.J.: Prentice-Hall, 1982), 24. Copyright 1982. Reprinted by permission of Prentice-Hall, Inc.

son's position (e.g., clerk, supervisor, or manager) helps shape his or her reaction to the organization. While factors such as sex and age are also influential, the position of the individual appears to be more important. In a similar vein, satisfaction with work is related to the position in the structure. Ivancevich and Donnelly (1975) found that salesmen were more satisfied and less anxious in organizations with fewer hierarchical levels.

Organizational characteristics and individual characteristics interact. Even in situations in which individual characteristics might seem crucial, organizational characteristics appear to be important, too. For example, the capacity for innovation, which is generally considered essential for organizational survival, has been found to be strongly linked to organizational characteristics. Baldridge and Burnham (1975) found that organizational size and complexity, together with environmental characteristics, were more related to organizational innovations than were individual factors, such as age, attitudes, and education. Individuals come up with innovative ideas, but organizational factors apparently determine whether they are developed and implemented.

There has been a great deal of research on the relationships among organizational characteristics. Indeed, a major concern of organizational research during the 1960s and early 1970s was the nature of, interrelationships among, and sources of organizational structural arrangements. The present discussion will include some selected examples from this literature, with more comprehensive statements available in Hage (1980), Scott (1981), and Hall (1982).

A major finding of Lawrence and Lorsch's (1967) classic study on contingency theory was that, in a set of plastics firms, high levels of differentiation or complexity, coupled with both integration and conflict among the departments, were associated with organizational effectiveness as measured by market and economic indicators. For our purposes, the key contribution of the study is its demonstration of the relationship of organizational characteristics to the critical-effectiveness outcome.

Blau and Schoenherr's (1971) important study of government agencies also deals with differentiation. They found that highly differentiated organizations faced problems in coordination and communications. Personnel in the managerial hierarchy spent more time on these problems than in actual supervision. There is pressure in complex organizations to add personnel for coordination and control operations, increasing the proportion of the total personnel devoted to such activities. This introduces an interesting paradox. Large organizations can achieve financial savings through economies of scale. At the same time, they experience cross-pressures to add personnel to handle control, coordina-tion, and conflict-resolution issues. Similarly, decisions to disperse operations physically, add divisions, or add hierarchical levels may be made in the interests of economy. But savings achieved by these decisions are counterbalanced by the costs of keeping the organization together.

Research along these lines has slowed in recent years, but the relationships among the organizational characteristics remain part of the reality of organizational behavior. My own opinion is that research on such relationships should continue, since we have not reached closure on the nature, sources, and consequences of organizational characteristics. At the same time, there is some agreement on the consequences of certain organizational characteristics for crucial processes within organizations, for example, communications.

It is generally recognized that hierarchical relationships influence the nature and content of communications. Brinkerhoff (1972) found that the form of communications differed by hierarchical level, with first-line supervisors engaging in spontaneous communications, and higher levels of management relying on staff conferences. Blau and Scott (1962) noted that hierarchical differences inhibited communications and generally interfered with the accuracy of the communication process, as subordinates sought to protect themselves and were unlikely to criticize their superiors. Katz and Kahn (1978) have also shown how the presence of hierarchy affects the communication process.

Communications are also affected by horizontal differentiation or specialization. Lawrence and Lorsch (1967) and Hage (1974) have pointed out that different departments can have very different views of the world, which interfere with the flow of ideas: As Hall notes,

> For example, in a petroleum company it is quite conceivable that the geological, engineering, legal, and public relations divisions could all come to different conclusions about the desirability of starting new oil-well drilling in various locations. Each would be correct in its own area of expertise, and the coordination of top officials would obviously be required when a final decision had to be made. During the period of planning or development, however, communications between these divisions would probably be characterized as nonproductive, since the specialists involved would be talking their own language, one that is unfamiliar to those not in the same profession. From the evidence at hand, each division would also be correct in its assessment of the situation and would view the other divisions as not understanding the "true" meanings of the situation.[3]

3. R. H. Hall, *Organizations: Structure and Process*, 3d ed. (Englewood Cliffs, N.J.: Prentice-Hall, 1982), 201. Copyright 1982. Reprinted by permission of Prentice-Hall, Inc.

These examples should have given some sense of the sociological approach to organizational behavior. The approach taken here is not without its critics, of course. Argyris (1972) argued that by ignoring the importance of individual personality, group dynamics, and interpersonal relationships, sociologists take an overly static view of the organizational world. More recently, Zey-Ferrell and Aiken (1981) suggested that the kind of approach taken here is overly rational, ideologically conservative, static, and ahistorical, and deemphasizes the role of power and power coalitions within organizations. These criticisms are to a large extent correct, at least as characterizations of the research of the 1960s and early 1970s. More recent developments, to be discussed in the next section, have moved the sociological analysis of organizational behavior away from a rather static emphasis on structure. This more recent literature has focused on organizations as responders to factors outside their own boundaries.

ORGANIZATIONS AS RESPONDERS

The literature reviewed in this section comes from a very different tradition from that which has been discussed so far. Indeed, much of it has been a response to the research examining internal organizational operations. Nevertheless, this literature tends to confirm the central argument of this chapter—that organizational behavior can be understood at the organizational level, and this understanding yields important contributions to a comprehensive view of organizational behavior.

The approach to be considered treats the organization as a member of a population. It draws on such concepts as the organizational "life cycle" (Kimberly and Miles 1980) or "births, deaths, and transformations" of organizational forms (Aldrich and Fish 1981). McKelvey (1978 and forthcoming) has attempted to develop an evolutionary taxonomy of organizations based on the view of organizations as units of analysis within a population of organizations.

This population-ecology or natural-selection approach to organizations (Aldrich and Pfeffer 1976; Hannan and Freeman 1977b; Aldrich, 1979; Kasarda and Bidwell 1979) focuses on the nature of the fit between the organization and its environment. Aldrich and Pfeffer identify three stages in the population-ecology of organizations. In the first stage, planned or unplanned variations in organizational forms occur. Then follows the selection stage. There is a strong biological analogy to mutations here. Organizational forms that fit are

selected by the environment over forms that do not. In the final retention stage, forms that have been selected are "preserved, duplicated, or reproduced" (p. 81). The emphasis here is on environmental selection and retention.

A key concept in the population-ecology approach is that organizational forms fill niches in the environment. Niches are viewed as distinct combinations of resources and other constraints that are sufficient to support an organizational form. For example, the corporate conglomerate—a set of unrelated industries under a single ownership—arose as a new organization form selected by the environment as appropriate within the constraints of economic, legal, and political conditions. The imagery here again is biological, with organisms moving into various niches, some to live and reproduce and others to die without progeny.

This approach has been criticized from several standpoints. Aldrich and Pfeffer (1976) themselves note that the sources of the original variations are not specified. The processes that lead to selection are ignored, including the managerial decisions to enter or not enter various niches. There is also an assumption of perfect economic competition (survival of the fittest), which scarcely ever occurs. Van de Ven (1979) and Hall (1982) argue that the population-ecology approach ignores factors related to effectiveness as an intervening variable between the environment and organizational form. It also ignores both internal and external political and moral considerations. But organizational forms do have an impact on internal and external participants and constituents, and these can be beneficial or detrimental.

The population-ecology model takes an extreme position, emphasizing the influence on organizational behavior of events beyond the control of the organization or its members. If the resources in an organizational niche begin to run dry, organizational behavior will be overwhelmingly dominated by the environment unless other actions are taken. But organizations are less passive than the preceding discussion may have suggested—a major consideration in an alternative approach to the issue of organizational-environment interactions.

The *resource-dependence* model of organizations is an attempt to bring organizational actors back into the picture. In this model (Aldrich and Pfeffer 1976; Pfeffer and Salancik 1978), the environment remains a major influence on organizations, but the organization itself is seen as an active participant. The model contains elements of the contingency approach (Lawrence and Lorsch 1967; Becker and Neuhauser 1975). It is also closely related to other recently proposed models, such as the political-economy model (Wamsley and Zald 1973; Benson 1975) and the dependence exchange model (Hasenfeld 1972; Jacobs 1974).

The resource-dependence approach begins by assuming that the environment, containing resources and a political structure, is crucial for organizational operations. It then adds in the notion that organizations deal actively with the environment and are not just passive recipients of pressures, as the population-ecology model would suggest. Organizations will attempt to manipulate other organizations to their own advantage. Pfeffer and Salancik (1978) emphasize the role of management in the process of actively dealing with the environment. Strategic choices have to be made. Also important as a basic premise of this model is the idea that all organizations are dependent upon the environment for resources. Even extractive industries that own the land from which their lumber or coal is taken depend on the environment for personnel and financial resources. Since the environment is largely composed of other organizations, the resource-dependence model is actually an interorganizational resource-dependence model.

The idea of strategic choice (Chandler 1962; Child 1972) is a key component in this approach. When faced with environmental contingencies, the organization makes decisions among a set of alternatives. The resource-dependence model emphasizes the importance of internal power arrangements in the decision process. Shifting coalitions can alter the direction taken by the organization. As it has been presented in the literature, the resource-dependence model makes no note of organizational goals, a point to which I will return shortly.

Like the population-ecology model, the resource-dependence approach deals with the variations, selection, and retention processes (Aldrich and Pfeffer 1976). Variations in organizations occur as the result of conscious efforts to respond to environmental contingencies—attempts to absorb interdependence and uncertainty, either completely, through merger, or partially, through cooperation or the movement of personnel among organizations (Aldrich and Pfeffer 1976; 87).

The selection process occurs as strategic choices are made. Decisions are not totally constrained by environmental pressures. Organizations attempt to manipulate the environment in their favor by creating demand for their products or services. They also operate through the state political process in seeking protective tariffs or other trade restraints. The same thing happens in the public sector. Public organizations have their own constituents and lobbying groups, as can be vividly illustrated by the various attempts that have been made to limit the size and scope of agencies such as the Defense Department or Environmental Protection Agency in the United States. So far the Defense Department has been vastly more successful than the Environmental Protection Agency in preserving its prerogatives, demonstrating that the manipulation of the environment by organizations is problematic and uncertain, and that organizations remain subject to environmental pressures even as strategic choices are made.

Perception represents an important component of the selection process. The way in which an organizational actor perceives its environment is shaped by factors such as organizational personnel policies (Starbuck 1976). Such policies can potentially leave the firm with a very homogeneous set of executives (Kanter 1977), in which case there would be more uniformity in environmental perceptions. In more differentiated organizations, perceptions would vary more widely, perhaps, making the organization more adaptive.

Even within the environment that is perceived, choice is limited. Legal and economic barriers can prevent an organization from moving in the directions that seem appropriate. A small firm may be unable to make inroads into a market dominated by large firms. Here again, the organization is a responder.

The retention process occurs as organizations set their forms and operations in place. This is bureaucratization. Documentation and filing systems are developed. Policies and procedures ensure uniformity of practice. Hierarchies are created and become bastions of power. Particular credentials are demanded for employment, and organizational socialization programs are implemented. Those who advance in the organization are screened and filtered.

Here the argument has come full circle. Because particular forms are retained through the bureaucratization process, organizational behavior becomes organizationally based. As environmental pressures force new variations, the new strategic decisions that are made will be heavily influenced by the existing organizational arrangements, although this point is not noted by advocates of the resource-dependence position.

The resource-dependence model is an important advance in organizational theory. Its recognition of the power of internal and external political and economic factors, although not yet well documented through systematic research, will probably shape organizational analyses for the next decade. To view organizations as active agents in their environments, although subject to the bureaucratization constraints I have noted, is to recognize the importance of decision making and decision makers. A comprehensive organization theory would incorporate the kinds of organizational behavior described in this chapter with the more individual organizational behavior of decision makers and other individuals.

One final observation about the resource-dependence model: its failure to acknowledge the role of organizational goals runs counter to the reality of actual decision making. To use a simple example, suppose that an organization pursues the single goal of a specified type of profit. It then considers environmental constraints *along with* the profit goal. Organizations do not simply respond to environmental pressures alone. Some resource-dependence theorists would argue that the organization seeks survival in the face of environmental constraints, rather than goals, but this appears to be too limited a view of the contents of decision making.

Bringing goals back into organizational theory makes no assumption about the rationality involved, nor is it assumed that organizations are only instruments designed to achieve goals. Rather, goals are added back in as part of the reason organizations act as they do. Organizations do face external pressures and they may be forced out of existence or have to alter their operations drastically. The models that emphasize organizational response to the environment are correct in pointing out the importance of the environment for the birth and death of organizations. They err, however, in their total dismissal of goal considerations.

The perspective taken here thus parallels that of Simon (1964), who noted that "goals are constraints on organizational decision making." While the purpose of his article was to argue against the rectification of the goal concept, his view of goals as constraints on decision making is exactly in line with the argument that has been presented here. *Both* goals and environmental constraints are major components of organizational behavior.

CONCLUSIONS

This chapter has not attempted a comprehensive view of organizational behavior. I have largely ignored the important literature on power relationships within organizations and that on the power of organizations as actors in the social system. Nor have I considered the manner in which individuals interpret organizational situations and how they actually act. Such foci are important for a total understanding of organizational behavior. But I hope the present discussion has given some sense of the degree to which purely organizational variables can explain observed reality.

What are the implications of the perspective presented here? To some extent, organizational sociology seems to be a new form of dismal science. It indicates that, because much individual behavior in organizations is organizationally based, efforts to train individuals are doomed to failure unless the organizations themselves are changed. Leadership training, behavior-modification efforts, and the like will have little impact unless the basic procedures in an organization are modified to reflect an altered view of human nature. When change strategies focus on modifying the individual and not the organization, operations will continue as before.

Moreover, the population-ecology model suggests that, since organizations reflect powerful forces in their environment, attempts to adopt organizational forms that are not congruent with that environment may be doomed to failure. The current strong interest in Japanese-style organizations would be a case in point. Unless Western social organization in general were modified, the Japanese form would not find support over the long run.

Two other implications of the sociological perspective have a more positive potential. First, the recognition that organizations have multiple goals that conflict to some degree provides a basis for introducing ethical considerations. To the goal configurations already present, organizations can add additional goals, perhaps involving treating members at all levels of the organization as complete human beings and examining the whole range of consequences of organizational actions. These would serve as additional constraints in the decision-making process, and make it more difficult. The difference would be one of degree, however, since the constraints on decision making are already complicated in certain contradictions.

A final implication is that organizational procedures should be reexamined in light of the assumptions that they make about the nature of individuals in organizations and in terms of the consequences they have for individuals and classes of individuals. In the recent past, such reexamination has led to pressures from public policy for affirmative action or environmental impact assessments. There is no real reason why the pressure has to come from the public-policy arena. Private policy could also involve such reexaminations.

REFERENCES

Aldrich, H. E. 1979. *Organizations and Environments.* Englewood Cliffs, N.J.: Prentice-Hall.

Aldrich, H. E., and D. Fish. 1981. "Origins of Organizational Forms, Deaths, and Transformations." Mimeograph, Cornell University.

Aldrich, H. E., and J. Pfeffer. 1976. "Environments of Organizations." *Annual Review of Sociology.* Vol. 2. Palo Alto, Calif.: Annual Reviews.

Argyris, C. 1972. *The Applicability of Organizational Sociology.* London: Cambridge University Press.

Baldridge, J. V., and R. A. Burnham. 1975. "Organizational Innovation: Individual, Organizational and Environmental Impacts." *Administrative Science Quarterly* 20, no. 2 (June): 165–76.

Baron, J. N., and W. T. Bielby. 1980. "Bringing the Firms Back In: Stratification, Segmentation and the Organization of Work." *American Sociological Review* 45, no. 5 (October): 737–65.

Becker, S. W., and D. Neuhauser. 1975. *The Efficient Organization.* New York: Elsevier Science. 1975.

Benson, J. K. 1975. "The Interlocking Network as a Political Economy." *Administrative Science Quarterly* 20, no. 2 (June): 229–49.

Blau, P. M. 1955. *The Dynamics of Bureaucracy.* Chicago: University of Chicago Press.

———. 1964. *Exchange and Power in Social Life.* New York: Wiley.

Blau, P. M., and W. R. Scott. 1962. *The Formal Organization.* San Francisco: Chandler.

Blau, P. M., and R. A. Schoenherr. 1971. *The Structure of Organizations.* New York: Basic Books.

Braverman, H. 1974. *Labor and Monopoly Capital.* New York: Monthly Review Press.

Brinkerhoff, M. B. 1972. "Hierarchical Status, Contingencies, and the Administrative Staff Conference." *Administrative Science Quarterly* 17, no. 3 (September):395–407.

Burrell, G., and G. Morgan. 1979. *Sociological Paradigms and Organizational Analysis.* London: Heinemann.

Chace, S. 1982. "Rules and Discipline, Goals and Praise Shape IBMers' Taut World." *Wall Street Journal.* 8 April, p. 10.

Chandler, A. D., Jr. 1962. *Strategy and Structure.* Cambridge, Mass.: MIT Press.

Child, J. C. 1972. "Organizational Structure, Environment, and Performance: The Role of Strategic Choice." *Sociology* 6, no. 1 (January): 1–22.

Clawson, D. 1980. *Bureaucracy and the Labor Process: The Transformation of U.S. Industry, 1860–1920.* New York: Monthly Review Press.

Clegg, S., and D. Dunkerly. 1980. *Organization, Class and Control.* London: Routledge & Kegan Paul.

Coleman, J. S. 1974. *Power and the Structure of Society.* New York: Norton.

Crozier, M. 1964. *The Bureaucratic Phenomenon.* Chicago: University of Chicago Press.

Denzin, N. K. 1977. "Notes on the Criminogenic Hypothesis: A Case Study of the American Liquor Industry." *American Sociological Review* 42, no. 6 (December): 905–20.

Edwards, R. C. 1979. *Contested Terrain.* New York: Basic Books.

Form, W. 1981. "Resolving Ideological Issues on the Division of Labor." In *Theory and Research in Sociology,* ed. H. M. Blalock, Jr. New York: Free Press.

Gouldner, A. 1954. *Patterns of Industrial Bureaucracy.* New York: Free Press.

Hage, J. 1974. *Communications and Organizational Control.* New York: Wiley.

———. 1980. *Theories of Organizations.* New York: Wiley.

Hall, R. H. 1982. *Organizations: Structure and Process.* 3d ed. Englewood Cliffs, N.J.: Prentice-Hall.

Hamilton, W., M. Adams, A. Abrahamson, H. E. Meiklejohn, I. Till, and G. Marshall. 1938. *Price and Price Policies.* New York: McGraw-Hill.

Hannan, M. T., and J. R. Freeman. 1977a. "Obstacles to Comparative Studies." In *New Perspectives on Organizational Effectiveness,* ed. P. S. Goodman and J. Pennings. San Francisco: Jossey-Bass.

———. 1977b. "The Population Ecology of Organizations." *American Journal of Sociology* 82, no. 5 (April): 929–64.

Hasenfeld, Y. 1972. "People Processing Organizations: An Exchange Approach." *American Sociological Review* 37, no. 3 (June): 256–63.

Herman, J. B., R. Dunham, and C. Hulin. 1975. "Organizational Structure, Demographic Characteristics, and Employee Responses." *Organizational Behavior and Human Performance* 13, no. 2 (April): 206–32.

Hills, F. S., and T. Mahoney. 1978. "University Budgets and Organizational Decision Making." *Administrative Science Quarterly* 23, no. 3 (September): 454–65.

Ivancevich, J. M., and J. H. Donnelly, Jr. 1975. "Relation of Organizational Structure to Job Satisfaction, Anxiety, Stress, and Performance." *Administrative Science Quarterly* 20, no. 2 (June): 272–80.

Jacobs, D. 1974. "Dependence and Vulnerability: An Exchange Approach to the Control of Organizations." *Administrative Science Quarterly* 19, no. 1 (March): 45–59.

Kahn, R. L., D. M. Wolfe, R. P. Quinn, J. D. Snoek, and R. A. Rosenthal. 1964. *Organizational Stress: Studies in Role Conflict and Ambiguity.* New York: Wiley.

Kanter, R. M. 1977. *Men and Women of the Corporation.* New York: Basic Books.

Kasarda, J. D., and C. E. Bidwell. 1979. "A Human Ecological Theory of Organizational Structuring." In *Sociological Human Ecology: Contemporary Issues and Applications,* ed. M. Micklin and H. M. Choldin. New York: Wiley.

Katz, D., and R. L. Kahn. 1978. *The Social Psychology of Organizations.* 2d ed. New York: Academic Press.

Kimberly, J. R., and R. A. Miles and Associates. 1980. *The Organizational Life Cycle.* San Francisco: Jossey-Bass.

Lawrence, P. R., and J. W. Lorsch. 1967. *Organization and*

Environment. Cambridge, Mass.: Harvard University Press.

Lazarsfeld, P. S., and H. Menzel. 1961. "On the Relationship Between Individual and Collective Properties." In *Complex Organizations: A Sociological Reader*, ed. A. Etzioni. New York: Holt, Rinehart and Winston.

Lincoln, J. R., and G. Zeitz. 1980. "Organizational Properties from Aggregate Data." *American Sociological Review* 45, no. 3 (June).

Lipset, S. M., M. A. Trow, and J. S. Coleman. 1965. *Union Democracy*. New York: Free Press.

Marglin, S. A. 1974. "What Do Bosses Do? The Origins and Functions of Hierarchy in Capitalist Production." *The Review of Radical Political Economics* 6, no. 2 (Summer): 60–112.

McKelvey, B. 1978. "Organizational Systematics: Taxonomic Lessons from Biology." *Management Science* 24, no. 13 (September): 1428–40.

———. 1982. *Organizational Systematics— Systematics, Taxonomy, Evolution, Classification*. Berkeley, Calif.: University of California Press.

Merton, R. K., A. P. Gray, B. Hockey, and H. Selvin, eds. 1957. *Reader in Bureaucracy*. New York: Free Press.

Michels, R. 1949. *Political Parties*. Glencoe, Ill.: Free Press.

Miles, R. E., C. C. Snow, and J. Pfeffer. 1974. "Organization-Environment: Concepts and Issues." *Industrial Relations* 13, no. 3 (October): 244–64.

Mohr, L. B. 1973. "The Concept of Organizational Goal." *American Political Science Review* 67, no. 2 (June): 470–81.

New York Times. 1981. 28 April, sec. A, p. 8, col. 3.

New York Times. 1982. 5 February.

Perrow, C. 1961. "The Analysis of Goals in Complex Organizations." *American Sociological Review* 26, no. 6 (December): 688–99.

Pfeffer, J., and G. R. Salancik. 1974. "Organizational Decision Making as a Political Process: The Case of a University Budget."

———. 1978. *The External Control of Organizations: A Resource Dependence Perspective*. New York: Harper & Row.

Quinn, R. E. 1977. "Coping with Cupid: The Formation, Impact, and Management of Romantic Relationships in Organizations." *Administrative Science Quarterly* 22, no. 1 (March): 30–45.

Scott, W. R. 1981. *Organizations: Rational, Natural, and Open Systems*. Englewood Cliffs, N.J.: Prentice-Hall.

Selznick, P. 1949. *TVA and the Grass Roots*. Berkeley, Calif.: University of California Press.

Simon, H. A. 1964. "On the Concept of Organizational Goal." *Administrative Science Quarterly* 9, no. 1 (June): 1–22.

Starbuck, W. H. 1976. "Organizations and Their Environments." In *Handbook of Industrial and Organizational Psychology*, ed. Marvin D. Dunnette. Chicago: Rand McNally.

Stolzenberg, R. M. 1978. "Bringing the Boss Back In: Employer Size, Employee Schooling and Socioeconomic Achievement." *American Sociological Review* 43, no. 6 (December).

Stone, K. 1974. "The Origins and Job Structures in the Steel Industry." *The Radical Review of Political Economics* 6, no. 2 (Summer): 113–73.

Swigert, V. L., and R. A. Farrell. 1980–1981. "Corporate Homicide: Definitional Processes in the Creation of Deviance." *Law and Society Review* 15, no. 1 (Fall): 163–82.

Van de Ven, A. H. 1979. "Howard E. Aldrich: Organizations and Environment." *Administrative Science Quarterly* 24, no. 2 (June): 320–26.

Wamsley, G., and M. N. Zald. 1973. *The Political Economy of Public Organizations*. Lexington, Mass.: Heath.

Weber, M. 1946. *From Max Weber: Essays in Sociology*. Trans. and ed. H. H. Gerth and C. W. Mills. New York: Oxford University Press.

———. 1947. *The Theory of Social and Economic Organization*. Trans. and ed. A. H. Henderson and T. Parsons. Glencoe, Ill.: Free Press.

Zey-Ferrell, M., and M. Aiken, eds. 1981. *Complex Organizations: Critical Perspectives*. Glenview, Ill.: Scott, Foresman.

7

The contribution of political science to organizational behavior

CYNTHIA HARDY

This chapter reviews the contribution of political science to organizational behavior (OB). The focus is on the models of power and politics that have been developed by political scientists. These developments form the basis of much of the research into power and politics that has been undertaken in organizational settings. In general, however, political perspectives have been ignored in OB, particularly by practitioners. Organization behaviorists have tended to explain behavior in ways other than political and, as a result, the potential contribution of a political framework remains untapped.

Why should power and politics be so neglected? One explanation is the negative connotations associated with these terms (see, for example, McClelland 1974). The application of "power" and "politics" seems slightly unethical (Pfeffer 1981). They are often felt to be used to further individual goals at the expense of the organization. A hint of corruption and malpractice is associated with the use of political strategies and, as a result, they are not deemed appropriate methods with which to manage and change organizations.

A second problem is that power and politics have proved difficult concepts to handle. Even in political science, where they have received long and careful scrutiny, there is little agreement as to exactly what they comprise (Partridge 1970; Allison 1974; Nagel 1975; Lukes 1977). Research has not been integrated enough to provide a general framework that can be applied to organi-

zations; consequently, these concepts are surrounded by controversy and confusion.

Such confusion is compounded by a third problem—the existence of competing well-established models of behavior within organizations. These often have a long tradition of use in organization and managerial contexts, which has reaffirmed their importance and refined their techniques. These models are usually far more consistent with the values associated with the practice of management in the Western world, typically conceiving of organizational members as a team working toward common goals. Their work may be hindered by such difficulties as bad communication, inadequate information, and unpredictable environments, but, if the manager or practitioner can remove these obstructions, harmony will be restored and both management and employees can get on with their jobs, benefiting themselves and the organization at the same time.

In contrast to this "win-win" situation, politics is more of a fixed-sum game: because of conflicts of interest, one group can benefit only at another's expense (Walton 1965). The explicit recognition of this condition makes managing a difficult job. It runs counter to the Western ideology that profit and efficiency benefit everyone. Selling new ideas is harder if it is apparent that someone is going to lose out. The political perspective thus embodies a threat: managers have a far greater chance of success if everybody can win; in a win-lose sit-

96

uation the losers are apt to become disenchanted, endangering the smooth functioning of the organization.

A further problem is that those proposing a political perspective often push too hard, seeing organizations as merely battlegrounds of competing factions: "Political scientists interested in organizations are sometimes bemused by the extreme self-consciousness with which sociologists and social psychologists approach the question of power and politics. . . . A political scientist can scarcely perceive of an organization as anything but political, as anything but a set of power relationships" (Wamsley 1970, 49). Such a view may characterize some organizations, some of the time, but it is not representative of the totality of organizational life.

Given all these problems, and given the existence of other tried and tested models, why should anyone bother with a political perspective? By trying to correct some of the problems discussed above, this paper will attempt to show how a political perspective can add to our understanding of organizations and practitioners.

First, the concepts of power and politics will be explored by tracing the roots of the political perspective within political science and linking it to developments in OB. Second, a perspective will be suggested that incorporates the recent developments of both disciplines. The fundamental assumption will be not that power is everything, but that, in certain circumstances, a political perspective is a useful way to understand and explain events. Rather than a ubiquitous, evil process, politics is seen as a phenomenon more likely to occur in some situations than others. When it does occur, it is not a pathology but an understandable reaction to certain pressures, which can and should be managed. Third, it will be demonstrated that when such circumstances arise, a political awareness is necessary. Pretending that power and politics do not exist will not make them go away; on the contrary, political ignorance may account for some of the failures experienced by managers.

The proposal is to explore the concepts of power and politics in order to offer a useful framework for understanding organizational behavior. The hope is that OB practitioners will be encouraged to adopt a political perspective if it is seen as a model like any other—a necessary but not sufficient mechanism for understanding organizations. The negative connotations associated with the concepts of power and politics are likely to remain a problem as long as political perspectives remain the prerogative of political science. These stigmas will disappear only as power and politics are incorporated more readily into organizational analysis.

Although it is by no means the only contribution of political scientists, the development of a political perspective is probably the most significant and far-reaching. Hence the focus of this paper. Certain develop-

ments and events from the political science area have not been given the attention they deserve, and there will be omissions that both political scientists and organization behaviorists may find disquieting. It is hoped that readers will accept these omissions as the result of necessity rather than neglect.

The chapter is divided into six sections. The first two examine the development of political decision-making models and the subsequent application and extension of these models to organizational contexts. Next we consider a broader definition of power and politics, extending beyond the decision-making arena, and trace its development in both political science and OB. The fifth section presents a political framework and the rationale for its conditions of use. Finally, an exploration of organizational development and strategy making will show how political ignorance can undermine efforts to manage and change organizations.

THE CONCEPT OF POLITICAL DECISION MAKING

Decision-making models have evolved from an early emphasis on a "rational-analytic" or synoptic (Braybrooke and Lindblom 1963) approach toward a political perspective. Many of the studies that criticized the synoptic model came from political science, but other disciplines also made important contributions.

Early decision-making literature typically assumed that decisions are made by choosing among "alternatives after careful and complete study of all possible courses of action and all their possible consequences and after an evaluation of these consequences in the light of one's values. That is to say, ideally one treats the policy question as an intellectual problem" (Braybrooke and Lindblom 1963, 40). This rational-analytic approach has its roots in the work of F. W. Taylor on scientific management and in Fayol's administrative principles. It was reaffirmed during the Second World War, when economists, mathematicians, statisticians, and industrial engineers cooperated to bring a quantitative and scientific approach to bear on the problem-solving needs of the war effort (Simon 1955; Gore and Silander 1959). The basis of this approach was a view of "economic man" who acts rationally and comprehensively to find optimal solutions to his problems.

Simon (1955) was one of the first to point out that cognitive constraints limit individuals' ability to act in this way. He introduced the notion of bounded rationality, through which individuals satisfice rather than optimize. Other studies also began to question the rational perspective (Lindblom 1959; Braybrooke and

Lindblom 1963; Gore and Dyson 1964; Leoni 1964; Lundberg 1964), and it became clear that the rational ideal seldom occurred in practice.

> Descriptive reports of administrative behavior and of the actual choices implemented soon lead the empirical investigator to believe that decision theories which confine themselves to the classical concept of rationality are so narrow that only a small part of daily administrative decisioning meets its standards. (Lundberg 1964, 21)

Although criticism pointed out the limits to rational decision making, the ideal of comprehensive rationality at first survived. Gradually, however, researchers began to insist that not only was the synoptic model descriptively inaccurate, it was prescriptively misguiding in a complex and unpredictable world. Braybrooke and Lindblom (1963) argued that attempts to optimize result in cognitive strains and time delays that can be counterproductive. The synoptic model lacks the adaptive measures necessary to take complex, uncertain, and time-constrained decisions. Simon's (1955) method of satisficing is not just a response to cognitive limits but an adaptive mechanism that allows decisions to be taken quickly when information is lacking. Popper (1945) has discussed "piecemeal" engineering in much the same way. Such mechanisms are often more effective than rational, comprehensive decision making, because information is costly to acquire (Meyers and Banfield 1955), and, under time constraints, it may be better to consider one rather than multiple alternatives (Snyder and Paige 1958). As a result of such criticisms, Braybrooke and Lindblom introduced the concept of disjointed incrementalism, in which issues and problems are dealt with one at a time, as they arise. They argue that this model is not only more accurate descriptively, but represents a better way to make decisions because it incorporates adaptive features to deal with limited problem-solving capabilities, inadequate information, costly analysis, and unsatisfactory evaluation methods.

Still it was assumed that actors are essentially trying to optimize as best they can under difficult conditions and with various corner-cutting methods. An implicit notion is that the decisions made are those best for the organization or institution (for example, Snyder, Bruck, and Sapin 1963). Political scientists in public administration, however, were starting to question whether behavior was actually guided by a desire for the "good of the organization" or by other, less altruistic considerations. They saw decision making as an arena of conflicting interest groups, in which decisions were the outcome of political negotiation and compromise. Actors were more concerned with their individual or group goals than those of the system (Lasswell 1936, 1951, 1971; Wildavsky 1961, 1964, 1969; Lindblom 1965, 1968; Dror 1967). As one writer commented, "A policy is sometimes the outcome of a political compromise among policy makers, none of whom had in mind quite the problem to which the agreed policy is the solution" (Lindblom 1968, 5).

Focusing on the political aspects of decision making, this multidisciplinary field of study came to be known as policy analysis. It has examined the policy issue area, the actors involved, their motives, beliefs, and resources (Dror 1967). Decision making is seen as inescapably political, characterized by bargaining and conflict, which can extend to the implementation phase (Gordon 1977).

Building on the work of political scientists and policy analysts, many organization analysts began to conceive of organizational decision making as a political process, and to examine the bases and uses of power in organizations. The following section describes these developments within OB.

POLITICAL DECISION MAKING IN ORGANIZATIONS

As a result of developments in political science and other areas, OB has moved away from synoptic models toward greater recognition and clarification of a political view of decision making.

March and Simon (1958) provided one of the earliest behavioral models of organizational decision making, which drew on Simon's concepts of bounded rationality, cognitive limits, and satisficing. They paint a picture of "a choosing, decision-making, problem-solving organism that can do only one or a few things at a time, and that can attend to only a small part of the information recorded in its memory and presented by the environment" (p. 11). The actor chooses among a limited number of alternatives, which are selectively perceived in accordance with his or her goals and definition of the situation. Alternatives and information have to be searched out, but this task is carried out on a limited and sequential basis. March and Simon acknowledge the existence of conflict but define it as a breakdown in decision making, arguing that it is not a stable condition because the motivation to reduce it is always prevalent. The possibility of inevitable, structural conflict or self-serving behavior is not discussed.

This work was followed by Cyert and March's *Behavioral Theory of the Firm* (1963), which develops a theory of search and choice in the face of complexity and uncertainty. These writers acknowledge organizations normally exist and thrive with considerable latent conflict of goals. Decision making is viewed as a political process in which coalitions of interest groups are formed to realize group goals. The basic premise is that interest groups emerge as a result of the division of labor. Because the goals of these groups often conflict, political behavior becomes necessary to safeguard and promote interests, and is intensified by competition for scarce resources (see, for example, Harvey and Mills 1970; Pettigrew 1973; Pfeffer 1981). Although Cyert and March acknowledge the existence of competing interest groups and political behavior, they do not describe how power is mobilized by these interest groups to achieve their ends (Pettigrew 1973). Subsequent work has focused more on the nature of political processes and on the sources of power.

Because it accrues to those who control scarce and valued resources, power is associated with dependency: those on whom others are dependent have power over them (Emerson 1962). Power is therefore entrenched in the relationship between actors, rather than being an attribute of a particular individual. This issue of resource interdependencies has formed the basis of research to uncover the power resources available to organizational members. For example, because they can restrict access to information and equipment (Mechanic 1962), lower-level participants can exercise power over members of higher echelons. The control of information has been found to be a particularly important source of power (Pettigrew 1973; Pfeffer 1981). Power has been related to the ability to control uncertainty (Crozier 1964; Hickson 1971; Pfeffer 1981), and to expertise (Pettigrew 1973). Credibility, stature, and prestige can also confer power (Pettigrew 1973; Pfeffer and Salancik 1974; Salancik and Pfeffer 1974). Other power sources include access to and contacts with members of higher echelons and the control of money, rewards, and sanctions (see, for example, French and Raven 1968).

Mere possession of scarce resources does not in itself confer power. Actors also have to be aware of pertinent resources and be able to control and use them tactically (Pettigrew 1973). In this dynamic view, political behavior can be defined as actions undertaken in order to mobilize power sources. "Political action takes place when an actor, recognizing that the achievement of its goal is influenced by the behavior of others' actions in the situation, undertakes action against the others to ensure that its own goals are achieved" (MacMillan 1978, 8).

This view of decision making as a political process has been attracting increasing interest, prompting a recent resurgence of research into the political aspects of organizational decision making (see, for example, Tushman 1977; Nord 1978; Madison et al. 1980; Farrell and Petersen 1982; Schilit and Locke 1982).

POWER AND POLITICS OUTSIDE THE DECISION-MAKING PROCESS

Early research in political science and many recent organizational studies have focused on power and politics in the decision-making process. The use of power is not, however, confined to this arena. Recent research has revealed the broader scope of power and politics. This section documents the main developments that have led to this view.

The pluralists

Early studies of community power typically focused exclusively on the decision-making process (see, for example, Dahl 1957, 1961; Polsby 1963; Wolfinger 1971). Researchers analyzed key decisions that seemed likely to illustrate the power relations prevailing in a particular community. The object was to determine who made these decisions. If the same groups were responsible for most decisions, the community could be said to be ruled by an elite. The researchers found, in contrast, that different groups were usually involved. Such a community was termed "pluralist," and it was hypothesized that America as a whole could perhaps be described as pluralist (see Lukes 1974; Parry and Morriss 1975).

Several assumptions underlay this research approach. It was believed that political conflict is resolved by political decisions—that power is only exercised in key decisions where conflict is clearly observable. Individuals are assumed to be aware of their grievances and to act upon them by participating in the decision-making process and trying to influence these key decisions. The researchers saw the decision-making arena as open to anyone with an interest in it, and interpreted an absence of participation as a sign of consensus (see Lukes 1974; Parry and Morriss 1975).

Radical writers quickly questioned the pluralist assumption that decision-making processes are readily accessible, and that nonparticipation reflects satisfaction with that system. A widespread doubt of the "permeability" of the American political system, however, may have been prompted by the urban riots and the backlash to the Vietnam War (Parry and Morriss 1975).

The two-dimensional approach

Researchers and political observers started to examine how full-and-equal participation might be constrained. Schattschneider (1960) argued that nonparticipation might be due to "the suppression of options and alternatives that reflect the needs of the nonparticipants. It is not necessarily true that people with the greatest needs participate in politics most actively—whoever decides what the game is about also decides who gets in the game" (p. 105).

Building on this insight, Bachrach and Baratz (1962, 1963, 1970) developed the concept of a "second face" of power—a process whereby issues are excluded from decision making, confining the agenda to "safe" questions. A variety of barriers can be used by more powerful groups to prevent subordinates from fully participating in the decision-making process, including force, sanctions, and the invocation of procedures and political routines. The use of these mechanisms has been termed nondecision making, because they allow the more powerful actors to determine outcomes without entering the formal decision-making arena. Such mechanisms are normally available to dominant groups because they support and reinforce existing biases that already benefit these groups.

The work of these authors highlights the fact that power is not exercised solely in the making of key decisions and that indeed the overt decision makers are not necessarily the most powerful groups (see Parry and Morriss 1975).

Some have argued that while the work of Bachrach and Baratz is an improvement on the pluralist model, it does not go far enough (Lukes 1974). They continue to assume that power is exercised only where there is some conflict of interest of which actors are aware. They ignore the possibility that power might be used to ensure that conflict does not arise at any level. But, as Saunders (1980) has pointed out,

> to assume genuine consensus in a situation where there is no apparent conflict (that is, to give the system—and the powerful—the benefit of the doubt) appears to be no more justifiable on theoretical grounds than to assume that such a situation necessarily indicates the existence of a widespread false consciousness. (p. 33)

The third dimension of power

Lukes (1974) has attempted to correct this deficiency by focusing on the use of power to prevent issues and conflict from arising at all. Power can be used to forestall grievances

> by shaping [people's] perceptions, cognitions, and preferences in such a way that they accept their role in the existing order of things, either because they can see or imagine no alternative to it, or because they view it as natural and unchangeable, or because they value it as divinely ordained and beneficial. (Lukes 1974, 24)

In other words, we can not confine our study of power to observable conflict, the outcomes of decisions, or even suppressed issues. We must also consider the question of political inactivity and quiescence: why grievances do not exist; why demands are not made; why conflict does not arise, since these negative phenomena may also be the result of power (Lukes 1974, 1977; Gaventa 1980; Saunders 1980). "We may, in other words, be duped, hoodwinked, coerced, cajoled or manipulated into political inactivity" (Saunders 1980, 22). Conflict may not exist because powerful actors have influenced the perceptions and desires of others to ensure that they will not be challenged.

Thus concepts of power have gradually become more comprehensive. The first two dimensions are concerned with the exercise of power in the face of competition, conflict, or opposition. Ranson, Hinings, and Greenwood (1980) remarked that, in the work of Bachrach and Baratz (1970), "the focus was very much upon 'issues' about which 'decisions' have to be made, albeit 'nondecisions.' Power in this view stands close to action, using the bases of power to ensure compliance" (p. 8). Parry and Morriss (1975) argue that most actions that fall under the heading of nondecision making are, in fact, decisions about which choices have to be made. Actors are aware of grievances and conflict and, as a result, use the available mechanisms to squeeze dangerous issues out. The third dimension of power, on the other hand, is its ability to ensure that conflict does not arise.

The most important distinction may be between the use of power to defeat competition and its use to prevent competition. Gamson (1968) has distinguished between two concepts of power and politics along these lines. Competing interest groups pursue a "strategy of conflict," each using power to achieve its own goals. The "management of conflict" refers to the use of power by the agents of the system to achieve system goals. Hardy (1985a) has distinguished between the overt use of power to defeat opponents, and unobtrusive power used to secure the acceptance and acquiescence of potential opposition groups.

Much of the work on power in organizations assumes, implicitly or explicitly, the overt use of power. The studies discussed in the previous section have typically focused on the use of power by actors who mobilize their resources to defeat opposition. Their efforts may be directed toward the decision-making process, they may circumvent decision making, or they may influence the implementation of previously made decisions. There has been little explicit research into nondecision making because of the difficulties of empirically verifying its existence (Bachrach and Baratz, 1975; Debnam, 1975). Studies by Crenson (1971) and Hunter (1980) provide two examples, and Plott and Levine (1978) have examined agenda control.

The overt exercise of power involves conflict and confrontation and necessarily poses a risk of losing. As Ranson, Hinings, and Greenwood (1980) point out, "power is most effective and insidious in its consequences when issues do not arise at all, when actors remain unaware of their sectional claims, that is, power is most effective when it is unnecessary" (p. 8). It is far safer to section off spheres of activity where actions remain unchallenged (Fox 1973). This use of power prevents opposition, by managing (rather than creating or exploiting) conflict. This theme will be discussed in terms of its development in political science and its application by organizational analysts.

THE MANAGEMENT OF CONFLICT

Harmony and stability, as Lukes has argued, may be the result of political maneuvers. Yet the successful management of conflict is seldom conceived of as a political process. One explanation may lie in the early work done on the subject of social control by systems theorists, notably Talcott Parsons (see Gamson 1968). Parsons talks of the power of the system to achieve collective goals, the assumption being that the fulfillment of system requirements meets the goals and desires of the constituents of that system.

The systems approach, borrowed from biological- and mechanical-system theories, attracted widespread interest in the social sciences, including political science (Easton 1965; Almond and Coleman 1960). It has been criticized, however, for its neglect of individual actors within the system. Some have argued that there is no such thing as "system" or "organizational" goals—only people have goals (Silverman 1970). As a result, some people have more to gain from the achievement of organizational goals than others. Selective entry, access, exit, the use of sanctions and persuasion, participation and cooptation do not just benefit the "system," they also protect the power positions of some individuals by reducing the chances of challenge from others (see Gamson 1968). The management of conflict may be an intensely political process.

The bias of the system

The third dimension of power, as described by Lukes (1974), lies in the unconscious acceptance of the values, traditions, cultures, and structures of a given institution or society. Although these characteristics are often seen as neutral, functional constructs, they also serve to protect the interests of dominant groups (Salaman 1979).

Structure, for example, has often been seen as determined by environmental constraints (Burns and Stalker 1961; Emery and Trist 1965; Lawrence and Lorsch 1967; Aldrich 1979) or other imperatives, such as technology (Woodward 1965), or size (Pugh et al. 1969). Child (1972) has criticized this functional-determinist approach, arguing that the nature of structure is to some extent a matter of choice. Dominant organizational members may be in a position to use this degree of freedom to choose a structure that protects and furthers their power positions. Structure thus becomes a product of both political processes and contextual constraints (Kimberley 1975) as "economic and administrative exigencies are weighed by the actors concerned against the opportunities to create a structure of their own preferences" (Child 1972, 16).

Structures embody certain assumptions, values, and practices which are taken for granted by organizational members, and which ensure that certain behaviors and actions are carried out without question (Ranson, Hinings, and Greenwood 1980). Behavior throughout the organization is directed to serve the interests of senior members by structures and technologies that although presented as neutral and utilitarian, are also political (Salaman 1979). Senior members thus have a vested interest in shaping the mechanisms that provide them with power, and "the organizational structures within which individuals both contribute to organizational performance and pursue sectional interests are in part the outcome of their own initiatives" (Watson 1980, 213).

Structure and technology are usually seen as the formal and official aspects of organizations, while the informal aspects are categorized under such terms as culture and ideology. Organizations may contain a variety of cultures and subcultures, which can be as important as the official structure in determining the nature of organizations and what goes on inside them (Salaman 1979).

Some researchers believe that the attitudes, expectations, beliefs, and values that make up a specific culture are formed primarily in response to contextual constraints and the wider societal culture. Relevant factors include characteristics of the organization, such as technology (Sayles 1958; Blauner 1964; Wedderburn and Compton 1972) and characteristics of the employees (Goldthorpe et al. 1968), the local community (Lane and Roberts 1971; Beynon 1973; Martin and Fryer 1973), and the wider society (Bendix 1954; Crozier 1964; Salaman 1979).

Other studies, in contrast, have highlighted the role of the entrepreneur in creating a culture (Lane and Roberts 1971; Beynon 1973; Martin and Fryer 1973). Entrepreneurs create ideologies and cultures to generate order, purpose, and commitment among organizational members, which in turn facilitate the achievement of their goals (Pettigrew 1977, 1979). And as a result, cultures and ideologies include a political element (Salaman 1979).

Power is institutionalized in the structures and cultures that make up an organization (Pfeffer 1981) and often protect the position of dominant groups. Lukes (1974) has defined such relationships as the exercise of power (see also Clegg 1975; Young 1978; Saunders 1980). But often the groups that benefit from the existing bias of a system were not the ones that created it. A distinction needs to be drawn between those who have the power to initiate a system and those who derive power from it (Parry and Morriss 1975). Furthermore, as systems evolve they may become bureaucratic and dysfunctional, serving the interests of no one in particular (Allison 1971). And it is difficult to measure exactly how much groups benefit from existing biases. In view of these problems, the bias of the system might be best described as the powerlessness of subordinate groups, rather than the power of dominant actors.

Cultures and structures do embody potential unobtrusive control mechanisms. The recent interest in the benefits of a Japanese or "Type Z" culture (Ouchi 1982) is a case in point. Behavior is guided by shared norms and values, instead of traditional formalized bureaucratic controls. Jaeger (1983) has found that the use of indirect cultural mechanisms is a viable alternative to bureaucratic structures. An implicit assumption is that culture is a power mechanism that can be manipulated by political actors.

The creation of legitimacy

The bias of the system is a subtle aspect of the management of conflict. Power can also be used in more concrete ways to prevent opposition by creating legitimacy for particular positions and actions. Political scientists have long recognized that a regime will be more stable if dominant groups can make the populace believe that existing institutions are best for society (Lipset 1959, 1963; Schaar 1969; Roelofs 1976; Rothschild 1979). Legitimacy can also be created for individual actions, thus reducing the chances of opposition to them. Edelman (1964, 1971, 1977) has pointed out that power

is mobilized not only to achieve physical outcomes, but also to give those outcomes meanings—to legitimize and justify them. Political actors use language, symbols, and ideologies to placate or arouse the public on specific issues.

> Political analysis must then proceed on two levels simultaneously. It must examine how political actions get some groups the tangible things they want from government and at the same time it must explore what these same actions mean to the mass public and how it is placated or aroused by them. In Himmelstrand's terms, political actions are both instrumental and expressive. (Edelman 1964, 12)

In an organizational context, Pfeffer has distinguished between substantive and sentiment outcomes of power. The former are physical outcomes, largely determined by resource interdependence in the face of competition. Political actors then try to mobilize support and quiet opposition by suing symbolic power (language, culture, symbols, ideology, and rituals) to produce favorable sentiments toward these outcomes.

Pfeffer argues that symbolic power has little to do with achieving substantive outcomes, but rather is used only to legitimize outcomes already determined by resource interdependencies. Hardy (1985a) has argued that if actors are able to legitimize their desired outcomes to the extent that they are accepted without opposition, they have in effect achieved substantive outcomes through the use of symbolic (or unobtrusive) power. Pettigrew (1977) calls this the management of meaning.

> Politics concerns the creation of legitimacy for certain ideas, values and demands—not just action performed as a result of previously acquired legitimacy. The management of meaning refers to a process of symbol construction and value use designed both to create legitimacy for one's own demands and to "delegitimize" the demands of others. (Pettigrew 1977, 85)

If successful, the process of legitimation prevents opposition from arising (see, for example, Mueller 1973; Abner Cohen 1975; Gaventa 1980; Hardy 1982a), and thus is a far safer way of using power than risking overt confrontation.

> Stable organizing power requires legitimation. To be sure, men can be made to work and to obey commands through coercion, but the coercive use of power engenders resistance and sometimes active opposition. Power conflicts in and between societies are characterized by resistance and opposition, and while the latter occur in organizations, effective operations necessitate

that they be kept at a minimum there and, especially, that members do not exhibit resistance in discharging their daily duties but perform them and comply with directives *willingly*. (Blau 1964, 199–200)

To be able to operate without risk of intervention, an organization must establish its legitimacy in the eyes of the external institutions that affect it, as well as its own members (Dowling and Pfeffer 1975). Organizations interact with their environment not only for the purpose of economic exchange but also to secure resources essential to their political survival (Zald 1970a; Wamsley and Zald 1973; Benson 1975).

Studies of the organization's relationship with its environment have often concentrated on economic transactions and the need to adapt to the pressures of a constraining environment (Emery and Trist 1965; Lawrence and Lorsch 1967; Terreberry 1968; Aldrich 1979). But by securing political resources from its environment, an organization may be able to modify and reduce economic constraints (Perrow 1970; Wamsley and Zald 1973; Pfeffer and Salancik 1978).

Mergers, joint ventures, cooperation, and cooptation may all occur for political reasons (Pfeffer and Salancik 1978). Organizational structures may be created to reflect the myths of the institutional environment rather than the requirements of efficiency (Meyer and Rowan 1977–78). Consultants may be hired to enhance legitimacy as much as to solve specific problems (Van Houten and Goldman 1981). Threatening elements may be coopted (Selznick 1949; Friedman 1977).

Cameron's study of the tobacco industry (Miles 1982) provides an example of how external legitimacy acts as a buffer against a hostile environment. When greater awareness of the hazards of smoking threatened their business during the 1970s, tobacco firms took a number of steps to protect themselves. They sought legitimacy for their products by taking actions to dilute the strong wording of health warnings, soliciting the support of senators and sponsoring medical research to enhance credibility. These measures (*domain defense*) bought the firms enough time to engage in *domain offense* (being more inventive and aggressive in existing businesses) and *domain creation* (diversification).

This section has discussed how power can be used to manage conflict and prevent it from arising. The existing bias of an organization's structures and cultures typically protects senior members from challenge. Although this effect may occur automatically, without deliberate action on the part of those who benefit from it, organizational bias remains a potential form of unobtrusive control. Conflict can also be prevented by consciously using symbols, language, rituals, or myths to convince potential opposition groups of the legitimacy of certain outcomes. Although the management of conflict is rarely discussed as a power issue, it can be a political process when actors deliberately use their sources of unobtrusive power to influence perceptions and legitimize outcomes that would not otherwise be accepted. In this case, quiescence is the result of power and politics.

A POLITICAL FRAMEWORK

Both economic and political factors influence behavior in organizations. As Burns (1961) has pointed out, people are both rivals and cooperators in common enterprises, and the success of individuals is bound up with the success of those enterprises. A political economy model of organizational behavior (Zald 1970b; Wamsley and Zald 1973) recognizes both types of constraint: external relations may be undertaken to acquire economic or political resources; internally, resources may be allocated, decisions taken and implemented on the basis of both economic and political criteria. The question is When are political factors likely to be most important?

It has been argued that political influences are likely to be particularly strong *when the existing pattern of resources is changing*, for it is then that opportunities to enhance power positions arise (Pettigrew 1973; Mumford and Pettigrew 1975; Mintzberg 1982). Large-scale innovative decisions typically fit this pattern. In such situations too there is often a significant amount of complexity, unpredictability, and uncertainty, which renders formal economic models less feasible and less likely to be used (Wilensky 1967). " . . . The relations between participants in routine decisions are typically characterized by cooperation, while conflict of some sort is the norm in innovative decisions" (Gore and Dyson 1964, 3)."

A reduction in resources has also been found to result in political behavior (Levine 1978, 1979; Levine, Rubin, and Wolohojian 1981; Jick and Murray 1982; Hardy 1982b; Mintzberg 1982). Threatened with the loss of resources, people may engage in political actions to safeguard them.

Finally, political behavior may be more prevalent in organizations that have a *history of conflict and cleavage*. As Gore and Dyson (1964) point out:

Different strategies are required to cope with various classes of response-demanding situations. The pattern of a decision where the situation is one of promise and where participants are happily inclined towards each other will differ from the pattern of a decision in a situation where there is little prospect of success and a history of conflict leads the participants to regard each other with suspicion. (p. 1)

Political actions thus are more likely in some situations than others. What is important is that the manager is able to recognize these situations and act accordingly. Political activity can be expected when cleavage between interest groups is high, particularly if the problem is also highly complex (see Astley et al. 1982). Complexity is usually associated with nonroutine, innovative decisions, while cleavage can be caused by the redistribution or reduction of resources.

How can the insight of political science help managers who recognize that a particular situation is likely to provoke political activity? First, they can prepare for a political backlash. Knowing the relevant power sources will suggest which groups will be in a position to oppose them, and how much damage they can inflict. Managers then have a choice: either they can mobilize resources to prepare for overt confrontation or they can use unobtrusive measures to gain acceptance for their actions and avoid conflict. For example, Hardy (in press) has studied how managers responsible for the implementation of plans to close factories and hospitals have been able to reduce the likelihood of employee resistance.

In circumstances where political activity is likely, managers may find they cannot rely on a political model of organizational behavior. Such models will not prepare them for the political difficulties that may obstruct their plans. The next section explores two specific examples—organizational development and strategy-making—to illustrate how the neglect of power and politics can undermine efforts to manage and change organizations.

THE NEGLECT OF POWER AND POLITICS

Traditional management literature has tended to ignore the political consequences of organizational development (OD) and strategy making. OD is based on a humanistic view of individuals that ignores the fact that they may have political motives. The prescriptive literature on strategy-making relies extensively on the rational-analytic model of decision making. Practitioners in both these areas might find it illuminating to adopt a political perspective on their efforts.

Organization development

OD has been defined as a method of facilitating change in people, technologies, structures, and processes (Fried-

lander and Brown 1974). Because such change involves the redistribution of resources, one might expect OD interventions to be susceptible to political influences by those who see opportunities in the changes or feel threatened by them.

OD theorists, however, have not adopted a political perspective (Friedlander and Brown 1974; Stephenson 1975; Beer 1976; Friedlander 1976). Instead OD has relied on humanistic values to guide interventions (for example, Beckhard 1969; French 1969; Margulies and Raia 1972; French and Bell 1973). The emphasis is on open problem solving, the delegation of decision making, personal growth, collaboration, trust, and consensus. Power is not considered a suitable mechanism with which to introduce change. As Margulies and Raia (1972) express it, "Planned change . . . does not include change which is . . . 'imposed' either by expertise or authority" (p. 57).

It has been argued, however, that theories of change need to incorporate an analysis of political forces (Pettigrew 1976) because of the redistribution of resources. OD interventions cause the release of political energy as individuals and groups work for or against planned change, according to their particular objectives.

A political perspective, however, contradicts many traditional OD values and suggests that very different actions are needed to promote and maintain change (Walton 1965; Huff 1980). The change-agent is only one of several actors with a view of desirable change: at some point he or she must be able to thwart incompatible ideas of change. Change-agents must also be aware of power sources so as to be able to select points of leverage from which to initiate change, to restructure the power relationships necessary to accommodate change, and to institutionalize power in new relationships to ensure that change persists (Huff 1980). It is unrealistic to assume tht resistance is an irrational act that can be overcome by improving communication and making people "see sense." Watson (1982) points out that "the definitions of situations which people develop and the actions which relate to these are informed by real and material differences of interest and experience between groups" (p. 270). The failure of OD to produce enduring and concrete changes in performance has been attributed to its failure to take political issues into account (Stephenson 1975; Nord 1978). "More effective OD," argue Friedlander and Brown (1974: 335), "will require more elaboration of the theory of power from the points of view of both the powerful and the powerless."

Change is a political act with political consequences that have to be dealt with if the change attempt is to be successful. But the humanistic model that guides research and practice in OD implicitly conceives of the organization as a team with everyone pulling together toward common objectives (Fox 1973). This model leaves managers ill-equipped to deal with the realities of change (Burns 1969; Fox 1973; Watson 1982).

Strategy making

Strategy making is another area in which relatively little attention has been paid to political factors. Most textbooks concentrate on the rational-analytic aspects of strategy formulation—for example, industry, competitor, and organizational analysis (Hardy 1982b). Strategic changes involve the redistribution of resources as new markets, new products, and new structures are introduced, and so may generate political energy.

Some studies have focused on the political aspects of strategy making (Murray 1978). MacMillan (1978) has conceived of strategic decision making as a political process. Bower (1970) argues that politics is a fact of life in the management of resource allocation processes in large organizations. Investment decisions are often subject to political factors (Aharoni 1966; Carter 1969; King 1976), as are budgets (Wildavsky 1964). Reorganizations can be used to manipulate structures and increase power (Kanter 1977). Consequently, managers have to pay attention to political factors if they are to formulate and implement strategies successfully (Wrapp 1967; Quinn 1980). Many organizations are currently having to deal with decline and must formulate retrenchment strategies, which have been found to be particularly susceptible to political influences (Levine 1978, 1979; Levine, Rubin, and Wolohojian 1981; Hardy 1982b; Jick and Murray 1982).

If strategic changes release political energy, managers need to be prepared for it. But the prescriptive literature on strategy making has largely ignored political developments in the field and may be recommending formal planning processes of limited value. Rational evaluations may produce "optimal" plans, but political skills may be necessary to ensure that those plans are accepted and implemented.

CONCLUSION

Power and politics have long been associated with successful leadership and management. Max Weber noted the various forms of power that characterized the management of earlier societies as well as more modern organizations. Many current books view management as a power game (for example, Jay 1970; Korda 1975; Ritti and Funkhouser 1977). Nevertheless, the literature that guides managers and practitioners in organizations has been generally loath to adopt a political perspective. One reason for this neglect of an important issue may be that successful "politicians" rarely admit their political motives. Nevertheless, power and politics are facets of organizational life that need to be taken into account.

This chapter has tried to clarify the nature of power and politics and the different ways in which they can be used by managers. Though political science has made vital contributions to OB, politics by itself is not enough to explain behavior in organizations—nor, for that matter is any one model, as Allison (1971) has pointed out. What is needed is the ability to use models eclectically.

To ignore political factors where they exist is likely to be counterproductive, as the experience of OD and strategy making suggests. In such circumstances, a political perspective can help managers and practitioners to achieve their objectives. It also enables them to choose intelligently between engaging in confrontation and trying to avoid it. A key to effective management is the ability to deal with conflict. The recognition of that task's inherent political component is more likely to help efforts to manage organizations than hinder them.

REFERENCES

Aharoni, Y. 1966. *The Foreign Investment Decision Process.* Cambridge, Mass.: Harvard University Press.

Aldrich, H. E. 1979. *Organizations and Environments.* Englewood Cliffs, N.J.: Prentice-Hall.

Allison, G. T. 1971. *Essence of Decision.* Boston: Little, Brown.

Allison, L. 1974. "On the Nature of the Concept of Power." *European Journal of Political Science* 2:131–41.

Almond, G. and J. S. Coleman, eds. 1960. *The Politics of the Developing Areas.* Princeton, N.J.: Princeton University Press.

Astley, W. G., R. Axelsson, R. J. Butler, D. J. Hickson, and D. C. Wilson. 1982. "Complexity and Cleavage: Dual Explanations of Strategic Decision Making." *Journal of Management Studies* 19, no. 4:357–75.

Bachrach, P. and M. S. Baratz. 1962. "The Two Faces of Power." *American Political Science Review* 56:947–52.

———. 1963. "Decisions and Nondecisions: An Analytical Framework." *American Political Science Review* 57: 641–51.

———. 1970. *Power and Poverty.* London: Oxford University Press.

———. 1975. "Power and Its Two Faces Revisited: A Reply to G. Debnam." *American Political Science Review* 69, no. 3:900–904.

Beckhard, R. 1969. *Organization Development: Strategies and Models*. London: Addison-Wesley.

Beer, M. 1976. "On Gaining Influence and Power for OD." *Journal of Applied Behavioral Science* 12, no. 1:44–51.

Bendix, R. 1954. *Work and Authority in Industry*. New York: Harper & Row.

Benson, J. K. 1975. "The Inter-Organizational Network as a Political Economy." *Administrative Science Quarterly* 20: 229–45.

Beynon, H. 1973. *Working for Ford*. London: Allen Lane.

Blau, P. 1964. *Exchange and Power in Social Life*. New York: Wiley.

Blauner, R. 1964. *Alienation and Freedom*. Chicago: University of Chicago Press.

Bower, J. L. 1970. *Managing the Resource Allocation Process*. Cambridge, Mass.: Harvard University Press.

Braybrooke, D., and C. E. Lindblom. 1963. *A Strategy of Decision*. New York: Free Press.

Burns, T. 1961. "Micro-politics: Mechanisms of Institutional Change." *Administrative Science Quarterly* 6:257–81.

———. 1969. "On the Plurality of Social Systems." In *Industrial Man*, ed. T. Burns. Harmondsworth, England: Penguin.

Burns, T. and G. M. Stalker. 1961. *The Management of Innovation*. London: Pergamon.

Carter, E. E. 1969. "*A Behavioral Approach to Firm Investment*." Ph.D. thesis, Carnegie-Mellon University.

Child, J. 1972. "Organizational Structure, Environment and Performance: The Role of Strategic Choice." *Sociology* 6: 1–22.

Clegg, S. 1975. *Power, Rule and Domination*. London: Routledge & Kegan Paul.

Cohen, Abner. 1975. *Two Dimensional Man*. London: Routledge & Kegan Paul.

Crenson, M. 1971. *The Un-Politics of Air Pollution*. Baltimore, Md.: Johns Hopkins University Press.

Crozier, M. 1964. *The Bureaucratic Phenomenon*. Chicago: University of Chicago Press.

Cyert, R. M. and J. G. March. 1963. *A Behavioral Theory of the Firm*. Englewood Cliffs, N.J.: Prentice-Hall.

Dahl, R. 1957. "The Concept of Power." *Behavioral Science* 20:201–15.

———. 1961. *Who Governs*. New Haven: Yale University Press.

Debnam, G. 1975. "Nondecisions and Power: The Two Faces of Bachrach and Baratz." *American Political Science Review* 64, no. 3:889–99

Dowling, J., and J. Pfeffer. 1975. "Organizational Legitimacy." *Pacific Sociological Review* 18:122–36.

Dror, Y. 1967. "The Policy Analyst." *Public Administration Review* 27:197–203.

Easton, D. A. 1965. *Systems Analysis of Political Life*. New York: Wiley.

Edelman, M. 1964. *The Symbolic Uses of Politics*. Champaign, Ill.: University of Illinois Press.

———. 1971. *Politics as Symbolic Action*. Chicago: Markham.

———. 1977. *Political Language*. London: Academic Press.

Emerson, R. M. 1962. "Power-Dependence Relations." *American Sociological Review* 27:31–41.

Emery, F. E., and E. L. Trist. 1965. "The Causal Texture of Organizational Environments." *Human Relations* 18: 21–32.

Farrell, D., and J. C. Petersen. 1982. "Patterns of Political Behavior in Organizations." *Academy of Management Review* 7, no. 3:403–12.

Fox, A. 1973. "Industrial Relations: A Social Critique of Pluralist Ideology." In *Man and Organization*, ed. J. Child. London: Allen and Unwin.

French, J. R. P., and B. Raven. 1968. "The Bases of Social Power." In *Group Dynamics*, ed. D. Cartwright and A. Zander. New York: Harper & Row.

French, W. L. 1969. "Organizational Development and Objectives: Assumptions and Strategies." *California Management Review* 12, no. 2:23–32.

French, W. L., and C. H. Bell. 1973. *Organization Development*. Englewood Cliffs, N.J.: Prentice-Hall.

Friedlander, F. 1976. "OD Reaches Adolescence: An Exploration of its Underlying Values." *Journal of Applied Behavioral Science* 12, no. 1:7–21.

Friedlander, F., and L. D. Brown. 1974. "Organizational Development." *Annual Review of Psychology* 25: 314–41.

Friedman, A. L. 1977. *Industry and Labour*. London: Macmillan.

Gamson, W. A. 1968. *Power and Discontent*. Homewood, Ill.: Dorsey Press.

Gaventa, J. 1980. *Power and Powerlessness*. London: Oxford University Press.

Goldthorpe, J. H., D. Lockwood, F. Bechhofer, and J. Platt. 1968. *The Affluent Worker: Industrial Attitudes and Behavior*. London: Cambridge University Press.

Gordon, I. 1977. "Perspectives on Policy Analysis." *Public Administration Bulletin* 25:126.

Gore, W. J., and J. W. Dyson, eds. 1964. *The Making of Decisions*. New York: Free Press.

Gore, W. J., and F. S. Silander. 1959. "A Bibliographical Essay on Decision Making." *Administrative Science Quarterly* 4, no. 1:97–121.

Hardy, C. 1985a. *Managing Organization Closure*. Aldershot, England: Gower Press.

———. 1985b. "The Nature of Unobtrusive Powers." *Journal of Management Structures* 22:4.

———. 1982a. "Organizational Closure: A Political Process." Ph.D. thesis. Montreal: University of Warwick.

———. 1982b. "Is Strategy Making a Political Process? The Example of Retrenchment." Paper presented at the Strategic Management Conference, Montreal, Canada.

Harvey E., and R. Mills. "Patterns of Organizational Adaptation: A Political Perspective." In *Power in Organizations*, ed. M. N. Zald. Nashville, Tenn.: Vanderbilt University Press.

Hickson, D. J., C. R. Hinings, C. A. Lee, R. E. Schneck, and J. M. Pennings. 1971. "A Strategic Contingencies Theory of Intraorganizational Power." *Administrative Science Quarterly* 16:216–29.

Huff, A. S. 1980. "Organizations as Political Systems: Implications for Diagnosis, Change and Stability." In *Systems The-*

ory for Organization Development, ed. T. G. Cummings. London: Wiley.

Hunter, D. J. 1980. *Coping with Uncertainty*. Chichester, England: Research Studies Press.

Jaeger, A. 1983. "The Transfer of Organized Culture Overseas: An Approach to Control in the Multi-national Corporation." *Journal of International Business Studies* 14, no. 2:91–114.

Jay, A. 1970. *Management and Machiavelli*. Harmondsworth, England: Penguin.

Jick, T. D., and V. V. Murray. 1982. "The Management of Hard Times: Budget Cutbacks in Public Sector Organizations." *Organization Studies* 3.141–69.

Kanter, R. M. 1977. *Men and Women of the Corporation*. New York: Basic Books.

Kimberley, J. 1975. "Environmental Constraints and Organizational Structure: A Comparative Analysis." *Administrative Science Quarterly* 20:1–9.

King, P. F. 1976. "An Investigation of the Process of Large-Scale Capital Investments: Decision Making in Diversified Hierarchical Organizations." Ph.D. thesis, University of London.

Korda, M. 1975. *Power*. New York: Random House.

Lane, T., and K. Roberts. 1976. *Strike at Pilkingtons*. London: Fontana.

Lasswell, H. D. 1936. *Politics: Who Gets What, When, How*. New York: McGraw-Hill.

———. 1951. *The Policy Sciences: Recent Developments in Scope and Method*. Stanford, Calif.: Stanford University Press.

———. 1971. *A Pre View of Policy Sciences*. New York: Elsevier Science.

Lawrence, P., and J. Lorsch. 1967. *Organization and Environment*. Cambridge, Mass.: Harvard University Press.

Leoni, B. 1964. "The Meaning of 'Political' in Political Decisions." In *The Making of Decisions*, ed. W. J. Gore and J. W. Dyson. New York: Free Press.

Levine, C. H. 1978. "Organizational Decline and Cutback Management." *Public Administration Review* 38, no. 4:316–25.

———. 1979. "More on Cutback Management: Hard Questions for Hard Times." *Public Administration Review* 39, no. 2:179–83.

Levine, C. H., I. S. Rubin, and G. S. Wolohojian. 1981. *The Politics of Retrenchment*. Beverly Hills, Calif.: Sage.

Lindblom, C. E. 1959. "The Science of Muddling Through." *Public Administration Review* 19:91–99.

———. 1965. *The Intelligence of Democracy*. New York: Free Press.

———. 1968. *The Policy Making Process*. Englewood Cliffs, N.J.: Prentice-Hall.

Lipset, S. M. 1959. "Some Social Requisites of Democracy: Economic Development and Political Legitimacy." *American Political Science Review* 53:69–105.

———. 1963. *Political Man*. New York: Doubleday.

Lukes, S. 1974. *Power: A Radical View*. London: Macmillan.

———. 1977. *Essays in Social Theory*. London: Macmillan.

Lundberg, C. C. 1964. "Administrative Decisions: A Scheme

for Analysis." In *The Making of Decisions*, ed. W. J. Gore and J. W. Dyson. New York: Free Press.

MacMillan, I. C. 1978. *Strategy Formulation: Political Concepts*. St. Paul, Minn.: West.

Madison, D. L., R. W. Allen, L. W. Potter, T. A. Fenwick, and B. T. Mayes. 1980. "Organizational Politics: An Exploration of Managers' Perceptions." *Human Relations* 33, no. 2:79–100.

March, J. G., and H. A. Simon. 1958. *Organizations*. New York: Wiley.

Margulies, N., and A. P. Raia. 1972. *Organizational Development: Values, Process and Technology*. London: McGraw-Hill.

Martin, R., and R. H. Fryer. 1973. *Redundancy and Paternalist Capitalism*. London: Allen and Unwin.

McClelland, D. S. 1974. "Two Faces of Power." In *Organizational Psychology*, ed. D. A. Kolb, I. M. Rubin, and J. M. McIntyre. Englewood Cliffs, N.J.: Prentice-Hall.

Mechanic, D. 1962. "Sources of Power of Lower Participants in Complex Organizations." *Administrative Science Quarterly* 7:349–64.

Meyer, J. W., and B. Rowan. 1977–78. "Institutionalized Organizations: Formal Structure as a Myth." *American Journal of Sociology* 83, no. 2:340–63.

Meyers, M., and E. C. Banfield. 1955. *Politics, Planning and the Public Interest*. New York: Free Press.

Miles, R. H. 1982. *Coffin Nails and Corporate Strategies*. Englewood Cliffs, N.J.: Prentice-Hall.

Mintzberg, H. 1983. *Power in and Around Organizations*. Englewood Cliffs, N.J.: Prentice Hall.

Mueller, C. 1973. *The Politics of Communication*. London: Oxford University Press.

Mumford, E., and A. M. Pettigrew. 1975. *Implementing Strategic Decisions*. London: Longman.

Murray, E. A. 1978. "Strategic Choice as a Negotiated Outcome." *Management Science* 24, no. 9:960–72.

Nagel, J. H. 1975. *The Descriptive Analysis of Power*. New Haven: Yale University Press.

Nord, W. R. 1978. "Dreams of Humanization and the Realities of Power." *Academy of Management Review* 3:674–9.

Ouchi, W. G. *Theory Z*. New York: Avon Books.

Parry, G., and P. Morriss. 1975. "When Is a Decision Not a Decision?" In *British Political Sociology Yearbook*, ed. I. Crewe. Vol. 1. London, England: Croon Helm.

Partridge, P. H. 1970. "Some Notes on the Concept of Power." In *Contemporary Political Theory*, ed. A. de Crespigny and A. Wertheimer. London: Nelson.

Perrow, C. 1970. *Organizational Analysis*. London: Tavistock.

Pettigrew, A. M. 1973. *The Politics of Organizational Decision Making*. London: Tavistock.

———. 1976. "Conference Review: Issues of Change." In *Personal Goals and Work Design*, ed. P. Warr. London: Wiley.

———. 1977. *The Creation of Organizational Cultures*. European Institute for Advanced Studies in Management, Working Paper 77-11:570–81.

———. 1979. "On Studying Organizational Cultures." *Administrative Science Quarterly* 24 (December): 570–81.

Pfeffer, J. 1981. *Power in Organizations*. Marshfield, Mass.: Pitman.

Pfeffer, J., and G. Salancik. 1974. "Organizational Decision Making as a Political Process." *Administrative Science Quarterly* 19:135–51.

———. 1978. *The External Control of Organizations*. London: Harper & Row.

Plott, C. R., and M. E. Levine. 1978. "A Model of Agenda Influence on Committee Decisions." *American Economic Review* 68:146–60.

Polsby, N. W. 1963. *Community Power and Political Theory*. New Haven: Yale University Press.

Popper, K. 1945. *The Open Society and Its Enemies*. London: Routledge.

Pugh, D., D. J. Hickson, C. R. Hinings, and C. Turner. 1969. "The Context of Organizational Structures." *Administrative Science Quarterly* 14:91–114.

Quinn, J. B. 1980. *Strategies for Change*. Homewood, Ill.: Irwin.

Ranson, S., R. Hinings, and R. Greenwood. 1980. "The Structuring of Organizational Structure." *Administrative Science Quarterly* 25, no. 1 (March):1–14.

Ritti, R. R., and G. R. Funkhouser. 1977. *The Ropes to Skip and the Ropes to Know: Studies in Organizational Behavior*. Columbus, Ohio: Grid.

Roelofs, H. M. 1976. *Ideology and Myth in American Politics*. Boston: Little, Brown.

Rothschild, J. 1979. "Political Legitimacy in Contemporary Europe." In *Legitimation of Regimes*, ed. B. Denitch. Beverly Hills, Calif.: Sage.

Salaman, G. 1979. *Work Organizations: Resistance and Control*. London: Longman.

Salancik, G., and J. Pfeffer. 1974. "The Bases and Use of Power in Organizational Decision Making." *Administrative Science Quarterly* 19:453–73.

Saunders, P. 1980. *Urban Politics*. London: Penguin.

Sayles, L. R. 1958. *Behavior of Industrial Workgroups*. New York: Wiley.

Schaar, J. H. 1969. "Legitimacy in the Modern State." In *Power and Community*, ed. P. Green and S. Levinson. New York: Pantheon.

Schattschneider, E. F. 1960. *The Semi-Sovereign People*. New York: Holt, Rinehart and Winston.

Schilit, W. K., and E. A. Locke. 1982. "Study of Upward Influence in Organizations." *Administrative Science Quarterly* 27:304–16.

Selznick, P. 1949. *TVA and the Grass Roots*. Berkeley, Calif.: University of California Press.

Silverman, D. 1970. *The Theory of Organization*. London: Heinemann.

Simon, H. A. 1955. "A Behavioral Model of Rational Choice." *Quarterly Journal of Economics* 69, no. 1:99–118.

Snyder, R. C., and G. D. Paige. 1958. "The United States Decision to Resist Aggression in Korea: The Application of an Analytical Scheme." *Administrative Science Quarterly* 3:341–78.

Snyder, R. C., H. W. Bruck, and B. Sapin, eds. 1963. *Foreign Policy Decision Making*. Glencoe, Ill.: Free Press.

Stephenson, T. F. 1975. "Organization Development: A Critique." *Journal of Management Studies* 12 (Oct.):249–65.

Terreberry, S. 1963. "The Evolution of Organizational Environments." *Administrative Science Quarterly* 13 (March): 590–613.

Tushman, M. 1977. "A Political Approach to Organizations: A Review and Rationale." *Academy of Management Review* 2:206–16.

Van Houten, D., and P. Goldman. 1981. "Contract Consulting's Hidden Agenda." *Pacific Sociological Review* 24, no. 4:461–93.

Walton, R. E. 1965. "Two Strategies of Social Change and Their Dilemmas." *Journal of Applied Behavioral Science* 1, no. 2:167–79.

Wamsley, G. L. 1970. "Power and the Crisis of the Universities." In *Power in Organizations*, ed. M. N. Zald. Nashville, Tenn.: Vanderbilt University Press.

Wamsley, G. L., and M. N. Zald. 1973. "The Political Economy of Public Organization." *Public Administration Review* 33:62–73.

Watson, T. J. 1980. *Sociology, Work and Industry*. London: Routledge & Kegan Paul.

———. 1982. "Group Ideologies and Organizational Change." *Journal of Management Studies* 19, no. 3:259–75.

Wedderburn, D., and R. Compton. 1972. *Worker Attitudes and Technology*. Cambridge: Cambridge University Press.

Wildavsky, A. 1961. "Political Implications of Budgetary Reform." *Public Administration Review* 21:183–90.

———. 1964. *The Politics of the Budgetary Process*. Boston: Little, Brown.

———. 1969. "Rescuing Policy Analysis from PPBS." *Public Administration Review* 29:189–202.

Wilensky, H. L. 1967. *Organizational Intelligence*. New York: Basic Books.

Wolfinger, R. E. 1971. "Nondecisions and the Study of Local Politics." *American Political Science Review* 65:1063–80.

Woodward, J. 1965. *Industrial Organizations*. Oxford: Oxford University Press.

Wrapp, H. E. 1967. "Good Managers Don't Make Policy Decisions." *Harvard Business Review* 45 (Sept.–Oct.):91–7.

Young, R. A. 1978. "Review Article." *Canadian Journal of Political Science* 11, no. 3:639–49.

Zald, M. N., ed. 1970a. *Power in Organizations*. Nashville, Tenn.: Vanderbilt University Press.

———. 1970b. "Political Economy: A Framework for Comparative Analysis." In *Power in Organizations*. Nashville, Tenn.: Vanderbilt University Press.

Zammuto, R. 1982. *Managing Decline in the Public Sector: Lessons from the U.S. Auto Industry*. Boulder, Colo.: National Center for Higher Education Management Systems.

8

Gestalt research: clinical-field-research approaches to studying organizations

PETER D. BLANCK AND ARTHUR N. TURNER

The general purpose of organizational behavior as a discipline is to improve useful knowledge and understanding of how members of real organizations actually behave. Accordingly, organizational behavior researchers need to get inside ongoing organizations to interview and observe their members at work. In this chapter, after defining and clarifying what we mean by the term *clinical field research*, we discuss several important issues that researchers face in designing and conducting clinical-field-research projects. We will give examples of how the issues have been handled by previous researchers, and in addition suggest answers to some of the questions raised by critics of this research strategy. In this way we hope to clarify the types of research questions and purposes most appropriate to clinical-field-research methods.

WHAT IS CLINICAL FIELD RESEARCH?

Perhaps the overriding purpose of clinical field research is to gain an in-depth understanding of the totality of a real, ongoing, and complex social situation. We use the term *gestalt research* to indicate the intention to capture this wholeness of ongoing complex social systems.

One distinguishing characteristic of gestalt or clinical field research is that typically only a very small num-

ber of situations (often only one) are studied. If the researcher's purpose is rigorously to test predefined hypotheses or theoretical propositions, or perhaps to discover whether phenomena occur within a statistically valid sample or similar social system, a "clinical" approach is usually inappropriate. However, when the researcher's purpose is to understand the internal dynamics and functioning of an organization or its members and to study in depth and over time one or a very small number of organizations, gestalt research is the sensible way to proceed.

Many criteria used to judge the validity of more experimental research methodologies are violated by gestalt or clinical-field-research approaches. One way to describe clinical research, or at least to describe what it is *not*, is to outline some of the standard rules of "scientific objectivity" that are normally violated by clinical field methodologies.

First, this approach violates the precept that the researcher should somehow be isolated or distanced from the phenomena being studied in order to avoid contamination effects. We believe the clinical and gestalt researcher is inevitably involved with the situation being studied; the researcher influences the situation and is influenced by it. The duty or essential skill of the clinical researcher is not to avoid involvement but to recognize and take account of the nature of that involvement. For example, the researcher's initial contact with the social system or organization that is the setting for the research project has subtle effects on that system. Observing how a system reacts to the researcher's presence, procedures, and questions is itself one of the most interesting sources of data for understanding how a system functions. Of course, researchers employing other methodologies—for example, those of the experimental social sciences—also recognize the extent to which they are influencing and being influenced by the phenomena they wish to understand. However, the issue of researcher involvement is especially unavoidable in clinical-field methodologies. Too often, it is suggested that the obvious involvement of clinical researchers in the setting of their research somehow makes their results less valid and reliable. We are suggesting, in contrast, that if clinical field researchers recognize the problems potentially created by researcher involvement, they may be able to capitalize on that involvement to learn more about how a social system functions when exposed to an external stimulus.

A second way in which clinical field research approaches may violate traditional rules of scientific inquiry is that this research is not, in the most basic form, designed to test hypotheses or to confirm a theory. Clinical field research may generate hypotheses that can be tested by other methods, and it may contribute, over time, to building useful theory. However, its immediate aim is usually more modest, but no less useful. This aim is to understand in depth how some aspect of a real-world social system actually functions and to describe this process in ways that will help others understand the functioning of this and other social systems. This purpose and working goal can be valued as highly in academia, when done well, as it has often been in the world of practice. As we will describe later in this chapter, several clinical-field-research studies have had a profound influence on both the theory and practice of organizational behavior.

Several other precepts of the scientific method are violated by clinical field researchers. Specifically, randomization procedures, statistical sampling procedures, reliability and internal validity questions (in the usual sense), and tests of statistical significance are not central concerns and are often regarded as peripheral questions of interest. Further, the quality of the description of phenomena is often regarded as more important than the quality of reported observations. In short, clinical field research is quite different from what many behavioral researchers have been trained to regard as "scientific." To some it is so different that it may not be regarded as research at all. To us it certainly is research, different, but no less valuable and no less rigorous when well practiced.

Before proceeding, two additional points need to be clarified. First, the word *clinical* should not be interpreted to mean that the researcher's role is primarily to heal or facilitate change. To us, clinical means that the researcher is closely interacting with, and trying to understand, real-world phenomena. The researcher's primary role is not that of consultant, change-agent, or interventionist. Certainly, the clinical field researcher intervenes, but only as a consequence of methodological procedures and not as a necessary part of the mission of clinical research. For this reason the term *gestalt research* may more accurately describe the research patterns discussed in this chapter.

The second introductory point we want to make is perhaps more obvious: the two major research tools for this methodology are interviewing and observation. Some interview and observation procedures are highly systematic and prescribed, and we will refer to some of these more structured approaches. However, many of the most respected clinical-field-research projects have employed unstructured interviewing and observation techniques which have been adapted to the characteristics of the particular field environment. Many regard this willingness to adapt methods of data collection to forces within the social system being studied as peculiarly nonscientific. Yet we believe this adaption is often necessary in order to obtain meaningful data.

Our discussion of clinical field or gestalt research methodology is organized around the issues raised in the different phases of this type of research project. We will consider in turn the following research steps: (1) developing the overall purpose and focus; (2) initial immersion in the field; (3) choosing and adapting specific types of field methodologies; (4) organizational entry and contracting approaches; (5) developing observation and interviewing techniques; and (6) processing these data and deriving findings and results. Various critical and strategic dilemmas associated with clinical-field-research approaches are also presented.

RESEARCH PURPOSE

As we have suggested, the appropriateness of any methodology depends, in part, upon the purpose of the research project. Whether a gestalt or clinical field approach should be chosen depends on what kind of knowledge is being sought and what kind of problem is to be investigated.

Kinds of knowledge

A gestalt approach is perhaps most obviously appropriate when the subject has not already given rise to established theory and clearly stated propositions. If little research has been done on the phenomena to be understood, it may make sense to go into the field with an exploratory and relatively open frame of mind to discover what can be learned through direct observation. Researchers may bring clinical data-gathering skills and perhaps a general way of thinking appropriate to the phenomena they want to understand, but no clearly formulated propositions to be tested. For example, a new kind of role in organizations may have emerged, and the researchers simply want to learn more about how members performing this function actually behave. Or they may be interested in a type of organization or set of organizational relationships about which little is known. In such cases it may be important to understand in depth how a particular role or set of relationships function in one or two instances before more systematic experiments or more broadly based surveys can sensibly be designed.

Often a clinical exploration of previously unresearched phenomena is the only way to begin to build a base of understanding necessary for subsequent development of theory leading to propositions that later can be tested by survey or experimental methods. In other words, the most obvious rationale for choosing a gestalt approach is that we lack the information needed to design other methodologies. But this is not the only rationale.

Occasionally clinical field research is used to test the validity of a specific theoretical proposition. However, most behavioral theories do not claim that their propositions usually hold true under all circumstances. Propositions are much more likely to describe tendencies or trends, or relationships valid only under relatively controlled circumstances. The discovery of one or two contrary instances, under complex environmental conditions that cannot all be controlled, does not necessarily discredit the proposition or the theory from which it is derived. This is why clinical field research is usually more appropriate for the hypothesis-generating phase than for the theory-testing phase in the development of knowledge. Does this mean that gestalt research in organizational behavior becomes less relevant as knowledge matures? We do not think so, if only because of the vast complexity of the field and the continual need for in-depth understanding of specific instances as new organizational forms develop and adapt to their ever-changing environment.

Kinds of problems

A gestalt approach is appropriate when the problem being investigated is related to how a social system, in all its complexity, actually functions. The underlying assumption is that by understanding the functioning of one system we can increase understanding of other similar systems. The history of organizational behavior as a field lends strong support to this notion.

Clinical field research in one or a small number of organizations over a relatively long period of time may be especially appropriate when the problem is related to how a social system adapts to various kinds of internal and external changes. The impact on organization functioning of management succession, consulting interventions, environmental challenge, structural redesign, and other changes, has been researched through clinical case studies. (For a review of research on organizational change, see Beer 1980.) Indeed, it is difficult to see how issues of this kind can be adequately understood by other approaches.

The nature of the problem to be researched influences the choice of methodology in another respect. A gestalt approach may be more appropriate when the main goal of the study is to improve practice, rather than to build knowledge. If the main intended audience of a research project is not the academic community but practitioners (government administrators, business managers, union leaders, consultants), a detailed description of how a problem was handled in one instance, based on careful clinical research, can have more face validity and therefore more influence than several more systematic and academically acceptable approaches. The story can teach important lessons, especially if it is real and well told. It can encourage the practitioner to test out for himself, in other situations, approaches that might otherwise never have been tried. A single case may not be a sufficient basis for developing a scientifically valid theory but may have great influence in the world of practice. It is therefore important that clinical field case studies be carefully conducted and responsibly reported, recognizing both the danger of overgeneralization and the potential value of experimentation *in practice* with their implications.

In spite of the practical implications of good clinical research, we close this section by reemphasizing its role in building validly generalizable knowledge. Before deciding on this approach, the researcher should ask, What kinds of knowledge about the problem I want to investigate already exist? Are there previously derived theoretical propositions that have been rigorously tested through an experimental or survey research design? Or do we need a more general understanding of the problem before testable propositions are relevant? In the latter case, the clinical or gestalt approach may be the most efficient way to explore relatively new territory. With the exception of propositions that can be disproved by discovering one contrary instance, clinical field research is usually less appropriate for testing the validity of existing theories than for discovering unknown propositions and developing new theories.

INITIAL IMMERSION

After deciding to employ a gestalt approach to a research project, but *before* deciding on the particular type of research design, the researcher needs to get out into the field and to begin to understand the phenomena under study and what way of learning about it may work best. Most experienced clinical researchers emphasize the importance of an initial exposure, or "immersion," in the field situation. During this period, the researcher is in a relatively unstructured, open frame of mind concerning what to look for and how to look for it.

We are suggesting that researchers go out into the field and have a look, even before the research concept and practices have been developed. For example, interview a manager before you know how many other interviews you will have or whether you will always be asking the same questions. See firsthand a group at work before you decide how many groups you will observe or what specific observational method you may use. Discover how something is actually done without necessarily knowing whether or not the thing you discover is related to the phenomena you want to study. Refrain from designing the project until you have had an initial direct exposure to at least part of the territory. Naïve, unstructured, unfocused, with open eyes and ears, learn *something* firsthand about what you want to study *before* you begin to study it more systematically.

Sometimes the result of this first immersion in the territory may be a decision not to pursue a clinical approach. The researcher may decide that an experimental or survey design is more appropriate to the question under investigation. On the other hand, it may be apparent that the researcher should look closely but briefly at one or two other field situations before deciding how to proceed. To produce useful results, clinical field research needs to be carefully designed. But the first step is a relatively *un*designed initial exposure to the reality of the field setting. The insights gained from unstructured observation and informal conversation will enable the researcher to select appropriate methods and develop a strategy for gaining permission to conduct subsequent structured phases of the research process.

RESEARCH DESIGN QUESTIONS

Methodological decisions made at the outset of the research process greatly influence the kind of analysis and sampling procedures of the study. This section describes several research design methodological alternatives and the determinants and consequences of these decisions. Finally, brief historical examples of research projects illustrating these alternatives are provided.

Level of analysis

As in most social research, the individual, the group, and the organization are the three basic levels of analysis available to the gestalt researcher. A general rule of thumb for deciding on the appropriate level of analysis is related to the population one wishes to generalize. For example, a researcher interested in studying the communication styles of chief executive officers could certainly use the individual CEO as the unit of analysis. If he or she were interested in studying communication styles in different organizations, the organization could be the appropriate unit of analysis. Aside from this obvious relationship, the focus of the inquiry—on the individual, group, or organization—will reflect the theoretical interest and subsequent generalizability of the research question.

Campbell and Stanley (1966) and Cook and Campbell (1979) have discussed two basic types of validity—internal and external—relevant to research in field settings. Internal validity refers to the extent to which a relationship between two variables could be described as meaningful, irrespective of theoretical predictions (Cook and Campbell 1979). Internal validity depends on the appropriateness of research operations and tests, statistical analyses, and randomization procedures. External validity, in contrast, refers to the generalizability of results or causal relationships to specific social settings or across many social settings. We believe external validity is the primary concern for research projects described in this chapter.

Cook and Campbell discuss three general techniques that researchers can use to increase the external validity of research projects. First, they might randomly select a sample from a larger population of cases. While considerable time and resources are required, results can then be generalized across similar social settings. Second, researchers can intentionally sample for heterogeneity, with the aim of deliberately selecting a wide range of instances from specific classes of behaviors. Finally, Cook and Campbell suggest a prototypical model, in which researchers seek to select the characteristic cases from a specific class of behavior or social settings.

These three models for increasing the external validity or generalizability of research results can also be effectively used in combination. For example, our researcher interested in the communication styles of CEOs might first randomly select a sample of CEOs from across the country and generally study their communication styles. Next, he or she might examine the general categories or classes of communication styles that emerge. Finally, a closer examination of the prototypical classes of CEO communication styles could be performed. All three approaches can help both to define and to refine generalizations concerning CEO communication styles.

The level of analysis of a research project can also influence the choice and flexibility of research methods. Clearly, interview techniques are more efficient and applicable when dealing with individuals over a long period of time. When the level of analysis of a research project is a group or organization, observation techniques become more and more essential in describing the social setting. Researchers need to be aware of the trade-offs they are willing to make, and understand how the level of analysis influences the degree of flexibility in choosing and practicing interview and observation techniques over the course of a research project.

Finally, the level of analysis of a research program also influences the researcher's relationship to the field setting. If only for logistical reasons, data sources and interrelationships among individuals, groups, and organizations become increasingly complex as the level of analysis increases. Researchers need to become increasingly selective in assimilating and analyzing incoming data as the scope of the research project expands. More important, an awareness of this editing process can lead to a more objective, and perhaps less personally biased, depiction of the social setting.

Number and types of cases

Three general sampling procedures are available to researchers for choosing the number and type of instances of social behavior to study. First, one can focus in depth on one instance of social behavior in a single case study. Alternatively, a comparative case study can be designed to assess and compare two or more cases of behavior that differ on theoretically relevant dimensions. ness of a single social setting. Alternatively, many

Finally, a representative sampling of case studies may be undertaken. The researcher examines several cases of social behavior in hopes of obtaining a representative view of the class of behaviors under study.

Sampling choices reflect the nature of the research question and influence a researcher's choice of method. In a very general sense, sampling choices are determined by an individual researcher's style and special competencies. For example, certain researchers may seek close, in-depth contacts with a single social setting over time. Here the goal is to understand the complexities and rich-researchers wish to examine diverse social settings or perhaps large organizations.

In a more theoretically central manner, the number and types of cases studied influences the nature and analysis of the research problem. As we have said, a major issue is whether the research project is designed to *build* theory or to *test* theory. We believe that as the primary purpose of the research moves from theory building to theory testing, it becomes appropriate to expand the number of cases of the research project. For example, the single-case-study method is best employed when the researcher's purpose is to describe, understand, and document rich and complex social behavior. The comparative case study can be used to build theory, but it can also be employed to test specific theory predictions. Such predictions can be directed toward specific target groups or general social settings. A representative sampling of case studies is a particularly effective means of testing theory predictions. By obtaining a representative view of the class of behaviors under study, the researcher can more confidently generalize the findings to other social settings.

Historical examples of level of analysis and sampling questions

The choice of a research methodology involves decisions as to both level of analysis and sampling procedures, as shown schematically in figure 8.1. Each of the nine cells

LEVEL OF ANALYSIS

NUMBER AND TYPES OF CASES		Individual	Group	Organization
	Single	Hodgson, Levinson, and Zaleznik	Zaleznik, Christensen, and Roethlisberger Homans	Selznick
	Comparative	Mintzberg	Roethlisberger and Dickson	Blau
	Sampling	Carlson	Whyte	Lawrence and Lorsch

Figure 8.1 Level of analysis and sampling design alternatives

in this matrix represents a particular research design or methodology that may be employed by the researcher. In each cell of the matrix appear the names of previous researchers who have chosen that particular methodological alternative.

Individual case study has long been practiced by psychologists and psychiatrists. Freud's case studies provide numerous examples of individual in-depth studies. Historical examples of individual work behavior are also available. Hodgson, Levinson, and Zaleznik's (1965) detailed analysis of three top executives in a hospital is one example of the individual case-study approach. In this study, the researchers conducted intensive observations of individual and interpersonal work behavior. The three executives' personalities and character structures were discussed in terms of specialized roles in the larger power constellation of the hospital. One executive, the hospital superintendent, was described as a domineering paternal figure, while the clinical director was described as a nurturant maternal figure. The third executive, the director of research, was said to be permissive and egalitarian, similar to the uncle figure in many family structures. Each executive was described as having a specialized role in the hospital power system. Power constellations in other organizations were hypothesized to be a product of similar individual and interpersonal role specialization.

Henry Mintzberg's (1973) description of the nature of managerial work provides a *comparative view* of the work of five chief executives. Mintzberg drew on a variety of data sources for each manager studied. He observed each manager for one week, examined a one-month record of their scheduled appointments, gathered information about the organization's environment, and conducted interviews with the managers' assistants to gain data on their personalities, work styles, and work-related activities. Mintzberg points out the basic characteristics of the work behavior of these five managers and describes the unique features of each individual. While his research was not specifically designed to compare different types of managers, Mintzberg suggests that the nature of the industry, organization, managerial style, and business needs all seem to influence the work of managers.

One of the first *in-depth sampling case studies* of individual work behavior was Sune Carlson's (1951) examination of nine Swedish company presidents. Carlson's explicit purpose was to describe executive behavior by studying a series of individual cases. He developed diaries for his executives to use in recording their daily behavior. He analyzed work time, communication patterns, and work content. Carlson found that the executives rarely were free to be alone and work without

interruption for more than fifteen minutes during the day. Communication obligations, such as answering mail and meeting with various subordinates, occupied most of the work day.

Researchers have also conducted a number of studies of small groups of people at work in organizations (work groups). An intensive *in-depth two-year study of work-group* membership, satisfaction, and productivity in a medium-sized manufacturing company was performed by Zaleznik, Christensen, and Roethlisberger (1958). This study explored the relationship between job-related and non-job-related group membership. Using Homans's (1950) theory of work group behavior, data about the "external system" were used to predict characteristics of the "internal system" or emergent behavior. In essence, a gestalt approach was used to test specific propositions of an existing theory. Satisfaction and productivity were primarily determined by position in the informal social organization and the degree to which an individual's activities and characteristics realized the group's norms and values. Some of the relationships between variables that appeared in the company were hypothesized to exist in other similar work groups.

In effect, if not in original design, one of the most extensive studies of *comparative work-group behavior* was conducted at the Hawthorne Works of the Western Electric Company between 1927 and 1932, as described in detail by Roethlisberger and Dickson (1939). The first group, known as the "relay assembly test room" group, was observed in order to assess the general effects of work conditions, such as rest pauses and changes in work hours, on worker and work-group behavior. Later, a second group, known as the "bank wiring observation room," was observed to discover more about the relationship between the technical and social organization of the work group. This study was designed to answer questions raised by the earlier relay-assembly-test-group observations, by closely examining a group that had not been established as an experiment, subject to unusual attention by management, but as it existed in its natural factory environment. In a comparative sense, while the first Hawthorne study was originally intended to explore the effects of physical conditions of work on worker behavior, the second was designed to focus on broader questions of human relations in the work setting.

Finally, an example of *sampling case studies* is provided by William Whyte's (1948) intensive field study of work-group behavior in twelve large urban restaurants in 1944 and 1945. People working in these restaurants formed social organizations that affected both customer service and worker morale. Whyte noted that the development of social groups was a primary need of restaurant employees. Further, where well-integrated social cliques existed, absenteeism and turnover were minimized.

Large formal organizations have also been studied by clinical researchers. An early example of a *sociological individual case study* was Selznick's (1949) study of the Tennessee Valley Authority (TVA). Selznick gathered data from 1942 to 1943 by means of personal interviews with TVA and Washington officials who had been intimately involved with the various programs discussed, by tapping "gossip channels," and by examining the written records and files of the TVA. Selznick checked his sources by verbal statements with the formal record and by using multiple data sources and informants. His work represents an early attempt at a case study on the sociology of formal organizations. He discussed the informal and formal structure of the TVA as well as the structural conditions that influenced organizational behavior, such as the "grass roots" ideology. The implications for democratic planning that emerged from this study, such as ideological context, power distribution, and bureaucratic functions, are also described.

A well-known example of the *comparative case study of organizations* is Peter Blau's (1955) study of the dynamics of bureaucracies. Blau examined the social patterns and work behavior of officials in two government agencies—a public employment agency and a federal enforcement agency—from 1948 to 1949. He used direct observation, interviewing, and the analysis of official records as data sources in both case studies. He also interviewed all the members of the two agencies at home in order to clarify the social patterns and practices in each case. Blau found that officials tended to extend the limited objectives of their work duties. He suggested that bureaucratic work conditions generate an increasing concern for the values of the larger society. Internal and external forces were shown to affect both agencies in different ways, and the more effective operations were able to respond flexibly to these forces. Blau also describes the administrators' perceptions of status and professional orientation in the bureaucratic organization.

Paul Lawrence and Jay Lorsch's (1967) examination of organizational characteristics and their environmental constraints provides an example of the *sampling approach to the study of organizations.* Six organizations in the plastics industry were studied. The researchers used both interviews and questionnaires to gather information about the specific demands placed on these six organizations by the plastics-industry environment. They described how environmental conditions, business context, and the domain of operation influence the internal structure and processes of organizations. Lawrence and Lorsch next performed a comparative analysis of a highly effective company and a less effective competitor in the standardized-container and processed-food industries, using a similar research design. This phase of the research project was designed to examine effective and less effective organizations in other industries and environments and to further examine how internal organizational structure was related to external environments. On the basis of these studies, the authors proposed a contingency theory of organizational structure, which suggested that the characteristics of internal organizational functions are related to specific environmental characteristics and interests. This theory has subsequently been tested and modified in a series of other clinical researches using similar methodologies.

ENTRY AND CONTRACTING

After deciding on the level of analysis and sampling procedures of the field research, on the basis of its general purpose and an initial exposure to some field settings, the researcher needs to find one or more sites in which the design can be carried out. How do gestalt researchers gain entry to suitable field settings and permission to proceed? In some ways this is the most problematic and crucial phase of the whole process. Unless it is handled with skill, the project, no matter how carefully designed to accomplish its purpose, may not produce valid data and useful results.

A first step is to stimulate interest in the research objectives on the part of influential persons in one or more target settings. Usually it is important to begin negotiations over entry at the highest feasible level of the organization in which the study is to be conducted. For some designs there are many potential settings; for others there may be only one or two. Sometimes the researchers will have already established a relationship of understanding and trust with influential members of appropriate settings; but often the design requires entry into organizations where the researchers and their institutions are relatively unknown. Because of these and other variations it is impossible to prescribe rules to follow in every case. Here we will merely suggest certain principles broad enough to apply to a wide range of circumstances.

First, explain in writing the purpose and design of the project in simple language that will make sense to practitioners. Sometimes this exercise even helps the researchers themselves become more clear about the project and leads to some useful simplifications in conceptualization and procedures. Present this general statement to one person in each potential site whose position indicates likely interest and influence in negotiating entry. Usually this initial statement should not be a formal request to conduct the study on this site, but should express a wish to discuss the project and to explore whether the particular site would be appropriate.

Second, if the person shows an interest in the project, arrange a meeting to explore the possibility of conducting the research at that site. Start by listening carefully and responding sensitively to the other person's reactions. What costs and benefits does he or she see in participating, and how realistic are these expectations? What constraints on your design will conducting the research at this site impose, and are they acceptable? How much time will your research require of members of the organization, and what will motivate them to help you to this extent?

These and similar questions need to be openly explored in the first and subsequent "contracting" sessions. Make it clear that this is a research, not a consulting, project. The principal motivation for cooperation should be to contribute generally to knowledge and understanding, not the expectation of immediate or competitive advantage for this organization or some members of it. Members at all levels may benefit simply by discussing their situations with an outsider who listens well to their concerns, but this should be explained as a potential by-product of the research process, not as its purpose. (For excellent advice on "contracting," addressed to consultants but relevant to researchers, see Block 1982.)

During contracting discussions, it is especially important to reach understanding and commitment concerning all relevant questions of confidentiality, release, and publication. Normally the researcher makes very clear that all data from interviews and observations will be held in strict confidence and that no information will be revealed to anyone in the organization in a way that makes it possible to identify the persons who provided that information. Also the researcher promises to conduct the research in every way so as not to bring harm to any member of the organization.

The results of the research belong to the researcher, who may or may not contract to share them with members of the organization before publication. Usually some sharing of general findings makes sense, because discussion with interested members of the organization greatly helps the researcher understand what the findings mean.

What agreement should be reached about publication and release? Normally, members of an organization expect and deserve the right to review the researcher's write-up of results before publication, and the researcher agrees to correct errors of fact and to disguise information regarded as harmful if published in undisguised form. When contracting, entry, and the whole relationship have been skillfully handled, differences about release and publication can almost always be reconciled without violating the organization's legitimate claim to privacy or the researcher's right to reach and publish his own conclusions.

METHODOLOGICAL STRATEGIES

After the entry and contracting phase, the researcher is in a position to develop appropriate methodological strategies. In capturing the wholeness of ongoing social systems, clinical and gestalt researchers are continuously developing testing and adapting research methods and data-gathering sources. In a real sense, over the course of the project, social scientists become street-wise researchers and develop methodological strategies appropriate for and adapted to the problem to be studied. Too often researchers, especially inexperienced ones, are not willing to adopt flexible methodological strategies and seem to overanalyze or "fight" their rich data sources, losing perspective on the larger social question. This tunnel vision may be due in part to a lack of social and/or interpersonal skills required to appreciate the totality of the social system. Many times, however, such resistance is due to an overreliance on and adherence to the standard rules of scientific objectivity that we have discussed. Additionally, we believe that this resistance may reflect the unnecessary and unfounded distinction often drawn between qualitative and quantitative research approaches. That is, clinical or gestalt research has often been portrayed as a qualitative and "soft" approach, while more experimental approaches have been deemed quantitative. Our intention here is to demonstrate that both qualitative and quantitative research-data-collection techniques and methodologies can be employed independently or in a complementary manner. Many qualitative and quantitative research strategies are available to the researcher and have been reviewed elsewhere (Bouchard 1976; Cannell and Kahn 1968; Weick 1968).

In the remainder of this section, we will briefly discuss several commonly employed methodological strategies. One difficult task that the researcher faces is to strike an appropriate balance of researcher involvement and structure in data-collection techniques. This balance needs to fit both the nature of the project and the researcher's own competence and preference to ensure meaningful and reliable findings.

Direct observation

Direct observation is perhaps the most complicated and yet most personally satisfying research methodology. In the most extreme form of direct observation—participant observation—the researcher actually becomes a member of the social system under study. Severyn Bruyn (1963, 222–23) has summarized the role of the participant observer:

1. The participant observer shares in the life activities and sentiments of people in face-to-face relationships.
2. The role of participant observer requires both detachment and personal involvement.
3. The researcher acquires a social role which is determined by the requirements of the research design and the framework of the culture.
4. The scientific interests of the participant observer are interdependent with the cultural framework of the people being studied.
5. The social role of the researcher is a natural part of the cultural life of the observed.

Several classic studies in organizational behavior have employed a wider range of observation techniques. (For example, in this chapter we have described Blau 1955 and Selznick 1949.) Still, the methodological foundations of this approach have been described by a number of social scientists as unscientific and epistemologically suspect. (For reviews, see Bruyn 1963, 1966.) The overriding advantage of this methodology, however, is precisely that it enables researchers to capture the wholeness and immediate reality of the ongoing social system.

Various observation and interviewing methods are used (see Zelditch 1962), and researcher participation ranges from a high level of involvement, such as William Foote Whyte's (1981) four year study of an Italian street group, to a very specialized and marginal level of involvement in a social system (see Bouchard 1976).

We have emphasized the importance of relatively unstructured initial exposure or immersion in the field setting. In the same view, Melville Dalton (1959, 62) described his use of participant-observer methodology: "No explicit hypotheses were formulated in *Men Who Manage*. . . . I never feel sure that it is relevant for hypothesizing until I have some intimacy with the situation." Once in the field, the observer can use direct-observation techniques, key informants, and natural and archival data sources in documenting the "natural history" of a social system.

Whether the researcher is employing a qualitative or more quantitative analytical method (e.g., the use of explicit measurement techniques) or both, direct observation techniques are subject to the rigorous concerns of reliability and validity, control, objectivity, and measurement. Bouchard (1976) and Bruyn (1963) have carefully summarized many of these concerns and research principles to guide the researcher's observations. The following list summarizes many of these general guidelines:

Focus on the Researcher

1. Be aware of your own biases and the bias you bring to each situation. Separate facts from artifacts.
2. Be sensitive to your own position in the social structure.
3. Be sensitive to changes in your values, attitudes, beliefs, and emotions.
4. Do not overidentify with any subgroup unless it is technically necessary; maintain sufficient distance to allow an uninhibited working style.
5. Be honest and candid with all informants and data sources.

Focus on the Participants

6. Be aware of participants' biases.
7. Examine all counter positions carefully.
8. Observe your subjects in as many different contexts as possible.
9. Strengthen interpretations with data from *multiple* data sources, such as other observers and informants, interviews, and archival data sources.

Focus on the Research Goals

10. Relate the research question to a larger social context or social problem.
11. Specify the procedures used so that other investigators can check and develop similar procedures. (A good example of this is William Foote Whyte's [1981] methodological appendix in the second edition of *Street Corner Society*.)
12. Specify the development of quantitative measures and analytical procedures.

Systematic observation

Qualitative and quantitative systematic observation techniques have also been employed by clinical researchers. Weick (1968, 360) has defined the observational method as "the selection, provocation, recording, and encoding of that set of behaviors and settings concerning organisms (in situ) which is consistent with empirical aims." Traditionally, direct observers have employed a "nondirective" observational field methodology. Weick's definition of systematic observation procedures, however, provides researchers with a more structured and quantitative model for observational methodologies. He notes several reasons for employing systematic observation methods:

1. A wide range of detailed data is provided.
2. Whole events are preserved.

3. The parameters of behavior are defined.
4. More than one individual can be studied.
5. Language may not be available to describe actions.
6. Individuals may not wish to serve as informants, or individual perceptions may be distorted or defective.

Many systematic or structured observation methods have been reviewed in detail elsewhere (e.g., Bouchard 1976; Weick 1968). Here we will briefly discuss three categories of behavior that have been studied by clinical and gestalt researchers: verbal behavior, nonverbal behavior, and overt/spatial behavior.

The analysis of verbal behavior involves studying and observing people talking in their natural surroundings (in situ). Robert Bales's well-known Interaction Process Analysis (IPA) system (1950) and his later System for the Multiple Level of Observation of Groups (SYMLOG) (1979) are based on peer and observer ratings of verbal statements, individual behavior, and group interaction. Mann (1967) has similarly developed a verbal coding system, which assesses individual behavior by studying the development of feelings toward a group leader. Borgatta (1963) and Argyris (1970) have also each developed a system of categories for coding interpersonal behavior. Verbal behavior has also been assessed by content analysis techniques. For example, Stone, Dunphy, Smith, and Ogilvie's (1966) *General Inquirer* computer programs are designed to assess, identify, and tabulate patterns of verbal behavior. Similarly, systematic studies have been made of nonverbal behaviors such as facial expressions, body movements, tone of voice, and speech patterns. For example, in *Unmasking the Face*, Ekman and Frieson (1975, 1977) provide a coding system for recognizing facial expressions of emotions based on the analysis of facial anatomy.

Finally, overt spatial behaviors have also been systematically observed. Investigators such as Hall (1964) and Sommer (1969) have coded individual use of personal and social space and territory, while other investigators have coded various human movements (for example, Birdwhistell 1970). The frequency of movements and interpersonal outcomes have been analyzed. These researchers, and others, have shown that individual spatial and overt behaviors are developed with regularity, and that violations of these patterns and boundaries affect social interaction.

The advantages of systematic observation techniques are especially great when multiple measures and multiple observers are employed. Verbal, nonverbal, and other descriptions of behavior can together provide a comprehensive view of social behavior. As we have emphasized, systematic techniques should be used to complement more qualitative observational approaches.

Interviewing strategies

Researchers ask questions. Whether a research problem is exploratory or intended to verify theory, a large part of the data will be collected through interviews, which may range from nondirective interviews to structured question-and-answer formats (for a review, see Cannell and Kahn 1968). Bouchard (1976) has classified four general types of interviews on the basis of the question-and-response format. First, in the "totally structured" or "directed" interview, the interviewer asked a specific set of questions requiring a specific set of responses. A second type of interview, often called the "open-ended" or "free response" interview, has specified questions but allows for any response. The third type of interview has no specified questions and allows for any response. Finally, the "nondirective," "exploratory," or "clinical" interview provides interviewers and respondents total freedom in discussing any materials or questions, with little structure to the interview process.

It seems clear that a genuinely nondirective interview is not practical for most research purposes. However, we believe that a tempered version of the open-ended and nondirective clinical interview, perhaps better called the nondirective research interview, is useful for the research process described by this chapter. Indeed, Whyte (1960) has described the inappropriateness of the genuinely nondirective clinical interview and has suggested that a modified version might be more applicable for field research. He describes his experience:

> Once, while studying human relations in restaurants, I decided that I would be just as nondirective as I could. I began each interview simply by asking the informant to tell me whatever he cared to that was important to him about the job situation. The usual answer was: "What do you want to know?" Some informants were willing to respond to questions, but no one poured out his feelings in response to my general invitation. Rather, the approach seemed to make the informants quite uneasy, and I quickly shifted to providing a good deal more structure in the interview. (p. 352)

The format of the nondirective *research* interview utilizes the general structure of the open-ended, free-response interview and the reflective and listening processes of the nondirective clinical interview. The nondirective research interviewer may come to the interview with a list of topics or general questions to be covered. The order and format of these questions is usually open-ended. Interview questions are designed to build on the respondent's confidence and comfort with the interviewer. The interviewer may also ask the respondent to clarify certain points during the interview process.

Gradually, confidence and rapport can be developed in this nonthreatening conversation.

Whyte (1960) has described several general rules for interviewing in field research. The rules are not meant to be exhaustive by any means, but reflect the goals and procedures of the nondirective research interview. The researcher is advised to

- listen more than talk;
- listen sympathetically and actively;
- summarize and reflect informant responses;
- avoid giving advice and passing moral judgment;
- generally do not interrupt;
- when an interruption is necessary, interrupt gracefully;
- design the questions to help the informants express themselves clearly (for example, use relevant language);
- ensure confidentiality of the interview.

Roethlisberger and Dickson (1939, 270–91) have similarly discussed "rules of orientation" and "rules for conducting the interview," which were developed during the Western Electric Hawthorne research program and subsequently modified for use in employee counseling. (For an account of the counseling program at Western Electric, see Dickson and Roethlisberger 1966.) A similar orientation to counseling and psychotherapy was developed by Rogers (1942, 1951).

There is no clear formula for deciding the types of questions, length of interview, whom to interview, and where and when to conduct the interview. Reviews of the interview process are available (Cannell and Kahn 1968), and we urge interested readers to examine them carefully.

During the interview, researchers are encouraged to probe participants. Certain topics may have been insufficiently covered. A degree of flexibility is also required. As Lofland (1971) suggests, this type of interview might be thought of as a "guided conversation." Finally, professional standards require a general introduction to participants, covering some of the essential points summarized by Lofland.

1. Explain the purpose of the study.
2. Assure anonymity and confidentiality.
3. Indicate that there are no right answers to the questions. Interest is in personal opinions.
4. Assure participants that it is all right to interrupt or ask for clarification.
5. Provide some background about own background and interests.

The collection of data from the interview generally follows the same rules that will apply in taking field notes. However, effective interpersonal and listening skills are mandatory in developing meaningful results.

We believe that the research aims reflected in this chapter are captured by the nondirective research interview. Clearly, the way to learn this technique is to get out in the field and question and listen, testing and improving the accuracy of your listening by occasionally reflecting back what you are hearing.

Unobtrusive research strategies

Eugene Webb and his associates (Webb, Campbell, Schwartz, and Sechrest 1966) have described a collection of unobtrusive research methods that can be used to supplement or cross-validate data collected through interviews, questionnaires, and systematic observation. Unobtrusive measures are a collection of nonreactive research tools—that is, these measures are not influenced by the biases and behavior of respondents, experimenters, or interviewers or by other sources of behavior that are influenced or not directly addressed by the research program. Webb and his associates argue for the necessity of employing multiple nonreactive methods as a supplement to the more traditionally employed social science data-gathering techniques (for example, the interview). Unobtrusive measures seem well suited to the clinical, gestalt, and "detective" aspects of the research process described in this chapter.

Webb and his associates discuss three general types of unobtrusive measures: physical traces, archival records, and observation techniques. Physical traces comprise natural erosion measures (for example, the physical wear of a library book can suggest its popularity and remnants of past behavior, or counting the number of liquor bottles in trash cans can be a measure of a town's sobriety). Archival records represent any data source (public and private) that was produced for other than scholarly purposes. Societal or organizational records, voting behaviors, budgets, birth rates, and appointment calendars all represent the archival record. Selznick's (1949) use of the TVA files and records illustrates the archival method. Finally, observational nonobtrusive measures can range from direct observation to more structured observation techniques. In the direct role, observers may simply code behavior and observe data in a nonobtrusive manner. They can code physical signs, for example, the spatial arrangement of furniture, or the verbal and nonverbal behavior of individuals. More intrusive (and ethically questionable) observation techniques include hidden cameras and recording devices, an intervening observer (for example, Allen Funt of "Candid Camera"), or entrapment studies (for example, the recent Abscam entrapment). In each case, although the social scientist may structure the situation, the individual is totally free.

Unobtrusive measures, by themselves, cannot eliminate bias and contamination in research projects, but they can be useful tools for supplementing more traditional approaches to social research. An integrative or multimethod approach seems well suited for the researcher whose goal is to capture the wholeness in an ongoing situation. Just as the researcher must become street-wise to understand the totality of the situation, he or she must play the detective, using all available clues and methods to understand the problem at hand.

PROCESSING AND ANALYZING RESEARCH DATA

Researchers are constantly collecting and interpreting data. Indeed, a major part of the ongoing learning process is comparing data sources and field notes during the course of a research project. This section discusses techniques that can be employed in processing and interpreting data.

Processing data

In their discussions of field research methods, Selltiz, Wrightsman, and Cook (1976) and Lofland (1971) each review numerous data-processing techniques. We will discuss several of these data-processing strategies, particularly those that are useful to the field or gestalt researcher.

Field notes are perhaps the most common way for researchers to process data. In describing the process of developing field notes, Lofland (1971, 102–3) emphatically writes:

> Without the sustained writing down of what has gone on, the observer is hardly in a better position to analyze and comprehend the workings of a world than are the members themselves. . . . Field notes provide the observer's raison d'être. If he is not doing them, he might as well not be in the setting.

Lofland carefully describes several fundamental steps in the development of field notes. A first step is to familiarize oneself with the culture, physical character, and natural events in the setting. Through relevant newspapers, observation of natural events, and informal discussions with participants, the researcher begins to develop descriptive *mental notes* on the nature of the field setting. After this initial immersion a second step is to preserve the natural sequence and importance of events through *jotted notes*. Key words, phrases, or quick

observations can be jotted on napkins over lunch or in small inconspicuous notebooks. Jotted notes serve to remind the field worker of key events and can jog memories when the time comes to write detailed notes. Finally, mental and jotted notes are used in developing *full field notes*. Lofland suggests that researchers promptly develop field notes at the end of each day, before memory lapses occur. Considerable personal discipline is required for accurately developing descriptive field notes.

Full field notes are meant to capture the ongoing events of the setting. For this reason, a chronological log of events and behaviors, described in a concrete and distanced manner, is suggested. Personal impressions, notes of future interests, previously forgotten material, and analytic suggestions can all be part of the full field notes. Selltiz and her associates also suggest that several common elements should be recorded in most field settings, including information on the participants, setting, purpose, social behavior, frequency and duration of behaviors, and the recording of behavioral anecdotes.

Data-processing techniques utilizing systematic observation are also available to the researcher. Weick (1968) has reviewed many of these more systematic recordings of behavior; we will focus only on techniques that may be useful to the field researcher. The first is the specimen record, a nonselective data-processing technique that sequentially and completely describes specific behaviors of interest. Similarly, observational data can also be collected by means of behavioral checklists. Brandt (1972) has distinguished between static and action checklists. Static checklists code stable characteristics of the participants and environment (for example, race, sex, and weather), while action checklists record actual behaviors. More elaborate checklists of behavior are represented by sign analysis—the sampling of specific predetermined behaviors of interest to the researcher (Brandt 1972)—and category systems, which are designed to yield mutually exclusive and independent dimensions of behavior (Weick 1968). Selltiz and her associates (1976) describe category systems as indicating whether a specific type of behavior has occurred, but not the frequency or intensity of an occurrence; Bales has studied groups using his SYMLOG category system (Bales 1979). Finally, behavior has also been recorded through field formats involving behavioral maps or notation techniques (Weick 1968). Hall (1964), for example, employs pictures, mnemonics, and number codes in describing social interaction.

The nondirective research interview also provides researchers with a rich descriptive data collection and processing technique. Lofland (1971) has outlined several steps in the development of interview topics. First, the researcher frames general topics of interest. This process may involve feedback and testing ideas, perhaps after the initial immersion in the setting. General clusters of topics may then emerge. The global structure of the topics is next considered. For example, more sensitive issues may be addressed toward the end of the interview. Finally, a general ordering of topics is developed.

Audiotaping and videotaping can be used to record interview and observational data. Most clinical researchers have relied primarily on their own notes, taken during the interview, from which they subsequently dictate or write up the interview. The advantages of note taking include the following:

- It communicates interest in what the subject says.
- It enables researchers to slow the pace of the interview when desirable.
- It helps researchers feed back interim summaries of what he or she is hearing.
- Stopping the note taking toward the end of the interview sometimes stimulates further exploration of sensitive subjects.
- Interviewees may be more comfortable and open than when the interview is taped.

The advantages of taping an interview are that it

- provides an accurate and complete record of what was said;
- minimizes selective bias and memory limitations;
- permits a permanent record that can be checked subsequently for other research purposes and by other researchers.

In all cases, taping interviews should only be conducted with the subjects' informed consent.

Analyzing data

The task of understanding patterns of behavior in organizations is perhaps the most difficult the researcher faces. Long after the interviews have been conducted, the hours of observation have been logged, and the relevant background resources have been reviewed, the researcher must decide how to process and analyze the data. Of course, if the researcher has been a careful detective and analyst all along, constantly questioning and analyzing the data inputs of the ongoing social systems, the process will be much easier.

Several concrete guidelines for processing and analyzing field data are available. Lofland's (1971) detailed analysis of the collection and management of field data, Whyte's (1960) discussion of indexing interview notes, and Mills's (1959) classic description of "fil-

ing" qualitative data are each helpful in this regard. These and other descriptions of field methodology all stress the importance of prompt development of a filing or indexing system. Whyte describes how he approached data processing and indexing in *Street Corner Society*.

> As I gathered my early research data, I had to decide how I was to organize the written notes. In the very early stage of exploration, I simply put all the notes in chronological order, in a single folder. As I was to go on to study a number of different groups and problems, it was obvious that this was no solution at all.
>
> I had to subdivide the notes. There seemed to be two main possibilities. I could organize the notes topically, with folders for politics, rackets, the church, the family, and so on. Or I could organize the notes in terms of the groups on which they were based. . . . Without really thinking the problem through, I began filing material on the group basis, reasoning that I could redivide it on a topical basis when I had better knowledge of what the relevant topics should be.
>
> As time went on, even the notes in one folder grew beyond the point where my memory would allow me to locate any given item rapidly. Then I devised a rudimentary indexing system: a page in three columns containing, for each interview or observation report, the date, the person or people being interviewed or observed, and a brief summary of the interview or observation record. Such an index would cover from three to eight pages. When I came to review the notes or to write from them, a five-to-ten minute perusal of the index was enough to give me a reasonably full picture of what I had and of where any given item could be located.[1]

Whyte (1960) suggests that it is not advisable to determine index categories before entering the field. Once the researcher has developed a sense of the culture and has become immersed in the setting, then meaningful categories may become apparent. Additionally, the indexing or filing system should reflect the substantive interests of the researcher.

Lofland (1971) has proposed that researchers may want to develop different types of files for storing, ordering, and retrieving information. A *mundane file* keeps track of such things as names, places, and documents. *Analytic files* contain brief summaries or reports on relevant observations or data sources. The analytic files are used to develop general coding schemes and track patterns of behavior. Finally, *field-work files* contain methodological strategies and choices that may be involved in conducting the research project. Indexes can

---

1. W. F. Whyte, *Street Corner Society*, 3d ed. (Chicago: University of Chicago Press, 1981), 307–8. © 1943, 1955 by The University of Chicago. Reprinted by permission.

also be used to cross-reference notes in these and other files. Additionally, computer-based storage and retrieval of files seem especially suited for field-research filing systems in light of the recent advances in the use of personal computers.

Field researchers quickly learn that processing and analyzing data sources go hand in hand. They must continuously summarize and process new data and compare new inputs with previous sources. The final analysis involves developing a plan or outline for organizing all these various learnings, and developing labels, categories, and patterns of behavior. We cannot stress too strongly that the final product is only as good as the researcher's *ongoing* analyses, learning, and reanalyses of the field data.

STRATEGIC AND ETHICAL QUESTIONS

Before closing our discussion of gestalt research methodologies, it is important to emphasize several strategic issues and ethical questions that characteristically arise in conducting and reporting field research. Some of these questions are not easy to answer, and the dilemmas have been resolved differently by different researchers. Because we believe these topics have been given insufficient attention in the literature of research methodology, we want to reemphasize here four characteristics of clinical field research.

1. The researcher has some special responsibilities to the members of the organization in which the research was conducted.
2. The research process itself is an intervention which produces some unintended change in the phenomena being studied.
3. The researcher's involvement inevitably raises questions about whether and how the results are biased by that involvement.
4. It is seldom clear whether the results of any one study contribute unequivocally to generalizable knowledge, even when they have a strong impact on practice.

Responsibility to members of the research site

To obtain valid data the researcher is given permission to enter an organization or other social system, to interview and observe its members, and in other ways to interfere with or inconvenience the people whose behavior

he or she wishes to understand. What responsibilities does the researcher have in return to the member of the site being studied? The answer to this question depends on the terms of the explicit and implicit contract under which permission to conduct the project is granted. But additional responsibilities are likely to arise during the research process, and general ethical considerations often imply responsibilities that may not be clearly specified during early negotiations. The most important responsibilities concern the confidentiality, clearance, and usefulness of the research project.

Normally the researcher undertakes to make available, before publication, all results of the research to the leaders of the organization, if not all its members. This is done for several reasons: as a check on validity, because the results will presumably be useful in some way to members of the organization, and in order to obtain clearance for publication. If the people whose behavior was studied do not perceive the findings as accurate descriptions of their experience, the validity of the results is certainly suspect. Of course, a distinction needs to be made between the perceived accuracy of reported facts and the perceived validity of the researcher's interpretations. During negotiations over entry, it should be made clear that members of the organization have a greater right to question reported facts than to veto the researcher's intrepretation of their significance. When there is strong disagreement over interpretation, the nature of this diagreement should be reported in published results. Sometimes this distinction is hard to make, and publication of the researcher's findings involves complicated negotiations or bad feelings. Obviously it makes sense to discuss these issues openly during the entire research process.

Negotiations over permission to conduct the research should include agreement about whether the identity of the organization is to be revealed. (Sometimes this decision is postponed until after the research report has been written.) If the organization is not to be identified, it may be necessary before publication not only to give the organization and its members fictitious names but also to alter the report in other ways (e.g., disguise the product or geographical location) so that readers cannot deduce the organization's identity. Sometimes it is difficult to reconcile a legitimate need to disguise identity with the researcher's obligation to report findings that will be regarded as valid.

Often the researcher also has to worry about revealing the identity or violating the confidence of individual informants. Researchers should, and usually do, undertake not to identify reported opinions or quotations from interviews with specific individuals. Sometimes this commitment will require the suppression of relevant data—

for instance, the fact that a certain opinion was only expressed by persons in a particular position. A good practice, not followed as often as it should be, is not to use any extensive quotation without showing it, and the context in which it is to be used, in advance to the informant and receiving explicit permission to use it in this way. When people are asked whether their opinions can be cited, they usually do not object and may agree or even want to be identified, provided they regard the opinion as accurate and valid.

If the research report is done well, it should be valuable to the organization and to the individuals who have been studied. If the results do not seem useful to the people with most knowledge of the situation, the researcher should wonder whether publication is appropriate. Obtaining clearance before publication, therefore, is not only a legitimate exchange for permission to conduct the research but also a valid check on the findings and the utility of the conclusions.

Occasionally there will be a disagreement between the researcher and members of the organizations studied as to whether publication of some of the findings will be useful. Organization members may feel that the findings, and the researcher's interpretation of them, put the institution in a bad light, but the researcher may believe, perhaps correctly, that publication will be useful in order to prevent other organizations from making the same mistake, and perhaps to prevent the studied organization from making similar errors in the future. Usually it is possible to agree on a form of publication and disguise that mediates effectively between these opposing opinions. Sometimes the organization may approve or even request publication of certain data that the researcher believes would harm some individuals in the organization. We believe a researcher should not publish data that will harm any of his informants even if, in terms of the formal contract, he has permission to do so.

Research and intervention

The clinical field research process itself is an intervention that inevitably alters to some extent the state of the social system being studied. The behavior observed and the attitudes recorded are unavoidably different, in ways that are not easy to define, from the behavior and attitudes that would have existed without the researcher's entry into the system he or she is trying to understand.

The extent of change in the system varies, because certain research procedures are more obtrusive than others. But some change in the preexisting state will probably be produced by the researcher's presence. The exact nature and extent of the change is quite difficult to determine accurately. The knowledge that gestalt research methods provide about behavior in real organizations is therefore knowledge about organizations that are being influenced by the fact that they are being studied. One consolation or rejoinder to this sobering thought is that knowledge about organizations responding to the inevitable intervention of field research is much better than no knowledge about real organizations at all.

There is, of course, an important exception that apparently avoids the problem: research may be conducted by a participant observer who conceals the fact that the purpose of his or her presence is research. For instance, one way of studying behavior in a factory is to get a job there and then use conversations and observations during work as data for a research study. There are obvious practical difficulties involved with this approach. Furthermore, we believe that deliberately hiding one's identity and purpose is unethical. People who are being studied for research purposes have a right to know that this is happening. Several important contributions to the literature of organizational behavior have been based on experience as a bona fide member of an organization. But in these cases the research contribution was a by-product of experience as a member of the organization, not its purpose, and hence no unethical concealment was involved.

Since data in the behavior of organization members should only be collected with their knowledge and permission, the research process will always influence the behavior being studied. Thus a primary requirement for competence as a gestalt researcher is a sensitive awareness of how one's presence and procedures interact with the data of interest. How a social system responds to outside influence is often the key to understanding the system's functioning. We believe that responses to the researcher's intervention are themselves data highly relevant to the researcher's purpose, *provided* he or she stays aware, of and carefully records the nature of, that response. For example, Whyte's observations of how different members of the groups he studied reacted to him in his acknowledged role as a researcher were essential data for his study. Similarly, the so-called "Hawthorne effect," far from being a flaw in research design, was in fact the central finding of the relay-assembly-test-room study at Western Electric.

To some critics, the most serious problem in clinical-field-research methodology is the contamination of the system studied by the researcher's intervention in it. But this inevitable circumstance can be turned to advantage. The important point to emphasize is that this kind of research paints a picture of a dynamic system responding to an outsider's presence. For this reason it is very important that the nature of the intervention, how it was arranged and responded to, should be an essential part of the report on the research results.

Involvement and bias

The best and most influential reports on field research have been made by researchers who spent months or even years inside the organizations they studied. The longer and more intense the time spent interacting with members of an organization, the more inevitably the researcher becomes personally involved with the behavior and attitudes he studies. He comes to know people, make real friends, find some members more congenial than others, sympathize with certain attitudes and react negatively to others, and perhaps find his own opinions modified by these experiences. It is important to remember that the researcher's role is to be an observer, not a group member. Of course, a certain level of personal involvement is an inevitable consequence of frequent and prolonged interaction.

What should researchers do about the danger that their involvement may bias their findings? Again, the most important advice that experienced field workers can give is not to pretend to have been uninvolved, but to remain as aware as possible of the nature of the involvement and to take this into account in reaching conclusions and reporting the results. As a practical matter, it can help if the researcher avoids continuous immersion over a long period in the same research site. It is important to alternate site visits with time in another site or back in the office, working on field notes and engaged in other kinds of work. It is also useful to exchange experiences and ideas with others engaged in the same or similar research projects. Discussions with an interested colleague about the meaning of observed events and how they interacted with the researcher's own feelings can be extremely valuable in understanding how those feelings are influencing and being influenced by what is heard and observed during field research. The relationship between what is going on inside the researcher and what is going on inside the organization he or she is studying is usually difficult to understand without the help of continuing conversations with others who share the problem and react to it in different ways.

Do results constitute generalizable knowledge?

Many of the considerations we have discussed in this chapter can lead one to question how the results of clinical field research contribute to a body of knowledge that can be generalized outside the particular setting in which the research is conducted. As a rule, this kind of research is not useful for testing specific propositions of a general theory of behavior. Its contribution to knowledge is much more likely to be generating ideas that may later be used to develop propositions that can more adequately be tested through experimental or survey methods. Most of the studies we have cited earlier in this chapter illustrate this role—perhaps a necessary but not sufficient function in the development of theoretical knowledge.

Finally, by contributing to practice, clinical field research has a power quite distinct from its ability to generate scientifically testable propositions. When well conducted and presented, a detailed case study of how an organization functions teaches the reader a useful way of understanding behavior in other organizations. Clinical research may influence practice less through its verifiable contribution to "knowledge" than through its direct contribution to the understanding and wisdom of practitioners. This power to influence practice in many situations underlines the importance of conducting gestalt or clinical research with professional responsibility and care.

REFERENCES

Argyris, C. 1970. *Intervention Theory and Method: A Behavioral Science View.* Reading, Mass.: Addison-Wesley.

Bales, R. F. 1950. *Interaction Process Analysis.* Chicago: University of Chicago Press.

Bales, R. F., and S. P. Cohen. 1979. *SYMLOG.* New York: Free Press.

Beer, M. 1980. *Organization Change and Development.* Santa Monica, Calif.: Goodyear.

Birdwhistell, R. L. 1970. *Kinetics and Context.* Phildelphia, Pa.: University of Pennsylvania Press.

Blau, P. 1955. *The Dynamics of Bureaucracy.* Chicago: University of Chicago Press.

Block, P. 1982. *Flawless Consulting: A Guide to Getting Your Expertise Used.* Austin, Tex.: Learning Concepts. (See chapters 4–6.)

Borgatta, E. F. 1963. "A New Systematic Interaction Observation System: Behavior Scores System (BSS System)." *Journal of Psychology Studies* 14:24–44.

Bouchard, T. J. 1976. "Field Research Methods: Interviewing, Questionnaires, Participant Observation, Systematic Observation, Unobtrusive Measures." In *Handbook of Industrial and Organization Psychology*, ed. M. D. Dunnette, 363–413. Chicago: Rand McNally.

Brandt, R. M. 1972. *Studying Behavior in Natural Settings*. New York: Holt, Rinehart and Winston.

Bruyn, S. 1963. "The Methodology of Participant Observation." *Human Organization*. 22, no. 3:222–35.

———. 1966. *The Human Perspective in Sociology; The Methodology of Participant Observations*, Englewood Cliffs, N.J.: Prentice-Hall.

Campbell, D. T., and J. C. Stanley. 1966. *Experimental and Quasi-Experimental Designs for Research*. Chicago: Rand McNally.

Cannell, C. F., and R. L. Kahn. 1968. "Interviewing." In *Handbook of Social Psychology*, rev. ed., vol. 2, ed. G. Lindzey and E. Aronson, 526–95. Reading, Mass.: Addison-Wesley.

Carlson, S. 1951. *Executive Behavior: A Study of the Work Load and the Working Methods of Managing Directors*. Stockholm: Strombergs.

Cook, T. D., and D. T. Campbell. 1979. *Quasi-Experimentation: Design and Analysis Issues for Field Settings*. Chicago: Rand McNally.

Dalton, M. 1959. *Men Who Manage*. New York: Wiley.

Dickson, W. J., and F. J. Roethlisberger. 1966. *Counseling in an Organization*. Boston: Division of Research, Graduate School of Business Administration, Harvard University.

Ekman, P., and W. V. Frieson. 1975. *Unmasking the Face*. Englewood Cliffs, N.J.: Prentice Hall.

———. 1977. *The Facial Action Coding System: A Manual for the Measurement of Facial Movement*. Palo Alto, Calif.: Consulting Psychologists Press.

Hall, E. T. 1964. *The Hidden Dimension*. New York: Doubleday.

Hodgson, R. C., D. J. Levinson, and A. Zaleznik. 1965. *The Executive Role Constellation*. Boston: Division of Research, Graduate School of Business Administration, Harvard University.

Homans, G. C. 1950. *The Human Group*. New York: Harcourt Brace and World.

Lawrence, P., and J. Lorsch. 1967. *Organization and Environment: Managing Differentiation and Integration*. Boston: Division of Research, Graduate School of Business Administration, Harvard University.

Lofland, J. 1971. *Analyzing Social Settings*. Belmont, Calif.: Wadsworth.

Mann, R. D. 1967. *Interpersonal Style and Group Development*. New York: Wiley.

Mills, C. W. 1959. *The Sociological Imagination*. New York: Grove Press.

Mintzberg, H. 1973. *The Nature of Managerial Work*. New York: Harper & Row.

Roethlisberger, F. J., and W. J. Dickson. 1939. *Management and the Worker*. Cambridge, Mass.: Harvard University Press.

Rogers, C. R. 1942. *Consulting and Psychotherapy*. Boston: Houghton Mifflin.

———. 1951. *Client-Centered Therapy*. Boston: Houghton Mifflin.

Selltiz, C., L. S. Wrightsman, and S. W. Cook. 1976. *Research Methods in Social Relations*. New York: Holt, Rinehart and Winston.

Selznick, P. 1949. *TVA and the Grass Roots*. Berkeley, Calif.: University of California Press.

Sommer, R. 1969. *Personal Space*. Englewood Cliffs, N.J.: Prentice-Hall.

Stone, P. J., D. C. Dunphy, M. S. Smith, and D. M. Ogilvie. *The General Inquirer: A Computer Approach to Content Analysis*. Cambridge, Mass.: MIT Press.

Webb, E. J., D. T. Campbell, R. D. Schwartz, and L. Sechrest. 1966. *Unobtrusive Measures: Nonreactive Research in the Social Sciences*. Chicago: Rand McNally.

Weick, K. E. 1968. "Systematic Observational Methods." In *Handbook of Social Psychology*, rev. ed., vol. 2, ed. G. Lindzey and E. Aronson, 357–451. Reading, Mass.: Addison-Wesley.

Whyte, W. F. 1960. "Interviewing in Field Research." In *Human Organizational Research*, ed. R. N. Adams and J. J. Press, 352–74. Homewood, Ill.: Dorsey Press.

———. 1948. *Human Relations in the Restaurant Industry*. New York: McGraw-Hill.

———. 1981. *Street Corner Society*. 3d ed. Chicago: University of Chicago Press.

Zaleznik, A., C. R. Christensen, and F. J. Roethlisberger. 1958. *The Motivation, Productivity, and Satisfaction of Workers: A Prediction Study*. Boston: Division of Research, Graduate School of Business Administration, Harvard University.

Zelditch, M. 1962. "Some Methodological Problems of Field Studies." *American Journal of Sociology* 67:566–76.

9

Experimental design in organizational settings

RICHARD S. BLACKBURN

Managers often make changes in their organizations in an effort to help them function more effectively. For example, they may institute training programs, modify reward systems, or redesign work flows. But in the complex world of the organization, where outcomes depend on multiple interacting variables, it can be difficult to know whether the deliberately introduced change has had the desired (or any) impact. Appropriately designed research can help managers trace cause-and-effect relationships and hence choose more promising interventions.

This chapter is intended to familiarize the personnel/human resources (P/HR) manager with the fundamentals of experimental design. As discussed in part I, an experimental approach may often be preferable to alternative ways of gathering information on the impact of managerial interventions on the organization. Part II describes some common pitfalls in designing experiments, which give rise to what might be called "pre-experimental designs." "True" experiments are defined in part III, which also explores the opportunities for conducting such experiments in an organizational setting. Even when a true experiment is not possible, "quasi-experimental" designs can provide a basis for valid inferences (part IV).

PART I: WAYS OF KNOWING IN ORGANIZATIONS

Suppose a manager wishes to evaluate whether a new training program has succeeded in improving managers' interpersonal skills and hence in improving performance in the organization. He or she has at least three options: to rely on observation and anecdote, to conduct a survey, or to take an experimental approach.

Anecdotal/observational approaches

In gathering information about a program's effectiveness, managers often rely on anecdotal or observational information collected from colleagues, subordinates, or "experts." The quality of the information generated by these procedures is suspect, however. Anecdotal reporting is often biased toward positive outcomes. No one likes to dwell on an unsuccessful effort at organizational improvement, and journals are more likely to publish reports of successful changes than of dismal failures. Within the organization, supervisors may hesitate to report decreases in performance following organizational changes, especially if top management has a vested interest in the implementation of a particular program.

Even when bias is not a problem, anecdote and observation cannot allow the manager to be confident that the new program actually caused the observed behavior. Simultaneous changes in other factors may have interacted with the planned change, either heightening or diminishing its effect. These interactions make it difficult to isolate the true causes of differences in particular outcomes.

Survey approaches

A second approach to acquiring information about the impact of a change is the organizational survey. (See chapter 10 in this volume as well as Dunham and Smith (1979) and Nadler (1977) for additional information on survey procedures.) Careful and continuing analysis of multiple survey results is more useful than anecdotal information for assessing the impact of changes on an organization. When used as a one-time measure, however, the survey does not provide a valid basis for making causal statements about the effects of a particular change on outcomes of interest. Too many alternative explanations are usually possible.

Suppose that survey results indicate a positive relationship between attendance at a training program, considerate supervisory behavior, and unit performance. One might be tempted to conclude that the training program caused the considerate behavior and the increase in unit performance. But it may be that the observed levels of considerate behavior and performance already existed in the units before the training program. In this case, the training program may have had no actual effect.

Similarly, a simple correlation in survey results cannot indicate the direction of causation. Instead of considerate behavior causing higher performance, it may be that the high performance levels already established in certain units led these supervisors to treat their employees more considerately.

The conclusion that training caused high performance may also be incorrect. Supervisors of high-performing units may be the ones chosen to participate in management training programs primarily because of the performance records of the units they manage.

Experimental approaches

In most cases, anecdotal and survey information can merely suggest possible causal relationships between variables of interest. Neither the anecdotal nor observational approach provides the kind of information needed to eliminate plausible alternative explanations for the relationships observed. The experimental approach, however, can give managers cogent evidence concerning causal relationships between changes made or planned and the outcomes of concern to the organization.

For the purposes of this chapter, the basic approach will be divided into three categories, only one of which is truly experimental in design. The first category, "preexperimental designs," includes both the anecdotal and survey approaches. The second category comprises designs that meet the criteria of manipulation, control, randomization, and observation required of "true" experiments. Experiments of this sort may be difficult to execute in organizational settings, but the underlying design criteria serve as models for feasible kinds of organizational research. "Quasi-experimental" designs, the third category discussed here, attempt to preserve as many of the properties of the true experiment as possible, subject to the constraints of the organizational research setting.

PART II: PREEXPERIMENTAL DESIGNS

Some definitions

Before considering the various experimental designs, it is necessary to define the fundamental concepts of validity, reliability, and generalizability.

VALIDITY: MEASUREMENT PERSPECTIVE

Organizational research may use various measurement techniques ranging from employee time cards to measure attendance, to interviews and survey questionnaires to measure attitudes. A valid technique is one that actually measures the variable of interest. Just as one would not use a bathroom scale to measure a person's height, job satisfaction, for example, should not be measured by procedures designed to measure turnover or absenteeism.

Finding valid measures for particular variables of interest in an organizational setting is not always easy. Standardized questionnaires need to be carefully and critically evaluated before they are used. (Additional information on questions of validity from a measurement perspective is available in Nunnally 1978, among others.)

VALIDITY: DESIGN PERSPECTIVE

The term *validity* is also used in the context of research design. *Internal validity* refers to the extent to which the results of a research study are unambiguous or unexplainable by alternative factors. A research design with good internal validity increases one's confidence in concluding that the input changes actually caused the observed outcome.

RELIABILITY

Reliability refers to the extent to which measurement procedures are free of systematic sources of errors (Stone 1978). If there are no real changes in the variables measured, reliable measurement instruments will yield similar results at different measurement times. Reliability is also said to exist if two or more individuals report similar levels of variables that are objectively identical—for example, if two supervisors observing the same employee provide similar performance evaluations.

While valid measures must by definition be reliable, the reverse is not necessarily true. A defective yardstick that is only thirty-five inches long will give the same reading every time it is used: it is reliable. But it is not a valid measure of a yard as usually defined.

GENERALIZABILITY

Also called *external validity*, generalizability refers to the extent to which the results of a research study can be generalized to groups of individuals other than those who participated in the original study. For example, some have argued that research that uses college students as subjects cannot be generalized to employees in organizations.

Relationships between internal and external validity

One way to increase internal validity is through control of the research setting. In a laboratory setting, nearly all aspects of a study can be controlled, eliminating factors that might suggest alternative explanations of the research results. But to achieve such control, one must often sacrifice generalizability. The resolution of this problem is an important aspect of the overall research strategy. The various quasi-experimental designs described below reflect an effort to optimize this trade-off between internal and external validity.

Designs

To discuss research designs efficiently, it is useful to employ a symbolic shorthand developed by Campbell and Stanley (1963). The letter O will stand for any observation of the outcome variables of interest. The letter X will represent any change or intervention that is of interest. In the jargon of experimental design, X represents the "treatment" or "manipulation" that is

given to a group of subjects in the research study. In the example discussed earlier, X would represent the organization's training program for managers.

Ideally, X should refer to a single change in a single factor. Thus, if a manager was interested in testing the impact of flexible working hours on performance, it would be a mistake to modify compensation systems at the same time.

The passage of time is indicated by reading the shorthand symbols from left to right. The symbolic description O X O says that first an observation was made, then a change occurred, and finally a second observation was made. When necessary, subscripts will be used to indicate explicitly the temporal ordering of observations and treatments. The simplest preexperimental design consists of a single set of observations:

$$O$$

This might represent general organizational information collected by either the anecdotal or survey procedure, or both.

A second preexperimental design measures certain outcome variables after a change is made:

$$X \quad O$$

Again, the observation can be made with either an anecdotal or survey approach, or both.

Because this second design does not incorporate any information about conditions preceding the change, it is difficult to determine if the change had a positive, negative, or neutral impact on the outcome. To address this problem, observations can be made, before the change is implemented, of certain variables that the change seems likely to affect:

$$O_1 \quad X \quad O_2$$

The two observations can be made using either the anecdotal or the survey approach, or both.

Even when this design detects a difference in the value of a variable before and after the change, it cannot support a conclusion about cause and effect. As discussed earlier, this design does not provide a basis for rejecting plausible alternative explanations, or "threats to internal validity."

Threats to internal validity

Several kinds of threats to internal validity can reduce the usefulness of preexperimental designs. Each is discussed briefly here, and a more detailed discussion is available in the literature (see, for example, Campbell and Stanley 1963; Cascio 1982; Cook and Campbell 1979; Spector 1981).

HISTORY

Events that occur during a research study, and which are unrelated to the change, X, may influence postchange outcomes. In the training program example, suppose that, between the prechange and postchange observations, the organization implements a new compensation system that more closely ties pay to performance.

Then posttraining performance increases may be due to the new pay system and not to the training program. The O X O design could not detect the effect of the new compensation system, and the experimenter might attribute the change in the outcome variable—performance—entirely to the training program.

TESTING

The actual measurement or observation process before a change may have an impact on the measurement or observations made after a change. Knowing that unit performance has been measured in the past, supervisors may take actions to improve their unit's performance in anticipation of another round of measurement; these actions may be independent of the effects of a training program. Similarly, when survey questionnaires are administered repeatedly, respondents may try to make their later answers consistent with the earlier ones, or may have learned how to respond to "look good" on a second administration. In short, the very act of taking a prechange measurement can influence the results of the postchange measurement.

INSTRUMENTATION

The nature of the instruments or procedures used to make observations can also affect the outcome variables. If different measurement techniques are used before and after an intervention, any change observed in the outcome variable may be due to the change in technique. Similarly, if the same individual reports on behavior before and after an intervention but improves his or her observation and evaluation abilities during the course of the experiment, observed changes may again be an artifact of the measurement process.

REGRESSION TO THE MEAN

Statistical regression (or "regression to the mean") threatens internal validity when a work unit is chosen to be the focus of some intervention or change because it represents an extreme case of one sort or another (extremely low or extremely high performance, for instance). An organizational unit might be chosen to participate in a training program, for example, because its performance was particularly poor. But the poor performance rating might reflect the fact that observations were made at atypical, inopportune times, such as the day after an office party. A second measurement would then be likely to show an improvement in performance quite independent of any training program. The measured level of performance will regress to the average level of "true" performance.

One way to counter the threats to internal validity is to use a control group of subjects—that is, to compare outcome levels for individuals who have and have not undergone some change. This new design is diagrammed as follows:

| Group A (training received) | X | O |
| Group B (no training) | | O |

One could argue that the history threat has been reduced because external events would presumably have similar influences on both groups. No pretesting is done, and we may assume that consistent measurement procedures are used in the observations. But even this more sophisticated design has not entirely solved the problem of assuring internal validity.

SELECTION

The internal validity of research results depends on how groups of subjects were selected for inclusion in the study. Postintervention outcomes may reflect preexisting characteristics of the subjects. In the two-group example just cited, Group A may have had a better performance record than Group B even before the training program.

MORTALITY

Often some proportion of participants drop out before a study is completed. If those who leave are somehow different from those who stay, the final observations may not reflect the impact of the intervention but rather the change in the population being observed.

Interaction threats to internal validity

Three of the threats to internal validity discussed above can interact with the selection process to create further difficulties.

SELECTION × MATURATION

We have already noted that research findings may be affected by subjects' maturing over the course of an experiment. To complicate the problem, people may mature at different rates, and those rates may be associated with membership, in particular groups that in turn may be a criterion for selection. Thus, if supervisors chosen for a training program are all young and inexperienced, they may be more willing to implement new ideas than older, more experienced people. Their attitudes, rather than the content of the training program, may then be responsible for changes in performance after the intervention.

SELECTION × HISTORY

History effects may also be linked to selection criteria. In the training-program example, suppose that postintervention performance is compared with performance in another plant where the program was not offered. Unless the two plants are very similar in their histories of pay raises, strikes, technology introductions, and so forth, it will be extremely difficult to tell if differential performance results should be attributed to the training program or to the difference in events occurring at the two sites.

SELECTION × INSTRUMENTATION

Sometimes the measurement method used prevents some group(s) of subjects from showing a change in the outcome variable. For example, the student who has already scored 100 percent on a test will not be able to improve his performance after a coaching session.

Threats to external validity

Problems of external validity should not be great for the P/HR manager conducting research in his or her own organization. But because research conducted outside the organization may suggest potential organizational changes, it is worth considering three possible threats to external validity.

SELECTION × TYPE OF CHANGE

Research results obtained with one group of employees may not be generalizable to another unless the two groups are similar with respect to such attributes as race, age, sex, site location, years of experience, and hierarchical level in the organization.

SETTING × TYPE OF CHANGE

Research results generated in one setting—say on a college campus—may not be valid for another, such as a business organization. Similarly, a training program conducted off-site may get better results than the same program when conducted on-site amid work-related interruptions.

HISTORY × TYPE OF CHANGE

Finally, it may not be possible to generalize from a relationship observed in the past to a prediction about the future. For example, an organization may respond to interventions quite differently during stable and turbulent periods. A training program that succeeded under favorable conditions may prove disappointing if repeated at a time of very severe production demands.

Summary

For various reasons, simple preexperimental research designs seldom allow managers to make confident assessments of the effectiveness of changes or programs in the organization. They will be better served by either true experimental designs or the quasi-experimental designs described in the following sections.

PART III: TRUE EXPERIMENTAL DESIGNS

Characteristics of experimental designs

In true experimental designs, participants are usually divided into two or more experimental groups. In the simplest experimental form, some subjects (the "experimental group") receive a "treatment" (undergo an intervention) and others (the "control group") do not. Four further conditions must be met before a research design can legitimately be called a true experiment.

First, certain aspects of the research setting must be subject to *manipulation*. That is, the manager must be able to vary some elements of the organization. Typically, manipulations are either "dichotomous" (an employee is or is not placed in a training program) or "multilevel" (training programs are of different durations or use different instruction methods).

Second, in a true experimental design, all factors not of interest in the research must be "controlled." Otherwise these factors could offer a variety of plausible alternative explanations for the changes that occur in the outcome variables. One way to achieve control is to hold certain variables constant across all subjects participating in the research. Particularly in an organizational setting, such an approach is difficult to implement, given the variety of participants. Moreover, such a research design would not permit generalizations to groups with different characteristics.

An alternative approach to controlling the extraneous factors is to let them vary, but to make a strictly "random assignment" of subjects to the various experimental groups. Individuals would have an equal, known, and finite chance of being assigned to either the treatment or the control group.

Finally, reliable and valid measurement/observation procedures are required. Measurements or observations must be made of both the intervention or change (to determine if the change was perceived as such by employees) and the outcome variables of interest (to assess if the change had any impact).

Experimental designs

PRETEST-POSTTEST CONTROL-GROUP DESIGN

The most straightforward of the true experimental designs, the Pretest-Posttest Control-Group Design, is diagrammed below. The R indicates that individual employees or work groups were randomly assigned to either the experimental group or the control group.

| Experimental Group | R O X O |
| Control Group | R O   O |

More than one experimental group could be used. For example, the effectiveness of a variety of training procedures could be evaluated by randomly assigning supervisors to training programs that use lectures (X_1), programmed learning (X_2), or case studies (X_3). For our purposes, however, the X/no-X distinction is satisfactory and greatly simplifies the discussion.

Random assignment of employees can eliminate threats caused by selection, maturation, and regression to the mean. If similar observation/measurement procedures are used in both groups at both observation times, there should be no problems associated with instrumentation. The impact, if any, of testing should be similar in both groups. Because random assignment should ensure that the two groups are essentially equivalent initially, one can determine if they differ in their mortality rates over the course of the experiment and, if so, whether such differences contributed to differences in outcome variables.

History is the only threat to internal validity not eliminated by this design. This issue may not be important if observations are made at the same time in both groups, and if the groups are physically close together. But in other situations various external or internal events could have different influences on the two groups.

OTHER EXPERIMENTAL DESIGNS

Two other experimental designs should be considered briefly. The first of these, the Solomon Four-Group Design, allows the researcher to determine whether pretesting affects outcomes. This design uses two experimental and two control groups. A preintervention measurement is made for just one of each pair, as in the following diagram:

Group A	R O X O
Group B	R O O
Group C	R X O
Group D	R O

The effects of testing, if any, can then be judged by comparing the four sets of outcome variables at the conclusion of the research.

In many organizational settings, it may be practically impossible to implement a randomly assigned four-group experimental design. Indeed, it may be impossible to conduct any pretesting. With random assignment, however, a true experiment is still possible, as in the diagram that follows:

| Group A | R X O |
| Group B | R   O |

This Posttest-Only Control-Group Design requires only two groups and one measurement session. Testing effects will not distort results, since there is no pretest. It will not be possible, on the other hand, to assess whether a pretest would have had an effect on the change itself.

Randomization

ASSETS

Randomization complicates the task of conducting an experiment in an organizational setting, but it serves at least four purposes (Cook and Campbell 1979). First, because randomly selected samples are more likely to be representative of the population from which they are drawn than are samples chosen in some other fashion, application of study results to the broader population of employees is more likely to be valid.

Randomization also results in samples that are initially comparable to one another, reducing the chance that outcomes are due to undetected differences between the experimental and control groups. A third rationale for random assignment is that the analytical procedures used in a randomized design are more powerful than the test associated with nonrandomized designs. Finally, from a pragmatic perspective, randomization may spare the organization some of the problems associated with unequal distribution of a desirable treatment. Organization members may accept the luck of the draw (random assignment) as a fair way to proceed.

In general, random assignment reduces the number of substantive assumptions that must be made in drawing inferences about causality. There are simply fewer plausible rival explanations for the observed results with random assignment than with a nonrandom process.

LIABILITIES

Research designs calling for random assignment can create some practical problems, but they are seldom insuperable (see Cook and Campbell 1979; Festinger 1953; Scott 1965; Seashore 1964; and Stone 1978).

1. Employees may resist a random-assignment procedure if they feel that participation in the experimental change program is likely to be beneficial to the individual. But if any systematic assignment process is used, randomization is lost. One way to resolve this problem is to eliminate the "no treatment" control group from the research design. Instead,

  a. a variety of experimental approaches to the same problem can be provided;
  b. a variety of experimental approaches aimed at a number of different problems can be provided; or
  c. a "placebo" control group can be formed that takes part in some type of change, but a change that is not expected to affect the variables of primary interest in the study.

In each case, while every employee participates in some type of change, the manager evaluates only the influence of the particular change(s) of interest. Without a true "no treatment" control group, however, the absolute impact of the change cannot be evaluated, but one can draw conclusions about the differential effects of the various programs involved.

2. Randomization must be accomplished through a procedure that guarantees that each employee has an equal probability of being assigned to a given experimental condition. The most straightforward process is to assign each available employee a number, making sure that no two receive the same number, and then draw samples by consulting a random-number table.

3. Randomization can be difficult if employees refuse to participate in a treatment that is viewed as undesirable. It is probably best to try to get subjects to participate before any random assignment is made.

Reichen et al. (1974) suggest that randomization can occur at any of three stages:

  a. once all eligible employees have been identified;
  b. once a subset of all employees has agreed to participate in the research study, regardless of assignment; or
  c. once a subset of employees has been given full explanation of possible conditions and has agreed to participate, regardless of assignment.

Clearly, if randomization is postponed to the last stage, fewer employees will refuse to accept the experimental change. But, the pool of potential participants will also be smaller and will more nearly approximate a group of volunteers. This limits the generalizability of the research results.

4. Some employess may withdraw from the experiment because of the treatment they receive. Such attrition reduces the comparability of groups initially achieved by randomization and undermines causal inferences. Cook and Campbell (1979) suggest several analyses that address this concern:

  a. Examine attrition in all groups of the research study. If a similar percentage drops out in each case, reason for leaving the study is probably not the experimental change, and there should be no systematic impact on the outcomes.
  b. Conduct exit interviews with those who leave the study to determine if reasons for leaving differ among the groups.
  c. Compare background/demographic information on those who remain after the treatment with similar information collected for the entire group initially.

5. When the experimenter does not fully control the implementation of a treatment—for example, if several managers each conduct a training program for a particular experimental group—the resulting differences in implementation procedures can reduce the internal validity of even a randomized experiment. As a practical matter, the organizational research can require that trained research personnel administer all treatments or can work closely with the supervisors/trainers responsible for implementing the change to encourage standardized procedures.

6. Finally, interactions between study participants may muddy the distinction between the experimental and control groups. Organization members may discuss their experience of the study, over lunch or in the office, in such a way that control-group members essentially get a diluted but real version of the experimental treatment. The control group may then no longer be a valid source of baseline information.

One approach to evaluating possible "contamination" between the two groups is to monitor carefully interactions between members of the groups. If the researcher believes that contamination did occur, the data should still be analyzed as though no contamination occurred. The results of the analyses would allow one of two conclusions to be made. It may be possible to conclude that while members of the control group were aware of the changes being made, even this knowledge was not sufficient to produce the kinds of outcomes seen in the experimental group.

If the results indicate no differences between the groups, then no conclusions can be made about the relative effectiveness of the change. In this case, the researcher may wish to combine the data from both groups and compare this larger "experimental" group with a third group that could act as a control.

Opportunities for experimental designs

Certain naturally occurring events in organizations can provide a convenient basis for conducting experimental research. There are times when random-assignment procedures will seem relatively uncontrived. For example, whenever demand for a particular program exceeds supply (e.g., not all qualified candidates can be included in a training program), random assignment will provide a natural foundation for an experimental study. Similarly, financial, personnel, structural, or temporal constraints may make it impossible to introduce a new technology or job design across the entire organization at the same time. Assigning employees randomly to the first group to receive the change may be appropriate and highly feasible.

There are also some fairly natural ways of keeping an experimental group temporarily isolated from the control group. Many organizations regularly conduct training sessions off-site, providing a good opportunity to implement treatment among those attending (or not attending) a program with reasonable assurance that the experimental group will not contaminate the control group. Similarly, an experimental design could randomly select participants from groups that work in different parts of a single plant, in different cities or countries, or on different shifts.

An opportunity to win top management's support for experimental research often arises when some organizational problem must be solved and experimentation seems to offer a way of finding the most appropriate solution. Highly sophisticated top-management teams who are aware of the potential problems associated with careless experimental designs may not just tolerate but actively demand a randomized experiment to resolve certain organizational questions.

Summary

Ideally, all organizational research would employ true experimental design. In reality, such an ideal is difficult, if not impossible, to attain. As a practical matter, certain quasi-experimental designs offer a reasonable compromise between the ideal and the realities of conducting research in organizations.

PART IV: QUASI-EXPERIMENTAL DESIGNS

If complete manipulation, control, and randomization are not possible, quasi-experimental designs may still allow the organizational researcher to generate valuable information. These designs lack the important ability to assign employees randomly to the various research conditions. Thus, the researcher's ability to draw substantive causal conclusions from the study findings is limited. On the other hand, carefully constructed quasi-experiments conducted with an awareness of the potential validity threats can be almost as good as true experiments, and may represent the only feasible means of rigorously investigating a change.

Two broad classes of quasi-experiments will be considered: nonequivalent-control-group designs and interrupted-time-series designs.

Nonequivalent-control-group designs

Without random assignment, one cannot assume that different experimental groups are equivalent at the beginning of a research study. Nevertheless a quasi-experimental design that includes a control group is preferable to the preexperimental designs, because it allows the researcher to rule out many of the threats to both internal and external validity. Cook and Campbell (1979) discuss designs in detail (see especially pages 103–46).

One of the most frequently used designs in organizational research is the Untreated Control Group Design with Pretest and Posttest, diagrammed below. The dashed line indicates the lack of random assignment.

| "Experimental" Group | O | X | O |
| Control Group | O | | O |

The presence of a control group, even though nonequivalent, allows the researcher to make less ambiguous interpretations of the study findings than is possible with preexperimental designs. The more similar the groups of subjects—in terms of pretest scores and how they were recruited (i.e., both volunteer groups preferable to one volunteer group and one commandeered group)—the more effective the control group becomes. This design is particularly useful when the research must be based on naturally occurring work groups. If the groups' pretest scores are sufficiently similar, there is little need to worry about threats to validity caused by history, maturation, testing, and instrumentation. These effects would probably be similar in all study groups. Unfortunately, any one of these threats may interact with the selection threat. Problems of local history may arise if different external events occur within the various research groups. Differences in posttest results may be due to differences in the groups' maturation rates. Or one group may be particularly "test wise," so that outcomes reflect an ability to provide the correct answers on the measurement instruments rather than the impact of the experimental intervention. Regression also represents a threat to internal validity with this experimental design.

These threats become more potent if the researcher attempts to match groups as a way of establishing preexperimental equivalence. It is highly unlikely that all of the variables that might influence the research outcomes can be identified and measured. Groups that are "matched" in some respects may differ substantially on important, but unmeasured, variables. If so, "the process of matching not only fails to provide the intended equation, but in addition insures the occurrence of unwanted regression effects" (Campbell and Stanley 1963, 49).

An alternative design can be used when some pretest measures are desired, but the researcher is concerned that a pretest may influence the results of the study. As indicated by the vertical line in the diagram,

$$\text{Group A} \quad \underline{\text{O}} \; \big| \; \text{X} \; \underline{\;\;} \; \underline{\text{O}}$$
$$\text{Group B} \quad \text{O} \; \big| \qquad \text{O}$$

the pretest is administered, not to the experimental and nonequivalent control groups, but to some other group(s). Care should be taken in choosing the groups. Again, the distinction between volunteered and commandeered groups should be noted. Moreover, the measurement procedures used in each group should be as nearly identical as possible. Finally, at least some variables unrelated to the research question should be measured to test comparability of the groups. Even if these precautions are observed, however, this experimental design remains weak, to be used only if no stronger design can be implemented.

Another quasi-experimental design administers two pretests to all groups in the study.

$$\text{Group A} \quad \underline{\text{O}_1} \; \underline{\text{O}_2} \; \underline{\text{X}} \; \underline{\text{O}_3}$$
$$\text{Group B} \quad \text{O}_1 \; \text{O}_2 \qquad \text{O}_3$$

This design reduces the threat of an interaction between selection and maturation, because differential maturation rates might be noted between the two pretests. Similarly, possible regression effects can be detected by comparing values of variables measured at time 2 and time 1.

Under certain conditions, a single group can serve as both an experimental group and a control group. One such quasi-experimental design involves first administering an intervention (X) and later removing it ($\overline{\text{X}}$):

$$\text{O}_1 \; \text{X} \; \text{O}_2 \; \ldots\ldots\ldots \; \text{O}_3 \; \overline{\text{X}} \; \text{O}_4$$

If the intervention has an effect, one would expect that the difference between the first and second observations would be opposite in direction from the difference between the third and fourth.

When this design is used in organizational settings, it is important that observations be made at equal time intervals both before and after the changes. Otherwise, differences in outcomes may simply reflect the length of time a change was or was not in effect. An additional consideration is that the removal of a popular intervention may so frustrate employees that their reactions to the loss may color the impact of the change itself on outcomes of interest.

A similar design makes only a single observation between the presentation of a change and its removal:

$$\text{O}_1 \; \text{X} \; \text{O}_2 \; \overline{\text{X}} \; \text{O}_3 \; \text{X} \; \text{O}_4 \; \text{etc.}$$

In this design every observation after the first serves as both a pretest and a posttest measurement. This design is most useful when it can be assumed that the effects of the change are transient, and that the removal of the change would not prevent the reoccurrence of results when the change is reintroduced.

The greatest threat to internal validity in this design comes from the possibility that cyclical organizational or environmental factors are influencing the observations. The evidence that X has an effect is most compelling if O_1 differs from O_2, O_2 differs from O_3, and the O_2–O_1 difference is in the same direction and of the same magnitude as the O_4–O_3 difference.

In a design of this sort, it is possible that employees might become aware that changes are being made. Their responses might then be primarily a function of their desire to see a particular policy returned or removed, rather than reflecting the actual impact of the change.

This problem can be reduced if changes are as unobtrusive as possible, and if a sufficient delay occurs between the presentations and removals of the intervention.

Interrupted-time-series designs

Time-series designs involve multiple pretest and posttest observations made over time. The intervals between such measures may range from an hour to a year or longer, depending on the nature of the change, the nature of the variables being measured or observed, and the resources required for each observation. To interpret these observations, the researcher must know just when a change or treatment will occur or has occurred.

If the treatment affects outcome of interest, observations made after it should differ from observations made before it. The simplest of these designs requires only a single group:

$$\ldots O_1 \; O_2 \; O_3 \; O_4 \; O_5 \; X \; O_6 \; O_7 \; O_8 \; O_9 \; O_{10} \ldots$$

Superficially an extension of the one-group pretest-posttest preexperimental design, the time-series design makes it possible to analyze potential effects of maturation, testing, mortality, and regression by examining the trends before and after the intervention.

The major threat to internal validity is the possibility of history effects. Some additional event may have occurred between the observations made immediately before and immediately after the intervention and may be responsible for the differences in the observations. This possibility can be reduced somewhat if the interval between observations is minimized and if the researcher carefully records external events that may affect the study results.

The fact that observations are made over a period of time increases the likelihood of instrumentation problems. For example, an organization may modify the definition of categories used in its record keeping so that two nominally identical measurements made early and late in the series are actually not equivalent. The interaction of selection and mortality is also a potential problem, if the composition of the group changes for some reason at the time of the intervention.

Finally, in all time-series designs the researcher must be sensitive to the impact of cyclical organizational patterns (such as seasonal fluctuations in sales or production) that might confuse the interpretation. If enough observations are recorded, it may be possible to capture any cyclical influences on the outcomes of interest. Effective treatments would be those that yield changes in outcomes beyond those attributable to cycles.

Two additional time-series designs can be viewed as extension of two nonequivalent-control-group designs. The first involves the implementation and removal of a change over a period of time, with multiple observations:

$$\ldots O_1 \; O_2 \; O_3 \; O_4 \; X \; O_5 \; O_6 \; O_7 \; O_8 \; O_9 \; \overline{X}$$
$$O_{10} \; O_{11} \; O_{12} \; O_{13} \ldots$$

In effect, this design is a combination of two interrupted time-series designs. The series of observations O_1 to O_9 is interrupted by X. This series assesses the impact of the intervention. The series of observations O_5 to O_{13} is interrupted by $\overline{X}$ and assesses the impact of removing the intervention. The strongest inferences about the impact of X could be made if the differences between O_4 and O_5 were in the opposite direction of the differences between O_9 and O_{10}.

In comparison with a simple time series, this design reduces the potential for history effects (because such an effect could arise only if an event exhibited opposite effects at two different times) or two different events operated in different directions at different times and also should mitigate mortality problems, which would occur only if different causes of attrition operated at different times.

In an alternative design, the intervention is presented and removed at irregular, random intervals:

$$\ldots O_1 \; O_2 \; X \; O_3 \ldots O_4 \; \overline{X} \; O_5 \ldots O_6 \; X \; O_7 \ldots$$
$$O_8 \; X \; O_9 \ldots$$

The random schedule of implementation and removal effectively rules out the threat of cyclical influences on research outcomes.

The last two time-series designs require two or more groups to participate in the research study. The first combines the logic of the nonequivalent-control-group designs with the multiple observations of the interrupted time-series designs:

Group A	$\ldots O_1 \; O_2 \; O_3 \; O_4 \; O_5 \; X$
Group B	$\ldots O_1 \; O_2 \; O_3 \; O_4 \; O_5$

$$O_6 \; O_7 \; O_8 \; O_9 \; O_{10} \ldots$$
$$O_6 \; O_7 \; O_8 \; O_9 \; O_{10} \ldots$$

Although more costly to carry out, this design has the advantage of reducing threats to the research results from general history effects, although the possible impact of local or unique events at the time of the change must be noted. This design should also permit an assessment of possible instrumentation effects and cyclical influences, because the two groups should show similar patterns. As with most of the nonequivalent-control-group designs, possible difficulties due to selection biases must always be considered.

Finally, if two nonequivalent groups are available, if multiple pretests and posttests measures can be made, and if both groups must eventually (but not necessarily simultaneously) implement the change in their operations, one can conduct an interrupted time-series design with switching replications, as illustrated below:

Group A $\ldots \overline{O_1} \; \overline{O_2} \; \overline{O_3} \; \overline{O_4} \; \overline{O_5} \; X$
Group B $\ldots \overline{O_1} \; \overline{O_2} \; \overline{O_3} \; \overline{O_4} \; \overline{O_5}$

$$\overline{O_6} \; \overline{O_7} \; \overline{O_8} \; \overline{O_9} \; \overline{O_{10}} \ldots$$
$$\overline{O_6} \; \overline{O_7} \; \overline{O_8} \; \overline{O_9} \; \overline{O_{10}} \ldots$$

One group initially serves as a nonequivalent control while the other group undergoes the intervention; at some later time these roles are reversed, and the second group undergoes the intervention. This design controls for most of the threats to internal validity; external validity is increased because the effect of the change has presumably been demonstrated at different times and with different groups of employees. This design might be appropriate when a change cannot be introduced for all work units at the same time.

Interrupted time-series designs (alone or in conjunction with nonequivalent control-group designs) are among the most powerful of the quasi-experimental approaches. For several reasons, however, they can be difficult to apply in an organizational setting. First, time-series designs assume that the necessary observations can be made before the change. But the timing of a change may be beyond the control of an organizational researcher, making such an assumption tenuous at best. These designs also assume that changes can be rapidly instituted between two of the observations, whereas in most organizational settings, many changes require a long time for implementation. Moreover, time-series designs assume that results of the change will manifest themselves quickly so that they can be measured at the ensuing observation. But the effect of changes in organizations may not be felt for some time, depending unpredictably on the nature of the change and the employees or work groups involved.

Finally, the use of interrupted-time-series designs imposes rather rigorous statistical requirements. Although the diagrams included here show only ten or twelve observations, at least fifty observations are required to conduct the appropriate statistical analyses adequately. The statistical procedures themselves are quite complex and demand a sophisticated understanding of time-series analyses. Professional assistance from a trained statistician is highly recommended for any manager undertaking such a study.

Some additional concerns

So far we have focused primarily on how to design an experiment so that one can be confident that outcomes are in fact attributable to the experimental intervention and not some other factor. Three additional problems in organizational research should also be considered.

COMPENSATORY EQUALIZATION

Problems can occur if employees in the control group feel that they are being treated unfairly in being denied a beneficial treatment (if, for example, participation in a training program is perceived [correctly or incorrectly] as a prerequisite for promotion). In such situations, organizations often abandon the experimental design and make the program available to everyone. An alternative is to provide acceptable alternative forms of training in addition to the program being examined. In this case, the experimental group can no longer be compared with a "no training" control group, but rather with a group that has gone through some different training program.

COMPENSATORY RIVALRY IN CONTROL GROUPS

Participants' feelings about their assignment to a particular experimental group can influence their performance. For example, if control-group employees are aware that they have not been chosen to participate in a new training program, they may take a "We'll show them" attitude, making a superhuman effort to outperform the experimental group. A comparison of the two groups would then probably not reveal significant differences, suggesting—incorrectly—that the intervention had no effect. This problem frequently arises when the various experimental conditions and the names of employees participating in each are made public.

One way to estimate the magnitude of this problem is to monitor the attitudes and behaviors of employees in the control group. Alternatively, a time-series design with a control group could reveal an unexpected increase in the outcome variables explainable only by this "underdog" effect.

RESENTFUL DEMORALIZATION

Control-group performance may also be adversely affected if employees resent being excluded from the experimental group. Rather than trying to vindicate their worth by doing a particularly good job, they may show poor motivation and lower performance levels. As a result, the differences in outcomes between the experimental and control groups could be significant. These differences should not be attributed to the intervention, however. Indeed, they may be due entirely to the control-group-morale effect rather than any change in the experimental group. Again, careful observation of the control group or use of a time-series design or both can help detect resentment and reduced motivation.

PART V: TEN COMMANDMENTS OF EXPERIMENTAL RESEARCH

A useful list of do's and don'ts for the manager interested in conducting organizational experiments was compiled by Cummings et al. (1977). What follows is an adaptation of those guidelines.

1. *Thou shalt assess the extent to which the change actually took effect.*

Valid measures must be made of the experimental intervention itself to determine whether the change "took." Allowing employees to vary their starting and finishing times by only five or ten minutes would probably not be an effective test of the impact of flexible working schedules on employee attitudes. More generally, if the change involves an activity that purports to alter employee perceptions or attitudes, evidence that such alterations actually occurred is needed before changes in the outcome variables are interpreted.

2. *Whenever possible, thou shalt use multiple measures.*

Some might argue that when only a single measurement procedure is used, the research results are peculiar to that measure. The use of multiple measures can provide evidence that the various procedures are indeed valid, measuring what they purport to measure. To the extent that the measurement procedures agree, one's confidence in what the measures reveal is increased.

3. *Whenever possible, thou shalt use unobtrusive measures.*

Entire books have been written on these measurement procedures, most notably Webb, Campbell, Schwartz, and Sechrest (1966). Unobtrusive measures are procedures of which participants remain unaware; thus the measurement process cannot influence their responses. Such procedures might include corporate historical information or physical evidence (e.g., the duration of break time inferred from the number of empty soda cups in the break room). For more detail on unobtrusive measures, the reader is referred to Webb, Campbell, Schwartz, and Sechrest.

4. *Thou shalt seek to avoid changes in measurement procedures.*

Every effort should be made to reduce the impact of instrument change on research outcomes. It may be necessary to continue using old forms or outdated processes in parallel with new procedures during the course of the experiment.

5. *Thou shalt endeavor to use a randomized experimental design whenever possible.*

Realistically, if resources and operating considerations preclude the use of a true experimental design, an effort should be made to use a nonequivalent-control group or data appropriate for a time-series design.

6. *In the absence of random assignment, thou shalt not select experimental or control groups on the basis of some characteristic that the group may possess to some unusual degree.*

If the researcher tries to determine the impact of organizational changes by providing these changes only to employees who perform particularly well or poorly, it will be difficult to eliminate alternative explanations of study results, including selection, maturation, and, most likely, regression to the mean.

7. *Thou shalt use appropriate statistical analyses to examine the differences between the experimental and control groups.*

The choice of appropriate statistical techniques is crucial to successful experimentation. The manager who wishes to conduct research within his or her organization may find it simplest to hire the requisite statistical expertise from within the organization or from an external professional source. Alternatively, discussions of analytical procedures appropriate for the designs presented here are available from a variety of sources (see, for example, Box and Jenkins 1976; Cook and Campbell 1979; Hays 1981; Kerlinger 1973; Kirk 1982; McDowall et al. 1980; Ostrom 1978; Spector 1981; Winer 1971).

The manager should proceed cautiously in interpreting statistical results. A statistically significant difference between pre- and postchange observations is not, by itself, sufficient proof that a causal relationship exists between the variables of interest. Moreover, there is a real distinction between statistical significance and practical significance in research results. Whenever sample sizes are large enough, statistically significant differences are generally discovered between experimental groups. The differences between the two groups may be negligible in any practical sense, however. Often the costs of implementing the change that produced the significant statistical differences would exceed the practical impact of the change on outcomes of interest to the organization.

8. *Whenever possible, thou shalt collect time-series data.*

Valid time-series data can greatly strengthen any of the quasi-experimental designs.

9. *To the greatest extent possible, thou shalt protect the employee, the organization, and the experiment, in that order.*

To protect the employees and the organization, the researcher must abide by an acceptable code of research ethics (see American Psychological Association 1981). Given the many legislative and union guidelines under which organizations operate, it would be unusual for serious ethical questions to arise in connection with research in an organizational setting. Nevertheless, it is essential that managers be aware of any experimental settings that might place employees in physical or psychological danger, such as using a new but untried technology or exposing employees to excessive (and unnecessary) stress.

Unanticipated and usually uncontrollable events can threaten the validity of an experiment by influencing the research results. To protect against these occurrences, the manager has several options. First, research schedules should include contingency plans. Should unforeseen events occur, data generated to that point in the study could be salvaged. Second, if potentially disruptive events can be predicted in advance, it may be possible to make appropriate adjustments to the initial design in terms of the choice of employees or work groups to participate, the nature and timing of measurements, or the nature and timing of the changes to be implemented. Third, while the research is in progress, the manager should make every effort to identify and record extraneous events that later may suggest alternative explanations for the research outcomes. Finally, once the data have been collected and analyzed, possible alternative explanations due to extraneous events should be evaluated and either rejected or incorporated in the final research report.

10. *Thou shalt report fully and honestly the procedures and results of the research.*

Disclosure and publication may spare others the task of reinventing the wheel. Often such disclosures must be limited to in-house constituents, particularly if the reports contain proprietary information. When possible, external publication of experimental research in organizations serves the broader community by improving the overall quality of the information available to managers.

Research results should be presented as objectively as possible. While managers may hope to find results of a certain sort, distortion of findings to provide support for a personal or corporate position is inappropriate and unethical.

CONCLUSIONS

This chapter has attempted to provide the P/HR professional with information about some of the major decisions that need to be made when conducting experiments in organizations, when supervising experiments conducted by subordinates or internal/external consultants, and when evaluating the presentation of such work in publications. Those managers interested in examining these topics in considerably greater detail are directed to any of the volumes or articles listed in the references.

True experimentation has long been considered the only acceptable way of learning and knowing in many scientific disciplines. In an organizational context, experimentation (both true and quasi) is but one way of learning and knowing about an organization. The use of appropriate experimental designs in organizational research should be given due consideration when research studies are being planned. The P/HR manager has a multitude of information-gathering tools available, and managerial effectiveness will be enhanced to the extent that the manager is able to choose the design most appropriate to the organizational setting and to the information required.

REFERENCES

American Psychological Association. 1981. *Ethical Principles of Psychologists.* Washington, D.C.: American Psychological Association.

Box, G.E.P., and G. M. Jenkins. 1976. *Time-series Analysis: Forecasting and Control.* San Francisco: Holden-Day.

Campbell, D. T., and J. C. Stanley. 1963. *Experimental and Quasi-experimental Designs for Research.* Chicago: Rand McNally.

Cascio, W. 1982. *Applied Psychology in Personnel Management.* 2d ed. Reston, Va.: Reston Publishing Company.

Cook, T. D., and D. T. Campbell. 1979. *Quasi-experimentation: Design and Analysis Issues for Field Settings.* Chicago: Rand McNally.

Cummings, T. G., E. S. Molloy, and R. Glen. 1977. "A Methodological Critique of Fifty-Eight Selected Work Experiments." *Human Relations* 8:675–708.

Dunham, R., and F. Smith. 1979. *Organizational Surveys.* Glendale, Ill.: Scott, Foresman and Company.

Festinger, L. 1953. "Laboratory Experiments." In *Research Methods in the Behavioral Sciences,* ed. L. Festinger and D. Katz, pp. 136–172. New York: Dryden Press.

Hays, W. L. 1981. *Statistics.* 3d ed. New York: Holt, Rinehart and Winston.

Kerlinger, F. 1973. *Foundations of Behavioral Research.* 2d ed. New York: Holt, Rinehart and Winston.

Kirk, R. 1982. *Experimental Design: Procedures for the Behavioral Sciences.* Belmont, Calif.: Brooks/Cole.

McDowall, D., R. McCleary, E. E. Meidinger, and R. A. Hay, Jr. 1980. *Interrupted Time Series Analysis.* Sage University Paper series on Quantitative Applications in the Social Sciences, 07–021. Beverly Hills and London: Sage Publications.

Nadler, D. A. 1977. *Feedback and Organization Development: Using Data-Based Methods.* Reading, Mass.: Addison Wesley Publishing Company.

Nunnally, J. 1978. *Psychometric Theory.* 2d ed. New York: McGraw-Hill.

Ostrom, C. W., Jr. 1978. *Time Series Analysis: Regression Techniques.* Sage University Paper series on Quantitative Applications in the Social Sciences, 07–009. Beverly Hills and London: Sage Publications.

Reichen, H., R. Boruch, D. Campbell, W. Coplan, T. Glennan, J. Pratt, A. Rees, and W. Williams. 1974. *Social Experimentation: A Method for Planning and Evaluating Social Innovations.* New York: Academic Press.

Scott, W. R. 1965. "Field Methods in the Study of Organizations." In *Handbook of Organizations,* ed. J. G. March, pp. 261–304. Chicago: Rand McNally.

Seashore, S. E. 1964. "Field Experiments with Formal Organizations." *Human Organizations* 23:164–170.

Spector, P. E. 1981. *Research Designs.* Sage University Paper series on Quantitative Applications in the Social Sciences, 07–023. Beverly Hills and London: Sage Publications.

Stone, E. F. 1978. *Research Methods in Organizational Behavior.* Glendale, Ill.: Scott, Foresman and Company.

Webb, E. J., D. T. Campbell, R. D. Schwartz, and L. Sechrest. 1966. *Unobtrusive Measures: Nonreactive Research in the Social Sciences.* Chicago: Rand McNally.

Winer, B. J. 1971. *Statistical Principles in Experimental Design.* New York: McGraw-Hill.

10

Surveys in organizations
STANLEY E. SEASHORE

This chapter raises some issues of strategic choice in the design, conduct, and interpretation or organizational inquiries using survey methods. These choices include, first, whether a survey is to be preferred over alternative methods. Other issues are related to the design and conduct of a survey plan and choice among alternative technical features. We also consider the formulation of the topics to be covered, ethical aspects of survey practice, and ways to link survey results to organizational purposes, policies, and plans of action. Throughout this chapter, our focus will be on interview or questionnaire surveys with organization members.

THE NATURE OF SURVEYS

Several methods are available for learning about an organization and its members (Seashore et al. 1983; Stone 1978). One can examine records (Is turnover rising?) or talk directly with members who are in a good position to observe and report their views on matters of interest (Are your people satisfied with the new wage agreement?). One can engage a consultant to conduct interviews exploring the adequacy of coordination between two departments and improvements, or monitor the organization's suggestion system to note the recurrent themes of dissatisfaction, preference, and problem solution. These and other methods are all familiar and commonly used ways to collect information about organization members' attitudes, opinions, beliefs, experiences, observations, or intentions with regard to policies, programs, facilities, persons, procedures, work environments, or external environments. These are all "surveys," in the limited sense that they seek to obtain information directly from or about members of the organization. Each has its own merits and limitations. The more thorough and systematic survey methods addressed here aim to strengthen the merits and moderate the limitations.

The employee survey approach to the assessment of organizations has been developing for four decades. The application expanded gradually during the 1950s and 1960s, in terms of both the number and the variety of employing organizations. Reliable current information is not available but it is apparent that a majority of the larger work establishments, both public and private, have made some use of employee surveys, that many now have provisions for continuous or recurrent surveys, and that smaller establishments increasingly find it feasible and useful to conduct employee surveys. The survey has long ceased to be a novelty or primarily a "research" rather than a "management" activity, and it has an established place among the practices associated with the information-getting, performance-surveillance, and policy-review functions of management. Many firms have in-house staff competence for such work and numerous consulting and research firms offer professional services to clients (Backstrom and Hursch-Cesar 1981).

No typical survey practice can be defined, for the variations in program, purpose, method, conceptual basis, and application strategies are many. However, the following brief description[1] treats one of the several common varieties of practice.

An example of an organizational survey

The establishment in question is a machine-manufacturing firm employing over three thousand people in four plants, all located in the same city. The firm is prosperous and technologically advanced, with an established place in its industry. There are three labor unions with jurisdiction over blue-collar, white-collar, and certain professional employees, respectively. The firm has a history of good employee relations, few occasions of organized labor dispute, and liberal employee benefit programs and services. Employee surveys had been conducted before, for special limited purposes, but not on a regular basis. The survey was not stimulated by any crisis or unusual issues but by a desire on the part of the management to have a comprehensive assessment of the current concerns of employees with respect to their employment, sources of satisfaction and dissatisfaction, and their opinions about various programs, policies, and working conditions then prevailing or planned.

While the firm had the staff capability for such a survey, they preferred in this instance to engage an outside group, partly to ensure neutrality and anonymity for the survey, and partly to avoid staff overload.

A general conception of the purposes, content, and methods of the survey was worked out jointly with the consultants and then discussed with each of the three labor unions. Consent to the survey was given by the offices of each of the unions, with the provision that each would have opportunity to review the specific questions to be asked of their members, and each would have equal access with management to the statistical summaries resulting from the survey, but not necessarily to the consultants' interpretive analyses and recommendations. Guarantees of anonymity were provided for all individuals participating in the survey. Participation would be voluntary. All categories of jobs and levels would be included.

The survey process included (1) preliminary interviews with a variety of employees to compose a roster of issues and topics of concern to employees, managers, and union officers; (2) a fifty-minute questionnaire completed at the workplace on paid time by a stratified random sample of employees and managers; (3) lengthy structured interviews with supervisors of major work departments and sections to obtain background, work organization, and work characteristics; and (4) information from firm records concerning absences, turnover, productivity, and product quality for selected departments and sections (not for individuals). The content of the survey focused upon the perceptions, beliefs, and reactions of individual respondents regarding their own specific jobs and work environment. Subsidiary information used as analytic and interpretive aids included demographic information, reports of family and community factors that might be associated with the individual's work life, and the "work group effectiveness" data taken from firm records. With respect to the respondents' questionnaire reports, there were produced about 250 specific questionnaire responses covering about 50 topical areas and recombined into about 40 generic conceptual variables representing environmental attributes (e.g., "physical discomfort," "job challenge," "pay equity," "work load," etc.) and individual responses to these attributes (e.g., "satisfaction," "preference," "motivation," "expectation," etc.).

The consultants' reports, planned jointly with the management and unions, provided statistical summaries for each question, each topical area, and each derived indicator. These data were shown in ways to allow comparison among work departments and sections and among demographic classes of employees (e.g., by sex, age, union membership, length of service, type and level of job, etc.). The reports were provided to the management and to each of the unions. The consultants provided technical explanations of the data (not interpretations) and suggested procedures for the further review, interpretation, and application of the results by various special-interest groups within the firm. The interpretive process included special attention to issues suggested by (1) relatively high rates of employee dissatisfaction or preference; (2) evidence of "importance" derived from association between attributes of the working environment and such consequences as relatively high individual satisfaction or relatively high work-group effectiveness; and (3) evidence of inequitable advantage to some group or beliefs about such inequity. Some limited attention was given to comparisons between the firm's own data and similar data from other unidentified firms provided by the consultant from previous studies.

The reader is reminded that this is but one example of several survey approaches to the assessment of a specific establishment, and is not to be regarded as typical or prevailing. The varieties of practice vary among several dimensions, including the source of initiative, the definition of objectives or purposes to be served, the ar-

---

1. This description is taken with permission, and with minor alterations, from S. E. Seashore, "Assessing the Quality of Working Life: The U.S. Experience," *Labour and Society* 1, no. 2:71-73.

rangements for control over the survey processes and outcomes, and the conceptual and methodological choices. It will serve, however, to illustrate issues to be discussed.

Advantages of the survey method

The survey method has several advantages over alternative methods of pursuing the same kind of information.

1. Surveys can be conducted with assured anonymity or confidentiality for individuals, this allowing (although not guaranteeing) candor in reporting private opinions, treatment of controversial topics that are not normally in management information systems and records, and access to information that does not exist except in the respondents' heads.

2. With sufficiently large samples of respondents, it is possible to apply statistical analysis techniques. The quality of the data can be assessed, subgroups can be compared, variations as well as consensus uniformities can be displayed, correlations can be determined, and so on.

3. Surveys with standardized questions and formats allow replication to detect changes over time, and extension to other parts or subgroups of the organization.

4. Cost effectiveness: a questionnaire survey can elicit, at relatively low cost, information from many people covering a wide range of topics. Interview surveys are much more costly per respondent but may be cost effective in other respects.

5. Appropriate sampling allows the selection of respondents in ways that ensure representativeness.

6. In some situations (with consent of respondents and tight confidentiality provisions), the survey data can be linked with open records (e.g., absences, productivity, subsequent turnover, pay, and the like) to allow the assessment of associations between what people say and what they do.

Some limitations and risks

Several limitations and risks often proscribe the conduct of an employee survey or reduce its potential scope and utility. Among them are the following:

1. Ambiguity of purpose: the initiators of a survey, usually an upper-management or staff group, may find it impossible to reach sufficient consensus about the purposes of the survey, the priorities of content, and the procedures for postsurvey review and interpretation of the results (Sirota 1974). Managements (and unions) may already be so committed to the policies and programs at issue that the results of a survey are unlikely to have any practical utility in forward planning.

2. Distrust: some initial level of trust in management and union leadership is needed for employees to volunteer freely, accept assurances of anonymity or confidentiality, and have confidence that sensible and considered interpretations and actions will follow.

3. Unacceptable topics: in any organization certain topics of great interest may be disallowed, on grounds that the employees have little information, context, or experience basis for forming opinions, or because they are too controversial. For example, management may prefer not to solicit employee views on practices that, for legal reasons, cannot be altered; unions may not want open information about members' views on issues under negotiation.

4. Organizational disturbance: the effective conduct of a survey requires consultation and information exchange with employees, scheduling of activities, and (usually) absence from workplace for interviews or questionnaires. Moreover, the survey is unavoidably a public event, which may call attention to latent issues or induce unrealistic expectations about subsequent actions.

Such considerations are not trivial. They often lead the knowledgeable professional staff member or an external consultant to dissuade the organization from undertaking a survey.

The utility of surveys

The preceding example of an organizational survey illustrates one common and relatively simple type of application. The aim was primarily to get a description of the current state of the organization on a broad spectrum of factors of interest to the management. Information was collected on the *employees'* opinions, intentions, and preferences; the *organization's* policies and programs; the *physical and social work environment* as seen by the employees; *management-union* relationships; and the like. The information was used in a rather simple form: tables and graphs showing the mean responses and distributions (variances) on each variable or index, set up to allow comparison of demographic subgroups. While some supplemental analysis was performed—for example, a search for patterns of work-group composition and attitudes associated with high group performance—the chief utility of the findings was to allow scanning for information that might suggest the existence of potential problems or that provided reassurance that things were in a satisfactory state.

Organizational surveys, however, have a wide range of potential uses, and a single survey can serve multiple purposes, reflecting the scope of information contained in the survey, the interpretational strategy, and the statistical treatment of the results.

PREDICTION

Managers often want a basis for estimating the future behavior of their employees or for understanding the conditions under which employees would do one thing or another. A few examples may be helpful. (1) How many employees, and what kinds, expect to be looking for a job elsewhere during the coming year? (2) Under new retirement policies, just introduced or being considered, how many think they would opt for early retirement, for deferred decision, or for continued employment beyond the traditional age limit? How many more would choose early (or deferred) retirement if attractive bonuses were offered? (3) If the firm moves its headquarters from an urban center to a suburb, about how many employees (and what kinds) would expect to commute from their present home, would move to a new home location, or would choose or be compelled to quit the firm? (4) How many of those eligible plan to sign up for a stock-purchase plan to be initiated next year?

Such questions can be asked directly, are persuasively related to sensible forward planning, and can be answered directly by the employees for themselves. Supplemental questions can be used to amplify the considerations they use in making their forward predictions. Of course some will be uncertain what they will do later, and some will change their minds. Changing external conditions (inflation, job market, etc.) may modify the future behaviors. Still, the information may be reassuring, or it may be arresting, as when a firm with a history of moderate voluntary turnover learned that over half of the work force definitely planned to quit and felt confident of finding acceptable jobs elsewhere.

The prediction of future behavior need not always rest upon poll-like self-reported intentions. If one has a confidently held theory about the correlates of the behavior of interest, then predictions can be made from these correlates. Such a model can often be discovered empirically by analyses of survey data in conjunction with firm records; the model can then be applied to estimating behavioral changes or comparative rates in the future. For example, the conditions associated with differential absenteeism rates in various plants or departments may be determined in this manner, and the model used to estimate the rates to be expected in the future under constant or changed conditions. The analytic procedures are analogous to those of operations research but applied to personnel rather than to a work system.

EXPLANATION

Quite often the aim to be served by a survey is not description or prediction, but rather the investigation of causes—a search for an understanding of the factors leading to favorable outcomes (to be fostered) or unfavorable outcomes (to be moderated). In one case, for example, an engineering design firm questioned its historical rates and high costs of rework—"finished" designs that had to be redone. Designers and draftsmen were surveyed to get a detailed description of the conditions and events associated with their most recent instances of rework. There resulted a short roster of frequently recurring "causes," some of which were inherent in the work and not controllable by the firm, and some of which suggested minor modifications of work flow, information-exchange practices, and location of responsibilities. Rework costs dropped substantially within a few months.

In another situation, a firm with many branch offices wanted to understand why some offices performed much more effectively than others. A survey of management practices reported by salespersons suggested a strong influence arising from the local support systems for new sales staff and variations in local approaches to coordination and decision making. Programs for coaching and training could then be designed to correct these previously unrecognized deficiencies.

In both these cases, other approaches might well have led to similar advantage, but the survey method was relatively quick and inexpensive, and the people affected by the changes responded well to the new information because it was their own, not imposed. To conduct such inquiries involving complex analyses of survey data, it is necessary to have information about some outcome or result that is of concern—rework costs in one example, and sales volume in the other—to which the survey data can be linked.

MONITORING CHANGE

Firms undergoing evolutionary changes (e.g., growth) or significant transitions (reorganization, new technologies) may experience unintended side effects. It may be judged worthwhile to monitor potential areas of impact to get early signals of gains to be preserved or losses to be moderated. In one case, for example, a firm composed of relatively autonomous units, attracted by the potential utility of new information-management technologies, set out to centralize the production planning, purchasing, and distribution scheduling for all units. Some feared that side effects might include a loss of local management initiatives, diminished sense of responsibility, "distance" from customers, delays in problem solving, and the like. To complement its established information systems for monitoring fiscal and production indicators, the firm introduced periodic questionnaire surveys of management people at all levels, making it possible to detect changes that might warrant some early corrective attention.

At least three large U.S. firms, and probably more, maintain a service unit in the corporate office to conduct employee surveys upon request of the local manager in any unit of the firm. A standard questionnaire with some local amendments is used, derived from some years of experience as to the kinds of variables that may change and that are most useful to managers. Many units, but not all, elect to take such a reading of their organizational health at intervals of two or three years.

Monitoring programs such as these may focus on a particular one-time set of issues and subgroups in the firm, or may be a more generalized, broadly based screening procedure to detect trends of change that require action or justify self-congratulation.

EVALUATING PROGRAMS

Most firms, from time to time, introduce programs of change intended to accomplish specific purposes, e.g., to reduce sexual harassment, to accelerate the promotion of outstanding junior staff, to improve understanding of policy changes, or to improve the generation and flow of ideas about work procedures. Some information is available from supervisory and managerial reports about the progress and success of such programs, but often the crucial information can be gathered earlier and more realistically through direct reports (i.e., a survey) from the people likely to be affected by a program. Early surveys can provide guidance in altering, fine tuning, or abandoning a program; later surveys can reveal the degree of success in attaining the intended purposes. Unanticipated problems in the conduct of the program may be revealed. Frequently, the needed information is not of a kind that can be observed and reliably reported by supervisors and managers. Often brief, small-sample surveys using interviews or questionnaires can serve to track the progress of the program, and there may be valuable by-products: the organization learns something about how to change itself effectively, and the employees gain some influence in helping to guide the programs.

DECIDING

Occasionally employee preferences are the crucial factor in a firm's choice between alternative and incompatible lines of action or policy. Shall we introduce flexitime? What additional fringe benefit is most preferred? How about the four-day week? These preferences may be assumed, or roughly estimated at some risk, or they may be measured through an advisory poll.

BASIC RESEARCH

All managers run their organizations on the basis of some set of values and some set of implicit or explicit theories about people and organizations. These are all subject to examination and change. Many issues can be illuminated by basic research procedures, which may include the use of surveys as one feature—perhaps a central feature—of the inquiry. Most of the progress made in the last decades in rethinking issues of organizational design, organizational policies, personnel practices, and the like has come from such basic research conducted by, or with the support and collaboration of, managers willing to question the contemporary folklore and inherited wisdom of managers. Such managers understand that the organization may be seen as a kind of "natural experiment," in which variations in practice can be measured against some criterion of organizational effectiveness, and that it may be purposely changed in an experimental way with provisions for evaluating the outcome. Such basic research is likely to be undertaken without any short-term commitment or even an expectation that a particular course of action will be demanded by the results; instead, the aim is to gain some insight into organizational functioning that may be applicable to future problems and decisions.

The number of such unresolved issues is still enormous. What is the optimum rate of turnover (renewal) for an organization? How are superior managers identified and advanced through a career line? Under what conditions do "participative" practices improve organizational performance? What are the main problems that arise when organizations are merged or divided?

PLANNING A SURVEY: DESIGN ISSUES

The technology of organizational surveys has become quite sophisticated, and a variety of books and journal articles cover the design issues in operational detail (Dunham and Smith 1979). The intent in the following pages is only to highlight the main areas of choice in design.

Interviews vs. questionnaires

The factors involved in this choice may be economic, conceptual, political, and technical, in some weighted mix. If a large population of respondents is to be surveyed, then the economic considerations are relatively important, for the questionnaire survey can be administered at a much lower cost per respondent. Hiring or training of skilled interviewers is costly; interviews usually take more time (and for two people) than a questionnaire of similar content; some travel or scheduling costs may be involved; and the costs of converting an interview record into quantified form for statistical analyses can be formidable. If the population of respondents is relatively small, on the other hand, cost may become a minor consideration, because the savings from a questionnaire administration tend to be offset by the costs of preparing and pretesting a sound questionnaire, which can be substantially more expensive than the preparation of a workable interview guide.

On the conceptual side, an inherent deficiency of the written questionnaire is that you must decide in advance just what you want to ask, how to ask it, and what constraints in interpretation you are willing to accept. The questionnaire is highly efficient in getting standardized responses to prescribed questions. The interview is highly efficient in accepting unanticipated responses, clarifying ambiguous meanings, and adapting the questions somewhat to the particular case.

Political considerations may involve issues of credibility, candor, and respect for respondents. For example, if the survey treats controversial topics and the results are to be subject to debate and challenge, the data should be drawn from a large and representative sample of respondents and should flow from response to statistical summary with minimal intervention for coding, screening, and interpretation of unique responses. A questionnaire or a questionnairelike poll is preferred. If privacy and confidentiality are especially important, the questionnaire procedure offers added assurance to skeptical respondents. In some situations, the relatively higher (or lower) status of the interviewer can inhibit candor. Matters of language, gender, culture, and ethnicity may demand the neutrality of a uniform questionnaire or, in some situations, the sympathy of an interview by "one of us."

The technical constraints on the choice between questionnaires and interviews are generally related to plans for analysis or comparison of the data. If trend data are required, or, for example, comparisons among organizational units, the procedures must be identical in all cases. If previously standardized scales and indexes are to be employed, the prior methods for getting the data must be replicated.

Most organizations with experience in organizational surveys use *both* interview and questionnaire procedures, in selective ways. They often are used in tandem, for example, an initial, small-scale interview survey to aid in the formulation of topics, questions, and response formats, which are then used in a larger-scale questionnaire survey.

Populations and samples

Many organizational surveys include all members of the organization, or all members of a given class (all supervisors), or a given organizational unit (engineering

department). No issues of sampling arise, as such a "total sample" cannot be improved upon. When the base population is large, however, or its size and boundaries unknown, some considered sampling procedure needs to be employed.

The elements to be sampled are usually persons, but quite often the interest is not in persons as such, but in some other kinds of "object," for example, jobs, events, decisions, groups, places, times, or products. In addition, the sampling need not seek representativeness, but may be purposefully nonrepresentative. Thus, an organizational survey may be designed to include all those people involved in a sample of product-redesign decisions, or those who are members of a representative sample of work groups. In some situations a purposive sample is most efficient even though not representative of the base population. For example, a firm that wanted to compare high-productivity and low-productivity branches might survey members of the top-ten and bottom-ten branches, ignoring the middle mass of "representative" branches. Similarly, a firm concerned about misinterpretations of its annual-leave policy statement might begin interviewing employees, chosen mainly on grounds of variety and convenience, and continue until it encountered a string of twenty interviews that produced no new information. The "sample" would be small and unrepresentative but sufficient to identify the small number of ways the existing policy statement could be misinterpreted.

When representative samples are needed, two main issues must be considered. First, how can a biased sample be avoided? Randomness is the key, but "random" does not mean merely "casual." Methods of varying convenience and precision are available for ensuring randomness. Second, how large a sample is needed? The answer to that question depends on the degree of sampling error that can be tolerated in the survey results and, more importantly, on the need to achieve adequate representation of any subgroups that will be singled out for comparisons or for special analyses. For example, if a special analysis of middle managers is planned, one must consider whether a simple random sample will produce the requisite number of respondents of this type.

Survey specialists have a useful bag of tricks that can be employed to obtain adequate samples without inflating the scale of a survey. An example is the purposeful oversampling of certain population categories that would otherwise produce too few respondents; this can be done without destroying the potential for random representation of the entire base population. Another possibility is a complex sample design that provides interlocking subsamples, thus achieving simultaneously and efficiently a good representation of the base population, of departments or work groups, and of jobs.

Instrument development and pretesting

Whether a questionnaire or an interview procedure is chosen, a crucial step in design is the preparation and pretesting of the instrument to be used (Belson 1981; Gorden 1969; Sudman and Bradburn 1982).

Whatever the survey is to be about, it is likely that some other organization with a similar purpose has already prepared and used a questionnaire or interview schedule. As a rule, it is better to adopt all or parts of such "pretested" instruments if they fit the case. The fit is seldom perfect, however, and it is likely that some modifications will be needed to conform to the local terminology practices and organizational structure or to include some topics unique to the new situation. Some general questionnaires and interview schedules are in the public domain, available to all. Others are proprietary and can be used only with permission or in connection with the owner's services. A number of topic-specific scales and indexes are in the public domain and can be incorporated in an instrument that is otherwise locally developed (for example, scales for measuring job satisfaction, motivational properties of jobs, job stress, organizational structure, or supervisory style). Such instruments or components are likely to have gone through several revisions, and their reliability and validity have most likely been documented (Cammann et al. 1983; Dunham, Smith, and Blackburn 1977; Smith, Kendall, and Hulin 1969).

Whether one opts for a standard or a tailor-made instrument or some combination of the two, it is wise to provide a pretest with a small number of diverse employees to ensure that the questions are unambiguous and the response categories clear, and that none of the questions are unnecessarily offensive or threatening.

PLANNING A SURVEY: ORGANIZATIONAL ISSUES

Several issues of organizational policy and practice should be considered as part of the survey-planning process. If not examined at the outset, such issues are likely to come up later in circumstances that make their resolution troublesome.

Confidentiality

Some surveys involve topics and respondent populations for whom confidentiality, privacy of views, and anonymity are not feasible or not a matter of great concern. Ordinarily, however, it is very important to assure respondents that their views cannot be used to help or hurt them personally. Some surveys contain hazardous information—for example, about the behavior of one's supervisor, evaluations of top management, intentions to quit, drug use at work, areas of dissatisfaction, and the like. Employees would be naïve or foolish to respond with candor unless they feel assured against harm and see no advantage in misrepresenting their views.

Anonymity usually can be assured with credibility if employees have a modicum of trust in the organization and if various symbolic and practical steps are taken. The usual minimum steps are to state clearly the firm's intention to respect anonymity, to omit respondents' names and identifying numbers from the questionnaires, to designate openly the persons responsible for maintaining anonymity, and to ask few questions of the sort that could conceivably identify a particular respondent. A further step might be to use an outside agency to collect, store, and analyze the data. In some few instances, organizations have formed committees of employees to oversee the arrangements for handling and protecting the data.

Total respondent anonymity may make certain legitimate and valuable uses of the survey data impossible. For example, to understand the delayed effects of different kinds of job stress upon individuals, it is desirable to resurvey the same individuals and analyze the two surveys jointly. But unless respondents are identified, it will not be possible to survey the same population again later. Similarly, to understand the conditions associated with absenteeism, high productivity, career progress, and the like, it might be necessary to draw on the organization's personnel and operating records. But a comparison of survey data with relevant organizational records will not be possible with anonymous respondents. It is possible, of course, to maintain confidentiality without anonymity, and employees will ordinarily assent to such an arrangement, provided their cooperation is voluntary and the procedures for protection are plausibly explained.

Participation in planning

The planning of a survey inevitably raises a fundamental question regarding the location of control over its purposes, design, and the use of the results. Top managers, staff specialists, supervisors, union officers, and other groups, all may feel that they have some right to a share in such control. Moreover, the quality and utility of the survey may be enhanced by their participation in the planning. Particularly in an organization with little past experience with surveys, there is a real risk that, unless they are consulted in advance, people will misunderstand features of the plan and be less confident that their concerns and interests will be taken into account.

Some considerations weigh heavily against broadly extended participation in the planning, however. Participation is likely to extend the planning time and to require diversion of some payroll hours from other work. Some ideas may be advocated that then have to be rejected, either on technical grounds, for policy or legal reasons, or simply because there is no way to accommodate an overabundance of suggestions.

On the positive side, early discussions with various interest groups or their representatives are likely to produce some good ideas, will certainly forestall some misunderstandings that otherwise would arise, and will very likely help to ensure cooperation in the conduct of the survey.

Voluntarism

Only rarely can an organization, with impunity, require employees to be interviewed or to fill out a questionnaire on matters that seem to intrude upon their sphere of privacy. In most organizations, employees (including managers) have rather clear ideas about the kinds of information management is entitled to demand (Can you work overtime next Saturday?, and the kinds employees may legitimately withhold (Why can't you work overtime on Saturday?). Accordingly, surveys are usually conducted in a way that makes it possible for an employee, without risk, to decline to participate.

The principle of voluntarism arises from respect for the prevailing norms of individual privacy but also reflects the practical fact that anyone so coerced will be free—and probably stimulated—to respond with less than total candor. The burden falls upon management to make sure that prospective respondents understand the nature and purposes of the survey and are informed about their safe option to decline. Some will do so. The proportion of decliners may be as low as 1–2 percent, under optimum conditions, or as high as 30 percent or even more if practical problems (illness, vacations, illiteracy) prevent some participation or if the levels of apathy or distrust are high. Participation rates of 85–95 percent are commonly attained; if they are much lower, and if representativeness is important, there is a need to evaluate the risk of distortion from selective, biased refusal to participate.

The steps taken to ensure cooperation are usually those customary for the organization, and may include some or all of the following: a letter of explanation to each prospective respondent; meetings to present the plan and respond to questions; supporting communications from union officials or the respondent's own supervisor; articles in the house organ; a "hot line" for anonymous queries about the survey plan; and assurance that interviews or questionnaire administration will be on company time, not on personal time.

Reporting the results

Questions inevitably arise about the reporting of results of an organizational survey. Who will get to see the results? In what detail? When? For what purposes? Some people will be merely curious to learn about the organization or to see how their own views compare with those of others. There is usually some sense of reciprocity: those who volunteer information may feel they are entitled to get some in return. In other cases, the organization member's's concern about the reporting and use of the results is much more intense and more closely linked with his or her role, status, and responsibilities in the organization. The results may reflect well or badly upon the individual's performance, or they may be highly pertinent to current organizational programs, problems, and tasks for which he or she is responsible. The data may contain some potential both for risk and for help.

Prudence requires that questions of reporting be anticipated and that some guiding principles be worked out and tested for acceptability as part of the early planning. The primary factors to be considered are the intended uses of the data by the organization and matters of respondent privacy and data confidentiality. The results must get to those who are to use them, in a form and detail suitable for the intended use. The information must be in a form that protects respondents against undue disclosure. Confidentiality must be weighed against the costs of secrecy and the possible gains from openness.

The resolution of these questions of reporting cannot be generally prescribed, because each survey has some unique features of content and context. An example can be offered for the common case of a questionnaire survey that covers a broad range of topics and diverse respondent populations.

Such a survey probably should not be undertaken at all unless the plans include review of the information by all or many of the people whose organizational performance and future actions are implicated. One form of reporting is to undertake a data-feedback program in a "waterfall" fashion designed to encourage understanding of the information, diagnosis of potential areas of action, and planning of feasible actions. In this procedure, survey data are summarized in statistical form, aggregated separately for each of the organizational units, and presented to each unit along with some assistance in its interpretation. Thus, a top-management group might get the data summarized for the organization as a whole and for a few of its major parts. At the next organizational level, each management group would get its own unit's data as well as the pooled data for the organization as a whole for comparison. Thus, like a waterfall, the pertinent information can flow to all levels of the organization, in a form and detail appropriate in each case, with great flexibility as to the topics reported and the exposure to information about others' units. Some selectivity as to topics covered is usually needed, either to highlight the more pertinent ones or simply to avoid information overload. Receiving groups may be invited to request any desired supplemental information from the survey and to report their interpretations, problem definitions, or proposed lines of response (Rickards and Bessant 1980; Dodd and Pesci 1977).

In addition to directing survey information to particular user groups, an organization may also wish to make public within the organization the results that are of general interest to employees. Here the objectives and methods are closer to those of public relations than of problem solving and action. Members of the organization are likely to be interested in knowing some of the general findings from the survey, and particularly in learning how the survey will be used for organizational benefit. Failure to report may feed the rumor mill or leave an impression that no one is paying attention to the views of those surveyed. Conducting a survey creates the expectation that something will be done with it, and no news may be considered bad news. As one manager put it, although with excessive drama, "A survey is like pulling the pin of a hand grenade . . . you can't just stand there holding it."

In most organizational surveys, the main problems of survey reporting arise from the sheer volume of information created, some of it inconsequential, and the fact that some issues will require extensive analysis before the meaning becomes clear. An effective strategy often is to proceed in stages, first allowing users with priority concerns to screen the results and later performing statistical analysis in collaboration with the user groups. For example, employees in one department may be particularly low in confidence that their career aspirations will be realized; the review group could then use the data base to determine what kinds of people in what kinds of jobs feel singularly disadvantaged, with the hope that this information will be useful in deciding what can be done about the problem, if anything.

To protect privacy, several conventions are often adopted in reporting survey data. Many follow the rule that no data will be aggregated and released for small subgroups or that remarks in interviews or write-ins on questionnaires will not be cited verbatim if they contain any potentially identifying features.

Professional help

While organizational surveys can be conducted by people without professional qualifications and experience—and sometimes with a satisfactory result—an organization is well advised to get qualified advice. At a minimum, a professional advisor should review the plans as to purpose, instrumentation, administration arrangements, analysis and reporting, and the intended interpretive and use strategies. Such a person is likely to have good ideas that will moderate risks and enhance effectiveness and efficiency. In addition, most organizations will want to have the survey managed, not merely inspected, by a professionally competent person, either an in-house staff specialist or one brought in from outside. Even firms that maintain an inside staff with survey qualifications often seek outside help. They may do so to balance staff work load or to have the help of people with special qualifications for a particular kind of survey or to gain the added assurance of respondent protection and cooperation by locating the survey data elsewhere.

The inside professional has the advantages of familiarity with the organizations, knowledge of past and concurrent events that might bear on effective planning, conduct of the survey, and applications of the results. The outside professional, on the other hand, is likely to have done a wide variety of surveys under different conditions and to be familiar with available resources and instruments; he or she can give full attention to the survey and can be dropped form the payroll when no longer needed.

Competent professional help is readily available. Some individuals and small firms specialize in such service. Larger general consulting firms are likely to have an appropriate capability. Many universities have staff and support facilities that can be made available to organizations; they are likely to be found in the department of psychology or the school of business administration. Organizations that wish further specialization might find a suitable person with expertise, for example, in hospital organizations, social agencies, public administrative organizations, and the like.

PLANNING A SURVEY: ANALYSIS AND INTERPRETATION

Organizational survey data can be interpreted at several different levels of complexity, each with distinctive features of convenience, cost, and analytic power. When planning the survey, it is essential to consider how the data will be used, and adjust the design accordingly (Sonquist and Dunkelberg 1977).

Much can be learned about an organization (or an issue) by simply scanning the raw aggregated data displayed graphically or in simple tables of means and distributions. One can make an intuitive judgment whether a given result seems good or bad, alarming or reassuring. It helps to compare observations among several scanners, and it is useful if they have had some prior experience in "reading" survey data.

Raw data can be deceptive, however. The meaning and action implications may not be apparent; the necessary collateral information may not be clearly defined or easily found; and the joint review of several related measures may become complex enough to require simplification through multivariate statistical analyses. Thus, a group of managers may have some difficulty arriving at a common view of what the aggregated data from their survey mean, and therefore what action they should take. They may observe that a substantial proportion, say 85 percent, of their people report general satisfaction with their jobs. Many managers will interpret this statistic to mean that satisfaction prevails and all is well. But someone will inevitably ask, "Shouldn't they *all* be satisfied? What are we doing wrong?" Someone else will ask, "What difference does it make to your year-end bottom line? None, I'd guess." Another will ask, "I wonder *what* they are dissatisfied about; maybe we need their ideas about some things that should be changed." In short, the interpretations may require assumptions and speculations. Many of the questions that will arise can be clarified by a more sophisticated look at the data. An experienced interpreter of survey findings, for example, might be able to point out that job satisfaction rates generally run a little higher than 85 percent, that job satisfaction—at least most of the time—is only weakly associated with productivity but is usually a factor in absences and turnover, that some dissatisfaction is inevitable and probably not a bad thing, provided it is a transient condition, with few people persistently and chronically dissatisfied.

Beyond such direct reading and interpretation of the survey news about one's organization, several further steps can be taken if the survey is well designed: (1) comparison among unlike or contrasting groups within the organization; (2) comparison with like groups—the same organization at an earlier time or other organizations; and (3) testing the meaning of the data against certain criteria, perhaps "outcomes" that represent the organization's values and goals, or other correlates of some organizational significance.

Comparing unlike groups

Ordinarily an organizational survey covers enough respondents of different kinds and in different parts of the organization to allow useful analytic comparisons. To pursue the job satisfaction illustration, one can examine the data set to determine whether dissatisfaction is higher in certain departments, among women or men, among younger or older employees, among low-, medium-, or high-level managers, or among employees who have spent a short or a long time in their present jobs. The possibilities are many. The patterns of association with demographic, organizational, and personal characteristics will often clarify what dissatisfaction means in the organization and suggest whether corrective steps are needed.

The same interpretive strategy can be applied to matters that may be of more importance to the organization than employee satisfaction. Suppose that a rather large number of people report that they have important skills and abilities that are not being used in their present jobs. No doubt some are overestimating the value of their unused skills, but the question arises whether such underutilization (certainly very costly) is distributed generally or is concentrated in certain organizational units or certain categories of employees.

One large organization, for example, found that nearly half of its people in technical positions felt that they had little or no chance to use their best skills. Comparison showed that this view was disproportionately reported by employees who were relatively young, had been recruited from universities during the last few years, and were employed in units other than research-and-development (R & D) and general business-management functions. Further, a comparatively large proportion of them felt their promotional opportunities were limited and they were considering a move to some other employer. The managers had known that there was some disaffection among these employees, but its strength surprised them. They wanted some turnover (those who left often joined customer firms), but felt they were at risk of losing too many and perhaps the best ones. As a result of the survey, the firm reconsidered its recruitment program and introduced a fast promotion program and more challenging jobs for a limited number of the more promising young employees.

Some users of survey data begin with a routine scan with an array of demographic, positional, and attitudinal variables to define subpopulations of interest. This produces a condensed summary showing which subgroups are significantly off standard in comparison with the firm-wide baseline or average responses. Such a procedure is unguided by theory or purpose, and risks turning up some information that will prove trivial upon examination, but it can uncover unanticipated problems or the absence of anticipated problems.

Comparing like groups

Users of organizational survey data often wish for some external norms that would help them evaluate their own survey results. How do we compare with other organizations? With other firms like ours? Such comparisons are a sensible idea and sometimes a practical one as well. While there is little reason to assume that the prevailing norm is optimum or a suitable standard for the organization in question, still it can be useful to know whether survey results are typical or unusually high or low.

Two conditions must be met if such comparisons are to be valid. First, one has to use an interview schedule or questionnaire that is at least partly standardized—that is, one that has been used in other organizations. Second, one has to have access to the survey results from other organizations, along with enough information to allow judgments about their comparability.

Access to appropriate data from other organizations is not always easy and not always useful, but should be considered as part of the early planning. A large multi-unit organization with a continuing survey program is likely to maintain a central data bank allowing comparison of the results for any unit with the norms from other similar units in the firm. Some service firms and agencies that have conducted surveys in diverse organizations maintain data banks that may make it possible to compare one's own data with those of other (unidentified) organizations of similar character. There are also a few public data banks from national sample surveys, cutting across all types of employment, which potentially allow comparisons based upon specific categories of employees—for example, secretaries, factory production workers, managers, teachers, and the like. In addition, members of some industry associations have agreed to use a common survey procedure and to pool their results, without member identification, to establish shared industry norms.

When planning such comparisons outside of one's own organization, it is essential to locate the source and arrange access in advance. It is also necessary to accept all or much of the standard instrument, sacrificing the flexibility to design an instrument tailored to local issues and conditions. As always, costs and benefits need to be weighed. The anticipated benefits are usually simple: to get a fix on whether one's own organization is roughly typical or significantly off standard. The interpretations often are not straightforward, as one has to assume that the compared organizations are really similar, without unique conditions that explain the differences that are found.

The most informative comparison, when feasible, is between the results of the current survey and those of an earlier survey of the same organization, using the same instrument. This comparison allows detection of trends of change. Managers are often more concerned about where their organization is going than about where it is now. Thus organizations are making increasing use of periodic surveys—say at intervals of two or three years—to monitor progress toward, or away from, their preferred organizational conditions.

Impact analysis and diagnosis

The foregoing approaches to the interpretation of survey results rest upon normative judgments and group comparisons. They invite and inform decisions about what issues to attend to, and they can identify some of the conditions that pertain to choosing a course of action. In many cases, this is sufficient. However, the survey method of inquiry also allows analyses directed to selected issues and designed to guide actions and policy changes. The procedures involve a multifactor analysis of the conditions associated with some valued criterion.

For example, one firm took pride in its salary program for middle-level managers, which emphasized individualized salary increases rather than across-the-board scaled increases, large differentials in salary increases based on merit, and a policy of confidentiality among peers about salaries. The program would be judged successful if two criteria were met: if organization members expected pay keyed to performance and if they were satisfied with their own salary levels. A survey asked, among other things, how satisfied each respondent was with the amount of his or her salary and with its fairness relative to the salary levels of others in the firm. It was expected that dissatisfaction would be limited to people who earned less than others of similar age, service, and rank. Analysis showed, however, that some well-salaried "high flyers" were also discontented.

A dozen possible explanatory variables were checked out singly and in various combinations; one stood out as a significant correlate of dissatisfaction that seemed to have no offsetting gain or constraint. This factor was the confidentiality policy, which apparently was being honored in some departments but not in others. Respondents who reported "knowing the salaries of most of the people in [their] group" tended strongly to be more satisfied with their own pay and with the equity of the salary determination system; this tendency was not related to individual salary level or work-group size, function, or average salary. It appeared that the effect of the confidentiality policy was the opposite of what the firm had intended. This problem could not have been discovered by direct inquiry or by debate among policy makers. The firm declared an "open information" policy and instructed the managers accordingly.

If survey data are to be used for such an impact analysis, one must ensure that the survey instrument contains questions that allow a reasonably inclusive analytic resolution of the issue. To ask the optimum questions, however, one should know in advance what variables are likely to be pertinent. Most survey designers are able to escape from this circularity to some extent. The issue is probably recognized as an issue because people on the scene have different ideas about it, which in turn suggest aspects of the issue that should be incorporated in the survey instrument. Many of the issues that are likely to arise have been researched by others or debated in print, and these sources can be used to help formulate an appropriate set of questions.

The criterion examined in an impact analysis can be almost any organizational state or outcome thought to be important, so long as it is variable (not a constant) within the organization and so long as it can be measured with some degree of accuracy. The issue may refer to individual employees, provided that the criterion can be measured for individuals and linked with their survey data, or provided it can refer to work groups, organizational units, or critical events. Impact analyses have been done to clarify such questions as the following: Why do some employees fail to attain the work effort and added pay that are available under an incentive pay system? What are the characteristics of work groups with low (or high) absence rates? How do employees in different categories weigh the trade-offs in a choice between more pay and an improved fringe benefit? Are the new CRT (cathode ray tube) work stations more or less stressful than those used in the old system?

Such analyses are likely to require some fairly sophisticated statistical and theoretical competence. It is generally necessary to control for personal and situational factors that might otherwise leave the results ambiguous, and perhaps to test for data quality. Often multivariate-analysis strategies are required to treat interacting factors simultaneously. This work is not for the novice. Professional help is needed.

Interpreting subjective measures

Users of organizational surveys, especially if inexperienced, are often skeptical about the accuracy and validity of survey data. Attitudes are unstable and likely to change, they may argue. There is no point in measuring opinions if the employees are not well informed about the complexities of the issue. Individuals often behave in ways incompatible with their expressed views. Many people seem to have an overall positive or negative mental set that colors their response to all questions. Questions often provide for vague answers, like "many" or "very little," with no reference to hard numbers.

These are grounds for skepticism. Managers should challenge the accuracy and validity of survey data at least as rigorously as they would challenge their other sources of information. The confidence with which managers use their familiar operating and fiscal data is due less to the intrinsic superior quality of the information than to managers' awareness of its limitations and experience in its use. They know that an index of quarterly profit may be as much a construction of art and policy as a report of "true" profit, and that a tally of in-process reject rates is, at best, a soft approximation of current quality problems. Both measures, however, have familiar limitations, and both serve reasonably well for detecting trends or unsatisfactory conditions.

In some respects, the quality of survey data can be assessed statistically. Professional and frequent users of such information routinely conduct checks for reliability, stability, concurrent validity, predictive validity, and internal consistency of response. The occasional user is not likely to undertake such tests, but will rely upon the counsel of someone who is familiar with the pitfalls, the ways of maximizing reliability, and the like.

Aside from the technology of data quality (which always shows the measures to be less than perfect and occasionally shows them to be unusable), some considerations of a conceptual sort may be useful. One point is statistical: while any individual respondent's report of opinion of fact may be exaggerated or distorted in some individualistic way (i.e., unreliable), the aggregation of reports from similar respondents can average out some of the error to produce a measure for the population that is highly reliable. Another issue has to do with interpretation: employees may hold attitudes and opinions that are uninformed, irrational, or naïve (or in other ways unlike those of the interpreter); still, these attitudes are the basis upon which people act. The attitude is a useful fact in itself, quite apart from its objective correctness. The stability of attitudes and opinions is highly variable. Many are highly resistant to change. In other cases, when there is little initial basis for taking a view when conditions change or new information is received, then attitudes do change—as anyone should know from following the presidential-election polls. The absence of anchored equal-interval scales (as in the case of dollars, linear feet, or pounds) can be distressing at first, but the experienced user of survey data soon learns that scales of variation (i.e., deviations from a norm or mean) work well when the interpretations rest upon relationships among measures more than upon their absolute scale values. There can be no zero point on a scale of employees' trust of top management, although there may be a neutral point meaning "no opinion."

Not all components of an organizational survey are subjective. Employee respondents may answer queries in several different roles: as subjects of inquiry (What is your opinion?), as part of a panel of expert observers (How frequently is the work in your area interrupted by parts-delivery failure?), or as sole sources of the objective facts (How do you usually get to work—on foot, personal auto, car pool, or public transportation?). The preference for objective information should depend entirely on the requirements of the issue addressed, not on a belief that objective data are inherently more reliable, more valid, or more useful. For example, in an inquiry about pay, it may be useful to know objectively how much the respondent is paid, but for some purposes it is more important to know whether the respondent regards the pay as "sufficient for your normal personal and family expenses." The two measures will be equally accurate, but will convey information that is different in meaning and possibly uncorrelated.

PLANNING A SURVEY: ACHIEVING AN INTEGRATED PLAN

A plan for an organizational survey has many component parts, each offering some choice among alternatives. Moreover, each organization offers distinctive constraints and opportunities. It would appear, in principle, that the variations are endless and the choice points very numerous.

In practice, matters are simpler. First, because of the interdependence of design features, a few key choices will preclude many of the related options that exist in theory and will make many of the remaining consequent

choices virtually self-determining. Second, not all options are really open to any given organization, for some constraints will arise from its own history, resources of time and money, readiness to handle information of an unfamiliar kind, and so on.

The starting point, of course, is to formulate some conception of purpose that might be served by an organizational survey. These purposes may be related to specific difficulties or problems that press for resolution. They may arise from speculations about trends and prospective future problems, or from an interest in an overview appraisal of the health of the organization. Thus, depending on the purpose to be served, one might choose a survey narrowly focused upon selected current issues, one that allows in-depth treatment of some aspects of organizational life that are of longer-range concern, or one that asks broadly, "How are we doing?". A survey can be tailored to the purpose, but the purpose must be known and must be acknowledged by those who will use the results. This self-evident truth is often overlooked, and then the survey is unlikely to match the needs, expectations, and capabilities of the users.

Design elements

The main elements in the technical design of a survey have already been mentioned: topical coverage, form of instrumentation, selection of samples or targeted categories of respondents, advanced planning for an analysis and reporting procedure, and preparation of the prospective users for their work of interpretation and action.

These elements are so interdependent that they have to be considered as a set, not as separate choices. For example, if the purpose is to get a broad reading of the conditions of the organization compared with external standards or norms, then the instrumentation should be a standard one; participative design is precluded; coverage should be broad, even if some depth of topical coverage must be forfeited; the respondents should be a representative or total sample of organization members; the analysis and reporting plan will be relatively simple and must conform to that established by the external source of norms; sophisticated analysis of specific issues is probably precluded; and so on.

Clearly some trade-offs must be made among design features. Each feature establishes some requirements, and forfeits some advantages, with respect to others. There is no objectively ideal or optimum design that fits all organizations. It is possible, however, to choose the best design for a particular set of priorities, values, or preferences. Ordinarily two or three (perhaps more) alternative overall designs are reviewed before a choice is made.

Fit to context

Quite independent of the technical design features is the question of fit to the particular organization. Both constraints and opportunties must usually be recognized. For example, if there is some doubt whether employees have full confidence in the protection of their anonymity or in the considered use of the survey results, some risky topics will probably be left untreated and no attempt will be made to link the survey returns to individual data of record. Similarly, if an earlier survey has been conducted in the same organization, there will be an opportunity to assess trends of change by replicating the earlier design in whole or in part. If there are many work groups of similar function but highly variable performance (a kind of natural experiment), then attention may turn to designing the technical features of the survey to allow examination in depth of the causes of higher and lower performance. All organizations offer some constraints and opportunities of such kinds.

Organizational linkages

An important early strategic choice has to do with the use of the survey in the organization. At one extreme, the survey may be regarded as a top-management activity primarily for informing the upper levels of management and selected staff groups. Alternatively, the survey may be embedded in the overall organization's review and decision-making system (Passmore and Friedlander 1978). Of course, intermediate approaches are also possible. The position taken on this issue has important implications for planning and the use of the survey results. Consider this example: a firm had a history of being relatively open with information and committed to engaging employees in matters that concerned them. A steering committee was formed to plan a survey—a rather large group, with half of the members nominated by the three unions and half by the management. External consultants worked with the steering committee to formulate and adapt the plans. A standard questionnaire was used, with numerous amendments and additions developed by the committee. It was agreed in advance that a number of smaller issue-oriented task groups would be formed to review the survey results (along with any other available and relevant information) and to recommend appropriate actions. The management reserved the right to accept or reject the recommendations, but plainly was predisposed to accept them unless there were strong contrary factors. The survey analysis and reporting were planned to be responsive to the special requirements of the various task groups, each of which could request additional analytic steps as their understanding of their task developed. Of the dozen task groups, a few reported that they had no recommendations to offer. The others, over a time span of eighteen months, produced a number of acceptable proposals for changes in the firm's policies and practices, including a successful major reorganization of one work unit.

Such an approach is not feasible or not desired in many organizations. But it is one way to get good value from an organizational survey.

REFERENCES

Backstrom, C. H., and G. Hursh-Cesar. 1981. *Survey Research.* New York: Wiley.

Belson, W. A. 1981. *The Design and Understanding of Survey Questions.* Aldershot, England: Gower Press.

Berdie, D., and J. Anderson. 1974. *Questionnaires: Design and Use.* Metuchen, N.J.: The Scarecrow Press.

Cammann, C., M. Fichman, G. Jenkins, Jr., and J. Klesh. 1983. "Assessing the Attitudes and Perceptions of Organizational Members." In *Assessing Organizational Change,* ed. S. E. Seashore et al. New York: Wiley.

Dodd, W. E., and M. L. Pesci. 1977. "Managing Morale Through Survey Feedback." *Business Horizons* (June).

Dunham, R. B., and F. J. Smith. 1979. *Organizational Surveys.* Glenview, Ill.: Scott, Foresman.

Dunham, R. B., F. J. Smith, and R. S. Blackburn. 1977. "Vali-

dation of the Index of Organizational Reactions with the JDI, MSQ and Faces Scales." *Academy of Management Journal* 20:420–32.

Gorden, R. 1969. *Interviewing: Strategy, Techniques, and Tactics.* Homewood, Ill.: Dorsey Press.

Passmore, W., and C. Friedlander. 1978. "An Action-Research Program for Increasing Employee Involvement in Problem Solving." *Administrative Science Quarterly* 27, no. 3: 343–62.

Rickards, T., and J. Bessant. 1980. "A Mirror for Change: Survey Feedback Experiences." *Leadership and Organizational Development Journal* 1:10–14.

Seashore, S. E. 1976. "Assessing the Quality of Working Life: The U.S. Experience." *Labour and Society* 1, no. 2:69–79.

Seashore, S. E., E. E. Lawler, P. H. Mirvis, and C. Cammann.

1983. *Assessing Organizational Change: A Guide to Methods, Measures and Practice.* New York: Wiley.

Sirota, D. 1974. "Why Managers Don't Use Attitude Survey Results." In Harmonds Worth, *Behavioral Science in Management*, ed. S. W. Gellerman. England: Penguin Books.

Smith, P. C., L. M. Kendall, and C. L. Hulin. 1969. *The Measurement of Satisfaction in Work and Retirement.* Chicago: Rand McNally.

Sonquist, J., and W. Dunkelberg. 1977. *Survey and Opinion Research: Procedures for Processing and Analysis.* Englewood Cliffs, N.J.: Prentice-Hall.

Stone, E. 1978. *Research Methods in Organizational Behavior.* Santa Monica, Calif.: Goodyear.

Sudman, S., and N. M. Bradburn. 1982. *Asking Questions: A Practical Guide to Questionnaire Design.* San Francisco: Jossey-Bass.

11

Individuals and careers

EDGAR H. SCHEIN

INTRODUCTION

The word *career* has many different connotations. Sometimes we attribute careers only to people who have a profession or whose occupational life is well structured and involves steady advancement. I prefer to use the word somewhat more broadly. All people develop some kind of picture of their work life and their own role in it. It is this "internal career" that I wish to explore.

This concept should be distinguished from other uses of the word *career* (Van Maanen and Schein 1977; Driver 1982). For example, the specific steps prescribed for progress through an occupation or an organization (Dalton, Thompson, and Price 1977) represent an "external career." The doctor has to go through medical school, internship, residency, and speciality board examinations. In some organizations the general manager must go through several business functions, gain experience in supervising people, take on a functional management job, and rotate through the international division before achieving a high-level division-head position. Some organizations talk of career paths, which define the necessary or at least desirable steps for the individual to take en route to a desired job (Walker 1980).

The word *career* also has some negative connotations. It can imply that the individual is too much involved in work or takes things too seriously ("Don't make

a career out of it"). One who jockeys for position may be accused of "careerism." Especially in Communist societies, "careerism" is viewed as undesirable because it implies too much personal ambition (Schein 1975).

In occupational psychology attempts have been made to predict career outcomes on the basis of various personal factors (Osipow 1973). These studies have usually found only small correlations between the independent variable and type of occupation entered or level of success attained, as measured by rank or money earned. A more useful approach may be to examine the internal career from a dynamic evolutionary perspective. In this chapter, after outlining some of the major stages of the career and some of the ways career progress can be measured, I describe in some detail the concept of the "career anchor," the self-image that a person develops around his or her career, which both guides and constrains career decisions. The implications of the career-anchor concept for human-resource management will be explored from the perspectives of the individual and the enterprise manager.

MAJOR STAGES OF THE CAREER

From the individual point of view, the career comprises a series of psychologically meaningful units. The length of time associated with each stage will vary immensely according to the occupation and the individual within it. The stages discussed here are an adaptation and elaboration of the major stages first identified by Super (1957)

This is an original paper prepared for this book. No parts of it may be reproduced without the written permission of the author. The research on which the paper is based was supported by the Office of Naval Research, Psychological Sciences Division (Code 452), Organizational Effectiveness Research, ONR, Arlington, Virginia, 22217, under Contract N00014-80-C0905, NR 170-911.

and described in detail in *Career Dynamics* (Schein 1978).

Stage 1. Growth, Fantasy, Exploration   The period when an occupation is merely thought about and a career has little meaning beyond occupational stereotypes and vague criteria of success. The person at this stage prepares to enter the necessary educational process for the chosen occupation.

Stage 2. Education and Training   Some occupations require minimal training, others a very elaborate process.

Stage 3. Entry into the World of Work   For most people, regardless of their preparation, this is a time of reality shock and major adjustment problems as they learn about the realities of work and their own reactions to it. Major personal learning begins at this point, leading to the emergence of an occupational self-concept.

Stage 4. Basic Training, Socialization   The length of this period will also vary immensely by occupation, organization, complexity of the work, and so on. Because the organization now begins to make some real demands on the individual, this stage involves significant personal learning.

Stage 5. Gaining Membership   At some point, individuals recognize, through the kinds of assignments they have been given, that they have passed beyond the trainee stage and have been accepted as full contributors. They can now develop meaningful images of themselves as members of the occupation or organization. Motives and values are clarified as they reflect on their own responses to different challenging situations. They begin to have a sense of their talents, strengths, and weaknesses.

Stage 6. Gaining of Tenure, Permanent Membership   Somewhere in the first five to ten years of the career, most organizations and occupations make a "tenure" decision, which tells the individual whether he or she can count on a long-run future in the organization. Tenure may be granted either explicitly or symbolically, with the proviso, of course, that tenure exists only so long as a job exists.

Mid-Career Crisis, Reassessment   There is mounting evidence that most people go through some kind of difficult self-reassessment when they are well into their career, asking themselves questions about their initial choice ("Have I entered the right career?"), their level of attainment ("Have I accomplished all I hoped to?" "What have I accomplished and was it worth the sacrifices?"), and their future ("Should I continue or make a change?" "What do I want to do with the rest of my life, and how does my work fit into it?") (Jacques 1965; Levinson et al. 1978; Vaillant 1978; Osherson 1980; Gould 1978).

Stage 7. Maintaining Momentum, Regaining It, or Leveling Off   The insights emerging from reassessment create a basis for deciding how to pursue the remainder of the career. At this stage each person develops a personal solution that will guide his or her next steps.

Stage 8. Disengagement   Eventually, the person slows down, becomes less involved, and begins to prepare for retirement. For some people, preparation takes the form of denial. That is, they deal with the tension of potential retirement by aggressively continuing business as usual and evading the attempts of others to get them involved in preparation for the next stage.

Stage 9. Retirement   Whether or not the individual has prepared, inevitably there will come a time when the organization or occupation no longer makes a meaningful role available. What happens to occupational self-image as the individual adjusts to the loss of this role is, of course, a major issue to be studied. Some people retire early because the occupation encourages it (e.g., the military or professional sports), or because they want to and have the opportunity to develop a "second career" in another occupation (Osherson 1980).

These nine stages provide a kind of internal timetable for every person, but it is important to recognize that the stages can be long or short, can repeat themselves if the person moves from one career to another, and are not related in any necessary fashion to age. Within a particular occupation, stages may be closely correlated with age, but a doctor, a clerk, a manager, a storekeeper, an engineer, and a consultant may reach a given stage at very different ages.

CAREER MOVEMENT, PROGRESS, OR SUCCESS

The standards by which an individual measures his or her own success may be quite different from those employed by another person or by society at large. In fact, as we shall see below, the subjective definition of success very much reflects the individual's career anchor or subjective career image. However, all progress can be measured along three basic dimensions or movements within an organization or occupation (Schein 1971, 1978; Van Maanen and Schein 1979).

Cross-functional movement: growth in abilities and skills

As we move into our careers, we change in terms of what we are able to do and how well we are able to do it. Such development may be the result of our own efforts or may depend on training opportunities provided by our employer or our profession. This kind of movement corresponds to cross-functional rotation within an organization or formal training that leads to a change in the work an individual does.

For most people, movement along this dimension is one measure of their success. Some recent developments in work redesign include creative compensation schemes that reward the worker according to the number of skills learned in a given job setting (Lawler 1981).

Movement up

In all occupations and organizations, there is some kind of hierarchy, some system of ranks or titles by which the individual's progress can be judged. In this sense, the successful person reaches or passes the level to which he or she aspires.

Again, others' judgments may differ from the individual's. An entrepreneur who has made $2 million told me he felt like a failure because his friends all own $300-million companies. Another person who has leveled off in middle management feels very successful because he has accomplished so much more than his father.

Without knowing the level of aspiration, one cannot judge subjective feelings of success. On the other hand, level of aspiration itself will be influenced by how society defines success, so there is likely to be some correlation between aspirations and external criteria. But the external criteria will be those relevant within a given occupation, not just those of society as a whole. Money may be a very general indicator of success in the United States, but for engineers the number of patents may be more important. Professors may care about the prestige of their university and their fame among colleagues; managers, about the size of the budget for which they are responsible. To understand the individual's success criteria and self-assessment, the appropriate reference group is the one in which that individual would place himself or herself.

Movement "in": attaining influence and power

One of the most important criteria of success is the individual's sense of how far he or she has penetrated the inner core of an organization or occupation. Such penetration is often correlated with hierarchical move-

ment, but may be achieved independently—for example, by a leveled-off employee who commands a strong "insider" position by virtue of seniority and personality, is consulted by high-ranking members of the organization, and thus can influence policy even from a low-ranked position. Many technical people enjoy this kind of influence in organizations; often secretaries have power and influence far beyond their formal position, resulting from informal contacts built up outside of work over the years (Dalton 1959).

Because such movement is invisible, it is difficult to judge its impact. Without asking the question directly, for example, one might have no idea that a certain person felt very successful because of his sense of being in the inner circle and having influence. This success criterion occasionally conflicts with movement upward, leading to such anomalies as the person who refuses a promotion because it would mean abandoning a carefully built up network of contacts.

THE DEVELOPMENT OF A CAREER ANCHOR

As the career progresses, and especially in stages 4, 5, and 6, described previously, every person develops a self-concept that embraces some explicit answers to the questions

1. What are my talents, skills, areas of competence? What are my strengths and what are my weaknesses?
2. What are my main motives, drives, goals in life? What am I after?
3. What are my values, the main criteria by which I judge what I am doing? Am I in the right kind of organization or job? How good do I feel about what I am doing?

This self-concept builds on whatever insight individuals have acquired from the experiences of their youth and education, but, by definition, no mature self-concept is possible until they have had enough occupational experience to know what their talents, motives, and values really are. And such learning may take anywhere from one to ten years or more of actual work experience.

If the person has many varied experiences and gets meaningful feedback in each, a self-concept will develop more quickly. If he or she has only a few jobs in the early years of the career or obtains minimal feedback, it may take longer.

Talents, motives, and values become intertwined as

we learn to be better at those things that we value and are motivated to do, and at the same time, learn to value and be motivated by the things we are good at. We also gradually learn to avoid things we do not do well, though without clear feedback we may cling to illusions about ourselves that set us up for repeated failure. If we have a talent but clearly no motivation to pursue it, the talent may gradually atrophy—yet often a new challenge can reveal latent talents that had simply not had an opportunity to appear earlier.

People differ in whether it is their talents, their motives, or their values that initially dominate their self-concept and provide a central career theme. As time goes on, however, our need for congruence makes us seek consistency and integration among the different elements of the self-concept. How is this consistency learned?

When people first enter the world of work they have many ambitions, hopes, fears, and illusions but relatively little good information about themselves, especially about their abilities and talents. Through testing and counseling they can get an idea of their interests, motives, and values, and of their intellectual and motor skills, but they cannot really determine how good they will be at a certain kind of work or how they will react to it emotionally.

This difficulty is particularly acute in the occupation of "management," because of the difficulty of simulating some of its key skills and abilities. Until one actually feels the responsibility of committing large sums of money, of hiring and firing people, of saying "no" to a valued subordinate, one cannot tell whether one will be able to do it or, even more important, whether one will like doing it.

The early years in an occupation are thus a crucial time of learning—both about the occupation or organization and about oneself in relation to the demands of the job. This process is often painful and full of surprises because of the misconceptions that people typically bring to their early work situations. Many of our dreams about ourselves and our work may have to be abandoned, for "reality shock" is one of the commonest phenomena observed in all occupations in the early years (Hughes 1958).

As people accumulate work experience, they have an opportunity to make choices, and it is from those choices that they begin to learn what is really important to them. Dominant themes emerge: a critical skill or ability that one really wants to exercise, an important need one has discovered, a crucial value that dominates one's orientation toward life. One may have known about these elements in a vague way, but until they have been tested in actual life experience, one does not know how important they are and how a given tal-

ent, motive, or value relates in a subjective hierarchy to other elements of the total personality.

With the accumulation of work experience and feedback come clarification and insight, which provide a basis for more rational and managed career decisions. Our self-concept begins to function more and more as a guidance system, in the sense of constraining career choices. We begin to have a sense of what is "me" and what is "not me." And this knowledge keeps us on course. In reviewing their career choices, people often talk of being "pulled back" to something if they have strayed, or figuring out what they "really want to do," or "finding themselves."

The career anchor, as defined here, is *that element in our self-concept that we will not give up, even if forced to make a difficult choice.* People typically manage to fulfill a broad range of needs through their careers, but those needs are not all equally important. If we cannot meet all our needs, it is important to know which ones have highest priority.

External constraints beyond the control of the individual may thwart the career anchor temporarily. For example, economic circumstances or illness in the family could prevent a person from pursuing an occupation consistent with his self-image. If interviewed, he would explain that what he is currently doing is "not really me, not really what I would like to be doing or am capable of doing." How do we know these are not just idle illusions talking? Because many people have actualized their self-concept the moment the external constraint was lifted.

The career anchor is the self-image, and it can remain remarkably stable even if there is no opportunity whatsoever to exercise it, as in the case of the starving artist who is driving a cab. The self-image will change if the person obtains systematic experience and feedback that make it impossible to maintain an illusion—in the case of the artist, for example, repeated failures to be able to create artistically even to one's own satisfaction. But the self-image may not change if the constraint is seen as merely external and temporary.

Early in his or her career, each person confronts the issue of how to integrate work, family, and personal priorities (Bailyn 1978; Evans and Bartolome 1980). Some will decide to deemphasize work, considering it merely instrumental to survival. Their experience is shaped primarily by what we might call a "life anchor." For our present discussion, we will focus on those people for whom work is important enough to warrant thinking in terms of career anchors. But as we will see, for many younger people the concept of "life anchor" makes more sense, and many older people significantly reassess their career commitments.

ORIGIN OF THE CAREER-ANCHOR CONCEPT

The concept of the career anchor grew out of a study that began in the early 1960s of managerial careers. To understand better how managerial careers evolved, and especially how people learned the values and procedures of their employing organizations, I undertook a longitudinal study of forty-four alumni of the Sloan School of Management at Massachusetts Institute of Technology (Schein 1975, 1978). The initial interviews and surveys of values and attitudes were conducted in 1961, 1962, and 1963, while the respondents were second-year students in the two-year master's program. All of them were interviewed at their place of work six months after graduation and again one year after graduation from MIT.

These interviews revealed a great deal about the problems of making the transition from school to work, the extensive reality shock that most graduates experienced as they faced the human problems of working in organizations, and the kinds of socialization processes that organizations employed. Important learning takes place during this first year: the organization learns about the graduate and, more important, the graduate learns not only about the organization but about himself.

This process of self-learning continued during the early career years, as we learned from a set of questionnaires completed five years after graduation and follow-up interviews conducted when alumni were approximately ten to twelve years into their careers. In these 1973 interviews, I elicited a detailed chronological career history, asking respondents not only to identify key choices and events, but also to speculate why they had occurred and how they felt about each change.

The actual events of the career histories proved to be highly variable. But the reasons that respondents gave for their actions and the pattern of their feelings about events revealed great regularities and themes of which the individual had often been unaware. Such themes reflected a growing sense of self— "This is me, and that is not me" —based upon the learning of the early years. I came to call this concept of self the career anchor.

TYPES OF CAREER ANCHORS

Based on this longitudinal study and subsequent career-history interviews of several hundred people in various career stages, several types of career anchors can be identified. Some of the career anchors (we identified) reflect basic issues in any career. For example, we must all re-

solve the question of *autonomy*: to what extent will we sacrifice independence for security and stability; in effect, letting our occupation and/or organization determine our career? A second issue has to do with the individual's definition of his or her basic abilities. Over time, a person may become more and more of a *technical* or *functional specialist* in some particular area, or may move increasingly toward administration, working with people, and *general management*, where a complex combination of motives, talents, and skills is the key to effective performance.

On both of these dimensions, because of the way in which the external career is structured in most organizations, the individual is typically forced to make a clear-cut choice (Maccoby 1976; Zaleznik et al. 1970). The more one seeks autonomy, the more one has to sacrifice security and stability; the more one seeks general management, the more one has to give up exercising one's technical or functional competence. For example, managers who try to cling to their technical competence are characteristically less effective in their general-manager role.

Our original sample included one other distinctive group of people—those whose overriding needs were to create some new product, service, or organization on their own. We termed their career anchor "entrepreneurial creativity." The more recent career-history studies have revealed that for some people, the focus of their career is *service or dedication to a cause*. For others it seems to be a kind of pure competitive drive, defining all work situations as self-tests that are won or lost against either an absolute standard or an actual competitor. We have adopted the label *pure challenge* as the essence of this anchor.

Affiliation with a powerful organization or identification with an occupation or organization seems to be a central theme for some people, suggesting "identity" as a possible anchor (DeLong 1982). Interviews indicate, however, that this group can be viewed as a variant of the security/stability anchor. Finally, more recent studies have identified a type defined by the belief that it should somehow be possible to integrate work, family, and self-concerns into a coherent life-style; we call this the *life-style* anchor.

Before examining the individual career anchors in detail, we should pause to consider their relative frequency. Table 11.1 shows the results of several studies of alumni, alumnae, and members of certain occupations (Albertini 1982; Anderson and Sommer 1980; Applin 1982; Burnstine 1982; Crowson 1982; Fowble 1982; Grzywacs 1982; Hall and Thomas 1979; Heller 1982; Hopkins 1976; Huser 1980; Janes 1982; Kanto 1982; Liebesny 1980; Senior 1982). The data in each study were

Table 11.1 Career anchor summary percentages for selected groups

Group		Security	Autonomy	Technical/Functional	Managerial	Entrepreneurial	Service	Challenge	Life-style	Un-clear
Managers (N 112)	%	12	3	39	41	4	1	0	0	0
Functional (N 58)	%	19	3	52	14	2	5	0	2	3
Alumni (N 84)	%	17	13	34	21	14	0	0	0	0
Alumnae (N 40)	%	10	5	8	32	12	8	0	5	20
Consultants (N 40)	%	2	20	8	15	2	12	20	8	13

Note: The managerial group includes 28 high-level program managers in the aerospace industry who might have been grouped with the functional group but for their level. If they are grouped with the functional group it exaggerates the differences in the table even more.

gathered by means of detailed biographical interviews. The results show a striking variability. Most of the anchor types occur in each group, but we also see biases that reflect the career path.

For example, in the group that has already or is clearly about to reach general management positions, we find, as expected, a preponderance of managerial anchors and virtually no autonomy or entrepreneurially anchored people. Perhaps more surprising is that this group also includes a good many people who are anchored in their technical/functional area. We might hypothesize that such people either would be unhappy in their managerial roles or would actually not be performing those roles, despite their job titles. We have seen both types in interviews: some who were successful general managers but never enjoyed the role and were happy to be promoted to a corporate level where they could again practice their speciality, and others who never made the adjustment and therefore did not perform the generalist role effectively. The "functional" group, which includes bank vice-presidents, data-processing managers, and financial managers, has a higher percentage of people anchored in their technical/functional speciality and relatively few whose anchors are managerial.

If we look at the more heterogeneous samples of male and female graduates, we notice first of all that the percentage of autonomy and entrepreneurial anchors is higher, as might be expected. Many of these people end up outside of traditional organizations and thus would not be found on typical surveys done in large organizations.

The men and women differ in some important ways. Alumnae are spread over more categories; more of them are hard to categorize into any one anchor group; more of them are managerially anchored; and noticeably fewer of them are technically/functionally anchored. It is not clear whether these differences are due to gender or to changes in social values, because the female samples were done more recently than some of the male ones.

The autonomy anchor is relatively prominent among the forty high-level management consultants studied. More interesting is the clear emergence in this

group of a new anchor category, *pure challenge*. For many of the consultants, the only thing that mattered about a job was whether it posed a significant, preferably insurmountable, challenge. In some respects their attitude resembles the pure competitive orientation found by Derr (1980) in his U.S. Navy sample. The only real goal of the group he called "warriors" was to prove themselves superior to a respected adversary.

Table 11.1 merges the results of more than a dozen samples, which are described individually in table 11.2. In several cases, a sample consisted entirely of people at a particular rank within a particular organization— yet still showed quite a diversity of career anchors. For example, a group of twenty fourth-level managers in a unit of the Bell System was found to have ten managerially anchored, seven technically/functionally anchored, two autonomy-anchored, and one security-anchored individuals. A group of twenty field-service managers who

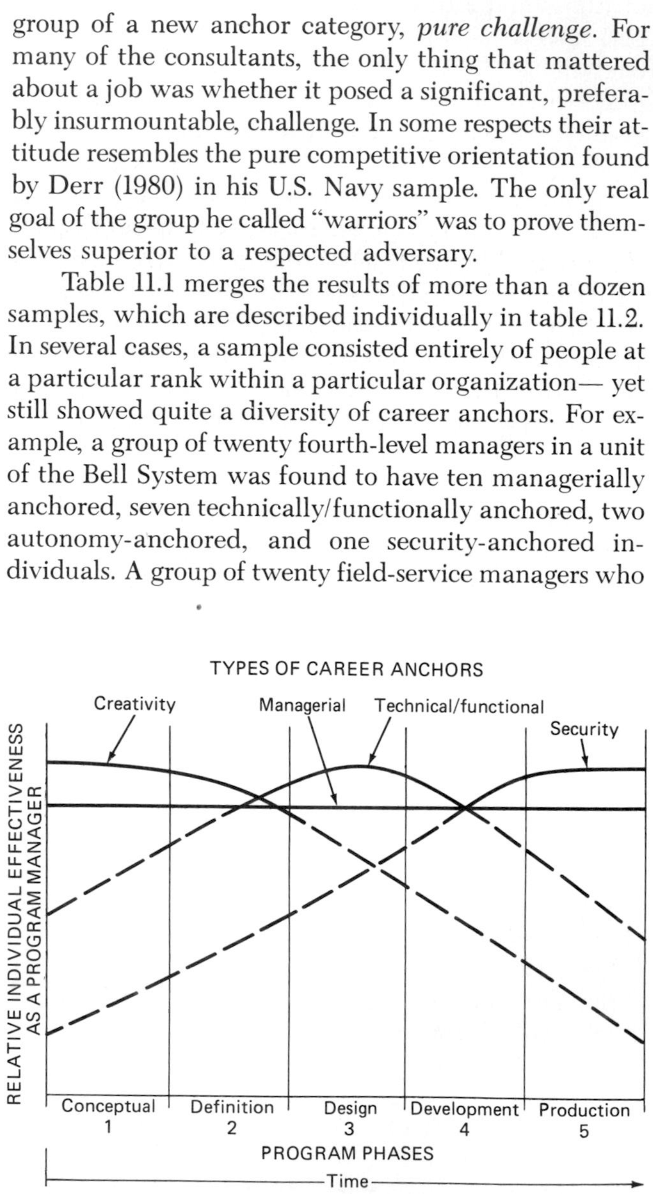

Figure 11.1 Program manager–career anchor model. (Reprinted from G. W. Hall and F. J. Thomas, "The Impact of Career Anchors on the Organizational Development of Program Managers in the Aerospace Industry," Master's thesis [Cambridge, Mass.: MIT Sloan School of Management, 1979], by permission.)

Table 11.2   Frequency of occurrence of different career anchors in different groups

Group studied	Anchor category (percentages)								
	Security	Autonomy	Technical/ functional	Mana-gerial	Entre-preneurial	Service	Challenge	Life-style	Identity
1961, 1962, 1963 Sloan School alumni panel (N 44)	9	16	43	18	14	0	0	0	0
Alumni of Sloan Fellows Program (5–10 years out; N 40)	25	10	25	25	15	0	0	0	0
MIT Senior Executive Program 1976 (N 20)	0	0	70	30	0	0	0	0	0
Sloan School alumnae (5 or more years out, 1980, 1981; N 40)	10	5	8	32	12	8	0	5	20
High potential women, middle managers (5–20 yrs. out; N 20)	0	35	0	35	15	5	0	0	10
Upper-middle managers in one Bell System co. (N 20)	5	10	35	50	0	0	0	0	0
Senior managers in five large companies (N 24)	0	0	42	58	0	0	0	0	0
Field service managers who started in 1969 (N 20)	25	0	10	60	0	5	0	0	0
Aerospace Program managers in five large companies (N 28)	29	4	39	14	14	0	0	0	0
Data-processing professionals in one large company (N 23)	13	0	48	26	4	0	0	0	9
Sloan School graduates in finance jobs (4 yrs. out; N 15)	7	0	67	0	0	20	0	7	0
Female bank vice-presidents in one large bank (5 yrs. out; N20[a])	20	0	35	20	0	5	0	0	0
Senior management consultants in one firm (N 20)	5	30	0	25	0	10	30	0	0
Strategy and management consultants, several companies (N 20)	0	10	15	5	5	15	10	15	25
Physicians who had left traditional medicine to go into management (N 14)	0	36	21	0	29	14	0	0	0

[a]This group included a number of minority members who had come in under affirmative-action programs.

had entered a single company in 1969 and were interviewed in 1982 was found to have twelve managerial, two technical/functional, five security, and one service-oriented individuals.

To illustrate the implications of this diversity for a given organization's career-management system, we should look in more detail at a study of twenty eight program managers in several large aerospace companies (Hall and Thomas 1979). Hall and Thomas postulated that the effectiveness and satisfaction of a program manager would vary according to how well his career anchor matched the requirements of the program phase. Their hypotheses are shown graphically in figure 11.1. During the creation phases of a large program, the more en-

trepreneurially oriented individual should be most effective and satisfied; during the design phase, it should be the technically/functionally anchored ones; and during the production phase, which often requires long periods of repetitive work, it should be the security/stability-anchored ones. Those with managerial anchors should be equally effective across all stages, but not most effective than the perfectly matched ones. Those with autonomy anchors would not work in program management in the first place, hence are not shown.

Interviews partially confirmed the authors' hypotheses. Table 11.3 shows the phases in which managers preferred to work and felt most effective. Though there is

Table 11.3   Percentage of program managers with different career anchors, who are working in different program phases, had prior experience in different phases, and feelings of effectiveness in different phases.

Career anchor		Phase				
		Conc.	Defin.	Design	Devel.	Prod.
1. Currently						
Entrepreneurial	(N 4)	25	50	25	0	0
Technical/functional	(N 11)	0	27	73	55	0[a]
Security	(N 8)	0	0	0	62	87
Manager	(N 4)	25	50	75	75	0
2. Prior experience						
Entrepreneurial	(N 4)	100	100	100	100	0
Technical/functional	(N 11)	100	100	100	100	9
Security	(N 8)	25	62	88	100	100
Manager	(N 4)	100	100	100	100	100
3. Felt most effective in						
Entrepreneurial	(N 4)	100	100	0	0	0
Technical/functional	(N 11)	0	36	100	64	0
Security	(N 8)	0	0	0	62	100
Manager	(N 4)	100	100	100	100	50

Note: Adapted from G. W. Hall and F. J. Thomas, "The Impact of Career Anchors on the Organizational Development of Program Managers in the Aerospace Industry," Master's thesis (Cambridge, Mass.: MIT Sloan School of Management, 1976), by permission.
[a]Numbers in a given row do not add up to 100 percent because managers were allowed to mention more than one phase in which they had worked, were working, and/or felt most effective. One manager with an autonomy anchor is not listed in the table.

some overlap, managers tended to report greater effectiveness and satisfaction in the phase most congruent with their anchor. Senior management in these companies recognized the need to match individual style and skill with job requirements, though they did not have the same kinds of labels for different types of program managers. What this line of research suggests is that mismatches between career anchors and job requirements not only lead to individual dissatisfaction but to poor job performance.

MANAGERIAL IMPLICATIONS OF CAREER-ANCHOR VARIETIES

We have seen that career occupants differ in their talents, needs, and values. Now we should look at each of the career-anchor types in some detail. What are these various kinds of people looking for in their careers, and what does this mean to the employing organization? How should each type be managed, motivated, and rewarded?

Security/stability/organizational identity as a career anchor

Some people feel a strong need to organize their careers in such a way that they will feel safe and secure, future events will be predictable, and they can relax in the knowledge that they have "made it." Everyone needs some degree of security and stability, and financial security can be particularly important at certain stages of life—when one is raising and educating a family, for example, or approaching retirement. But for some people, security, stability, and identification with a larger organizational unit become an overriding concern, which guides and constrains all major career decisions.

We have identified at least two kinds of people whose careers are anchored in security concerns. One kind becomes strongly identified with a given organization, welcomes the "golden handcuffs," and turns over all responsibility for career management to the employer. In exchange for tenure, these people will loyally do as they are told, letting the employer determine how much they travel, where they live, how often they switch assignments, and so on.

Another kind of security-oriented person links himself or herself to a particular geographic area, putting down roots in the community, investing in a house and a stable life-style. People of this type may sacrifice their standard of living to some degree, moving from one company to another if necessary to remain in one area.

TYPE OF WORK

The security-anchored person prefers stable, predictable work and is more concerned about the context of the work than the nature of the work itself (Katz and Van Maanen 1976; Hackman and Oldham 1980). Job enrichment, job challenge, and other intrinsic motivational tools would matter less than extrinsic factors such as improved pay, working conditions, and benefits. Nevertheless, highly talented members of this group may move to fairly high-ranking managerial or functional jobs within organizations. For example, in the group of aerospace managers studied by Hall and Thomas, it was the security anchored ones who were seen by themselves and their companies as best suited for the manufacturing phase of large programs.

Less talented, security-oriented people may level off in middle-level managerial or functional jobs and gradually become less involved in their work. If they get the security they are seeking, they will be content with the level they have attained. For some, that level will fulfill their ambition, especially if they have exceeded the socioeconomic level of their own parents; they feel quite successful even though they know others would not agree. They may feel guilty for not having more ambition, but we should not assume that everyone continues to want to rise in the organization. If they have unused talents, they may prefer to express them through activities unrelated to work.

PAY AND BENEFITS

The person anchored in security/stability prefers to be paid in steady predictable increments based on length of service. Such a person would prefer benefit packages that emphasize insurance and retirement programs.

PROMOTION SYSTEM

This kind of person prefers a seniority-based promotion system, and would probably welcome a published grade or rank system that spells out how long one must serve in any given grade before promotion. Obviously, he or she would welcome a formal tenure system such as exists in schools and universities.

TYPE OF RECOGNITION

The security-oriented person wants to be recognized for his or her loyalty and steady performance, preferably with reassurances of further stability and continued employment. Above all, this person needs to believe that loyalty makes a real contribution to the organization's performance.

Most personnel systems are geared to the kind of person described here although guarantees of tenure are rare. As we will see, other career-anchor types encounter more difficulty with the personnel policies of the typical company.

Autonomy/independence as a career anchor

Some people discover early in their working lives that they cannot stand to be bound by other people's rules, by procedures, by working hours, dress codes, and other norms that arise in almost any organization. Whatever they are working on, such people have an overriding need to do things their own way, at their own pace, and against their own standards. They find organizational life restrictive, irrational, or intrusive into their own private lives, and therefore prefer to pursue more independent careers on their own terms.

If they are genuinely interested in business or management, they may go into consulting or teaching. Or they end up in those areas of work where autonomy is relatively possible even in large organizations: research and development, field sales offices, plant management (if the plant is geographically remote), data processing, market research, financial analysis, management of geographically remote units or divisions, and so on.

Just as all need some stability, everyone requires a certain amount of autonomy, which may vary with stage of life. And everyone must resolve the dependence-independence dilemma in life, or remain in perpetual conflict over the issue. The autonomy-anchored person is one whose need for independence is so strong that he begins to organize his entire career around it. If such a person has a job that permits autonomy, he or she will decline the offer of a much better job that would impinge on his or her independence.

Sometimes these extreme autonomy needs are associated with high levels of education; the individual's professional training has made him or her totally self-reliant and responsible. Sometimes such feelings are developed very early in life by child-rearing methods that emphasize self-reliance and independence of judgment. Whatever the origins, autonomy-anchored people are found in organizations, and they are often valued contributors.

TYPE OF WORK

The autonomy-anchored person prefers clearly delineated, time-bounded kinds of work within his or her area of expertise. Thus contract or project work, either part-time or full-time, or even temporary work would be acceptable and often desirable. In addition, this type of person likes work that clearly defines goals but leaves the means of accomplishment to the individual. The autonomy-anchored person cannot stand close supervision, but might be happy to agree to organizationally imposed goals or targets. Once those goals are set, he or she wants to be left alone.

PAY AND BENEFITS

The autonomy-anchored person is terrified of the "golden handcuffs." He or she would prefer merit pay for performance, immediate payoffs, bonuses, and other forms of compensation with no strings attached. On the benefits side, this group would prefer the portable benefits and the cafeteria style that would permit them to select the options most suitable for their life situation at a given point in time.

PROMOTION SYSTEM

This type of person would want a promotion that reflects past accomplishments and gives even more freedom than he or she had before. In other words, promotion means getting more autonomy. Greater rank or responsibility could actually be threatening, because that might entail loss of autonomy. The autonomous salesperson knows very well that the sales manager may have less freedom, so he or she turns down the promotion.

TYPE OF RECOGNTION

The autonomy-oriented person would respond best to forms of recognition that are "portable." Thus medals, testimonials, letters of commendation, prizes, awards, and other such rewards would probably mean more than promotion, title change, or even financial bonuses.

Most organizational reward systems are not at all geared to dealing with autonomy-anchored people. Hence, we should not be surprised when they leave in disgust, complaining about organizational "mickey mouse," and "red tape." If their talents are not needed, no harm is done. But if some of the key people on whom the organization depends happen to have autonomy anchors, it will become more important to redesign personnel systems to make organizational life more palatable to this group.

Technical/functional competence as a career anchor

Some people discover as their careers unfold that they have both a strong talent and high motivation for a par-

ticular kind of work. What turns them on is the exercise of their talent and the satisfaction of knowing that they are expert. This can happen in any kind of work: an engineer discovers he or she is very good at design; a salesperson discovers real selling talent and desire; a marketer gets better at and enjoys developing product promotions; a manufacturing manager finds greater and greater pleasure in running complex plants; a financial analyst gets increasing satisfaction out of solving complex financial-modeling problems; a computer programmer becomes very skilled at writing certain kinds of software; and so on.

As these people move along in their careers they discover that other areas of work are less satisfying and they feel increasingly pulled back to the area of expertise they enjoy. They begin to build their sense of identity around the content of their work, the technical or functional skill in which they excel—their craft (Maccoby 1976).

Every occupation has its craftsmen: the doctor who wants to be the world's best neurosurgeon; the professor who becomes a world authority in some esoteric research area; the consultant who specializes in certain types of clients; the lawyer who becomes a tax expert; the functional manager who prides himself on running the best functional department of its kind in the industry; and so on. They commit themselves to a life of specialization and begin to devalue the generalist concerns of the administrator and manager, though they are willing to be functional managers if it enables them to pursue their craft.

Most careers start out being technical/functional in their orientation, and the early phase of most careers is involved with the development of a speciality (Dalton, Thompson, and Price 1977; Super 1957; Schein 1978; Driver 1982). But not everyone is turned on by his or her speciality. For some people the job is a means to organizational membership or security rather than an end in itself. For others it is simply a stepping-stone to higher rungs on the organizational ladder, an entry into general management. For still others, it is an opportunity to learn some skills that will be needed to launch into independent or entrepreneurial activities. So while most people start out specializing, only some find this focus so intrinsically rewarding that it becomes their career anchor.

TYPE OF WORK

Above all, this group wants work to be challenging. If the work does not test the individual's ability, it quickly becomes boring and demeaning, and he or she will seek some other assignment. Since the self-esteem of this person hinges on exercising talent, he or she needs tasks that permit such exercise. In contrast to the security-oriented person, who is primarily concerned about the context of work, this type of person focuses on the intrinsic content of the work.

Technical/functional people who have committed themselves to an organization (as opposed to autonomous professionals) are willing and anxious to share in goal setting (Pelz and Andrews 1966; Schein 1978; Bailyn 1982), but once goals have been agreed upon, they demand maximum autonomy in execution. They generally also want "unlimited" facilities, budgets, and resources of all kinds, to enable them to perform their job properly. There is thus often a conflict between general managers, who are trying to limit the cost of specialized functions, and specialists, who need a certain level of investment to enable them to do their jobs.

The person anchored in this way will tolerate administrative or managerial work so long as he or she believes that it is a requirement for getting the job done, but such work is viewed as painful and necessary, not intrinsically fun or desirable. Promotion into a more generalist job is emotionally unwelcome, because it will force the person out of the speciality with which he or she identifies.

PAY AND BENEFITS

Technical/functional people want to be paid according to their skill level, often defined by education and work experience. A person who has a Ph.D. wants higher pay than someone who has an M.A., no matter what their actual accomplishments may have been. This group is oriented to "external equity" in that they will compare their pay level to what others with the same qualifications are earning in other organizations. Even if they are the highest-paid people in their own organizations, they will feel that they are not being treated fairly if they are underpaid relative to their peers in other organizations.

Technical/functional people are more concerned about their absolute pay level than about special incentives such as bonuses or stock options, except as the latter are forms of recognition. They probably prefer cafeteria-style, portable benefits because they view themselves as highly mobile and want to be able to take as much with them as possible. Like the autonomy group, they are frightened of the "golden handcuffs" because they might get stuck in unchallenging work.

PROMOTION SYSTEM

These people clearly prefer to have a professional promotional ladder that parallels the typical managerial ladder, and promotional systems that make "advancement" equivalent to moving into administration or management. While this pattern has been recognized in some

R & D and engineering organizations, it is just as applicable to all the other functional specialities that exist in organizations—finance, marketing, manufacturing, sales, etc.—yet few organizations have created viable multiple career systems that are genuinely responsive to the needs of the technically/functionally anchored person.

Promotion need not be in terms of rank. If pay meets the criteria of external equity, this kind of person would be responsive to an increase in the scope of his or her job, greater access to senior management and the policy-making functions, a larger budget or more technical support or subordinates, and so on (Bailyn 1982).

TYPE OF RECOGNITION

The specialist values most the recognition of his or her professional peers and cares relatively less for uninformed rewards from members of management. In other words, a pat on the back from a boss who does not really understand what was accomplished is worth a lot less than acknowledgment from a professional peer or subordinate who knows exactly what was accomplished and how difficult it may have been.

Forms of recognition that would be valued by the technical/functional person would include opportunities for self-development in the speciality: educational programs, organizationally sponsored sabbaticals, encouragement to attend professional meetings, budgets for buying books and equipment, and so on. Beyond that, this person values the formal recognition of being identified to colleagues and other organizational members as a specialist. Thus awards, publicity, and other public acknowledgments might be more important than an extra percentage point in the raise (provided the basic pay level is considered equitable).

Organizational careers tend to be designed by general managers, who put a high value on learning several functions, being a generalist, internal equity in pay, organizational loyalty, and getting along with all kinds of people—considerations which may be irrelevant to the technically/functionally anchored. He or she is thus particularly vulnerable to organizational mismanagement. If these people are a valued resource in the organization, some redesign of the career-development system will be called for.

Managerial competence as a career anchor

Some people discover as their careers progress that they really want to become general managers. Management per se interests them; they have the range of competences required to be a general manager, and they have the ambition to rise to a level at which they will be responsible for major policy decisions and at which their own efforts will make the difference between success and failure.

This group views specializations as a trap, though they recognize the need to get to know several functional areas well, and they accept that one must be expert in one's business or industry to function well as a general manager (Kotter 1982). Key values and motives for this group of people are advancement up the corporate ladder to ever-increasing levels of responsibility, opportunities for leadership, contribution to the success of the total organization, and high income (Bailyn 1980).

When they first enter an organization, most people have aspirations to "get ahead" in some generalized sense, and many of them talk explicitly of ambitions to "rise to the top." Few, however, have a realistic picture of what is actually required in the way of talents, motives, and values. With experience it becomes clearer to them, especially those who have committed themselves to general management as a career anchor, that they will not reach the top unless they have a high level of motivation and a mixture of talents and skills in three basic areas: analytical, interpersonal, and emotional competence (Schein 1978).

ANALYTICAL COMPETENCE

The ability to identify, analyze, and solve problems under conditions of incomplete information and uncertainty is analytical competence. All of the general managers we have talked with commented that it is important for someone in their position to be able to decipher what is going on, to cut through a mass of possibly irrelevant detail to get to the heart of the matter, to judge the reliability and validity of information when clear verification is not possible, and ultimately to pose the problem or question in such a way that it can be worked on. What is involved here is not so much decision making itself as managing the decision-making process. And it is the management of this process which requires the next set of skills.

INTERPERSONAL AND INTERGROUP COMPETENCE

The ability to influence, supervise, lead, manipulate, and control people at all levels of the organization toward organizational goal achievement is known as interpersonal and intergroup competence. The manager's task is not ordinarily to tell people what to do, because the correct line of action may not be clear in any case. Rather, he or she must be able to elicit information from others, communicate clearly the goals to be achieved,

get them to behave in a synergistic manner, motivate them to contribute what they know to the problem-solving process, facilitate the decision-making process and decision implementation, monitor progress and elicit corrective action if people are going off target. Because much of this work goes on in and between groups, group skills are very relevant to general managers.

Young managers on their way up the ladder talk vividly about the importance of early experiences in supervising others. Would they be any good at it? Almost equally important, would they like it? Most people do not know what their people skills are unless they have played leadership roles in school, which is probably why management recruiters are so anxious to know about extracurricular activities when they assess a candidate. Any evidence of track record in this area is of great value to both the individual and the organization.

Those who discover either that they are not talented in supervision or that they do not really like that kind of work, gravitate toward other pursuits and build their career anchor around technical/functional competence, autonomy, or even entrepreneurial activity. It is crucial for organizations to create career systems that enable such people to move out of supervisory roles if they are not suited to them, preferably without too much penalty. All too often the best engineer or salesperson is promoted to be supervisor, fails in the role but is then stuck in it, leading the organization to admit ruefully, "We not only lost a good engineer, but we gained a bad supervisor."

EMOTIONAL COMPETENCE

Emotional competence includes the capacity to be stimulated, rather than exhausted or debilitated, by emotional and interpersonal issues and crises, the capacity to bear high levels of responsibility without becoming paralyzed, and the ability to exercise power and make difficult decisions without guilt or shame.

All of the general managers we have interviewed commented that learning how to make the tough decisions had been a painful process. Almost all of them said they had not anticipated what it would be like or how they would react. Only as they gained confidence in their ability to handle their own feelings did they feel sure they could really succeed at being general managers. As examples they cited such problems as laying off a valued older employee; deciding between two programs, each of which is backed up by valued subordinates; committing large sums of money to a project, knowing that the fate of many people rides on success or failure; asking subordinates to undertake a difficult assignment they do not want to do; inspiring a demoralized organization; fighting for a project at a higher level; and delegating to subordinates and leaving them alone enough to learn how to do things.

The most difficult aspect of the general manager's job is to keep functioning day after day without giving up, getting an ulcer, or having a nervous breakdown. The essence of the general manager's job is to absorb the emotional strains of uncertainty, interpersonal conflict, and responsibility. It is this aspect of the job that often repels the technically/functionally anchored individual but excites and motivates the managerially anchored individual. This is what makes the job meaningful and rewarding.

General managers differ from the other groups primarily in that they have significant competence in all three areas. They cannot function without some analytical, some interpersonal, and some emotional competence, though no one area has to be developed to a very high level. It is the combination of skills that is essential, while in the technical or functional person it is the high development of one skill element that is crucial.

TYPE OF WORK

Managerially anchored people want high levels of responsibility; challenging, varied, and integrative work; leadership opportunities; and opportunities to contribute to the success of their organization. They will measure the attractiveness of a work assignment in terms of its importance to the success of the organization, and they will identify strongly with the organization and its success or failure as a measure of how well they have done. In a sense, they are real "organization people," whose identity rests on having an effective organization to manage.

PAY AND BENEFITS

Managerially anchored people measure themselves by their income level and expect to be very highly paid. In contrast to the technically/functionally anchored people, they are oriented more toward internal than external equity. In other words, they want to be paid substantially more than the level below them and will be satisfied if that condition is met even though someone at their level in another company is making much more. They also want short-run rewards, such as bonuses for achieving organizational targets, and, because they identify with the organization, they would be very responsive to such things as stock options.

With regard to benefits, managerially anchored people share with security-oriented people a willingness if not a positive desire to accept "golden handcuffs," particularly in the form of good retirement benefits, because so much of their career is tied up with a given company. Their particular skills may not be portable in mid-life

or later, and recent research by Kotter (1982) suggests that their particular effectiveness rests in the combination of a generalist orientation and an intimate knowledge of a particular industry or company. Thus, the mobile manager who claims to be able to manage anything, and would therefore want highly portable benefits, may not represent the typical effective general manager.

PROMOTION SYSTEM

Managerially anchored people insist on promotion based on merit, measured performance, or "results." Even though it is acknowledged that personality, style, seniority, politics, and other factors play a role in who gets promoted, the official ideology to which general managers subscribe emphasizes the ability to get results as the only important criterion.

TYPE OF RECOGNITION

The most important form of recognition is promotion to a position of higher responsibility, and managerially anchored people measure such positions by a combination of rank, title, salary, number of subordinates, size of the budget they are responsible for, and less tangible factors defined by their superiors (i.e., the "importance" of a given project or department or division to the "future of the company"). They expect promotions frequently. If they remain too long in a given job, it is assumed that they are not performing adequately. Every organization seems to have such a timetable, and managers measure their success partly by whether they are moving along at the "right" pace (Lawrence 1984). Thus movement itself becomes an important form of recognition unless it is clearly lateral or downward.

Organizations sometimes develop implicit career paths that become known informally to the more ambitious general managers. It may be commonly understood, for example, that one should move from finance to marketing, then take over a staff function in an overseas company, then move to headquarters, and eventually take over a division. If promotions do not follow the path, these people will worry that they are "off the fast track" and are losing their "potential." So movement to the "right" job is another important form of recognition.

This group of people is highly responsive to monetary recognition in the form of raises, bonuses, and stock options; they enjoy titles, status symbols such as large offices, cars, special privileges; and, perhaps most important, they appreciate the approval of their superiors. Whereas the technically/functionally anchored person only values approval from someone who really understands his or her work, the general manager values approval specifically from his superiors because they control his or her most important incentive—the promotion to the next higher level.

In summary, the person who is anchored in managerial competence has a very different orientation from others in the typical organization, even though they all begin in very similar kinds of jobs. In our interviews we found that such an orientation developed as soon as the person had enough data to determine whether he or she had the analytical, interpersonal, and emotional skills to be a general manager. Some people had this insight early and, if the organization did not respond to their need to rise quickly, they went to another organization that would permit them to reach a responsible level rapidly.

Entrepreneurial creativity as a career anchor

Among the several hundred people we have interviewed so far, we have found only twenty-three entrepreneurs, but this group is clearly very different from all the other anchor groups. These people discovered early in life that they had an overriding need to create a new business of their own by developing a new product or service, by building a new organization through financial manipulation, or by taking over an existing business and reshaping it in their own image. We are not talking about the inventor or the creative artist here, though some of them may become entrepreneurs. Nor should this group be confused with the creative researcher, market analyst, or advertising executive. The entrepreneur's creative urge is specifically toward creating a new organization, product, or service that can be identified closely with his or her building efforts, that will survive on its own, and that will permit the making of a fortune by which the success of the enterprise can be measured.

Many people dream about founding their own business and express those dreams at various stages of their career. In some cases these dreams express needs for autonomy—to get out on one's own. The people we identified as entrepreneurially anchored began early to pursue these dreams relentlessly. Often, they had started small moneymaking enterprises while still in high school. They found they had both talent and an extraordinarily high level of motivation to prove to the world that they could do it. Often, an older member of their own family had already established himself as a successful entrepreneur. These people did not stay with traditional organizations very long, or they kept organizational jobs only as a sideline while their real energy went into the building of their own enterprise.

TYPE OF WORK
Entrepreneurially anchored people are obsessed with the need to create, and they get easily bored. If they are in

their own enterprise they may keep inventing new products or services, or they may lose interest in the business, sell it, and start a new one. But they are restless and require constant new challenge.

PAY AND BENEFITS
For this group of people, ownership is the most important issue. Often they do not pay themselves very well, but they retain control of the organization's stock. If they develop new products, they want to own their own patents. They want wealth, not primarily for its own sake but as a way of proving to the world what they have accomplished. Benefits are probably not a very meaningful issue to them one way or the other.

PROMOTION SYSTEM
This type of person would want a system that permits being wherever he or she wants to be at any given point during his or her career. He or she would want the power and the freedom to move into whatever roles would meet personal needs. And he or she would probably pick those roles that best permitted exercise of creativity.

TYPE OF RECOGNITION
I have already mentioned the building of a fortune and a sizable enterprise as two of the most important ways that this group gets its sense of recognition. In addition, it should be noted that the entrepreneur is rather self-centered, seeking high personal visibility and public recognition, often symbolized by putting his or her own name on the product or the company.

The people in the three remaining anchor categories—service, pure challenge, and life-style—represent a small but potentially growing pool to be considered. They will not be analyzed in as much detail because we do not yet have enough information about them.

Sense of service, dedication to a cause as a career anchor

So far we have encountered fourteen people whose careers are organized around their sense of service. Two of these people are physicians who became entrepreneurial and left traditional medicine, three are in financial analysis jobs, five are consultants, and the rest are in varied other positions.

These people all chose their careers and made subsequent career decisions primarily on the basis of working toward some important values, some cause that they considered paramount—improving the world in some fashion. We think of people like this in the "helping professions," such as nursing, teaching, or the ministry, but clearly such central concerns are also characteristic of some people in business management and in organizational careers.

The small number of cases that fall into this anchor category does not permit very clear generalizations about what is important to this group, but some of their characteristics can be stated. Clearly, they value work that permits them to be instrumental in realizing their essential values. The prototype of this kind of person was a professor of agriculture who left a tenured university position to accept a job as manager of environmental planning for a large mining company. He stated that he would continue to work for this company as long as he was allowed to do some of the key environmental planning and continued to have clout and get things done.

One would presume that people anchored in this fashion would want "fair" pay for their contribution and portable benefits, because they would not have any *a priori* organizational loyalty, but that money per se would not be central to them. More important would be a promotional system that recognized their contribution and moved them into positions where they would have more influence and the freedom to operate relatively autonomously.

They would want recognition and support both from their professional peers and from their superiors, and would want to feel that their values were shared by higher levels of management. If they did not get such support they would probably operate in more autonomous professional roles— like the consultants in our sample who had this anchor.

Pure challenge as a career anchor

Some people anchor their career in a sense that they can "lick anything or anybody." Some seek jobs in which they face perpetually tougher challenges or more difficult problems, but in contrast to the technically/functionally anchored group, they seem not to care what kind of problem is involved. Some of the high-level strategy/management consultants seemed to fit this pattern, in that they relished more and more difficult kinds of strategic assignments (Applin 1982; Burnstine 1982).

Derr (1980) found a number of naval aviators whose sole purpose in life and career seemed to be to prepare themselves for the ultimate confrontation with an enemy. In that confrontation, these "warriors" prove to themselves and to the world their own superiority in competitive combat. Though the military version of this anchor might seem somewhat overdramatized, we have met others who define life very much in competitive terms. One can speculate that a good many salespersons, professional athletes, and even managers define their careers essentially as a daily combat or competition in which "winning" is everything.

The managerial issues involved in motivating and developing such people are intrinsically complex. On the one hand, they are already highly motivated to develop themselves and probably very loyal to an organization that gives them adequate opportunities for self-tests. But they can also be very single-minded and can certainly make life difficult for others around them who do not have comparable aspirations. The movie *The Great Santini* is an excellent depiction of the difficulties created by a "warrior," both for his bosses and for his family. The career has meaning only if the competitive skill can be exercised; if there is no opportunity the person can become demoralized and hence a problem to himself and others.

Life-style as a career anchor

At first glance this concept seems like a contradiction in terms. People who organize their existence around "life-style" are, in effect, saying that their career is less important to them and therefore that they do not have a career anchor. They are included in this discussion, however, because a growing number of graduates who are highly motivated toward meaningful careers are insisting that the careers be meshed with total life-style. It is not enough to *balance* personal and professional life (Evans and Bartolome 1980) as many have traditionally done; it is more a matter of finding a way to *integrate* the needs of the individual, the family, and the career.

Because such an integration is itself an evolving characteristic, this kind of person wants flexibility more than anything else. But unlike the autonomy-oriented person, he or she is quite willing to work for an organization provided the right options are available at the right time. Such options would include traveling or moving some of the time when family issues permit it, part-time work if life concerns require it, sabbaticals, paternity and maternity leaves, day-care options (which are becoming especially relevant for the growing population of single parents), flexible working hours, and so on. Those with a life-style anchor are looking more for an organizational attitude than for a specific program, an attitude that reflects respect for personal and family concerns and that makes genuine renegotiation of the psychological contract possible (Schein 1978).

This anchor was first observed in women graduates of the Sloan School but is increasingly found in male graduates, especially those who have gone into management and strategy consulting (Applin 1982; Burnstine 1982). It probably reflects a number of social trends in our society and is an inevitable effect of the dual-career family. It is not at all clear at this point what organizational responses are appropriate, except to become more flexible. What this group requires most from managers is understanding.

CONCLUSION: MATCHING INDIVIDUAL AND ORGANIZATIONAL NEEDS

This paper has focused on the individual, internal side of the career. We have looked at the characteristic stages of career development, considered some ways of thinking about career movement and success, and used the concept of career anchors to illuminate the self-images that people develop as their careers evolve. It remains to focus on the ultimate dilemma of how to match individual and organizational needs.

Because individual career needs vary so widely, self-insight is critically important. Constructive career management is impossible unless the individual knows his or her own needs and biases. Such comprehension is essential both to communicate clearly with the organization, and to make intelligent choices. It is unrealistic to expect our bosses and our organizations to understand us at the level of individuality that is relevant to career choices. Ultimately, we must manage our own careers. Abdicating that responsibility to others is a gamble unlikely to yield a successful outcome.

How then can organizations and their managers help the indvidual? They can do three things.

1. Create more flexible career paths, incentive systems, and reward systems to meet a wider range of individual needs, even within a particular job category.
2. Stimulate more self-insight and self-management, starting with themselves, that is, analyze their own career anchors, manage their own careers more actively, and only then ask their subordinates to do the same.
3. Be clearer about what the organization needs from the individual. If career seekers and job incumbents can be given a more accurate picture of the work to be done in a given job and of career patterns overall, they will be better able to set a constructive course for themselves. Implied in this is also clearer performance appraisal and career relevant feedback.

If I know myself well but cannot get good information about what I will have to do in a given job, I cannot make an intelligent choice. For the organization to help me and help itself set the right talent in the right place, it must be clearer about what it needs from me (Schein 1978). The matching process can be improved only if both the organization and the individual understand themselves well, communicate clearly, and respond flexibly to each other. This is the challenge for the future.

REFERENCES

Albertini, W. O. 1982. "Organization Managers: A Career Study." Master's thesis, MIT Sloan School of Management, Cambridge, Mass.

Anderson, M. E., and F. F. Sommer. 1980. "Career Evolution of Sloan Fellows." Master's thesis, MIT Sloan School of Management, Cambridge, Mass.

Applin, M. R. 1982. "A Study of the Careers of Management Consultants." Master's thesis, MIT Sloan School of Management, Cambridge, Mass.

Bailyn, L. 1978. "Accommodation of Work to Family." In *Working Couples*, ed. R. Rapoport and R. N. Rapoport. pp. 159–86. New York: Harper & Row.

——. 1982. "Resolving Contradictions in Technical Careers; or What if I Like Being an Engineer?" *Technology Review* 85:40–47.

Bailyn, L. with E. H. Schein. 1980. *Living with Technology*. Cambridge, Mass.: MIT Press.

Burnstine, R. 1982. *Career Anchors of Management and Stra-*

tegic Consultants. Master's thesis, MIT Sloan School of Management, Cambridge, Mass.

Crowson, L. 1982. *Career Anchors of Finance Executives*. Master's thesis, MIT Sloan School of Management, Cambridge, Mass.

Dalton, G. W., P. H. Thompson, and R. L. Price. 1977. "The Four Stages of Professional Careers." *Organizational Dynamics* (Summer).

Dalton, M. 1959. *Men Who Manage*. New York: Wiley.

DeLong, J. 1982. "The Career Orientation of MBA Alumni: A Multidimensional Model." In *Career Issues in Human Resource Management*, ed. Ralph Katz, pp. 50–64. Englewood Cliffs, N.J.: Prentice-Hall.

Derr, C. B. 1980. "More About Career Anchors." In *Work, Family, and the Career*, ed. C. B. Derr, pp. 166–87. New York: Praeger.

Driver, M. J. 1982. "Career Concepts—A New Approach to Career Research." In *Career Issues in Human Resource*

Management, ed. R. Katz, pp. 23–32. Englewood Cliffs, N.J.: Prentice-Hall.

Evans, P., and F. Bartolome. 1980. *Must Success Cost So Much?* New York: Basic Books.

Fowble, W. F. 1982. "The Relationship Among Managers' Career Anchors, Subordinate Evaluation, and Organizational Socialization." Master's thesis, MIT Sloan School of Management, Cambridge, Mass.

Gould, R. 1978. *Transformations.* New York: Simon & Schuster.

Grzywacs, J. M. 1982. "Career Anchors of Sloan Alumnae." Master's thesis, MIT Sloan School of Management, Cambridge, Mass.

Hackman, J. R., and G. R. Oldham. 1980. *Work Redesign.* Reading, Mass.: Addison-Wesley.

Hall, G. W., and F. J. Thomas. 1979. "The Impact of Career Anchors on the Organizational Development of Program Managers in the Aerospace Industry." Master's thesis, MIT Sloan School of Management, Cambridge, Mass.

Heller, E. E. 1982. "Physicians in Management: Why Are They There?" Master's thesis, MIT Sloan School of Management, Cambridge, Mass.

Hopkins, A. D. 1976. "Managers at Mid-Career—Where Are They Going?" Master's thesis, MIT Sloan School of Management, Cambridge, Mass.

Hughes, E. C. 1958. *Men and Their Work.* Glencoe, Ill.: Free Press.

Huser, E. A. W. 1980. "The Motivation of Managers: A Study of the Basic Motivations that Determine the Career Decisions of Female Executives." Master's thesis, MIT Sloan School of Management, Cambridge, Mass.

Jacques, E. 1965. "Death and the Mid-life Crisis." *International Journal of Psychiatry* 46:502–13.

Janes, M. J. 1982. "Career Anchors of Business and Professional Women." Master's thesis, MIT Sloan School of Management, Cambridge, Mass.

Kanto, J. J. 1982. "Career Choices: A Study of Career Anchors in Female Bank Officers." Master's thesis, MIT Sloan School of Management, Cambridge, Mass.

Katz, R., and J. Van Maanen. 1976. "The Loci of Work Satisfaction." In *Personal Goals and Work Design*, ed. P. Warr. New York: Wiley.

Kotter, J. P. 1982. *The General Managers.* New York: Free Press.

Lawler, E. E., III. 1981. *Pay and Organization Development.* Reading, Mass: Addison-Wesley.

Lawrence, B. S. 1984. "Age Grading: The Implicit Organizational Timetable." *Journal of Occupational Behavior* 5:23–35.

Levinson, D. J., with C. N. Darrow, E. B. Klein, M. H. Levinson, and B. McKee. 1978. *The Seasons of a Man's Life.* New York: Knopf.

Liebesny, C. B. 1980. "Career Paths for Data Processing Professionals." Master's thesis, MIT Sloan School of Management, Cambridge, Mass.

Maccoby, M. 1976. *The Gamesman.* New York: Simon & Schuster.

Osherson, S. D. 1980. *Holding On or Letting Go.* New York: Free Press.

Osipow, S. H. 1973. *Theories of Career Development.* 2d ed. New York: Appleton-Century-Crofts.

Pelz, D. C., and E. M. Andrews. 1966. *Scientists in Organizations.* New York: Wiley.

Schein, E. H. 1971. "The Individual, the Organization, and the Career: A Conceptual Scheme." *Journal of Applied Behavioral Science* 7:401–26.

———. 1975. "How Career Anchors Hold Executives to Their Career Paths." *Personnel* 52, no. 3:11–24.

———. 1978. *Career Dynamics.* Reading, Mass.: Addison-Wesley.

Senior, K. W. 1982. "A Study of Career Anchors of Field Service Engineers." Master's thesis, MIT Sloan School of Management, Cambridge, Mass.

Super, D. E. 1957. *The Psychology of Careers.* New York: Harper & Row.

Vaillant, G. 1978. *Adaptation to Life.* Boston: Little, Brown.

Van Maanen, J., and E. H. Schein. 1977. "Improving the Quality of Work Life: Career Development." In *Improving Life at Work*, ed. J. R. Hackman and J. L. Suttle, pp. 30–95. Santa Monica, Calif.: Goodyear.

———. 1979. "Toward a Theory of Organizational Socialization." In *Research in Organizational Behavior*, ed. B. Staw. Vol. 1. Greenwich, Conn.: Jai Press.

Walker, J. W. 1980. *Human Resource Planning.* New York: McGraw-Hill.

Zaleznik, A., G. W. Dalton, L. B. Barnes, and P. Laurin. 1970. *Orientation and Conflict in Career.* Boston, Mass.: Graduate School of Business Administration, Division of Research, Harvard University.

12

The development of working relationships

JOHN J. GABARRO

Human relationships are a fact of life for people of every occupation, situation, rank, and status, but they are an especially critical and pervasive aspect of a manager's life. The executives who were the subject of Mintzberg's now-classic study of managerial work spent 78 percent of their working time interacting with others, and as much as 50 percent of that time in interactions with subordinates (Mintzberg 1973, 39–45). More recent studies by Stewart (1982) and Kotter (1982) provide further support for the importance of two-person ("dyadic") relationships in managerial work. Kotter found that developing a network of interpersonal relationships was critical to a general manager's ability to formulate and implement an agenda and that the quality of these relationships was a key determinant of managerial effectiveness (Kotter 1982, chaps. 2, 3, 4). Similarly, Liden and Graen (1980) found that subordinates reporting good relationships with superiors were better performers, assumed more responsibility, and contributed more to their units than those reporting poor relationships. The importance of interpersonal relationships as an aspect of management is documented in study after study of managerial behavior, regardless of national culture or type of management job.[1] Indeed, Weick (1969, 57) has argued that from a social-psychological point of view, relationships are the principal means through which organizations are controlled. Most experienced managers would agree.

Any manager, regardless of position, is dependent on subordinates, peers, and superiors for his or her unit's performance. This dependency is especially important for general and upper-level managers because they typically cannot be experts in all of the functions that report to them and thus must rely on the competence of subordinates and others. Moreover, the greater the size or complexity of a manager's organization, the more difficult it is for him or her to influence all of the key variables directly, regardless of how good the company's information, control, and reward systems are. Thus much of the work of managing complex organizations occurs in the individual relationships that make up the networks described by Kotter and others.

Given the importance of these relationships, it is surprising that relatively little research has focused on the topic of how working relationships actually develop in organizations and what behaviors lead to effective relationships (Wortman and Linsenmeier 1977). There are some notable exceptions to this generalization, such as the early work of Hodgson, Levinson, and Zaleznik (1965) on the executive role constellation; Levinson's (1964, 1968) work on the psychodynamic aspects of superior-subordinate relations; and Gabarro's (1978, 1979) research on the development of managerial working relationships. But relatively little research within organizational behavior has focused explicitly on the

The author gratefully acknowledges the assistance of Colleen Kaftan for her insights and help in reviewing the basic literature on relationship formation.

1. Mintzberg (1973, nn. 103–4), for example, cites studies conducted by Stieglitz (1969) on non-U.S. executives; Inkson et al. (1970) on English and U.S. executives; Stewart (1967) on British executives; and Dubin and Spray (1964) on U.S. executives.

development of two-person relationships as such. Most of the research that has addressed the topic of working relationships has done so within the context of broader processes, such as managerial work, group behavior, or leadership.

This chapter presents a brief overview of the existing literature on working relationships and compares their characteristic development with that of other types of social relationships. It draws on two literatures relevant to the development of two-person working relationships. The first is the literature on the broader topic of relationship formation, which has focused almost exclusively on social and intimate relationships rather than on task-based relationships. The second is the much smaller literature within organizational behavior that has dealt with aspects of task-based relationships. Viewing the topic from these two perspectives allows us to deal with the conundrum that although "relationships are relationships," as Weick (1969) has put it, task-based relationships are likely to differ from social relationships because they are subject to different situational and contextual forces (Wortman and Linsenmeier 1977; Triandis 1977).

Any interpersonal relationship involves both some degree of interaction between two people and some degree of continuity between successive interactions (Hinde 1977; Swensen 1973). The term *working relationship* is used here to mean an interpersonal relationship that is task-based, nontrivial, and of continuing duration. Working relationships like social relationships develop over time and can vary in their stability, mutuality, and efficacy (Gabarro 1978). Although working relationships have not been studied as a substantive area of inquiry, the more general topic of relationship formation in social and intimate relations has been treated extensively. The topic occupies a significant place in the literatures on interpersonal attraction and two-person relationships. Accordingly this review will begin with these more general literatures.

Several conceptual and methodological problems are inherent in studying and describing interpersonal relationships of any kind. The most basic of these problems is that although they can be defined in terms of dyadic characteristics, such as shared meaning, content of interaction, "quality," patterning of behavior, and context (Hinde 1979), relationships are themselves the consequence of interactions amongst individuals and are heavily permeated by the effects of individual personality and predispositions (Sullivan 1953; Carson 1969, Hodgson, Levinson, and Zaleznik 1965). Moreover the processes involved in the evolution of a relationship are multifaceted (Huston 1974) and involve different levels and types of behavior. Triandis (1977), for example, has differentiated among attributive, affective, and overt behaviors, while Huston (1974) has distinguished among evaluative, cognitive, and behavioral components. Altman and Taylor (1973) have described the relevant processes as consisting of internal subjective processes (including expectations, attribution processes, and evaluative judgments) and overt behaviors, which they define as including verbal and nonverbal behaviors and the use of objects and space. Altman has further argued that the process of relationship formation is sufficiently complex, in terms of the variables that influence it over time, that the phenomenon should be studied from a social-ecological point of view (Altman 1974, 121–25).

A final question that arises in discussing relationship formation is what distinguishes a "developed" relationship from a partially developed one. As Hinde (1979) has pointed out, even the distinction between "interaction" and "relationship" is by necessity somewhat arbitrary. The question is a particularly difficult one because most theoretical descriptions of the development of relationships include not only a temporal dimension but also hierarchical dimensions of mutuality and pair relatedness (Levinger 1974) and commitment (Secord and Backman 1964).

These problems are further compounded when we focus our attention on working relationships as a substantive category. All of the research and theory on the general topic of relationship formation strongly indicates that the situational and role-related factors that distinguish working relationships from social ones are likely to make a difference in their development.

This chapter obviously cannot examine in depth all of the processes and issues just described. It is possible, however, to address some of these questions one at a time, beginning with a discussion of the dimensions along which relationships develop as indicated by the general literature on social relationships. Then, after considering the stages that characterize relationship formation and the underlying social processes that drive it, we can turn to working relationships as a substantive category and explore the issues involved in their development in more detail.

DIMENSIONS ALONG WHICH RELATIONSHIPS DEVELOP

Although scholars differ in their definitions of a developed relationship, there is a remarkable degree of convergence in the literature on the dimensions that characterize the development of relationships. Several of these dimensions are summarized in figure 12.1, which draws heavily on the integrative review of Altman and Taylor (1973) and to a lesser degree on those of Levinger and Snoek (1972) and other authors referenced in figure 12.1. Let me briefly describe each of these dimensions as characteristics, while postponing my discussion of the underlying processes, such as social exchange, that move relationships along the various dimensions.

The first three dimensions listed in figure 12.1 are perhaps the most frequently cited as characteristics of mature, stabilized relationships: the *degree of self-*

disclosure present in a relationship; the degree and richness of *knowledge that each party has of the other*; and the ability of both parties to *predict and anticipate each other's reactions and responses*. It is no accident that these three characteristics are interrelated. The higher the level of mutual self-disclosure in a relationship, the greater the knowledge base each person has of the other; the more extensive this knowledge base, the easier it is

From	To
OPENNESS AND SELF-DISCLOSURE[1,2,3,4,6]	
Limited to "safe," socially acceptable topics	Disclosure goes beyond safe areas to include personally sensitive, private, and controversial topics and aspects of self
KNOWLEDGE OF EACH OTHER[2,4,5,6]	
Surface, "biographic" knowledge; impressionistic in nature	Knowledge is multifaceted and extends to core aspects of personality, needs, and style
PREDICTABILITY OF OTHER'S REACTIONS AND RESPONSES[2,4,5,6]	
Limited to socially expected or role-related responses, and those based on first impressions or repeated surface encounters	Predictability of other's reactions extends beyond stereotypical exchange and includes a knowledge of the contingencies affecting the other's reactions
UNIQUENESS OF INTERACTION[1,2,5]	
Exchanges are stereotypical, guided by prevailing social norms or role expectations	Exchanges are idiosyncratic to the two people, guided by norms that are unique to the relationship
MULTIMODALITY OF COMMUNICATION[1,2]	
Largely limited to verbal channels of communication and stereotypical or unintended nonverbal channels	Includes multiple modalities of communication, including nonverbal and verbal "shorthands" specific to the relationship or the individuals involved; less restrictiveness of nonverbal
SUBSTITUTABILITY OF COMMUNICATION[1,2]	
Little substitution among alternative modes of communication	Possession of and ability to use alternative modes of communication to convey the same message
CAPACITY FOR CONFLICT AND EVALUATION[1,2,3,5]	
Limited capacity for conflict; use of conflict-avoidance techniques; reluctance to criticize	Readiness and ability to express conflict and make positive or negative evaluations
SPONTANEITY OF EXCHANGE[1,2,3]	
Interactions tend to be formal or "comfortably informal" as prescribed by prevailing social norms	Greater informality and ease of interaction; movement across topical areas occurs readily and without hesitation or formality; communication flows and changes direction easily
SYNCHRONIZATION AND PACING[1,2]	
Except for stereotyped modes of response, limited dyadic synchrony occurs	Speech and nonverbal responses become synchronized; flow of interaction is smooth; cues are quickly and accurately interpreted
EFFICIENCY OF COMMUNICATION[1,2]	
Communication of intended meanings sometimes requires extensive discussion; misunderstandings occur unless statements are qualified or elaborated	Intended meanings are transmitted and understood rapidly, accurately, and with sensitivity to nuance
MUTUAL INVESTMENT[2,7]	
Little investment in the other except in areas of role-related or situation interdependencies	Extensive investment in other's well-being and efficacy

1. Altman and Taylor 1973, 129–36.
2. Levinger and Snoek 1972; Levinger 1974, 100–109.
3. Jourard 1971.
4. Hinde 1979, 133–34.

5. Swensen 1973, 105–6, 455, 230–37.
6. Triandis 1977, 191–93.
7. Secord and Backman 1964.

Figure 12.1 Summary of dyadic dimensions among which relationships develop

for each party to anticipate the other's responses and reactions correctly. Even without extensive self-disclosure, two people will get to know each other better (and therefore predict each other's reactions better) simply through the residual personal learning that results from the repeated interactions that occur in sustained relationships.

The next three dimensions noted in figure 12.1 are also manifestly related to how well both parties know each other and are to some degree a natural product of cumulative and sustained interaction. *Uniqueness of interaction* is the extent to which exchanges are idiosyncratic to a dyad and guided by norms unique to the relationship, as compared with the more stereotypical exchanges that occur in casual relationships, which tend to be guided by prevailing social norms (Altman and Taylor 1973) or by role expectations (Kelvin 1970). *Multimodality of communication* refers to the number of modalities of communication that are available and used by a dyad, including verbal and nonverbal shorthands specific to the relationship. The general finding has been that mature and stable relationships are characterized by greater multimodality than casual or less intense relationships. *Substitutability of communication* concerns a dyad's ability to use alternate modes of communication to convey the same message. Such substitutability is a characteristic of mature, developed relationships, because it requires considerable mutual knowledge and experience to develop a shared repertoire of meanings and ways of expressing those meanings.

The next three dimensions listed in figure 12.1 can also be seen as parts of a related constellation. A dyad's *capacity for conflict and evaluation* refers to the readiness and ability of two people to express conflict and to make positive or negative evaluations of each other. Although this capacity requires more than the mere passage of time and sustained interaction, it is more likely to be found in developed relationships than in those involving surface encounters (Levinger 1974), in which social norms prescribe the polite avoidance of conflict and criticism (Altman and Taylor 1973). *Spontaneity of exchange* refers to the informality and ease of interaction characteristic of a relationship and the ability of a dyad to move across topical areas readily (Altman and Taylor 1973; Levinger 1974). This type of spontaneity seldom occurs between people whose relationship remains at a superficial level, because it assumes a high degree of shared meaning and interpersonal comfort. *Synchronization and pacing* refers to the degree to which verbal and nonverbal responses are coordinated, the smoothness of interaction, and the extent to which cues are quickly and accurately interpreted. All three of these characteristics presume a depth of familiarity and

mutual knowledge that is seldom found in casual acquaintanceships, and it should not be surprising that they become more prevalent as a relationship grows in importance and experience.

Efficiency of communication refers to the degree to which intended meanings are transmitted and understood with rapidity, accuracy, and sensitivity to nuance. Again, it is not surprising that as a relationship develops, its efficiency of communication increases. Progress along this dimension is presumably closely related to progress along the other nine dimensions. For example, a high degree of substitutability and multimodality of communication cannot help but increase the efficiency with which two people can exchange meanings. Similarly the development of norms and shorthands unique to a relationship, a capacity for conflict, spontaneity, and synchronization all help two people communicate more quickly and accurately.

Finally, *mutual investment* refers to each party's interest in the other's well-being and efficacy. This dimension derives principally from the work of Levinger and Snoek (1972), who directly relate it to several of the other dimensions already discussed, as well as to underlying dynamics of social exchange.

Before proceeding further, it is useful to underscore several observations concerning the characteristics we have just reviewed. First, they are not pure dimensions, because they are closely interrelated and appear to emerge from common underlying processes, such as social exchange, evaluation, and attribution, which have not yet been discussed. Second, these dimensions are progressive in nature and are treated as such in the literature (see Altman and Taylor 1973). They are progressive even when the nature of the relationship is pathological, and increased movement along such dimensions as mutual investment and uniqueness and synchrony of interaction can result in destructive outcomes for one or both parties (Carson 1969; Lidz et al. 1957; Lidz and Fleck 1960). Third, as will be discussed later, progression along these dimensions is moderated by three general classes of factors, which Altman and Taylor (1973) term *individual factors*, *situational context*, and the *outcomes of the exchange* for each party.

Although the dimensions just described are based almost exclusively on research conducted on dyads of a social and intimate nature, they have face validity and relevance for task-based relationships, at least at a descriptive level. Everyday observation would suggest that individual working relationships differ from each other along these dimensions and progress along these dimensions as they develop. Moreover, barring underlying psychodynamics of a pathological nature, progression along these dimensions should enable the two parties to work better together, if only because of the increased efficacy of exchange that characterizes more developed relationships.

STAGES IN THE RELATIONSHIP-FORMATION PROCESS

Implicit in the dimensions just reviewed is progression not only of a qualitative nature but also of a temporal and cumulative nature as well. A number of authors have suggested that relationships typically progress through stages as they develop. Although Hinde (1971, 1979) has argued that such stages cannot be distinguished by observable discontinuities and that any definitions of stages are likely to depend on arbitrary criteria, he also

suggests that it can be useful to describe changes in a relationship as involving a succession of stages (pp. 289–90). Stage paradigms of the relationship-formation process have been postulated by several researchers. Simmel (1950), for example, implied a progression through stages of casual acquaintanceships, friendships, reciprocated love, and established dyads; Newcomb (1961) postulated differences in stages in terms of balance theory; Kerckhoff and Davis (1962) described differences in terms of similarity and complementarity of attitudes; and Murstein (1977) postulated stages in terms of stimulus, value comparison, and role compatibility. This review, however, will focus only on the three stage paradigms that figure most prominently in the literature on relationship formation (see, for example, reviews in Swensen 1973; Huston 1974; Triandis 1977; Hinde 1979). These three are Secord and Backman's (1964) reciprocal-

---

I. Reciprocal exchange paradigm (Secord and Backman 1964; Thibaut and Kelley 1959)

Stages or levels of relationship

1. *Sampling*: Selection process by which a person chooses another with whom he will have a more involved relationship; requires propinquity; appearance, attractiveness, similarity are used to evaluate potential payoffs.

2. *Bargaining*: Each party tests and negotiates to see if "a more permanent trading relationship would be to mutual advantage." In a sense, this starts the moment two people begin to interact; rewards come from ease of interaction, similarity of values, and complementarity of needs.

3. *Commitment*: Relationship becomes more central and, in social and romantic relationships, intimate. Each party forgoes relations with others to engage in relationship with the other party.

4. *Institutionalization*: Formal ratification of the commitment takes place (if deep and appropriate). Legal, symbolic, or other ratification and mutual acknowledgment of the commitment occurs.

Underlying processes

The "motor" for both the formation and termination of the relationship is each party's desire to *maximize personal outcomes*. Each person's comparison level (Thibault and Kelley 1959) and comparison level of alternatives change over time with experience and learning, and therefore the evaluation of payoffs is evolutionary.

II. Mutuality and pair-relatedness paradigm (Levinger and Snoek 1972; Levinger 1974)

Levels of relationship

1. *Unilateral Awareness*:(Level 1) Other is seen entirely in terms of external characteristics. Attraction based on perception of favorable and *potentially* rewarding attributes (expected favorable outcomes before extended interaction occurs). Knowledge of each other is superficial.

2. *Bilateral Surface Contact*: (Level 2) Interactions primarily superficial and stereotyped; defined by socially determined roles. Relationships typically segmented in that they deal with partial aspects of living; attraction based on *actual* reward-cost outcomes and expected future outcomes. Variables are important at this stage, not necessarily so for later stages. Knowledge of each other is partial.

Underlying processes

Dyads develop through stages of increasing *mutuality* of rewarding exchanges. Processes include

1. *Mutual Disclosure*: Disclosure of selves and sharing of significant attitudes, feelings, and experiences result in a "spiral of shared assumptions."

2. *Mutual Investment*: As a relationship unfolds, each party takes increasing pleasure in the other's satisfaction. Mutual investment includes learning how to accommodate each other's responses and preferences. The deeper the relationship, the larger the cargo of joint experiences, shared feelings, and behavior coordination.

Figure 12.2 Major stage paradigms of the relationship-formation process

exchange-stage paradigm, which is heavily based on Thibaut and Kelley's (1959) work; Levinger and Snoek's (1972) and Levinger's (1974) pair-relatedness model; and Altman and Taylor's (1973) social-penetration model. Figure 12.2 describes these stage paradigms in terms of both the stages postulated and the underlying processes thought to move relationships through these stages.

The reciprocal-exchange model

Secord and Backman (1964) postulated that social relationships can progress through four stages, which they called *sampling, bargaining, commitment,* and *institutionalization* (see figure 12.2). Their view of the underlying social processes that account for progress through these stages is based on social-exchange theory. A rela-

tionship's progress through these stages, they argue, will depend on each person's ability to maximize personal rewards in the relationship as compared with external alternatives. A relationship will develop if doing so increases personal outcomes, given each person's internal comparison level and comparison levels of alternatives (Thibaut and Kelley 1959). They further argue that each person's comparison levels will change over time and that the evaluation of payoffs is evolutionary in nature.

Mutuality and pair-relatedness

Levinger and Snoek (1972) see the potential evolution of relationships in terms of three levels of pair relatedness, which are in turn based on the degree of mutual-

---

3. *Mutuality:* (Level 3) A continuing evolution toward greater shared meanings; attraction is based on the satisfactions of levels 1 and 2 and also on unique dyad emotional investments, interdependencies, and mutuality of need satisfactions. Partners possess shared knowledge of each other and assume responsibility for furthering each other's outcomes. Both parties share private norms for regulating their association.
(Advanced level 3) The prior history of the pair's interactions serves to increase the "number of its actual and potential joint behavior repertoires."

III. Social-penetration paradigm (Altman and Taylor 1973)

Stages of social penetration
1. *Orientation:* Interactions are stereotyped in nature; exchanges lack breadth, depth, or richness. Information exchanged at superficial level. Little open evaluation, criticism, or expression of conflict; indirect techniques used for conflict avoidance. Interactions limited to outer, public areas of personality. "Social actors scan one another and communicate according to conventional formula."

2. *Exploratory affective exchange:* Interpersonal behavior is still at periphery of self. Relations flow more smoothly and are more relaxed. Commitments are limited or temporary.

3. *Full affective exchange:* Both parties know each other well; fairly extensive history of association; exchange more spontaneous; considerable interpersonal synchrony, permeability, and substitutability; readiness to make positive and negative evaluations; increased uniqueness in patterns of communication. Knowledge of intermediate levels of each other's self, many barriers to intimacy down, but exchange still retains restrictedness and caution.

4. *Stable exchange:* Achieved in only a few relationships. Exchanges involve richness, spontaneity. Parties know each other well and can readily interpret and predict feelings and probable behavior of other; considerable knowledge and dialogue involving core areas of personality.

Underlying processes
1. *Social penetration involves* (1) *overt interpersonal behaviors,* (2) *internal subjective processes* (including attribution, assessment) which precede, accompany, and follow overt exchange. Interactions are "critiqued" to see if further contact or penetration is worth pursuing.

2. Penetration is a systematic, orderly *process of mutual self-disclosure,* which proceeds gradually from superficial to deeper areas of personality.

3. The rate and stage of penetration *varies as a function of interpersonal rewards and costs* (absolute magnitude and reward/cost ratio), both immediate and expected.

4. Depenetration is the reverse process and is also systematic.

5. The process is moderated by personal characteristics of the two people involved, outcomes of exchange, situational context.

ity present in a relationship (see figure 12.2). Like that of Secord and Backman, their model is based on social-exchange theory (Homans 1950, 1961; Thibaut and Kelley 1959) in that dyads are seen as developing through stages of increasingly rewarding mutual exchanges. However, Levinger and Snoek go well beyond the simple concept of rewards and costs and describe mutual self-disclosure (Jourard 1959) and mutual investment in a common bond as important underlying processes that move a relationship through these stages. Thus their stage paradigm goes significantly beyond the social-exchange paradigms of Secord and Backman (1964) and Thibaut and Kelley (1959).

"breadth" dimension (how many aspects of one's personality become known to the other), a "breadth-frequency" dimension, and a "depth" dimension (disclosure of central versus peripheral aspects of self). In these terms, the social-penetration process proceeds toward greater depth, breadth, and interconnectedness, resulting in greater vulnerability and access to "socially undesirable" characteristics as well as greater understanding of the whole personality. A surface relationship would tend to be segmented (low breadth) and peripheral (low depth), while a more advanced relationship would be characterized by mutual disclosure and knowledge of a broader, deeper, and more interconnected nature.

Social-penetration model

Perhaps the most inclusive, integrated, and detailed stage paradigm of the relationship-formation process has been presented by Altman and Taylor (1973) (see figure 12.2). They postulate four stages of social penetration, which involve increasing degrees of mutual knowledge, openness, uniqueness of exchange, spontaneity, synchrony, and substitutability. Although they emphasize that any attempt to categorize the social-penetration process into clearly delineated stages is artificial, their four stages differ markedly in their central activities, exchanges, and characteristics. They see the social-penetration process as including both overt interpersonal behaviors and internal subjective processes (including attribution, assessment, and expectations), which take place before, during, and after exchanges. Interactions are "critiqued" over time to see if further penetration is worth pursuing.

Altman and Taylor define social penetration as a systematic and orderly process of mutual self-disclosure, which proceeds gradually from superficial to deeper areas of exchange involving more central aspects of each person's personality. In this respect, their view of the underlying dynamics is similar to Levinger and Snoek's. Similarly, they also view the rate and stage of social penetration as a function of interpersonal rewards and costs (in terms of absolute magnitude and reward/cost ratio), both immediate and expected.

Altman and Taylor's social penetration model is quite inclusive and extends to aspects of personality and self. Like Levinger and Snoek, they believe the development of a relationship is closely related to self-disclosure and the breadth and depth of each person's knowledge of the other. Critical to their conception of the social-penetration process, however, is the degree of access each person has to core aspects of the other's personality. They visualize both disclosure and access in terms of a

Commonalities

These three stage models have several important underlying similarities. The first is that early stages largely involve interactions that are socially "safe" or stereotypical, concerning topics that are routine, superficial, or prescribed by role expectations. Commitment tends to be tentative; knowledge of the other is superficial and segmental; and the focus of each party's concerns tends to be principally unilateral rather than bilateral. In contrast, later stages are characterized by richer and more penetrating exchanges, more commitment to the other and to the relationship itself, and finally greater permanence and stability.

Underlying processes

The three stage paradigms are all rooted in social-exchange theory, in that movement from one stage to another is based on the prospect that greater social penetration, mutuality, or commitment will be, on balance, more rewarding. All three models also presume the presence of what Altman and Taylor have described as internal subjective processes, such as attribution, the development of expectations, assessment, and evaluation. Finally, several common overt processes are involved in moving from one stage to another. These include selective self-disclosure, exploration, testing, and negotiation.

In their shared view of the direction of movement and the underlying processes, the three stage models are readily applicable to the development of working relationships. It is not clear, however, that the *particular configurations* of the stages postulated by these authors are as applicable to working relationships as they are to social and intimate relationships. Let us now turn our attention to working relationships as a substantive category to explore these differences and their implications in more detail.

WORKING RELATIONSHIPS AS A SUBSTANTIVE TYPE

One should not draw too sharp a line between working relationships and social relationships. Working relationships are, after all, a form of social relationship; they employ social modalities, develop between two social beings, and exist in organizational contexts that are themselves social structures. For these reasons we will treat them as a substantive type of social relationship. Nonetheless, it also seems clear that working relationships are not the same as purely social or intimate relationships. The stage paradigms reviewed in figure 12.2 do not apply easily to most working relationships, except as they pertain to their purely personal aspects. A key question thus is what characteristics of working relationships distinguish them from other types of social relationships.

Interpersonal setting and relationship goals

An important factor affecting the development of any relationship is the behavioral setting itself (Barker 1968; Wicker 1972) and the expectations that people bring to it as an interpersonal setting (McCall 1974). Interpersonal settings have been described in terms of a number of dimensions. These include such contextual cues as time, space, and objects (Athos and Gabarro 1978) and place, imagery, and nonverbal clues (McCaskey 1978). Altman and Taylor (1973) have argued that the purpose of a relationship is itself a basic aspect of the interpersonal setting. They cite earlier work by Bennis et al. (1964) in which interpersonal settings are defined in terms of relationship goals, that is, the purposes inherent in why a given relationship is formed in the first place. Using this definition, Bennis et al. identified four different types of relationships that act as interpersonal settings: (1) relationships formed to fulfill themselves (such as love, friendship, and marriage); (2) those formed for self-confirmation or situational definition; (3) those formed to influence or bring about change; and (4) those formed to focus on task achievement. Although working relationships often meet two or more of these goals simultaneously, their primary purpose is usually the achievement of a task, and the wider setting is typically an organizational or task-based context. Because of their distinctive purpose and interpersonal setting, several factors are much more important in working relationships than in purely social ones. These factors include task and task instrumentality, the degree of affect, the role of competence, the nature of self-disclosure, and the importance of role.

TASK AND TASK ACHIEVEMENT

One result of the centrality of the task dimension is that the social component of a working relationship is less important than it is in an intimate relationship (Triandis and Davis 1965; Goldstein and Davis 1972). In terms of underlying social-exchange dynamics, the principal rewards and costs concern task achievement. Similarly, although the affective component is important to all relationships, it is less so in task-based, formal relationships than in purely social ones (Triandis 1977). In part, this is because people seek out other interpersonal settings to attain other kinds of rewards (McCall 1974) and form working relationships principally to focus on task completion.

TASK INSTRUMENTALITY

When task attainment is the basis for a relationship, people can be expected to value attributes in the other that are consistent with task accomplishment (Wortman and Linsenmeier 1977). Research by Wall and Adams (1974) and others shows clearly that in task-based dyads, a person's ability to perform effectively influences a number of interpersonal outcomes, including the other person's willingness to grant autonomy, the development of trust, and the other person's evaluation—all of which are important to the relationship-formation process. Similarly, other research has shown that successful task performance is a basis for both liking and attraction (Farris and Lim 1969) and satisfaction and cohesion (Staw 1975).

Conversely, some research on working relationships also suggests that some conventional sources of interpersonal attraction are less important in working relationships than they are in social or intimate relationships. In a three-year longitudinal study of the evolution of managerial relationships, Gabarro (1978) found that initial liking and attraction were not predictive of the longer-term strength of the relationship. Other more instrumentally relevant attributes, such as judgment, competence, and task consistency, were far more important to the development of a working relationship and its resulting quality, but these attributes did not emerge until after the two parties had worked together for some time. Gabarro also found that if a superior or subordinate was an effective working partner, managers would overlook social traits that they would have considered undesirable in a personal relationship (Gabarro 1978, 290–92).

Elsewhere, I have referred to the task-based instrumentality found in managerial relationships as a "pragmatic imperative," arguing that it shapes interactions profoundly but not always with the best outcomes (Gabarro 1980).[2] The pragmatic imperative influences how a relationship develops and what is valued in it. It has particular implications for competence and for the nature of self-disclosure in working relationships.

COMPETENCE

Task-specific competence plays a much greater role in the development of working relationships than it does in purely social ones. Considerable research suggests that competence has a direct effect on the development of both interpersonal trust and influence (see the review by Walton et al. 1968; Bachman 1968; Wall and Adams 1974; Gabarro 1978, 1979; Schwarzwald and Goldenberg 1979). Demonstrated competence has also been found to influence liking and interpersonal evaluation in working relationships (Lowin and Craig 1968; Farris and Lim 1969; Fromkin, Klimoski, and Flanagan 1972) as well as how much a person is willing to invest in a relationship (Gabarro 1978). Thus competence can be expected to be a very powerful personal attribute in the development of working relationships.

SELF-DISCLOSURE

In all three of the major stage paradigms reviewed earlier, self-disclosure, especially of a personal or intimate nature, figures prominently both as a characteristic of a relationship and as an underlying process involved in the development of relationships. The limited work that has been done on the role of self-disclosure in working relationships suggests that disclosure about self is less important than openness concerning task or organizational issues (Gabarro 1978), but that openness concerning task-related issues is quite critical (Gaines 1980; Sgro et al. 1980). Current research also suggests that interpersonal trust as related to openness is a two-factor variable comprising a person-specific, attitudinal factor, which is broad-based and stable, and a situation-specific factor, which is less stable and is situationally contingent (Archer 1979; Scott 1980). Indeed, Gabarro (1978) found examples of working relationships that were perceived by both parties as highly effective and satisfying but that involved very little disclosure of a personal or intimate nature. This should not be surprising, because working relationships are, in Altman and Taylor's (1973) terms, segmental in nature: they do not necessarily involve all aspects of a person's life. Disclosure of one's intimate thoughts and feelings is not as important to the development of a working relationship as openness about variables that directly influence the relationship. In fact, personal disclosures may have a negative effect if seen as inappropriate (Jones and Gordon 1972; Derlega and Grzelak 1979; Wortman et al. 1976) or poorly timed (Jones and Archer 1976).

Role as a factor

If task instrumentality is an important consequence of the purposive nature of working relationships, the presence of organizational roles is an equally important aspect of their interpersonal setting (Biddle and Thomas 1966). Roles and role expectations are part of the context of all social interaction, but they are even more pervasive and are more explicitly defined in working relationships, particularly when they occur within or across organizational hierarchies. Most working relationships develop between people by virtue of their roles. In this respect, people begin with an institutionalized role relationship, often before they have begun to develop an actual working relationship. For example, superiors and subordinates begin their interactions with a "ratified role relationship," which is the final stage in the Secord and Backman paradigm of relationship development (see figure 12.2). In a perverse way, they are at stage 4 before they have begun the activities that Secord and Backman describe as occurring in earlier stages. The operational question for such a dyad is not whether to get "married," but rather how to make the marriage work (Gabarro and Kotter 1980).

---

2. In using the expression *pragmatic imperative* I am calling attention to the desire of managers to focus on aspects of causality that are instrumentally relevant in achieving the ends they are most concerned with, i.e., creating effects that contribute to task attainment and personal and organizational performance. But in a more basic sense *all* relationships are pragmatic in that people see their situations and act upon them in ways that help them attain what they want or what they think is important (Lecky 1945). Part of this pragmatism in everyday life is that people tend to perceive their situations in ways that simplify them so they can focus on what is *salient* to and what is important. The need for this selective simplification is a recurrent theme in virtually every school of psychology and social psychology, and the concept of the pragmatic imperative as a variable in human interaction is an old and pervasive one. Weick (1969, 67) explicitly describes the predominant orientation of the human actor as pragmatic and identifies this pragmatism as the essential determinant of what a person attends to and what meanings he makes of his experiencing. Thus, in using the term *pragmatic imperative*, I am only highlighting an essential aspect of all human interaction in managerially specific terms.

A second consequence of roles in hierarchical organizations is that the distribution of power in working relationships tends to be far clearer and more asymmetric than in relationships of a purely social and voluntary nature. Asymmetry in power has a negative effect on self-disclosure and the development of trust (Walton et al. 1968; Walton, 1969) unless such self-disclosure is legitimized by role-related social norms, such as those pertaining to relationships with psychiatrists, physicians, social workers, and priests (Derlega and Grzelak 1979). Thus working relationships are likely to develop in a more guarded and monitored fashion than those described in the general literature on relationship formation. On the other hand, work by Tedeschi (1974) and others suggests that asymmetry in power can sometimes be a basis of attraction if a foundation of trust or credibility exists.

A final and rather direct way in which role definitions can affect the development of working relationships is that people's reactions to each other and the attributions they make about each other are clearly influenced by role expectations (Davis 1973; Guiot 1977; Triandis 1977). Guiot has argued convincingly that attributions about intention and behavior are made quite differently if one is viewed "in role" rather than "*qua persona*," and that behavior that leads to the attribution of sincerity or trustworthiness "*qua persona*" will not lead to the same attribution if a person is seen "in role." Guiot further argues that because of this distinction many findings in the attribution literature are not applicable to role-based situations.

Salient differences

As the preceding discussion makes clear, working relationships differ from more purely social relationships in a number of ways that are likely to influence their development. First, they are more *segmental* in nature than intimate or personal relationships. Both the mutuality of exchange and the breadth of that mutuality can be expected to be narrower and less inclusive than in personal relationships; relationship development is more likely to involve depth of mutual understanding concerning task-related issues rather than breadth along a fuller range of issues. Second, *openness* concerning task-salient issues can be expected to be more important than self-disclosure per se. Third, specific *competencies* that are task relevant will be an important influence on attributions, liking, and evaluation. Finally, *role definitions* can be expected to temper openness, trust, and self-disclosure as a working relationship progresses and, all other things

being equal, retard the degree of social penetration that is likely to occur (Altman and Taylor 1973).

THE DEVELOPMENT OF WORKING RELATIONSHIPS

With these differences in mind, let us now turn our attention to the question of how working relationships develop. Although the particular configurations and content of the stages summarized in figure 12.2 do not fit working relationships easily, the underlying processes and directionality of these paradigms do have applicability if we consider the differences just reviewed as moderating variables. For example, working relationships clearly evolve toward the greater shared meanings of Levinger and Snoek's pair-relatedness model, though this development may not occur along all of the dimensions described in figure 12.2. The underlying process of self-disclosure is also applicable if we consider self-disclosure in terms of task-relevant openness. The related notion of a "growing spiral" of shared assumptions also applies if we construe it in terms of assumptions salient to task. Similarly the process of mutual investment has manifest applicability in terms of mutual accommodation and investment in common goals, if not along the other dimensions shown in the figure. The same argument can be made about the directionality of Altman and Taylor's stages of orientation, exploration, and stabilized exchange, if one views progression as occurring segmentally in terms of depth.

We can expect therefore that working relationships that develop beyond role-specified surface encounters will progress along the dimensions summarized in figure 12.1 and with the directionality of movement indicated in figure 12.2. Thus for a working relationship to develop effectively, we can expect that mutual understanding and richness of knowledge will increase, and that the nature of this mutual knowledge will move from being general and impressionistic to specific and concrete. The underlying processes of expectation formation, attribution, assessment, and evaluation will operate in the development of working relationships just as they do on other types of relationships. Finally, we can expect that task-relevant openness will play a role analogous to that of self-disclosure in intimate relationships, and depth of mutual investment will not occur unless doing so is on balance more rewarding (or less costly) than not doing so.

Although little field-based research has been done on the actual development of working relationships, there is some evidence suggesting that the development of mutual expectations is an important factor influencing both the effectiveness of working relationships (Liden and Graen 1980; Baird and Wieting 1979) and how satisfying they are (Klimoski and Hayes 1980; Valenzi and Dessler 1978). These findings are similar to those reported in the leadership literature suggesting that the structuring of expectations is the single pattern that contributes positively to productivity and satisfaction (Stogdill 1974).

The findings of the longitudinal study cited earlier are consistent with these findings. In a three-year study of the evolution of managerial relationships, Gabarro (1978, 1979) found that over time, expectations about performance, goals, and each party's role became not only more mutual but more concrete and specific as well. Interestingly, the exceptions to this pattern were either relationships that involved relatively little interdependence or ones in which one or both parties were dissatisfied with the relationship once it became stabilized. In the latter cases, Gabarro concluded that these were relationships in which insufficient openness, testing, or exploration had occurred.

The findings of this study also suggested, however, that individual relationships varied greatly in the rate at which mutuality and concreteness of expectations developed. Because of the small sample (thirty-three president/vice-president dyads in four sites) it was not possible to identify why this variation occurred. One can, however, postulate a number of reasons why some relationships develop more quickly or with greater depth than others, including differences in personal style, variations in interdependency, the relative performance of the subordinate's unit (e.g., poor performance would create greater interaction and scrutiny), and proximity (a subordinate located five hundred miles away is not likely to interact as often with his or her superior as one on the same floor).

Just as mutual expectations tended to become more specific over time, Gabarro also found that attributions about such interpersonal variables as trust and influence became more differentiated with continued interaction. In early stages, attributions of the other's trustworthiness were typically general and impressionistic, while at later stages they were quite differentiated and specific, for example, "His sense of the market is excellent but he's consistently too optimistic [on sales forecasts]" (Gabarro 1979, 12). On the basis of cross-time interview comparisons, Gabarro identified several dimensions along which attributions of trust were differentiated; these fell into two broad groups: character-based sources of trust (trust in the other's integrity, motives and intentions, consistency of behavior, openness and discreetness) and competence-based sources of trust (trust in the other's

functional or specific competence, interpersonal competence, and "general business judgment") (Gabarro 1978, 295–98). Also identified were several dimensions along which attributions of influence were differentiated in terms of both positional and personal bases.

In comparing the evolution of these relationships over the three years of the study, Gabarro postulated a four-stage model of the development of working relationships: (1) orientation and impression formation; (2) exploration; (3) testing and working through; and (4) stabilization. Figure 12.3 presents Sathe's (1985) overview of these stages, which summarizes the interpersonal tasks, issues, and dilemmas characteristic of each stage. The model is quite similar in many respects to those presented by Altman and Taylor and by Secord and Backman. The important difference is that the stages presented in figure 12.3 are described in terms of archetype issues that emerge with continued interaction rather than in terms of the "goodness" of a relationship. Gabarro postulated that management dyads progress through these stages regardless of the quality of their relationships, unless one party quits or is fired before the relationship becomes stabilized. For this reason, some working relationships that reached the stabilization stage were seen by one or both parties as not fully effective or satisfying (Gabarro 1979, 9–17).

Using a "contract" metaphor (Levinson 1968; Lawless 1972; Thomas 1976), Gabarro postulated that managers go through these stages in the process of forming a unique interpersonal contract. He also argued, however, that a relationship's effectiveness is not determined by whether a dyad progresses through these stages, but rather by how well the dyad deals with the archetypical problems and dilemmas presented by each stage. Thus, unlike the stage paradigms reviewed earlier, Gabarro's stages are defined simply by the interpersonal tasks and issues that emerge with sustained interaction. It should be clear, however, that working relationships could also be configured in terms of stages defined along hierarchical dimensions of mutuality or other qualitative aspects of relationships, which would be more directly analogous to the stage paradigms of Altman and Taylor and Levinger and Snoek.

Despite these differences, the general directionality of Gabarro's stages is essentially the same as that described in the Secord and Backman and Altman and Taylor stage paradigms. Moreover, the content and process issues described as characterizing each of the stages in figure 12.3 require the same types of exploration, openness, and reward/cost assessments as those described by Altman and Taylor and Levinger and Snoek, as well as the implicit testing and negotiating described by Secord and Backman. Indeed, figure 12.3 implies that these interpersonal processes must occur if a working relation-

Figure 12.3   Stages in the development of new working relationships: characteristics, tasks, and issues.

Stage	Characteristics	Major tasks	Issues and questions
I. Orientation: Impression formation	Brief period, perhaps lasting the first several weeks.	Deal with the question of the other's motives.	How competent, reliable, and open is the other person?
	Mutual sizing up beginning with first impressions, and continuing with more extended and less stereotyped interactions.	Exchange an initial set of expectations at a general level concerning objectives, roles, and needs.	What are the other's concerns, motives, and intentions? How open and forthright to be with the other person?
	Trust is impressionistic and undifferentiated.	Develop initial understanding of how both parties will work together in the future.	
	Personal influence not yet developed.		
II. Exploration: Beyond impressions	Longer period than Stage I, perhaps lasting the first several months. General and tentative expectations of Stage I become more specific and concrete.	Explore in more detailed and concrete terms other's expectations about goals, roles, and priorities.	How much can the other person be trusted in terms of integrity, motives, competence, judgment, and consistency of action?
	Rapid learning to search out the other's important assumptions and expectations, and to communicate one's own.	Surface and clarify differences in expectations. Explore and identify questions and sources concerning trust in terms of motives, competence, consistency, and openness.	How safe is it to be open with the other person in terms of problems or differences of opinion?
	Both parties begin to assert their personal identities, styles, and values.	Explore and identify questions and sources concerning influence in terms of positional and personal attributes.	What is the other person's credibility and decisiveness?
	Leads to confirmation or rejection of initial impressions.		
III. Testing: Testing and defining the interpersonal contract	A long period, perhaps six months to a year in duration, but could be longer.	Test the mutuality of expectations, and the bases and limits of trust and influence.	To what extent is the situation (e.g., environment, structure, culture) rather than the other person the cause of the difficulties in the relationship?
	Testing concerning minimal expectations, areas in which trust exists, and limits of each person's influence on the other are tacitly and overtly tested.	Work through and negotiate basic unresolved differences. Assess the degree to which mutual accommodation is possible, and whether the costs of achieving it are acceptable.	How long should the testing continue? How to know when enough is enough?
	As a result, limits of the evolving interpersonal contract are defined for better or for worse.	Define stabilized set of expectations concerning each other's role, and the bases for trust and influence in the relationship.	How to insure an adequate testing to avoid a superficial and unsatisfactory relationship, without pressing too hard and risking unnecessary or unproductive confrontation?
IV. Stabilization	Interpersonal contract becomes defined.	If events or episodes lead to negative feelings (e.g., conflict over a decision, slight, or oversight), take steps to repair the damage.	Is the interpersonal contract appropriate given changes in the individuals or the situation?
	Little further effort goes into learning about or testing each other.	Insure that the relationship continues to be productive, adaptive, and satisfying as the needs of the situation and the parties change.	How to keep the interpersonal contract viable in the face of major individual and situational changes?
	Aspects of the relationship such as expectations, trust, and influence undergo little additional changes.		

Figure 12.3 *continued*

Stage	Characteristics	Major tasks	Issues and questions
IV. Stabilization *continued*	Major event or change needed to destabilize the relationship.	If a major episode (e.g., one party's actions violate the level of trust built up) or a significant environmental change destabilizes the relationship, rework the earlier stages of the relationship-building process from the point of regressions.	

Reprinted from V. Sathe, *Culture and Related Corporate Realities* (Homewood, Ill.: Irwin, 1985), by permission.

ship is to develop effectively. Otherwise the relationship will stabilize at a relatively superficial level.

THE DEVELOPMENT OF MUTUAL EXPECTATIONS

Working relationships vary in their mutuality, efficacy, and intensity. Some stabilize at a relatively superficial level of exchange, others at rather deep levels of mutuality and synchrony. For purposes of this discussion, the development of working relationships has been seen as a progression from role-specified surface encounters to a greater degree of mutual exchange and task-related efficacy. The process involves both temporal dimensions (such as the sequential phases shown in figure 12.3) and qualitative dimensions (such as those summarized in figure 12.1). An implicit assumption has been that when the work of two people makes them highly dependent on each other, it is desirable to develop a relationship that is mutual and robust enough to be rewarding and effective.

How can this process be facilitated? Several implications can be drawn from the work we have just reviewed. The first is that developing a robust working relationship takes time. The internal subjective processes of attribution, expectation formation, and assessment, described earlier as underlying the relationship formation process, all occur over time, are interactive, and typically involve extended sequences of interactions (Altman 1974). To accelerate or influence the process (i.e., actually "develop" a working relationship rather than let it evolve) will require purposive "interpersonal work." Identifying and dealing with important differences of opinion, for example, requires emotional energy and action, as well as a level of awareness, of self and other, that does not occur naturally for most people.

A second implication is that the development of mutual expectations plays a key role in this process. In terms of task instrumentality and effectiveness, the relevant areas of mutuality in expectations concern (1) expectations about what the task is and what the outcomes of the joint endeavor should be; (2) expectations about how the two parties should actually work with each other (which include assumptions about process as well as responsibility); and (3) expectations about how the two people work singly and independently on the joint task. Thus the task-salient aspects of mutuality include not only expectations about outcomes but also about interpersonal processes involving interdependence, autonomy, and individual influence, which are in turn affected by each person's assumptions about trust and power within a relationship (Deutsch 1962; Argyris 1962; Jacobson 1972; Barnes 1981).

Both the general literature on relationship formation and the field-based research reviewed earlier suggest that the development of mutual expectations requires a great deal of exploration, testing, and negotiation of individual expectations. These processes occur at both tacit and overt levels of behavior. It also requires considerable internal subjective work by each party, involving attributional processes, the formation and revision of individual expectations, and evaluative processes of the type described by social exchange theorists. To work actively toward developing shared expectations therefore requires a clear communication of initial expectations, where possible, and the exploration and testing of any difference in expectations. Exploration is also required when it is not clear to one or both parties what should be done or how to proceed (as is often the case at the outset of a joint endeavor). Finally either tacit or overt negotiation of differences is required before mutual expectations can be formed.

Although mutual expectations are sometimes negotiated or clarified as a result of critical and occasionally dramatic events, they are more typically worked out over time during a succession of routine interactions, such as *ad hoc* encounters, meetings, progress reviews, and discussions of task-based problems (Gabarro 1978).

Thus much of the work of developing mutual expectations will appear to be routine, invisible, or tacit, except where differences in initial expectations are clear.

The difficulty involved in clarifying, exploring, testing, and negotiating expectations will depend on the *a priori* differences between the two people involved. In this respect, working relationships are no different from purely social relationships, in which similarities in values and attitudes affect the ease with which further mutuality can develop (Berscheid and Walster 1969). Considerable evidence suggests that the more similar two people are in background and attitudes, the easier and more satisfying a task-based relationship will become (Wexley et al. 1980; Ross and Ferris 1981; Posner and Munson 1979; Weiss 1978). The literature on organization theory also suggests that differences in functional backgrounds result in different cognitive orientations concerning task achievement and different attitudes toward structuring, which are themselves natural sources of conflict (Lawrence and Lorsch 1967; Lorsch and Allen 1973). Thus we can expect that differences in social attitudes and values as well as functionally based task predispositions will influence the amount of interpersonal work needed to develop an effective working relationship. This will be especially true in early stages, when initial expectations are "traded" and explored, and in later stages when mutual expectations are tested and negotiated.

Most of the research on working relationships (as well as much of the work done on the dynamics of task-based groups) suggests that openness in the confrontation of differences can make the outcomes of these processes more effective. The dilemma, of course, is that although openness tends to be reciprocated (Chaikin and Derlega 1974), some threshold amount of interpersonal trust is needed before it seems safe to be open with another person (Rubin 1975), especially where differences involve emotionally charged issues. No doubt this is why people "test" apparent differences incrementally and why modeling of openness by one or both parties is seen by many scholars of two-person relationships as a major explanation of why two people become more open over time (Bandura 1977). In working relationships, it seems clear that the superior or the higher-status member of the dyad is in the safer position to model such behavior (Levinson 1968; Gabarro 1979).

The process of developing mutual expectations is further complicated by the reality that often one or both parties do not know what they want at the outset of a working relationship. One's expectations often do not become clear until after one has had some experience working with another person. In this respect, most differentiated expectations result from a process that

Weick (1979) has called "retrospective sense-making" involving the "reflective glance." Much of the work of developing mutual expectations is therefore episodic and iterative. Even if early agreement on initial expectations is easily attained, subsequent renegotiation is needed as relationships develop. Several large U.S. corporations, such as General Electric and Exxon, have used "assimilation meetings" to facilitate the clarification and negotiation of mutual expectations between newly assigned managers and their new subordinates. These meetings have been very effective in clarifying initial expectations, developing a basis of trust, and accelerating the process by which initial mutual expectations are agreed upon. Experience with these interventions suggests, however, that subsequent meetings are needed after six to eight months to deal with issues that neither party could anticipate at the outset.

The development of mutual expectations is an extended process. Concrete differentiation of these expectations takes time and requires interpersonal work. As for the development of influence and trust, one-time interventions are insufficient (Scott 1980). The research reviewed in this chapter, however, suggests that greater attention on the part of one or both parties can greatly influence the success and effectiveness of this process, and that certain interventions of the type just described can help focus and accelerate the process. My own belief is that they also legitimize the confrontation and resolution of differences early in the relationship-formation process, thereby making it easier and safer for both parties to be open with each other as the relationship develops.

IMPLICATIONS FOR FURTHER RESEARCH

The development of working relationships is a vital aspect of organizational life. Nevertheless, although a large number of scholars trained in social psychology have recently entered the field of organizational behavior, it remains a neglected area of inquiry.

The thinness of existing research applicable to understanding how working relationships develop has at least three implications for further work. The first is that more research is needed on the development of working relationships as a substantive area of knowledge. The second is that more field-based work is needed so that working relationships can be studied in context. The third is that more work of a longitudinal nature is needed because the development of working relationships is an evolutionary social phenomenon.

Substantive area of inquiry

Research on phenomenal causality of behavior within two-person relationships is a strong tradition within social psychology, dating back to the early 1930s. This tradition has included work on interpersonal perception as well as phenomenal causality, and has yielded several major theories, including balance theory, other consistency theories, exchange theories, and, most recently, attribution theory. Yet for our purposes, this impressive body of knowledge has two significant limitations. First, although these theories are potent in their general explanatory power, they are of less value in predicting behavior and outcomes in *specific types of relationships*. This is not because they are poorly constructed theories. Rather, it is because they are so general that they cannot be usefully applied unless one first understands the situational context and purpose of a relationship. As Levinger (1974, 117) has pointed out in a critique of exchange and reinforcement theories, the strengths of these theories are simultaneously their weaknesses: "that which explains everything explains nothing; the 'laws' of [such theories] must be moved toward greater specificity and their elements differentiated." What is salient in a relationship obviously depends in part on its nature and context (From 1957; Tagiuri 1969; Jones and Thibaut 1958). Situational forces are sufficiently complex and variable in and of themselves that one cannot understand what is important to two people in a relationship without understanding the context and how it impinges on the people involved (Kerckhoff 1974). For example, attribution theory is clearly germane to the question of how two managers make attributions about each other in forming working relationships. But it is not very useful in understanding how working relationships develop unless one understands what traits, dispositions, behaviors, and contextual entities are salient to managers in their working relationships.

Indeed, several theories emerging from the literature on phenomenal causality—most notably attribution theory, cognitive-dissonance theory, and exchange theory—have been taught for some time in most graduate business schools and are included in most current textbooks on organizational behavior. Yet practicing managers seldom use these concepts to inform their decisions. I suspect that one reason for this disjunction between theory and practice is the lack of situationally grounded substantive theory. The importance of this gap between general and substantive theory has been pointed out by Wortman and Linsenmeier (1977) in their review of research on interpersonal attraction and ingratiation and its applicability to organizational settings. They note that the importance of competence and power in working relationships significantly affects the extent to which existing theory and findings are useful in predicting outcomes, and they conclude that considerably more research is needed on the particular "vicissitudes of the phenomena in organizational settings" before existing research on interpersonal attraction and ingratiation can be applied to the substantive issues and problems of organizational and managerial behavior (p. 173).

Clearly, certain basic underlying dynamics of relationships transcend situational settings. But the manifestation of these dynamics and the particular contextual factors that affect them vary from setting to setting. Further work of an integrative and substantive nature is needed to learn how these processes take place between people within organizations.

Field-based longitudinal research

As we attempt to learn more about the development of working relationships, there is a great need for field-based, longitudinal research. Very little research so far has focused on how "natural" working relationships evolve over time. By natural relationships, I mean real, ongoing relationships as they exist in everyday life. Most research on relationship formation has involved "synthetic" relationships created for purposes of laboratory experimentation.[3] Such synthetic relationships are by their very nature carefully constrained, controlled, and short-lived (as brief as thirty minutes; typically no longer than a couple of hours). Usually the person with whom the subject interacts in the relationship is a confederate of the experimenter, so that even if the subject's reactions are "natural," those of the confederate are not.

Obviously laboratory experimentation has many advantages, the principal one being that it enables the researcher to focus on specific variables under controlled conditions. Most of the advances in attribution theory and interpersonal attraction have been based on such work. But the results of laboratory research have only limited applicability to our understanding of the dynamics of developing relationships. Natural relationships are ongoing and evolutionary in nature, and people's interactions are less constrained than in a laboratory setting. In real relationships people are free to seek additional information, and, more important, they are able to "proact" on each other over time. As Weick (1979) and others have pointed out, people learn from their actions and the consequences of their actions and make cause-

---

3. See, for example, Swensen's (1973) review of various approaches to the study of interpersonal relations and the data and methods employed within these approaches (144–47). There are, of course, some exceptions to this generalization, especially in regard to social exchange theory (245–56).

effect attributions in terms of past history (Jones and Goethals 1972). Laboratory subjects are really objects, in the literal sense of the word, because they are one of the variables being manipulated and their ability to proact is severely constrained. In real relationships people are both subjects and objects. They can seek more information, act, and learn from their actions, and they do this over time (Bugental 1969, 1978). To my knowledge, little empirical research within organizational behavior has focused on the development of natural working relationships and on how attributions change or develop over time as two people work together.

A related limitation of much of the work on relationship formation in general is that it is largely devoted to the verification and development of general theory (or what Glaser and Strauss [1967] and others have called formal theory). Thus, although some of it has dealt with specific aspects of behavior, the resulting findings are still at a very general level of abstraction and thus of limited utility in substantive areas such as working relationships. Unfortunately, this is particularly true of research on attribution, which is a central aspect of the relationship-formation process.

In stressing the need for more field-based longitudinal research and for more substantive theory, I do not wish to reinforce further the polarity that currently exists between field-based, middle-range theory and laboratory-based general theory. Clearly, further substantive research on the topic needs to be informed by existing formal theory, and conversely the development of more grounded, substantive theory cannot help but inform and articulate the larger base of general theory.

REFERENCES

Altman, I. 1974. "The Communication of Interpersonal Attitudes: An Ecological Approach." In *Foundations of Interpersonal Attraction*, ed. T. L. Huston, p. 121. New York: Academic Press.

Altman, I., and D. A. Taylor. 1973. *Social Penetration: The Development of Interpersonal Relationships*. New York: Holt, Rinehart and Winston.

Archer, R. L. 1979. "Role of Personality and the Social Situation." In *Self-Disclosure*, ed. G. J. Chelune. p. 28. San Francisco: Jossey-Bass.

Argyris, C. 1962. *Interpersonal Competence and Organizational Effectiveness*. Homewood, Ill.: Dorsey Press.

Athos, A. G., and J. J. Gabarro. 1978. *Interpersonal Behavior*. Englewood Cliffs, N.J.: Prentice-Hall.

Bachman, J. G. 1968. "Faculty Satisfaction and the Dean's Influence: An Organizational Study of Twelve Liberal Arts Colleges." *Journal of Applied Psychology* 52:55–61.

Baird, J. E., Jr., and G. K. Wieting. 1979. "Nonverbal Communication Can Be a Motivational Tool." *Personnel Journal* 58, no. 9 (September): 607–25.

Bandura, A. 1977. *Social Learning Theory*. Englewood Cliffs, N.J.: Prentice-Hall.

Barker, R. 1968. *Ecological Psychology. Concepts and Methods for Studying the Environment of Human Behavior*. Stanford, Calif.: Stanford University Press.

Barnes, L. B. 1981. "Managing the Paradox of Organizational Trust." *Harvard Business Review* (March-April).

Bennis, W. G., E. H. Schien, D. E. Berlew, and F. I. Steele. 1964. *Interpersonal Dynamics*. Homewood, Ill.: Dorsey Press.

Berscheid, E., and E. Walster. 1969. *Interpersonal Attraction*. Reading, Mass.: Addison-Wesley.

Biddle, B. J., and E. J. Thomas. 1966. *Role Theory: Concepts and Research*. New York: Wiley.

Bugental, J. F. T. 1969. "Someone Needs to Worry: The Existential Anxiety of Responsibility and Decision." *Journal of Contemporary Psychotherapy* 2, no. 1:41–53.

———. 1978. "Intentionality and Ambivalence." In *Interpersonal Behavior: Communication and Understanding in Relationships*, ed. A. G. Athos and J. J. Gabarro, p. 512. Englewood Cliffs, N.J.: Prentice-Hall.

Carson, R. C. 1969, *Interaction Concepts of Personality*. Chicago: Aldine.

Chaikin, A. L., and V. J. Derlega. 1974. *Self Disclosure*. Morristown: N.J.: General Learning Press.

Davis, M. S. 1973. *Intimate Relations*. New York: Free Press.

Derlega, V. J., and J. Grzelak. 1979. "Appropriateness of Self-Disclosure." In *Self-Disclosure*, ed. G. J. Chelune, p. 151. San Francisco: Jossey-Bass.

Deutsch, M. 1962. "Cooperation and Trust: Some Theoretical Notes." In *Nebraska Symposium on Motivation*, pp. 275–319. Lincoln, Neb.: University of Nebraska Press.

Dubin, R., and S. L. Spray. 1964. "Executive Behavior and Interaction." *Industrial Relations*, no. 3:99–108.

Farris, G. F., and F. G. Lim, Jr. 1969. "Effects of Performance on Leadership, Cohesiveness, Influence, Satisfaction, and Subsequent Performance." *Journal of Applied Psychology* 53:490–97.

From, F. 1957. "The Experience of Purpose in Human Behavior." Paper read at Fifteenth International Congress of Psychology, Brussels. Cited in Tagiuri and Petrullo 1958.

Fromkin, H. L., R. J. Klimoski, and M. F. Flanagan. 1972. "Race and Competence as Determinants of Acceptance of Newcomers in Success and Failure Work Groups." *Organizational Behavior and Human Performance*, pp. 25–42.

Gabarro, J. J. 1978. "The Development of Trust, Influence, and Expectations." In *Interpersonal Behavior*, ed. A. G. Athos and J. J. Gabarro, p. 290. Englewood Cliffs, N.J.: Prentice-Hall.

———. 1979. "Socialization at the Top: How CEO's and their Subordinates Evolve Interpersonal Contracts." *Organizational Dynamics* (Winter), p. 2.

———. 1980. "The Evolution of Managerial Working Relationships." Working Paper, Harvard University International Senior Management Program Center, Vevey, Switzerland.

Gabarro, J. J., and J. P. Kotter. 1980. "Managing Your Boss." *Harvard Business Review* (January-February).

Gaines, J. H. 1980. "Upward Communication in Industry: An Experiment." *Human Relations* 33, no. 12 (December): 929–42.

Glaser, B., and A. L. Strauss. 1967. *The Discovery of Grounded Theory: Strategies for Qualitative Research.* Chicago: Aldine.

Goldstein, M., and E. E. Davis. 1972. "Race and Belief: A Further Analysis of the Social Determinants of Behavioral Intentions." *Journal of Personality and Social Psychology* 22:346–55.

Guiot, J. M. 1977. "Attribution and Identity Construction: Some Comments." *American Sociological Review* 42:692–704.

Hinde, R. A. 1971. "Some Problems in the Study of Development of Social Behavior." In *The Biopsychology of Development,* ed. E. Tobach, L. R. Aronson, and E. Shaw. New York: Academic Press.

———. 1977. "On Assessing the Bases of Partner Preferences." *Behavior* 62:1–9.

———. 1979. *Towards Understanding Relationships.* London: Academic Press.

Hodgson, R. C., D. J. Levinson, and A. Zaleznik. 1965. *The Executive Role Constellation.* Boston: Division of Research, Graduate School of Business Administration, Harvard University.

Homans, G. 1950. *The Human Group.* New York: Harcourt, Brace and World.

———. 1961. *Social Behavior: Its Elementary Forms.* New York: Harcourt, Brace and World.

Huston, T. L. 1974a. *Foundations of Interpersonal Attraction.* New York: Academic Press.

———. 1974b. "A Perspective on Interpersonal Attraction." In *Foundations of Interpersonal Attraction,* ed. T. L. Huston, p. 3. New York: Academic Press.

Inkson, J. H. K., J. P. Schwitter, D. C. Pheysey, and D. J. Hickson. 1970. "A Comparison of Organizations Structure and Managerial Roles: Ohio, U.S.A., and the Midlands, England." *The Journal of Management Studies* no. 7:347–63.

Jacobson, W. D. 1972. *Power and Interpersonal Relations.* Belmont, Calif.: Wadsworth.

Jones, E. E., and R. L. Archer. 1976. "Are There Special Effects of Personalistic Self-Disclosure?" *Journal of Experimental Social Psychology* 12, no. 2:180–93.

Jones, E. E., and G. R. Goethals. 1972. "Order Effects in Impression Formation: Attribution Context and the Nature of the Entity." In *Attribution: Perceiving the Causes of Behavior,* ed. E. E. Jones, D. E. Kanouse, H. H. Kelley, R. E. Nisbett, S. Valins, and B. Weiner. Morristown, N.J.: General Learning.

Jones, E. E., and E. M. Gordon. 1972. "Timing of Self-Disclosure and Its Effects on Personal Attraction." *Journal of Personality and Social Psychology* 24, no. 3:358–65.

Jones, E. E., and J. W. Thibaut. 1958. "Interaction Goals as Bases of Inference in Interpersonal Perception." In *Person Perception and Interpersonal Behavior,* ed. R. Tagiuri and L. Petrullo, p. 151. Stanford, Calif: Stanford University Press.

Jourard, S. M. 1959. "Self-Disclosure and Other Cathexis." *Journal of Personality and Social Psychology,* p. 59.

———. 1971. *Self-Disclosure: An Experimental Analysis of the Transparent Self.* New York: Wiley-Interscience.

Kelvin, P. 1970. *The Bases of Social Behaviour: An Approach in Terms of Order and Value.* London: Holt, Rinehart and Winston.

Kerckhoff, A. C. 1974. "The Social Context of Interpersonal Attraction." In *Foundations of Interpersonal Attraction,* ed. T. L. Huston, p. 61. New York: Academic Press.

Kerckhoff, A. C., and K. E. Davis. 1962. "Value Consensus and Need Complementarity in Mate Selection." *American Sociological Review,* 27.

Klimoski, R. J., and N. J. Hayes. 1980. "Leader Behavior and Subordinate Motivation." *Personnel Psychology* 33, no. 3 (Autumn): 543–55.

Kotter, J. P. 1982. *The General Managers.* New York: Macmillan.

Lawless, D. J. 1972. *Effective Management: A Social Psychological Approach.* Englewood Cliffs, N.J.: Prentice-Hall.

Lawrence, P. R., and J. W. Lorsch. 1967. *Organization and Environment.* Boston: Harvard Business School.

Lecky, P. 1945. *Self-Consistency: A Theory of Personality.* New York: Island Press.

Levinger, G. 1974. "A Three-Level Approach to Attraction: Toward an Understanding of Pair Relatedness." In *Foundations of Interpersonal Attraction,* ed. T. L. Huston, p. 100. New York: Academic Press.

Levinger, G., and J. D. Snoek. 1972. *Attraction in Relationship: A New Look at Interpersonal Attraction.* Morristown, N.J.: General Learning.

Levinson, H. 1964. *Emotional Health in the World of Work.* New York: Harper & Row.

———. 1968. *The Exceptional Executive.* Cambridge, Mass.: Harvard University Press.

Liden, R. C., and G. Graen. 1980. "Generalizability of the Vertical Dyad Linkage Model of Leadership." *Academy of Management Journal* 25 (September): 451–65.

Lidz, T., A. Cornelison, S. Fleck, and D. Terry. 1957. "The Intra-familial Environment of Schizophrenic Patients: II. Marital Schism and Marital Skew." *American Journal of Psychiatry* 114:241–48.

Lidz, T., and S. Fleck. 1960. "Schizophrenia, Human Integration, and the Role of the Family." In *The Etiology of Schizophrenia,* ed. D. D. Jackson. New York: Basic Books.

Lorsch, J. W., and S. A. Allen. 1973. *Managing Diversity and Interdependence.* Boston: Harvard Business School.

Lowin, A., and J. R. Craig. 1968. "The Influence of Level of Performance on Managerial Style: An Experimental

Object-lesson in the Ambiguity of Correlational Data." *Organizational Behavior and Human Performance* 3:440–58.

McCall, G. J. 1974. "A Symbolic Interactionist Approach to Attraction." In *Foundations of Interpersonal Attraction*, ed. T. L. Huston, p. 217. New York: Academic Press.

McCaskey, M. B. 1978. "Place Imagery and Nonverbal Cues." In *Interpersonal Behavior*, ed. A. G. Athos and J. J. Gabarro. Englewood Cliffs, N.J.: Prentice-Hall.

Mintzberg, H. 1973. *The Nature of Managerial Work.* New York: Harper & Row.

Murstein, B. I. 1977. "The Stimulus-Value-Role (SVR) Theory of Dyadic Relationships." In *Theory and Practice in Inter-Personal Attraction*, ed. S. Duck. London: Academic Press.

Newcomb, T. M. 1961. *The Acquaintance Process.* New York: Holt, Rinehart and Winston.

Posner, B. Z., and J. M. Munson. 1979. "The Impact of Subordinate-Supervisor Value Consensus." *Akron Business and Economic Review* 10, no. 2:37–40.

Ross, J., and K. R. Ferris. 1981. "Interpersonal Attraction and Organizational Outcomes: A Field Examination." *Administrative Science Quarterly* 26, no. 4 (December): 617–32.

Rubin, Z. 1975. "Disclosing Oneself to a Stranger: Reciprocity and Its Limits." *Journal of Experimental Social Psychology* 11, no. 3:233–60.

Sathe, V. 1985. *Culture and Related Corporate Realities.* Homewood, Ill.: Irwin.

Schwarzwald, J., and J. Goldenberg. 1979. "Compliance and Assistance to an Authority Figure in Perceived Equitable or Nonequitable Situations." *Human Relations* 32, no. 10 (October): 877–88.

Scott, C. L., III. 1980. "Interpersonal Trust: A Comparison of Attitudinal and Situational Factors." *Human Relations* 33 (November): 805–12.

Secord, P. F., and C. W. Backman. 1964. *Social Psychology.* New York: McGraw-Hill.

Sgro, J. A., P. Worchel, E. C. Pence, and J. A. Orban. 1980. "Perceived Leader Behavior as a Function of the Leader's Interpersonal Trust Orientation." *Academy of Management Journal* 23, no. 1 (March): 161–65.

Simmel, G. 1950. *The Sociology of Georg Simmel*, trans. K. H. Wolff. New York: Free Press of Glencoe.

Staw, G. M. 1975. "Attribution of the 'Causes' of Performance: A General Alternative Interpretation of Cross-sectional Research on Organizations." *Organizational Behavior and Human Performance* 13:414–32.

Stewart, R. 1967. *Managers and Their Jobs.* London: Macmillan.

———. 1982. *Choices for the Manager: A Guide to Managerial Work and Behavior*, Englewood Cliffs, N.J.: Prentice-Hall.

Stieglitz, H. 1969. *The Chief Executive—And His Job.* Personnel Policy Study no. 214. New York: National Industrial Conference Board.

Stogdill, R. M. 1974. *Handbook of Leadership.* New York: Free Press.

Sullivan, H. S. 1953. *The Interpersonal Theory of Psychiatry.* New York: Norton.

Swensen, C. H., Jr. 1973. *Introduction to Interpersonal Relations.* Glenview, Ill.: Scott, Foresman.

Tagiuri, R. 1969. "Person Perception." In *Handbook of Social Psychology*, vol. 3, ed. G. Lindzey and E. Aronson. Reading, Mass.: Addison-Wesley.

Tagiuri, R., and L. Petrullo. 1958. *Person Perception and Interpersonal Behavior.* Stanford, Calif.: Stanford University Press.

Tedeschi, J. T. 1974. "Attributions, Liking, and Power." In *Foundations of Interpersonal Attraction*, ed. T. L. Huston. New York: Academic Press.

Thibaut, J., and H. H. Kelley. 1959. *The Social Psychology of Groups.* New York: Wiley.

Thomas, R. 1976. "Managing the Psychological Contract." In *Organizational Behavior and Administration*, ed. P. Lawrence, L. Barnes, and J. Lorsch, p. 465. Homewood, Ill.: Irwin.

Triandis, H. C. 1977. *Interpersonal Behavior.* Monterey, Calif.: Brooks/Cole.

Triandis, H. C., and E. E. Davis. 1965. "Race and Belief as Determinants of Behavior Intentions." *Journal of Personality and Social Psychology* 2:715–25.

Valenzi, E., and G. Dessler. 1978. "Relationships of Leader Behavior, Subordinate Role Ambiguity, and Subordinate Job Satisfaction." *Academy of Management Journal* 21, no. 4 (December): 671–78.

Wall, J. A., and J. S. Adams. 1974. "Some Variables Affecting a Constituent's Evaluations of and Behavior Toward a Boundary-Role Occupant." In *Organizational Behavior and Human Performance* 2:290–408.

Walton, R. E. 1968. *Social and Psychological Aspects of Verification, Inspection, and International Assurance.* Lafayette, Ind.: Purdue University Press.

———. 1969. *Interpersonal Peacemaking: Confrontations and Third-Party Consultation.* Reading, Mass.: Addison-Wesley.

Weick, K. E. 1969, 1979. *The Social Psychology of Organizing* (2d ed., 1979). Reading, Mass.: Addison-Wesley.

Weiss, H. M. 1978. "Social Learning of Work Values in Organizations." *Journal of Applied Psychology* 63, no. 6 (December): 711–18.

Wexley, K. N., R. A. Alexander, J. P. Greenawalt, and M. A. Couch. 1980. "Attitudinal Congruence and Similarity as Related to Interpersonal Evaluations in Manager-Subordinate Dyads." *Academy of Management Journal* 23, no. 2:320–30.

Wicker, A. W. 1972. "Processes Which Mediate Behavior-Environment Congruence." *Behavior Science* 17:265–77.

Wortman, C. B., and J. A. W. Linsenmeier. 1977. "Interpersonal Attraction and Techniques of Ingratiation in Organizational Settings." In *New Directions in Organizational Behavior*, ed. G. Salancik and B. M. Staw, p. 133. Chicago: St. Clair Press.

Wortman, C. B., P. Adesman, E. Herman, and R. Greensburg. 1976. "Self-Disclosure: An Attributional Perspective." *Journal of Personality and Social Psychology* 33, no. 2:184–91.

13

An intergroup perspective on group dynamics

CLAYTON P. ALDERFER

INTRODUCTION

The study of intergroup relations brings to bear a variety of methods and theories from social science on a diverse set of difficult social problems (Allport 1954; Merton 1960; Sherif and Sherif 1969; Van Den Berge 1972; Pettigrew 1981). Taken literally, intergroup relations refer to activities *between* and *among* groups. Note that the choice of preposition is significant. Whether people observe groups only two at a time or in more complex constellations has important implications for action and for understanding. Intergroup concepts can explain a broader range of phenomena than just what go on at the intersection of two or more groups. The range of concern is from how individuals think as revealed in studies of prejudice and stereotyping to how nation states deal with each other in the realm of international conflict. A central feature of virtually all intergroup analysis is the persistently problematic relationship between individual people and collective social processes.

The argument in this chapter proceeds in four major steps. The first section describes several prominent historical developments that set the stage for intergroup theory and method as we know it today. Included in this section are accounts of limitations in the early works as well as contributions. The second section explores several

dimensions along which contemporary versions of intergroup theory may be compared. The perspectives in this section pertain to concepts, methods, and social problems. The third section presents a version of intergroup theory. This particular formulation deals explicitly with organizations and provides answers to questions raised about early and contemporary formulations. The final section applies the particular theory to a variety of problems of practice and theory in organizational behavior. Here the aim is to show how application of intergroup theory leads to potentially different interpretations and actions than suggested by other writers. Throughout the paper, concepts from intergroup theory address statements and actions by individuals from a wide diversity of organizational roles, including researchers, politicans, teachers, managers, publicists, and consultants. The aim of the chapter is to explain and to explicate intergroup theory.

HISTORICAL BACKGROUND

The roots of contemporary social scientific thinking about intergroup relations can be found in the period between the 1890s and the 1930s. This era contains the origins of theory, method, and technique that influence much of today's work. Here I identify four key developments: (1) Le Bon's (1895) theory of *the crowd*, (2) Sumner's (1906) concept of ethnocentrism, (3) Roethlis-

This research was sponsored by the Organizational Effectiveness Research Programs, Office of Naval Research (Code 442OE, Contract No. N00014-82-K-0715).

berger and Dickson's (1939) empirical work on management and the worker, and (4) the social invention of group treatment methods. Taken together the focus of attention ranges from the political behavior of nations, to the feelings and actions of clans and tribes, to the work activities of profit-making organizations, to the treatment of psychologically disturbed individuals.

Le Bon and *The Crowd*

Social scientists mark the beginning of intergroup studies with the publication of Gustave Le Bon's *The Crowd* in 1895 (Turner and Giles 1981). Le Bon used political events of nineteenth-century France as the basis for a series of propositions about individual and crowd behavior. Many of the issues and problems he addressed remain central to the study of intergroup relations today. These include

1. the effects of race in human affairs;
2. the substitution of unconscious action by groups for the conscious actions of individuals;
3. the impact of social scientists' group memberships on the views they espouse;
4. the stimulation of creativity and altruism in individuals by groups;
5. the tension between elites and masses;
6. the utility of group psychology for those who exercise leadership;
7. the manner in which groups shape the meaning of words and concepts for their members;
8. the role of leaders in groups; and
9. the variation in types of groups based on their composition and purpose.

These subjects were analyzed differently than they would be today. Le Bon was not a twentieth-century social scientist. Nevertheless the breadth of his vision was notable. Contemporary intergroup research is far more precise in both theory and data than Le Bon's pioneering effort. But the extent of intergroup phenomena to which he attended is rarely matched by current scholars. Le Bon's work was also important because it provided a stepping-off place for Sigmund Freud's *Group Psychology and the Analysis of the Ego* (1922), a small book that has been highly influential in many efforts to use knowledge about groups for the treatment of individual psychopathology. Yet there is a double paradox in this connection. Le Bon was rather unsure about whether his knowledge could or should be used to bring about change, and Freud did not conduct group treat-

ment, even though his analysis has been quite influential among those who do (Anthony 1971).

Sumner's concept of ethnocentrism

Just after the turn of the century, William Graham Sumner (1906) formulated the idea that intergroup relations in a state of conflict took on a predictable syndrome-like pattern, which he called "ethnocentrism." According to Sumner, ethnocentrism became the term to identify the "view of things in which one's own group is the center of everything, and all others are scaled and rated with reference to it. . . . Each group nourishes its own pride and vanity, boasts itself superior, exalts its own divinities, and looks with contempt on outsiders" (Sumner 1906, 13). Related to ethnocentrism were the concepts of in-group and out-group. The in-group is one's own group, and an out-group is any group with which one is in conflict.

Sumner's concepts have proved to be extraordinarily influential. Recently Levine and Campbell (1972) built an entire comparative theoretical analysis about theories of conflict, ethnic attitudes, and group behavior around the concept of ethnocentrism. Brewer and Campbell (1976) then conducted an extensive empirical study covering more than thirty groups to test hypotheses derived from comparing theories related to Sumner's propositions.

In both theoretical analysis and empirical study, Campbell and his associates demonstrate an awareness of the inability of investigators to escape being influenced by the phenomena they study. Examining Sumner's (1906; Sumner, Keller, and Davie 1927) literature searches, Levine and Campbell (1972, 19) note, "We must assume that the very great preponderance of the ethnographers available for Sumner to read were themselves unconsciously ethnocentric." Brewer and Campbell (1976, 125–26) describe a "triangulation" model for achieving what they term "objectivity" by having several observers describe several cultures. In employing this multigroup multiobserver model, Brewer and Campbell use a common interview format, which they themselves brought to the study. Thus, while they are able to see a version of researcher-group identification in reviewing Sumner's (1906) work, they seem unaware that their instrument, however carefully translated and used by different observers of diverse groups, is still *their* questionnaire. The issues they ask about are based on the theory of a white male Yale professor, vintage early-twentieth century (i.e., William Graham Sumner). How likely are the concepts embedded in the interview to be relevant, or, perhaps equally important, how likely are they to be similarly relevant to all groups in an array of thirty tribes in eastern Africa in 1965? How likely were Brewer and Campbell, using the methodology that they did, to determine whether there were different degrees of relevance of their questions to the groups they studied?

The tradition of intergroup research set in motion by Sumner, even though subject to criticism for the ethnocentrism of its author and in spite of its conceptual power, has been one whereby investigators are *not* prodded to examine searchingly their own group identifications and their likely effect on research results.

Management and the worker

Roethlisberger and Dickson's (1939) work moves the arena of attention from national politics and tribal warfare to business organizations. There was no question about pragmatic motives. The Western Electric Company cooperated with researchers from the Harvard Business School because both organizations were concerned with determining the factors in the work place that influenced the morale and productive efficiency of workers. But their effort did not explicitly contribute to intergroup theory, despite the book's title. Rather, the importance of their work, in my opinion, rests with the empirical results they produced, even though the interpretation of their findings remains problematical. In addition, the research process demonstrated a long-term commitment to understanding and a repeated willingness to revise methods and interpretations in light of unanticipated findings.

The Hawthorne studies began with the aim of investigating the "relation of quality and quantity of illumination to efficiency in industry" (Cass and Zimmer 1975). It ended by proposing that industrial organizations be viewed as social systems in which every part bears a relation of interdependence to every other part (Roethlisberger and Dickson 1939). The initial orientation was largely based on the disciplines of physics and engineering, and the concluding position set the stage for several generations of work in psychology, sociology, and organizational behavior. Beginning hypotheses were concerned with one-way causality between illumination and productivity. The final conceptualization emphasized multiple levels of analysis, multidirectional causes and effects, and multiple theories of explanation.

The steps from opening to closing modes of understanding included experimental, survey, and interventionist methodologies, but neither the original writers nor their contemporary interpreters were as catholic in their perceptions of intergroup effects. Despite several revisions in concept and method, the investigators did not arrive at an explicitly intergroup formation of social system dynamics even though the data for such a position were abundant. Data relevant to gender, age, and ethnicity were reported throughout the study (see Roethlisberger and Dickson 1939, e.g., pp. 349, 360, 491), yet they did not enter into the final conceptual analysis. As recently as 1975, commentators on the Hawthorne legacy continued to refer to people who participated in the illumination experiments as "the girls" (Cass and Zimmer 1975, 279ff.).

In the chronology of methodologies employed in the Hawthorne studies were several efforts to isolate work groups in order to observe their behavior carefully. This occurred both in the illumination studies and in the bank wiring-room research. The investigators report evidence concerning reactive effect of these moves in both instances. Yet they miss the opportunity to conceptualize their experimental interventions as changes in the intergroup relations between the factory as a whole and the research participants and between the isolated groups and themselves as a "research group" with a position related to the organization hierarchy. As open as they were in methodological strategy, they did not have the conceptual or technical equipment to examine the consequences of their own group behavior on the system they were learning to study. Unwittingly they may have begun a tradition of experimental research on small groups that closed off the groups under study and the researchers from being aware of their intergroup relationships. The study of "group dynamics" as mainly internal relations among group members without attention to how the groups under study related to the larger social system in which they were embedded accelerated in the years after Hawthorne.

There are clues in Roethlisberger's (1977, 14–15) autobiography about the origins of the Hawthorne researchers' blindness to intergroup issues. Describing his decision to "disinherit" (his word) himself from his family, he wrote,

> I was an American—an isolationist by factors then unknown to me . . . who was not going to have anything to do with the mighty battles fought in Switzerland between the Canton de Bern and the Canton de Vaux or with the Franco-Prussian War. This was America, where race, color, creed, birth, heredity, nationality, family, and so forth, did not count and where individual merit, skill, competence, knowledge, liberty, freedom, and so on did. I believed it with all my heart and in a crazy way, *in spite of many subsequent experiences to the contrary, I still do* [emphasis added].

Is it possible that Roethlisberger could not permit his theory of organization to contain concepts that he was unable to integrate within his own self-perception?

Le Bon, the Frenchman who was able to talk about group differences, made an observation that anticipated Roethlisberger's difficulty many years before the American reported it. Le Bon (1895, 107–8) wrote,

I shall confine myself to observing that it is precisely the words most often employed by the masses which among different people possess the most different meanings. Such is the case, for instance, with the words "democracy" and "socialism" in such frequent use nowadays.

In reality they correspond to quite contrary ideas and images in the Latin and Anglo-Saxon mind. For the Latin peoples the word "democracy" signifies more especially the subordination of the will and the initiative of the individual to the community represented by the State. Among Anglo-Saxons, and notably in America, this same word "democracy" signifies, on the contrary, the intense development of the will of the individual, and as complete a subordination as possible of the State . . .

From Le Bon's perspective the changed relationship between the individual and the collective signified by "democracy" was quite different for Latin and Anglo-Saxon people. Perhaps for Latins democracy was an alternative to anarchy, while for Anglo-Saxons democracy was preferred to totalitarianism. In the conceptual language of intergroup theory, Latins were responding to democracy as an adjustment to underbounded conditions, and Anglo-Saxons were reacting to democracy as an improvement to overbounded conditions (Alderfer 1980). If this interpretation is valid, it suggests that the meaning of an important term (in this case, *democracy*) depends in part on the group condition of the people using it.

Roethlisberger's life history included parental struggles between a German-Swiss father and a French-Swiss mother. His method of coping with this conflict was flight, and it may have set limits on how able he was to incorporate ethnic differences into his theory of social systems. These two ethnic groups tend to evolve different roles for men and women in the family and therefore may also have influenced how Roethlisberger saw the relations between men and women in his research (McGoldrick 1982).

Group-treatment methods

According to Anthony (1971), the use of groups by therapists to treat individuals' emotional difficulties may have begun as early as 1907. Using groups for clinical intervention adds an important element to the foundation of intergroup perspectives. The practice is only reasonable if one has a working hypothesis that group forces can be harnessed for constructive ends. In *The Crowd*, Le Bon recognized that groups can have constructive effects, but his emphasis was heavily on destructive irrationality. Moreover, his restrained attitude toward how knowledge of group processes might be used certainly did not suggest that pragmatic values could be served by group-level intervention. Apparently physicians—some of whom were psychiatrists—first used groups for treatment purposes (Anthony 1971). From the beginning, the emotional life of groups became the central feature in their potential role in effecting cures. One early experiment by Joseph Pratt, for example, involved group treatment for individuals with tuberculosis, who were known to be emotionally difficult for people close to them (Anthony 1971).

As soon as a number of individuals are brought together for treatment, the professional faces a choice. To what degree does he or she treat individuals in the group? To what degree does he or she treat the group as a whole? When one moves from the customary one-on-one relationship to a group setting, the natural tendency is to continue working one-on-one with individuals in the group. However, the combination of the intellectual growth of *group* psychology during this period and the living experience of group life in the here-and-now led some of the early group workers to recognize that they could aim their interventions toward the group as a whole rather than, or in addition to, individuals. Interventions aimed at individuals take the form of the therapist's commenting about people by name, for example, "I wonder what it means when Mary sits with her head down, arms tightly clasped, and back bent over." Interventions with the group as a whole take the form of the consultants commenting impersonally on group events, for example, "The group might wish to examine why only the male members have been talking for the last ten minutes."

Advances in psychoanalytic theory and methods in this period also carried important implications for the conduct of group work. From the earliest experiences with their treatment procedures, psychoanalysts had learned the importance of paying careful attention to patients' emotional reactions to them as significant and powerful figures and, in turn, of their analogous feelings toward clients. The terms given to these two classes of emotional process were *transference*, when the origin seemed to be with the patient, and *countertransference*, when the beginning seemed to be with the analyst. In either case, the fundamental idea was that both parties had tendencies to "transfer" or to reproduce the emotional dynamics of relationships with other important people (e.g., parents, lovers) in the therapeutic activities. Without proper attention, transferential effects interfered with therapeutic progress. When the transference was "positive" and unexamined, clients showed dramatic improvements, which did not last when the relationship with the analyst changed. When the transference was "negative" and inadequately worked through, treatment terminated prematurely without significant gains for the client; however, when properly understood and effectively managed, transferential phenomena became a major force in effective treatment. Analysts learned how to be attentive to patients' reactions to them and in turn to their reactions to patients and to comment on these data in ways that could advance treatment. Originally, the discovery of transferential phenomena occurred in the one-on-one relationship between Freud and a female patient (Freud 1905 in Freud 1963). Freud's (1922) *Group Psychology and the Analysis of the Ego* brought the same underlying psychological reasoning to the study of group as well as interpersonal behavior.[1]

The book begins with a critique of Le Bon's *The Crowd*. The Austrian founder of psychoanalysis was rather mixed in his reactions of the French sociologist's work. Le Bon's attention to the powerful and pervasive operation of unconscious emotional processes "in" (the preposition becomes important) groups drew Freud's approval. But the psychoanalyst was not pleased with how the sociologist explained these effects. The dissatisfaction became an opportunity for Freud to present his own views, and, in the process, to begin the kind of theoretical arguments that would bring the transferential reasoning into the realm of group behavior. One succinct formulation provided by Freud (1922, 99–100) is,

> The uncanny and coercive characteristics of group formations, which are shown in their suggestion phenomena, may therefore with justice be traced back to the fact of their origin from the primal horde. The leader of the group is still the dreaded primal father; the group still wishes to be governed by unrestricted force; it has an extreme passion for authority; in Le Bon's phrase, it has a thirst for obedience. The primal father is the group ideal which governs the group in place of the ego ideal. Hypnosis has a good claim to being described as a *group of two* [emphasis added]; there remains as a definition for suggestion—a conviction which is not based upon perception and reasoning but upon an erotic tie. . . . We have come to the conclusion that suggestion is a partial manifestation of the state of hypnosis, and that hypnosis is solidly founded upon a predisposition which has survived in the unconscious from the early history of the human family.

---

1. My uses of the terms *transference* and *countertransference* here are broader than those of classical psychoanalysis (Singer 1963). They have most in common with the formulation of Frieda Fromm-Reichmann (1950) and have also been significantly affected by Sullivan (1953) and Jung (1946).

Freud's formulation makes explicit the unconscious emotional ties from members to leader and from members to one another. From time to time his work also makes allusion to intergroup forces by the portions of Le Bon to which he refers or by the concrete examples he selects to illustrate his theoretical points (e.g., Freud 1922, 44, 50, 90). Fundamentally, however, Freud's analysis of unconscious emotional processes derives from the one-on-one relationship (the "group of two"). It shall remain for others to carry the analysis of unconscious emotional dynamics more fully into the realm of intergroup relations.

An additional problem posed by the practical application of group work is composing membership. The professional deciding to work with a group for curative purposes must determine who shall be members. Answering this question can hardly escape giving some attention, however implicitly, to intergroup dynamics. By deciding who is to be inside the group, the professional also determines who is outside. Whether conscious of it or not, members of the treatment group will have to deal with nonmembers; their relations with nonmembers will be changed somewhat—and possibly dramatically—by their participation in the treatment.

In 1923 Harry Stack Sullivan undertook a most significant experiment in the treatment of schizophrenics at the Sheppard and Enoch Pratt Hospital, where he established a special ward in which only male schizophrenics were to receive care. Staff for the special ward were men carefully selected by Sullivan. Many staff were former patients. There was also evidence that Sullivan himself had been a hospitalized patient, although he is not known to have acknowledged his patienthood to more than a few friends (Perry 1982, 3ff). To create the innovative setting, Sullivan had special permission from the administration of the hospital. Part of the "training" for his staff involved meetings at Sullivan's home and included attention to the personal tensions of the staff as well as those of the patients. Sullivan's innovation changed the customary intergroup relationship between male schizophrenics and female nursing staff as well as between his particular patients and the hospital administration as a whole. He did this, of course, without an explicit theory of intergroup relations (see Perry 1982, 189–200). Like some other organization innovations to be described later, Sullivan's "successful" program was eventually terminated. Within the hospital itself he faced difficulties with the nurses (a predominantly female group), and eventually the senior administration of the hospital, which had been most supportive of Sullivan, was pressed by the board of trustees to discontinue Sullivan's activity. Perhaps if Sullivan or others in the setting had been thinking about his innovation from an intergroup perspective in addition to the intrapsychic and interpersonal viewpoints, he could have found mechanisms to deal with the concerns of the other groups that eventually acted to impede his work.

The fact that many of Sullivan's carefully selected male staff were former patients probably greatly aided their effectiveness in the unit. If Sullivan himself was a recovered patient, that experience probably gave him an understanding, that would be difficult to obtain in any other way, of the male patient group. But, paradoxically, it may also be that Sullivan's reluctance to acknowledge his own patienthood interfered with his capacity to conduct intergroup negotiations on behalf of his unit and thereby was a factor in the demise of the innovation.

CONTEMPORARY ISSUES AMONG INTERGROUP PERSPECTIVES

Today there is no single intergroup theory. Instead, there are a variety of conceptual and methodological positions. Clarity about the dimensions on which intergroup perspectives differ sets the stage for understanding the contributions and limitations of any one. Here I shall identify four dimensions on which intergroup perspectives differ. *Level of analysis* pertains to the degree that the group as a unit is central to the conceptual formula. Groups *isolated or embedded* refer to the degree that investigators take into account the contexts in which groups exist. Empirical investigations into group life may be *active or passive* in terms of how investigators relate to the material they study. Finally, researchers may or may not be *reflective* about their own individual position and group memberships in relation to those they study.

Level of analysis

Taken at face value, of course, intergroup theory deals with relations among groups. But intergroup perspectives have varied in the degree of attention they have given to individual, group, and intergroup phenomena. Foci for attention have ranged from personality psychology (e.g., Adorno et al. 1950) to economic sociology (Blalock and Wilken 1976) and cultural anthropology (Otterbein 1977). Intergroup theorists generally accept the validity of multiple levels of analysis; the theory is often attractive because it offers intellectual equipment for cross-level reasoning (Rice 1969).

Given the variations in levels to which intergroup theory might be applied, researchers cannot be equally attentive to everything. They make choices according to their interests. Often these choices reflect preferences for methods as well as for data.

For the purposes of this article, a crucial choice pertains to whether group-level phenomena become central. Although the group is the intermediate level in the range addressed by intergroup theory, it does not necessarily follow that all intergroup researchers thoroughly attend to the group as a unit worthy of attention in its own right. The idea of "group as a whole" usually includes several elements: (1) a group is different from simply a linear sum of individual members; (2) groups share collectively unconscious assumptions about members' relations to the group's leadership and to one another; and (3) words spoken and actions taken by group members represent the whole group or subgroup of the whole group (Bion 1959; Wells 1980; Agazarian and Peters 1981).

The question of whether the group becomes a unit in intergroup theory has both intellectual and cultural determinants. During the early part of the twentieth century, for example, there was considerable controversy among academic researchers about the concept of "group mind." Le Bon (1895) had started the idea that groups had properties that transcended and, in some cases, overwhelmed individual functioning. At the other pole was a view that vigorously disputed the utility of group-level concepts that existed apart from the functioning of individuals. Floyd H. Allport (1924; cited by Brown and Turner 1981, 33) made the case against group-level concepts as follows:

> There is no psychology of groups which is not essentially and entirely a psychology of individuals. Social psychology must not be placed in contradistinction to the psychology of the individual; *it is a part of the psychology of the individual,* whose behavior it studies in relation to that sector of his environment comprised by his fellows.

Brown and Turner (1981, 34) note that Allport's influence was substantial and that "many social psychologists . . . especially in North America . . . conceptualize such phenomena as group prejudice and social conflict as interpersonal or intrapersonal processes simply writ large." Scholars writing from a North American perspective, and perhaps particularly from the United States', may unwittingly have their "theories" shaped by the national ideology. The U.S. Constitution vigorously defends the rights of individuals; it addresses some questions of "rights" by saying that *individuals* may *not* be denied the privileges conveyed by citizenship because of their membership in racial, ethnic, or gender groups. Thus, the very ideology of the United States pits the individual against the group. It is not surprising that scholars embedded within this cultural context would promote theories that were consistent with the national ideology; however, there are empirical findings that support the concept of group-level phenomena independent of (not versus) individual effects (Alderfer 1971; Klein 1977; Alderfer et al. 1983; Smith 1982).

The extent of this cultural influence is illustrated by a recent article from the front page of the *New York Times* entitled "Japan's Schools Stress Group and Discourage Individuality." The article begins with an example from a seventh-grade mathematics class in a Japanese junior high school. A 13-year-old girl is called upon and is unable to answer a question. The *Times* reporter describes the situation.

> She stood beside her desk staring at the floor, obviously at a loss to understand the problem. She tried a couple of guesses, then fell silent. Finally the teacher allowed her to sit down.
>
> In an American school, the student would probably have been placed in a slower class where she could work alongside students of comparable ability. In Japan there is no such thing as "tracking."
>
> The social cost of a student's being removed from her peers is viewed as far greater than the frustration of sitting day after day in a class where the pupil does not understand what is going on. . . .
>
> The incident is indicative of how schools here in Japan are inextricably tied to distinctly Japanese values such as the primacy of the group rather than the individual.[2]

Fiske's implicit theory in the article is clearly of the individual versus group variety. The same events would be reported differently if the reporter used group-level concepts. He might have written,

> The Japanese choose not to make separate groups of students according to their apparent levels of ability. They believe that the damage to individuals caused by assigning them to an out-group deemed to be of lesser ability is far greater than whatever gains might be achieved in educational efficiency by such group splitting. In the United States, we are witnessing changes of a similar kind. People with disabilities have organized to persuade school systems not to separate them into "tracks" but rather to include them in the "mainstream" of educational activities.

The rewritten story reflects several aspects of using group-level concepts. First, it recognizes that separating a category of individuals (apparently less-able students)

is a group-level event making at least two groups where formerly there was one. Second, the rewritten account suggests that group-level interventions may help as well as hurt *individuals*. Third, it implicitly seeks to join rather than divide the United States and Japan by showing that similar logic is being used in both countries. Needless to say, the degree of subtlety in all this is not slight. The quoted piece was a news article, not an analysis, column, or editorial.

Within the field of organizational behavior, group-level concepts are employed unevenly. Some researchers give the group a central place in their thinking, while others deal with the phenomena of group life without giving attention to the group per se. Katz and Kahn, for example, in their *Social Psychology of Organizations* (1978) give almost no attention to group-level dynamics. They deal with some of the phenomena of group life by two alternative conceptual devices—the analysis of leadership and the detailed formulation of the concept of role. Both these concepts lend themselves nicely to a substitution for dealing with group effects for investigators who seem to prefer dealing with individual and interpersonal units of analysis rather than with groups as wholes.

One sees similar conceptual assumptions in the presentation of handbook chapters. In the *Handbook of Organizations* (March 1965) there is a chapter called "Small Groups and Large Organizations" by Golembiewski. Despite the suggestive title, the political scientist makes the links from micro to macro levels by the use of supervisor-to-subordinate relations and by subordinate-to-subordinate relations; he thus stays "inside" the group by relying on interpersonal relations as the key mediating process. Later in the same book, Shepard reports on the processes for changing interpersonal and intergroup relationships in organizations. Again there is a suggestion that group-level concepts might be employed, and to a limited extent, they are. The major distinction is between a coercive-compromise mentality and a collaboration-consensus mentality. As Shepard conceives of these states of mind they seem to apply to both individuals and groups. It is clear that the state-of-mind analysis is more fully developed for individuals than for groups. Shepard is able to draw on a variety of studies about healthy individuals to specify what collaborative-consensus mentality means for individuals. He has no similar material for groups. It is also clear that he had at least the beginning of such ideas for groups, because he talks about how groups develop a strategic sense of their relationship to the whole organization, and he recognizes that how members can function in temporary task forces depends on how the groups they represent relate to one another.

2. E. B. Fiske, "Japan's Schools Stress Group and Discourage Individuality," *New York Times*, 11 July 1983. Copyright © 1983 by The New York Times Company. Reprinted by permission.

The preference for individual and interpersonal concepts among organizational psychologists did not show notable change by the time the *Handbook of Industrial and Organizational Psychology* (Dunnette 1976) was prepared. In that collection there was just one paper with *group* in the title, and that was a chapter by Hackman, "Group Influences on Individuals." There was some attention to group-level effects in a chapter on conflict by Thomas, and on change processes by Alderfer.

Researchers from the Tavistock Institute in Great Britain have had a long history of attending to group-level effects. The earliest efforts began with changes in the technology of coal mining (Trist et al. 1963), which in turn induced alterations in the structure of work groups. Later the theory and methods taken from the coal mining work was transferred to weaving mills in India (Rice 1963).

Thus within both academic social psychology and organizational behavior we find differences between those who utilize group-level concepts and those who do not. For theorists who prefer only individual and interpersonal constructs, the notion of group is missing or, in the extreme, actively denied. The converse, however, does not seem to apply. Theorists who attend to group-level phenomena tend also to use individual level. As shown in figure 13.1, we seem to have two distinct modes of conceptualizing individual and group effects. The first emphasizes individual in opposition to group concepts. The operation of group forces as a threat to individuals is incorporated into the theory in such a way that group dynamics are absent if individual consciousness is present. The second approach sees the individual and group as more orthogonal. According to this view, group and individual concepts may exist comparatively autonomously. At the very least, this orientation allows for the separate measurement and testing of individual and group effects. It allows for empirical data rather than the declaration of theorists to determine the relative potency of individual and group effects.

Isolated or embedded

The question of isolation or embeddedness depends on whether the theory has a way to deal with how a particular intergroup relationship stands relative to its environment. An illustration may be helpful. One of the most significant studies of intergroup relationships were those conducted by Muzafer Sherif and Carolyn Sherif (1969). In these studies the investigators constructed a series of competitive games between teams of twelve year-old boys at summer camps. The phenomena they documented pertained to how the external conditions of group competition or cooperation affected the internal dynamics of the groups. As the investigators went about their work, they seemed to take no cognizance of the fact that their groups consisted entirely of boys. Replications were conducted across time, in different geographical settings, and with variation in either the age or the gender of the respondents. The research implicitly assumed that gender has some bearing on their results or on their ability to carry out and replicate their results, or they would not have held gender constant in their studies. But it is not obvious what their assumptions were. The studies were carried out in the late 1940s and early 1950s in the United States. During this period there was relatively little explicit questioning of the relationship between men and women or boys and girls. The pattern of having males as participants in the primary research activities in studies of the Sherif paradigm was also followed by Blake, Shepard, and Mouton (1964), who extended the work to industrial settings.

What is especially interesting about the role of women in the Sherif studies is that both the camp studies and the industrial extensions included women on the research team. The Sherif studies were frequently reported in different places by Carolyn *and* Muzafer Sherif. The industrial extensions were written by Robert Blake *and* Jane Mouton. In a summary of the work written for a general audience, Muzafer Sherif discusses various replications of the work and includes references to doctoral dissertations that employed female respondents (Sherif 1966, 96–7). In at least two reports Sherif (1966) and Sherif and Sherif (1969) discuss the nature of gener-

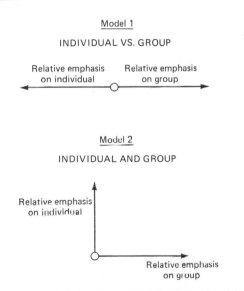

Model 1

INDIVIDUAL VS. GROUP

Relative emphasis on individual — Relative emphasis on group

Model 2

INDIVIDUAL AND GROUP

Relative emphasis on individual

Relative emphasis on group

Figure 13.1 Two models of conceptualizing the relationship between individual and group effects

alizations to other forms of intergroup relations that might be made from their research. Included in these discussions are extensions to international relations, labor management conflict, and inter-ethnic relations. No mention was made of extensions to male-female relations, and I know of no attention by the Sherifs to how their paradigm might respond to mixed gender groups and to studies that varied the proportion of men and women in experimental groups. There are, however, interesting data on the Carolyn-Muzafer relationship in the 1966 report of their work, entitled *In Common Predicament*. Muzafer Sherif (p. xiii) writes in the preface,

> Carolyn Sherif shared with me all the effort of putting together the material to go into this book, in organizing it through long hours of discussion, in writing much of what are probably its best chapters, and, not least, in going through the prolonged efforts and pain of revision. In spite of this she has resisted my urging that she share the title page with me. Yet I want to make it clear that this is a Sherif and Sherif work like several others published earlier.

From these words, one may suggest that the way the Sherifs handled their female-male differences may have affected how they conducted, reported, and interpreted their research. There does seem to be a context—characteristic of both the times in which they did their work and in the collaboration itself—in which the pattern of relations between men and women working together are not examined or conceptualized.

Suppose the Sherifs had given more thorough and explicit attention to their own work relationship in terms of female-male dynamics; how might that have affected their research? The answers to this question are, of course, speculative. They are given to explain what it means to conduct research with consciousness of the embeddedness of intergroup relations and how that awareness can affect various elements of the investigation, not to criticize Carolyn and Muzafer Sherif personally. In fact, the responses to this question should be viewed as *group-level* interpretations and predictions.

Here then are the changes that might have occurred in the Sherif and Sherif paradigm: (1) There would have been explicit discussion about the proportions of boys and girls in the original studies and of men and women in the adult extensions. (2) These discussions would probably have led to some systematic variation in the female-male proportions in the series of studies employing the Sherif and Sherif paradigm. (3) As a result, there would be data on how the intergroup dynamics, so clearly documented by the studies, are affected by varying the proportions of men and women in the groups. (4) There would be data on whether female and male participants experienced the phenomena in similar or different ways as a function of the proportions of each gender in the groups. (5) Discussion of how the findings apply to practical problems would include attention to male-female relations. (6) Authorship and acknowledgments of the research reports would include cases where Carolyn was the first or only author and would not include prefatory comments by one of the partners that explained why one of the partners deserved but did not accept joint authorship.

Research and development or clinical methods

At the outset I noted that intergroup research has a long tradition of being concerned about social problems. Most intergroup research people take their subjects for investigation from "the real world" and aim to influence practical affairs with their findings. There is little in any facet of intergroup research that works *only* toward knowledge for its own sake; however, within the general orientation of seeking understanding both for the advancement of understanding and for improving social conditions there are important differences in research methods.

In a paper reviewing research on stereotyping and intergroup behavior, Thomas Pettigrew (1981) identified three wings of social psychology. He called them "experimental social psychology," "symbolic interactionism," and "contextual social psychology." The chief differences among these subgroups turn on their methods and the journals in which they publish their research. Pettigrew was also alert to how generational differences among social scientists and organizational locations also are associated with their intellectual products. According to Pettigrew (1981), experimental social psychologists focus on individual-level properties, operate in the laboratory chiefly with college sophomores as "subjects," and thereby achieve internal validity at the expense of external generalizability. Symbolic interactionists work in the field of naturally occurring events, attend to dynamics of social process, and collect data by observing, interviewing, and retrieving. From Pettigrew's perspective the symbolic interactionists achieve external validity at the price of internal rigor. Finally, there is the third subgroup of contextual social psychologists in whose membership Pettigrew places himself. This group seems to share in the best of both worlds—achieving internal validity through probability samples and quasi-experimental designs and attaining external validity by the variety of settings in which members act as researchers.

From my perspective, there is also a fourth subgroup, which Pettigrew's analysis omits. All the subgroups that he describes share a similar idea of "application." When research results have achieved the appropriate degree of validity, they are to be transferred to policy makers, who, in turn, will be guided by them in making or changing public policy. A good example of this sort of application is the use of Clark and Clark's (1947) race research in the shaping of the 1954 U.S. Supreme Court decision to end the *separate but equal* doctrine of public education. I give the term research and development to the orientation that establishes research results separately from utilization and then applies the findings to social and organizational problems. Investigators who work in this manner are similar to many physical scientists who develop their innovations comparatively independently of the people who will use them. An alternative approach, representing a fourth group, which Pettigrew omits is clinical research.

Erik Erikson (1964) has put it this way: "One can study the nature of things by doing something *to* them, but one can really learn something about the essential nature of living beings only by doing something *with* them or *for* them. This, of course, is the principle of clinical science." For the research and development orientation to intergroup research something is done *to* one set of people (often called subjects) so that something might be done *with* and *for* another set. For the clinical orientation to intergroup research something is done with and for respondents.

A key difference between research and development versus clinical social psychologists turns on beliefs (and, for some, theories) about how much and in what ways the different styles contaminate the phenomena they study. The R & D position is that by taking a "scientific" role and by exercising careful controls researchers can minimize their contamination of the phenomena under study. In this manner they more closely approximate objectively reliable and reproducible findings. Their criticism of clinical methods is that investigators become excessively involved with their data and thereby lose objectivity. According to the R & D group, the products of clinical methods are not research data, but anecdotal accounts that, however interesting, do not qualify as valid research findings. Thus, Pettigrew omits clinical social psychologists from his subgroup delineation.

The clinical critique of R & D social psychology is that research is intervention (and often intrusion). The question is not *whether* to influence the phenomena under study but *how* (Berg 1980). Laboratory social psychologists create temporary social systems to do their research work. They exercise legitimate authority by virtue of university faculty roles when they invite or require sophomores to participate in experiments. They alter existing group membership and authority relations when they join existing social systems as participant observers. They represent private or public organizations when they conduct survey interviews. For clinical social psychologists, objectivity is sufficiently elusive as not to be a primary goal, regardless of method or subject matter. Rather than attempting to produce bias-free research, we attempt to understand and acknowledge the inevitable bias in any research and seek, rather, to specify the conditions for reproducing the results we report. According to this reasoning, reproduction of research results is not just an empirical exercise whereby the same laboratory instructions, the same questionnaire, the same interview questions, or the same kind of people are repeatedly studied. Rather, reproduction of results is a theoretical *and* empirical matter in which theory is used to develop methods of research as well as to predict and interpret findings (Alderfer and Smith 1982; Alderfer et al. 1983).

Thus, for clinical organizational psychologists, research is not separated cleanly into investigation and application phases. The alternative mode is continuing exchange between intervention and understanding. Clinical organizational psychologists believe that research data are importantly shaped by the relationships between investigators and respondents as well as by the phenomena being studied. They believe that the goal of excellence in research is best served by being conscious of those relationships and by altering them as appropriate and possible.

Individual and group reflection

In conducting research, investigators vary significantly in whether they have a theory-based method for examining and managing relationships with the people they study. It is probably fair to say that most social scientists have some awareness of their entanglements with what they study, yet few have a disciplined, systematic way of understanding and managing how they affect and are affected by their work. Data-generation methods implicitly shape researcher-respondent relationships either by aiming for minimal influence (participant observation, survey-interviewing) or by exercising tight control (laboratory experimentation).

Preceding sections contained a variety of examples in which researchers seemed to shape their investigations in important ways without being aware of what they were doing. Here, I summarize the more important episodes for two reasons. First, putting several cases in one place gives a clearer sense of their frequency. My own experience is that most investigators prefer not to think too hard about or observe too carefully these matters. Second, having several instances together helps a reader test the utility of concepts that will be proposed to explain and predict researcher-respondent relationships.

The aim of reviewing these episodes is not, however, to criticize the investigators whose work is cited. We would not have an opportunity to learn from their experience if they had not reported it. The fact that the "data" I cite, for the most part, do not come from the "results" sections of their research reports is much more of a statement about the ideology of the research culture in which they worked than an assessment of them as individuals.

1. Marilyn Brewer and Donald Campbell (1976) did not seem to notice that their questionnaire for studying East African tribes emerged from a predominantly white male, northern European–American scientific culture. The research team did show cognizance of how *other* investigators' group identifications might have affected their perceptions of intergroup relations. They also did not reflect upon how their own gender differences, and how they managed them, might have influenced the research.

2. Fritz Roethlisberger and William Dickson omit consideration of age, gender, and ethnicity in their social systems conception of the Hawthorne plant. In his "intellectual autobiography," Roethlisberger describes his own commitment to "individual merit" to the extrusion of group-level variables.

3. Harry Stack Sullivan did not seem to be aware of the female-male and administration-patient dynamics he altered when he created an innovative treatment setting for male schizophrenics. As a result, an innovation that many people today consider successful was terminated. Sullivan himself left the setting and turned away from hospital psychiatry.

4. Muzafer and Carolyn Sherif omit explicit consideration of female-male differences in their account of the boys' camp experiment on intergroup conflict and cooperation. Muzafer Sherif later gives a report on Carolyn Sherif's dropping authorship for an overview report of these studies despite clear acknowledgment of her extensive contribution to the work. In generalizing the implications of their work to an array of intergroup circumstances, the Sherifs omit discussion of men and women.

5. A counterexample seems to be Gustave Le Bon. The French sociologist gave attention to how the concept of democracy varied between Northern European and Latin peoples. He did this in the context of reflecting upon the consequences of revolution and its aftermath in his own country. In the process, he gave especially detailed attention to power of unconscious forces in group life; however, Le Bon's acknowledgment of group-level forces on his own work was more implicit than explicit. He did not offer a set of concepts or methods for investigators to follow in order to take account of the impact of their own individual and group identifications on their research.

Among sociologists who do participant observation, there is a literature reporting researcher-respondent relationships in some detail (Whyte 1955b; Adams and Preiss 1960; Filstead 1970; McCall and Simmons 1969). An interesting effect of the phenomena is that reporting seems to be dominated by relatively junior investigators describing experiences associated with dissertations. In sociology, Bill Whyte may have started it all by publishing an appendix to *Street Corner Society* in 1955.

In clinical psychology and psychiatry, however, the tradition is much older, beginning with Freud's work on transference and countertransference (Menninger 1958). Within the classical psychoanalytic tradition, transference and countertransference are interpreted in terms of unconscious personality and interpersonal dynamics. Initially, the reaction to the phenomena by Freud himself was to call upon the analyst to become surgeon-like—cool and aloof. As the phenomena became more fully understood and accepted, attitudes changed. Rather than something to be denied and avoided, countertransference feelings in the analyst became an important source of treatment data, which can provide clues about the interaction between the personalities of analyst and patient, and can serve both, if effectively examined and utilized (Searles 1955).

Group-level transference, however, has received far less thorough attention. Thanks to Whyte and others who follow his lead, there is an empirical literature identifying the empirical phenomena, although Whyte himself provides no conceptualization. The tendency for this material to come from younger people and to be reported without theoretical commentary, however, has worked against its being incorporated into the main currents of social-research method and theory. When senior people do not report their personal experiences, it is as if the collective assumption among social scientists is that group-level transference and countertransference go away as investigators mature. One could hardly argue that investigators stop having gender, ethnicity, age, and organizational affiliations or that people stop noticing these attributes as researchers become more established professionals. There is, however, another view that takes account of both group- and individual-level transference and incorporates the phenomena into what is viewed as the natural ongoing activities of the social scientist.

The first person I know of to incorporate the two levels of understanding was George Devereux, who decided to conduct and report psychotherapy with a Plains Indian with a conscious awareness of both personality development and of areal culture patterns (Devereux 1968). In conducting therapy, Devereux (1968) dealt with both individual- and group-level transference. In writing his book, he perceptively managed his intergroup relationship between the Plains Indian culture, which he entered as an employee of the Veterans Administration, and the white-male-dominant European-American culture that he belonged to by birth.

Conceptually, Devereux called upon anthropological analyses of Plains Indians to provide the group-level knowledge necessary to understand the group membership of his patient. He integrated this group-level knowledge with classical psychoanalytic personality theory to form a notion of the ethnic personality. In the therapy itself he examined and utilized the transference phenomena of the patient to him in terms of behaviors characteristic of the patient's tribal life. Thus, the concrete content of the transference was therapist as "guardian spirit." In terms of therapeutic objectives and outcomes, the intergroup differences between Devereux's own culture and his patient's were made very explicit. His general aim was "to restore the person to himself." In this particular case that self was a Plains Indian substantially identified with his tribal culture, and it was a culture that was in acute distress in response to its historically determined destructive relationship with the dominant white American culture.

Presenting his material to a predominantly white American culture, Devereux (1968) took account of that culture's relationship to Indians. He addressed the key elements in the classical perception of Indians by whites as inferior. In the 1968 edition of the book, he also dealt with critical reactions to the book from members of the dominant culture.[3] In the process, he took the opportunity to refuse certain laudatory comments while interpreting the group-level basis of their origin. An especially poignant example is his reaction to words from Karl Menninger, who is one of the most widely respected practitioner-theorists of individual-interpersonal psychoanalysis. "In his Preface to the first edition, Dr. Karl Menninger commended my willingness to shoulder my share of America's guilt toward the Indian. But I feel no more guilty of these crimes than for the Athenians massacre of the Melians" (Devereux, 1967, xxxiv).

Here Menninger apparently makes a group-level attribution to Devereux, who refuses to accept it. The interesting question is whether Devereux refuses because he does not believe he is influenced by group-level forces (i.e., he is *just* an individual) or because he believes that Menninger has given him the wrong group membership (i.e., he identifies more with the continental French than

with Americans). My own impression is that the matter is more of Menninger's getting the wrong group than of Devereux's denying the effects of his own group memberships; however, in the Plains Indian study, the matter is not clarified. In that book, Devereux is much more explicitly attentive to transference than to countertransference issues. Devereux devotes an entire volume to countertransference reactions in social research and, in that volume, draws on many concrete examples from his own experience, which includes *both* individual- and group-level processes.

In taking Devereux's (1967) work with the Plains Indian as a clear example of an investigator's using group and individual transference, one should also be clear that his target for intervention was the individual. As therapist, Devereux observed and utilized the effects of group-level forces on his client and on himself in relation to his client. The target for intervention, however, remained the person. There was no attempt to work with his client's tribal group. Nor was there any indication that the group-level concepts Devereux used fruitfully to assist his patient could have been employed to aid the Indian's tribe.

Having posited the observation of group-level transferences, I wish to conclude this section by suggesting why the phenomena have been so widely overlooked. The reasons are several. None are particularly comfortable to hear if accepted. Most call for some degree of reorientation in feeling, thinking, and acting among social researchers.

To accept the validity of these processes is to take on an unending task of self- and group-scrutiny. In the extreme, it means one should be regularly asking the question, "How is what I am as a person and group representative shaping what I am finding?" This is a demanding undertaking often characterized by emotional turbulence.

To acknowledge the force of transferential and countertransferential processes is to revise significantly the meaning of objectivity. In the extreme, it means that it may be impossible to separate data from the relationship among parties associated with data collection (Berg 1984). The pursuit of objective information therefore requires relationship skills—both interpersonal and intergroup—and a new degree of tentativeness that takes account of the limits of any person's or group's capacity to influence the nature of a relationship with other parties.

To face the effects of group-level transference is to recognize that there may be circumstances in which one person alone cannot advance knowledge. One solution to the effects of group forces is to form groups that are capable of reflecting upon themselves in order to under-

---

3. The original edition of the Plains Indian study was published in 1951.

stand group and intergroup relations. The well-worn model of a single investigator alone in search of understanding must be complemented by teams of individuals composed to reflect the group-level differences among members (Alderfer and Smith 1982). Faced with this alternative, investigators may confront a new level of awareness concerning both how and why our knowledge of human behavior is limited. On this point, the difference between individual- and group-level transference becomes particularly significant. Working only with individual dynamics, one can maintain a realistic goal of continuously expanding self-awareness. Given an array of techniques for self-scrutiny, an investigator can at least approach the ideal of full self-understanding, even though in practice all accept the human limits of such a quest. But at the group level, there are sharper limits. There are groups to which we all belong that cannot change (e.g., gender, family, ethnicity). It is especially difficult for groups to engage in self-examination under conditions of intergroup conflict. To the extent that group memberships and relations among groups shape how others react to us and how we perceive those reactions, we are indeed captured by the groups to which we belong. We are, of course, most fully prisoner of those groups of whose membership we remain unaware (Smith 1982).

A THEORY OF INTERGROUP RELATIONS AND ORGANIZATIONS

In the two preceding sections I sought to establish two metatheoretical points. The first was to establish intergroup theory in general as a way of thinking about problems of human behavior; the aim was to distinguish intergroup theory from nonintergroup theory. The second was to determine dimensions on which particular versions of intergroup theory varied from one another; the objective was to differentiate among versions of intergroup theories. This section now presents a particular version of intergroup theory.

According to the dimensions of difference among intergroup theories, it has the following properties:

1. The group is the primary level of analysis.
2. Groups appear embedded in social systems.
3. The orientation toward research is clinical.
4. Concepts from the theory apply to researchers as well as to respondents.

Historically, the theory evolved inductively from anomalous research findings and mistakes in social inter-

vention. Studies crucial to identifying the need for such a theory have been concerned with generational struggles in management development (Alderfer 1971; 1977a), leadership struggles in labor-management relations (Lewicki and Alderfer 1973), and organization development in a boarding school (Alderfer and Brown 1975). Research that has proved fruitful in establishing the deductive utility of the theory addressed labor-management cooperation (Alderfer 1977b) and race relations in management (Alderfer et al. 1980; Alderfer et al. 1983). The theoretical perspective has also proved useful in understanding the behavior of behavioral scientists in their roles as research interpreters, teachers, and investigators (Alderfer 1970a; 1971). The chief intellectual ancestor of the formulation is A. K. Rice's (1969) effort to explain the interdependence among individual, group, and intergroup processes. Material presented in this section closely follows formulations elsewhere (Alderfer 1977b; Alderfer and Smith 1982; Alderfer et al. 1984).

Definition of groups in organizations

Within the social psychology literature there is no shortage of definitions of groups, but there is also no clear consensus among those who propose definitions (Cartwright and Zander 1968). Because much of the work leading to these definitions has been done by social psychologists studying internal properties of groups in laboratories, the resulting concepts have been comparatively limited in recognizing the external properties of groups. Looking at groups in organizations, however, produces a definition that gives more-balanced attention to both internal and external properties.

> A human group is a collection of individuals (1) who have significantly interdependent relations with each other, (2) who perceive themselves as a group, reliably distinguishing members from nonmembers, (3) whose group identity is recognized by nonmembers, (4) who, as group members acting alone or in concert, have significantly interdependent relations with other groups, and (5) whose roles in the group are therefore a function of expectations from themselves, from other group members, and from non-group members. (Alderfer 1977a)

This idea of a group begins with individuals who are interdependent, moves to the sense of the group as a significant social object whose boundaries are confirmed from inside and outside, recognizes that the group as a whole is an interacting unit through representatives or by collective action, and returns to the individual members whose thoughts, feelings, and actions are deter-

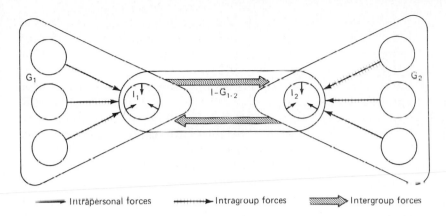

Intrapersonal forces   Intragroup forces   Intergroup forces

Figure 13.2   Intergroup transaction between individuals

mined by forces within the individual and from both group members and nongroup members. This conceptualization of a group makes every individual member into a group representative wherever he or she deals with members of other groups and treats transactions among individuals as at least, in part, intergroup events (Rice 1969; Smith 1977).

Figure 13.2 shows an "intergroup transaction between individuals." This is another way of reconceptualizing what may usually be thought of as an interpersonal transaction. In the diagram, there are three classes of forces corresponding to intrapersonal, intragroup, and intergroup dynamics. The general point is that any exchange between people is subject to all three kinds of forces; most people (including behavioral scientists) tend to understand things mainly in intrapersonal or interpersonal terms. Which class of forces becomes most dominant at any time depends on how the specific dimensions at each level of analysis differentiate the individuals. Suppose I_1 is a male engineering supervisor and I_2 is a female union steward. Intrapersonally I_1 prefers abstract thinking and demonstrates persistent difficulty in expressing feelings; I_2 prefers concrete thinking and shows ease in expressing feelings. G_1 is a predominantly male professional group that communicates to I_1 that he at all times should stay in control and be rational. G_2 is a predominantly female clerical group that communicates to I_2 that she should be more assertive about the needs of the G_2's. The I-G_{1-2} relationship includes ten years of labor-management cooperation punctuated by a series of recent strike (from the labor side) and termination (from the management side) threats. The tradition in much of behavioral-science intervention is to focus on the I dynamics and to give little or no attention to G or I-G forces (Argyris 1962; Walton 1969).

By viewing transactions between individuals from an intergroup perspective, an observer learns to examine the condition of each participant's group, the relationship of participants to their groups, and the

relationship between groups represented by participants as well as their personalities in each "interpersonal" relationship. Thus, in the earlier example reporting Devereux's psychotherapy with a Plains Indian, the investigator described the patient's personality, his relationship to his tribe, and the relationships among his tribe, other tribes, and the dominant U.S. culture.

Properties of intergroup relations

Research on intergroup relations has identified a number of properties characteristic of intergroup relations, regardless of the particular groups or the specific setting where the relationship occurs (Sumner 1906; Coser 1956; Van Den Berge 1972; Levine and Campbell 1972; Billig 1976; Alderfer 1977). These phenomena include

1. Group boundaries. Group boundaries, both physical and psychological, determine who is a group member and regulate transactions among groups by variations in their permeability (Alderfer 1977b). Boundary permeability refers to the ease with which boundaries can be crossed.

2. Power differences. Groups differ in the types of resources they can obtain and use (Lasswell and Kaplan 1950). The variety of dimensions on which there are power differences and the degree of discrepancy among groups on these dimensions influence the degree of boundary permeability among groups.

3. Affective patterns. The permeability of group boundaries varies with the polarization of feeling among the groups; that is, to the degree that group members split their feelings so that mainly positive feelings are associated with their own group and mainly negative feelings are projected onto other groups (Sumner 1906; Coser 1956; Levine and Campbell 1972).

4. Cognitive formations, including "distortions." As a function of power differences and affective patterns,

groups tend to develop their own language (or elements of language, including social categories), condition their members' perceptions of objective and subjective phenomena, and transmit sets of propositions—including theories and ideologies—to explain the nature of experiences encountered by members and to influence relations with other groups (Sherif and Sherif 1969; Blake, Shepard, and Mouton 1964; Tajfel 1970; Billig 1976).

5. Leadership behavior. The behavior of group leaders and of members representing a group reflects the boundary permeability, power differences, affective patterns, and cognitive formations of their group in relation to other groups. The behavior of group representatives, including formally designated leaders, is both cause and effect of the total pattern of intergroup behavior in a particular situation.

Group relations in organizations

Every organization consists of a large number of groups, and every organization member represents a number of these groups in dealing with other people in the organization. The full set of groups in an organization can be divided into two broad classes: identity groups and organizational groups. An identity group may be thought of as a group whose members share some common biological characteristic (such as gender), have participated in equivalent historical experiences (such as migration), currently are subjected to similar social forces (such as unemployment), and as a result have consonant world views. The coming together of world views by people who are in the same group occurs because of their having like experiences *and* developing shared meanings of these experiences through exchanges with other group members. As people enter organizations they carry with them their ongoing membership in identity groups based on variables such as their ethnicity, gender, age, and family. An organizational group may be conceived of as one whose members share (approximately) common organizational positions, participate in equivalent work experiences, and, as a consequence, have consonant organizational views. Organizations assign their members to organizational groups based on division of labor and hierarchy of authority. One critical factor in understanding intergroups in organizations is that identity-group membership and organizational-group membership are frequently highly related. Depending on the nature of the organization and the culture in which it is embedded, certain organizational groups tend to be populated by members of particular identity groups. In the United States, for example, upper-management positions tend to be held by older white males, and certain departments and ranks tend to be more accepting of females and minorities than others (Loring and Wells 1972; Purcell and Cavanagh 1972).

Considering the definition of a human group given above, we can observe how both identity groups and organizational groups fit the five major criteria. First, identity-group members have significant interdependencies because of their common historical experiences, and organizational groups, because of their equivalent work or organizational experiences, which result in their sharing similar fates even though members may be unaware of their relatedness or even actively deny it. Second, organization-group and identity-group members can reliably distinguish themselves as members from nonmembers on the basis of either identity factors (ethnicity, gender, etc.) or of location in the organization. However, the precision of this identification process can vary, depending on both the permeability of group boundaries and the fact that many groups overlap significantly, with individuals having multiple group memberships. A similar point applies to the third definitional characteristic, the ability of nonmembers to recognize members; this again will vary, depending on the permeability of the group's boundaries. The less permeable the boundaries, the more easily recognizable are members. The fourth and fifth aspects of the definition are highly linked when applied to identity and organizational groups. For example, members may be more or less aware of the extent to which they are acting, or being seen, as group representatives when relating to individuals from other groups. Every person has a number of identity- and organizational-group memberships. At any given moment an individual may be simultaneously a member of a large number, if not all, of these groups. However, which group will be focal at the moment will depend on who else representing which other groups is present and what identity-group and organizational-group issues are critical in the current intergroup exchanges. A white person in a predominantly black organization, for example, can rarely escape representing "white people" at some level, regardless of performance. But the same white person placed in a predominantly white organization will not be seen as representing "white people," but rather some other group, such as a particular hierarchical level. Rarely are individuals "just people" when they act in organizations. When there are no other group representatives present, individuals may experience themselves as "just people" in the context of their own group membership, but this subjective experience will quickly disappear when the individual is placed in a multiple-group setting. How group members relate to each other within their group, and to the expectations placed upon them by others, is highly dependent on the nature of both the intragroup and intergroup forces active at that time.

The concepts of identity groups and organizational groups do not permit an exhaustive listing of the elements in either set. In any particular setting, the relevant identity groups and organizational groups can be determined only by detailed study using intergroup methods. But it is possible to specify the more frequently observed identity groups and organizational groups and to note major issues around which those intergroup relations develop.[4]

IDENTITY GROUPS

The essential characteristic of identity groups is that individuals join them at birth. While there is little choice about physical membership in identity groups, there is some degree of "negotiation" about psychological membership. A person may behave, think, and feel more or less as if he or she is a member of an identity group. Identity-group membership precedes organizational-group membership. The identity groups to which we give attention are gender, ethnicity, family, and age.

Gender differences between men and women in organizations reflect the effects of unequal influence, stereotypical perceptions, and sexuality. Although we are living in an era of significant social change, the historical and contemporary relationships between men and women in the United States are unequal. In general, women tend to have less access to a variety of resources (e.g., income, position, and information) than men. There are views held by many men about the fitness of women for certain kinds of responsibilities, and there are increasingly successful efforts on the part of women and men to identify and change the consequences of these perceptions both for themselves and for the total culture. Research on female-male dynamics in organizations has documented structural, interpersonal, and personal effects of the power and perception inequalities between men and women (see Kanter 1977; Filene 1974).

Male-female dynamics in organizations are also determined by sexual dynamics, an area in which there has been little research, for understandable reasons. There are cultural taboos against discussing sexual behavior, except under relatively narrowly defined circumstances (e.g., with one's sex partner, in a therapy setting, or as part of legal proceedings to determine whether sex-

ual harassment has occurred). But these prohibitions and inhibitions do not keep sexual feelings from arising and influencing the behavior and perceptions of men and women in organizations.

Ethnic differences are closely tied to the historical relationships between the most numerous ethnic groups in a region (Van Den Berge 1972; Te Selle 1973; Glazer and Moynihan 1975). Specific kinds of work and organizational roles tend to be available only to members of particular ethnic groups. Struggles among ethnic groups for control of material, positional, and informational resources are more visible at some times (e.g., when violence breaks out or when nonviolent demonstrations occur) than at others (e.g., when surface appearances suggest peace). The potential for serious conflict among ethnic groups is present as long as access to resources is understood to be inequitably distributed and group members believe that their ethnic identity is the basis for their losing or not receiving access to resources. In the United States some of the most severe ethnic conflicts have been between blacks and whites (Kerner and Lindsay 1968).

As a result of cultural traditions and contemporary experiences, ethnic groups develop different ways of explaining what happens to themselves and to others: they have different "theories" to explain the world. Dominant groups tend to assume that their theories are correct. They either define other groups' views as wrong or they remain largely unaware that alternative theories exist. Less-dominant groups tend to be aware of both majority and minority theories, they expect their theories to be ignored or devalued by dominant groups, and they may try to make their theories dominant (Billig 1976).

Family groups play an especially prominent role in business enterprises that were built around the contributions of family members (see Sofer 1961; Miller and Rice 1967). Family groups become a significant force shaping intergroup relations after the business grows to the point where nonfamily people are necessary to maintain or enhance the human capacities of the organization. When a substantial proportion of nonfamily members become organization members, the intergroup relationship between family and nonfamily members takes on the dynamics of an overbounded system (i.e., the family) dealing with an underbounded system (i.e., the nonfamily).[5] Family members face questions about whether they wish to share or give up control of the

---

1. The treatment given to each of these in the following paragraph is inevitably incomplete. A more extended analysis of ethnicity, gender, and age as they relate to organizations and organizational groups may be found in Alderfer (1977a), which also includes an extended bibliography. Guzzo and Epstein (1979) provide an analogous bibliography on family business, and Paolino and McCrady (1978) present a most useful collection of essays on families.

5. Clearly not all families are overbounded systems. But it seems unlikely that members of a family who work in the same family-owned business can escape being overbounded as a result of their internal dynamics and their relations with nonfamily members.

enterprise to nonfamily members. Nonfamily members struggle with whether they wish to remain psychologically outside the family or strive to earn the status of adopted daughters or sons, thereby enhancing their influence as individuals while maintaining the dominance of the founding family.

The pattern of relations between family members and nonfamily members is also related to generational intergroup dynamics. Nonfamily members often must compete with daughters and sons of the entrepreneur for positions of influence in the enterprise. Children of the entrepreneur, depending on the nature of their family relationships, must struggle more or less with their parents about whether they stay in or leave the business and with the implications of that decision for their standing in the family and in the business.

Generational groups, unlike the other identity groups, have the property that everyone who lives long enough will inevitably belong to several. As a result, members of older groups have the potential for developing empathy for members of younger groups because they inevitably have had some of the same experiences. But members of younger groups, because of their more limited experience, have far less potential for understanding the experiences of members of older groups. Levinson et al. (1978), for example, have noted the rather profound ways that individuals do not understand the significance of life events until they have passed through identifiable phases.

The patterns of dominance and subordination characteristic of generational groups are also unique in relation to other identity groups. In the culture of the United States, members of the middle-aged group (roughly late-thirties to late-fifties) tend to dominate both younger and older groups. But the younger people contend with their subordination knowing that at least some of their members will reach more influential positions, while the older people face the reality that their influence is determined to decrease with the passage of time. Generational groups tend to be bound together by their members' sharing a common historical experience that in some material and symbolic way resulted in their members' sharing a common deprivation (Feurer 1969). The loosely defined ideology that evolves from the generational experience provides the rationale both for one generational group's rebelling or resisting another and for one group's dominating the others.

ORGANIZATIONAL GROUPS

The essential characteristic of organizational groups is that individuals belong to them as a function of negotiated exchange between the person and the organization. Often the exchange is voluntary, as when a person decides to work to earn a living or volunteers to work for a community agency. But the exchange may also be involuntary, as when children must attend school, draftees must join the military, and convicted criminals must enter a prison. Regardless of whether the exchange about entry is mainly voluntary or involuntary, becoming an organizational member assigns a person to membership in both a task group and a hierarchical group. A person who stops being an organization member, for whatever reason, also gives up membership in the task and hierarchical groups. In this way task-group and hierarchical-group memberships differ from identity-group affiliations.

Task-group membership arises because of the activities (or, in some unusual cases, such as prisons or hospitals, the inactivities) members are assigned to perform. The activities typically have a set of objectives, role relationships, and other features that shape the task-group members' experiences. As a result, people develop a perspective on their own group, other groups, and the organization as a whole, which in turn shapes their behavior and attitudes.

Membership in task groups also tends to be transferable from one organization to another because people can carry the knowledge and skills necessary to perform particular tasks with them if they leave one system and attempt to join another. As a function of developing and maintaining certain knowledge and skills, people may belong to known professional or semiprofessional organizations outside their employing (or confining) organizations. Support from these "outside interest groups" may help people achieve more power within the system where they are working, and it may make it more possible for them to leave one system and join another.

Hierarchical-group membership is assigned by those in the system with the authority to determine rank in the system. The determination of a member's hierarchical position in an organization is typically a carefully controlled, and often highly secret, process. One's place in the hierarchy determines one's legitimate authority, decision-making autonomy, scope of responsibility, and, frequently, access to benefits of membership. Group effects of the hierarchy arise from the nature of the work required of people who occupy the different levels, from the various personal attributes that the work calls for from incumbents, and from the relations that develop between people who occupy different positions in the hierarchy (Smith 1982; Oshry 1977).

People at the *top* of the hierarchy carry the burden of responsibility for large segments of the institution (or for the whole organization). They have access to more resources than lower-ranking members, including relatively more autonomy in determining how to define and conduct their assignments. They also tend to maintain a larger network of relationships with key people outside the institution than lower-ranking members.

By the very nature of the hierarchy, people at or near the top have more potential power than lower-ranking people. However great their actual power, higher-ranking poeple tend to be seen by lower-ranking members as possessing more power than they experience themselves as being able to use effectively. The world confronted by higher-ranking people is typically very complex, and the untoward effects of misusing their power is often much clearer to them than to lower-ranking people, who typically face less complicated environments.

The positional attributes of higher-ranking people affect communications with people below them in the system. Because there are hazards to bearing bad news, lower-ranking people tend to censor information flowing upward so that it has a positive flavor. Because of the complexity of their work and the public visibility of controversial events, higher-ranking people naturally prefer good news. Thus, an unwitting collusion develops between higher- and lower-ranking people, which tends to keep higher-ranking people better informed about good news than about bad.

People in the *middle* of the organization have the task of holding the organization together in an uneasy alliance between the highest- and lowest-ranking members. They are truly people in the middle. They are more in touch with the concrete day-to-day events than those above them, and they have more power, authority, and autonomy than those below them. They are aware of the tensions and pressures faced by those at the top, and they can be conscious of the deprivations and struggles faced by those below them. They must exercise some control over those below them in the system, and they must satisfy those above them if they are to retain their positions.

The middle holds the system together by dispensing rewards and punishment downward and by exchanging information upward. They send information upward on the basis of judgments of what serves the joint needs of upper and middle people. The exercise of control is a balancing process: too much restriction foments rebellion, and too little permits chaos. The balance of rewards and punishments depends on the quality of interaction between middle and lower people. The more the affective balance is positive, the more rewards are used to influence behavior (and conversely). The more the affective balance is negative, the more punishments are used to shape behavior (and conversely).

People at the *bottom* of the system execute the concrete work for which the system was created. In terms of material needs and formal influence, they are the most deprived (Argyris 1957). They have fewer material resources, and, as individuals working alone, wield less power than any other class of individuals in the system. There is a sense of anonymity about being at the bottom of large systems—a consequence that encourages people to lose their individuality in groups and not to feel responsible for their actions.

The people at the bottom of the system cope with their relative deprivation and alienation by both passive and aggressive means. When times are "calm," they withhold some of their potential involvement in objectives set for them by middles in order to retain a modicum of control over their lives. They may also covertly undermine vulnerable parts of the larger system. When times are "turbulent," they organize and openly resist initiatives and structures set out by the middles (Brown 1978). A portion of the lower group also identifies with the middle and upper groups; they are most susceptible to the rewards and punishments offered by the middle, and they often share and support the control of their "peers" by the middle group (Bettelheim 1960).

No one who belongs to an organization escapes the effects of hierarchy. Finer differentiations than the three offered here (e.g., upper upper, lower middle, etc.) can be made, but the same basic structure will be repeated within the microcosm of finer distinctions. The effects of hierarchy are "system" characteristics; anyone occupying a particular position in the hierarchy will tend to show the traits associated with that level.

Figure 13.3 provides a schematic to show the intersection of identity and organization groups. There is an inevitable tension between the two classes of groups as long as there are systematic processes that allocate people to organization groups as a function of their identity groups. Sometimes these processes are called "institutional discrimination." (Thought question: how many 30-year-old-[age group too young] Greek [ethnic group nondominant] women do you know of who are presidents of major corporations?) There is usually enough tension among organization groups to occupy the emotional energies of the top group, who have the task of managing group boundaries and transactions. Thus, unless there are special forces to strengthen the boundaries of identity groups within organizations (i.e., give them more authority), the inclination of those in senior positions will be to manage only in terms of organization groups. The manner in which an organization is embedded in its environment and the relations among identity groups in that environment will affect the degree to which management processes respond to identity *and* organization groups or just to organization groups.

A *Time* magazine article described IBM as "the colossus that works" (Greenwald 1983). With profits of

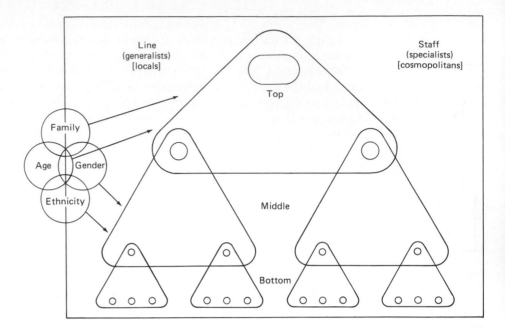

Figure 13.3 Identity and organization groups

$4.4 billion on sales of $34.4 billion, the corporation was called the most profitable U.S. industrial company. This assessment can be only in terms of the values of organization groups. Late in the article, the writer notes, "Despite increased efforts to recruit women and minorities, there are still few of either in management ranks. Only 3,089 of IBM's more-than-29,000 managers are women." Numbers are not mentioned at all for minority-group members. If identity-group values were considered relevant to *Time's* assessment of IBM, whether the "colossus . . . works" would be far more conditional. They might say the corporation is effective in satisfying investors and energetic employees who accept the corporate culture and perform (conform) well according to IBM's special set of values.

Embedded-intergroup relations

Any intergroup relationship occurs within an environment shaped by the suprasystem in which it is embedded. In observing an intergroup relationship one has several perspectives.

1. The effects on individuals who represent the groups in relation to one another
2. The consequences for subgroups within groups as the groups deal with one another
3. The outcomes for groups as a whole when they relate to significant other groups
4. The impact of suprasystem forces on the intergroup relationship in question

Regardless of which level one observes, the phenomenon of "interpenetration" among levels will be operating. Individuals carry images of their own and other groups as they serve in representational roles (Berg 1978; Wells 1980). Subgroup splits within face-to-face groups reflect differing degrees of identification and involvement with the group itself, which are in turn shaped by the relationship of the group as a whole to other groups. Then the group as a whole develops a sense—which may be more or less unconscious—of how its interests are cared for or abused by the suprasystem. The concept of embedded-intergroup relations applies to both identity and task groups (Alderfer and Smith 1982).

Figure 13.4 provides a diagram to illustrate how to think about embedded-intergroup relations from a system's perspective. The picture shows how to contruct an embedded-intergroup analysis from an understanding of a particular group's place in a given social system. As group members look toward the suprasystem, they make assessments as to whether their own or another group is in control of distributing scarce resources. When one's own group is in charge or has significant influence, the situation is less hazardous than when the other group dominates. The effects of one's own group's occupying a favorable position in a system may be muted by its being at a relative disadvantage in the suprasystem (Alderfer and Smith 1982).

In the particular example shown in figure 13.4, the relationship is between two task groups, sales and engineering. Both groups do work that is essential for their corporation and, since they are "functional" groups,

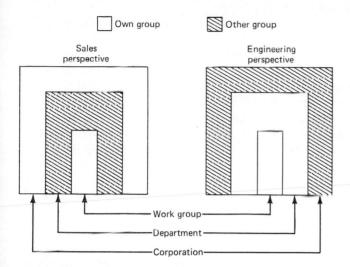

Figure 13.4 Organization-level analysis of embedded-intergroup relations

group. The work group has four subgroups identified by dashed lines. Viewed exclusively from the perspective of intragroup dynamics, the work group is affected only by the individual and subgroup processes inside the group. An intergroup perspective, however, suggests that the subgroups inside the work group represent memberships in groups that exist beyond the boundaries of the work unit as indicated by the dotted lines. Suppose I_3 is a new female group leader, having recently joined the group from outside; I_1 and I_2 are men closely associated with the former male group leader; I_4, I_5, and I_6 are junior male members of the work team; and I_7, I_8, I_9, and I_{10} are junior female members of the work team. During the period of transition, and probably subsequent to it as well, embedded-intergroup theory would predict that the relationship between the new female leader and the senior men would be affected by the authority of women in the total system, and that the relationship between the junior men and junior women in the work group would be changed by the group as a whole gaining a female leader.

might be conventionally viewed as having about equal standing in the corporation. But close examination would probably reveal a pattern of differences. The diagram shows the relationship between sales and engineering work groups in a department dominated by engineers, which, in turn, is in a corporation dominated by sales. Any understanding of the relationship between the groups would be limited if it did not take account of different patterns of embeddedness of the groups in the larger system.

Figure 13.5 shows how intergroup dynamics might be exhibited in the dynamics within a ten-person work

Parallel and unconscious processes

In earlier sections I discussed transferential and countertransferential phenomena, mainly as these processes have been observed in psychotherapeutic situations and almost exclusively as they have been applied in one-to-one relationships. Previous examples have also included concrete illustrations from the lives of social researchers

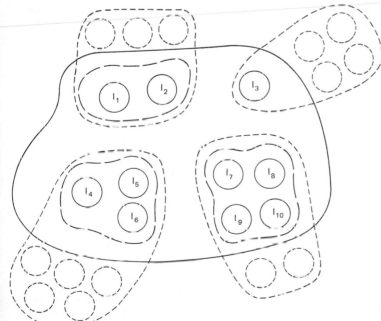

Figure 13.5 Intergroup dynamics embedded in a small group

in which unexamined aspects of these people's lives have apparently shaped their work in ways that seem both meaningful and unrecognized by the authors. I have suggested, but not actually proposed, that these processes have both individual- and group-level components. The terms "parallel process" and "unconscious process" signify concepts for dealing with the somewhat puzzling, and often overlooked, processes whereby two or more human systems in relationship to one another seem to "infect" and become "infected" by one another.

The basic proposition concerning parallel processes is that the dynamics of a system tend to reflect processes in the suprasystem and in its subsystems. Therefore, a system can face reinforcing or conflictual pressures as the outside affects the inside, and the inside, in turn, affects the outside.[6]

From the group-level perspective, parallel processes refer to the ways in which group representatives (i.e., individual people) or groups as a whole having significant *and* changing relationships tend toward showing similar affect, behavior, and cognition. The primary mechanism by which parallel processes occur is generally emotional and frequently involves unconscious processes at both individual and group levels. Conventionally defined transferential and countertransferential processes between two individuals are special cases of parallel processes at the individual and interpersonal levels. When a therapist begins to show reactions to a patient as a result of unconscious dynamics set off in the therapist, the process is termed "countertransference" (Searles 1955). When a patient begins to show similar reactions to a therapist as a result of unconscious reactions set off in the patient, the process is termed "transference." At the group level, analogous phenomena occur. After interaction between groups, members may find that their characteristic pattern of roles and subgroups change to reflect the roles and subgroups of the group with whom they were relating.

An organizational diagnosis team had assigned its members to each of five departments in a small manufacturing company. Members of the team had interviewed each department head and several department members. They had also observed department meetings. The team was preparing to observe their first meeting of department heads and were trying to anticipate the group's behavior in advance. At first they seemed to have no "rational" basis for predicting the top group's behavior because they "had no data" from direct observation. Their

interview questions had not asked about department head meetings. Reasoning from the theory of parallel processes, they decided to role play the group meeting they had never seen. Diagnostic team members behaved as they thought the department heads would, and the result was almost uncanny. Team members found that they easily became engaged with one another in the simulated department-head meeting; emotional involvement occurred quickly for all participants. When the team actually was able to observe a department-head meeting, they were amazed at how closely the simulated meeting had approximated the actual session.

When parallel processes are set in motion from inside to outside, the unit in the dominant position is engaged in some sort of projection. Accordingly, the process-dominant (i.e., the inside) unit acts toward the other unit as if it were some part of itself, and the other unit responds as if it were indeed that part. The benefit to the sending unit of this happening is that it can release troublesome emotions to another unit. When parallel processes are set in motion from outside to inside, the unit with the submissive process is engaged in some sort of absorption. Accordingly, the process-submissive (i.e., the inside) unit reacts to the other unit as if it were a part of its own, and accepts the offered conditions. The benefit to the receiving unit of this happening is that it can avoid having to differentiate itself from its outside environment.

Without reference to content or purpose, parallel processes may be constructive or destructive. For the purposes of diagnosis, for example, it may be advantageous for a diagnosing unit (person or group) to absorb temporarily a client's condition. For the purposes of change, it may be beneficial for a more optimally functioning system to project its condition onto a related unit. Constructive absorption of parallel processes may be aided by the submissive system's taking an empathic and receptive attitude. Destructive absorption of parallel processes may occur when the submissive system fails to maintain adequate control over its own boundary. Constructive projection of parallel processes may occur when a system with substantial awareness of its own and other system dynamics consciously plans to effect the relationship between the parties for the benefit of both parties and with the conscious consent of the other party. Destructive projection of parallel processes may occur when a system with limited awareness of its own internal dynamics begins to attribute these characteristics to others in order to damage or destroy them (see Alderfer 1981; Alderfer et al. 1984).

Understanding parallel processes requires a willingness to contend explicitly with emotional reactions—both one's own and others'. Included among the emo-

---

6. To be able to observe parallel processes takes special training and may not be accessible to everyone even with training (see Alderfer et al. 1984 for a review of the literature identifying parallel processes and for detailed studies documenting the phenomena).

tional reactions are conscious and unconscious processes that may occur at both individual and group levels. Inevitably any direct dealing with the range of emotions characteristic of parallel processes involves being disturbed and giving up some degree of control. To accept parallel processes as phenomena worthy of attention is to be willing to face anxiety and uncertainty.

The mechanisms by which parallel processes may be altered differ for the projective and the absorptive positions.

1. Projective mechanisms are reduced when the origins—whether individual or group—own, rather than share, responsibility for what is happening. Concretely, at the individual level, this means making "I" statements such as, "I was feeling nervous when . . . " The analogue at the group level is "we" statements pertaining to characteristics of a group in which the speaker acknowledges membership.
2. Absorptive mechanisms are reduced when the targets raise questions about why particular messages are being sent to them as they are. The question identifies the parallel process and inquires about its meaning or purpose. For example, "I wonder why members of the red group treat members of the green group as if we are untrustworthy."

Parallel processes are dynamic rather than static. They may affect relationships across levels of analysis (individual to group; group to organization) and between comparable units (individual to individual; group to group). Observation and management of parallel processes provide key avenues for understanding and changing systems from group and individual levels. Thus, parallel processes are not only phenomena that investigators observe in systems they attempt to understand and change, but they are also dynamics that play out in the lives of investigators as they do their work. The behavioral aspects of methodology become the means by which researchers actively engage, or unwittingly suppress, the parallel processes set off by their activities (Alderfer and Smith 1982).

APPLICATION OF THE INTERGROUP THEORY TO SELECTED PROBLEMS

As a general perspective on group behavior in organizations, the intergroup theory may be used to address a

variety of human problems. In this concluding section, I shall discuss what the theory has to say about four problems that face organizational psychologists. The list of problems is short and by no means exhaustive; particular problems vary in the degree to which "the problem" is conceptional (i.e., developing a more fruitful way of thinking) or practical (i.e., establishing a more useful way of acting). I selected each of the problems because it has been a subject of my attention during the last several years. The problems are,

1. developing effective teams;
2. understanding organizational culture;
3. responding to minorities and white women in predominantly white male organizations;
4. teaching organizational behavior in management schools.

Developing effective teams

For purposes of this work, a team is an officially sanctioned collection of individuals who have been charged with completing a mission by an organization and who must depend upon one another for successful completion of that work. The life of the team may be finite (e.g., a task force with a particular due date for its product) or infinite (e.g., a top-management group). According to the concept of group given above, a team so defined is also a group.

Traditionally "team building," as the social technology is usually called, has focused inward toward the interpersonal relationships among team members. The question is what difference, if any, the intergroup theory would make to conventional team building. Suggestive answers can be formed in two of the earliest reports on team building interventions.

In *Money and Motivation*, Whyte (1955a, 90–96) reports one of the earliest experiments in team building among hourly workers that failed because "it succeeded too well." The target for change was a group of "girls" who operated along an assembly line that produced wooden toys. The external consultant was a male as was the women's foreman.[7] Changes were brought about by the consultant's talking with the foreman, who in turn consulted with his subordinates and other key people in the system. Especially significant seemed to be the foreman's recognition of and working with the "informal leader" of the women's group. As a result of these consultations two sociotechnical innovations were introduced within the work group. First, the women asked

---

7. In this case Whyte himself was not the consultant.

to improve the condition of the air in the setting where they worked. After much talk and considerable hesitation by management, they were given two fans. The work group as a whole decided how to locate the fans. Once the group had satisfied itself about the location, their morale increased dramatically. Second, they asked for and received—again, with great reluctance, this time from the quality control engineers and senior management—the right to control the pace of their assembly line. Again, there was a period of testing, but eventually the group established a pattern to their liking. After the changes were made, notable productivity gains were realized. The average pace of the line set by the team was higher than the rate originally established by the plant engineers. The team was paid on a group piece rate incentive, so they benefited financially from the productivity gains. Rationally, one might think that the program was a great success for the employees and for the factory.

In fact, the experiment was unilaterally discontinued by the foreman's boss. The work group's success apparently was very disturbing to several other groups in the organization. Similar work teams were bothered by the experimental team's autonomy and income. The work-study engineers were embarrassed by their exceeding the predicted production rates. Senior management was upset by the range and intensity of the complaints they received. Thus, the "successful" innovation was terminated. Within several months, most of the original team members and the foreman left the group in order to find work elsewhere.

In *Interpersonal Competence and Organizational Effectiveness*, Argyris (1962) reports one of the earliest experiments in team building among senior managers.[8] The consulting program brought about changes within the group that received consultation, but eventually these changes eroded because the intervention failed to alter significantly the relationships of these men to others in their organization. The chief problems that face senior management groups differ from those encountered at lower levels in the organization. Argyris's (1962) executives acted to suppress emotions in their dealings with each other, demonstrated an inability to listen receptively, and withheld information relevant to interdependent tasks.

The intervention with the all-male group included on-site interviews coupled with observations, a feedback meeting giving the group a diagnosis of its interpersonal patterns, an intensive off-site T-group workshop, and follow-up sessions to assess the impact of these activities. Roger Harrison (1962) conducted an independent assessment of the program using different methods than

Argyris; Harrison's findings were mainly congruent with Argyris's own evaluation.

Despite major differences in method and minor differences in theory, both researchers found that the executives who took the program reported and demonstrated substantial and significant changes in their perceptions of each other. Argyris also found behavior changes among the executives who had participated in the off-site workshop. Harrison found that the executives changed their perceptions only of those individuals who also attended the workshop. Both investigators explain the limited efforts of the change as arising from counterforces in the organization. The exact words used by Argyris (1962, 247) were, " . . . The biggest difficulties encountered by the experimental group was [*sic*] in their relationship with their peers (who had not attended the laboratory) and subordinates (who also had not attended the laboratory) as well as the pressures from 'above' and 'outside.' " Furthermore Argyris reported a dampening of the effects of the program as time passed, even for those who attended the off-site sessions.

Both the Whyte and the Argyris interventions show an awareness of external group forces acting on their innovative groups. In Whyte's case, the forces came from individual engineers, higher-level management, and other work groups. In Argyris's case, the forces came from other groups of managers above, below, and beside the target group. For Whyte's group the innovation was ended by a single spectacular action taken by senior management. For Argyris's group, the gains of the intervention were slowly and subtly eroded by interactions with individuals representing groups who had not participated in the intervention program. From my perspective, the difficulties with both interventions call out for intergroup interpretation. Both programs had intergroup data from the outset, gave primary attention to intragroup events during the intervention period, and then encountered difficulties that can be explained readily by the operation of intergroup dynamics.

Both the Whyte and the Argyris reports were pioneering efforts carried out before the technology and theory of applied behavioral science were as well developed as they are today. The question naturally arises as to whether recent technology and theory of team development has begun to take more complete account of intergroup forces. In a book summarizing the social technology of team building, Dyer (1977) wrote 139 pages; of those, six were devoted to reducing inter-team conflict, the only portion of the book explicitly addressing intergroup dynamics. In that section, he gives five different "inter-team" designs. All these approaches deal only with the external boundaries between interdependent groups. None considers the effects of individuals within a group serving as group representatives (such as

---

8. In this case Argyris was a consultant to the group.

the effects of a single male in an all-female group) or of the larger organization context consisting of many identity and organization groups. His work shows no awareness of embedded-intergroup relations. In short, Dyer's review and summary of team development shows little more awareness of intergroup concepts or intergroup intervention than the original work by Whyte and Argyris. An alternative view may be found in Alderfer and Brown (1975), which reports the failure of a team-development effort that initially relied only on intragroup concepts followed by success in the same system with the same group after the theory and method were changed to include intergroup concepts and technology.

Alderfer and Brown (1975) faced the difficulties of an exclusively intragroup orientation from the outset of the intervention. Unlike the projects described by Whyte and Argyris, they were not permitted to start without taking account of the other groups in the system. Originally, the target for their efforts was the group of senior student leaders in a boarding school who had responsibilities for managing dormitory life. When initially invited to participate in an intervention, the students resisted because they viewed the consultation as an effort sponsored by the school administration to control them. Later, when the intervention design was altered to include faculty *and* students who had dormitory responsibilities, both groups responded enthusiastically to the invitation to participate.

In general, the problem of managing the intergroup relations of several identity and organization groups who may have an interest in a team-development intervention can be addressed by creating a microcosm group of representatives from the interested units (Alderfer 1977b; Alderfer et al. 1980; Alderfer 1981; Alderfer and Smith 1982).

Understanding organizational culture

As investigators and consultants have shifted their concerns from small groups to the organization as a whole, there has been a corresponding search for concepts that offer the possibility of giving a holistic formulation to the total system. The notion of an organizational culture has, in part, emerged from this quest.[9] From the standpoint of this paper, the key question is What sort of intellectual conversation might occur between the theorist of organizational culture and the intergroup theorist? As a response to this question I examine the work of Schein (1983a) and of Martin and Siehl (1982).

Schein's analysis is especially useful because he approaches the concept of organizational culture from the standpoint of group dynamics and learning theory. He provides a formal definition of culture, as follows:

> Organizational culture is the *pattern of basic assumptions* which a *given group* has *invented, discovered, or developed in learning to cope* with its *problems of external adaptation and internal integration*, which have *worked well enough to be considered valid*, and, therefore, to be *taught to new members* as the correct way to *perceive, think and feel* in relation to those problems.

Schein's view of culture is that, "there cannot be any culture unless there is a group which 'owns' it. Culture is created by groups, hence the creating group must always be clearly identified." In his conceptual work, Schein is *mainly* associating organizational culture with a single group, but there is also a sense that he is not quite sure that it is one group; he said, "Culture is created by groups" (plural). Yet the main focus of his attention is on *a* group—the set of individuals who work with the founder to establish the organization (Schein 1983b). However, even within that orientation, Schein's empirical work describing three different founder cultures indirectly reports intergroup phenomena. One of the three founders he describes in detail established a family business that included nonfamily members in the founder's group. As it turned out, the behavior of the founder was different toward nonfamily members than toward family members. Family members received stock options, easy access to developmental assignments, and ready excuses for errors—none of which were available to nonfamily members. As a result "subcultures" formed around "groups of younger managers who were . . . insulated from the founder" (Schein 1983a).

Martin and Siehl (1982) also use the concept of subculture. In their case, they propose the notion of a "counterculture" formed around a charismatic figure who provides a sensitively balanced set of assumptions and behaviors that offer an alternative to the dominant culture. Their empirical material is drawn from the activities of John DeLorean when he was a senior executive with General Motors.

The notion of subcultures, of course, suggests an intergroup perspective, but it does not explicitly propose that view. Rather the term *subculture* implies that the diversity of cultures is really *subordinate* to the main culture, or perhaps, that subculture is the theorist's way of accommodating to data that are obviously present but do not quite fit a "one-group" view of cultural dynamics. What if the idea of organizational culture were viewed as a multiple-group phenomenon?

9. The concept of organizational culture serves other functions as well, and not all organizational culture researchers are concerned with viewing organizations holistically.

A study by McCollom (1983) provides data that were gathered and analyzed from a multiple-group perspective. Her work is especially interesting because she initially expected to find a single culture but emerged from her research to write about the cultures of the BCD School. Her own words state,

> I began this study expecting to be able to identify a culture which typified BCD. Instead, I found a number of distinct subcultures residing in the major groups in the School (students, faculty, and staff). The interaction of these cultures seemed to produce an organizational culture that was far from homogeneous. In fact, conflict between the groups seemed to become part of the culture of the whole system (e.g., the generally held expectation that staff and faculty would disagree). My hypothesis is that the relative power of each of the groups over time in the organization is a major factor in determining the culture.

This statement exemplifies an intergroup view of organizational culture. It makes the culture of the whole system a product of the cultures of key groups in the system *in interaction with one another.* In McCollom's study the predominant pattern of interaction between at least two of these groups was conflictual. Conflict, however, need not be the major style of intergroup transaction for the organization culture to be usefully conceptualized as dynamic intergroup pattern.

An important difference between the work of McCollom and that of Schein (1983a) and Martin and Siehl (1982) may be their own roles and group memberships in relation to the cultures they described. Schein was an outsider with direct access (perhaps as a consultant?) to his founders and their groups. Martin and Siehl were outsiders who read published materials about GM and DeLorean and who interviewed people who had been close to the scene. McCollom was a member of the organization she studied and was committed to examining the perspectives her group memberships gave her on the system she studied. It is likely that Schein and Martin and Siehl were prevented from fully seeing the multiple-group qualities of the organizations they studied, because they permitted themselves to become mainly associated with just one group. I suggest again that the intergroup relationships of investigators and how those relationships are managed are likely to shape the data they obtain and the concepts derived from those findings.

Responding to white women and minorities in predominantly white male organizations

Speaking before the American Bar Association on August 1, 1983, the president of the United States said,

> We aim for a cross-section of appointments that fully reflects the rich diversity and talent of our people. But we do not, and we will never, select individuals just because they are men or women, whites or blacks, Jews, Catholics or whatever. I don't look at people as members of groups, I look at them as individuals and as Americans. I believe you rob people of their dignity and confidence when you impose quotas. The implicit, but false, message of quotas is that some people can't make it under the same rules that apply to everyone else. . . .
>
> When an opening appeared on this nation's highest court, I selected the person I believed the most outstanding candidate. I'm proud that, for the first time in our history, a woman, named Sandra Day O'Connor, now sits on the Supreme Court of the United States. But I am proudest of this appointment, not because Justice O'Connor is a woman, but because she is so well qualified.
>
> We are committed to appointing outstanding blacks, Hispanics and women to judicial and top level policy-making positions in our administration. Three women are members of my Cabinet. . . . [10]

The president shows in this speech that he consciously holds the individual *versus* group view of intergroup dynamics. Yet careful observation of his words suggests a more complex picture. "We are committed to appointing outstanding blacks, Hispanics and women . . . " is a statement that suggests that blacks and Hispanics are not women or that women are not black or Hispanic. The statement could also imply that the adjective "outstanding" applies in his thinking only to blacks, Hispanics, and women. Applying a kind of tough-minded logic to the president's words, one could deduce that people who are not black, Hispanic, or women might not be subject to the criterion of "outstanding" when considered for appointments. All of this is to suggest that the president is using group-level concepts perhaps more than he understands or acknowledges.

There is a variety of ways that his statement could be rewritten to make the implicit group concepts more explicit. But to clarify what he meant requires the addition of at least two more group identifications—white and male. The president himself is a white man; the senior people in his administration are primarily white men; and a basis on which listing blacks, Hispanics, and women in a series makes sense is if they are to be contrasted (implicitly) with white men. So perhaps the more precise—though possibly more politically volatile—form of the statement is, "We are committed to appointing outstanding blacks, Hispanics, and white women. . . . "

10. Excerpts from President's Address to American Bar Association, *New York Times*, 2 August 1983. Copyright © 1983 by The New York Times Company. Reprinted by permission.

Sandra Day O'Connor and the three cabinet-level people he alludes to are *white women*. With such a change, the terms "black" and "Hispanic" would less ambiguously imply black men and women and Hispanic men and women. However, it is also not completely clear that the president means to appoint Hispanic and black women to senior positions.

The president says he does not look at people as members of groups but as individuals and *as Americans*. Being an American is usually thought of as being a member of a national group. Here again the president gives a conflicted message about whether he prefers to look at people solely as individuals or as individuals and as members of some groups. The president is also reasonably well known for wishing to distinguish between Republicans and Democrats.

Finally there are his words about quotas: "The implicit, but false, message of quotas is that some people can't make it under the same rules that apply to everyone else. . . . " I believe the president had a particular kind of quota in mind when he made that assertion. He probably meant quotas in the form of affirmative-action targets such that by a particular date there will be a specific number of white women, Hispanics, blacks, Asian-Pacific Islanders, native American Indians in positions formerly held only by white men. But quotas as goals are not the only form of quotas that have operated, and continue to operate, in the United States. There are also quotas such as restrictions that a private club shall have no black members. Viewing quotas from the perspective of restrictions, review the president's words: "The implicit, but false, message of quotas is that some people can't make it under the same rules that apply to everyone else. . . . " The message of restrictive quotas is exactly that: some groups of people do not make it under the same rules that apply to white men.

The point of this detailed examination of the president's words is mainly to view them as statements by a group representative. We select the president of the United States as our primary national-group representative. As it turns out, the history of the United States is that only white men have been elected to that office, and for a significant proportion of our history, only white men were permitted to vote for people to serve in that office. Because the president is our national group spokesperson, his words not only can, but should, be taken to reflect the views of the country as a whole. The complex mix of assertions and denials, of rejecting and accepting the use of group and individual concepts, is deeply established in our national unconscious.

The president's formulation, therefore, is not his alone. He speaks from the group perspective of the

United States. But perhaps more accurately, he speaks for older white men who hold senior positions in large organizations. The president's words in all their nuance are understandable as coming from a political leader reflecting the coalition that brought him to office. The failure to acknowledge white men as a group, the omission of "white" from the identification of his most senior women, and the ambiguity about whether black and Hispanic include men and women are elements of a larger pattern characteristic of white men as a group (Alderfer et al. 1983).

These sorts of considerations become part of the analytic framework when intergroup theory is used to understand and to act in relation to what are today called "affirmative action issues." In fact, the words *affirmative action*, even though they were created by a political administration whose ideology was different from that of the current administration, have considerable latent textual ambiguity. The converse of the two words taken together is *passive inaction*, which is so often what affirmative action becomes in practice, because the administrative systems that have the power to carry out the policy are in charge of senior white men whose theory in practice is very similar to the president's.

An intergroup perspective on affirmative action notably heightens the complexity of thinking and of action. Perhaps the beginning is to recognize and to accept that a white male is not only an individual but also a group condition (see figure 13.2). The term *affirmative action* interpreted progressively means recognizing and changing the exclusively white-male domination of a large proportion of U.S. institutions. Acknowledging only the individual differences among white men (or any other group) and denying the group effects seriously limits what can be understood and what can be done. These limits often serve the material interests of certain groups and individuals—perhaps especially white men but also individual white women and individual members of minority groups who unconsciously or consciously have decided to cope with their group's position by using white men as models (see Davis and Watson 1982; Davis 1983; Joseph and Lewis 1981).

However, once one begins to take a multiple group perspective, the answers do not come easily nor do the actions become obvious. In fact, there is probably an increase in group-level psychic pain associated with an increase in consciousness about both the historical and contemporary relations of one's own group to other groups. For some, there may be a wish that all oppressed groups can unite in challenging the oppressor group of white males. But then new awareness develops. An historical examination of the relation between white women and blacks reveals some periods of serious cooperation *and also* many evidences of deep-seated racism in the (white) women's movement (Joseph and Lewis 1981; Davis 1983). History also includes episodes when black men spoke against immediately developing voting rights for women (Davis 1983). Contemporary research shows evidence of black women ready to capitalize on the difficulties of black men in order to advance in predominantly white male corporate cultures (Davis and Watson 1982) and of white women in totally female interracial organizations apparently oblivious to racial dynamics unless directly confronted with the issues (Van Steenberg 1983).

I began this section with a detailed examination of a statement by the president of the United States. He is a white male, as am I. Intergroup theory applied normatively indicates that a group can begin to reverse destructive parallel processes based on projection by questioning and examining itself. The process of scrutinizing one's own group represents the first step in a process that can lead to cross-group interaction and intergroup cooperation. Beginning with an analysis of one's group and returning periodically to such work can provide a basis for seeing realistic differences in priorities among groups and for discovering sound bases for cooperation (see Alderfer et al. [1980] for the description of such a process applied to race relations in management).

Teaching organizational behavior in management schools

At one time there was a single normative model of *the* learning-teaching process, which had roughly the following form:

One began with *the material* to be learned. Usually this had the form of a mix of abstract generalizations and concrete applications. In some settings, such as professional schools, the material also included knowledge not only of how to think but also of how to act. In addition to the material, the normative model included two other components: the teacher who had access to the material and the student who did not, at least initially. The task of the teacher was to transfer the material from wherever it was (e.g., in her or his mind, in lecture notes, in books, in cases) into the minds of students. The task of the student was to absorb the material. The learning-teaching process succeeded to the degree that the teacher was able to transfer and the student was able to absorb the material.

I believe this normative model was both correct as far as it went and extraordinarily limited, especially when the material is human behavior in organizations.

In the history of teacher education there has been a long-standing tension between people who gave primary (or exclusive) attention to the material versus those who gave primary (or exclusive) attention to the transfer (Sarason, Davidson, and Blatt 1962). I believe the normative model was correct because its fundamental elements were sound, and it was limited because it failed to deal adequately with the great variety of transfer and absorption processes or with the complex interactions between different kinds of material and alternative transfer and absorption processes. The tension between those who emphasize the material versus those who emphasize the transfer is made more understandable if one assumes that the underlying functional relationship is interactive (i.e., multiplicative); it takes *both* knowledge of the material and of transfer-absorption processes to effect learning-teaching. Tension arises because individuals and groups have difficulty holding such tensions; they find a certain degree of relief from their own anxiety if they can escape from one aspect of the conflict. Choosing to emphasize either knowledge of the material or of transfer-absorption processes provides at least short-term relief.

When the material is organizational behavior, interactions between the material and transfer-absorption processes have special qualities because every learning-teaching event is also a concrete here-and-now event in the organizational lives of teachers and students. Organizational behavior teachers vary substantially in the degree to which they show awareness of this property and of how they take account of it, should they be aware of it (see Bradford, Benne, and Chin 1964; Rice 1965; Alderfer 1970a; Gillette and Van Steenberg 1983; issues of *Exchange: The Organizational Behavior Teaching Journal* 1975–83).

Intergroup theory treats the classroom as an organization embedded in larger suprasystems (i.e., the school and the university). Teachers represent their organizational groups by rank and discipline and their identity groups. Students represent their organizational groups by seniority (year in program) and position in the university (program member versus non–program member) and their identity groups. Classrooms usually include intergroup transactions among organization groups of students (e.g., first- and second-year students) and among identity groups of students (e.g., men and women) and between teachers and students. When faculty work as teams within a classroom or by having several sections of large courses, then complex interactions among organization and identity groups develop and exert powerful effects on the learning-teaching process.

An especially lucid case of the interaction between organization groups of faculty and students has been reported by Cohen and Miaoulis (1978). They describe the consequences of their efforts to coordinate the teaching of organizational behavior and marketing in two successive years within a graduate school of business. In the first year, the course "evaluations" favored the organizational behavior instructor and demeaned the marketing professor. In the second year, exactly the opposite pattern was observed; the marketing professor "won," and the OB professor "lost." Part of the descriptive data from the courses were the self-assessments of the instructors, who in both years believed that the student assessments were exaggerated. Regardless of whether the instructor was on the favorable or unfavorable side of the split, he believed the student perceptions were significantly polarized. In my own teaching, I have observed similar phenomena. The course consisted of a weekly lecture of ninety minutes and a section meeting of similar duration. I gave the weekly lectures and took one section. The other five sections of the course were taken by teaching assistants. An evaluation questionnaire administered at the end of course showed significant differences in evaluations *of the lectures* as a function of section membership. My own section gave the lectures the most favorable evaluation. The most unfavorable evaluation came from a section whose teaching assistant had the most strained relationship with me. The traditional normative model of the learning-teaching process has no way to explain the Cohen and Miaoulis (1978) data or my own. According to conventional notions of objectivity, the organizational behavior and marketing teachers are unlikely to be good or bad teachers one year and virtually the opposite the next. A "good" teacher (property of the person without group-level concepts) is a good teacher, period, and similarly for a "bad" teacher. Even if one allows that a person might have good and bad years, it is unlikely that a team of people, as a function of their *individual* life fortunes, would have good and bad years in such an obviously complementary fashion. Furthermore, the data from my lecture-discussion course carry similar dynamics. According to the individually based, traditional normative model, a large lecture setting involves communications from the lecturer to the student. There is no place in the model for the intergroup effects of different section membership in explaining why groups of students evaluate the same lectures differently as a function of their section-group memberships. Moreover, the concept of parallel processes offers an explanation of how stress in the relationship between the teaching assistant and me (i.e., an interpersonal dynamic) can be projected into a difference in evaluations by section (i.e., an intergroup effect). Intergroup theory applied to these events and others like them does offer an explanation; the relevant proposition is that the permeability of group boundaries varies with the polarization of feel-

ing among the groups; that is, to the degree that members split their feelings so that mainly positive feelings are associated with their own group and mainly negative feelings are projected onto other groups.

Probably without awareness (i.e., unconsciously), the students participated in an ethnocentric process as they provided their evaluations. Faculty members generally have more control over their own behavior than over students'. An understanding of these dynamics suggests a more complex evaluation process. To the extent that faculty choose to work directly with each other in their teams on the affective, as well as on the cognitive, aspects of their relationships, it is less likely that tensions that originate in the faculty-to-faculty relationships (whether intergroup, e.g., OB to marketing, or interpersonal, e.g., rivalry between individuals of similar identity and organization group memberships) are to be projected into the student-faculty intergroup relationship. The traditional normative model's focus on the transaction between *the* teacher and *the* student provides no reason to examine relationships among groups of faculty to understand how they might affect the learning-teaching process.

The affective-patterns proposition from intergroup theory has implications for other aspects of the learning-teaching process as well. It offers insight regarding some effects of teaching by "the" case method. It suggests connections between how organizational behavior groups are embedded in management schools and events in the classroom.

The chief difficulty that intergroup theory raises with the case method is that it encourages projection of destructive parallel processes and discourages owning up to the effects of one's individual and group dynamics. In carrying out a case discussion, students discuss the events in the lives of *other* people in *other* groups and organizations. The method is a continuing invitation for the student to dissociate herself or himself from uncomfortable feelings and thoughts and attribute them to the characters in the cases. Inadvertently, instructors "teach" students to explain the difficulties and dilemmas of human affairs in organizations by projecting onto others. People so taught are less likely to examine their own behavior and relationships as a means of dealing with situations they face. The extent of this subtle encouragement to avoid dealing with one's own condition in the here-and-now is suggested by reflections offered by Anthony Athos (1979), who is one of the better-known and well-respected case-method teachers. He describes his own thoughts on preparing for the first day of his course on interpersonal behavior.

> They (the students) look at your clothes because they know that is what you chose to put on to present your-

self to them. I do not know about you, but the first day I go to class, I have a strategy. Remember, it's Interpersonal Behavior but I dress like I was going down to do some consulting at McKinsey in New York City. I have a suit I used to wear to do that—I bought it for that purpose. It is dark gray. It's a business suit and I walk in dressed like a businessman. I do not come in dressed like a professor. I do that from my understanding of where they are coming from out of the first year and what they think about soft Organizational Behavior–type courses. I want the first day so organized so that they see a lot of the instrumental side of me.

An intergroup interpretation of Athos's strategy suggests that he expects to be the object of an ethnocentric reaction by the students—a soft organizational behavior professor. By his clothes he attempts to join another group—(presumably) hard McKinsey consultants. One can wonder what Athos's response would be if faced with student questions such as, "Professor Athos, why do you dress like a McKinsey consultant? Is it because you belong to that group? [I thought you were mainly a professor.] Is it because you represent the McKinsey group's values and concepts? [I have never thought of McKinsey as especially progressive in its understanding of human behavior.]" Intergroup theory also predicts that it is extremely unlikely that Athos would be asked these questions on the first day of class, which is not to say students would overlook his dress. How they would interpret that observation depends on how they relate their own groups to Athos. If he is correct, the most straightforward prediction (at least for the male students) is that they would infer, "He is a member of our group in good standing; he will not be disruptive to our existing ways of thinking and acting; it will be a comfortable and cohesive class among us McKinsey people." Perhaps that is what Athos wants.

Then again, it may not be quite, or even mainly, what Athos wants. The article from which I quoted was published in the organizational behavior teaching journal. Thus, there are clearly circumstances under which Athos is willing to acknowledge his membership as an organizational behavior professor. Perhaps the explanatory process is less Athos's relationship to his own group of organizational behavior teachers and more the relationship of his group to the suprasystem in which it is embedded. Roethlisberger's (1977) autobiography provides a detailed account of the difficulties and struggles encountered by the organizational behavior group at the Harvard Business School, which is where Athos was teaching when he wrote the article. Beyond the special circumstances of Harvard, however, there is also evidence that organizational behavior groups in general face difficulties within the context of schools of business (Fil-

ley, Foster, and Herbert 1979). Another intergroup interpretation of Athos's preparation for his first day in class is that it reflected his attempt to cope with systemic processes that reject and depotentiate his group. His own words say, "I do that from my understanding of where they are coming from . . . and what they think about soft Organizational Behavior–type courses. . . . " Intergroup theory applied to the problem of OB groups facing intellectual ideologies that wish to deny the existence of behavioral phenomena—especially feelings—does not support denying one's own group membership or the group's potential for making a unique contribution to management-school culture. Doing that colludes with destructive parallel processes whose unconscious (and sometimes conscious) aim is to prevent managers and management teachers from having to face the difficult emotional and behavioral issues characteristic of complex organizations.

The alternatives offered by intergroup theory are either to invite the students to give their perceptions (rather than operating on inferences) and thereby own up to whatever they think and feel or to have the instructor own up to his behavior and beliefs rather than dealing with his group membership covertly by dressing to disown his OB-faculty group membership. Learning and teaching about the nonrational side of organizations is one major reason why organizational behavior groups exist. When organizational behavior professors act like McKinsey consultants, we provide support to groups who argue that OB does not have a novel and worthwhile contribution to make to management education. The alternative is to be clear about one's group boundaries and group membership in the classroom and in embedded disciplinary group negotiations, and from that clarity to demonstrate in here-and-now events that organizational behavior contributes uniquely from its own methods and theories to the overall multidisciplinary culture of management education.

Intergroup theory applied to teaching organizational behavior in management schools modifies the normative model of learning-teaching.

One begins with the material, which is constantly being enacted among organization and identity groups of students and faculty. Abstract generalizations and concrete applications about the material become part of the cognitive formations that student and faculty groups develop as a function of their power differences and affective patterns in order to explain the nature of experiences encountered by group members and to influence relations with other groups. The degree of change in cognitive formations for individuals depends upon their intrapsychic conditions, their relations with members of their own groups, and the relations between their groups and other interdependent groups in the system in which they are embedded.

CONCLUSION

Intergroup perspectives began to shape the understanding of human behavior from the beginning of the twentieth century. Scholars reflecting upon such diverse events as political revolution, tribal warfare, labor-management relations, and mental illness showed an awareness of group-to-group relations in their thinking and action. In the last thirty years, numerous intergroup theories have evolved and shaped methodological traditions. Currently, these theory-method combinations can be distinguished by their relative focus on group-level concepts, attention to groups in context or in isolation, acceptance of interventionist behavior by researchers, and tendency toward examining the individual and group behavior of investigators.

Intergroup theory provides interpretations for individual, interpersonal, group, intergroup, and organizational relations. The version of intergroup theory given here uses a definition of group that is concerned with both internal and external properties. It explains intergroup dynamics in terms of group boundaries, power, affect, cognition, and leadership behavior. It examines the nature of identity and organization groups. It relates the state of intergroup relations to the suprasystem in which they are embedded. It presents an understanding of the changing relations among interdependent groups and their representatives through the operation of parallel and unconscious processes.

The theory relates to a wide array of social and organizational problems, including the development of effective work teams, the definition and management of organizational culture, the analysis and implementation of affirmative action, and the teaching of organizational behavior in management schools.

The most important implication of intergroup theory may be the reorientation it offers to those who study and teach about human behavior in groups and organizations. Mannheim was among the most prominent of twentieth-century scholars who connected the sociology of knowledge with the group memberships of writers.

> Accordingly, the products of the cognitive process are already . . . differentiated because not every possible aspect of the world comes within the purview of the members of a group, but only those out of which difficulties and problems for the group arise. And even this common world (not shared by any outside groups in the same way) appears differently to subordinate groups within the larger group. It appears differently because the subordinate groups and strata in a functionally differentiated society have a different experiential approach. . . . (Mannheim 1936, 29).

Intergroup theory proposes that both organization groups (e.g., being a researcher versus being a respondent) and identity groups (e.g., being a person of particular gender, age, ethnicity and family) affect one's intergroup relations and thereby shape one's cognitive formations. The body of data supporting this general proposition grows as changes in society broaden the range of identity groups with access to research roles (see Balmary 1981; Eagly and Carli 1981; Herman 1981), and consequently the content of "well-established" empirical generalizations and conceptual frameworks are called into question. These new developments affect research and development as well as clinical methods. None of the accepted methods in their implementation escapes potential intergroup effects between researchers and respondents. Investigators who accept this idea cannot avoid questioning the part they and their groups play in the knowledge-making process. Understanding one's intergroup relationships may become a key ingredient for all who wish to study people effectively.

REFERENCES

Adams, R. N., and J. J. Preiss. 1960. *Human Organization Research.* Homewood, Ill.: Dorsey.

Adorno, T. W., E. Frenkel Brunswik, D. J. Levinson, and R. N. Sanford. 1950. *The Authoritarian Personality.* New York: Harper.

Agazarian, Y., and R. Peters. 1981. *The Visible and Invisible Group.* London: Routledge and Kegan Paul.

Alderfer, C. P. 1970a. "Teaching Organizational Change to 'Insiders' and 'Outsiders.'" *Professional Psychology* 1:397–401.

——. 1970b. "Subcultures in Behavioral Science and the In-

terpretation of Research on Experiential Methods." *Proceedings of the Industrial Relations Research Association* 22:98–108.

——. 1971. "Effect of Individual, Group, and Intergroup Relations on Attitudes toward a Management Development Program." *Journal of Applied Psychology* 55:302–11.

——. 1976. "Change Processes in Organizations." In *Handbook of Industrial and Organizational Psychology,* ed. M. D. Dunnette, pp. 1591–1638. Chicago: Rand-McNally.

——. 1977a. "Group and Intergroup Relations." In *Improv-*

ing Life at Work, ed. J. R. Hackman and J. L. Suttle, pp. 227–96. Santa Monica: Goodyear.

———. 1977b. "Improving Organizational Communication through Long-Term, Intergroup Intervention." *Journal of Applied Behavioral Science* 13:193–210.

———. 1980. "Consulting to Underbounded Systems." In *Advances in Experiential Social Processes*, vol. 2, ed. C. P. Alderfer and C. L. Cooper, pp. 267–95. New York: Wiley.

———. 1981. "Intergroup Relations and Organizational Diagnosis." In *Making Organizations Humane and Productive*, ed. H. Meltzer and W. R. Nord, pp. 355–71. New York: Wiley.

———. 1982. "The Problems of Changing White Males' Belief and Behavior in Race Relations." In *Change in Organizations*, ed. P. Goodman, pp. 122–65. San Francisco: Jossey-Bass.

Alderfer, C. P., C. Alderfer, L. Tucker, and R. C. Tucker. 1980. "Diagnosing Race Relations in Management." *Journal of Applied Behavioral Science* 16:135–66.

Alderfer, C. P., and L. D. Brown. 1975. *"Learning from Changing.* Beverly Hills, Calif.: Sage.

Alderfer, C. P., L. D. Brown, R. E. Kaplan, and K. K. Smith. 1984. *Group Relations and Organizational Diagnosis.* New York: Wiley.

Alderfer, C. P., and K. K. Smith. 1982. "Studying Intergroup Relations Embedded in Organizations." *Administrative Science Quarterly* 27:35–65.

Alderfer, C. P., R. C. Tucker, D. Morgan, and F. Drasgow. 1983. "Black and White Cognitions of Changing Race Relations." *Journal of Occupational Behavior* 4:105–36.

Allport, F. H. 1924. *Social Psychology.* New York: Houghton Mifflin.

Allport, G. W. 1954. *The Nature of Prejudice.* New York: Doubleday.

Anthony, E. J. 1971. "The History of Group Psychotherapy." In *Comprehensive Group Psychotherapy*, ed. H. I. Kaplan and B. J. Sadock, pp. 4–31. Baltimore: Williams and Wilkins.

Argyris, C. 1957. *Personality and Organization.* New York: Harper.

———. 1962. *Interpersonal Competence and Organizational Effectiveness.* Homewood, Ill.: Richard D. Irwin.

Athos, A. G. 1979. "Contingencies Beyond Reasoning." *Exchange* 4:7–12.

Balmary, M. 1981. *Psychoanalyzing Psychoanalysis.* Baltimore: Johns Hopkins University Press.

Berg, D. N. 1978. "Intergroup Relations in Out Patient Psychiatric Facility." Ann Arbor, Mich.: University of Michigan.

———. 1980. "Developing Clinical Field Skills: An Apprenticeship Model." In *Advances in Experiential Social Processes*, vol. 2, ed. C. L. Cooper and C. P. Alderfer, pp. 143–64. New York: Wiley.

———. 1984. "Objectivity and Prejudice." *American Behavioral Scientist* (January).

Bettelheim, B. 1960. *The Informed Heart.* New York: Free Press.

Billig, M. 1976. *Social Psychology and Intergroup Relations.* London: Academic Press.

Bion, W. R. 1959. *Experiences in Groups.* New York: Basic Books.

Blake, R. R., H. A. Shepard, and J. Mouton. 1964. *Managing Intergroup Conflict in Industry.* Houston: Gulf.

Blalock, H. M., and P. H. Wilken. 1976. *Intergroup Processes.* New York: Free Press.

Bradford, L., K. Benne, and R. Chin. 1964. *T-Group Theory and Laboratory Method.* New York: Wiley.

Brewer, M. B., and D. T. Campbell. 1976. *Ethnocentrism and Intergroup Attitudes.* New York: Wiley.

Brown, L. D. 1978. "Toward a Theory of Power and Intergroup Relations." In *Advances in Experiential Social Processes*, vol. 1, ed. C. L. Cooper and C. P. Alderfer, pp. 161–80. New York: Wiley.

Brown, R. J., and J. C. Turner. 1981. "Interpersonal and Intergroup Behavior." In *Intergroup Behavior*, ed. J. C. Turner and H. Giles, pp. 33–65. Chicago: University of Chicago Press.

Caplette, M. 1981. "Women in Publishing: A Study of Careers in Organizations." Ph. D. dissertation, Department of Sociology, SUNY, Stony Brook.

Cartwright, D., and A. Zander. 1968. *Group Dynamics.* 3d ed. Evanston, Ill.: Row-Peterson.

Cass, E. L., and F. Zimmer, eds. 1975. *Man and Work in Society.* New York: Van Nostrand Reinhold.

Clark, K. B., and M. P. Clark. 1947. "Racial Identification and Preference in Negro Children." In *Readings in Social Psychology.* 3d ed., ed. E. Maccoby, T. M. Newcomb, and E. L. Hartley. New York: Holt, Rinehart and Winston.

Cohen, A. R., and G. Miaoulis. 1978. "MBA Student Anxiety and Overreactions: Learning from Linking the Required OB and Marketing Courses." *Exchange: The Organizational Behavior Teaching Journal* 3, no. 2:11–19.

Coser, L. A. 1956. *The Functions of Social Conflict.* Glencoe, Ill.: Free Press.

———. 1984. "The Greedy Nature of *Gemeinschaft.*" In *Conflict and Consensus: Essays in Honor of Lewis A. Coser*, ed. W. W. Powell and R. Robbins. New York: Free Press.

Cooley, C. H. 1929. "Case Study of Small Institutions as a Method of Research." In *Personality and the Social Group*, ed. E. W. Burgess. Chicago: University of Chicago Press.

Davis, A. Y. 1983. *Women, Race, and Class.* New York: Vintage Books.

Davis, G., and G. Watson. 1982. *Black Life in Corporate America.* Garden City, N.Y.: Anchor Press/Doubleday.

Devereux, G. 1967. *From Anxiety to Method in the Behavioral Sciences.* Paris: Mouton.

———. 1968. *Reality and Dream.* Garden City, N.Y.: Anchor Books.

Dunnette, M. D. 1976. *Handbook of Industrial and Organizational Psychology.* Chicago: Rand-McNally.

Dyer, W. G. 1977. *Team Building: Issues and Alternatives.* Menlo Park, Calif.: Addison-Wesley.

Eagly, A. H., and L. L. Carli. 1981. "Sex of Researchers and Sex-Typed Communications as Determinants of Sex Differences in Influenceability: A Meta-Analysis of Social Influence Studies." *Psychological Bulletin* 90:1–20.

Erikson, E. H. 1964. *Insight and Responsibility.* New York: W. W. Norton.

Excerpts from President's Address to American Bar Association. *New York Times.* 2 August 1983.

Exchange: The Organizational Behavior Teaching Journal. 1975–1983.

Feurer, L. S. 1969. *The Conflict of the Generations.* New York: Basic Books.

Filene, P. G. 1974. *Him, Her, Self.* New York: Harcourt Brace Jovanovich.

Filley, A. C., L. W. Foster, and T. C. Herbert. 1979. "Teaching Organizational Behavior: Current Patterns and Implications." *Exchange: The Organizational Behavior Teaching Journal* 4:13–21.

Filstead, W. J., ed. 1970. *Qualitative Methodology.* Chicago: Markham.

Fiske, E. B. 1983. "Japan's Schools Stress Group and Discourage Individuality." *New York Times,* 11 July.

Freud, S. 1922. *Group Psychology and the Analysis of the Ego.* New York: Liveright.

———. 1963. "Fragment of an Analysis of a Case of Hysteria (1905)." In *Dora—An Analysis of a Case of Hysteria,* ed. P. Reiff, New York: Collier.

Fromm-Reichmann, F. 1950. *Principles of Intensive Psychotherapy.* Chicago: University of Chicago Press.

Gillette, J., and V. Van Steenberg. 1983. A Group-on-Group Design for Teaching Group Dynamics in a Management School Setting. Yale School of Organization and Management Working Paper.

Glazer, N., and D. P. Moynihan. 1975. *Ethnicity: Theory and Experience.* Cambridge, Mass.: Harvard.

Golembiewski, R. T. 1965. "Small Groups and Large Organizations." In *Handbook of Organizations,* ed. J. March, pp. 87–141. Chicago: Rand-McNally.

Greenwald, J. 1983. "The Colossus that Works." *Time* 122, no. 2:44ff.

Guzzo, R. A., and G. Epstein. 1979. *Behavioral Issues in Family Businesses: An Annotated Bibliography.* Montreal: School of Management, McGill University.

Hackman, J. R. 1976. "Group Influences on Individuals." In *Handbook of Industrial and Organizational Psychology,* ed. M. Dunnette, pp. 1455–1526. Chicago: Rand-McNally.

Harrison, R. 1962. "Impact of the Laboratory on Perceptions of Others by the Experimental Group." In *Interpersonal Competence and Organizational Effectiveness,* ed. C. Argyris. Homewood, Ill.: Dorsey Press.

Herman, J. L. 1981. *Father-Daughter Incest.* Cambridge, Mass.: Harvard University Press.

Joseph, G. I., and J. Lewis. 1981. *Common Differences: Conflicts in Black and White Feminist Perspectives.* Garden City, N.Y.: Anchor Press/Doubleday.

Jung, C. G. 1946. *The Psychology of the Transference.* Princeton, N.J.: Princeton University Press.

Kanter, R. 1977. *Men and Women of the Corporation.* New York: Basic Books.

Katz, D., and R. L. Kahn. 1978. *The Social Psychology of Organizations.* 2d ed. New York: Wiley.

Kerner, O. and J. Lindsay. 1968. *Report of the National Advisory Commission on Civil Disorders.* New York: Dutton.

Klein, E. G. 1977. "Transference in Training Groups." *Journal of Personality and Social Systems* 1:53–64.

Lasswell, H. D., and A. Kaplan. 1950. *Power and Society.* New Haven: Yale.

Le Bon, G. 1895. *The Crowd.* New York: Macmillan.

Levine, R. A., and D. T. Campbell. 1972. *Ethnocentrism.* New York: Wiley.

Levinson, D. J., C. N. Darrow, E. B. Klein, M. H. Levinson, and B. McKee. 1978. *The Seasons of a Man's Life.* New York: A. A. Knopf.

Lewicki, R., and C. P. Alderfer. 1973. "The Tensions Between Research and Intervention in Intergroup Conflict." *Journal of Applied Behavioral Science* 9:424–49; 463–68.

Loring, R., and T. Wells. 1972. *Breakthrough: Women into Management.* New York: Van Nostrand Reinhold.

Mannheim, Karl. 1936. *Ideology and Utopia.* New York: Harcourt Brace Jovanovich.

March, J. G. 1965. *Handbook of Organizations.* Chicago: Rand-McNally.

Martin, J., and C. Siehl. 1982. "Organizational Culture and Counterculture: An Uneasy Symbiosis." Working paper, Stanford University.

McCall, G. J., and J. L. Simmons, eds. 1969. *Issues in Participating Observation.* Reading, Mass.: Addison-Wesley.

McCollom, M. 1983. "Organizational Culture: A Case Study of the BCD School." Yale School of Organization and Management Working Paper.

McGoldrick, M., J. K. Pearce, and J. Giordano, eds. 1982. *Ethnicity and Family Therapy.* New York: Guilford Press.

Menninger, K. 1958. *Theory of Psychoanalytic Technique.* New York: Harper Torchbooks.

Merton, R. K. 1960. "The Ambivalences of Le Bon's *The Crowd.*" In *The Crowd,* ed. G. Le Bon, pp. v–xxxix. New York: Viking.

Miller, E. J., and A. K. Rice. 1967. *Systems of Organization.* London: Tavistock.

Oshry, B. 1977. *Power and Position.* Boston: Power and Systems Training.

Otterbein, K. F. 1977. *Comparative Cultural Analysis.* New York: Holt, Rinehart and Winston.

Paolino, T. J., and B. S. McCrady. 1978. *Marriage and Marital Therapy.* New York: Brunner/Mazel.

Perry, H. Swick. 1982. *Psychiatrist of America.* Cambridge, Mass.: Harvard Press.

Pettigrew, T. P. 1981. "Extending the Stereotype Concept." In *Cognitive Processes in Stereotyping and Intergroup Behavior,* ed. D. Hamilton, pp. 303–32. Hillsdale, N.J.: Lawrence Erlbaum Associates.

Purcell, T. V., and G. F. Cavanagh. 1972. *Blacks in the Industrial World.* New York: Free Press.

Rice, A. K. 1963. *The Enterprise and Its Environment.* London: Tavistock.

———. 1965. *Learning for Leadership.* London: Tavistock.

———. 1969. "Individual, Group, and Intergroup Processes." *Human Relations* 22:565–84.

Roethlisberger, F. J. 1977. *The Elusive Phenomena*. Cambridge, Mass.: Harvard Press.

Roethlisberger, F. J., and J. Dickinson. 1939. *Management and the Worker*. New York: Wiley.

Sarason, S. B., K. Davidson, and B. Blatt. 1962. *The Preparation of Teachers*. New York: Wiley.

Schein, E. H. 1983a. "Organizational Culture: A Dynamic Model." *Office of Naval Research: Technical Report*, TR-ONR-13.

———. 1983b. "The Role of the Founder in the Creation of Organizational Culture." *Office of Naval Research: Technical Report*, TR-ONR-12.

Searles, H. J. M. D. 1955. "The Informational Value of the Supervisor's Emotional Experiences." *Psychiatry* 18:135–46.

———. 1962. "Problems of Psycho-Analytic Supervision." In *Science and Psychoanalysis*, ed. J. H. Masserman, vol. 5.

Sherif, M. 1966. *In Common Predicament*. Boston: Houghton Mifflin.

Sherif, M., and C. Sherif. 1953. *Groups in Harmony and Tension*. New York: Harper & Row.

———. 1969. *Social Psychology*. New York: Harper and Row.

Singer, E. 1965. *Key Concepts in Psychotherapy*. New York: Random House.

Smith, K. K. 1977. "An Intergroup Perspective on Individual Behavior." In *Perspectives on Behavior in Organizations*. 2d ed., ed. J. R. Hackman, E. E. Lawler, and L. W. Porter, pp. 397–407. New York: McGraw-Hill.

———. 1982. *Groups in Conflict: Prisons in Disguise*. Dubuque, Iowa: Kendall-Hunt.

Sofer, C. 1961. *The Organization from Within*. London: Tavistock.

Sullivan, H. S. 1953. *The Interpersonal Theory of Psychiatry*. New York: W. W. Norton.

Sumner, W. J. 1906. *Folkways*. New York: Ginn.

Sumner, W. G., A. G. Keller, and M. R. Davie. 1927. *The Science of Society*. New Haven: Yale University Press.

Tajfel, H. 1970. "Experiments in Intergroup Discrimination." *Scientific American* 223:96–102.

Te Selle, S., ed. 1973. *The Rediscovery of Ethnicity*. New York: Harper.

Thomas, K. 1976. "Conflict and Conflict Management." In *Handbook of Industrial and Organizational Psychology*, ed. M. Dunnette, pp. 889–936. Chicago: Rand-McNally.

Trist, E. L., G. W. Higgin, H. Murray, and A. B. Pollock. 1963. *Organizational Choice*. London: Tavistock.

Turner, J. C., and H. Giles, eds. 1981. *Intergroup Behavior*. Chicago: University of Chicago Press.

Van Den Berge, P., ed. 1972. *Intergroup Relations*. New York: Basic Books.

Van Steenberg, V. 1983. "Within White Group Differences on Race Relations at CTCGS." Yale School of Organization and Management Working Paper.

Walton, R. E. 1969. *Interpersonal Peacemaking*. Reading, Mass.: Addison-Wesley.

Wells, L. J. 1980. "The Group-as-a-Whole." In *Advances in Experiential Social Processes*, vol. 2, ed. C. P. Alderfer and C. L. Cooper, pp. 165–200. London: Wiley.

Whyte, W. F. 1955a. *Money and Motivation*. New York: Harper & Row.

———. 1955b. *Street Corner Society*. Chicago: The University of Chicago Press.

14

The study of organization:
toward a biographical perspective

JOHN R. KIMBERLY

This is an interesting time to be observing, managing, consulting to, or writing about organizations. It is a time of transition in both theory and practice. At the level of theory, it is a time of questioning existing paradigms and methodologies and of searching for interesting and viable alternatives.[1] Theories based on classical assumptions of rationality appear to have serious deficiencies; models of organizations that emphasize stability, either explicitly or implicitly, omit important dimensions of organizational life.[2]

In the domain of practice, there is a real sense of dissatisfaction with existing organizational technology spurred by widespread discussion of the performance problems of U.S. industry, and a genuine search for new combinations of structure and process both within and among enterprises. People are groping for new organizational solutions to a variety of problems, some new and some age-old, as evidenced by the current fascination with Japanese management.[3] We have been giving new

thought to the impact of rewards systems that place a premium on short-run performance measures,[4] and experimenting with a variety of arrangements intended to nurture rather than stifle innovation and creativity.[5] There has been widespread debate about how senior managers are best developed: what is the appropriate balance between professional (and presumably transferable) managerial training and experience specific to a given industry or organization?[6] The startling sales of *Theory Z*[7] and *In Search of Excellence*[8] are indicative of managers' thirst for solutions.

The range of issues raised by researchers, consultants, and managers is broad, yet at least one theme cuts across virtually all discussions, whether of theory or of practice. As managers know, and as researchers are learning, organizations are fluid entities. They are created, grow, shrink, grow again, change shape, and sometimes pass completely from the scene. The volatility of organizations, sometimes masked by the appearance of in-

Preparation of this chapter was supported in part by a grant from the National Institute of Education Program on Educational Policy and Organization, School Management and Organization Studies, John R. Kimberly and Janet A. Weiss, co-principal investigators.

1. See, for example, Jeffrey Pfeffer, *Organizations and Organizations Theory*, (Marshfield, Mass.; Pitman, 1982).

2. John R. Kimberly and Robert H. Miles, *The Organizational Life Cycle* (San Francisco: Jossey-Bass, 1980).

3. See, for example, Richard Turner Pascale and Anthony G. Athos, *The Art of Japanese Management* (New York: Warner Books, 1981).

4. Robert Hayes and William Abernathy, "Managing Our Way to Economic Decline," *Harvard Business Review* 60, no. 4 (July-August 1975).

5. See, for example, William G. Ouchi, *Theory Z* (New York: Avon Books, 1981).

6. See, for example, John P. Kotter, "What Effective General Managers Really Do," *Harvard Business Review* 60, no. 6 (November-December 1982): 156–67.

7. See note 5

8. Thomas J. Peters and Robert H. Waterman, Jr., *In Search of Excellence* (New York: Harper & Row, 1982).

ertia, assumptions of ponderousness, and stereotypes of bureaucratization, needs to be better appreciated in theory and better managed in practice.

The chapter is based on the premise that useful knowledge[9] can be developed by studying organizations as such. Previous chapters in this section of the handbook have focused on the individual, interpersonal, group, and intergroup levels of analysis. Such a division is somewhat artificial, because it is virtually impossible to bound real-world phenomena in that way. On the other hand, the approach may force us to consider what phenomena are most usefully analyzed at a particular level. This chapter, in contrast, will focus on what can be learned by studying organizations as entities in their own right.

The chapter begins by arguing that ownership is what distinguishes organizations from other arenas of collective action. Various approaches to the study of organizations are reviewed briefly. The next division emphasizes the development of perspectives on organization-environment relationships. Finally, a biographical approach to the analysis of organizations is described—an approach that highlights the influence of an organization's past on its present and future behavior.

OWNERSHIP DISTINGUISHES ORGANIZATIONS?

Most people have an intuitive sense of what an organization is. At the very least, most people can define by example. A bank, a university, an insurance company, a shoe factory, a hospital—what do these entities have in common? And what sets them apart from other social aggregates? What, in other words, makes it worthwhile to study organizations in their own right?

No one wants to spend time splitting definitional hairs. On the other hand, it is important to be clear about the point of reference and its distinctive attributes. If there are none, then one would do better to think in terms of other entities, whether individuals or groups, that do have analytically meaningful and theoretically distinctive characteristics.

I want to make the case that *ownership* is what distinguishes organizations from other collectivities or arenas for collective action. Following the lead of Becker

and Gordon,[10] I define organizations as systems of resources (of many kinds) and procedures for coordinating and controlling those resources to which an owner has property rights.

The notion of ownership is central to the essence of organization because our legal system has defined (and continues to elaborate) a set of rights and obligations between owners and others, both within the organization (e.g., employees) and outside it (e.g., competitors). An important aspect of twentieth-century social and economic arrangements at the macro level has been the evolution of organizations as legally defined entities (with the legal definition having both legitimating and constraining effects). Organizations are what they are today because of the continuing interplay among social and economic forces as mediated by the legal system over time.[11]

The forms of ownership

The three basic forms of ownership are private, public, and nonprofit.[12] Interestingly, research and professional education on the structure, management, and performance of institutions in our society has tended to divide along ownership lines. Business and management schools have grown up around the analysis of privately owned enterprises; schools of public administration, around the analysis of federal, state, and local government organizations; while the nonprofits have generally not been the object of separate educational efforts.[13] As one might expect, there is substantial disagreement as to whether the same managerial skills are needed in both publicly and privately owned organizations, and whether theories of organization are relevant for all organizations regardless of their ownership form.[14] Thus ownership and its

---

9. There are many perspectives on what constitutes "useful knowledge" about organizations. See the December 1982 and March 1983 issues of the *Administrative Science Quarterly* for a sampling of views. For a different perspective on this issue, see William McKelvey and Howard Aldrich, "Population, Natural Selection and Applied Organizational Science," *Administrative Science Quarterly* 33 (March 1983): 101–28.

10. Selwyn Becker and Gerald Gordon, "An Entrepreneurial Theory of Formal Organizations," *Administrative Science Quarterly* 11, no. 3 (December 1966): 315–44.

11. Space does not permit a more detailed analysis of this evolution. What is important for present purposes is the idea that organizations are relatively recent social inventions. Particularly in Western societies, the evolution of increasingly complex legal institutions is at least positively correlated with the proliferation of organizations as vehicles for the advancement of various interests. Whether this trend will continue is a matter of considerable interest and speculation.

12. A detailed discussion of various forms of ownership and their implications in business organizations can be found in William A. Klein, *Business Organization and Finance: Legal and Economic Principles* (Mineola, N.Y.: Foundation Press, 1980).

13. There are a few important exceptions. The Nonprofits Program in the Institution for Social and Policy Studies at Yale is particularly noteworthy.

14. It would be interesting to examine patterns of name changes in professional schools. Such changes reflect adaptations to continuing debates over the characteristics and requirement of "public" and "private" management.

consequences are a significant concern in professional education and managerial (if not organizational) research.

An illustration may suggest the significance of ownership for the analysis of organizations as organizations. In the most rudimentary form of organization—the sole proprietorship—ownership is private. A single individual owns the resources of the organization and is responsible for deciding how they are to be used (i.e., formulating strategy), for making sure they are being used properly (coordinating and controlling), and perhaps for actually doing the work (producing). Ownership, management, and production are vested in a single person.

As growth occurs, additional employees may be hired to do the work. That is, ownership and management are still vested in one person, but production is delegated to others. The owner has the right to expect certain levels of performance from the workers and also has certain obligations toward them. These rights and obligations are legally defined, or at least both parties have legal recourse in the event of disputes. The advantage to the owner of this arrangement is obvious: the possibility to increase the rate of production. The cost is also obvious: the behavior of the workers is problematic and must be managed.

As more growth occurs, the owner may need to hire not only additional workers but also someone to help keep track of orders and deadlines and to schedule work in such a way that customers are satisfied. Soon a group of managerial and support personnel develops. The owner is unable to monitor production directly and entrusts this function to others. Reports become the medium of communication between owner and operations. The owner has to determine, with management perhaps, the content of those reports. What needs to be known? How frequently? What level of accuracy is required? As ownership and management become differentiated, the owner has to decide how to define the relationship with management. How much autonomy do the managers need? How much can they handle? How much is the owner willing to grant?

Assume continued growth. The owner wants to expand. The necessary capital is unavailable. Financing (through debt or equity) needs to be arranged. If an equity strategy is pursued, the sole proprietorship may become a limited partnership. The infusion of capital makes expansion possible. But now ownership is no longer vested in a single person. Others are now involved in decisions about how the enterprise is to be run, what opportunities it should pursue, and whether its performance is adequate. A new dynamic is added. Strategic decision making becomes more complex.

At some point later, a public offering of stock is made. Several million shares are sold to several thousand investors. Ownership is now widely dispersed. And the dynamics associated with control of the enterprise become yet more complex. A board of directors mediates between owners and managers. Two principal questions emerge: What are the dynamics within the board? and What are the dynamics between the board and senior management? Who, in other words, exercises effective control over the resources to which the owners have property rights?

As ownership becomes more dispersed, some very interesting and significant changes occur. The distance (both psychological and physical) between owners and workers increases enormously. Owners come to rely on and care about increasingly abstract, aggregated, surrogate measures of what is occurring in the technical core of the organization. Return on investment and stock-price performance are light-years away from actual experience of the organization's production subsystem. Workers, on the other hand, come to confuse owners, whom they never see, with managers. Because managers are in authority positions, workers tend to attribute to them many of the rights, prerogatives, and responsibilities of owners.

Control becomes increasingly problematic. Owners must rely on managers for information on how effectively and how efficiently the resources they own are being used. A vocabulary for communicating needs to be developed, as do criteria and decision rules. The greater the distance between owners and workers, and the less interest owners have in what is actually occurring in the technical core of the organization, the more willing they will be to rely on abstract measures, increasing the potential for managers to influence how owners see the performance of the system. Thus, to the extent that managers control owners' perceptions of the organization and workers attribute ownerlike prerogatives to management, the dynamics of systems with dispersed ownership are likely to be strongly tilted in favor of managers rather than owners.[15]

The importance of ownership as a distinctive attribute of organizations, then, lies in the dynamics of the interplay among owners, managers, and workers over who has *effective* control of the organization's resources. From a narrowly defined legal point of view, the answer is clear: the owners have control. In practice, however,

---

15. Workers' cooperatives and recent efforts by workers to purchase failing businesses represent interesting experiments in changing the structure of ownership and its consequences. A variety of perspectives on these developments can be found in Frank Lindenfeld and Joyce Rothschild-Whitt, eds., *Workplace Democracy and Social Change* (Boston: Porter Sargent, 1983).

the answer is often very different. Much of the behavior we observe within organizations, including major structural changes, can be explained in terms of the continual working out—sometimes quietly and sometimes not—of the control problem created by the fact of ownership.[16]

The implications of public ownership are perhaps less obvious. As a general rule, under democratic forms of government, the owners of public organizations are the people empowered to vote in a particular jurisidiction, be it federal, state, or local. Thus, the owners of the myriad agencies that together make up the U.S. government are those who are authorized by the U.S. Constitution to vote. An empowering document identifies the owners by specifying a set of eligibility criteria for voting in elections.

This definition of ownership may sound farfetched, but an illustration may clarify the analogies with the private form of ownership described previously. Proposition 13 in California and Proposition 2½ in Massachusetts can be viewed as attempts by owners to exert effective control over the resources to which they have property rights. They are using their proxies. They are saying to their managers that organizational performance is poor and that changes need to be made.

Governmental organizations represent extreme cases of dispersed ownership and its consequences. And they are good examples of the tendency of managers to usurp the prerogatives of ownership. Just as stockholders elect representatives to the board of directors of a private corporation, so voters elect representatives to bodies that presumably advance their (the voters') interests as decisions are made about resource utilization. There are analogous problems of control. The voter is generally far removed from the actual operations of the organization. The voter's representative is somewhat closer, but still has limited familiarity with fundamental activities. Management under these circumstances can become extraordinarily powerful, particularly when the owners fail to exercise their prerogatives (perhaps because they do not think of themselves as owners or feel that they as individuals have the power to influence outcomes).

Periodic elections provide the owners an opportunity to change the mix of representatives but do not guarantee changes in management policy or direction. Strategic reorientations are theoretically possible, and the theoretical possibility is reinforced with a barrage of rhetoric. But the problems of effectively penetrating the managerial core in governmental organizations are well

known to many of us. To use the jargon of organization theory, the technical core of the organization is effectively sealed off from external uncertainty.

The fundamental issue in both the public and the private form of ownership is who *effectively* controls decisions about how resources will be used. Formal lobbying efforts in Washington are paralleled by analogous processes in privately owned organizations. I would argue strongly that the fact of ownership creates a series of dynamics that are fundamentally the same in both publicly and privately owned systems.

The nonprofit form of ownership presents a minor conceptual dilemma in that there are no analogues to stockholders in a for-profit corporation or voters in a public organization. But there is little difference between nonprofits and other organizations in the dynamics of the struggle for effective control within the board or the relationships between the board and senior management, and between these two groups and workers.

APPROACHES TO THE STUDY OF ORGANIZATIONS

Since 1960, and particularly since 1970, there has been a virtual explosion in research and writing on the subject of organizational analysis, broadly defined. Other chapters in this volume, particularly those in this section and in section II, together provide a comprehensive overview of the contributions that have been made. The title of the volume itself, with its focus on organizational behavior (rather than, for example, organizational theory), indicates the orientation of most of the research reviewed and the perspectives and issues discussed. The dominant thrust has been toward describing, analyzing, explaining, predicting, and perhaps improving behavior *in* organizations rather than the behavior *of* organizations or groups of organizations.[17]

The study *of* organizations is characterized by a multiplicity of approaches differing in disciplinary roots, substantive interests, units of analysis, settings, and fundamental conceptions of how and why (and occasionally whether) organizations behave. In this part of this chapter we will expand briefly on each of these issues to provide an indication of the diversity that exists, the debates that currently appear to preoccupy organization

16. Most organization theorists have examined this question under the theoretical rubric of "power." See, for example, Jeffrey Pfeffer, *Power in Organizations* (Marshfield, Mass.: Pitman, 1981).

17. This distinction was made some time ago in Peter Blau, "The Comparative Study of Organizations," *Industrial and Labor Relations Review* (April 1965), pp. 323–38.

theorists, and the directions in which research and theory are likely to move in the next few years.

Disciplinary roots

Historically, research with organizations as the unit of analysis was done primarily by sociologists. Others may not agree with this interpretation, but I believe that the work done by Peter Blau and his students in the early and middle 1960s provided a major impetus for the development of organization theory as it exists today.[18] The comparative structuralists' approach, developed by sociologists Richard Hall,[19] Stanley Udy,[20] Jerald Hage,[21] and Michael Aiken,[22] among others, was a reaction against the limitations of both the human-relations tradition emerging from the work of Elton Mayo[23] and his colleagues and the institutional school shaped by Phillip Selznick[24] and some of his students. Displeased with the softness and theoretical quality of much of the human-relations research, bothered by the problems of external validity associated with the richly descriptive work of the institutionalists, and intrigued by the possibilities of applying some of the statistical techniques beginning to capture the imagination of many social scientists, the comparative structuralists began collecting and analyzing data about the properties of organizations as such. This marked a real turning point in the field.

The comparative analysis of organizations did not remain the province of sociologists for long. Joan Woodward published her influential analysis of technology and organizational structure in 1964,[25] and shortly afterward Derek Pugh and his colleagues began publishing the results of their comparative analysis of industrial enterprises in England.[26] The study of organizations then moved quickly into professional business and management schools. Although trained in a traditional discipline, the faculty members in these schools were typically earning a living and training their students in multidisciplinary, applied settings.

Another powerful contemporary influence on the development of organization theory was the writings of James March, Herbert Simon, and Richard Cyert.[27] Difficult to classify in traditional disciplinary terms, their work stimulated a good deal of thinking about organizations as such, and March's *Handbook of Organizations*,[28] published in 1965, did as much as any other single volume to establish intellectually the legitimacy of the organizational level of analysis.

Recently, after occasional flirtations over the years,[29] organization theory has begun to converge with both industrial organization and institutional economics. As organization theorists begin to consider more carefully what "environment" means for organizations, and as economists begin both to question traditional assumptions about human behavior and to explore why organizations are the locus for so many economic transactions, a genuine interdisciplinary development is likely to continue.

Sociology, economics, and management theory have all made important contributions to the study of organizations, which cannot be adequately described here. This disciplinary diversity has been both a strength in research done at the organizational level of analysis, and a source of tensions, as described below.

Substantive interests

Researchers at the organizational level have been concerned primarily with performance and configuration.

18. The Comparative Organization Research Program headed by Blau while he was at the University of Chicago was the center of gravity for much of this work. A particularly good example of the epistemological character of that work is Peter M. Blau and Richard Schoenherr, *The Structure of Organizations* (New York: Basic Books, 1971).

19. See, for example, Richard H. Hall, "The Concept of Bureaucracy: An Empirical Assessment," *American Journal of Sociology* 58 (July 1963): 32–40.

20. Stanley H. Udy, Jr., " 'Bureaucracy' and 'Rationality' in Weber's Organization Theory," *American Sociological Review* (December 1959), pp. 791–95.

21. Jerald Hage and Michael Allen, "Relationship of Centralization to Other Organizational Properties: A Comparative Analysis," *Administrative Science Quarterly* (June 1967), pp. 72–92.

22. Michael Aiken and Jerald Hage, "Organizational Alienation: A Comparative Analysis," *American Sociological Review* 65 (August 1966): 497–507.

23. Elton Mayo, *The Human Problems of Industrial Civilization* (New York: Macmillan, 1933).

24. Phillip Selznick, *TVA and the Grass Roots* (New York: Harper & Row, Torchbooks, 1966).

25. Joan Woodward, *Industrial Organizations* (London: Oxford University Press, 1964).

26. Derek A. Pugh et al., "A Conceptual Scheme for Organizational Analysis," *Administrative Science Quarterly* 8, no. 3 (December 1963): 301–7.

27. See James G. March and Herbert A. Simon, *Organization* (New York: Wiley, 1958); Richard M. Cyert and James G. March, *A Behavioral Theory of the Firm* (Englewood Cliffs, N.J.: Prentice-Hall, 1963).

28. James G. March, ed., *Handbook of Organizations* (Chicago: Rand McNally, 1965).

29. Oliver E. Williamson, *Markets and Hierarchies; Analysis and Antitrust Implications* (New York: Free Press, 1975).

For years people have been trying to identify the factors that characterize high-performing organizations (and which, it is hoped, "cause" high performance). The brisk sales of *Theory Z* and *In Search of Excellence* reflect managers' hope that there are formulae for success, that researchers will discover mechanisms, structures, and/or processes through which managers can enhance organizational performance.

Other researchers have been curious about patterns in organizational structure and the causes and consequences of variations in these patterns over time. Research begun in the 1960s on patterns of relationships among structural attributes of organizations has evolved in the direction of research on the characteristics of populations of organizations and how and why characteristics change over time.

At the intersection of economics and sociology, a serious intellectual interest has developed recently in the subject of strategy, at the levels of single organizations, clusters of organizations, and entire industries. Stimulated by Alfred Chandler's writing in the 1960s about the relationships between strategy and structure,[30] more recent work has moved in a number of directions. One stream, exemplified by the work of Michael Porter, attempts to characterize the basic ingredients of successful competitive strategies within and between industries at the firm level.[31] Another stream, developed primarily by Henry Mintzberg, has questioned the textbook assumption that organizations consciously develop strategies and then pursue them.[32] Mintzberg contends that strategy can only be inferred after the fact, by identifying patterns in the flow of decisions that have already been made. Differences in these two approaches reflect major differences in conceptualizations of how and why organizations behave as they do, and they subsequently will be described more fully.

Units of analysis

As organization theory has evolved, the unit of analysis has begun to change. Instead of focusing on the individual organization, researchers have begun to turn their attention to groups, clusters, or populations of organizations and their attributes.[33] This shift is not merely a change in the *level* of analysis, but represents the beginning of a more complex appreciation of the relationships between organization and environment, as discussed later in this chapter.

Settings

Organizational research has been conducted primarily in business enterprises, but also in other institutional settings, as discussed in section VI of this handbook. It may be that too much attention has been devoted to the peculiarities of individual settings. The ownership perspective suggests that there is a set of core issues that confront *all* organizations. If so, we should be looking for resemblances, not differences, between business enterprises and educational and health-care institutions. If we want to create a general theory of organizations rather than theories of universities, hospitals, banks, or manufacturing firms, we need to ask whether apparent differences among "types" of organizations are fundamental or marginal in a theoretical sense.[34] Are they differences of kind or of degree? As research shifts its focus from single organizations to clusters of organizations, I believe that interest in more general theories will revive. Focus on single organizations almost inevitably leads to an emphasis on the apparently idiosyncratic. Focus on clusters will force serious consideration of theoretical similarity.

Conceptions

Two fundamentally different conceptions of how and why organizations behave have dominated approaches to their study. One perspective posits a central role for managerial choice. In this view, behavior is the result of conscious, deliberate, goal-directed action. In this sense, organizations behave "rationally." Choices are the result of search undertaken in the context of explicitly defined goals, weighing of alternatives, and selection of the alternative most likely to produce the desired result. Managers and their choices make major differences in organizational outcomes.

30. Alfred D. Chandler, Jr., *Strategy and Structure* (New York: Doubleday, Anchor Books, 1966).

31. Michael E. Porter, *Competitive Strategy* (New York: Free Press, 1980).

32. See, for example, Henry Mintzberg, D. Raisinghani, and A. Thoret, "The Structure of 'Unstructured' Decision Processes," *Administrative Science Quarterly* 21 (March 1976): 246–75.

33. See, for example, Michael T. Hannan and John H. Freeman, "The Population Ecology of Organizations," *American Journal of Sociology* 82 (1977): 929–64.

34. For an interesting discussion of organizational "types," see William McKelvey, *Organizational Systematics* (Los Angeles: University of California Press, 1982).

The second perspective sees the behavior of organizations as determined primarily by external forces, over which managers have very little control. In this view, organizational behavior is explained not by the choices that managers make but by external constraints and conditions. The population-ecology approach, as exemplified in the writing of Howard Aldrich, Michael Hannan, and John Freeman, is the most vivid example of this more heavily deterministic view of organizational life.

Three recent reviews of the literature on organization theory are available for the reader interested in pursuing in depth the various approaches to the study of organizations. Scott classifies the various approaches into rational, natural, and open-systems models.[35] Pfeffer distinguishes both perspectives on action and levels of analysis.[36] He identifies three perspectives on action: (1) purposeful, intentional, goal-directed, rational; (2) externally constrained and controlled; and (3) emergent, almost random, socially constructed. For research at the "total organization" level of analysis, Pfeffer cites structural-contingency theory, the market-failures/transaction-costs perspective, and Marxist or class perspectives as examples of the first category; population ecology and resource-dependence perspectives as examples of the second; and organizations as paradigms, decision process and administrative theories, and institutionalization theory as examples of the third.

The third review, by Astley and Van de Ven, classifies schools of organizational thought by level of analysis (micro versus macro), on one hand, and assumptions about human nature (deterministic versus voluntaristic), on the other.[37] For them, "micro" approaches are ones that focus on individual organizations. "Macro" approaches focus on populations and communities of organizations. Deterministic assumptions essentially view organizational outcomes as the result of environmental pressures; voluntaristic assumptions see behavior as a reflection of individuals' choices about preferences. Cross-classification of these two dimensions yields four schools of thought: the system-structural view (micro/deterministic), the strategic-choice view (micro/voluntaristic), the natural-selection view (macro/deterministic), and the collective-action view (macro/voluntaristic).

Because all three reviews focus on essentially the same body of literature, it is not surprising that there should be some similarities in the classificatory schemes developed. That the Astley and Van de Ven paper, which is the most recent of the three, should focus exclusively on the single and multiple organization levels of analysis is perhaps indicative of a trend in current organization research toward more probing analysis of organizational environments and their impacts. Because of the increasing interest in and research on organization-environment relations it would be worthwhile to describe briefly the evolution of thinking in this area.

ORGANIZATION AND ENVIRONMENTS

In 1976, William Starbuck published an extensive critical review of the literature on organization-environment research, which included references to more than six hundred books, monographs, and articles.[38] Likening his efforts to an attempt by Jonah to swallow the whale, he claimed to have been unable to include, because of space limitations, two-thirds of the material collected for his review. Since that review appeared, publication on organization-environment relations has accelerated. A number of major books and scores of articles have appeared.

Examined in a historical perspective, seven primary clusters of work stand out in the literature. Each is discussed under the heading of its principal contribution.

Environments are important to organizational function

As obvious as this statement may seem today, it was relatively big news to organizational researchers in the late 1940s and early 1950s. Perhaps the single greatest stimulus to examination of organization-environment relations was the development of general-system theory and the application of the system-theoretic paradigm to the analysis of organizations. Particularly influential was the work of Ludwig von Bertalanffy.[39] With its now-familiar (and to some, time-worn) emphasis on inputs, throughputs, and outputs, system theory forced researchers to

35. W. Richard Scott, *Organizations: Rational, Natural and Open Systems* (Englewood Cliffs, N.J.: Prentice-Hall, 1981).

36. Pfeffer, *Organizations and Organization Theory.*

37. Graham Astley and Andrew H. Van de Ven, "Central Perspectives and Debates in Organization Theory," *Administrative Science Quarterly* 28 (June 1983).

38. William H. Starbuck, "Organizational Environments," in *Handbook of Industrial Psychology,* ed. Marvin D. Dunnette (Chicago: Rand McNally, 1976).

39. Ludwig von Bertalanffy, "General Systems Theory," In *General Systems Yearbook,* Society for the Advancement of General System Theory (1956).

ask questions like Where do inputs come from? and Where do the outputs go? The "environment" was, of course, the answer.

The most prominent influence of system theory in the 1950s and early 1960s was linguistic. Researchers quickly adopted the system-theoretic lexicon and, as a result, included the concept of environment in their discourse. The new idea, however, had little immediate impact on what researchers did. They continued to focus primarily on internal structures and processes, acknowledging the importance of environment conceptually but not incorporating it empirically. It was a sort of conceptual residual category; variance in performance not explained by internal structures and processes was attributed to "environmental factors." Still, the groundwork had been laid. No longer was it possible to view organizations in isolation from the world around them.

Environments constrain organizations

Some researchers began to examine the ways in which environments were important. The first efforts to examine the nature of environmental influence were guided by an implicitly deterministic view of the relationships. Environments were seen as controlling the fate of organizations,[40] which were relatively passive actors, buffeted by external forces over which they had no control. They were reactive entities, struggling to cope with a variety of essentially negative external influences. The environment was a threat to survival, and the effective organization was one that successfully warded off external intrusions by, in James Thompson's terms, "buffering" itself or "sealing off its core technology."[41] Indeed, this orientation has persisted and is found in much contemporary research concerned with, for example, the effects of governmental regulation.[42]

Unequal prominence of environmental aspects

As researchers began to reflect systematically on the question of how environments affect organizations, it became clear that it was misleading to think of environment in holistic terms. It was necessary to distinguish conceptually (and empirically) between more- and less-salient aspects of the outside world. Thus Thompson and William Dill began, in the 1960s, to speak of an organization's "task environment."[43] Because of the goals it pursues, the work it performs, and the resources it requires, an organization attends much more carefully and intensively to certain aspects of the outside world than to others. William Evan's work on organization "sets" moved in a similar direction,[44] as did Sol Levine and Paul White's early work on organizational domains.[45] Richard Hall ten years later used the terms *general* and *specific environments* to make the same conceptual point.[46] Any organization faces some external factors that are relevant in a very general sense, such as cycles of activity in the economy or changes in the demography of the labor force, and others that are relevant in a very immediate and specific sense, such as product competition in particular markets or municipal effluent ordinances.

Different environments for different organizations

Research on organization-environment relations has taken an increasingly variegated view of environments. In a very influential article in the mid-1960s, Fred Emery and Eric Trist developed a taxonomy of organizational environments, arguing that not all environments are similar for all organizations and further that environments may shift for particular organizations.[47] The notion that different types of environments pose different problems for organizations was an important theoretical advance. A similar theme was developed by Paul Lawrence and Jay Lorsch in their work on contingency theory.[48] They argued that organizations in different industries face different environmental contingencies and, to be effective, require different internal structures. And

---

40. For a more extended discussion, see Richard J. C. Roeber, *The Organization in a Changing Environment* (Reading, Mass.: Addison-Wesley, 1973).

41. James D. Thompson, *Organizations in Action* (New York: McGraw-Hill, 1967).

42. See, for example, B. Mitnick, *The Political Economy of Regulation* (New York: Columbia University Press, 1980).

43. Thompson, *Organizations in Action;* William R. Dill, "Environment as an Influence on Managerial Autonomy," *Administrative Science Quarterly* (March 1958): 409–43.

Interorganizational Relations," in *Approaches to Organization Design*, ed. James D. Thompson (Pittsburgh: University of Pittsburgh Press, 1966).

45. Sol Levine and Paul E. White, "Exchange as a Conceptual Framework for the Study of Interorganizational Relationships," *Administrative Science Quarterly* 8 (March 1962): 583–601.

46. Richard H. Hall, *Organizations: Structure and Process* (Englewood Cliffs, N.J.: Prentice-Hall, 1972).

47. Fred E. Emery and Eric L. Trist, "The Causal Texture of Organizational Environment," *Human Relations* (February 1965), pp. 21–32.

48. Paul R. Lawrence and Jay W. Lorsch, *Organizations and Environment* (Homewood, Ill.: Irwin, 1968).

they were able to demonstrate empirically the utility of their view.

Organizations shape environments

For a number of years the predominant view was that organizations were essentially passive in their relations with the external world. In the late 1960s and 1970s, however, certain researchers began to argue that organizations are often proactive in these relations and develop a variety of strategies for shaping and molding their environments. Charles Perrow noted the extraordinary influence wielded by a few large corporations on patterns of legislation and regulation.[49] Mayer Zald was instrumental in formulating a political-economy approach to organizational analysis, which incorporated a more proactive vision of organizations' transactions with the outside world.[50] And Jeffrey Pfeffer and Gerald Salancik noted that organizations attempt to influence their environments through strategies such as mergers, joint ventures, trade associations, lobbying efforts, and political contributions.[51] In their view, although organizations are dependent on external sources for resources critical to their continued existence, they can reduce this dependence substantially by anticipating environmental shifts and by acting collectively vis-à-vis, for example, sources of supply or the state.

Environments are enacted

When researchers moved from concept to measure, they encountered some interesting problems. Uncertainty had emerged as a central theme in theorizing about organization-environment relations. It was argued that where there was little uncertainty about environmental influences, bureaucratic forms of organization were appropriate. Where uncertainty about these influences was high, organizational structures needed to be more flexible to permit relatively rapid response to events as they occurred. The measurement of environmental uncertainty, however, proved to be quite a challenge. Were there "objective" characteristics of organizational environments that were both measurable and valid as in-

dexes of uncertainty? Or was uncertainty not a property of environments but rather an interpretation made by beholders?[52]

In the midst of this debate Karl Weick proposed the notion that environments are selectively created by organizational members.[53] The "reality" of organizational environments that is significant for organizational outcomes is that which is perceived by members and acted upon. This notion of enactment dovetailed nicely with John Child's strategic-choice approach, which highlighted the role of organizational decision making as the link between external conditions and organizational structure and outcomes.[54] This view suggests that while there may be discrepancies between "real" and enacted environments, it is *perceptions* of environmental threats and opportunities that have consequence.

Environments are organizations

As more researchers became interested in organization-environment problems, different approaches were taken. Some examined the problem from the perspective of perception, decision, and action. Others argued that fields, sets, or populations of organizations are the settings for organizational action. They move beyond the conception of a focal organization struggling to hold its own in a hostile environment and began to examine patterns of transactions among classes of organization, and such phenomena as the expansion and contraction of populations of organizations. Howard Aldrich, Michael Hannan, John Freeman, Johannes Pennings, Graham Astley, and Charles Fombrun all moved in this more macro direction.[55] They were more interested in the structure and distribution of a field of organizations than in what happened to a particular organization. Whereas the enactment perspective was a view of the outside world from the interior of a particular organization, the popu-

---

49. Charles Perrow, *Organizational Analysis: A Sociological View* (Belmont, Calif.: Wadsworth, 1970).

50. Mayer Zald, *Organizational Change: The Political Economy of the YMCA* (Chicago: University of Chicago Press, 1970).

51. Jeffrey Pfeffer and Gerald Salancik, *The External Control of Organizations* (New York: Harper & Row, 1978).

52. For a good discussion of the issues, see Robert H. Miles, *Macro Organizational Behavior* (Santa Monica, Calif.: Goodyear, 1980).

53. Karl Weick, *The Social Psychology of Organizing* (Reading, Mass.: Addison-Wesley, 1969).

54. John Child, "Organization Structure, Environment and Performance: The Role of Strategic Choice," *Sociology* 6 (1972): 2–22.

55. See Howard E. Aldrich, *Organizations and Environments* (Englewood Cliffs, N.J.: Prentice-Hall, 1979); Hannan and Freeman, "Population Ecology of Organizations"; Johannes M. Pennings, "Environmental Influences on the Creation Process," in *The Organizational Life Cycle*, eds. John R. Kimberly and Robert H. Miles (San Francisco: Jossey-Bass, 1980); W. Graham Astley and Charles J. Fombrun, "Collective Strategy: The Social Ecology of Organizational Environment," *Academy of Management Review*, (October 1983).

lation ecology or organizational-community perspective obviated the need for research on internal views.

Much current research on organizations emphasizes external forces as shapers of organizations and their behavior. Pfeffer described the implications of this emphasis well. "Focus on explanation of behavior in the conditions and constraints of the environment saves the analyst from the often intractable task of exploring internal decision-making processes and, in particular, of trying to build a theory of organizational action premised on rational, decision-making theory when there is clear evidence that the production of organization-level rationality is quite problematic and can certainly not be assumed."[56]

Organizations are purposive, goal-oriented entities only in the broadest sense of those terms. The rational model and its assumptions about behavior fit more closely with theorists' normative beliefs than with observations of organizational life. Management texts may hold out goal-directed action as the ideal toward which tomorrow's leaders must strive, but research on the behavior of managers reveals patterns very different from what the texts advocate.

On the other hand, organizations *do* produce a variety of tangible and intangible benefits for a variety of parties. Researchers have been stymied by the problems involved in defining and measuring organizational effectiveness, and theorists from economics, sociology, and other disciplines have not yet been able to account satisfactorily for the pervasive continued existence of organizations. Ownership may be the key. To the extent that owners' interests are satisfied by whatever activities the organization pursues, it is likely to continue. Organizations create value, whether or not they behave "rationally" in the eyes of an external observer. That in itself is reason enough to be concerned with why they work the way they do on an individual basis, and how, why, and with what consequences linkages among them are created, nurtured, and dissolved.[57]

I do not wish to argue that any of Pfeffer's three perspectives on action is right or wrong in any ultimate sense or that any one of Astley and Van de Ven's four perspectives on organization and management is inherently and demonstrably superior. Rather, I would like to sketch out some of the basic elements of a different perspective, a biographical perspective, a framework for thinking about organizations that helps to order some

observations about how they behave and to suggest some important questions about their development.

A BIOGRAPHICAL PERSPECTIVE

The perspective discussed in the following pages is based on my belief that useful knowledge about organizations should both inform theory and have some relevance for practicing managers.[58] This is a strictly personal view, shared by some but certainly not all, perhaps not even most, organizational researchers.

To view the organization as a sort of black box, as the determinists do, is to argue that managers' choices and actions are without consequence. If important outcomes are externally determined, it makes virtually no difference *who* managers are, *what* they do, or what *decisions* they make. The mechanisms that underlie change then take on a particular significance. How does change in and of individual organizations and clusters take place? How are the forces that result in change shaped and controlled? Neither the rational model nor the external-control model provides adequate answers to these questions. The biographical perspective is useful, in part, because it specifically addresses the problem of change, particularly at the level of individual organizations.

The basics of biography

Every organization is in some ways unique. A particular set of circumstances surrounded its creation. A unique set of people was responsible for putting it together. The major events that shaped its subsequent development are not precisely replicated anywhere else. The combination of resources accumulated to further the owners' interests is never the same from one setting to the next. And every organization has a particular set of connections and relationships with the world it inhabits. The evolving configuration of ownership, people, events, resources, and external connectedness is never precisely the same from one organization to the next.

All organizations are alike in some ways. Every organization is owned. Every organization faces the problems of internal social control, of designing work, and of managing relations with the environment. Every or-

56. Pfeffer, *Organizations and Organization Theory*, p. 179.

57. John R. Kimberly, Frederick Norling, and Janet A. Weiss, "Pondering the Performance Puzzle: Effectiveness in Interorganizational Settings," in *Organizational Theory and Public Policy*, ed. Richard H. Hall and Robert E. Quinn (Beverly Hills, Calif.: Sage, 1983).

58. By "relevance" I mean research that may help managers think in new ways about old problems.

ganization has certain measurable attributes: a demographic structure, a physical design, and a technological configuration.

Organizations in this respect are like individual people. Every human being shares certain attributes as a consequence of being a person; he or she also has a unique genetic makeup and a unique set of life experiences. No effort to understand individual behavior would be complete without taking both the unique and the common into account.

Organizations are like individual people in another important respect: yesterday's events shape today's behavior. Just as it is helpful to know certain things about an individual person's past in understanding and predicting his or her behavior today (different theories, of course, suggest very different dimensions of a person's past as relevant), so it would be helpful to know certain things about an organization's past to understand and predict its current behavior.

The analogy between people and organizations should not be pushed too far. The differences are obvious and substantial. Organizations are not biological organisms. They do not have finite life-spans. Neither do they have emotions and reasoning capacities in the same way that individual people do. We do not wish to engage here in anthropomorphism. Yet the similarities are intriguing. At the time of its creation, the organization does not have fully developed capacities. It experiments and "learns," often by trial and error, in ways that parallel the ways in which people learn.[59] Events and traditions in the organization's youth influence its subsequent development. Over time, a relatively distinctive "personality" emerges, which is not easily changed and which may give the organization a unique identity.[60] Identity is symbolically important, as the prominence of corporate logos and school mascots suggests. Who can imagine Merrill Lynch without its bull, Princeton without its tiger, or Arkansas without its razorback? Identity also allows the organization to draw coherence from its past and establish direction for the future. In this respect, a sense of identity is every bit as important for an organization as for a person.

Biography is a vehicle for illuminating the lives of individual people. The astute biographer places the subject in a historical context and traces how the person both shaped and was shaped by external events and forces.

When we read good biography, we become acutely aware of how the values, thought processes, and behavior of the subject evolved and how they were connected to the surrounding world. We understand that individual personalities evolve and that the evolutionary process is only partially controlled by the individual. We understand further that some individuals are more aware than others of the possibilities for controlling their destinies and more aggressive in their efforts to act upon this awareness.

There is a substantial literature on the methodology of biography. The potential weaknessess of the medium are well known. It is not "scientific." It is potentially subject to the biases of the biographer. The biographer can become so involved with the subject that detachment is impossible. There are problems with assessing the quality of the product. How do you compare the work of one biographer with that of another? What criteria distinguish excellent from mediocre or poor biography?

These are serious questions, but ones that can be raised about any effort to enhance understanding. A full discussion of all of the issues here is far beyond the scope of this chapter. For present purposes, I would like to argue that "rigor" is every bit as relevant for the biographer as for any other person using any other set of techniques to enhance understanding of a given phenomenon. I would also like to suggest that biographies of organizations represent a potentially useful way of understanding some important and underappreciated aspects of organizational life. Using the logic of biography would force researchers and managers to think explicitly about how the past has shaped the present and could enrich their ability both to understand the present and to hypothesize about the future (and to intervene sensibly in shaping it). Furthermore, it would focus attention on the interplay between internal and external forces and the flows of events and decisions that shape an organization and its relationship with the world it inhabits. Such a focus would no doubt lead to the development of more sophisticated theories of organization-environment relations. Finally, thinking about organizations in biographical terms should help us develop increasingly sophisticated theories of organization change and more effective approaches to producing change.

---

59. For an interesting discussion, see Chris Argyris, *Reasoning, Learning and Action* (San Francisco: Jossey-Bass, 1982).

60. I invoke the concept of personality with considerable misgivings, for what I assume are obvious reasons. On the other hand, the concept helps to open up to examination and discussion some underexplored aspects of organizational life as people experience it.

Biography and life cycle

The term *biography* is intended to focus research attention on a particular set of issues in organizational life. It is also intended to move thinking beyond the concept of organizational life cycles. The life-cycle analogy is only partially appropriate in the analysis of organizations.[61] While most organizations may go through a limited number of relatively predictable stages in their early years, the remainder of their life course is much less predictable. If we could observe them over long enough periods of time, centuries in some cases, we might detect in organizations cyclic patterns similar to those we observe in biological organisms.[62] As a practical matter, however, our observational capabilities are limited, and there is no well-developed theory of organizational life that presupposes the inevitability of decay and death.

The concept of transition seems to fit better with our experience of "postadolescent" organizations than the concept of life cycle.[63] Transitions are significant changes in organization mission, strategy, or structure. Changes in executive leadership are often signals that a transition has taken or is taking place. Central to the development of organizational biographies is the identification of major transitions in an organization's life and an effort to understand both their causes and their implications. Unlike the imagery of life cycles, then, the notion of organizational biography, makes no assumptions about temporally ordered stages or about the inevitability of death.

Organizational biography and corporate history

Corporate histories are not new. Many large corporations have commissioned histories, particularly to commemorate important milestones in their development, such as the fiftieth anniversary of their founding. Generally, corporate histories are part of the overall image-management process. They tend to emphasize the positive and to reinforce dominant symbols and myths, particularly those that illustrate the vision, forcefulness, and wisdom of the founders. They are typically heavy on description and light on analysis. Though interesting as components of organizational culture, corporate histories are not likely to provide insight into the complex questions of how and why the organization has evolved as it has. These questions are the essence of biography.

An organizational biography, in contrast to a corporate history, is both skeptical and analytical. Its objective is to assemble, assess, and interpret evidence on the life course of its subject. Done well, it is neither a testimony to nor a diatribe against the overall mission or accomplishments of its subject. It is geared toward understanding and explanation. Ideally, it would be a vehicle both for enriching theory and for helping managers in the subject organization achieve a better understanding of the context in which they work, which would help them be more effective.

The structure of organizational biography

Many variables have been used to describe, analyze, and model organizations and their behavior. What is generally missing, as noted earlier, is an appreciation for the implications of ownership as the distinctive feature of organizations and for the developmental quality of organizational life.

The framework for organizational analysis proposed here focuses particular attention on decisions made relatively early in an organization's life. These decisions, we hypothesize, set the organization on a course from which it is difficult to diverge. Myriad forces reinforce chosen courses, and major transitions are generally infrequent. Change occurs, but is typically incremental rather than revolutionary. Thus there is the outward appearance of stability, even rigidity.[64] An organization characterized by many transitions in a relatively short period of time is exceptional, and its behavior would merit special attention.

Not all decisions made early in the life of an organization are of equal significance. The biographical perspective highlights the importance of four kinds of choices in shaping future behavior: decisions about governance, domain, expertise, and design.

GOVERNANCE DECISIONS

The fact of ownership and the need for control underline the significance of governance decisions. Yet governance questions are frequently surrounded by ambiguity—more operational than legal—and uncertainty. Rights and responsibilities among partners, for example, may not be clearly defined at the outset, potentially creating numerous problems at later points. Investors in a corporation may be more interested in return on investment than in sound business practice and thus may be willing to overdelegate responsibilities to

61. Some of these limitations are discussed in John R. Kimberly, "The Life Cycle Analogy and the Study of Organizations," in *The Organizational Life Cycle*, ed. John R. Kimberly and Robert H. Miles (San Francisco: Jossey-Bass, 1980).

62. John H. Freeman, "Organizational Life Cycles and Natural Selection Processes," in *Research in Organizational Behavior*, vol. 4, ed. Barry M. Staw and L. Cummings (Greenwich, Conn.: Jai Press, 1982).

63. See John R. Kimberly and Robert E. Quinn, eds., *Managing Organizational Transitions* (Homewood, Ill.: Dow Jones-Irwin, 1984).

64. This idea might usefully be explored in the context of J. B. Quinn, *Logical Incrementalism.*

management. This tendency is amplified in technology-intensive situations where the investors may be relatively unsophisticated about the organization's business and hence may be unwilling or unable to ask hard questions. Mystified by the technology, they may fail to assert their ownership prerogatives forcefully.

Boards of directors may be composed of people who differ in their motivations, conceptions of their role, and understanding of the organization's business. This is most often the case in (though certainly not limited to) community-oriented nonprofit organizations, where altruistic commitments to community service help to explain both board composition and board ineffectiveness.[65]

Initial decisions about the *structure* of governance and early experience with the *process* of governance together create a set of expectations about how internal control will be exercised. Expectations are powerful constraints on subsequent behavior. The consequences of early decisions and actions around governance thus become amplified later in an organization's life.

DOMAIN DECISIONS

The owners of every organization have to decide what business they are in. They have to stake out a domain, which includes the "products" they will produce, the clientele they will serve, and the markets they will enter. Initial decisions imply subsequent decisions about technology, structure, and, perhaps most important, expertise. Once an organization has begun to invest in particular technologies, configurations, and people, it becomes increasingly difficult to change course. Theoretically, of course, such changes are possible. But in practice they are the exception rather than the rule. A key task of the biographer, then, is to identify the initial decisions made with respect to domain.

EXPERTISE DECISIONS

Every organization in one way or another represents a concentration of expertise. A key to understanding how an organization has evolved is to examine patterns of early hiring. In the most immediate sense, the early hires represent the owners' (or managers') efforts to accumulate the kind of expertise needed to get the organization moving. Early hires also play a vital role in defining the culture and central values of the organization.[66] The background and experience of those who are hired into

senior management positions will influence how the organization does its work and shape the internal climate and style of the system. Their priorities and the way in which they work together are the building blocks of culture, that elusive yet powerful influence on organizational behavior.[67] To the extent that it is reasonable to think of the organization as having a distinctive personality, initial choices of key managers create its fundamental personality characteristics. The way in which it learns (or does not learn, as the case may be), its propensity to take risks, its level of commitment to excellence, its tolerance of failure, and its creative potential are all substantially determined by early hires and soon-established patterns of working relationships among them.

DESIGN DECISIONS

Information is at the heart of effective control. Initial decisions about organizational design affect what information is available, where it is located, and how accessible it is to various parties. They also help to determine who talks to whom about what, and, just as important, how the organization interacts with its environment. Thus, both performance and subsequent alternatives are influenced by initial decisions about the decision-making process, the kinds and extensiveness of various controls, flows of information, reporting relationships, and the nature of the physical environment.

Initial decisions about governance, domain, expertise, and design together define the basic conditions of the early life experience of every organization. External forces undoubtedly influence early decisions to some extent. But, however these choices were made, they strongly influence the future course of the organization, by limiting the range of feasible alternatives, shaping the internal culture, and defining the organization's identity.

In a rough way, decisions about expertise and governance shape culture, and decisions about domain and design define identity. And all four determine how the organization is connected to its environment. Ownership (governance) defines both a set of major stakeholders and potential sources of legitimation and support; domain defines both market niches and clientele; the early hires define a network of contacts with other people and organizations; and design reflects how the organization chooses to define its interdependence with its task environment. None of these factors is immutable; however,

---

65. See, for example, Deborah H. Harrison and John R. Kimberly, "HMOs Need Not Fail," *Harvard Business Review* 60, no. 4 (July-August 1982): 115–24.

66. A counterexample in Seymour B. Sarason, *The Creation of Settings* (San Francisco: Jossey-Bass, 1972).

67. Research on organizational culture is booming. The concept is empirically difficult to pin down, but widely acknowledged to be a significant influence on behavior. Some hard thinking would be welcome on the conceptual connectedness of organizational culture and organizational personality.

the effort required to change how an organization thinks of itself and the world around it (and vice versa) should not be underestimated.

It is impossible to define precisely the temporal frame within which these four decisions are made. The sequence and timing will vary from one organization to the next. In most cases, however, these decisions will be made within the first year, or possibly two, of an organization's life. Later on, from a biographical perspective, the most interesting questions have to do with the precipitants and consequences of major transitions.

Organization theory can predict neither the precise nature nor the timing of these transitions. They may be precipitated internally by contradictions, in content or process, between the fundamental decisions described above. Other transitions may be externally precipitated by environmental inductions beyond the focal organization's peripheral vision or control. Good organizational biography will identify the transitions, trace their origins, and describe their consequences. Researchers will examine the connections among transitions and how the consequences of one may contain the seeds of another. Good biography will appreciate the interplay of individual personalities, organizational culture, identity structure, process, and connections with the external environment. It will necessarily counterpose micro and macro levels of analysis, and it will embrace rather than ignore history and context.

A note on method

Biographical approaches are hardly in the mainstream of current research and theory on organizations. Hence, the literature includes no real discussions on how to *do* biography.[68] However, a number of my associates and I are currently developing a methodology for this purpose. Our approach is retrospective and thus is subject to all of the problems and opportunities, well documented elsewhere, associated with retrospective research. From our perspective, it is an attractive option because it is resource-efficient. It obviates the need for real-time analysis and opens the way for comparative studies. At this stage in our work, it appears to provide a vehicle for dealing with many concerns about the state of contemporary organizational research.

The methodology is being developed in the context of two studies. The first is an examination of the crea-

tion and development of educational service centers; the second is a pilot study of the creation of academic health centers. These are extraordinarily complex institutions, and they provide a critical test. If the approach proves viable in these settings, it is difficult to imagine that it would not work in other settings as well.

A three-stage process is involved. Stage I employs a combination of interviewing and document analysis to produce a Significant Event Chronology for the institution. The aim here is to identify key events in the creation and development of the organization, events whose existence can be fully and unambiguously chronicled. The resulting historical record should not in itself produce controversy. A secondary objective is to identify key individuals and constituencies whose actions appear to have given shape to the institution. They may have been employees, sponsors, or critics. They may or may not have had a direct financial interest in the outcomes. But they are persons whose perspectives on the existence of the institution need to be appreciated in order to understand how events unfolded.

Interpretive flesh is added to the historical skeleton in stage II. In interviews, respondents are asked for their views of the various events pieced together in stage I. We seek out their perceptions, motivations, reservations, anxieties, and aspirations. We are particularly interested in instances of conflicting information, whether caused by self-serving accounts or faulty memories. An extensive literature in social psychology suggests that people tend to reinterpret past events in ways that minimize the dissonance they feel about outcomes, distort their own roles in influencing those outcomes, and/or justify or rationalize their previous behavior, particularly with respect to outcomes with negative consequences.

There is obviously no way to eliminate conflicting accounts, nor would we want to do so even if we could. Differences in perceptions and interests are a driving force in the behavior of institutions. To assume consensus and convergence is to miss one of the central engines of the organization's behavior. Thus, our strategy is to seek out areas of convergence *and* divergence in perceptions of particular events and/or processes and then to attempt to understand why such convergence or divergence exists as a function of the actors' differing relationships to the issue at hand. The task of the organizational biographer is to distill from the welter of individual accounts an explanation that takes account of widely varying personal agendas and stakes in particular outcomes. The researcher must be part scientist, part detective, and part investigative reporter. If done well, historical reconstruction can provide a basis for comparative organizational analysis very different from the structural approach.

68. For an interesting discussion of a methodology for longitudinal research on strategy formulation, see Henry Mintzberg and Jim Waters, "Steps in Research on Strategy Formation" (Montreal: McGill University, 1982, mimeographed).

Archives can also be a rich source of data for the organizational biographer. In stage III, documents are the principal data source, and efforts are made to obtain copies of written records surrounding significant events. Our experience also strongly suggests that in many cases more than one interview with certain people will be necessary. Such interviews are carried out in stage III, when a clearer picture of the issues as well as the events begins to emerge.

There is thus no particular magic in the construction of a useful organizational biography. It requires strong interviewing skills, an ability to remain analytically outside any single person's interpretation of events, and a good deal of patience. By focusing explicitly on questions of motivation, politics, strategy, and tactics, and how they changed over time, the methodology can move us beyond relatively sterile and static views of organizations in general and organization-environment relations in particular. And by forcing us to confront rather than avoid many of the more complex problems associated with the functioning of any human system, it raises questions that are likely to generate useful knowledge.

Beyond the single organization

On the surface, one of the most serious problems with the biographical approach to organizational analysis may appear to be its focus on the innards of single organizations. If taken seriously, however, the emphasis on ownership and developmental processes inevitably forces the researcher outside the focal organization and into its connections with individuals, groups, and organizations in its environment. Because control of resources is the principal theoretical concern, careful analysis of any single organization will reveal important influences on control that derive from its connectedness to others. Joint ventures, mergers, and hostile take-overs are only the most obvious examples. More subtle and more pervasive forms of control deriving from and influencing ownership abound. Professional-standards organizations, accrediting bodies, regulatory agencies, funding sources, formal professional associations, informal networks, even direct competitors in a given market—all represent potentially important influences in the life course of a single organization.

More interesting, perhaps, is what they represent collectively as actors in a particular social and economic arena. Although the term *biography* suggests a focus on the development of single organizations, the sociological reality is that single organizations are players in a larger game whose structure is itself an important arena for analysis. The developmental histories of single organizations are interdependent with those of other organizations. This observation leads in to the final chapter in this section on the interinstitutional level of analysis. As noted earlier, distinguishing among levels of analysis creates some phenomenologically artificial—though practically necessary—boundaries. The study of organizations and their behavior neither starts nor stops with biography. Biography merely enriches our analytical armamentarium.

POSTSCRIPT

No single approach to the study of organizations is wholly satisfactory; each leaves many questions unanswered and still others unasked. The biographical approach bridges the worlds of organizational behavior and organization theory by inquiring into the interplay among people, the structures and systems they create, and the constraints that affect what they create and how their creations fare over time.

Biographies are not corporate histories. They are more analytic and more critical. They are theory-driven, in the sense that the structure of inquiry reflects what is already known about influences on organizational creation, growth, and change. And their task is not to justify and perhaps glorify but to illuminate and perhaps explain.

Most managers have their own personally developed sense of the biographies of the institutions in which they work. To the extent that biographies illuminate the past and to the extent that the past shapes the present and constrains the future, more explicit attention to the dynamics of organizational evolution is likely to be diagnostically useful to practicing managers.

There is no danger that organizational biographies will become commonplace. They are time-consuming and hence expensive to produce. But the questions they raise, the methods by which they seek answers, and the answers themselves all will help to inform both theory and practice in the world of organizations.

15

Interorganizational relations

DAVID A. WHETTEN

It is a basic axiom that industrialization increases the need for coordinated action in a society. As a consequence, improving relations between organizations has long been a common concern of organizational behavior researchers and practitioners. As the emphasis in organizational theory and research shifted in the 1960s from controlling internal activities to managing external constraints, discussions of resource control became prominent (Phillips 1960; Katz and Kahn 1967). The emphasis placed on the organization/environment interface during this period drew attention to the options available to an organization for increasing its control over the uncertainty of environmental exigencies. Chief among these options is collaborative agreements with other organizations.

This chapter reviews the research conducted on these agreements, beginning with a discussion of the various research traditions that have emerged in the field of interorganizational relations (IOR) and of some key studies of particular forms of IOR. The latter half of the chapter reviews one aspect of interorganizational relations—improving coordination—in greater detail because of its practical significance. The structural forms of coordination are discussed, as well as its antecedents,

some of its unintended side effects, and one specific model for improving coordination.

RESEARCH ON INTERORGANIZATIONAL RELATIONS

Scholars from a variety of disciplines have interested themselves in different facets of the phenomenon of interorganizational relations. As a result, four distinct research traditions have emerged in the field. As shown in table 15.1, these approaches differ in their orientation, the organizations studied, type of linkage, the dominant issues examined, and the type of data collected.

The *public administration* approach has primarily been interested in ways to improve coordination within a service-delivery system, such as mental health. More specifically, the interest of this group is in the improvement of lateral coordination at the local level—for example, between local units of state or federal mental-health programs. Researchers in this area have examined the impact of mandating interorganizational coordination (Aldrich 1976; Hall et al. 1977), the perceived costs of coordination to the participating organizations (Whetten and Leung 1979), and alternative forms of coordination (Aiken et al. 1975; Landau 1969).

This chapter is a substantially revised version of David A. Whetten, "Interorganizational Relations: A Review of the Field," *Journal of Higher Education* 52 (January/February 1981): 1–28, copyright © 1981 by the Ohio State University Press, and is used by permission.

Table 15.1 Four approaches to research on interorganizational relations

Orientation	Type of organization	Type of linkage	Dominant issue	Type of data
Public administration	Service agencies in a delivery system	Lateral dyadic	Enhance coordination	Surveys
Marketing	Businesses linked in a "channel of distribution"	Vertical	Sources of power and effects of conflict	Surveys
Economic	Businesses (e.g., *Fortune* 500, chemical industry, and government)	Vertical & lateral dyadic	Expose illegal linkages	Secondary data— aggregated statistics
Sociological	All organizations in a community	Lateral network	Describe overall pattern of relations—especially distribution of power	Surveys and secondary data

In contrast, researchers with a *marketing* orientation have primarily examined vertical linkages between business organizations. A great deal of research has examined channels of distribution, such as the chain from chemical producer to paint manufacturer to paint wholesaler to paint retailer. This research has examined the relationship between control over valued resources and perceived power, and the causes and consequences of interorganizational conflict along the distribution channel. One of the principal outcomes of this line of research has been the formulation of several models of interorganizational conflict management (Simon 1969; Stern, Sternthal, and Craig 1975; Stern and Heskett 1969).

Relatively little research has been conducted on vertical relations in the public sector, although the linkages between the federal, state, and local levels of government could logically be treated as a channel for distributing public goods. Authors such as Porter and Olsen (1976) and Kunde and Berry et al. (1979) have written on vertical intergovernmental relations, but it would be instructive for public-sector researchers to investigate more systematically the perceived sources of conflict and power between various levels of government, so that the dynamics of vertical interorganizational relations in the public and private sectors could be compared (Reve and Stern 1979).

Both the public-administration and the marketing-research approachs have tended to focus on dyadic relations between a relatively small number of organizations and have relied primarily on survey data. The *economic* and *sociological* orientations, in contrast, have allowed for the examination of much larger organizational networks, using a variety of data-gathering methodologies. Several researchers interested in the economic structure of society have examined the linkages between large businesses. For example, the number of interlocking boards of directors between business firms has been examined by Pennings (1980); Allen (1974); Dooley (1969); Burt, Christman, and Kilburn (1980); and Galaskiewicz and Wasserman (1981). The number of mergers and joint ventures between businesses in the same, versus different, industries has been studied by Pfeffer (1972) and Pfeffer and Nowak (1976). And the movement of personnel between major corporations has been examined by Pfeffer and Leblebici (1973) and Endstrom and Galbraith (1977). In general these studies have found extensive interbusiness networks centered on the banking industry. They have also shown that interorganizational agreements are an effective means of gaining control over uncertain environmental conditions.

While research conducted on interorganizational relations in the public sector and on channels of distribution tends to explore ways to improve coordination, research on the economic structure tends instead to search for evidence of inappropriate collaboration between businesses. This interest in the power structure undergirding a network of organizations is also reflected in the sociological research on communities. Sociologists and political scientists have debated for decades the question of whether communities are governed by an elitist or a pluralistic power structure (Dahl 1961; Hunter 1953). When community researchers found that the members of a community who are perceived as most influential tend to occupy positions in several organizations (e.g., Perrucci and Pilisuk 1970), research on community power began focusing on the analysis of interorganizational network structures (Galaskiewicz 1979a; Laumann, Galaskiewicz, and Marsden 1978a; Laumann, Marsden, and Galaskiewicz 1978b).

A related strain of community-based IOR research has examined the community contextual factors that influence the overall pattern of relations between community organizations. For example, Turk (1973) found that the city's form of governance (i.e., strong mayor, city council, city manager) and the degree of social integration in the community influence the amount of interorganizational coordination, and Galaskiewicz and Shatin (1981) found that the stability, homogeneity, and income level of Chicago neighborhoods influenced the number of cooperative ties established between community-based human-service organizations.

This comparison of the four approaches indicates the diversity of IOR research and suggests some important practical implications. First, a search of the IOR literature can be streamlined by identifying the appropriate research orientation. In addition, it is important to recognize that comparing results from studies within one of the four approaches is more legitimate than across the approaches. Moreover, this typology makes explicit the assumptions and limitations of the various research orientations, thereby suggesting ways to improve traditional research designs. For example, there is a significant need for those conducting economically oriented research to make use of the data-gathering techniques more commonly associated with the public-administration approach. Because IOR research on business organizations has relied primarily on secondary data in the past, we know considerably more about the frequency of interlocking directorates than about their substantive meaning. While it is widely assumed that interlocking boards of directors act to thwart the natural forces of competitive markets, relatively little research has tested this assumption directly. To do this effectively, future research in this topic should collect primary data through personal observation and intensive interviews.

FORMS OF INTERORGANIZATIONAL RELATIONS

Researchers from each of these scholarly disciplines studied various types of interorganizational linkage. We will examine four forms of interaction: dyadic linkages. organization sets, action sets, and networks.[1]

Dyadic linkages

The simplest kind of interaction—dyadic linkage—is formed when two organizations find it mutually benefi-

---

1. See Aldrich and Whetten (1981) for a more elaborate discussion of these forms.

cial to collaborate in accomplishing a common goal. For example, joint ventures are often created to share the risk of innovation. Two universities may share the expense of installing a new research computer, or two oil companies may form a partnership to explore a remote section of the earth for natural resources. Dyadic linkages tend to grow out of interpersonal associations between organizational representatives. Once established, joint ventures tend to be project specific in focus and duration.

A less formal model of dyadic interaction entails simple coordination of various aspects of two organizations' production activities. For example, people-processing organizations (Hasenfeld 1972) often develop interorganizational agreements to improve the quality of service provided to a common client pool. In the education and training sector, one organization may provide intake, screening, and placement services, while another offers the actual educational services. These dyadic linkages differ from joint ventures because they do not create a unique organizational entity or project. Instead, organizations simply agree to coordinate their respective activities to increase efficiency. Because the commitment of organizational resources is modest, the relationship is typically less formal and consequently more difficult to maintain. It is generally dependent on the informal agreements between the initiators; as a result, it is vulnerable to turnover in organizational personnel. To counteract this inherent problem some organizations draft nonfinancial agreements specifying the details of their coordination activities as a means of institutionalizing what otherwise would be basically an interpersonal commitment between boundary spanners.

Because this is the most fundamental form of IOR, a great deal of research has examined the antecedents and consequences of dyadic coordination. This body of research is discussed in detail in later sections.

Organization sets

A related form of interorganizational interaction has been identified by Evan (1972), who defines an "organizational set" as the total sum of interorganizational linkages established by an organization. The term is derived from Merton's concept of the "role set," the collection of role relationships a person has by virtue of his or her social status (e.g., a professor is connected to students, administrators, family, and so on.) It is important to point out that an organization set is constituted around a focal organization. Therefore it is not a true network, because although the dyadic linkages between the focal and interacting organizations are examined, the relations between the interacting organizations are ignored.

The research on organization sets has focused primarily on two issues. First, what factors affect the size and composition of the set? Second, how does the focal organization cope with the conflicting expectations of set members?

It seems likely that a large and diverse set of relationships increases the power and discretion of the focal organization; the more options an organization has, the less it must depend on any single relationship. Research on organization-set size and diversity is exemplified by Whetten and Aldrich's (1979) study of manpower programs. They found that the best predicators of set size and diversity (number of different types of organizations represented) were factors over which the local agency administrator had little control. These included the size of the organization's budget, the number of different services it was mandated to provide, and the range of occupational specialties represented in the staff. Interorganizational relations were less significantly influenced by factors that could be more readily manipulated by local administrators, such as the degree of centralization in the decision-making process, the level of continuing professional training and activity of staff members, the number of staff meetings, and the formalization of work rules and procedures.

The problem of conflicting expectations from multiple constituencies was discussed by Evan in his original treatise on organization set and documented by Whetten (1978). For each of sixty-seven manpower organizations, Whetten obtained a rating of organizational effectiveness from three constituencies: internal staff members, federal-level administrators, and heads of other community organizations. These three evaluations were negatively correlated for the sample as a whole. Further, when the expectations of these three groups were correlated with various characteristics of the focal organization it became clear that an administrator could not satisfy the expectations of one group without violating those of another. For example, if an administrator responded to the pressure of the federal-level administrators to process more clients, then the bureaucratic procedures required to reach that objective would run counter to the expectations of both staff, who preferred a highly professional working environment emphasizing quality client relationships, and other community organizations, which hoped for extensive local interorganizational activity.

The salience of these conflicts has been noted in other organization set studies. For example, Evan's (1966) study of the organization set of federal regulatory commissions focused on the pressures that eventually turned the Interstate Commerce Commission and the Food and Drug Administration into the defenders, rather than the regulators, of the industries they were created to monitor. Similarly, Hirsch (1972) examined how publishing houses, movie studios, and record companies changed their relations with their organization sets because of demand uncertainty for their products. Producers responded to these pressures by proliferating boundary-spanning roles, differentially promoting products, and attempting to co-opt media gatekeepers. In a similar study Elesh (1973) investigated the strategies used by universities in competing with members of their organization set for new students.

The most extensive study of the strategies used by a focal organization to manage its relations with other organization-set members was conducted by Metcalfe (1976) in England. He studied the National Economic Development Council, which performs a central role in facilitating coordination between management, labor, and government on economic matters. Faced with the challenge of molding the conflicting objectives of these interest groups into an integrated plan of action, the council used several strategies: (1) mobilizing the support of third parties; (2) securing peer-group support for regulating organization-set demands; (3) making conflicting demands of organization-set members observable; (4) forming coalitions between less powerful members; (5) promulgating an overarching ideology; and (6) co-opting leaders of member organizations into the council's decision-making strategy.

Action sets

Action sets are essentially purposive networks, coalitions of organizations working together to accomplish a specific purpose. The concept denotes an interacting group of organizations, in contrast to the organization set, which is explicitly centered on a single focal organization. An action set can be centered on a single organization, however, as in the case of a price leader in an oligopoly or the largest university in a state higher-education system.

Phillips (1960) identified four conditions that affect the degree to which an interfirm action set will be able to achieve coordinated behavior: (1) the number of organizations in the action set; (2) the extent to which a single powerful organization assumes a leadership role; (3) similarity in values and attitudes among the members; and (4) the impact of other action sets' behavior. Developing this concept further, Hirsch (1975) examined the effect of forming an action set on the profitability of the ethical-drug and the record industries. The drug industry succeeded in forming a cohesive action set that co-opted the American Medical Association and lobbied successfully for favorable changes in state and federal laws affecting the drug industry, whereas the record industry was singularly unsuccessful.

Organizational federations represent a specific form of action sets. Stern's (1979, 1981) research on the National Collegiate Athletic Association has provided useful insights into the development and operation of one of the strongest federations in our country. Starting out as a loose, voluntary confederation of universities, the NCAA was transformed into the dominant control agent in intercollegiate athletics when the member schools granted it regulatory power in 1952. As Stern's research points out, it is difficult for a federation to serve simultaneously as both coordinator and regulator. As the member institutions invested more and more regulatory power in the NCAA, its role as a coordinator was impaired by member distrust and at times open contempt and hostility.

Networks

A network consists of all interactions between organizations in a population, regardless of how the population is organized into dyads, organization sets, or action sets. There are two types of interorganizational networks: attribute and transaction. Attribute networks consist of organizations that possess common characteristics, such as resource requirements or outputs. Transaction networks focus on the exchange relationships that link organizations (Fombrun 1982).

As represented in graph or matrix form, a network is a static entity. To understand the significance of this pattern of interorganizational relations, it is important to consider the dynamic processes that generated the present configuration. This requires an in-depth understanding of both the contextual factors impinging on the entire network and the evolutionary processes occurring within the dyadic and action-set components of the network (Stern 1979).

To date, more research has been conducted on the determinants of network structure than on network evolution. In both contexts, however, the concept of "loose coupling" has commanded attention. Systems theorists such as Granovetter (1973), Glassman (1973), and Simon (1969) have posited that systems evolve in such a way that critical functions are performed in subsystems that consist of densely coupled linkages between internal elements. These subsystems in turn are joined to each other only loosely, by means of "linking-pin" relationships between a few representatives. Such a system, it is argued, has the greatest posssible adaptive capacity, because changes can be made in one subsystem without seriously

disrupting the performance of other subsystems. In contrast, introducing change into a richly joined system with numerous linkages between and within subsystems creates considerable turbulence, because a change in one subsystem produces ripple effects throughout the system.

In network analysis, stable action sets are the typical subnetwork units in a loosely joined system, although the type of subsystems identified depends on the scope of the network studied. For example, at the national level of the economy, industries can be treated as the subsystems that are aggregated into a loosely joined system through resource interdependence. At the industry level, stable action sets are oligopolistic coalitions and cartels, while studies of local community structure often treat power elites or other groupings of vested interests as the building blocks of a community power structure.

To date most of the research on loosely joined structures has been descriptive, that is, investigators have utilized sociometric techniques to identify the degree to which a network is richly or loosely joined. Typically a statistical technique such as "block modeling" (Knoke and Rogers 1979) is used to analyze a transaction matrix. This program identifies the blocks (or cliques) of organizations that are tightly interconnected but loosely coupled with the rest of the network. The more blocks found in a network, the more loosely coupled it is. For example, in a study of seventy-eight organizations in a midwestern community, Galaskiewicz (1978) found four blocks that essentially represented different community-interest groups (business, government, social services, labor, and political parties).

Block-modeling studies have increased our awareness of the diversity of relations present in a large network. For example, Van de Ven, Walker, and Liston (1979) identified three distinct clusters of social-service agencies in a Texas community. In one cluster the dominant purpose for interorganization linkages was providing direct services; in another, it was planning and coordination; in the third, resource exchange.

While block modeling is useful for identifying pockets of intense interaction between members, it does not examine the relationship between these clusters. To determine the extent to which richly joined clusters are hierarchically arranged in the nested fashion suggested by Simon (1969), Leblebici and Whetten (1982) classified interorganizational linkages in seventeen community social-service networks into first-, second-, and third-order clusters, with the first-order clusters representing the most intense level of interaction. They found that in all networks at least 85 percent of the linkages could be classified into one of the three levels.

In the future, as more descriptive network studies are conducted and a more complete knowledge of the intricacies of network configuration is developed, the field will probably move on to the next analytical step of predicting the degree of loose coupling across a large sample of networks.

Researchers who view networks as loosely joined systems are naturally interested in the role of linking-pin organizations. These organizations have established ties to more than one action set and consequently play a key role in integrating the entire organizational population. For example, they serve as communication channels between clusters and provide services that link third parties to one another by transferring resources, information, or clients. Their critical role often gives linking-pin organizations considerable status in the network. Because other network members are dependent on them for obtaining critical resources, and because of their high status, linking-pin organizations exert a considerable influence on the overall pattern of activities in the network—either directly, by manipulating the flow of information and other resources, or indirectly, by serving as a role model for other organizations to imitate (Boje and Whetten 1981).

Research on network centrality has examined the determinants of an organization's location in the pattern of exchanges. In a study of the linkages between seventy-three organizations in a single community, Galaskiewicz (1979b) discovered that control over economic resources was a better predictor of network centrality than control over political resources. In a similar study conducted in seventeen countries, Boje and Whetten (1981) found that local administrative discretion, abundant organizational resources, and informal acquaintances with members of other organizations were the best predictors of network centrality. This study also showed that network centrality is associated with reputational influence, which had previously been demonstrated at the interpersonal and interdepartmental levels of analysis.

The degree to which the network is hierarchically organized, is reflected in the concentration of power in a few organizations. While loose coupling measures horizontal configuration, hierarchy measures vertical configuration. In a completely competitive market structure, in which no organization has authority over other network members and no organization controls a disproportionately large share of the network's resources, the network has only minimal hierarchy. In practice, however, a pure market structure is seldom found, because a few members of the network typically emerge to form a dominant elite. This can be done in several ways: (1) By establishing extra-network connections (for example, as a member of a national association), an organization can reduce its dependence on other network members for obtaining vital resources. (2) An organiza-

tion may be granted formal authority to coordinate the activities of other network organizations. This authority may derive either from the consent of the other members (as when one party is elected chairman of a coordination council) or from an outside authority source, such as the state or federal government. (3) An organization may gain control over internal network resources by shrewd political maneuvering or as a consequence of occupying a naturally strategic position in the network (such as linking-pin organizations).

INTERORGANIZATIONAL COORDINATION

Although much of the interorganizational-relations research has been descriptive, a significant portion is devoted to seeking ways to improve interorganizational coordination. We will review this prescriptive material by organizing it into four categories: structural forms of coordination, antecedents of coordination, a model for creating coordination, and the unintended side effects of coordination.[2] Because most of this literature has focused on relations between local public-service-delivery organizations, our discussion will assume that context.

Structural forms of coordination

The phenomena included in the concept of "coordination" are extremely broad, ranging from simple *ad hoc* agreements between two organizations to participation in formally organized coordinating councils. Most of the literature on coordination focuses on a limited part of this spectrum, namely the periodic coming together of two or more organizations to plan future activities or to work on joint projects. The more *ad hoc* side of this continuum often is conceptualized as interorganizational cooperation.

The wide range of coordinating structures is best described by Warren (1967), Thompson (1967), and Lindblom (1965). We have chosen to collapse these structures into three types, following Clark (1965) and Adams (1976): mutual adjustment, corporate, and alliance. As shown in table 15.2, these three categories vary in intensity, form of social power, formalization, and scope of the coordination activity. Mutual adjustment is the weakest form of coordination, while corporate is the strongest. We will discuss the two extreme models first.

2. For a more extensive review of the interorganizational-coordination literature, see Rogers and Whetten et al. (1982). This section has drawn extensively on that work.

Table 15.2 Coordination structures

	Type of structure		
	Corporate	Alliance	Mutual adjustment
Some differentiating characteristics			
Social power	Authority	Negotiation	Influence
Formalization	Central authority develops written expectations	Participating organizations develops written expectations	Informal unwritten expectations
Sanctions	High	Some	Almost none
Example	Agency	Coordinating council	Informal committee

Note: Adapted from G. E. Klonglan, C. L. Mulford, R. D. Warren, and J. M. Winkelpleck, "Creating Interorganizational Coordination: Project Report," Sociology Report No. 122A, Department of Sociology, Iowa State University, Ames, Iowa, 1975, by permission.

MUTUAL ADJUSTMENT

The mutual-adjustment structure typifies the type of coordination that occurs in a competitive market. Consequently, the orientation in mutual-adjustment situations is on the interests of the participating agencies or their clients (Haas and Drabek 1973; Lehman 1975; Warren 1967). There are few if any shared goals toward which the units work. When common goals do emerge, they are apt to be only temporary. Coordination tends to focus on specific cases rather than on the development of a comprehensive delivery system.

Agency representatives in this situation are generally professionals or administrative staff at the supervisory level, rather than the top administrator. Individuals who are involved in the day-to-day activities of an agency often attend meetings or make phone contact with their counterparts in other agencies as the need arises. Because few if any resources are being committed through the joint activity, it is unnecessary to involve those with higher authority.

The rules used in this strategy are developed as the need arises in the process of interaction; interpersonal concerns are likely to be as important as organizational issues. Consequently, the violation of rules and norms is not regarded as severely as in other coordinating strategies, nor are the types of punishment or sanctions for violation nearly as severe. Further, there is no central unit to monitor or detect violations.

This strategy provides the narrowest range of benefits but also the fewest costs. Funding arrangements are made only at the convenience of the contracting parties, and complete authority is retained by the participating organizations. In a system of peers, attempts to change the balance of power among organizations tend to be resisted. Control over organizations, when it occurs, is achieved through mutual agreement. In this context, differences of opinions regarding goals and program administration can be resolved only through negotiation and bargaining between participants.

CORPORATE

In the corporate structure, coordination occurs under the umbrella of an overarching formal authority structure. Units being coordinated are members of an encompassing organization or system. Examples are departments of a state government, or campuses in a statewide higher-education system (Warren 1967; Lehman 1975; Lindblom 1965).

In a corporate system, the objective of each unit is to achieve the interagency system's goals. Activities are divided among specialized units, and each performs in accordance with a central plan. The basis of control resides in the legitimacy of collective decisions. Thus interagency decisions are accepted and become part of the program repertoire of the member organizations. A strong central administration establishes systemwide policies and monitors their implementation by member organizations. Control is achieved through regulations that constrain the actions of member units or through conventional sanctions such as funds, manpower, and promotion.

A corporate interorganizational design closely approximates the control features (incentives, decision-making structure) of a single multi-unit organization. Naturally, this approach is generally resisted by participating organizations; consequently an ongoing tension between allegiance and sovereignty is a hallmark of most corporate interorganizational systems.

ALLIANCE

Between the corporate and mutual-adjustment structures are strategies containing elements of both; they represent efforts to coordinate autonomous organizations without the authority of a formal hierarchy (Clark 1965; Warren 1967; Mott 1968; Lindblom 1965). This intermediate category is very wide and includes a range of strategies, such as federations, councils, and coalitions.

There are two major variations in the distribution of power within this intermediate strategy. One possibility is to form a central unit to develop programs and administer day-to-day operations as responsibilities are delegated by the member agencies. For example, a central staff may mediate between the member agencies to facilitate agreements and resource transfers. The second variation is represented by a coalition or council. Coalitions, unlike federations, typically do not create a central administrative unit. Here the authority system is more informal, and the power is lodged in each member agency. Coordination is more difficult to orchestrate because of the absence of a third-party mediator.

Within the alliance structure, both the system and the member units exercise power. In federations some decisions are made at the top, but authority is retained at the unit level. Thus systemwide decisions must be ratified by member units. Federative structures are also characterized by formalized systems of rules. Although the rules may be negotiated initially, they become more formal over time as the roles of central staff and member agencies are clarified and adapted.

Coalitions and councils, in contrast, tend to assign extremely restricted decision-making powers to a central staff. Further, the rules and procedures tend to be more *ad hoc* and are constantly being renegotiated. Policies formulated by councils and coalitions tend to focus on procedural matters (e.g., how decisions are made) and thus have little regulatory effect on the participating organizations.

Antecedents of coordination

The three forms of coordination described above represent only structural configurations and authority relationships between organizations. The structure creates the context for coordination, but does not represent the process of coordination itself. This process must be induced within the constraints of each of the three structural forms. Consequently, it is instructive to examine the factors influencing an organization's decision to enter into a coordination agreement.

Both assets and liabilities are inherent in every interorganizational agreement (Schmidt and Kochan 1977). The principal asset is access to the resources controlled by other organizations, but resource-exchange agreements also represent obligations that restrict administrators' flexibility. The more agreements in force, the more commitments and obligations must be considered in making subsequent decisions. Thus administrators must be convinced that the benefits of entering into a new coordination agreement outweigh the inherent costs (Whetten and Leung 1979).

A variety of perceptual and situational factors influence this assessment. As shown in table 15.3, five conditions must be met for voluntary coordination to occur, but only three when coordination is mandated by law (for example, between two federal social-service agencies). In the case of voluntary coordination it is necessary first of all for administrators to have a positive attitude toward interorganizational coordination. Otherwise they will define their organizational problems in such a way that coordination does not appear to be a useful solution. Next, they must recognize and organizational need for coordination that justifies absorbing the associated costs. Then the search for potential coordination partners is initiated. After the likely candidates have been identified, they are evaluated in terms of desirability and compatibility. Finally, the participating organizations must assess their capacity to manage the ongoing coordination process.

POSITIVE ATTITUDE TOWARD COORDINATION

A positive attitude toward coordination can stem from a number of various sources. For example, Whetten (1978) found that staff members with a strong professional background who placed a high value on meeting client needs tended to encourage coordination activities. Becker (1970) found that staff members with a cosmopolitan ethos were willing to take greater risks with unfamiliar staff members from other organizations. A staff member's natural inclination to value coordination can be reinforced by organizational norms and rewards. For example, Schermerhorn (1975) and Akinbode and Clark (1976) found that organizations that encouraged group-centered client treatment fostered greater interorganizational coordination. In state and federal service-delivery systems the attitude of top-level administrators toward collaboration between local organizations is reflected in organizational policies and rewards. For instance, one service-delivery system might openly encourage local coordination by providing planning money to local leaders for developing an interorganizational

Table 15.3   Preconditions for successful coordination

VOLUNTARY COORDINATION

Positive attitude towards coordination	Recognized need for coordination	Awareness of potential coordination partners	Assessment of compatibility and desirability	Capacity for maintaining coordination process
Cosmopolitan ethos	Interdependence	Informal contact	Status congruity	Adequate resources and staff
Strong professional background and values	Broad goals	Geographic proximity	Compatible ideology and definition of problems	Adequate communication channels
	Diverse clients	Formal communication	Domain consensus	Flexible rules and procedures
Organizational policies and rewards provide positive reinforcement	Wide range of services		Complementary organizational structures and procedures	Professional staff

MANDATED COORDINATION

Awareness of mandate		Assessment of compatibility and desirability		Capacity for maintaining coordination process
Understanding of mandate		Status congruity		Adequate resources and staff
Knowledge of interacting organizations		Compatible ideology and definition of problems		Adequate communication channels
		Domain consensus		Flexible rules and procedures
		Complementary organizational structures and procedures		Professional staff
		Goal compatibility		

coordination council, while another system might unintentionally discourage coordination by maintaining strong central control and providing resource support only for internal administrative activities (Whetten 1977).

RECOGNIZING A NEED FOR COORDINATION

Akinbode and Clark (1976) and Davidson (1976) found that a necessary prerequisite for interorganizational coordination is the recognition of partial interdependence. When organizations share the same client pool, the same resource base, or provide the same type of services, the need for coordination becomes apparent. Van de Ven (1976) has argued that there is an optimal level of interdependence for fostering coordination. If organizations have too little in common, there is little incentive to collaborate. On the other hand, if they share too much, they perceive one another as strong competitors and refuse to work together. Whetten and Aldrich (1979) found that

an organization is likely to perceive interdependence with a large number of other members of its population if it has broad goals, provides diverse services, and serves a wide range of clients.

KNOWLEDGE OF POTENTIAL PARTNERS

Coordination will not occur unless two organizations become aware of their complementary needs. This awareness may emerge from informal contacts between staff-members, perhaps at professional training meetings or community-based voluntary association meetings, or in smaller communities between neighbors who work in related organizations. Friendships formed while working in previous jobs are particularly salient communication channels (Boje and Whetten 1981; Galaskiewicz and Shatin 1981). Geographical proximity may also lead to coincidental interactions between staff members of different organizations that build awareness of common needs. Reid (1969) and Schermerhorn (1975) report that coordination is more likely to occur between nearby organizations for this reason. Finally, formal communications from one organization to another convey useful information about resource availability, client needs, and service opportunities. Klonglan et al. (1976) found that newsletters, bulletins, letters, and program announcements were effective tools for stimulating interest in coordination.

ASSESSMENT OF COMPATIBILITY AND DESIRABILITY

The costs of coordination increase as a function of differences between the collaborating organizations. Hence organizations tend to seek partners that have roughly equal status (Paulson 1976), share a common definition of the problems to be addressed (Rogers and Glick 1973), have an encompassing professional ideology (Benson 1975), do not present a threat to respective domain claims (Hall et al. 1977), and have compatible organizational structures and procedures (Form and Nosow 1958).

CAPACITY FOR MAINTAINING COORDINATION LINKAGE

Successful coordination programs often break down because one or both of the partners are incapable of maintaining the relationship. The problem may be a resource cutback, a small staff overloaded with internal administrative responsibilities, staff inefficiency or ineptitude, inadequate internal and interorganizational communication channels, or a lack of flexibility in organizational policies (Whetten and Aldrich 1979; Aiken and Hage 1968).

In summary, successful voluntary coordination depends upon both *favorable staff assessments* (conditions 1–4) and *resource and structural adequacy* (condition 5) (see table 15.3). Both are necessary and neither is sufficient for the initiation and maintenance of a voluntary coordination linkage.

The preconditions for a mandated linkage are somewhat different. As shown in table 15.3, when coordination is required by legal mandate the staff's attitude toward coordination and its knowledge of available coordination partners is no longer a necessary precondition. Awareness of the mandate substitutes for recognition of a need to coordinate. However, assessment of compatibility and organizational capacity are still salient factors. If an organization's staff members perceive that they are being forced to interact with an undesirable organization and that this interaction will severely tax their resources, they will probably attempt to undermine the mandate. On the other hand, if staff members required to implement a coordination mandate perceive that it will produce desirable outcomes with acceptable costs, then the coordination linkage is likely to be stronger than if the relationship were not mandated (Raelin 1980; Al-

drich 1976; Hall et al. 1977). Therefore, the critical components of a successful mandated relationship are (1) *justifying the need for coordination to the implementers*, and (2) *providing them with sufficient resources to maintain the coordination process in addition to their other responsibilities*. If these conditions are not met—if the organization is forced to establish a large number of coordination linkages that staff members feel are of little use in meeting the organization's objectives— mandated coordination creates a negative, fatalistic attitude that sharply limits the organization's effectiveness (Whetten and Leung 1979).

A model for creating coordination

With an understanding of the necessary conditions for voluntary coordination, it is possible to outline a proactive strategy for creating coordination. One such approach has been developed by a group of sociologists at Iowa State (Klonglan et al. 1975). The coordination model contains five steps, as shown in table 15.4.

1. *Analyze the present situation.* The first step is to specify the problem to be addressed, the geographical boundaries within which it occurs, and the organizations in that area that can provide support (personnel, information, endorsements, materials, and agreements).

2. *Manage organizational decisions.* Once the relevant population of organizations has been identified, then the person initiating the coordination program should call key administrators in each organization. At this point private discussions should be held one-on-one so that the coordinator can build a commitment to his or her ideas and ascertain each organization's level of support. Support for a coordination program is most likely to be obtained if the organizations agree that there is a genuine, pressing problem. If organizations are committed to solving a problem, they will be more willing to absorb the costs inherent in interorganizational coordination. To build commitment, the coordinator can exploit a crisis, make comparisons (e.g., "other counties are working on this problem"), present figures documenting the seriousness of the problem, emphasize reciprocal ongoing obligations, set up demonstration projects, present evidence based on citizen preferences, and explicitly discuss the costs and benefits of ignoring (versus solving) the problem.

3. *Manage interorganizational decisions.* Once the coordinator feels that a critical mass of support has been developed for the coordination program, the next step is to organize a group meeting. The purpose of these joint sessions is to solidfy commitment to the problem and de-

Table 15.4 Five steps for creating coordination

Analyze the present situation	Manage organizational decisions	Manage inter-organizational decisions	Take action	Measure impact on objectives
Specify the problem	Obtain problem commitment	Outline the objectives	Monitor fulfillment of responsibilities	Changes in target population
Specify the relevant geographical boundaries	Obtain coordination commitment	Specify the flow of resources	Monitor delivery of resources	Changes in participating organizations
Identify the key organizations	Achieve consensus	Specify the structure	Monitor meeting deadlines	Changes in larger context
		Outline a plan for work		

Note: Adapted from Klonglan et al. 1975, by permission.

sign a coordination program with a broad base of support. This can best be done by outlining the objects to be accomplished, specifying the flow of resources between participating organizations, establishing a structural arrangement to guide the flow of resources, and outlining a concrete plan for work that specifies each participant's responsibilities.

4. *Take action.* Once the program is operational it is important that the coordinator follow up on the participants' commitments. Specifically, the organizations should be monitored regularly to ensure that they have delivered promised resources and met agreed-upon deadlines.

5. *Measure impact on objectives.* Periodically it is important that participants evaluate and discuss the outcomes of the program. The short- and long-term effects of the program on specific target populations, the participating organizations, and the encompassing social and political environments should be assessed. This feedback may prompt the group to make changes in the program design or the mix of participating organizations; it also helps reinforce the participating organizations' commitment to the program. Particularly because organizations are always sensitive to the cost inherent in any coordination program, it is important that they frequently receive information about the benefits of their participation.

This coordination model has been used extensively in a variety of institutional contexts, because it is both theoretically sound and practically useful. One reason for its success is that the model addresses all five of the preconditions for coordination shown in table 15.3. In the process of analyzing the present situation, a pool of potential coordination partners is generated (precondition 3). Then, as the leader develops commitment to a specific problem and the need for coordination, he or she can assess administrators' general attitude about coordination and articulate a justification for its application (preconditions 1 and 2). During both the dyadic and the group discussions, the coordinator can assess the compatibility of participating organizations and their capacities for supporting the coordination program. This information can then be used in designing the coordination program, selecting the participating organizations, and specifying the level and type of resource commitment requested from each organization (preconditions 4 and 5).

Consequences of coordination

The IOR literature generally assumes that the most problematic aspect of coordination is that it does not happen as often as it should. But coordination projects can have some serious negative side effects. To provide a balanced perspective for evaluating the benefits of interorganizational coordination, this section discusses some of the most common dysfunctional consequences of coordination.

IMPACT ON ADAPTIVE POTENTIAL

Tighter systemic integration reduces adaptive potential. A joint program forms a dyadic linkage between two organizations that, when placed in a larger context of an encompassing action set, tends to increase the interconnectedness of all members of the network. Hence the more joint programs established in a network, the more richly joined it becomes. In richly joined networks, as mentioned earlier, a change in one organization creates turbulence throughout the network because the interconnected organizations are forced to adapt. Because each organization must be responsive to slightly different environmental contingencies while maintaining linkages with other organizations, the result is instability in the network.

This negative side effect of coordination is minimized when three conditions are met: (1) network members all interface with essentially the same (or at least compatible) environmental conditions; (2) the network's environment consists of homogeneous elements that do not change frequently; and (3) there is a central authority structure in the network that can be used to coordinate internal change and reconcile conflicts between members. Unfortunately, these conditions are difficult to obtain in most service-delivery systems. Consequently, while encouraging extensive coordination between network members may improve their respective effectiveness, the long-run adaptive capacity of the network as a whole may be reduced.

IMPACT ON PROGRAM INNOVATION.

Joint programming may reduce program innovation. Conventional wisdom holds that "striking two unlike substances together produces a spark." Does this mean that a program is most likely to be innovative if it is designed by representatives from a diverse group of organizations? This intuitively appealing proposition often does not hold in practice, for two reasons. First, the more diverse the background and orientations of joint program planners, the more difficult the planning process becomes. Establishing a common language, a set of working assumptions, and a high degree of trust between dissimilar people is very difficult. Consequently, as the joint program planning process advances, frustrations created by communication difficulties mount, and pressures from superiors to reach a decision increase. As a result, despite the potential for cross-fertilization of ideas, there is a natural tendency for participants to search for safe solutions—which also turn out to be rather mundane.

Joint ventures are typically subject to intense political bargaining. At least one of the participating organizations is likely to have a "hidden agenda" for the new program, which consequently becomes a pawn in some larger chess game. The resulting bargaining and compromising often leads to a watered-down program inferior to what either organization could have produced on its own. This outcome is especially likely when participating organizations enter the planning process with unequal power, because the wishes of a dominant actor typically prevail in a bargaining situation.

The negative side effects of collaboration on program innovation can be reduced by selecting organizational representatives with some common background,

so that they can relate to one another, form a trusting relationship, and establish a common language for discussing their common objectives. In addition, participating organizations should have comparable resources and reputations, so that the power bases of their representatives will be similar. And it will be helpful to obtain outside seed money to support the joint venture planning process. If the participating organizations are compensated for the staff time required to design a joint venture, there will be less pressure on the organizational representatives to complete the design process quickly.

IMPACT ON SERVICE QUALITY

Extensive coordination may reduce the quality of services provided by the network as a whole. Warren, Bergunder, and Rose (1974) have argued that extensive coordination between members of a service-delivery system reinforces the status quo by hindering entrance of new organizations, technologies, and ideologies. Their study of "war on poverty" programs found that while members of this action set frequently criticized one another and disagreed on points of program administration, they all subscribed to an underlying ideology that the problems of the poor could best be addressed by using the programs of the current human-services system. Hence these organizations typically responded to criticisms of ineffective service delivery by proposing to increase coordination between existing organizations, and opposed innovative propositions grounded in a private-sector model of competition (such as issuing a social-services credit card to clients for purchasing services from the organizations of their choice).

Extensive coordination may also reduce the overall quality of services provided by an action set because it eliminates useful redundancy. One of the major reasons for increased coordination in delivery systems, particularly those administering federal and state categorical programs, is to reduce the overlap in services provided. However, as Landau (1969) has noted, reductions in redundancy decrease performance reliability, because all back-up systems are eliminated. In a human-services-delivery setting it is difficult to maintain a high level of client access and service quality without some redundancy. If the system is a completely nonredundant system, with each service provided by only one source, clients' access can be limited by their ignorance or by staff error or prejudice, and service quality can be reduced by a lack of competition.

The best way to counter this negative side effect of coordination is to establish an extra-network monitor—perhaps a legislative committee, a regulatory body, an advisory board, a citizen's-action group, or a client-advocacy organization. The purpose of one of these bodies would be to ensure that the system maintains an appropriate balance between efficiency and reliability and to guard against the possiblity that organizations would collaborate to protect their vested interests at the expense of innovation and service quality.

COSTS

The maintenance of interorganizational relations represents a substantial cost to the exchange partners. The organizational cost of initiating and maintaining interorganizational coordination linkages have received relatively little attention in the literature. These costs include increased expenditures for boundary-spanning personnel, reduced internal decision-making autonomy, and increased conflict. As one would expect, the perceived costs associated with maintaining a given linkage vary with the perceived instrumental value of the linkage. Organizations tend to avoid interacting with organizations of marginal utility (Schmidt and Kochan 1977), reduce the intensity of their interactions with mandated linkages perceived as liabilities (Hall et al. 1977; Whetten and Leung 1979), and enlarge and diversify their organization set to reduce dependence on any particular linkage (Provan 1982; Whetten and Aldrich 1979).

There is, however, a limit to an organization's ability to mold its network of interorganizational linkages to its advantage. It may find itself forced to honor contracts for services that are no longer useful, or feel obligated to interact with external interest groups or participate in federations and associations with no direct payoffs in order to maintain a desirable status or image. Or it may be impractical to diversify the organization's linkages enough to reduce its dependence on a principal source of resources. For example, Salancik's (1979) study of a sample of national corporations found that one of the best predictors of the degree to which a firm complied with affirmative-action-employment regulations was the percentage of its business contracted with government agencies. Fearing the cancellation of contracts if they were found in noncompliance, the firms altered their employment practices to accommodate the dictates of the federal government.

Because interorganizational linkages represent both assets and liabilities, researchers should avoid the trap of assuming that all exchange relationships are equally advantageous to both partners or that interorganizational linkages in general represent a cost-free opportunity for the focal organization. While these false assumptions have been challenged directly (Provan, Beyer, and Kruytbosch 1980; Whetten and Leung 1979), a lingering positive bias persists in the interorganizational literature. A systematic analysis of the factors affecting the costs versus benefits of interorganizational relations represents a much needed line of research.

SUMMARY AND CONCLUSIONS

Efforts to improve our understanding of interorganizational relations began with a number of case studies several decades ago. These were typically written by practitioners who had participated in a collaborative venture and sought an opportunity to reflect on the problems encountered and the lessons learned. Large-scale empirical research expanded during the 1960s and attracted researchers from a variety of orientations, such as public administration, economics, marketing, and sociology. Research in this field has examined various forms of interorganizational relations, including dyadic linkages, organization sets, action sets, and networks. The most commonly researched question has been How can we improve coordination between interdependent organizations? In attempting to answer this question, researchers have sought to document the antecedents of effective coordination programs, and in the process various forms of coordination have been identified and several prescriptive models have been proposed.

Researchers have perhaps been too much concerned with improving coordination. With the exception of the studies on illegal interlocks between businesses, they have consistently avoided examining the positive outcomes of competition and conflict between organizations. One reason for the dominant pro-coordination bias in the literature is that researchers have typically approached their work from the perspective of the elites in the system under investigation. Few studies have examined coordination from the point of view of clients, taxpayers, or organizational staff members. Research conducted from the vantage point of these interest groups would focus on a different set of issues, such as the loss of worker autonomy and efficiency due to the added paperwork and staff meeting requirements imposed by large-scale coordination programs, and the loss of multiple access points into a service-delivery system resulting from the elimination of useful program overlap. Because they have adopted the pro-coordination model of administrators, researchers have overlooked some important questions: Do public organizations use the recommendation of increasing interorganizational coordination to mask organizational ineffectiveness and administrative ineptitude? Is coordination a legitimating mechanism used by current actors to divide the turf and collude to prevent the entry of competition and dampen innovation?

To adopt a more balanced perspective, future research should draw on the insight of other disciplines. Sociology, for example, has long emphasized that conflict can improve the vitality of a system (Coser 1956; Gouldner 1959), and political science has established the importance of examining a program from the vantage of all its critical constituencies (Wamsley and Zald 1973).

These perspectives can both increase the sophistication of future research on interorganizational relations and greatly enrich our understanding of the phenomena by expanding the range of issues examined.

Our approach to the study of interorganizational relations needs to be broadened in at least two other ways. First, most research to date has been conducted at a single level of analysis (e.g., boundary spanners, dyadic linkages, networks, or populations). This approach yields an oversimplified view of a very complex interaction between processes occurring at multiple levels. For example, an organization's position in its network affects its ability to establish new dyadic linkages, the contextual conditions surrounding a network affect the ties between network members, and the quality of the relationships between individual boundary spanners affects the likelihood that their organizations can maintain a viable long-term relationship. Studies that include data on interorganizational activity at multiple levels of analysis both increase the amount of variance explained and, more importantly, improve our understanding of the coordination process (Whetten 1982; Fottler et al. 1982). Recent examples of this approach include Boje and Whetten (1981), Galaskiewicz and Shatin (1981), and Miller, Lincoln, and Olson (1981).

Second, more longitudinal analysis is needed. To date, few investigators have directly examined the de-velopmental aspect of interorganizational linkages. Studies typically assume that all linkages under investigation are at a common, mature level of development. In fact, it may be significant that some linkages have only recently been established (possible only on a trial basis), while others have been in existence so long that their value is taken for granted (independent of their actual current utility). Because of our inattention to developmental processes, we know very little about why relationships are dissolved or what factors influence organizational leaders' decisions to institutionalize agreements arranged between their boundary spanners. For several reasons it is particularly difficult to test process, rather than variance, models in studies involving multiple organizations (Whetten 1982); as these problems are overcome, however, important new insights will result (see Stern 1979; Metcalfe 1976).

In summary, substantial progress has been made during the past two decades in the investigation of interorganizational relations. We have moved from writing about isolated cases to conducting large-scale field studies. The new frontiers in this area appear to include (1) examining dysfunctional, or at least unintended, consequences of interorganizational relations, (2) focusing on interorganizational relations at multiple levels, and (3) conducting longitudinal studies of the initiation, maintenance, and dissolution processes.

REFERENCES

Adams, J. S. 1976. "Organization Boundary Behavior: Toward a General Model." Paper presented at Annual Meeting of the American Psychological Association, Washington, D.C.

Aiken, M., R. Dewar, N. DiTomaso, J. Hage, and G. Zeitz. 1975. *Coordinating Human Services.* San Francisco, Calif.: Jossey-Bass.

Aiken, M., and J. Hage. 1968. "Organizational Interdependence and Intra-Organizational Structure." *American Sociological Review* 33:912–30.

Akinbode, I. A., and R. C. Clark. 1976. "A Framework for Analyzing Interorganizational Relationships." *Human Relations* 29:101–14.

Aldrich, H. E. 1976. "Resource Dependence and Interorganizational Relations: Local Employment Service Offices and Social Services Sector Organizations." *Administration and Society* 7:419–54.

Aldrich, H. E., and D. A. Whetten. 1981. "Organizational Sets, Action Sets, and Networks: Making the Most of Simplicity." In *Handbook of Organization Design*, ed. P. Nystrom and W. Starbuck, vol. 1: 385–408. London: Oxford University Press.

Allen, M. P. 1974. "The Structure of Interorganizational Elite Cooptation: Interlocking Corporate Directorates." *American Sociological Review* 39:393–496.

Becker, M. H. 1970. "Factors Affecting Diffusion of Innovations Among Health Professionals." *American Journal of Public Health* 60 (February): 294–304.

Benson, J. K. 1975. "The Interorganizational Network as a Political Economy." *Administrative Science Quarterly* 20:229–49.

Boje, D. M., and D. A. Whetten. 1981. "Effects of Strategies and Contextual Constraints on Centrality and Attributions of Influence in Interorganizational Networks." *Administrative Science Quarterly* 26:378–95.

Burt, R. S., K. P. Christman, and H. C. Kilburn, Jr. 1980. "Testing a Structural Theory of Corporate Cooptation: Interorganizational Directorate Ties as a Strategy for Avoiding Market Constraints on Profits." *American Sociological Review* 45:821–41.

Clark, B. R. 1965. "Interorganizational Patterns in Education." *Administrative Science Quarterly* 10:224–37.

Coser, L. 1956. *The Functions of Social Conflict.* New York: Free Press.

Dahl, R. 1961. *Who Governs?* New Haven: Yale University Press.

Davidson, S. M. 1976. "Planning and Coordination of Social Service in Multi-Organizational Centers." *Social Service Review* 50:117–37.

Dooley, P. 1969. "The Interlocking Directorate." *American Economic Review* 59:314–23.

Elesh, D. 1973. "Organization Sets and the Structure of Competition for New Members." *Sociology of Education* 46:371–95.

Endstrom, A., and J. R. Galbraith. 1977. "Transfer of Managers as a Coordination and Control Strategy in Multinational Corporations." *Administrative Science Quarterly* 22:248–63.

Evan, W. 1966. "The Organization Set." In *Approaches to Organizational Design*, ed. James Thompson. Pittsburgh: University of Pittsburgh Press.

———. 1972. "An Organization Set Model of Interorganizational Relations." In *Interorganizational Decision Making*, ed. M. Tuite, R. Chisholm, and M. Radnor. Chicago: Aldine.

Fombrun, C. J. 1982. "Strategies for Network Research in Organizations." *Academy of Management Review* 7:280–91.

Form, W. H., and S. Nosow. 1958. *Community in Disaster*. New York: Harper & Row.

Fottler, M. D., and J. R. Schermerhorn, Jr., J. Wong, and W. H. Money. 1982. "Multi-Institutional Arrangements in Health Care: Review, Analysis, and Proposal for Future Research." *Academy of Management Review* 7:67–79.

Galaskiewicz, J. 1978. "Hierarchical Patterns in a Community Interorganizational System." Paper presented at the American Sociological Association Meetings in San Francisco (August).

———. 1979a. *Exchange Networks and Community Politics*. Beverly Hills, Calif.: Sage.

———. 1979b. "The Structure of Community Organizational Networks." *Social Forces* 57:1346–64.

Galaskiewicz, J., and D. Shatin. 1981. "Leadership and Networking among Neighborhood Human Service Organizations." *Administrative Science Quarterly* 26:434–48.

Galaskiewicz, J., and S. Wasserman. 1981. "A Dynamic Study of Change in a Regional Corporate Network." *American Journal of Sociology* 46:474–84.

Glassman, R. 1973. "Persistence and Loose Coupling." *Behavior Science* 18:83–98.

Gouldner, A. W. 1959. "Reciprocity and Autonomy in Functional Theory." In *Symposium on Sociological Theory*, ed. Llewellyn Gross. New York: Harper & Row.

Granovetter, M. 1973. "The Strength of Weak Ties." *American Journal of Sociology* 78:1360–80.

Haas, J. E., and T. E. Drabek. 1973. *Complex Organizations: A Sociological Perspective*. New York: Macmillan.

Hall, R. H., J. P. Clark, P. Giordano, P. V. Johnson, and M. Van Roekel. 1977. "Patterns of Interorganizational Relationships." *Administrative Science Quarterly* 22:457–74.

Hasenfeld, Y. 1972. "People Processing Organizations: An Exchange Approach." *American Sociological Review* 37:256–63.

Hirsch, P. 1972. "Processing Fads and Fashions: An Organization Set Analysis of Cultural Industry Systems." *American Journal of Sociology* 77:639–59.

———. 1975. "Organizational Effectiveness and the Institu-

tional Environment." *Administrative Science Quarterly* 20:327–44.

Hunter, F. 1953. *Community Power Structure*. Chapel Hill, N.C.: University of North Carolina Press.

Katz, D., and R. L. Kahn. 1967. *The Social Psychology of Organizations*. New York: Wiley.

Klonglan, G. E., C. L. Mulford, R. D. Warren, and J. M. Winkelpleck. 1975. "Creating Interorganizational Coordination: Project Report." Sociology report no. 122A, Department of Sociology, Iowa State University, Ames, Iowa.

Klonglan, G. E., R. D. Warren, J. M. Winkelpleck, and S.K. Paulson. 1976. "Interorganizational Measurement in Social Services Sector: Differences by Hierarchical Level." *Administrative Science Quarterly* 21:675–87.

Knoke, D., and D. L. Rogers. 1979. "A Blockmodel Analysis of Interorganizational Networks." *Sociology and Social Research* 64:28–52.

Kunde, J. E., D. E. Berry and Associates. 1979. "Negotiating the Cities Future." *Nation's Cities Weekly*, 26 November.

Landau, M. 1969. "Redundancy, Rationality, and the Problem of Duplication and Overlap." *Public Administration Review* 39:346–58.

Laumann, E. O., J. Galaskiewicz, and P. V. Marsden. 1978a. "Community Structure as Interorganizational Linkages." *Annual Review of Sociology* 4:455–84.

Laumann, E. O., P. V. Marsden, and J. Galaskiewicz. 1978b. "Community-Elite Influence Structures: Extension of a Network Approach." *American Journal of Sociology* 83:594–631.

Leblebici, H., and D. A. Whetten. 1982. "The Concept of Horizontal Hierarchy and the Organization of Interorganizational Networks: A Comparative Analysis." Working paper, College of Commerce and Business Administration, University of Illinois.

Lehman, E. W. 1975. *Health Care: Explorations in Interorganizational Relations*. Beverly Hills, Calif: Sage.

Lindblom, C. E. 1965. *The Intelligence of Democracy*. New York: Free Press.

Metcalfe, J. L. 1976. "Organizational Strategies and Interorganizational Networks." *Human Relations* 29:32–7, 327–43.

Miller, J., J. R. Lincoln, and J. Olson. 1981. "Rationality and Equity in Professional Networks: Gender and Race as Factors in the Stratification of Interorganizational Systems." *American Journal of Sociology* 87:308–35.

Mott, B. J. F. 1968. *Anatomy of a Coordinating Council: Implications for Planning*. Pittsburgh: University of Pittsburgh Press.

Paulson, S. K. 1976. "A Theory and Comparative Analysis of Interorganizational Dyads." *Rural Sociology* 41:311–29.

Pennings, J. 1980. *Interlocking Directorates*. San Francisco: Jossey-Bass.

Perrucci, R., and M. Pilisuk. 1970. "Leaders and Ruling Elites: The Interorganizational Bases of Community Power." *American Sociological Review* 35:1040–56.

Pfeffer, J. 1972. "Merger as a Response to Organizational Interdependence." *Administrative Science Quarterly* 17:382–94.

Pfeffer, J., and H. Leblebici. 1973. "Executive Recruitment and the Development of Interfirm Organization." *Administrative Science Quarterly* 18:445–61.

Pfeffer, J., and P. Nowak. 1976. "Joint Ventures and Interorganizational Interdependence." *Administrative Science Quarterly* 21:398–418.

Phillips, A. 1960. "A Theory of Interfirm Organization." *Quarterly Journal of Economics* 74:602–13.

Porter, D. O., and E. A. Olsen. 1976. "Some Central Issues in Government Centralization and Decentralization." *Public Administration Review* 36:72–84.

Provan, K. G. 1982. "Interorganizational Linkages and Influence over Decision Making." *The Academy of Management Journal* 25:443–51.

Provan, K. G., J. M. Beyer, and C. Kruytbosch. 1980. "Environmental Linkages and Power in Resource-Dependence Relations Between Organizations." *Administrative Science Quarterly* 25:200–25.

Raelin, J. A. 1980. "A Mandated Basis of Interorganizational Relations: The Legal-Political Network." *Human Relations* 33:57–68.

Reid, W. J. 1969. "Interorganizational Coordination in Social Welfare: A Theoretical Approach to Analysis and Intervention." In *Readings in Community Organizations Practice*, ed. R. M. Kramer and H. Specht, 188–200. Englewood Cliffs, N.J.: Prentice-Hall.

Reve, T., and L. W. Stern. 1978. "Interorganizational Relations in Marketing Channels." *Academy of Management Review* 4:405–16.

Rogers, D. L., and E. Glick. 1973. "Planning for Interagency Cooperation in Rural Development." *Card Report U.S. Center for Agricultural and Rural Development*. Ames, Iowa: Iowa State University Press.

Rogers, D. L., and D. A. Whetten and Associates. 1982. *Interorganizational Coordination: Theory, Research, and Implementation*. Ames, Iowa: Iowa State University Press.

Salancik, G. S. 1979. "Interorganizational Dependence and Responsiveness to Affirmative Action: The Case of Women and Defense Contractors." *Academy of Management Journal* 22:375–94.

Schermerhorn, J. R., Jr. 1975. "Determinants of Interorganizational Cooperation." *Academy of Management Journal* 18, no. 4 (December): 846–56.

Schmidt, S. M., and T. A. Kochan. 1977. "Interorganizational Relationships: Patterns and Motivations." *Administrative Science Quarterly* 22:220–34.

Simon, H. 1969. "The Architecture of Complexity." In *Organizations*, ed. Joseph Litterer, vol. 2. New York: Wiley.

Stern, L. W., and J. Heskett. 1969. "Conflict Management in Interorganizational Relations: A Conceptual Framework." In *Distribution Channels: Behavior Dimensions*, ed. L. Stern. Boston: Houghton Mifflin.

Stern, L. W., B. Sternthal, and C. S. Craig. 1975. "Strategies for Managing Interorganizational Conflicts: A Laboratory Paradigm." *Journal of Applied Psychology* 60:472–82.

Stern, R. N. 1979. "The Development of Interorganizational Control Network: The Case of Intercollegiate Athletics." *Administrative Science Quarterly* 24:242–418.

———. 1981. "Competitive Influences in the Interorganizational Regulations of College Athletics." *Administrative Science Quarterly* 26:15–32.

Thompson, J. D. 1967. *Organizations in Action*. New York: McGraw-Hill.

Turk, H. 1973. "Comparative Urban Structure from an Interorganizational Perspective." *Administrative Science Quarterly* 18:37–55.

Van de Ven, A. H. 1976. "On the Nature, Formation and Maintenance of Relations Among Organizations." *Academy of Management Review* 4:24–36.

Van de Ven, A. H., G. Walker, and J. Liston. 1979. "Coordination Patterns Within an Interorganizational Network." *Human Relations* 32:19–36.

Wamsley, G., and M. N. Zald. 1973. "The Political Economy Model of Public Organizations." *Public Administration Review* 33:62–73.

Warren R. L. 1967. "The Interorganizational Field as a Focus of Investigation." *Administrative Science Quarterly* 12:396–419.

Warren, R. L., A. Bergunder, and S. Rose. 1974. *The Structure of Urban Reform*. Lexington, Mass.: Heath.

Whetten, D. A. 1977. "Toward a Contingency Model for Designing Interorganizational Service Delivery Systems." *Organization and Administrative Sciences* 8:77–96.

———. 1978. "Coping with Incompatible Expectations: An Integrated Model of Role Conflict." *Administrative Science Quarterly* 23:254–71.

———. 1982. "Issues in Conducting Research." In *Interorganizational Coordination: Theory, Research and Implementation* by David Rogers and David Whetten and Associates. Ames, Iowa: Iowa State University Press.

Whetten, D. A., and H. Aldrich. 1979. "Organization Set Size and Diversity: Links Between People Processing Organizations and Their Environments." *Administration and Society* 11:251–82.

Whetten, D. A., and T. K. Leung. 1979. "The Instrumental Value of Interorganizational Relations: Antecedents and Consequences of Linkage Formation." *Academy of Management Journal* 22:325–44.

16

The design of effective reward systems

EDWARD E. LAWLER III

Reward systems are one of the most prominent and frequently discussed features of organizations. Indeed, the organizational behavior and personnel-management literature is replete with examples of their functional and dysfunctional roles (see, for example, Whyte 1955). Too seldom, however, do writers examine thoroughly the potential impact of reward systems on organizational effectiveness and how they relate to the strategic objectives of the organization.

This chapter will focus on the strategic design choices that are involved in managing a reward system, and their relationship to organizational effectiveness, rather than on specific pay-system technologies. The details of pay-system design and management have been described in numerous books (e.g., Henderson 1979; Patten 1977; and Ellig 1982). The underlying assumption in this chapter is that a properly designed reward system can be a key contributor to organizational effectiveness. But careful analysis is required of the role reward systems should play in the strategic plan of the organization.

OBJECTIVES OF REWARD SYSTEMS

Reward systems in organizations have six kinds of impact that can influence organizational effectiveness: at-

Financial support for this paper was provided by the Office of Naval Research under Contract N00014-81-K-0048; NR 170-923.

traction and retention of employees, motivation of performance, motivation of skill development, cultural effects, reinforcement of structure, and cost.

Attraction and retention

Research on job choice, career choice, and turnover clearly shows that the rewards an organization offers influences who is attracted to work for it and who will continue to work for it (see, for example, Lawler 1973; Mobley 1982). Overall, organizations that give the greatest rewards tend to attract and retain the most people. High reward levels apparently lead to high satisfaction, which in turn leads to lower turnover. Individuals who are currently satisfied with their jobs expect to remain so, and thus want to stay with the same organization.

The relationship between turnover and organizational effectiveness is not simple. It is often assumed that the lower the turnover rate, the more effective the organization is likely to be. Turnover is expensive. Replacing an employee can cost at least five times his or her monthly salary (Macy and Mirvis 1976). However, not all turnover is harmful to organizational effectiveness. Organizations may actually profit from losing poor performers. In addition, if replacement costs are low, as they may be in unskilled jobs, it can be more cost effective to keep wages low and accept high turnover. Thus, the effect of turnover depends on its rate, the employees affected, and their replacement cost.

The objective should be to design a reward system that is very effective at retaining the most valuable employees. To do this, the system must distribute rewards in a way that will lead the more valuable employees to feel satisfied when they compare their rewards with those received by individuals performing similar jobs in other organizations. The emphasis here is on *external* comparisons, for it is the prospect of a better situation elsewhere that induces an employee to leave. One way to accomplish this is to reward everyone at a level above that prevailing in other organizations. This strategy can be very costly, however. Moreover, it can cause feelings of intraorganizational inequity. The better performers are likely to feel unfairly treated if they are rewarded at the same level as poor performers in the same organization, even though they fare better than their counterparts elsewhere. They may not quit, but they are likely to be dissatisfied, complain, look for internal transfers, and mistrust the organization.

The best solution is to have competitive reward levels and to base rewards on performance. This should satisfy the better performers and encourage them to stay with the organization. It should also attract achievement-oriented individuals, because they like environments in which their performance is rewarded. However, it is important that the better performers receive *significantly more* rewards than poor performers. Rewarding them only slightly more may simply make the better and poorer performers *equally* dissatisfied.

In summary, managing turnover means managing anticipated satisfaction. Ideally, rewards will be effectively related to performances. When this difficult task cannot be accomplished, an organization can try to reward individuals at an above-average level. If turnover is costly, this should be a cost-effective strategy, even if it involves giving out expensive rewards.

Research has shown that absenteeism and satisfaction are related, although not as strongly as satisfaction and turnover. When the workplace is pleasant and satisfying, individuals come to work regularly; when it isn't, they don't.

One way to reduce absenteeism is to administer pay in ways that maximize satisfaction. Several studies have also shown that absenteeism can be reduced by tying pay bonuses and other rewards to attendance (Lawler 1981). This approach is costly, but sometimes less costly than absenteeism. In many ways such a system is easier to administer than a performance-based one, because attendance is more readily measured. It is a particularly useful strategy in situations where both the work content and the working conditions are poor and do not lend themselves to meaningful improvements. If such improvements are possible, they are often the most effective and cost-efficient way to deal with absenteeism.

Motivation of performance

Under certain conditions, reward systems have been shown to motivate performance (Lawler 1971; Vroom 1964). Employees must perceive that important rewards are tied in a timely fashion to effective performance. Individuals are inherently neither motivated nor unmotivated to perform effectively. Rather, they each use their own mental maps of what the world is like to choose behaviors that lead to outcomes that satisfy their needs. Thus, organizations get the kind of behavior that leads to the rewards their employees value. Performance motivation depends on the situation, how it is perceived, and the needs of people.

The most useful approach to understanding how people develop and act on their mental maps is called "expectancy theory" (Lawler 1973). Three concepts serve as the key building blocks of the theory.

PERFORMANCE-OUTCOME EXPECTANCY

Each individual mentally associates every behavior with certain outcomes (rewards or punishments). In other words, people believe that if they behave in a certain way, they will get certain things. Individuals may expect, for example, that if they produce ten units, they will receive their normal hourly pay rate, while if they produce fifteen units, they will also receive a bonus. Similarly, they may believe that certain levels of performance will lead to approval or disapproval from members of their work group or their supervisor. Each performance level can be seen as leading to a number of different kinds of outcomes.

ATTRACTIVENESS

Each outcome has a certain attractiveness for each individual. Valuations reflect individual needs and perceptions, which differ from one person to another. For example, some workers may value an opportunity for promotion because of their needs for achievement or power, while others may not want to leave their current work group because of needs for affiliation with others. Similarly, a pension plan may have much greater value for older workers than for young employees on their first job.

EFFORT-PERFORMANCE EXPECTANCY

Individuals also attach a certain probability of success to behavior. This expectancy represents the individual's perception of how hard it will be for him or her to achieve such behavior. For example, employees may have a strong expectancy (e.g., 90 percent) that if they put forth the effort, they can produce ten units an hour, but may feel that they have only a 50-50 chance of producing fifteen units an hour if they try.

Together, these concepts provide a basis for generalizing about motivation. An individual's motivation to behave in a certain way is greatest when he or she believes that the behavior will lead to certain outcomes (performance-outcome expectancy), feels that these outcomes are attractive, and believes that performance at a desired level is possible (effort-performance expectancy).

Given a number of alternative levels of behavior (ten, fifteen, or twenty units of production per hour, for example), a person will choose the level of performance with which the greatest motivational force is associated, as indicated by a combination of the relevant expectancies, outcomes, and values. In other words, he or she considers questions such as Can I perform at that level if I try? If I perform at that level, what will happen? and How do I feel about those things that will happen? The individual then decides to behave in a way that seems to have the best chance of producing positive, desired outcomes.

On the basis of these concepts, it is possible to construct a general model of behavior in organizational settings (see figure 16.1). Motivation is seen as a force impelling an individual to expend effort. Performance depends on both the level of the effort put forth *and* the individual's ability—which in turn reflects his or her skills, training, information, and talents. Effort thus combines with ability to produce a given level of performance. As a result of performance, the individual attains certain outcomes (rewards). The model indicates this relationship in a dotted line, reflecting the fact that people sometimes are not rewarded although they have performed. As this process of performance reward occurs repeatedly, the actual events provide information that influences an individual's perception (particularly expectancies) and thus influences motivation in the future. This is shown in the model by the line connecting the performance-outcome link with motivation.

Rewards can be both external and internal. When individuals perform at a given level, they can receive positive or negative outcomes from supervisors, coworkers, the organization's reward system, or other environmental sources. A second type of reward comes from the performance of the task itself (e.g., feelings of accomplishment, personal worth, achievement). In a sense individuals give these rewards to themselves when they feel they are deserved. The environment cannot give them or take them away directly; it can only make them possible.

The model also suggests that satisfaction is best thought of as a result of performance rather than as a cause of it. Strictly speaking, satisfaction does influence motivation in some ways. For instance, when it is perceived to come about as a result of performance, it can increase motivation because it strengthens people's beliefs about the consequences of performance. Also, satisfaction can lead to a decrease in the importance of certain outcomes (a satisfied need is no longer a motivation), and as a result, it can decrease motivation.

The expectancy model is a deceptively simple statement of the conditions that must exist if rewards are to motivate performance. It suggests that all an organization has to do is relate pay and other frequently valued rewards to obtainable levels of performance. But if the reward system is to be an effective motivator, the connection between performance and rewards must be visible, and a climate of trust and credibility must exist in the organization. The belief that performance will lead to rewards is essentially a prediction about the future. Individuals cannot make this kind of prediction unless they trust the system that is promising them the rewards. Unfortunately, it is not always clear how a climate of trust in the reward system can be established. However, as will be discussed later, research suggests that a high level of openness and the use of participation can contribute to trust in the pay system.

Skill development

Just as reward systems can motivate performance they can motivate skill development. They can do this by tying rewards to skill development. To a limited degree most pay-for-performance systems do this indirectly by re-

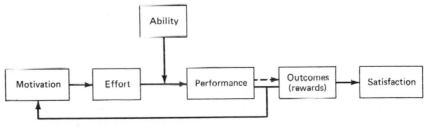

Figure 16.1   The expectancy-theory model

A person's motivation is a function of:

1. Effort-to-performance expectancies
2. Performance-to-outcome expectancies
3. Perceived attractiveness of outcomes

warding the performance that results from the skill. Pay systems that pay the holders of higher level, more complex jobs also reward skill development when and if it leads to obtaining a higher level job.

Technical ladders, which are often used in research and development settings, are intended to reward skill development more directly. As will be discussed later, some skill-based pay plans have recently been installed in some settings. They give individuals more pay as they develop specific skills. Like merit pay systems these systems are often difficult to manage because skill acquisition can be hard to measure. When they are well designed and administered, however, there is little question that they can motivate skill development (Lawler 1981).

The relationship between skill development and organizational effectiveness is not always a direct one. The nature of the technology an organization deals with or the availability of skilled labor may make this a low priority for an organization. Thus, although the reward system may be used to motivate skill development, in some instances this may not have a positive impact on organizational effectiveness.

Culture

Reward systems contribute to the overall culture or climate of an organization. Depending upon how they are developed, administered, and managed, reward systems can help create and maintain a human-resources–oriented, entrepreneurial, innovative, competence-based, bureaucratic, or participative culture.

Reward systems can shape culture precisely because of their important influence on motivation, satisfaction, and membership. The behaviors they evoke become the dominant patterns of behavior in the organization and lead to perceptions about what it stands for, believes in, and values.

Perhaps the most obvious connection between reward systems and culture concerns the practice of performance-based pay. A policy of linking—or not linking—pay and performance can have a dramatic impact on the culture because it so clearly communicates what the norms of performance are in the organization. Many other features of the reward system also influence culture. For example, relatively high pay levels can produce a culture in which people feel they are an elite group working for a top-flight company, while innovative pay practices such as flexible benefits can produce a culture of innovativeness. Finally, having employees participate in pay decisions can produce a participative culture in which employees are generally involved in

business decisions and as a result are committed to the organization and its success.

Reinforcement and definition of structure

The reward system can reinforce and define the organization's structure (Lawler 1981). Because this effect is often not fully considered in the design of reward systems, their structural impact may be unintended. This does not mean it is insignificant. Indeed, the reward system can help define the status hierarchy, the degree to which people in technical positions can influence people in line-management positions, and the kind of decision structure used. As will be discussed later, the key issues here seem to be the degree to which the reward system is hierarchical and the degree to which it allocates rewards on the basis of movements up the hierarchy.

Cost

Reward systems are often a significant cost factor. Indeed, the pay system alone may represent over 50 percent of the organization's operating cost. Thus, it is important in strategically designing the reward system to focus on how high these costs should be and how they will vary as a function of the organization's ability to pay. For example, a well-designed pay system might lead to higher costs when the organization has the money to spend and lower costs when it does not. An additional objective might be to have lower overall reward-system costs than business competitors.

In summary, reward systems in organizations should be assessed from a cost-benefit perspective. The cost can be managed and controlled and the benefits planned for. The key is to identify the outcomes needed for the organization to be successful and then to design the reward system in such a way that these outcomes will be realized.

RELATIONSHIP TO STRATEGIC PLANNING

Figure 16.2 presents a way of viewing the relationship between strategic planning and reward systems. It suggests that once the strategic plan is developed, the organization needs to focus on the kinds of human resources, climate, and behavior that are needed to make it effective. The next step is to design reward systems that will

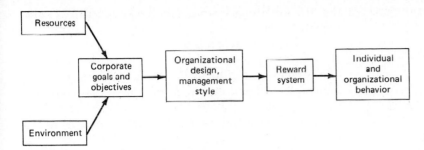

Figure 16.2 Goals and reward-system design

motivate the right kind of performance, attract the right kind of people, and create a supportive climate and structure.

Figure 16.3 suggests another way in which the reward system needs to be taken into consideration in strategic planning. Before the strategic plan is developed, it is important to assess a variety of factors, including the current reward system, and to determine what kind of behavior, climate, and structure they foster. This step is needed to ensure that the strategic plan is based on a realistic assessment of the organization's current condition and the changes likely to be needed to implement the new strategic plan. This point is particularly pertinent to organizations that are considering going into new lines of business, developing new strategic plans, and acquiring new divisions.

Often, new lines of business require a different behavior and therefore a different reward system. Simply putting the old reward system in place can actually lead to failure in the new business. On the other hand, developing a new reward system for the new business can cause problems in the old business because of the comparisons that will be made between different parts of the same organization. The need for reward system

changes must be carefully assessed before an organization enters into new business sectors.

DESIGN OPTIONS

Organizational reward systems can be designed and managed in virtually an infinite number of ways. A host of rewards can be distributed in a large number of ways. The rest of this chapter focuses on the visible extrinsic rewards that an organization can allocate to its members on a targeted basis: promotion, status symbols, and perquisites. Little attention will be given to such intrinsic rewards as feelings of responsibility, competence, and personal growth and development.

All organizational systems have a content or structural dimension as well as a process dimension. In a reward system, the content is the formal mechanisms, procedures, and practices (e.g., the salary structures, the performance-appraisal forms)—in short, the nuts and bolts of the system. Its communication and decision processes are also important. Key issues here are how much is revealed about how the reward system operates and how people are rewarded, and how much participation is allowed in the design and administration of the system. Many organizations administer rewards in a top-down, secretive way. Often this practice does not reflect a conscious choice. As discussed subsequently, organizations may wish to consider other ways that rewards can be administered.

Reward systems play important roles in organizational change efforts. They can aid or inhibit efforts to increase effectiveness. Ordinarily, major changes in other important organizational systems require a modification of the reward systems to ensure that all systems work well together. A key design decision then concerns the coordination of reward-system changes with other changes (for example, should they lead or lag?).

To begin the discussion of design choices, we will look at some key structural choices and then some key

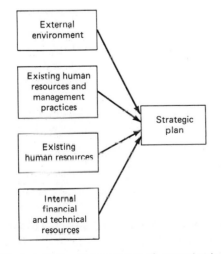

Figure 16.3 Determinants of strategic plan

process choices. Finally the issue of pay and organizational change will be considered.

STRUCTURAL DECISIONS

Bases for rewards

JOB BASED

Traditionally in organizations such rewards as pay and perquisites have been based on the type of job a person does. Indeed, with the exception of bonuses and merit salary increases, the standard policy in most organizations is to evaluate the job, not the person, and then to set the reward level. This approach is based on the assumption that job worth can be determined and that the person doing the job is worth only as much to the organization as the job itself is worth. This assumption is in many respects valid, because such techniques as job-evaluation programs make it possible to determine what other organizations are paying people to do the same or similar jobs. A job-based reward system assures an organization that its compensation costs are not dramatically out of line with those of its competitors, and it gives a somewhat objective basis to compensation practices.

SKILL BASED

An alternative to job-based pay that has recently been tried by a number of organizations is to pay individuals for their skills. In many cases this approach will not lead to pay rates very different from those of a job-based system. After all, people's skills are usually matched reasonably well with their jobs. A skill approach can, however, produce some different results in several respects. Often people have more skills than the job uses, in which case they would be paid more than under a job-based system. In other cases, newly appointed jobholders do not initially have all the skills associated with the position; they would have to earn the right to be paid whatever it is the job-related skills are worth.

Perhaps the most important changes introduced with skill-based or competence-based pay are in organizational climate and motivation. Instead of being rewarded for moving up the hierarchy, people are rewarded for increasing their skills and developing themselves. This policy can create a climate of concern for personal growth and development and produce a highly talented work force. It also can decrease the attractiveness of upward mobility and the traditional type of career progression. In factories where this system has been used, many people learn to perform multiple tasks, so that the work force becomes highly knowledgeable and flexible.

Skill-based pay tends to produce an interesting mix of positive and negative features as far as the organization is concerned (Lawler 1981). It typically produces somewhat higher pay levels for individuals, but this higher cost is usually offset by greater work-force flexibility. Lower staffing levels are also possible, there are fewer problems when absenteeism or turnover occur, and indeed absenteeism and turnover may be reduced, because people like the opportunity to utilize and be paid for a wide range of skills. On the other hand, skill-based pay can be rather challenging to administer. There is no easy way of determining how much a skill is worth, and skill assessment can often be difficult. Several systems have been developed for evaluating jobs and comparing them to the marketplace, but there are no analogous systems for workers' skills.

There are no well-established rules to determine which organizational situations best fit job-based pay and which best fit skill- or competence-based pay. In general, skill-based pay seems best suited to organizations that want to have a flexible, relatively permanent work force that is oriented toward learning, growth, and development. It also seems to fit particularly well with new plant start-ups and other situations in which the greatest need is for skill development. Despite its newness and the potential operational problems, skill-based pay seems to be a system that more and more organizations will be using.

PERFORMANCE BASED

Perhaps the key strategic decision made in the design of any reward system is whether or not it will be based on performance. Once this decision is made, other features of the system tend to fall into place. The major alternative to basing pay on performance is to tie it to seniority. Many government organizations, for example, base their rates on the job the person does and then on how long he or she has been in that job. In Japan, individual pay is often based on seniority, although individuals may receive bonuses based on corporate performance.

Most business organizations in the United States say that they reward individual performance and describe their pay system and their promotion system as merit-based. A true merit pay or promotion system is often more easily aspired to than done, however. It has been observed that many organizations would be better off if they did not try to relate pay and promotion to performance, but relied on other bases for motivating performance (Kerr 1975; Goldberg 1977; Hills 1979). It is difficult to specify what kind of performance is desired and often equally difficult to determine whether that performance has been demonstrated. There is ample evidence that a poorly designed and administered reward system can do more harm than good (see, for example, Whyte 1955; Lawler 1971). On the other hand, when pay is effectively related to the desired performance, it clearly helps to motivate, attract, and retain outstanding performers. Thus, when it is feasible, it is usually desirable to relate pay to performance.

How to relate pay to performance is often the most important strategic decision an organization makes. The options are numerous. The kind of pay reward that is given can vary widely, and many include such things as stock and cash. In addition, the interval between rewards can range from a few minutes to many years. Performance can be measured at various levels. Each individual may get a reward based on his or her own performance. In addition, rewards based on the performance of a particular group can be given to each of its members. Or everyone in the organization can be given an award based on the performance of the total organization. Finally, many different kinds of performance can be rewarded. For example, managers can be rewarded for sales increases, productivity volumes, their ability to develop their subordinates, their cost-reduction ideas, and so on.

Rewarding some behaviors and not others has clear implications for performance. Thus decisions about what is to be rewarded need to be made carefully and with attention to the overall strategic plan of the business (see, for example, Galbraith and Nathanson 1978; Salscheider 1981). Consideration needs to be given to such issues as short- versus long-term performance, risk taking versus risk aversion, division performance versus total corporate performance, ROI (return on investment) maximization versus sales growth, and so on. Once key performance objectives have been defined for the strategic plan, the reward system needs to be designed to motivate the appropriate performance. Decisions about such issues as the use of stock options (a long-term incentive), for example, should be made only after careful consideration of whether they will encourage the kind of behavior that is desired (see, for example, Crystal 1978; Ellig 1982). In large organizations, it is quite likely that the managers of different divisions should be rewarded for different kinds of performance. Growth businesses call for different reward systems from those of "cash cows," because the managers are expected to produce different results (see Stata and Maidique 1980, for an example).

A detailed discussion of the many approaches to relating pay and performance is beyond the scope of this chapter. Table 16.1 gives an idea of some of the design features that are possible in a reward system, and some of the advantages and disadvantages of each.

The first column in the table rates each plan in terms of its effectiveness in creating the perception that pay is tied to performance. In general, this indicates the degree to which the approach leads employees to believe that higher pay will follow good performance. Second, each plan is evaluated in terms of whether it produced the negative side effects often associated with performance-based pay plans (such as social ostracism of good performers, defensive behavior, and giving false data about performance). Third, each plan is rated as to its ability to encourage cooperation among employees. Finally, employee acceptance of the plan is indicated. The ratings were developed on the basis of a review of the literature and my experience with the different types of plans (see, for example, Lawler 1971).

Several patterns appear in the ratings. Pay to performance are seen as most closely linked in the individual plans; group plans are rated next; and organizational plans are rated lowest. In organizational plans, and to a lesser extent in group plans, an individual's pay is not directly a function of his or her behavior, but depends on the behavior of many others. In addition, when some types of performance measures (e.g., profits) are used, pay is influenced by external conditions that employees cannot control.

Bonus plans are generally seen as more closely tied to performance than pay-raise and salary-increase plans. The use of bonuses permit substantial variation in an individual's pay from one time period to another. With salary-increase plans, in contrast, such flexibility is very difficult because past raises tend not be rescinded.

Approaches that use objective measures of performance are rated higher than those that rely on subjective measures. In general, objective measures enjoy higher credibility; that is, employees will often accept the validity of an objective measure, such as sales volume or units produced, when they will not accept a superior's evaluation of their performance. When pay is tied to objective measures, therefore, it is usually clearer to employees that it is determined by performance. Objective measures are also often publicly measurable. Thus the relationship between performance and pay is much more visible than when it is tied to a subjective, nonverifiable measure, such as a supervisor's rating. Overall, the data suggest that individually based bonus plans that rely on objective measures produce the strongest perceived connection between pay and performance.

The ratings indicate that most plans have little tendency to produce negative side effects. The notable exceptions here are individual bonus and incentive plans below the management level. These plans often lead to situations in which good performance leads to social rejection and ostracism, so that employees present false per-

Table 16.1 Ratings of various pay-incentive plans

		Tie pay to performance	Negative side effects	Encourage cooperation	Employee acceptance
Salary reward					
Individual plan	Productivity	4	1	1	4
	Cost effectiveness	3	1	1	4
	Superiors' rating	3	1	1	3
Group plan	Productivity	3	1	2	4
	Cost effectiveness	3	1	2	4
	Superiors' rating	2	1	2	3
Organizational plan	Productivity	2	1	3	4
	Cost effectiveness	2	1	2	4
Bonus					
Individual plan	Productivity	5	3	1	2
	Cost effectiveness	4	2	1	2
	Superiors' rating	4	2	1	2
Group plan	Productivity	4	1	3	3
	Cost effectiveness	3	1	3	3
	Superiors' rating	3	1	3	3
Organizational plan	Productivity	3	1	1	4
	Cost effectiveness	3	1	3	4
	Profit	2	1	2	4

Note: On a scale of 1 to 5, 1 = low and 5 = high.

formance data and restrict their production. These side effects are particularly likely to appear where trust is low and subjective productivity standards are used.

In terms of the third criterion—encouraging cooperation—the ratings are generally higher for group and organizational plans than for individual plans. Under group and organizational plans, it is generally to everyone's advantage that an individual work effectively, because all share in the financial fruits of higher performance. This is not true under an individual plan. As a result, good performance is much more likely to be supported and encouraged by others when group and organizational plans are used.

Most performance-based pay plans achieve only moderate employee acceptance. The ratings show individual bonus plans to be least acceptable, particularly among nonmanagement employees, presumably because of their tendency to encourage competitive relationships between employees and the difficulty of administering such plans fairly.

No one performance-based pay plan represents a panacea, and it is unlikely that any organization will ever be completely satisfied with the approach it chooses. Furthermore, some of the plans that make the greatest contributions to organizational effectiveness do not make the greatest contributions to quality of work life, and vice versa. Still, the situation is not completely hopeless.

When all factors are taken into account, group and organizational bonus plans that are based on objective data receive high ratings, as do individual-level salary-increase plans.

Many organizations employ multiple or combination reward systems. For example, they may use a salary-increase system that rewards workers for their individual performance while at the same time giving everybody in the division or plant a bonus based on divisional performance. Some plans measure group or company performance, calculate the bonus pool generated by the performance of a group, and then divide it among group members on the basis of individual performance. By rewarding workers for both individual and group performance, the organization tries to motivate individuals to perform all needed behaviors (see, for example, Lincoln 1951; Fox 1979).

A common error in the design of many pay-for-performance systems is the tendency to focus on measurable short-term operating results because they are quantifiable and regularly obtained in any case. In particular, many organizations reward their top managers on the basis of quarterly or annual profitability (Fox 1979). Such a scheme can make managers very short-sighted in their behavior and encourage them to ignore strategic objectives important to the long-term profitability of the organization. A similar error is the tendency to depend on completely subjective performance appraisals for the allocation of pay rewards. There is considerable evidence that these performance appraisals are often biased and invalid, and instead of contributing to positive motivation and a good work climate that improves superior-subordinate relationships, they do just the opposite (see, for example, DeVries et al. 1981; Latham and Wexley 1981). Other common errors include the giving of too small rewards, failure to explain systems clearly, and poor administrative practices.

In summary, decision of whether to relate pay to performance is a crucial one in any organization. It can be a serious error to assume automatically that they should be related. A sound linkage can contribute greatly to organizational effectiveness. But a poor job can be harmful. Specifically, if performance is difficult to measure and/or rewards are difficult to distribute on the basis of performance, a pay-for-performance system can motivate counterproductive behaviors, invite lawsuits charging discrimination, and create a climate of mistrust, low credibility, and managerial incompetence. On the other hand, to declare that pay is unrelated to performance would be to give up a potentially important motivational tool and perhaps condemn the organization to a lower level of performance. The ideal, of course, is to foster conditions in which pay can be effectively related to performance and as a result contribute to the effectiveness of the organization.

Promotion, training opportunities, fringe benefits, and status symbols are important extrinsic rewards that, like pay, can be linked to performance. When they are linked to pay and are important, they, like pay, can motivate performance. The issues involved in relating them to performance are very similar to those involved in relating pay to performance, thus they will not be discussed in detail. As a general rule they are not usually tied to performance in organizations to the degree that pay is. They also are less flexible than is pay. This is, they are harder to give in varying amounts and to take away once they have been given.

Market position

The reward structure of an organization influences behavior partially as a function of how the size of its rewards compares to what other organizations give. Organizations frequently have well-developed policies about how their pay levels should compare with the pay levels in other companies. For example, some companies (e.g., IBM) feel it is important to be a leader and consciously pay more than any of the companies with which they compete. Other companies are content to set their pay levels at or below the market for the people they hire. This structural issue in the design of reward systems is

a critical one because it can strongly influence the kind of people that are attracted and retained by an organization as well as the turnover rate and the number of job applicants. Simply stated, organizations that pay above market end up attracting and retaining more people. From a business point of view this policy may pay off for them, particularly if turnover is a costly factor in the organization and if the business strategy requires a stable, highly talented staff.

On the other hand, if many of the jobs in the organization are low skilled and people are readily available in the labor market to do them, then a corporate strategy of high pay may not be effective. It can increase labor costs without offsetting benefits. Of course, organizations need not pay above market for all their jobs. Indeed, some organizations identify certain key skills that they need and pay generously for them, while offering average or below-average pay for other skills. This approach has some obvious business advantages, because it allows the organization to attract critically needed skills and at the same time to control costs.

Although it is not often recognized, the market position that a company adopts with respect to its reward systems can also affect organization climate. For example, a policy of paying above market can make people feel that they are members of an elite organization that employs only competent people and that they are indeed fortunate to be there. A policy that awards extra pay to certain skilled employees but leaves the rest of the organization at a lower pay level can cause divisive social pressures within the organization.

Finally, some organizations try to offer more noncash compensation than the average as a way of competing for the talent they need. They talk in terms of producing an above-average quality of work life, and stress not only hygiene factors but interesting and challenging work. This stance potentially can be a very effective one and could give the organization a competitive edge, at least in attracting people who value these things. Still other organizations stress such noncash rewards as status symbols and perquisites. This approach also can be effective in attracting certain kinds of people.

In summary, the market position and mix of an organization's total reward package has a critical effect on both the behavior of members and the climate of the organization. This decision needs to be carefully related to the general business strategy of the organization, in particular, to the kind of human resources needed and the organization climate desired.

Internal/external—pay-comparison oriented

Organizations differ in the degree to which they strive toward internal equity in their pay and reward systems.

An internal-equity-oriented company tries to see that individuals doing similar work will be paid the same even though they are in very different parts of the country and/or in different businesses. Some corporations (e.g., IBM) base their national pay structure on the highest pay that a job receives anywhere in the country. Organizations that do not stress internal equity typically focus on the external labor market as the key determinant of what somebody should be paid. Although this approach does not necessarily produce different pay for people doing the same job, it may. For example, two industries—say, electronics and automobiles—may differ significantly in what they pay for the same job.

The internal-equity approach has both advantages and disadvantages. It can facilitate the transfer of people from one location to another, because there will be no pay difference to contend with. Similarly, it avoids the problems of rivalry and dissatisfaction that can develop within the organization if one location or division pays more than another. In addition, it can produce an organizational climate of homogeneity and the feeling that all work for the same company and all are treated fairly.

On the other hand, a focus on internal equity can be very expensive, particularly if pay rates across a diversified corporation are set at the highest level that the market demands anywhere in the corporation (Salscheider 1981). If it pays much more than is necessary to attract and retain good people, the organization may become noncompetitive in certain businesses and find that it has to limit itself to businesses in which its pay structures permit competitive labor costs. Overly high labor costs have, for example, often made it difficult for auto and oil and gas companies to compete in new business areas.

In summary, the difference between focusing on external equity and internal equity is a crucial one in the design of pay systems. It can influence the organization's cost structure as well as its climate and behavior. The general rule is that highly diversified companies are pulled more strongly toward an external market orientation, while organizations that are based on a single industry or single technology typically find themselves more comfortable with an internal-equity emphasis.

Centralized/decentralized reward strategy

Closely related to the issue of internal versus external equity is the question of centralization. Organizations that adopt a centralized-reward-system strategy typically make the corporate staff responsible for seeing that such things as pay practices are similar throughout the organization. They ordinarily develop standard pay grades and pay ranges, standardized job-evaluation systems, and perhaps standardized promotion systems. In decentralized organizations, decisions about pay, promotion, and other rewards are left to local option. Sometimes the corporations suggest broad guidelines or principles to follow, but the day-to-day administration and design of the system is left up to the local entity.

The advantages of a centralized structure rest primarily in the expertise that can be accumulated at the central level and the homogeneity that is produced in the organization. This homogeneity can lead to a clear image of the corporate climate, feelings of internal equity, and the belief that the organization stands for something. It also eases the job of communicating and understanding what is going on in different parts of the organization. The decentralized strategy allows for local innovation and for closely fitting reward practices to the particular business.

There is no one right choice between the centralized and decentralized approaches to reward system design and administration. Overall, the decentralized system tends to make the most sense when the organization is involved in businesses that face different markets and perhaps are at different points in their life cycles (Greiner 1972; Galbraith and Nathanson 1978). It allows variation in practices that can give a competitive advantage to one part of the business but may prove to be a real hindrance in another. For example, such perquisites as cars are often standard operating procedure in one business but not in another. Similarly, extensive bonuses may be needed to attract one group of people, for example, oil-exploration engineers, but not others, for example, research scientists. Overall, then, an organization needs to look carefully at its mix of businesses and the degree to which it wants a single set of principles or policies to prevail across all its operating divisions, and then decide whether a centralized or decentralized reward strategy is likely to be more effective.

Degree of hierarchy

Closely related to the issue of job-based versus competence-based pay is the strategic decision concerning the hierarchical nature of the organization's reward systems. Often no formal decision is ever made to have a relatively hierarchical or relatively egalitarian approach to rewards. A hierarchical approach simply happens because it is so consistent with the general way organizations are run. Hierarchical systems usually pay people more money and give them greater perquisites and symbols of office as they move higher up the organization ladder. This approach strongly reinforces the traditional hierarchical power relationships in the organization and fosters a climate of different status and power levels. In some cases, a hierarchical reward system may include more levels than the formal organization chart, creating additional status differences in the organization.

The alternative to a hierarchical system is one that downplays differences in rewards and perquisites based only on hierarchical level. For example, in large corporations that adopt an egalitarian stance to rewards (e.g., Digital Equipment Corporation), such privileges as private parking spaces, executive restrooms, and special entrances are eliminated. People from all levels in the organization eat together, work together, and travel together. Further, high levels of pay are not restricted to managers but can be earned by those who have worked their way up a technical ladder. This approach to rewards produces a distinctive climate in an organization, encouraging decision making by expertise rather than by hierarchy position, and minimizing status differentials in the organization.

In general, a steeply hierarchical system makes the most sense when an organization needs relatively rigid bureaucratic behavior, strong top-down authority, and a strong motivation for people to move up the organizational hierarchy. A more egalitarian approach fits with a more participative management style and the desire to retain technical specialists and experts in nonmanagement or lower-level-management roles. It is not surprising, therefore, that many of the organizations that emphasize egalitarian perquisites are in high-technology and knowledge-based industries.

Reward mix

The kind of rewards that organizations give to individuals can vary widely. Monetary rewards, for example, can take many forms, from stock to medical insurance. When cash rewards are translated into fringe benefits, perquisites, or other trappings of office, they may lose their value for some people and as a result may be a poor investment for the employer (see, for example, Nealy 1963; Lawler 1971). On the other hand, certain benefits can best be obtained through mass purchase, and therefore many individuals want the organization to provide them. In addition, certain status symbols or perquisites may be valued by some individuals beyond their actual dollar cost to the organization and thus represent good buys. Finally, as was mentioned earlier there often are some climate and organizational structure reasons for paying people in the form of perquisites and status symbols.

One interesting development in the area of compensation is the flexible or cafeteria-style benefit program (Fragner 1975; Lawler 1981). The theory is that if individuals are allowed to tailor their own reward packages to fit their particular needs, the organization will get the best value for its money, because it will give people only those things that they desire. Such an approach also has the advantage of treating individuals as mature adults rather than as dependent people who need their welfare looked after in a structured way. While flexible benefit programs have not yet been widely implemented, the results of experiments to date have been favorable, and there is reason to believe that other organizations may adopt this approach in the near future, because it can offer a strategic cost-benefit advantage in attracting and retaining certain types of employees.

Overall, the forms in which the organization rewards its members should be consistent with the climate of hopes to foster. For example, a flexible compensation package is highly congruent with a participative open organization climate that treats individuals as mature adults and wants to attract talented mature people. A highly status-symbol-oriented approach, on the other hand, may appeal to people who value position power and need a high level of visible reinforcement for their position. This would seem to fit best in a relatively bureaucratic organization that relies on position power and authority to carry out its actions.

PROCESS ISSUES AND REWARD ADMINISTRATION

Reward system design and administration raise numerous process issues. Indeed, process issues are confronted more frequently than structure and content issues, because organizations must constantly make reward-system management, implementation, and communication decisions while structures tend to be relatively firmly fixed in place. Rather than discussing specific process issues here, the focus will be on broad process themes that can be used to characterize the way reward systems are designed and administered.

Communication policy

Organizations differ widely in how much information they communicate about their reward systems. At one extreme, some organizations are extremely secretive, particularly in the area of pay. They forbid people to talk about their individual rewards, give minimal information to individuals about how rewards are decided upon and allocated, and have no publicly disseminated policies about such things as market position, the approach to gathering market data, and potential increases and rewards for individuals. At the other extreme, some organizations are so open that everyone's pay is a matter of public record, as is the overall organization pay philosophy (many new high-involvement plants operate this way; see, for example, Lawler 1978; Walton 1980). In addition, all promotions are subject to open job postings, and in some instances peer groups discuss the individual's eligibility for promotion.

The difference between an open and a closed communication policy in the area of rewards is enormous. There is no clear right or wrong approach. The issue is rather to choose a position on the continuum from open to secretive that is supportive of the overall climate and types of behavior needed for organizational effectiveness. An open system tends to encourage people to ask questions, share data, and ultimately be involved in decisions. A secretive system tends to put people in a more dependent position, to keep power concentrated at the top, and to allow an organization to keep its options open with respect to commitments to individuals. Secrecy can lead to considerable distortion in people's beliefs about the rewards given to other organization members, and can create a low-trust environment in which the relationship between pay and performance is not clear (see, for example, Lawler 1971; Steele 1975). Thus, a structurally sound pay system may end up being rather ineffective because its strong secrecy policies open it to misperceptions.

Open systems put considerable pressure on organizations to do an effective job of administering rewards. Thus, if such difficult-to-defend policies as merit pay are to be implemented, considerable time and effort needs to be invested in pay administration. If such policies are poorly administered, strong pressures usually develop to eliminate discrimination and pay everyone the same (see, for example, Burroughs 1982). Ironically, therefore, if an organization wants to spend little time administering rewards but still wants to base pay on merit, secrecy may be the best policy, although secrecy in turn may limit the effectiveness of the merit pay plan.

Decision-making practices

Closely related to the issue of communication is the matter of how decisions about compensation are to be made. If individuals are to be actively involved in decisions concerning reward systems, they need to have information about policy and actual practice. Open communication makes it possible to involve a wide range of people in the decision-making process. Secrecy by its very nature limits the number of people who can be involved in pay decisions.

It is important to distinguish between decisions concerning the design and ongoing administration of reward systems. Traditionally, of course, organizations have made both design and administration decisions in a top-down manner. But it is possible to adopt a different decision-making style for each type of decision.

Systems typically have been designed by top management with the aid of staff support and administered by strict reliance on the chain of command. The assumption has been that this approach provides the proper checks and balances in the system and locates decision making where the expertise rests. In many cases this is a valid assumption and certainly fits well with an organizational management style that emphasizes hierarchy, bureaucracy, and control through the use of extrinsic rewards. It does not fit, however, with an organization that believes in more open communication, higher levels of employee involvement, and control through individual commitment to policies. Nor does it fit when expertise is broadly spread throughout the organization, as is often true in companies that rely heavily on knowledge workers or spend a great deal of effort training their people to become expert in technical functions.

Some organizations have experimented with involving employees in the design of pay systems (Lawler 1981). Favorable results have generally been achieved when employees help design their own bonus system. They tend to raise important issues and provide expertise not normally available to the designers of the system. And perhaps more importantly, once the system is designed, it is well accepted and understood. Employee involvement often makes possible a rapid start-up of the system and creates a commitment to see it survive long-term. In other cases systems have been designed by line managers, because they are the ones that need to maintain it. Unless they have had an opportunity for design input, it often is unrealistic to expect line people to have the same level of commitment to the pay system as the staff people have.

Some organizations have also experimented with having peer groups and low-level supervisory people handle the day-to-day decision making about who should receive pay increases and how jobs should be evaluated and placed in pay structures. The best examples are the new participative plants that use skill-based pay (see, for example, Walton 1980). In these plants, the work group typically reviews an individual's performance and decides whether he or she has acquired the new skills. This approach appears to work well. Peers often have the best information about performance and thus are in a good position to make a performance assessment. In traditional organizations their expertise is of no use, because they lack the motivation to give valid feedback and to respond responsibly. In more participative open systems, this motivational problem seems to be less severe, and as a result involvement in decision making is more effective.

In a few cases, executives have been asked to assess each other in a peer-group reward system (e.g., in Graphic Controls Corporation). Again, this approach can apparently work well in an organization that has a history of open and effective communication. Deciding on rewards is clearly not an easy task, and thus should not be assigned to a group unless members have good confrontation skills and can talk openly and directly about each other's performance.

Overall, there is evidence that some participative approaches to reward systems can be effective because of their congruence with the overall style and because the skills and norms needed to make them work are already in place. In more traditional organizations, the typical top-down approach to reward-system design and administration probably remains the best. From a strategic point of view, then, the decision about how much participation is desirable in reward-system design and administration depends on whether a participative, high-involvement type of organization is best suited to accomplish the strategic objectives of the business. If so, then participation in pay decisions and reward-system decisions should be considered.

In these situations the initial change effort is the installation of a system of bonuses based on improvements in productivity. In the case of the Scanlon Plan, attempts are also made to build participative problem-solving groups into the organization, but the clear emphasis is on the gain-sharing formula and the financial benefits of improved productivity. The participative management structure is intended to facilitate productivity improvement, which in turn will result in gains to be shared. Not surprisingly, once gain-sharing starts and factors inhibiting productivity are identified, other changes follow. Typical of these are improvements in the organization structures, the design of jobs and work, and additional training programs. The gain-sharing plan itself provides a strong motivation to swiftly and effectively deal with those issues.

Other reward system changes can also lead to broader organizational change efforts. For example, the introduction of skill-based pay can potentially prompt a broad movement to participation because it gives people the skills and knowledge they need to participate. The movement to a more flexible fringe-benefit program can change organizational climate by creating one of innovation in the area of human-resource management.

In a somewhat different vein, a dramatic change in the pay-for-performance system can be very effective in shaping an organization's strategic directions. For example, installing bonus systems that reward previously neglected performance indicators can dramatically shift the directions of an organization. Similarly, a long-term bonus plan for executives can lead them to change their time horizons and their decision-making practices in important ways.

REWARD SYSTEMS AND ORGANIZATIONAL CHANGE

In many major organizational changes, it is difficult to alter all the relevant systems in the organization simultaneously. Typically one change leads to another. Modification of the reward systems may either lead or lag in the overall change process.

Reward as a lead

Perhaps the most widely discussed example of pay as a lead change is the use of a gain-sharing plan to improve plant productivity (Moore and Ross 1978; Lawler 1981).

Rewards as a lag

In most major organization change efforts, pay is a lag factor. As an organization moves toward participative management, for example, the initial thrust often comes in such areas as team building, job redesign, and quality circles. It is only after these practices have been in place for some time that the organization makes the associated changes in the reward system. Often, the organization does not originally anticipate a need to revise the reward system. But because all organizational systems are interconnected, it is almost inevitable that major changes in strategic direction or management style and practices will require that changes be made in the reward system as well.

New participative plants represent an interesting example of the simultaneous installation of participative reward systems and other participative practices (Lawler 1981). The success of these plants is probably due in part to the fact that all their systems have operated in a participative manner from the outset.

Rewards as a motivator of change

Major strategic changes are often difficult to accomplish even though they don't involve a change in management style. The forces of equilibrium have the effect of canceling out many changes. To the extent that changing one component of an organizational system reduces its congruence with other components, energy will develop to limit, encapsulate, or reverse the change. In addition, attention may be diverted from other important tasks by the need to direct a change, deal with resistance, and cope with the problems created by change.

Management is therefore faced with two key tasks if change is to be brought about. The first is *motivating change*—overcoming natural resistance and encouraging individuals to behave in ways that are consistent with both the immediate change goals and long-range corporate strategy. The second major task is *managing change.*

It is useful to think of organizational changes in terms of transitions (Beckhard and Harris 1977). The organization exists in a current state (C). An image has been developed of a future state of the organization (F). The period between C and F can be thought of as the transition period (T). The question is how to manage the transition. Too often, however, managers overlook the transition state, assuming that all that is needed is to design that best possible future. They think of change as simply a mechanical or procedural detail.

In most situations, the management systems and structures developed to manage either C or F are simply not appropriate for the management of T. They are steady-state management systems, designed to run organizations already in place rather than transitional management systems. During the transition period, different systems, and specifically different reward systems, may be needed temporarily. Many change efforts are resisted because organization members see them as a threat to their pay level. Particularly when the present system is highly standardized and tied to objective measures, such as the number of subordinates, people may resist a reorganization or other type of change whose impact on their pay is unclear but potentially negative. There is no magic formula for overcoming this resistance, but two approaches can help.

First, a floor should be put under individual pay rates throughout the transition period. That is, no one should have to fear losing pay during the change process. This point is critical in the case of a major reorganization, which may require some people to give up some subordinates and responsibilities, and to accept a lower salary if their jobs were reevaluated. If this problem is likely to be severe, the organization may want to assure individuals that their pay will not be cut, even after the change is in place.

A second important step is to appoint a group of high-level managers to develop an approach to compensation that will fit the new organization. This group should articulate a corporate rewards philosophy that includes the following:

1. The goals of the pay system
2. How the pay system will fit the new organizational structure
3. The fit between the management style of the organization and the process used to administer the pay system
4. How the pay system will be managed once it is developed

There are several reasons for developing a compensation system in this way. First, a philosophical base is needed for an effective pay system. More and more evidence is accumulating that, unless supported by some sort of widely accepted philosophy, corporate pay administration ends up being haphazard and a source of internal conflict. A philosophy cannot answer all the problems associated with rewards, but it can at least provide a touchstone against which new practices, policies, and decisions can be tested.

A second advantage of the group approach is that it will give key individuals a chance to influence how they will be paid in the future. A big unknown in the new organization thus becomes something under their control, rather than a potentially threatening factor about the reorganized structure. Moreover, by seriously considering how the pay system will have to change to fit other changes, the group can prevent "surprise" pay-system problems from occurring once the other changes have been implemented. Finally, as discussed further below, by assuring that an acceptable supporting pay system will exist, the group can promote institutionalization of the new organization structure.

Putting a floor under existing salaries helps reduce resistance, but it does nothing to encourage good implementation of change. It is possible, however, to use the reward system to support implementation of the reorganization. First of all, the organization needs to make it clear that the jobs and associated rewards given to managers after the transition will depend on their contribution to an effective transition process. One-time bonuses and payments may also ease the transition. In most cases, it makes sense to award these one-time financial payments on a group basis rather than on an individual basis.

It is important that transition goals specify, as precisely as possible, both the rate at which change is introduced and the process used to introduce it. One-time bonuses should be tied to meeting these goals, which can be a critical ingredient in the effective motivation of change. The organization should specify target dates for particular implementation events, such as having a new unit operating or completing the relocation of personnel. In addition, measures should be defined for the process used to implement change; examples might include people's understanding of the new system, the degree to which it was explained to them, the level of turnover among people that the organization wished to retain, signs of stress among people involved in the transition, and the willingness of managers to give up people to other parts of the organization where they can make a greater contribution.

Rewards, goals, and performance measures are critical tools in managing the transition process. They can help to assure that the change strategy is implemented rapidly and in a way that minimizes the dysfunctional

consequences for both the organization and the people who work in it.

REWARD SYSTEM CONGRUENCE

For simplicity, we have so far treated each reward-system design feature as an independent factor. Overall system congruence is an important consideration, however. There is considerable evidence that reward-system design features affect each other and thus should be supportive of the same types of behavior, the same business strategy, and reflect the same overall managerial philosophy.

Table 16.2 illustrates one effort to define congruent sets of reward-system practices (Lawler 1977). The two management philosophies portrayed here are the traditional bureaucratic management style and a participative employee-involvement strategy. Their reward-system practices are different in every respect. The practices associated with traditional bureaucratic models tend to be more secretive, top-down, and oriented toward producing regularity in behavior. The participative practices, in contrast, encourage self-development, openness, em-

Table 16.2 Appropriate reward-system practices

Reward system	Traditional or theory X	Participative or theory Y
Fringe benefits	Vary according to organizational level	Cafeteria—same for all levels
Promotion	All decisions made by top management	Open posting for all jobs; peer-group involvement in decision process
Status symbols	A great many carefully allocated on the basis of job position	Few present, low emphasis on organization level
Pay		
Type of system	Hourly and salary	All salary
Base rate	Based on job performed; high enough to attract job applicants	Based on skills; high enough to provide security and attract applicants
Incentive plan	Piece rate	Group and organization wide bonus; lump sum increase
Communication policy	Very restricted distribution of information	Individual rates, salary-survey data, and all other information made public
Decision-making locus	Top management	Close to location of person whose pay is being set

ployee involvement in reward-system allocation decisions, and ultimately more innovation and commitment to the organization.

Greiner (1972) and Galbraith and Nathanson (1978) have pointed out that reward-system practices need to be congruent with the maturity of the organization and the market in which the business operates. For example, rapidly developing businesses need to stress skill development, attraction, high-potential individuals, and incentives tied to business growth, while declining businesses need to reward expense reduction and to have a formalized job-evaluation system that closely tracks the market.

The reward system also needs to fit other features of the organization to ensure congruence in the total human-resource-management system. The reward system should be consistent with the way jobs are designed, the leadership style of the supervisors, and the types of career tracks available in the organization, to mention just a few examples. Unless this kind of fit exists, the organization will be riddled with conflicts, and the reward system practices may be canceled out by practices in other areas. For example, even the best performance-appraisal system will be ineffective unless accompanied by interpersonally competent supervisory behavior and jobs designed to allow for good performance measure (see DeVries et al. 1981).

CONCLUSION

An effective reward system should be designed to fit well with the other design features of the organization as well as with its business strategy. Thus there is no one best set of reward practices; indeed, it is impossible to design an effective reward system without knowing how other features of the organization are arrayed. Decisions about the reward system should be made in an interactive fashion: shaped by the business strategy, tentative reward-system design choices would then be tested against how other features of the organization are being designed. The ultimate goal is to develop an integrated human-resource-management strategy that is consistent in the ways it encourages people to behave, attracts the kind of people that can support the business strategy, and encourages them to behave appropriately.

REFERENCES

Beckhard, R., and R. Harris. 1977. *Organizational Transitions: Managing Complex Change.* Reading, Mass.: Addison-Wesley.

Burroughs, J. D. 1982. "Pay Secrecy and Performance: The Psychological Research." *Compensation Review* 14, no. 3:44–54.

Crystal, G. S. 1978. *Executive Compensation.* 2d ed. New York: AMACOM.

DeVries, D. L., A. M. Morrison, S. L. Shullman, and M. L. Gerlach. 1981. *Performance Appraisal on the Line.* New York: Wiley, Interscience.

Ellig, B. R. 1982. *Executive Compensation—A Total Pay Perspective.* New York: McGraw-Hill.

Fox, H. 1979. *Top Executive Bonus Plans.* New York: Conference Board.

Fragner, B. N. 1975. "Employees' 'Cafeteria' Offers Insurance Options." *Harvard Business Review* 53:2–4.

Galbraith, J. R., and D. A. Nathanson. 1978. *Strategy Implementation: The Role of Structure and Process.* St. Paul, Minn.: West.

Greiner, L. 1972. "Evolution and Revolution as Organizations Grow." *Harvard Business Review* 50, no. 4:37–46.

Goldberg, M. H. 1977. "Another Look at Merit Pay Programs." *Compensation Review* 3:20–28.

Henderson, R. I. 1979. *Compensation Management: Rewarding Performance.* 2d ed. Reston, Va.: Reston.

Hills, F. S. 1979. "The Pay-for-Performance Dilemma." *Personnel*, no. 5:23–31.

Kerr, S. 1975. "On the Folly of Rewarding A, While Hoping for B." *Academy of Management Journal* 18:769–83.

Latham, G. P., and K. N. Wexley. 1981. *Increasing Productivity Through Performance Appraisal.* Reading, Mass.: Addison-Wesley.

Lawler, E. E. 1971. *Pay and Organizational Effectiveness: A Psychological View.* New York: McGraw-Hill.

———. 1973. *Motivation in Work Organizations.* Monterey, Calif.: Brooks/Cole.

———. "Reward Systems." In *Improving Life at Work*, ed. J. R. Hackman and J. L. Suttle, pp. 163–226. Santa Monica, Calif.: Goodyear.

———. 1978. "The New Plant Revolution." *Organizational Dynamics* 6, no. 3:2–12.

———. 1981. *Pay and Organization Development.* Reading, Mass.: Addison-Wesley.

Lincoln, J. F. 1951. *Incentive Management.* Lincoln Electric Co., Cleveland, Ohio.

Macy, B. A., and P. H. Mirvis. 1976. "A Methodology for Assessment of Quality of Work Life and Organizational Effectiveness in Behavior-Economic Terms." *Administrative Service Quarterly* 21:217–26.

Mobley, W. H. 1982. *Employee Turnover: Causes, Consequences, and Control.* Reading, Mass.: Addison-Wesley.

Moore, B. E., and T. L. Ross. 1978. *The Scanlon Way to Improved Productivity*. New York: Wiley, Interscience.

Nealy, S. 1963. "Pay and Benefit Preferences." *Industrial Relations* 3:17–28.

Patten, T. H. 1977. "Pay: Employee Compensation and Incentive Plans." New York: Free Press.

Salscheider, J. 1981. "Devising Pay Strategies for Diversified Companies." *Compensation Review* 58, no. 6:15–24.

Stata, R., and M. A. Maidique. 1980. "Bonus System for Balanced Strategy." *Harvard Business Review* 58, no. 6:156–63.

Steele, F. 1975. *The Open Organization*. Reading, Mass.: Addison-Wesley.

Vroom, V. H. 1964. *Work and Motivation*. New York: Wiley.

Walton, R. E. 1980. "Establishing and Maintaining High Commitment Work Systems." In *The Organization Life Cycle*, ed. J. R. Kimberly, R. N. Miles, and associates. San Francisco: Jossey-Bass.

Whyte, W. F., ed. 1955. *Money and Motivation: An Analysis of Incentives in Industry*. New York: Harper.

17

Prediction, understanding, and control as antidotes to organizational stress

ROBERT I. SUTTON AND ROBERT L. KAHN

This article proposes prediction, understanding, and control as antidotes to stress, examines their relevance for organizational research, and describes their implications for managerial practice. By using the term *antidote* we do not mean to imply that all stresses are poisonous or that they can be completely counteracted. Rather, we mean that prediction, understanding, and control act in a variety of specific ways to reduce organizational stress or to relieve its negative effects.

Studies of stress have become numerous in organizational and medical research; investigators are apparently undeterred by the vagueness of the concept and the disparate definitions and measures in current use. Such problems, however, persist. Even the fundamental question of whether stress is to be regarded as an external stimulus (Lazarus 1966) or as a reaction of the organism (Selye 1956, 1971) remains unresolved.

We concur with Lazarus in finding the engineering analogy clarifying for theory and suggestive for empirical research. Engineers define a stress as an external force applied to some object or construction, and strain as the resultant change (distortion, compression, destruction) in that object. Applying this definition in organizational settings, we will distinguish between objective stresses (demands and pressures, constraints and deprivations) imposed on individuals and the consequent strains (dissatisfactions, performance decrements, psychological and somatic symptoms).

Research along these lines, despite methodological and definitional problems, has discovered consistent and significant relationships between various organizationally generated stresses and individual strains. Much of this research has been summarized, with varying degrees of enthusiasm, by McGrath (1976), Kasl (1978), Katz and Kahn (1978), Beehr and Newman (1978), McLean (1979), and House (1981). In 1982, the *Journal of Occupational Behavior* devoted an entire issue to studies of stress (Jick and Burke 1982), and the Institute of Medicine published a major evaluation of stress research and its prospects (Eisdorfer and Elliott 1982). Stress research is reported on a continuing basis in *The Journal of Human Stress*, which began publication in 1975, and in two book series on occupational stress, one edited by McLean for Addison-Wesley and the other by Cooper and Payne for Wiley.

As might be expected, this quantity of stress research has discovered a formidable number of stress-strain relationships that are relevant for organizational theory, for example, between role conflict and psychological tension (Kahn et al. 1964); between machine-paced work and adrenaline levels (Frankenhauser and Gardell 1976), and between responsibility for the well-being of others and the prevalence of such diseases as hypertension, peptic ulcer, and diabetes (Cobb and Rose 1973). The many studies of stress and strain vary greatly in the adequacy of their population samples, the specificity with which stress and strain are defined, and the objectivity with which they are measured. In some studies, stress is wholly inferred from occupational titles. In others, both stress and strain are measured entirely by self-report. Moreover, the findings tend to be weaker when the measures of stress and strain are methodologically independent of each other rather than based on self-report, a pattern that is strongly suggestive of correlated error. Kasl (1978) describes some painful examples of overreliance on self-reported data in stress research, and of the resulting trivialities.

Setting aside such problems, however, students of stress and strain have had to confront the fact that the relationship between the two, while often significant, is seldom large; correlations in excess of .40 are rare, and correlations around .20 are common. Researchers have sought to account for these persistent but limited findings in two main ways: by demonstrating that certain personal characteristics (gender or age or type A personality) make some individuals "strain-prone" and others "strain-resistant," and by identifying situational variables that have similar interactive effects. Social support is by far the most studied of these situational stress-buffering variables.

For example, in a study of scientists, engineers, and administrators, French (1974) reported a correlation of .35 between role ambiguity (an organizationally imposed stress) and serum cortisol (an indicator of physiological strain) among employees whose relations with their subordinates were poor, but a correlation of only .06 among those whose relations with their subordinates were good. The difference between these two correlations was interpreted as the buffering effect of supportive relations. In the same study, similar findings were reported between workload and systolic blood pressure, with a correlation of .33 among the scientists, engineers, and administrators whose relationships with their own supervisors were poor, but a correlation of only .06 among those who reported good relations with their supervisors. In a number of parallel analyses the stress-strain correlations for people with poor relations to their colleagues were significantly higher than the correlations for those with good relations.

Cobb (1976) reviewed a broader literature of stressful events and associated indicators of strain to see whether the stress-strain relationship was regularly reduced in the presence of social support. He reported that buffering effects of social support were apparent in the relationship between intrusive situational changes and pregnancy complications (Nuckolls, Cassel, and Kaplan 1972), between hospitalization and psychological reactions among children (Jessner, Blon, and Waldfogel 1952), between surgical operation and speed of recovery (Egbert et al. 1964), between severe life stresses and affective disorder (Brown, Bhrolchain, and Harris 1975), between job stress and escapist drinking (Quinn, cited in Katz and Kahn 1978), between job loss and symptoms of rheumatoid arthritis (Gore 1973), and between job loss and elevation of cholesterol level (Cobb 1974). More recent studies in work settings (Cobb and Kasl 1977; House and Wells 1978) have presented additional evidence for the stress-buffering effects of social support.

This line of research is not without problems, however. First, the buffering effect, when measured as an interaction term in the stress-strain equation, is not always observable (Pinneau 1975; Andrews et al. 1978; LaRocco and Jones 1978; Lin et al. 1979). Second, many of the studies reporting significant buffering effects of support present serious methodological deficiencies—a fact that has been pointed out mainly by scholars who sought such effects unsuccessfully in their own data. LaRocco, House, and French (1980) have done a great deal to clarify these inconsistencies in research findings and to explicate the mechanisms or pathways by which social support works. They present evidence that the buffering hypothesis is supported for physical- and mental-health variables such as somatic complaints but not for job-specific strains such as job dissatisfaction. Such research on social support will continue, and should. In this chapter, however, we wish to urge an additional line of research. The discovery of social support as a variable that can moderate the relationship between stress and strain should stimulate a search for other variables with stress- or strain-reducing properties. Support is not a sovereign remedy for stress, and there is no reason to think that it is unique in its antidotal effects.

We propose three variables that deserve investigation as stress-strain antidotes in organizational life: *prediction, understanding,* and *control.* We hypothesize, for example, that a stress of a given type and magnitude will create less strain when the affected individual can predict the time of its onset, its magnitude, and its duration. We would also expect that the understandability of the stress—that is, knowledge of its causes, origins, and pathways—will have effects similar to those of predictability, yet independent of them. Finally, we expect that control by the stressed individual—for example, control over the timing of the stress—will have both main effects (stress reduction, strain reduction) and interaction effects (reduction of the stress-strain relationships).

The triad of prediction, understanding, and control is of course not new to research workers. These concepts are the alleged and reiterated aims of research itself, of science. It is not unreasonable, we believe, to propose that the goals and motives of men and women everywhere, as they try to make sense of their world and anticipate the opportunities and hazards it presents, are like those of scientists in these important respects. Scientists and other citizens engage in tasks of some underlying similarity, although that similarity is masked by differences in conceptual language, apparatus, and modes of investigation. And, of course, scientists and nonscientists share the unavoidable human limitation of bounded rationality in their efforts to predict, explain, and control their world.

In the remainder of this chapter we will review the wide-ranging research literature that encourages us to consider prediction, understanding, and control as hypothetical antidotes to stress in organizational settings; we will present a model for the relationship of these antidotes to stress and strain; and we will discuss the implications of this model for organizational theory and research, as well as for managerial practice.

PREDICTION

Prediction is the ability to forecast the frequency, timing, duration, and quality of events in one's environment. The main effects of the *lack* of predictability at work are well established in the literature on role ambiguity (for reviews see Kahn, 1974; Katz and Kahn 1978, chap. 17; or Pearce 1981). Pearce (1981) observes that most studies of role ambiguity (e.g., Rizzo, House, and Lirtzman 1970; Lyons 1971; Ivancevich and Donnelly 1974) operationalize the concept as a generalized information deficiency rather than as the unpredictability of specific events. However, some rigorous research (e.g., Caplan 1971; Caplan et al. 1975; Beehr 1976) has employed measures of role ambiguity that emphasize the unpredictability component.

This research on the lack of prediction has uncovered potent main effects on behavioral, psychological, and physiological strain. Of particular interest is Caplan's (1971) finding that the frequency of unscheduled work interruptions is related to such strains as elevated heart rate and serum cholesterol level. Unpredictable events tend to disrupt organized response sequences, and such disruption has been described as stressful to all organisms (Mandler and Watson 1966).

While the association of unpredictability and strain has been fairly well documented in cross-sectional research on organizations, the potential of predictability as an antidote to job stress has not been demonstrated experimentally in organizational settings. Data from laboratory research, however, suggest that the ability to forecast the frequency, timing, and qualities of a stres-

sor considerably reduces its negative impact. Seligman's (1975) experimental work on predictability and unpredictability has been especially influential. He presents the signal/safety hypothesis: when a stressful event can be predicted, the absence of the stressful event can also be predicted. Thus, the person knows when he or she can relax, and need not be in a constant state of vigilance or anxiety. As an example of the signal/safety phenomenon, Seligman cites the function of air-raid sirens during the bombing of London in World War II. The air-raid sirens worked so well as a signal that people could go about their business without immediate fear (i.e., in safety) a large percentage of the time; vigilance and protective action were required only when the sirens sounded.

Empirical support for the signal/safety hypothesis is provided by a number of laboratory studies with animals (Seligman 1968; Weiss and Strongman 1969; Seligman and Meyer 1970; Byrum and Jackson 1971) and with human beings (Glass and Singer 1972; Price and Geer 1972; Staub and Kellet 1972). The setup of these experiments varied, but a common arrangement in the animal research involved the delivery of electrical shocks at irregular intervals through a metal grid or floor and, for a random subset of animals, the use of a buzzer or light as a warning signal just before the shock. In all these experiments, aversive stimuli were found to have a weaker negative impact on subjects, both animal and human, that were able to predict the onset, duration, magnitude, or nature of the stress. This research appears to have profound implications for stress at work.

Job stressors that cannot be predicted may, by definition, appear at any time. According to the signal/safety hypothesis, this fact implies a constant state of anxiety, because the person never receives a "signal" that he or she is safe, even for a short period of time. Such unpredictability, however, requires further specification. Any aspect of a stimulus may be unpredictable—its nature or quality, its time of onset, its strength or magnitude, its duration, and the like. Seligman emphasizes timing and strength. If both are predictable, persons at risk can relax most of the time and marshal their resources appropriately when required. The strain of continual vigilance or inappropriate mobilization is obviated.

Organizational researchers have not attempted to test the signal/safety hypothesis explicitly in any of its aspects. Nevertheless, some organizational research can be interpreted as supporting the proposition that predictable job-related stressors are less threatening than unpredictable stressors. Studies of organizational socialization (Van Maanen 1976; Schein 1978) indicate that the frustration and anxiety of new members are related to the gap between their initial expectations about the job and the actual attributes of the new role. In other words, lack of ability to forecast events increases the stress associated with a life change that is already threatening for most people—entry into a new social system. Perhaps this is one of the reasons that realistic job previews appear to reduce turnover among new employees (Wanous 1973; Ilgen and Seely 1974).

Indirect evidence for the value of predictability as an antidote is also found in research on job transfers. Brett (1980) has recently conducted an excellent review of the literature on job transfer. She reports that, as one would expect, transfers are more disruptive when the new job and work environment are dissimilar to the old. Brett suggests that disruption may be greater because dissimilarity implies lack of knowledge about behavior-outcome contingencies in the new setting. In other words, unpredictable stimuli (both threatening and benign) are more stressful than predictable stimuli.

UNDERSTANDING

Understanding, in this context, is knowledge about the causes of significant events in the workplace. If predictability involves questions of *what* and *when*, understanding involves questions of *how* and *why*. Little organizational research has been conducted directly on understanding. Studies that explore opportunities for learning on the job (Rousseau 1978), task identity and feedback (Hackman and Oldham 1975), and social support as information from others (Caplan et al. 1975) are relevant, however. Information from co-workers and from task performance itself may increase knowledge about the causes of events at work. For instance, the positive relationships observed between feedback and job satisfaction (Hackman and Lawler 1971; Hackman and Oldham 1975) may involve understanding as an unmeasured intervening variable. This is a testable, but as yet untested, hypothesis.

Until such hypotheses have been tested in organizational settings, arguments for the antidotal effects of understanding must come from other sources. Three are of particular relevance: (1) the conceptual distinction between prediction and understanding as it has been made in other fields, (2) the substantial body of research that implies a human need to understand, and (3) the suggestion in some laboratory research that understanding and prediction have different empirical consequences even for animals.

The conceptual distinction between prediction and understanding is explicit in our definitions; it is the difference between (1) knowledge of the timing, dura-

tion, magnitude, and quality of a future stimulus; and (2) knowledge of its causes and the mechanisms by which it acts. The distinction is familiar to research workers, who often find that they can predict an outcome but cannot specify the pathways or mechanisms by which it is produced. In medicine, for example, the pain-relieving effect of aspirin and the contraceptive effect of intrauterine devices are established beyond doubt, but research biochemists and physiologists are not yet able to specify fully the pathway or sequence of physiological events by which either of these effects is created. They say, and we concur, that in these cases prediction exceeds understanding and that the two are distinct.

Theorists' postulations of universal human needs have generally produced more long lists than good theory; nevertheless, the assumption of a motive to understand significant aspects of one's environment underlies a great deal of research and practice. The "Aha!" experience of gestalt psychology—the momentary feeling that accompanies the recognition of a pattern or the sudden grasping of the solution to a problem—implies a drive to understand and a release of tension when understanding is attained (Kohler 1929). Another example comes from psychoanalytic theory and practice, which assume that insight into the causes of one's own behavior (understanding) is not only a necessary step in altering behavior but is itself a means of relieving neurotic symptoms (Dollard and Miller 1950). In social psychology, the tendency of human beings to create causal explanations, even from the most meager perceptual cues, was demonstrated in Heider's (1958) classic experiments. More recently, cognitive social psychology has become the dominant subfield of that discipline, and the attribution of cause under conditions of uncertainty is a central issue in cognitive psychology.

For example, experimental subjects who are required to make predictions under conditions of uncertainty, drawing on data provided by the experimenter, rely most on those facts that enable them to make causal attributions (Ajzen 1977; Nisbett and Ross 1980; Tversky and Kahneman 1980). So powerful is the propensity to seek causal explanations that experimental subjects tend to neglect information that would enhance their predictions but would not contribute to their implicit theories about the causes of events.

Finally, some research with animals also suggests that understanding is empirically distinct from prediction. Animals that have been trained to work for food by pressing a lever show adverse physiological reactions (elevated plasma corticoids) when reinforcement contingencies are changed so that regular lever pressing no longer produces food (Coover, Goldman, and Levine 1971). This finding is interpreted by Levine (1982) as an effect of unpredictability rather than deprivation, because the animals continue to be fed regularly. When the experiment was varied by removing the lever itself, however, the animals did not show the same adverse physiological responses. Kahn (1981a) suggests that in the latter case the animals were able to "understand" the situation; they noticed that the food-producing lever had been removed. This research implies that understanding the cause of a stress may serve as an antidote independent of control or prediction.

CONTROL

Our concept of control in organizational settings is straightforward; it consists of a dependent relationship between the behavior of an organizational member and the subsequent occurrence of outcomes in the work environment desired by that member. Control is thus the exercise of effective influence over events, things, and persons. Its opposite, as Seligman's (1975) work makes clear, is helplessness.

The importance of control over one's immediate environment is a persistent theme in the behavioral science. Adler stated in 1930 that the control of one's relevant environment is "an intrinsic necessity of life itself" (cited in Langer and Rodin 1976, 398). In more recent years, Seligman's (1975) work on learned helplessness in animals and humans, Rotter's (1966) research on locus of control, Lazarus's (Lazarus 1966; Lazarus and Launier 1978) investigations of "direct action" in coping with stress, and Bandura's (1977) experiments on self-efficacy all emphasize that dependence between behavioral responses and preferred outcomes in one's environment has important consequences for well-being.

Such dependence is also a persistent theme in the literature of occupational stress, although the label "personal control" is rarely used. Writings on participation in decision making (Alutto and Belasco 1972; Caplan et al. 1975), autonomy (Hackman and Lawler 1971; Hackman and Oldham 1975), authority (Kay 1974), power (Kahn et al. 1964), and alienation (Blauner 1964; Seeman 1972) focus on the relationships among organizational properties, individual behavior, and desired outcomes in the work environment.

Additional evidence that links control with well-being, at least by implication, comes from research that demonstrates the negative consequences of lack of control. Laboratory research on learned helplessness suggests that independence between outcomes and responses may directly reduce motivation (Thornton and Jacobs 1971), interfere with cognitive processes (Kemler and Shepp

1971), and lead to emotional disturbances such as depression (Roth and Kubel, cited in Seligman 1975).

The link between lack of control and poor mental and physical health is also visible in the job-stress literature. Caplan et al. (1975), found substantial relationships between lack of participation in decision making, boredom, and job dissatisfaction. These latter variables in turn predicted anxiety, depression, and somatic complaints. Similar patterns are found in research on lack of autonomy (Hackman and Oldham 1975) and on alienation (Blauner 1964).

The persistence of such "control effects" and their diffusion across different life roles have yet to be fully explored. Most of the relevant field studies are cross-sectional, attempt to assess chronic conditions of control or its absence, and do not measure off-the-job consequences. Nor have the field studies made explicit the pathways through which control has its effects.

Many such paths are possible. For example, the perception of control may cause an individual to construe an aversive event as less threatening independently of any main effects of control on strain. A number of experiments indicate that subjects with control over an aversive stimulus are more likely to tolerate higher levels of that stimulus than subjects who do not have control. Experiments of this type have been conducted with stimuli such as shock (Bowers 1968), cold pressor pain (Kanfer and Seidner 1973), and noise (Glass, Singer, and Friedman 1969). In fact, Thompson (1981) reports that perceived control has been consistently linked to tolerance for adverse stimuli, although not to arousal at impact of the stimulus and not to perceived pain caused by the stimulus.

Most laboratory experiments on control do not measure postexperimental behaviors. Some experimenters (Glass and Singer 1972; Mills and Krantz 1979), however, have done so. They report that lack of control has a negative impact on the performance of tasks attempted *after* the experiment has been completed. Seligman (1975) would interpret these findings as short-term examples of learned helplessness. Thus, both laboratory research on general stress, and field research on organizational stress suggest that control has potent main effects on well-being. Some studies indicate that control can also reduce strain through indirect mechanisms as well.

A field experiment by Langer and Rodin (1976) provides compelling evidence both for the indirect benefits of personal control on well-being and for the complex paths by which such benefits are attained. Members of the experimental group in the Langer-Rodin study of nursing-home patients attended a "pep talk" that encouraged them to take greater control over their lives. They were then asked to care for a house plant that was placed in their room, and to choose which night they would attend movies shown by the nursing-home staff. Members of the control group attended a lecture emphasizing all the things the staff could do to help them. They were told that the plants in their rooms would be cared for by the staff, and they were also told on which nights they were to attend the movies.

The results of this seemingly modest experimental intervention were impressive. Members of the experimental group chose to participate in more recreational activities and expressed more positive attitudes toward life in general. Moreover, an eighteen-month follow-up by Rodin and Langer (1977) indicated that a lower percentage of patients in the experimental group had died during the intervening period. We assume that control over mundane matters in life, such as which night to watch a movie or when to water a plant, do not have powerful main effects on stress or strain. The other demands and constraints of nursing-home routine were not directly affected by the experimental manipulation. The Langer Rodin findings tell us not that these threats to well-being were eliminated but that they had fewer negative effects on members of the experimental group. The relationship between these stresses and the consequent strains (negative attitudes and mortality) was reduced or buffered by the experimental intervention.

Both the direct stimulus-modifying effects of control on stress and the indirect moderating effects of control on the stress-strain relationship have been well demonstrated in organizational settings. Pasmore and Friedlander (1982) describe a field experiment in which increased employee control appears to have produced what Averill (1973) called "stimulus modification," that is, the direct elimination or reduction of stressful stimuli.

This action-research project addressed a recalcitrant problem of high on-the-job injury rates by increasing the level of employee participation. A representative group composed of five workers, two supervisors, and the manager of employee relations was chosen to work on the problem. This group and the action-research team together conducted interviews and designed a questionnaire to identify causes and possible solutions, as seen by the workers themselves. The questionnaire data were then used to develop a list of suggestions for reducing injuries at work. After some resistance from management, many of these suggestions were implemented. In some cases they addressed the causes of injuries directly, by altering or adjusting mechanical equipment. In areas where injuries had been most frequent, methods-redesign groups of managers and employees were established to develop additional proposals. The results were dramatic. The number of injuries in the plant dropped from almost eighty during the first year of intervention to less than ten during the fourth year following the change effort. While other factors, including a change in management, may have influenced these data, they are suggestive of the power of stimulus modification. It appears that, as they acquired increased control, employees drastically reduced on-the-job injuries by the design and implementation of changes that had a direct impact on physical threats to their well-being.

Karasek's (1979) excellent study of employees in Sweden and the United States suggests that control may also be a potent modifier of the stress-strain relationship. This study was based on national survey data from both countries. A primary finding was that employees who had heavy job demands (measured as role overload and conflict) suffered mental strain when they had *low* decision latitude (i.e., little potential control over their tasks and conduct throughout the working day). In contrast, Karasek reported that the relationship between heavy job demands and strain was not present among those employees who had *high* decision latitude.

There are at least two possible explanations for the finding that control attenuated the stress-strain relationship among these respondents. First, as in the nursing-home study, the ability to control relevant aspects of the environment may have changed the meaning of certain stressors that could not be eliminated. For example, employees who have both high levels of control and high levels of role overload may suffer less mental strain than similarly overloaded workers without such control because the high-control workers feel that working sixty hours a week is their own choice, or at least that they had some input in the decision. In contrast, employees compelled to labor sixty hours may suffer mental strain because the workload is inconsistent with their wishes, quite apart from the fatiguing effect of the overtime itself.

Second, employees with higher levels of control in the Karasek study may have been able to alter when and in what way the stressors were received. This kind of control corresponds to Averill's (1973) concept of regulated administration—that is, regulated by the subject. Averill's review of laboratory research with animals and humans suggests that regulated administration independently reduces the negative impact of stress. Although it is impossible to reduce the level of some stressors, control may enable a person to regulate where, when, and in what way the stress is encountered. The overloaded employee with a high level of control may choose to work sixteen hours one day and eight hours the next. The overloaded employee with a low level of control may be forced to work twelve hours each day. The ability to regulate when the overload occurs increases both the predictability of the stressor and the dependence between the member's responses and outcomes in his or her relevant environment.

The virtues of regulated administration can also be inferred from the small body of literature on flexi-time (Elbing et al. 1974; Golembiewski, Hilles, and Kagno 1974; Walker, Fletcher, and McLeod 1975; Hicks and Klimoski 1981). Research on this topic suggests that dull and repetitive jobs create less subjective stress and strain when workers can control the days and hours that they work. An essential attribute of flexi-time is that the number of hours worked (i.e., the overall level of the stressor) remains constant; only the worker's power to regulate when the stimuli are received is altered.

SUMMARY

Our central assertion is that less strain will be suffered by organization members who can forecast the type of frequency of a stressor, who know the causes and mechanisms of that stressor, and who can produce responses that change significant aspects of that stressor. The cognitive limits of the human species restrict the degree to which anyone can predict, understand, and control job-related threats to his or her well-being. Yet these three elements are variables rather than constants. As they increase, so does the success of organization members in interpreting, avoiding, and mastering stressors in their work environment.

The specific ways in which prediction, control, and understanding may serve as antidotes to occupational stress are shown in figure 17.1. This figure builds on the ISR model of social-environmental determinants of health (French and Kahn 1962; Katz and Kahn 1978) and on the model of the relationships among occupational stress, social support, and health proposed by Larocco, House, and French (1980). We propose that objective organizational (work) stress leads to subjective stress (link a), which in turn leads to strain (link b). Strain is any

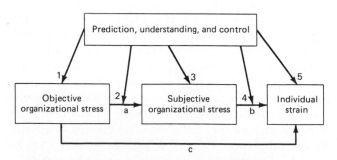

Figure 17.1   Five pathways by which prediction, understanding, and control serve as antidotes to organizational stress. (Adapted from French and Kahn 1962; Katz and Kahn 1978; LaRocco, House, and French 1980.)

diverse behavioral, psychological, or physiological response by a person. For instance, a person whose daily hours of work have been increased from eight to twelve (an objective stress) may report role overload (a subjective stress). This subjective role overload may lead to strains such as excessive smoking (a behavioral response), depression (a psychological response), or elevated blood pressure (a physiological response). The figure also indicates that some forms of objective work stress can lead directly to strain (link c). For example, the presence of lead particles in the work environment (an objective stressor) may cause a wide range of adverse physiological conditions independent of the worker's perceptions (Ledford 1981). The relationships among objective stress, subjective stress, and strain are firmly established in the literature on work and health (for reviews see Cooper and Marshall 1978; Katz and Kahn 1978, chap. 17; and Schuler 1980).

The primary emphasis in the preceding discussion has been on the links that are numbered 1 through 5 in figure 17.1. We have proposed a variety of different ways in which prediction, understanding, and control can serve as antidotes to job stress. As mentioned above, control over a stressor can reduce such objective stress directly (link 1). Further, it appears that all three of these antidotes can weaken the relationship between objective stress and subjective stress (link 2), reduce subjective work stress directly (link 3), and weaken the relationship between subjective stress and strain (link 4). In addition, a wide-ranging body of empirical research suggests that prediction, understanding, and control have main effects upon strains (link 5).

IMPLICATIONS FOR ORGANIZATIONAL RESEARCH

The basic proposition of this chapter is that prediction, understanding, and control in work settings act as buffers or antidotes to stress, both by directly reducing certain stressful aspects of work and by weakening the complex relationship between such stressors and the resulting physiological and psychological strains. The application of this proposition in organization life involves two major assumptions: first, that jobs and organizations can be modified so that people become more able to predict, understand, and control significant aspects of their immediate work environment, and, second, that people want such changes. There are, of course, subsidiary assumptions, for example, that organizations can increase the predictability, understandability, and controllability of jobs without incurring unacceptable costs, and that most people not only want such increases but can handle them appropriately. Whether these assumptions are justified remains to be discovered, but discovery is possible; the assumptions are testable.

They have not yet been tested, however. In emphasizing the potential for stress reduction through the design of jobs and organizations, we are urging a line of research and application that is different from and complementary to the thrust of most current investigations of stress. Researchers and proponents of meditation, diet, exercise, and other diverse regimens all focus on the individual and his or her vulnerability to life's stressful events, at work and elsewhere. They offer advice and activity patterns that are intended to increase the individual's ability to endure such stressful events without physical or psychological damage or decrements in performance.

Specialists in personality measurement and personnel selection are similarly individualistic in their orientation; they are trying to see to it that, to paraphrase Harry Truman's often-quoted dictum, people who can't stand the heat are kept out of the organizational kitchen. And conventional programs of counseling and psychotherapy, insofar as they address organizational impacts on individual behavior and well-being at all, concentrate on increasing individual resilience and resistance to job-imposed stress. Individualistic approaches to organizational stress bear about the same relationship to our approach as individual medicine does to public health. For the most part, they are remedial rather than preventive, and they are expensive. The difference between the two approaches, individual and organizational, is well illustrated by two recent field experiments. In one (Ganster et al. 1982), employees of a public agency were involved in an eight-week training program designed to help them recognize and alter their cognitive interpretations of stressful stimuli; results were favorable in direction but modest in magnitude. Attempts at replication were unsuccessful, and the authors do not recommend the adoption of such programs of stress management.

This experiment can be compared with that of Pasmore and Friedlander (1982), in which the injury rate was dramatically reduced by a series of employee-initiated changes in methods, equipment, and the like. This experiment in participative decision making and hazard reduction is especially impressive because it had been preceded by unsuccessful attempts to achieve similar results by making individuals more safety conscious. In terms of both impact on employee well-being and cost effectiveness, it was better to reduce stressful elements in the workplace through increased employee control than to try to increase employees' tolerance level for stress at work.

We suspect that this would often be the case, and that the best way to deal with organizationally induced stressors would generally be to begin by reducing the stressors themselves, then introduce moderating factors, and only later consider the difficult and costly effort to increase individual tolerance for stress. We propose this preference ordering for both practice and research. The current concentration on individual stress tolerance creates a tendency in both arenas to treat stressors as constant or irreducible even where modification is possible.

For those who find this argument plausible, we offer four researchable questions: (1) What are the relationships among the proposed antidotes—prediction, understanding, and control? (2) What is the relationship between social support and these three antidotes? (3) What is the relationship between these variables and the explication of stress in terms of episodes (stressful life events)? (4) How do individual differences enter into our approach to stress, strain, and antidotes?

Relationships among the three antidotes

We have discussed separately the stress- and strain-reducing properties of prediction, understanding, and control. The relationships among them are also relevant for a comprehensive theory of stress and for organizational practice. Competing hypotheses about these relationships are easily framed. First, in organizational life, as in science, it may be that prediction, understanding, and control constitute a continuum of increasing power. Control, according to this view, incorporates prediction and understanding. By controlling a stress or a stress-strain relationship, we show that we understand it. As for prediction, by definition a stress or a stress-strain sequence that we control occurs only when we permit it.

An alternative hypothesis about the relationship among the proposed antidotes accepts control as the most potent of the three but does not rank the other two. Understanding may lead to and may be tested by prediction, but prediction may stimulate the kind of speculation that leads to understanding. Still another possibility is that the three stress antidotes are to some extent interchangeable, so far as their stress-reducing effects are concerned. If so, we would expect the three to share a common antidotal effect and each to have an additional unique effect of its own.

It is likely, of course, that none of these hypotheses will hold without qualification, and that the effectiveness of a given antidote will be contingent on properties of the specific stress-strain sequence under consideration. For example, if Malkiel (1973) is correct in his assertion that investing in the stock market constitutes a "random walk," efforts at prediction and control will be useless. Understanding the chance nature of the enterprise, however, might still provide some relief from strain.

Our main point here, however, is not the relative plausibility of these alternative hypotheses; it is the importance of determining the degree of independence, the substitutability, and the relationship under varying conditions of the three stress-reducing variables—prediction, understanding, and control. These are research tasks.

Relationship between social support and antidotes

To the extent that social support is defined as the expression of positive interpersonal affect—direct expression of fondness, liking, love, or esteem for another person—its relationship to the other stress antidotes is a matter for empirical determination. To the extent that social support is defined more broadly (and it often is), its relationship to prediction, understanding, and control becomes in part a definitional issue.

For example, House (1981) includes in his definition a form of support that he calls informational, which incorporates advice, suggestions, directives and relevant factual material. If the information is accurate and appropriate to the problem at hand, one would expect it to increase the ability of the receiver to predict and understand the confronting stressors. Information can also increase control, especially when the information describes strategies that have been controlling in similar situations. House also describes a class of supportive behaviors that he calls instrumental, which involves direct assistance in effort, material, or money. The apparent intent of such actions is to increase the recipient's control over his or her immediate situation.

Assuming that informational and instrumental support indeed operate in these ways, either of two interpretations seems appropriate. One can say that these kinds of support reduce strain because they make the situation more predictable, understandable, and controllable. Or one can say that prediction, understanding, and control are actually forms of social support. They may thus provide a basis for classifying several kinds of supportive acts. Both views imply a more proactive model of stress management than is usual in the literature of social support, much of which treats support as alleviating strain without affecting the external stresses that cause it.

Relationship between antidotal variables and episodic approach to stress

We have discussed stress and stress antidotes as continuous variables, that is, as if each of them could be rated on a scale ranging from zero to some maximum. We agree with Lazarus (Lazarus 1966; Lazarus and Lau-

nier 1978) however, that stress occurs through a series of discrete transactions or episodes between the individual and the immediate environment, and we believe that the reduction of stress and strain occurs in similar fashion. Prediction, understanding, and control as variables are useful summaries of specific transactions between an individual and others in his or her environment. When we say, for example, that a person has a great deal of control over his or her workload, that statement is reducible to a specific set of transactions in which that person's behavior is linked to certain outcomes (reduced workload, altered pacing, or the like).

The fact that measures of stress and of stress antidotes ultimately reduce to transactional episodes reminds us of an additional issue that requires theoretical and empirical attention—the gross differences in the importance of different episodes. To be told, for example, that one may be laid off for a month is a work-related stress; to be told that one may be dismissed is a much greater stress, although both pose problems of uncertainty and possible loss. If these episodes are combined in a single count of "uncertainty episodes," such distinctions of importance and magnitude are lost. One can, of course, assign weights to different episodes, according to the magnitude of the stress that they involve. The more general point is that the language of variables, for all its convenience and quantitative advantage, has its costs. As abstractions from episodes, variables are a form of data reduction; and the more different and complex the episodes, the more drastic the data reduction.

Role of individual differences in the proposed stress framework

The core proposition in our model is that work-imposed stresses cause individual strains. We have proposed that three additional attributes of the work setting (the predictability, understanding, and controllability of the stress) act in several ways to reduce such strains. Almost nothing has been said about individual differences, although different people, of course, respond differently to most stresses.

To elaborate our model to recognize individual differences, we would begin with personality variables that are linked theoretically to the three stress antidotes—prediction, understanding, and control. For example, research on the distinction between type A and type B personalities (Chesney and Rosenman 1980) indicates that the type A's—who are competitive, often hostile and aggressive, and oppressed by the urgency of time—have a greater need for control than the type Bs (usually defined as people who are not type A). We would predict, therefore, that lack of control would create more strain for a type A than for a type B person, and that the antidotal effect of increased control would be greater for the type A.

Similar predictions can be made involving other measures of the need for control. Rotter's (1966) work on locus of control would be especially interesting, because it suggests two conflicting hypotheses. Rotter's concept of locus of control is a measure of a person's perception of the degree to which people's lives are controlled by the individuals themselves as opposed to external forces. If a person's sense of locus of control is interpreted as a direct measure of need for control, then the "internals" on Rotter's scale should respond like the type A's in Rosenman's categories. If, on the other hand, the perception of internal control is regarded as a defense mechanism, Rotter's "internals" will relieve the strain of low-control jobs by distorting their real properties.

Understanding and prediction could be treated in analogous fashion. For example, tolerance for ambiguity (Kahn et al. 1964), is a personality attribute that would enter into an elaborated form of our model. Organization members with a low tolerance for ambiguity would be hypothesized to suffer more strain from unpredictable stresses than members with a high tolerance for ambiguity. The research task is to discover which enduring characteristics of individuals should be incorporated into the subsequent development of the prediction-understanding-control framework.

IMPLICATIONS FOR MANAGERIAL PRACTICE

In this chapter we have reaffirmed the relevance of stress research for organizational theory, acknowledged the importance of social support as a "buffer" or partial antidote to stress, and proposed the investigation in organizational settings of three other hypothesized antidotes—prediction, understanding, and control.

These are not perfect antidotes, that will work in all circumstances, for all individuals, and in all amounts. On the contrary, their effectiveness is likely to vary, depending on the nature of the stress and the personality of the individual. Moreover, it is likely that, as with other good things, one can get too much of prediction, understanding, and control in one's life. We do not assert that these variables reduce stress in linear fashion, but rather that their stress-reducing properties in organizational life deserve exploration. A further proposal is that the theoretical and empirical search for stress antidotes be extended. Prediction, understanding, and control do not exhaust the set of antidotes. We wish to stimulate the search, not end it.

Finally, we have used examples and cited research that suggest the importance of stress antidotes for organizational practice as well as theory. Their introduction into organizational life should be a task for the designers and managers of organizations. We shall therefore conclude this chapter by considering the implications of prediction, understanding, and control for managerial practice. As stress antidotes, these three factors assume special importance when some new organizational stress threatens an existing equilibrium. The following proposals should therefore be particularly useful to managers who must deal with severe retrenchment, transformation of factory and office procedures by computer-directed technology, and other major organizational changes.

Be generous with information

There is an understandable tendency among managers to husband information. Communication in large organizations is often costly and occasionally disruptive. Research has shown that human beings have a limited capacity for processing information and are prone to "information input overload." The managerial rule of thumb is therefore to give people only the information they need to do their jobs. This limitation is debatable under most conditions, but it is almost certainly wrong when some profound organizational change is imminent. At such times, our framework implies that people will need and seek information to help them understand the causes of potentially threatening events, to predict when they will occur, and to discover which aspects of the change can be avoided, controlled, or used to advantage.

An administrator who managed the closing of a government facility used this tactic of deliberate "information overload" and multiple communication channels to reduce fear, anger, denial, and low performance among employees. He sent out a detailed newsletter each week that included the reasons for the closing, the dates on which individual employees would be laid off, and the employment opportunities that might be available in other government facilities and in the private sector. The information was repeated in memoranda that were posted in each department. Moreover, for especially important announcements, a letter was mailed to each employee. In addition, the administrator met with department heads almost every day to convey new information and respond to questions, and he met each week with all employees for the same purpose.

An enormous amount of information was given to employees affected by this closing. Yet they did not complain; in fact, they sometimes demanded still more. They sought this quantity of information because it concerned some of the most important aspects of their lives—when, why, and how they would lose their source of income and the community of workers to which they belonged. Moreover, this information helped them discover some steps they might take to cope with these stresses in their environment.

Acknowledge the information functions of the informal organization

The arrival of a new machine, a change in organizational structure, or news of impending layoffs will cause employees to spend time watching and discussing the change, perhaps interrupting their work to do so. Managers may be tempted to break up such activities with immediate orders to return to work. Yet these displays of human curiosity may serve to enhance prediction, understanding, and control in ways that are beneficial to both the organization and the employees. This is most easily illustrated with the example of new machines. Employees inevitably want to stand around and watch a new paper copier, word processor, or industrial robot for a while. This period of observation and discussion may help employees understand how the machine operates, predict the impact it will have on their own work, and learn the steps required to operate the machine.

In one organization we observed, a group of fourteen people spent about an hour watching one person operate a new word processor. Although some working time was lost during that hour, the period of observation helped secretaries who would be using the new machine feel less threatened by its arrival. Moreover, professional staff members learned some tips for their own manuscript preparation that would enable secretaries to use the new machine more efficiently.

Don't hold back bad news too long

Managers often postpone delivering news about layoffs, unwanted transfers, forced retirement, demotions, or pay cuts because they do not wish to face angry or depressed employees. But the framework presented here implies that, during times of imminent change, it is best for affected employees if they are notified early enough to act intelligently in their own interest. Such knowledge is especially useful if presented along with reasons why the organizational change is thought necessary, detailed information about when the change will occur, and descriptions of action alternatives available to employees.

The organization also benefits in some respects if it announces bad news as soon as possible. The prediction-understanding-control framework teaches us that people have a strong need for information about stressful events. This is one of the reasons that rumors are rampant among employees in declining organizations where top-down communication is poor. Employees who are placed in such an information vacuum are trying to make sense—to predict and understand—potential threats in the work environment. Because the sense-making process is inevitable in any group of human beings, it may be useful for management to announce bad news as soon as possible. False rumors are often more threatening than the truth, and they motivate coping behaviors that may be both costly and inappropriate.

The closing of the government facility described previously illustrates that bad news is better than no news. Rumors were numerous during the period just before the closing was announced. Some employees were saying that the facility was going to be closed without notice. Some said that it would never be closed. And still others warned that it would be impossible for union members to collect severance pay if a closing did occur. The decision to announce the closing was made, in part, because the true closing date was much further off than many of the rumors suggested. Moreover, union employees were to receive severance pay.

This closing also illustrates that it is best to provide detailed information about bad news. A list showing each employee's last day was compiled and distributed months before the first layoff occurred. This helped employees predict the onset of this stressor in their own lives, so they could plan to search for a new job, prepare for retirement, or learn the steps required to collect unemployment benefits (which many were forced to do). In other words, this knowledge enabled employees to exercise control over some aspects of an event fundamentally beyond their control.

Minimize the duration of those periods in which organization members experience loss of prediction, understanding, or control

Although not explicitly included in our framework, duration is a relevant variable. Long exposure to stressors that cannot be predicted, understood, or controlled will cause more damage than brief exposure. Long-term exposure to some stressors can lead to illness; brief exposure to the same stressors may cause only short-term psychological and physical discomfort. This is a simple truth and its managerial implications seem obvious. They are, however, frequently ignored.

The current "down-sizing" of many American universities illustrates these points. When a unit within a university is considered for elimination or large budget cuts, a complex, protracted, formal process of review usually ensues. This procedure conforms to major aspects of our framework and has some advantages for members of the university unit under review. The steps and time frame for the review are usually made explicit (prediction); the reason for the review is announced (understanding); and the steps that can be taken to defend the unit are made explicit (control). Nonetheless, this review period is stressful. Members are uncertain of the fate of their work group. They may be uncertain of their own employment status; even tenured faculty have been at risk in some schools. Members of the affected units may not believe the announced reason for the review, and often feel they can do little to influence the decision.

It is probably impossible to remove the profound loss of prediction, understanding, and control that usually accompanies such ordeals. The very act of questioning the right of a social unit to exist will cause much stress for members. Much can be done, however, to shorten the period of distress. In our experience, such reviews move at an agonizingly slow pace. Committees have monthly meetings. Reports take months to write. Public hearings are spread over a long period of time. After all recommendations are received from various subcommittees, administrators may take several more months to reach a final decision. Thus, the members of the unit under scrutiny are often forced to endure this profound stress for a year or longer.

We suggest that steps can be taken to compress the review period. Committee meetings can be held more frequently. Public meetings can be held at shorter intervals. Severe deadlines can be established for the preparation of reports, as well as for decisions made by executive officers. Changes such as these would not reduce the force of the stress experienced by those who are the target of review, but they could reduce the duration and therefore the cumulative effects of the stress experience.

The last two sections of this chapter, on the implications of the prediction-understanding-control framework for research and for management, epitomize a persisting tension between theory and application. Research workers, entranced with their theories but keenly aware of the limitations of their data, want more research. Managers, who must act on some mixture of evidence and intuition, want data-based advice *now*. We have concluded our chapter with four advisory statements, even though we regard each of them as a hypothesis yet to be fully tested. May they be useful in their present form and improved by the research that awaits them.

REFERENCES

Ajzen, I. 1977. "Intuitive Theories of Events and the Effects of Base-Rate Information on Prediction." *Journal of Personality and Social Psychology* 35:303–14.

Alutto, J. A., and J. A. Belasco. 1977. "A Typology for Participation in Organizational Decision Making." *Administrative Science Quarterly* 17, no. 1:117–25.

Andrews, G., C. Tennant, D. M. Hewson, and G. E. Vaillant. 1978. "Life Stress, Social Support, Coping Style, and Risk of Psychological Impairment." *Journal of Nervous and Mental Disease* 166:307–16.

Averill, J. R. 1975. "Personal Control over Aversive Stimuli and Its Relationship to Stress." *Psychological Bulletin* 80:286–303.

Bandura, A. 1977. "Self Efficacy: Toward a Unifying Theory of Behavioral Change." *Psychology Review* 54:191–215.

Beehr, T. A., "Perceived Situational Moderators of the Relationship Between Subjective Role Ambiguity and Role Strain." *Journal of Applied Psychology* 61:35–40.

Beehr, T. A., and J. E. Newman. 1978. "Job Stress, Employee Health, and Organizational Effectiveness: A Facet Analysis, Model and Literature Review." *Personnel Psychology* 31:665–99.

Blauner, R. 1964. *Alienation and Freedom: The Factory Worker and His Industry.* Chicago: University of Chicago Press.

Bowers, K. 1968. "Pain, Anxiety and Perceived Control." *Journal of Clinical and Consulting Psychology* 32:596–602.

Brett, J. M. 1980. "The Effects of Job Transfer on Employees and Their Families." In *Current Concerns in Occupational Stress,* ed. C. L. Cooper and R. Payne. Chichester, England: Wiley.

Brown, G. W., M. N. Bhrolchain, and T. Harris. 1975. "Social Class and Psychiatric Disturbance Among Women in an Urban Population." *Sociology* 9:225–54.

Byrum, R. P., and D. E. Jackson. 1971. "Response Availability and Second-Order Conditioned Suppression." *Psychonomic Science* 23:100–8.

Caplan, R. D. 1971. "Organizational Stress and Individual Strain: A Social-Psychological Study of Risk Factors in Coronary Heart Disease Among Administrators, Engineers, and Scientists." Ph.D. diss. University of Michigan.

Caplan, R. D., S. Cobb, J. R. P. French, R. V. Harrison, and S. R. Pinneau. 1975. *Job Demands and Worker Health.* U.S. Department of Health, Education & Welfare (NIOSH) publication 75-160.

Chesney, M. A., and R. Rosenman. 1980. "Type A Behavior in the Work Setting." In *Current Concerns in Occupational Stress*, ed. D. L. Cooper and R. Payne. Chichester, England: Wiley.

Cobb, S. 1974. "Role Responsibility: The Differentiation of a Concept." In *Occupational Stress*, ed. A. McLean. Springfield, Ill.: Thomas.

———. 1976. "Social Support as a Moderator of Life Stress." *Psychosomatic Medicine* 38, no. 5.

Cobb, S., and S. V. Kasl. 1977. *Termination: The Consequences of Job Loss.* U.S. Department of Health, Education & Welfare (NIOSH) publication no. 77-224.

Cobb, S., and R. M. Rose. 1973. "Hypertension, Peptic Ulcer, and Diabetes in Air Traffic Controllers." *Journal of the American Medical Association* 224:489–92.

Cooper, C. L., and J. Marshall. 1978. "Sources of Managerial and White Collar Stress," in *Stress at Work*, ed. C. L. Cooper and R. Payne, pp. 81–106. Chichester, England: Wiley.

Coover, G. D., L. Goldman, and S. Levine. 1971. "Plasma Corticosterone Increases Produced by Extinction of Operant Behavior in Rats." *Physiology and Behavior* 6:261–3.

Dollard, J., and N. E. Miller. 1950. *Personality and Psychotherapy.* New York: McGraw-Hill.

Egbert, L. D., D. E. Battit, C. E. Welch, and M. K. Bartlett. 1964. "Reduction of Post-Operative Pain by Encouragement and Instruction of Patients." *New England Journal of Medicine* 270:825–7.

Eisdorfer, C., and G. Elliott, eds. 1982. *Research on Stress in Health and Disease.* Washington, D.C.: Institute of Medicine, National Academy of Sciences.

Elbing, A. O., H. Gadon, and J. Gordon. 1974. "Flexible Work Hours: It's About Time." *Harvard Business Review* 52:18–33.

Frankenhauser, M., and B. Gardell. 1976. "Underload and Overload in Working Life: Outline of a Multidisciplinary Approach." *Journal of Human Stress* 2:35–46.

French, J. R. P., Jr. 1974. "Person-Role Fit." In *Occupational Stress*, ed. A. McLean. Springfield, Ill.: Thomas.

French, J. R. P., Jr., and R. L. Kahn. 1962. "A Programmatic Approach to Studying the Industrial Environment and Mental Health." *Journal of Social Issues* 18, no. 3:1–47.

Ganster, D. C., B. T. Mayes, W. E. Sime, and G. D. Tharp. 1982. "Managing Organizational Stress: A Field Experiment." *Journal of Applied Psychology* 67:533–42.

Glass, D. C., and J. E. Singer. 1972. *Urban Stress: Experiments on Noise and Social Stressors.* New York: Academic Press.

Glass, D. C., J. E. Singer, and L. N. Friedman. 1969. "Psychic Costs of Adaptation to an Environmental Stressor." *Journal of Personality and Social Psychology* 12:200–10.

Golembiewski, R. T., R. Hilles, and M. S. Kagno. 1974. "A Longitudinal Study of Flexi-time Effects: Some Consequences of an O.D. Structural Intervention." *Journal of Applied Behavioral Science* 10, no. 4:503–32.

Gore, S. 1973. "The Influence of Social Support and Related Variables in Ameliorating the Consequences of Job Loss." Ph.D. diss., University of Pennsylvania.

Hackman, J. R., and E. E. Lawler III. 1971. "Employee Reactions to Job Characteristics." *Journal of Applied Psychology Monograph* 55:259–86.

Hackman, J. R., and G. R. Oldham. 1975. "Development of the Job Diagnostic Survey." *Journal of Applied Psychology* 60:159–70.

Heider, F. 1958. *The Psychology of Interpersonal Relations.* New York: Wiley.

Hicks, W. D., and R. J. Klimoski. 1981. "The Impact of Flexitime on Employee Attitudes." *Academy of Management Journal* 24:333–41.

House, J. S. 1981. *Work Stress and Social Support.* Reading, Mass.: Addison-Wesley.

House, J. S., and J. A. Wells. 1978. "Occupational Stress, Social Support, and Health." In *Reducing Occupational Stress: Proceedings of a Conference*, ed. A. McLean, G. Black, and M. Colligan. U.S. Department of Health, Education & Welfare (NIOSH) publication no. 78-140: 8–29.

Ilgen, E. W., and W. Seely. 1974. "Realistic Expectations as an Aid in Reducing Voluntary Resignations." *Journal of Applied Psychology* 59:452–5.

Ivancevich, J. M., and J. H. Donnelly, Jr. 1974. "A Study of Role Clarity and Need for Clarity for Three Occupational Groups." *Academy of Mangement Journal* 17:28–36.

Jessner, L., G. E. Blom, and S. Waldfogel. 1952. "Emotional Implications of Tonsillectomy and Adenoidectomy on Children." *Psycho-analytic Study of the Child* 7:126–69.

Jick, T. D., and R. J. Burke, eds. 1982. *Journal of Occupational Behavior* 3:1.

Kahn, R. L. 1974. "Conflict, Ambiguity and Overload: Three Elements in Job Stress." *Occupational Mental Health* 3:1.

Kahn, R. L., D. M. Wolfe, R. P. Quinn, J. D. Snoek, and R. A. Rosenthal. *Organizational Stress: Studies in Role Conflict and Ambiguity.* New York: Wiley.

Kanfer, F., and M. L. Seidner. 1973. "Self-Control: Factors Enhancing Tolerance of Noxious Stimulation." *Journal of Personality and Social Psychology* 25:381.

Karasek, R. A., Jr. 1979. "Job Demands, Job Decision Latitude, and Mental Strain: Implications for Job Redesign." *Administrative Science Quarterly* 24:285–308.

Kasl, S. V. 1978. "Epidemiological Contributions to the Study of Work Stress." In *Stress at Work* ed. C. L. Cooper and R. Payne. Chichester, England: Wiley.

Katz, D., and R. L. Kahn. 1978. *The Social Psychology of Organizations.* 2d ed. New York: Wiley.

Kay, E. 1974. "Middle Management." In *Work and the Quality of Life*, ed. J. O'Toole. Cambridge, Mass.: MIT Press.

Kemler, D., and B. Shepp. 1971. "The Learning and Transfer of Dimensional Relevance and Irrelevance in Children." *Journal of Experimental Psychology* 90:120–7.

Kohler, W. 1929. *Gestalt Psychology.* New York: Liveright.

Langer, E. J., and J. Rodin. 1976. "The Effects of Choice and Enhanced Personal Responsibility for the Aged: A Field Experiment in an Institutional Setting." *Journal of Personality and Social Psychology* 34:191–8.

LaRocco, J. M., J. S. House, and J. R. P. French, Jr. 1980. "Social Support, Occupational Stress, and Health." *Journal of Health and Social Behavior* 21:202–18.

LaRocco, J. M., and A. P. Jones. 1978. "Co-worker and Leader

Support as Moderators of Stress-Strain Relationships in Work Situations." *Journal of Applied Psychology* 63:629-34.

Lazarus, R. S. 1966. *Psychological Stress and the Coping Process.* New York: McGraw-Hill.

Lazarus, R. S., and R. Launier. 1978. "Stress-Related Transactions Between Person and Environment." In *Perspectives in Interactional Psychology*, ed. L. A. Pervin and M. Lewis. New York: Plenum.

Ledford, G. E., Jr. 1981. "A Layman's Guide to Some Medical Issues in Occupational Exposure to Lead." Lead Industries Association, New York.

Levine, S. 1982. "A Psychobiological Approach to Stress and Coping." In *Research on Stress in Health and Disease*, ed. C. Eisdorfer and G. Elliott. Washington, D.C.: Institute of Medicine, National Academy of Sciences.

Lin, N., R. S. Simeone, W. M. Ensel, and W. K. Kuo. 1979. "Social Support, Stressful Life Events, and Illness: An Empirical Test." *Journal of Health and Social Behavior* 20:108-19.

Lyons, T. F. 1971. "Role Clarity, Need for Clarity, Satisfaction, Tension, and Withdrawal." *Organizational Behavior and Human Performance* 6:99-110.

Malkiel, B. G. 1973. *A Random Walk Down Wall Street.* New York: Norton.

Mandler, G., and D. L. Watson. 1966. "Anxiety and the Interruption of Behavior." In *Anxiety and Behavior*, ed. C. D. Spielberger. New York: Academic Press.

McGrath, J. E. 1976. "Stress and Behavior in Organizations." In *Handbook of Industrial and Organizational Psychology*, ed. M. D. Dunnette. Chicago: Rand McNally.

McLean, A. A. 1979. *Work Stress.* Reading, Mass.: Addison-Wesley.

Mills, R. T., and D. S. Krantz. 1979. "Information, Choice, and Reactions to Stress: A Field Experiment in a Blood Bank with Laboratory Analogue." *Journal of Personality and Social Psychology* 37:608-20.

Nisbett, R., and L. Ross. 1980. *Human Inference: Strategies and Shortcomings of Social Judgement.* Englewood Cliffs, N.J.: Prentice-Hall.

Nuckolls, K. P., J. Cassel, and B. H. Kaplan. 1972. "Psychosocial Assets, Life Crisis, and the Prognosis of Pregnancy." *American Journal of Epidemiology* 95:431-41.

Pasmore, W., and F. Friedlander. 1982. "An Action Research Program for Increasing Employee Involvement in Problem-Solving." *Administrative Science Quarterly* 27:343-62.

Pearce, J. L. 1981. "Bringing Some Clarity to Role Ambiguity Research." *Academy of Management Review* 6:665-74.

Pinneau, S. R. 1975. "Effects of Social Support on Psychological and Physiological Stress." Ph.D. diss. University of Michigan.

Price, K. P., and J. H. Geer. 1972. "Predictable and Unpredictable Aversive Events: Evidence for the Safety Signal Hypothesis. *Psychonomic Science* 26:215-16.

Rizzo, J. R., R. J. House, and S. I. Lirtzman. 1970. "Role Con-

flict and Ambiguity in Complex Organizations." *Administrative Science Quarterly* 15:150-63.

Rodin, J., and E. J. Langer. 1977. "Long-Term Effects of a Control-Relevant Intervention with the Institutionalized Aged." *Journal of Personality and Social Psychology* 35:897-902.

Rotter, J. B. 1966. "Generalized Expectancies for Internal Vs. External Control of Reinforcement." *Psychological Monographs* 80:609.

Schein, E. H. 1978. *Career Dynamics: Matching Individual and Organizational Needs.* Reading, Mass.: Addison-Wesley.

Schuler, R. S. 1980. "Definition and Conceptualization of Stress in Organizations." *Organizational Behavior and Human Performance* 24:115-30.

Seeman, M. 1972. "Alienation and Engagement." In *The Meaning of Social Change*, ed. A. Campbell and P. E. Converse. New York: Russell Sage Foundation.

Seligman, M. E. P. 1968. "Chronic Fear Produced by Unpredictable Shock." *Journal of Comparative and Physiological Psychology* 66:402-11.

———. 1975. *Helplessness.* San Francisco: Freeman.

Seligman, M. E. P., and B. Meyer. 1970. "Chronic Fear and Ulcers as a Function of the Unpredictability of Safety." *Journal of Comparative and Physiological Psychology* 73:202-7.

Selye, H. 1956. *The Stress of Life.* New York: McGraw-Hill.

———. 1971. "The Evolution of the Stress Concept—Stress and Cardiovascular Disease." *Society, Stress, and Disease: The Psychosocial Environment and Psychosomatic Diseases*, ed. L. Levi, vol. 1. London: Oxford University Press.

Staub, E., and D. S. Kellet. 1972. "Increasing Pain Tolerance by Information About Aversive Stimuli." *Journal of Personality and Social Psychology* 21:198-203.

Thompson, S. C. 1981. "Will It Hurt Less If I Can Control It? A Complex Answer to a Simple Question." *Psychological Bulletin* 90:89-101.

Thornton, J. W., and P. D. Jacobs. 1971. "Learned Helplessness in Human Subjects." *Journal of Experimental Psychology* 87:369-72.

Tversky, A., and D. Kahneman. 1980. "Causal Schemas in Judgments under Uncertainty." In *Progress in Social Psychology*, ed. M. Fishbein, vol. 1. Hillsdale, N.J.: Erlbaum.

Van Maanen, J. 1976. "Breaking In: Socialization at Work." In *Handbook of Work, Organization and Society*, ed. R. Dubin. Chicago: Rand McNally.

Walker, J., C. Fletcher, and D. McLeod. 1975. "Flexible Working Hours in Two British Government Offices." *Public Personnel Management* 4:216-22.

Wanous, J. P. 1973. "Effects of a Realistic Job Preview on Job Acceptance, Job Attitudes, and Job Survival." *Journal of Applied Psychology* 58:327-32.

Weiss, K. M., and K. T. Strongman. 1969. "Shock-Induced Response Bursts and Suppression." *Psychonomic Science* 15:238-40.

18

Performance appraisal

MICHAEL BEER

The outboard motor "completely refused to run a) when the waves were high, b) when the wind blew, c) at night, early in the morning, and evening, d) in rain, dew, or fog, e) when the distance to be covered was more than 200 yards. But on warm, sunny days when the weather was calm and the white beach close by—in a word, on days when it would have been a pleasure to row, it started at a touch and would not stop."[1]

Steinbeck's description of an outboard motor makes an apt introduction to a chapter on performance appraisal. When performance has been good, when superiors and subordinates have an open relationship, when promotions or salary increases are abundant, when there is plenty of time for preparation and discussion—in short, whenever it's a pleasure—performance appraisal is easy to do. Most of the time, however, and particularly when it is most needed and most difficult (e.g., when performance is substandard), performance appraisal refuses to run properly.[2]

This article is based on Michael Beer, Note on Performance Appraisal (9-478-019), Harvard Business School. Copyright © 1977 by the President and Fellows of Harvard College.

1. John Steinbeck, *The Log from the Sea of Cortez* (New York: Viking, 1962). This quote was first used in connection with performance appraisal by McCall and DeVries, "Performance Appraisal and Feedback: Flies in the Ointment."

2. Morgan W. McCall and David L. DeVries, "Appraisal in Context: Clashing with Organizational Realities." Paper presented in symposium, "Performance Appraisal and Feedback: Flies in the Ointment." 84th Annual Convention of the American Psychological Association, Washington, D.C., 5 Sept. 1976.

WHAT IS PERFORMANCE APPRAISAL AND WHY IS IT A PROBLEM?

The evaluation of individual performance is an inevitable part of organizational life. Everyone is constantly evaluated by his or her boss, peers, and subordinates. Much of the evaluation is informal, but most organizations have a formal appraisal system designed to collect systematic information about the performance of employees. The formal system usually includes a form on which supervisors indicate their evaluations of subordinates' performances. The form may be a blank sheet of paper on which the supervisor's views are noted, a guide for setting objectives and checking on their attainment (commonly referred to as Management by Objectives, or MBO), or a series of ratings on how the subordinate goes about his or her job. Regardless of the format, appraisals become part of the individual's formal record and are used to make decisions about his or her pay and career. The supervisor is usually expected to sit down with the subordinate once a year to discuss the appraisal.

For a number of very important reasons, almost all organizations maintain appraisal systems. Managers need data about performance and potential in order to make decisions and to justify them. It is also important to have these data in corporate personnel-department records, so that personnel decisions can be made with some objectivity, equity, and fairness. Without corporate involvement, inequities can lead to dissatisfaction among employees and, increasingly, to costly lawsuits under fair-employment legislation. Such lawsuits by disgruntled employees who have been fired, passed over for promotion, or demoted are becoming more frequent in the United States.[3] The corporate personnel department also requires data on employee performance and potential to determine how many employees will be available to fill future openings assuming a certain turnover, retirement, and growth rate, and to help line managers decide who will be promoted. It should be clear that central recording of objective data is a necessity in managing large aggregates of employees, because personal knowledge of all employees by all managers is virtually impossible. Centrally maintained records are the means by which the corporation attempts to remove favoritism, subjectivity, and politics from personnel decisions. Unfortunately, many systems do not accomplish these lofty goals, because employee perceptions of equity and objectivity in personnel decisions depend on a climate of trust and open communication. Such a climate can only be created by managers who are interpersonally competent in their dealings with employees.

Evaluation is also needed to improve the performance and potential of employees. Feedback is essential if performance is to improve. People must develop and grow in their skill as the company grows or business conditions change, if the organization is to have the competencies required to compete. That objective can be met in part through better selection, but more importantly it requires continuing growth in the competence of employees. Thus, performance-evaluation data and the process of feedback and discussion with employees are necessary to help employees develop. Because this process of feedback and discussion is highly dependent on individual manager-subordinate relationships and skills in discussing difficult problems, it presents the corporation with significant implementation problems.

Despite their value, managers and subordinates alike seem to be ambivalent about performance appraisal. Managers recognize performance appraisal as a potentially useful tool for improving the performance of subordinates and the effectiveness of their organizational units; yet they also sense that performance appraisal inherently poses some danger to the motivation of their subordinates and their relationship with them. Like tax payments, performance appraisal is something managers feel obligated to do but don't really want to. On the other hand, subordinates want, and often ask for, feedback about how they are doing, because they want to know where they stand, but they prefer feedback that is consistent with their image of themselves as good performers. Thus,

both managers and subordinates have ambivalent feelings about performance appraisal and share a natural tendency to underplay or avoid dealing with the negative aspects of the procedure.

In this chapter we will explore some reasons for managers' and subordinates' difficulties with performance appraisal and some ideas for dealing with these difficulties. Performance appraisal is one of the oldest management tools available, and the problems associated with it are equally well established. This chapter cannot hope to identify or solve all of these age-old problems.

Performance appraisal is both a system of papers and procedures designed by the organization for use by its managers (we will refer to this as the "appraisal system," and an interpersonal process in which manager and subordinate communicate and attempt to influence each other (we will refer to this as the "appraisal process" or interview). Many of the problems in performance appraisal stem from the appraisal system itself—the objectives it is intended to serve, the administrative system in which it is embedded, and the forms and procedures that make up the system. We will not discuss these system design problems in any depth, but will refer to them as needed to explain problems in the appraisal process. (The design of performance-appraisal systems is discussed extensively in several recent books.[4]) We will focus instead on performance appraisal as a process in which boss and subordinate meet to discuss issues relating to the latter's performance. The focus will be on what we know about this process, the difficulties it presents, and how these might be overcome.

GOALS OF PERFORMANCE APPRAISAL

Both the organization and the individual employee have certain goals they wish fulfilled by performance appraisal. In some cases these objectives are compatible, in others not. We will briefly explore these goals and the potential for conflict between them.[5]

The organization's goals

Performance evaluation is an important element in the information and control system of most complex organi-

3. R. D. Arvey, "Fairness in Selecting Employees" (Reading, Mass.: Addison-Wesley, 1979).

4. Gary P. Latham and Kenneth N. Wexley, *Increasing Productivity Through Performance Appraisal* (Reading, Mass.: Addison-Wesley, 1981); Stephen J. Carroll and Craig E. Schneider, *Performance Appraisal and Review Systems* (Glenview, Ill.: Scott, Foresman, 1982).

5. This discussion of performance-appraisal goals draws extensively on Lyman W. Porter, Edward E. Lawler III, and J. Richard Hackman, *Behavior in Organizations* (New York: McGraw-Hill, 1975).

zations. It provides information about the performance of organizational members used in decisions about placement, promotions, firing, and pay. Not having the right person available to fill an important job can be as serious as not having the money to expand physical facilities or buy equipment. An evaluation system can help track those people who have potential so that they can be placed in developmental positions. The organization's personnel department is usually responsible for coordinating these activities, and the performance-appraisal system serves them in this purpose.

Performance-appraisal systems and, more important, the discussions between supervisor and subordinate about performance can also be aimed at influencing the behavior and performance of individuals. This is true of MBO systems, as well as various performance-rating systems in which the employee's skills to carry out specific parts of the job are evaluated. The process of influencing behavior is important to the development of human resources, and it is of utmost importance to managers' efforts to obtain the results for which they are accountable. The performance appraisal process can help motivate employees, point out needed changes in the way they do things, and help them grow and develop competence needed now and in the future. It is thus a major tool for changing individual behavior.

From the organization's point of view, then, performance appraisal serves two sets of goals, as summarized here:

EVALUATION GOALS

1. To give feedback to subordinates so they know where they stand
2. To develop valid data for pay (salary and bonus) and promotion decisions and to provide a means of communicating these decisions
3. To help the manager in making discharge and retention decisions and to provide a means of warning subordinates about unsatisfactory performance

COACHING AND DEVELOPMENT GOALS

1. To counsel and coach subordinates so that they will improve their performance and develop future potential
2. To develop commitment to the larger organization through discussion of career opportunities and career planning
3. To motivate subordinates through recognition and support
4. To strengthen supervisor-subordinate relations

5. To diagnose individual and organizational problems

The most important thing to note about this list is that there are many goals and they are in conflict.[6] When the goal is evaluation, managers use the appraisal system as a tool for making difficult judgments that affect their subordinates' future. When they communicate these judgments they must justify their appraisal in response to or in anticipation of disagreement by subordinates. The result can be an adversary relationship, poor listening, and low trust—conditions that work against the coaching and development objectives of performance appraisal. When coaching and development are the goals, managers must play the role of helper. If they are to help, they must listen, draw out subordinates about their problems, and get subordinates to understand their weaknesses. The fact that different communication processes are required to achieve the conflicting goals of performance appraisal creates difficult problems for the manager.

The individuals' goals

Like the organization, the individual has conflicting goals in performance evaluation. Individuals want feedback about themselves because it helps them learn.[7] Research on how managers find out about their performance suggests that they rely most often on self-evaluation based on personal criteria. They also rely on informal signals from their superiors about how they have done on given tasks. But a very significant source of feedback is the performance-appraisal interview. Though it is less frequently used than the other sources and not always accurate, it represents the bottom line on how the organization values the individual.[8]

The performance-appraisal situation is an opportunity for employees to get such feedback and to learn how they are progressing in their careers. If this information is favorable, it helps satisfy their needs for competence and psychological success; if it is not, they tend to experience failure, and the feedback is often difficult to accept. Thus, even when people in organizations ask

6. Michael Beer and Robert A. Ruh, "Employee Growth Through Performance Management," *Harvard Business Review* (July-August 1976).

7. L. Festinger, S. Schachter, and K. Back, *Social Pressures in Informal Groups* (Stanford, Calif.: Stanford University Press, 1950); T. F. Pettigrew, "Social Evaluation Theory: Convergences and Applications," in *Nebraska Symposium on Motivation*, J. D. Levine ed. (Lincoln, Neb.: University of Nebraska Press, 1967).

8. Margret Pennybacker and David DeVries, "Developing a Sixth Sense," *Center for Creative Leadership Newsletter* 5, no. 2 (June 1978).

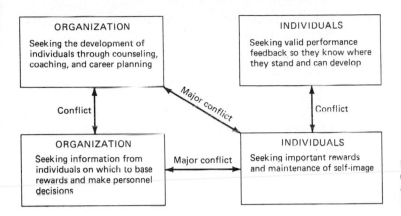

Figure 18.1 Conflicts in performance appraisal. (Adapted from Lyman W. Porter, Edward E. Lawler III, and J. Richard Hackman, *Behavior in Organizations*, [New York: McGraw-Hill, 1975], by permission.)

for and sometimes demand feedback, down deep they are hoping for feedback that will affirm their concept of themselves. When rewards such as pay and promotion are tied to the evaluation, employees have a further reason for wanting to avoid unfavorable evaluations. They may gloss over problems, if not deny them. Often without realizing it, the individuals may present themselves in a favorable light to gain valued organizational rewards.

There are obvious conflicts between individuals' desire for personal development and their wish for rewards and feedback consistent with their self-image. Self-development requires openness to feedback and real receptivity to alternative approaches to the job. Subordinates must be willing to drop their defenses and consider accepting the manager's view of their performance, taking an exploratory attitude about their performance and what might be done about it. However, this openness may not always serve the subordinate's objective of gaining raises, bonuses, and promotions when these are in scarce supply.

portant influence on their rewards (pay, recognition), their career (promotions and reputation), and their self-image, they will be reluctant to engage in the kind of open dialogue required for valid evaluation and personal development. The poorer the performance of the individual involved, the worse the potential conflict and the less likely the exchange of valid information. Figure 18.1 depicts graphically the several kinds of conflict involved in performance appraisal.

It is these conflicts that suggest an analogy to Steinbeck's outboard motor. Performance appraisal runs well and is a pleasure in the case of good performers who are eager to give and receive valid data. It does not run well and is very uncomfortable when the individual is a poor performer and the conflicts between his or her own self-interest and those of the organization are high.

PROBLEMS IN PERFORMANCE APPRAISAL

Conflicting individual and organizational goals

Because the organization is pursuing conflicting objectives (evaluation and development), the manager must use performance appraisal in two quite contradictory ways. Similarly, individuals have conflicting objectives as they approach a performance appraisal. The most significant conflict, however, is between the individual and the organization. The individual desires to confirm a positive self-image and to obtain organizational rewards of promotion or pay. The organization wants individuals to be open to negative information about themselves so they can improve their performance. It also wants individuals to be helpful in supplying this information. The conflict is over the exchange of valid information. As long as individuals see the appraisal process as having an im-

Ambivalence and avoidance

Given the inherent conflicts, it is not surprising that supervisors and subordinates are often ambivalent about participating in the performance-appraisal process.[9] Superiors are uncomfortable because their organizational role places them in the position of being both judge and jury. They must make decisions that affect people's careers and lives in significant ways. Furthermore, most managers are not trained to handle the interpersonally difficult situations that are likely to arise when feedback is negative. This is particularly a problem because

9. D. T. Hall and E. E. Lawler, III, "Job Design and Job Pressures as Facilitators of Professional-Organization Integration," *Administrative Science Quarterly* 15 (1970): 171–281.

managers would like to maintain good relations with their subordinates in order to carry on with their jobs. All this leads to uncertainty about their subjective judgments and anxiety about meeting with subordinates to discuss performance. Yet supervisors also know that both the organization and the subordinate want such a discussion to be held. Finally, supervisors often feel personally bound to let people know where they stand. If they are not open with their subordinates, the knowledge that they have been less than truthful keeps them from building a relationship of mutual trust. In short, supervisors are likely to be extremely ambivalent about the performance-appraisal process.

At the same time, subordinates are likely to be very ambivalent about receiving negative feedback. They may well want to discuss negative aspects of their performance so they can improve and develop, but will not want to jeopardize promotions, pay, or their own self-image.

The ambivalence of superiors and subordinates has led to the vanishing performance appraisal.[10] In many organizations, supervisors report that they hold periodic appraisal interviews and give honest feedback, while their subordinates report they have not had a performance appraisal for many years or that they heard nothing negative.[11] It is probable that supervisors, fearful of the appraisal process, have expressed themselves in such a way that subordinates do not receive the unwelcome messages. The supervisor may carefully package the negative feedback between heavy doses of positive feedback (the sandwich approach) or may make only very general statements, without referring to specific problems. That is, supervisors provide negative feedback, but immediately counterbalance it with positive statements when their own anxiety or the defensiveness of the subordinate signals potential problems. Because of their fear of learning things that will affect their self-image, subordinates collude with the supervisor in avoiding negative feedback. This sometimes results in long conversations only marginally related to the purpose of the appraisal interview. Sometimes avoidance is manifested in small talk or humor that conveys an oblique message, or the use of phrases that do not have clear meaning to either the supervisor or subordinate. Thus, negative feedback is often not explored in depth and is not fully understood and internalized by the subordinate.

As a result, no real appraisal occurs or, more likely, a shallow appraisal just skims the surface. Both parties collude in meeting the organization's requirements for

appraisal but avoid the tough issues. Is it surprising then that subordinates do not think they have been given negative feedback, or had an appraisal at all?

Defensiveness and resistance

The conflict in appraisal between the organization's evaluation objectives and its coaching and development objectives tends to place the manager in the incompatible roles of *judge* and *helper*. Some managers feel obligated to fulfill their organizational role as judge by communicating to the subordinate all facets of their evaluation. They want to be sure they fulfill their obligation of letting the subordinate know where he or she stands by detailing all shortcomings in performance. This naturally can elicit resistance on the part of subordinates as they defend against threats to their self-esteem. The defensiveness may take a variety of forms.[12] Subordinates may try to blame their unsatisfactory performance on others or on uncontrollable events; they may question the appraisal system itself or minimize its importance; they may demean the source of the data; they may apologize and promise to do better in the hope of shortening their exposure to negative feedback; or they may agree too readily to the feedback while inwardly denying its validity or accuracy.

The important point is that supervisors find themselves communicating their evaluation to the subordinate at the very time they are also trying to develop an open two-way dialogue leading to valid information exchange and development. The defensiveness that results may take the form of open hostility and denials or may be masked by passivity and surface compliance. In neither case does the subordinate really accept or understand the feedback. Thus, the very subordinates who need development most may learn least.

The worst of all interviews: avoidance and defensiveness combined

The worst situation is one in which the problems created by ambivalence and avoidance of performance appraisal are combined with the problems of feedback and defensiveness. This can happen when managers go through a *pro forma* performance appraisal to fulfill their duty as supervisors. Their ambivalence leads them to avoid

10. Porter, Lawler and Hackman, *Behavior in Organizations.*
11. Hall and Lawler, "Job Design and Job Pressures."

12. Alvin Zander, "Research on Self-Esteem, Feedback and Threats to Self-Esteem," in *Performance Appraisals: Effects on Employees and Their Performance*, ed. A. Zander (Ann Arbor, Mich.: Foundation for Research in Human Behavior, 1963).

direct and meaningful talk about performance. But because of their need to fulfill their role, they go through a mechanical yet complete review of the evaluation form. Without getting deeply into problems of subordinates' performance, they nevertheless elicit defensive behavior by covering the evaluation form in detail. Thus, neither the benefits of avoidance (i.e., maintenance of good relations and personal comfort), nor the benefits of accurate feedback (i.e., clear understanding and development) are realized, while all the problems of avoidance and defensiveness remain.

Nonevaluative evaluation

The central dilemma in the appraisal process is how to have an open discussion of performance that meets the individual's need for feedback and the organization's personnel-development needs while preventing damage to the individual's self-esteem and to his confidence about organizational rewards. Both goals cannot be fully achieved, but the remainder of this chapter suggests some ways of dealing with this paradox.

POTENTIAL SOLUTIONS TO APPRAISAL PROBLEMS

Several approaches to the problems we have outlined are possible. A manager seeking to improve performance appraisal should examine each of the three major factors influencing appraisal outcomes (see figure 18.2) to see where changes might be helpful. First, the appraisal system can be designed to minimize the negative dynamics discussed previously. The manager often has only marginal control over these matters. Second, the ongoing

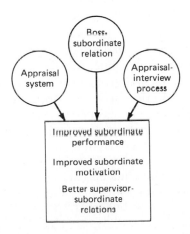

Figure 18.2 Factors influencing appraisal outcomes

relationship between boss and subordinate will have a major influence on the appraisal process and outcome. Third, the interview process itself, the quality of communication between boss and subordinate, can help to minimize problems.

The appraisal system

UNCOUPLING EVALUATION AND DEVELOPMENT

Less defensiveness and a more open dialogue are likely if the manager distinguishes his roles as helper and judge.[13] Two separate performance-appraisal interviews can be held—one focused on evaluation and the other on coaching and development. The open, problem-solving dialogue required for building a relationship and developing subordinates would come at a different time of the year from the meeting in which the supervisor informs the subordinate of his overall evaluation and its implications for retention, pay, and promotion. This split recognizes that a manager cannot be simultaneously a helper and a judge, because the behavior required by one role interferes with the other.

CHOOSING APPROPRIATE PERFORMANCE DATA

A manager can minimize defensiveness and avoidance by narrowly focusing feedback on specific behaviors or specific performance goals. For example, an unsatisfactory rating on a characteristic as broad as motivation is likely to be perceived as a personal attack and could threaten self-esteem. Feedback about specific incidents or aspects of job performance is more likely to be heard than broad generalizations and will also be more helpful to the individual in terms of changing behavior. Thus, an appraisal discussion that relies on a report-card rating of traits or performance is doomed to failure because it leads the supervisor into general evaluative statements that threaten the subordinate.

Fortunately, some appraisal techniques can guide the supervisor toward more specific behavioral observations. A behavioral rating scale, for example, asks supervisors to indicate the degree to which subordinates fulfill certain behavioral requirements of their job (e.g., participating actively in meetings or communicating sufficiently with other departments). In the Critical Incident Method, the supervisor records important examples of effective or ineffective performance.[14] Similarly, various

13. H. H. Meyer, E. Kay, and J. R. P. French, Jr., "Split Roles in Performance Appraisal," *Harvard Business Review* (Jan.–Feb. 1965); Beer and Ruh, "Employee Growth."

14. John C. Flanagan and Robert K. Burns, "The Employee Performance Record," *Harvard Business Review* (Sept.–Oct. 1955).

MBO techniques can be used to guide the appraisal discussion toward reviewing specific accomplishments. Some experts on performance appraisal have suggested that a comprehensive performance-management system should include both MBO and behavioral ratings.[15] They see these techniques as complementary tools in managing and appraising performance. MBO is a means of managing *what* employees should do, while behavioral rating is a means of helping them see *how* they should do it.

It is generally acknowledged, however, that behavioral data are more relevant than data on goal accomplishment when the purpose is employee development. *Outcomes* such as sales or profits are a function of many factors beyond the individual's control. Moreover, focusing on subordinates' failure to achieve goals may bias supervisor's evaluations and limit their ability to develop a constructive dialogue.[16]

SEPARATING EVALUATION OF PERFORMANCE AND POTENTIAL

Current performance, as measured by the attainment of results, is not necessarily correlated with potential for promotion. Yet many appraisal systems do not adequately provide for separate evaluations of these dimensions. If a subordinate rates high in current performance and low in potential for advancement (or vice versa), a manager must average his or her assessments of these qualities and then defend an evaluation that may be inconsistent with the subordinate's perception of either performance or potential alone. Even if separate evaluations of these dimensions do not reduce subordinate defensiveness, they will relieve the manager of the need to defend a composite rating that he or she cannot justify. Systems that separate assessments of performance and potential increase the likelihood of a constructive dialogue and therefore reduce the likelihood of avoidance.

RECOGNIZING INDIVIDUAL DIFFERENCES IN SYSTEM DESIGN

Individuals differ in their needs for performance evaluation and development. Upwardly mobile employees may desire and need more feedback about performance and promotability than less upwardly mobile employees. They will also need longer and more frequent developmental discussions. Similarly, more confident and open employees will be able to handle these discussions better than will employees who lack self-esteem and are

defensive. Performance-appraisal policies should permit managers to use different methods for different employees. An appraisal every two or three years may be enough for an employee who has reached the peak of his or her capabilities. Such an appraisal could be limited to a rating and discussion of current performance, but omit any discussion of promotion potential. Uniform systems and procedures stand in the way of such differential treatment.

UPWARD APPRAISAL

One of the appraisal dynamics that contributes most to defensiveness and/or avoidance is the authoritarian character of the supervisor-subordinate relationship. The simple fact that one person is the boss and is responsible for evaluation places him or her in a dominant role and induces submissive behavior on the part of the subordinate. Furthermore, the boss holds and controls rewards. To develop the open two-way dialogue required for coaching and development, power must be equalized or at least brought into better balance during the interview. Physical arrangements can contribute to this goal, but the adoption of a rate-your-boss appraisal process may be even more effective. Before the interview, subordinates are given a form on which to rate the supervisor's performance, with a clear understanding that their ratings and views will be reviewed in the appraisal meeting.

An upward appraisal can help a supervisor create the conditions needed for an effective performance-appraisal interview. It gives subordinates a real stake in the appraisal interview and an opportunity to influence a part of their environment that ultimately influences their performance. Thus, it makes them more equal and less dependent, increasing their motivation to enter the appraisal process with an open mind. It also offers the supervisor an opportunity to model nondefensive behavior and to demonstrate a willingness to engage in a real two-way dialogue (assuming the supervisor is capable of behaving nondefensively).

The rate-your-boss appraisal process can give superiors data they will find extremely useful in adjusting their approach to managing. As a result of one such program reported by Maloney and Hinrichs, 25 percent of subordinates said they had seen lasting changes in their supervisors, 88 percent of supervisors said they had tried to change, and 60 percent of the supervisors and subordinates agreed that productivity had increased as a result of the program.[17]

The use of subordinate feedback is increasing in corporations. Morrison, McCall, and DeVries reviewed

---

15. Beer and Ruh, "Employee Growth."

16. T. R. Mitchell and R. E. Wood, "Supervisor's Responses to Subordinate Poor Performance: A Test of an Attributional Model," *Organizational Behavior and Human Performance*, 25 (1980): 123–38.

17. P. W. Maloney and J. R. Hinrichs, "A New Tool for Supervisory Self-Development," *Personnel* 36 (1959): 46–53.

twenty-four instruments used in organizations to facilitate subordinate evaluations of their managers.[18] Most organizations, however, still do not have rate-your-boss forms. In such a situation, supervisors can develop their own or seek informal feedback sometime during the appraisal interview.

Supervisor-subordinate relations

Not surprisingly, the quality of the appraisal process is dependent on the nature of the day-to-day boss-subordinate relationship. In an effective relationship, the supervisor is providing feedback and coaching on an ongoing basis. Thus, the appraisal interview is merely a review of issues that have already been discussed. Moreover, expectations for the appraisal interview are likely to be shaped by the broader supervisor-subordinate relationship, of which it is only a small part. If a relationship of mutual trust and supportiveness exists, subordinates are more apt to be open in discussing performance problems and less defensive in response to negative feedback.

There are no easy techniques for changing a boss-subordinate relationship. Nor is the development of these relationships the subject of this chapter. It is important to note, however, that the context within which the boss and subordinate work, the broader culture of the organization, and the climate of the primary work group will have important influences on the boss-subordinate relationship.

If the organization culture encourages participative management, open communication, supportiveness accompanied by high standards of performance, a concern for employees, and egalitarianism, it is more likely that these values will characterize the culture of the primary work group and therefore the relationship between boss and subordinate. Many companies launch programs to improve the performance-appraisal process without recognizing that the very culture of the organization will have to change to obtain desired improvements. And this change will require reexamination of fundamental values and assumptions about management by top executives who have a strong influence on corporate culture by their example and the policies they develop.

Just as important is the culture of the primary work group. Managers can materially improve their relationship with subordinates by developing an open and supportive environment in which trust is high. Clearly,

autocratic management will not achieve this result. It is for this reason that upward appraisals were suggested earlier as a way of improving the appraisal process. Managers who want to improve their relationships with subordinates might also schedule regular team-building meetings with all of their subordinates. Such meetings, sometimes facilitated by consultants, are aimed at involving all members of the group in a discussion of how effectively the group is functioning and what and who might change to improve that functioning.[19] In fact, the aggregate results of upward appraisals have been used as data in team-building meetings. The supervisor might discuss the negative comments he or she had received from subordinates, grouping these comments into three categories: 1) areas that I cannot change (citing the reasons), 2) areas that I can change immediately, and 3) areas that through discussion and help from you (subordinates) we can change together.[20] Sometimes discussion covers the behavior of each group member and how it affects group performance. Managers who open themselves to influence through this process provide clear signals that they are not arbitrary, and thus can develop more trust. At the same time they can help establish standards for constructive criticism in the group and skills in giving and receiving feedback that will support the performance-appraisal process between manager and subordinate.

The appraisal interview

The best techniques for conducting a particular appraisal interview depend on the mix of objectives pursued and the characteristics of the subordinate. Employees differ in their age, experience, sensitivity about negative feedback, attitude toward the supervisor, and desire for influence and control over their destiny. If the subordinate is young, inexperienced, and dependent, and looks up to the supervisor, and if the supervisor's objective is to let the subordinate know that performance improvement is needed, it may be appropriate to have the supervisor do most of the talking. On the other hand, if the subordinate is older, more experienced, and sensitive about negative feedback, and has a high need for controlling his or her destiny, the same objective is best met by a less directive approach to the interview.

18. A. M. Morrison, M. W. McCall, Jr., and D. L. DeVries, "Feedback to Managers: A Comprehensive Review of Twenty-Four Instruments," tech. report no. 8 (Greensboro, N.C.: Center for Creative Leadership, 1978).

19. W. G. Dyer, *Team Building: Issues and Alternatives* (Reading, Mass.: Addison-Wesley, 1977).

20. Gary P. Latham and Kenneth N. Wexley, *Increasing Productivity Through Performance Appraisal* (Reading, Mass.: Addison-Wesley, 1981), 91–92.

Norman Maier[21] describes three types of appraisal interviews, each with a distinct specific objective. The differences are important in determining the skills required by the supervisor and the outcomes for employee motivations and supervisor-subordinate relationships. The three methods—termed *tell-and-sell, tell-and-listen,* and *problem-solving*—can be combined if several objectives must be met by the same interview.

THE TELL-AND-SELL METHOD

The aim of the tell-and-sell method is to communicate evaluations to employees as accurately as possible. The fairness of the evaluation is assumed and the manager seeks (1) to let the subordinates know how they are doing, (2) to gain their acceptance of the evaluation, and (3) to get them to follow the manager's plan for improvement. In the interview, supervisors are in complete control; they do most of the talking. They decide what subordinates need to do to improve and attempt to persuade subordinates that their observations and recommendations are valid. Clearly, this method can lead to defensiveness, lack of trust, lack of open communication, and exchange of invalid information. It can hurt supervisor-subordinate relations (because the employees feel hostile and angry when they must accept a supervisor's views that are inconsistent with their self-perceptions) and may not motivate employees to change (because they are placed in a dependent position and do not contribute to the plan).

Nevertheless, there may be situations in which this approach is the only way. For example, there may be an urgent need to be clear about what is expected from an employee who remains resistant to change, especially after less directive approaches have been used.

THE TELL-AND-LISTEN INTERVIEW

The purpose of this interview method is to communicate the evaluation to the subordinate and then let him or her respond to it. The supervisor describes the subordinate's strengths and weaknesses during the first part of the interview, postponing points of disagreement until later. The second part of the interview is devoted to exploring the subordinate's feelings about the evaluation. Thus, the supervisor functions as a judge but also listens to objectives from the subordinate without refuting them. In fact, the supervisor encourages the subordinate to disagree, to drain off any negative feelings the appraisal arouses. The verbal expression of frustration is assumed to reduce the hostility resulting from negative feedback.

The tell-and-listen interview differs substantially from the tell-and-sell method in how disagreement and resistance are handled. While both interviews start with a one-way communication from the supervisor to the employee, in the tell-and-listen interview the supervisor then sits back and assumes the role of a nondirective counselor.[22] This role requires the supervisor to (1) *listen actively*—accepting and trying to understand the employee's attitudes and feelings; (2) *make effective use of pauses*—waiting patiently without embarrassment for the subordinate to talk; (3) *reflect feelings*—responding to and restating feelings in a way that shows understanding of them; and (4) *summarize feelings*—helping subordinates understand themselves. This approach is not intended to communicate agreement or disagreement with subordinates. Rather, it acknowledges the subordinates' viewpoints and helps them decide which part of the feedback to accept.

The tell-and-listen approach is apt to result in better understanding between supervisor and subordinate than the tell-and-sell. The subordinate is less likely to be defensive and therefore more likely to accept feedback. Supervisors are likely to learn a lot about subordinates if they listen. However, the interview may not give subordinates a clear understanding of where they stand and how to improve, and may not inspire a commitment to improving behavior.

THE PROBLEM-SOLVING INTERVIEW

This interview approach takes the manager out of the role of judge and puts him or her in the role of helper. The objective is to help subordinates discover their own performance deficiencies and lead them to take the initiative in developing a joint plan for improvement. The problem-solving interview is best suited to coaching and development objectives. It has no provision for communicating the supervisor's evaluation. The assumption is that subordinates' self-understanding and motivation to improve performance can best be achieved in a climate of open communication and mutual influence.

Because the objective is to allow subordinates to discover their own developmental needs, the manager cannot specify areas for improvement—that would be an evaluative judgment. The supervisor helps employees examine themselves and their jobs and must be willing to consider their ideas for performance improvement. In this regard, the skills required in the problem-solving interview are similar to those required in the latter half of the tell-and-listen interview. However, the objective is to go well beyond listening and help subordinates dis-

21. Norman R. F. Maier, "Three Types of Appraisal Interviews," *Personnel* (March-April 1958).

22. Carl R. Rogers, "Releasing Expression," in *Counseling and Psychotherapy* (Cambridge: Houghton Mifflin, 1942).

cover and explore alternative solutions to problems identified. Supervisors may suggest their own ideas for solution, but in the pure problem-solving interview, the supervisor works from the subordinates' initiatives. Supervisors may stimulate subordinate initiative by asking questions about how a job problem can be eliminated. The questions should not put subordinates on the spot but should indicate an interest in helping them develop the best plan. Maier gives the following examples:

> "Can this plan of yours deal with an emergency situation, in case one arises?"
>
> "Would you rather have other people at your level participate in the plan?"
>
> "What kinds of problems do you anticipate in a changing market?"[23]

Exploratory questions can draw the person out, help clarify thinking, and direct analysis to areas that may have been overlooked.

The problem-solving interview eliminates defensiveness because the issues raised and the ideas for solution are primarily the subordinate's. He or she is therefore more willing to accept the problems and better motivated to accomplish personal and job-related plans for improvement. This interview method also encourages creative thinking by subordinates, and both supervisor and employee are more likely to arrive at new discoveries about the job and themselves. Thus, there is the potential for changes in the job, the organization, and the supervisor's own style. All of these can affect the performance of the individual.

THE MIXED MODEL INTERVIEW

The three interview models we have reviewed are a convenient way of categorizing stylistic strategies for an appraisal interview. As noted earlier, the ideal way of dealing with the inherent conflict between evaluation (judging) and development (helping) is to separate these interviews and choose the appropriate method for each. If this were done, the tell-and-sell or tell-and-listen interview would be used for evaluation and the problem-solving interview for developmental objectives. However, such factors as time, organizational practice, and subordinate expectations may dictate that one interview serve both purposes.

The most effective way of implementing a mixed-model appraisal interview is to begin with the open-ended problem-solving interview and end with the more directive tell-and-sell or tell-and-listen approach. The re-

INTERVIEW BEGINS

Open-ended discussion and exploration of problems: the subordinate leads and the supervisor listens

Problem-solving interview: the subordinate leads, but supervisor takes somewhat stronger role

Agreement on performance problems and a plan for improvements needed

The supervisor summarizes his or her views using Tell-and-Listen or Tell-and-Sell methods if the subordinate has not dealt with important issues

INTERVIEW ENDS

Figure 18.3 Mixed-model interview

verse order is unlikely to work.[24] If the supervisor starts off with one-way communication, the subordinate is likely to become defensive or passive, and real two-way communication and in-depth exploration of personal and job-performance issues are unlikely to follow. Thus, as figure 18.3 shows, the interview should start with an open-ended exploration of perceptions and concern, with the subordinate taking the lead, and finish with a more narrowly defined agreement on what performance improvements are expected. If a mutual agreement on performance problems and improvements is not possible, ultimate responsibility for closure on these matters rests with the supervisor. The supervisor may choose to tell the subordinate what is expected if crucial problems have not been discussed or solutions agreed to.

A mixed-model interview can be implemented in many ways. We will outline one possible pattern for an effective appraisal interview with multiple purposes. This procedure, which assumes an interview similar to that outlined in figure 18.3, can make the climate of the interview more conductive to coaching and problem solving, while at the same time allowing a more directive role for the supervisor is needed. The goal is to improve employee performance and motivation as well as boss-subordinate relations, while leaving subordinates with a clear understanding of what is expected and where they stand.

The assumption is that subordinate participation in

---

23. Maier, "Appraisal Interviews."

24. Ibid., Herbert H. Meyer, "The Annual Performance Review Discussion—Making it Constructive," undated paper, University of South Florida.

all facets of the performance-appraisal interview will improve all of these desired outcomes. While we have no direct evidence that participation in the performance-appraisal interview will improve performance, there is considerable evidence that, with most employees, it improves satisfaction with the interview and the supervisor, facilitates acceptance of the supervisor's feedback, and increases the subordinate's motivation to improve.[25] A sequence of ten steps in a mixed-model interview will now be described in the order in which they would be taken.

1. *Scheduling*: Notify the subordinate well before the meeting date that an appraisal discussion is scheduled. The time of the interview should be such that both parties are alert and undisturbed by external organizational or family matters. The side effects of unrelated upsetting events can affect the interview process needlessly.

2. *Agreeing on content*: Discuss with the subordinate the nature of the interview and work toward agreement on what will be discussed in the interview (i.e., rating forms to be used or performance issues to be discussed). This gives the subordinate a chance to prepare for the meeting (including rating the supervisor if this is to be part of the session), and to come into the interview on a more equal footing with the boss. It also underscores the importance of the performance appraisal. Research has shown that when employees prepare for appraisal interviews by analyzing their jobs and the problems they are encountering, the amount of time spent in such preparation is positively correlated with performance improvement.[26]

3. *Agreeing on process*: Before the interview, agree with the subordinate on the process for the appraisal discussion. For example, agreement should be reached on the sequencing of interview phases (e.g., first an open exploratory discussion, followed by problem solving, action planning, and upward appraisal). Similarly, ground rules for communication can be established that will ensure constructive feedback and good listening (see step 7.) The important point is that both parties understand and agree to the interview process before the interview starts.

4. *Location and space*: If possible, meet on neutral territory or in the subordinate's office. This helps establish a relationship of more equal power, so crucial to open communication. Using the supervisor's office gives him or her an edge. Similarly, it is best that the supervisor not sit behind a desk, which often symbolizes authority and can be a barrier to communication.

5. *Opening the interview*: Review the objectives of the appraisal interview as previously agreed to. This sets the stage and allows supervisor and subordinate to prepare themselves psychologically. It is a warm-up for the more important communication to come.

6. *Starting the discussion*: Give the initiative to the subordinate in the discussion that follows the opening statement. Specifically, start the discussion by asking, "How do you feel things are going on the job? What's going well and what problems are you experiencing? How do you see your performance?" Such general questions will stimulate the subordinate to take the initiative in identifying and solving problems. A useful technique may be to ask the subordinate to appraise his or her own performance on the form provided by the organization. Research suggests that such a self-appraisal results in more subordinate satisfaction with the appraisal interview, less defensiveness, and more improvement in performance.[27] Organizations that have tried this approach have found that it works best if the manager and subordinate simply make a note of ratings that are only one point apart on the final corporate form, but discuss larger differences in depth. If the manager starts by expressing views about the employee's performance, the interview almost inevitably develops into a tell-and-sell session in which the subordinate participates very little. Only an unusually strong and skilled subordinate could regain the initiative. When subordinates fill out a self-appraisal form, on the other hand, they are more likely to ask questions and make suggestions.[28]

7. *Exchanging feedback*: Follow well-accepted ground rules for giving and receiving feedback.[29] A supervisor who models these methods for effective communication encourages the exchange of valid information. In giving feedback, a supervisor can reduce employee defensiveness by being specific about the performance and behavior-causing problems (i.e., what was said and done). Citing examples of behavior observed and describing the effects of that behavior on others, on the supervisor's feelings, and on the performance of the department can help an employee identify what needs

25. David L. De Vries, Ann M. Morrison, Sandra L. Shullman, and Michael L. Gerlach, *Performance Appraisal on the Line* (New York: Wiley, Interscience, 1981) 74–75; Latham and Wexley, *Increasing Productivity*, 150–52.

26. R. J. Burke, W. Weitzel, and T. Weir, "Characteristics of Effective Performance Review and Development Interviews: Replication and Extension," *Personnel Psychology* 31 (1978): 903–19.

27. G. A. Bassett and H. H. Meyer, "Performance Appraisal Based on Self-Review," *Personnel Psychology* 21 (1968): 421–30.

28. K. S. Teel, "Self Appraisal Revisited," *Personnel Journal* (1978): 364–67.

29. John Anderson, "Giving and Receiving Feedback," paper prepared for Proctor & Gamble, Cincinnati, Ohio.

to be changed. Following this procedure allows the supervisor to give feedback without being overly evaluative. To prevent defensive reactions, the supervisor should avoid making general statements, imputing motives to behavior (i.e., saying he or she is lazy, or isn't committed), blaming, or accusing.

The supervisor should also model and encourage the subordinate to follow ground rules for receiving feedback. Negative feedback is usually cut off by the giver when signs of defensiveness appear in the receiver, thus reducing the amount of information transmitted. Active listening, on the other hand, can enhance the value of negative feedback. The receiver can maintain openness and keep information coming by exploring negative feedback and showing a willingness to examine himself critically. He may paraphrase what is being said, request clarification, and summarize the discussion periodically. In contrast, justifying actions, apologizing, blaming others, explaining, or building a case tends to cut off feedback and reduce understanding.

The ground rules for receiving feedback are not meant to imply that supervisors and subordinates should not help each other understand why they are doing what they are doing. However, the timing of explanations is critical in signaling openness versus defensiveness. Active listening should precede explanations. The communication in an appraisal interview can be much improved if both boss and subordinate follow these ground rules, which should be agreed to before the interview begins.

8. *The manager's views*: Provide a summary of the subordinate's major needs for improvements based on the previous discussion. This summary sets the agenda for jointly developing plans for improvement. It should also include the subordinate's strengths, however—those things that should be continued.

9. *Developing a plan for improvement*: Let the subordinate lead with what he or she thinks is an adequate plan for improvement, given the previous discussion and summary. It is much easier to prevent defensiveness if the supervisor reacts to and perhaps expands on plans that the subordinate has for changing rather than making such suggestions directly. A problem-solving rather than blame-placing approach should be maintained. However, if the subordinate cannot formulate good action plans, or seems to be unmotivated to do so, the supervisor can take a more directive approach at this point. It is critical that the interview end in a concrete plan for performance improvement; otherwise no change is likely to occur. The plan should pinpoint specific goals to behavior change. There is considerable evidence that when such goals are set in a participative manner, and when subsequent goal accomplishment is acknowledged with praise, improved performance and

other desired consequences follow.[30] A plan may include certain task assignments, training programs, subordinate experimentation with new approaches in specific settings, a change in the subordinate's role, working closely with others who are skilled in a certain area, or a shift of goals and objectives.

10. *Closing the discussion*: Close the interview by discussing what the future might hold for the individual. (This assumes that opportunities for promotion exist and the employee clearly has potential, or that the individual raises the issue.) If the employee needs to be told where he or she stands, this should occur at the very end of the interview by way of a summary of the appraisal discussion. As stated earlier, it is preferable that such a judgment be delivered in a separate interview or review.

This proposed interview sequence assumes that the primary objective of the appraisal discussion is counseling and coaching, with a secondary goal of letting subordinates know where they stand. It is also assumed that the appraisal interview is a culmination of ongoing performance discussions. The most effective coaching is associated immediately and directly with behavior as it occurs on a day-to-day basis. The formal interview is an attempt to improve working relations, encourage upward communication, develop deeper understanding, and define developmental plans.

Guidelines for assessing the effectiveness of an interview

During and/or after the interview, participants should ask themselves several questions as a check on the effectiveness of the appraisal process. Indeed, an effective appraisal interview should probably include at least one examination of the process sometime during the interview. Organizational consultants have found that groups that periodically examine their own process can more readily make the adjustments needed to improve the effectiveness of their meetings.[31] The following questions might be helpful:

At the beginning

1. Did the supervisor create an open and accepting climate?

30. G. P. Latham and E. A. Locke, "Goal Setting: A Motivational Technique That Works," *Organizational Dynamics* 8 (Autumn 1979): 68–80; G. P. Latham and S. B. Kinne, "Improving Job Performance Through Training in Goal Setting," *Journal of Applied Psychology* 59 (1974): 187–91; G. P. Latham and J. J. Baldes, "The Practical Significance of Locke's Theory of Goal Setting," *Journal of Applied Psychology* 60 (1975): 122–24.
31. S. H. Schein, *Process Consultation: Its Role in Organization Development* (Reading, Mass.: Addison-Wesley, 1969).

2. Was there agreement on the purpose and process for the interview?
3. Were both parties equally well prepared?

During the Interview

4. To what extent did the supervisor really try to understand the employee?
5. Were broad and general questions used at the outset?
6. Was the supervisor's feedback clear and specific?
7. Did the supervisor learn some new things—particularly about deep feelings and values of the subordinate?
8. Did the subordinate disagree and confront the supervisor?
9. Did the interview end with mutual agreement and understanding about problems and goals for improvement?

Appraisal Outcomes

10. Did the appraisal session motivate the subordinate?
11. Did the appraisal build a better relationship?
12. Did the subordinate come out with a clear idea of where he or she stands?
13. Did the supervisor arrive at a fairer assessment of the subordinate?
14. Did he or she learn something new about the subordinate?
15. Did the subordinate learn something new about the supervisor and the pressures he or she faces?
16. Does the subordinate have a clear idea of what actions to take to improve performance?

ORGANIZATIONAL IMPLICATIONS

Performance appraisal is inevitably difficult to implement in organizations. The problems of avoidance by the supervisor and defensiveness by the subordinate are inherent in any evaluation process and cannot be eliminated easily. There are no magic systems or techniques. Ultimately managers and subordinates must learn to negotiate the difficult dilemmas of discussing a performance evaluation in a nonevaluative manner. They must learn how to agree on shortcomings and set goals for performance improvement to which both are committed. For without that commitment, employee satisfaction with performance appraisal will be low and the likelihood of change will be small.

Unfortunately, few organizations have succeeded in institutionalizing the type of performance-appraisal process described in this chapter. Too often the system has been confused with the process. Organizations have assumed that the introduction of a new system, perhaps one that meets higher technical standards for reliable and valid measurement of performance, will mean wider use. Better systems with more reliable and valid measurement methods are important, but they are not sufficient. An effective informal and formal appraisal process requires a fundamental change in the interpersonal competence of managers and subordinates, which in turn requires a change in managerial behavior and organization culture. Experience suggests that cultural change in an organization requires a rearrangement of several important elements, including staff, skills, management style, structure, superordinate goals, strategy and, of course, systems.[32] Such massive changes will typically not take place unless pressures in the organization's business or social environment produce enough dissatisfaction among managers to unleash the energy required for change.[33]

Clearly it will not be enough to install a performance-appraisal system mandated by the personnel department because it needs the data or believes the process is important. Managers and subordinates must see the system and process as meeting their needs; more effective means for implementation will also be needed. Furthermore, we will have to go beyond the traditional model of boss-subordinate appraisal to deal with some of the inherent problems of avoidance and defensiveness. A brief summary follows of key changes that will probably have to occur if better performance appraisals are to be institutionalized in organizations.

MORE SOURCES OF DATA

More data about performance and potential wil have to be developed to avoid putting the manager in the difficult position of being both judge and helper. Some years ago a study at General Electric indicated that a boss-subordinate discussion based on self-appraisal alone compared favorably with the more traditional approach.[34] Managers rated self-appraisals as more satisfying and constructive than the traditional supervisor-prepared appraisals. Moreover, they noted less defensiveness and resistance on the part of subordinates, and job performance

---

32. R. Waterman, T. Peters, and J. Phillips, "Structure Is Not Organization," *Business Horizons* (June 1980).

33. M. Beer, *Organization Change and Development: A System View* (Glenview, Ill.: Scott, Foresman [Goodyear] 1980).

34. G. A. Bassett and H. H. Meyer, "Performance Appraisal Based on Self-Review," *Personnel Psychology* 21 (1968): 421–30.

improvements were more likely to follow. Low-rated employees, the ones for whom performance appraisal is most difficult, were especially likely to show an improvement in performance, as rated by managers, after a self-review discussion. Similarly, there is overwhelming evidence that peer ratings are more reliable and valid than any other sources of performance evaluation.[35] In fact, such ratings are implicit in most team-building meetings, and these have been found to change behavior. Perhaps a manager who uses data generated by others, say peers, can more easily play the role of helper and coach. The manager is then not placed in a position of defending an evaluation. It remains to be seen if employees will accept these sources of data as legitimate or if they will be willing to supply the needed information. Given the general movement toward more participative and egalitarian organizational cultures, it is likely that they will.

PROBLEM-CENTERED INTRODUCTIONS

If performance-appraisal systems and processes mandated by the personnel department are unsatisfactory, it may make sense to begin by designing a system and implementation strategy to solve a particular organizational problem. Experience suggests that managers will embrace the basic need for improving interpersonal competence, for learning how to give feedback and set goals, when they perceive a need for these skills.[36] Many problems—turnover, inadequate productivity, poor communication and commitment, for example—can lead to the same basic performance-appraisal process. But starting with the problem rather than the system or process increases organization members' sense of ownership. If this approach results in the adoption of different systems or processes in various parts of the organization, these can be standardized much later after the basic process is understood and accepted.

PARTICIPATION IN SYSTEM/PROCESS DESIGN

Commitment to performance appraisal can be enhanced and the content made more relevant if the managers and employees who will use the system also design it and introduce it. For example, a task force of employees in a given department might be assigned the responsibility for introduction and follow-up. A system or process so designed is likely to be perceived by subordinates as fair and valid, an important consideration in employee ac-

ceptance of their evaluations and their willingness to change.

TOP-DOWN CHANGE PROCESS

An effective performance-appraisal process cannot be successfully introduced without the support of higher-level management. The chances for success are also enhanced if managers have an opportunity to learn from models. Too often performance-appraisals processes are introduced quickly across all levels of the organization. Institutionalization is much more likely to occur if a slower, cascading process is used, in which introduction at any given level is contingent on effective implementation and institutionalization at the next higher level. In this approach, a manager and subordinates at one level would design, discuss, and train with a new appraisal system or process to make sure they get it right before pushing it down another level in the organization.[37]

MORE EMPHASIS ON DEVELOPING SKILLS

Much more emphasis is needed on helping both managers and subordinates learn behavioral skills required to conduct effective performance-appraisal interviews. Without these skills, managers and subordinates will be threatened by systems that ask them to be more complete and open in their dialogue. In one organization, a performance-appraisal system was introduced with a two-day training program that included learning to conduct a problem-solving interview by means of role playing, skill development in giving and receiving feedback, and other interview skills.[38] Behavior modeling programs, in which participants are shown films that demonstrate key behaviors required in responding to particular situations, have been found quite effective in improving the skills needed in performance appraisal.[39] More interpersonally competent managers will perform more effective performance appraisals. Unfortunately, this obvious connection has not been reflected in most introduction efforts.

BOTTOM-UP PRESSURE

Most efforts to introduce an effective performance-appraisal process have relied on top-down pressure. For example, managers are sometimes required to show that they have conducted appraisal interviews with subor-

35. Latham and Wexley, *Increasing Productivity*, 84–89.

36. M. Beer, R. Ruh, J. A. Dawson, B. B. McCaa, and M. J. Kavanagh, "A Performance Management System: Research, Design, Introduction and Evolution," *Personnel Psychology* 31 (Fall 1978): 505–35. Latham and Wexley, *Increasing Productivity*, 198–201.

37. H. Levinson, "Appraisal of What Performance?" *Harvard Business Review* 54, no. 4 (1976): 30–32.

38. M. Beer et al., "Performance Management Systems," 59–66.

39. G. A. Latham and L. M. Saail "The Application of Social Learning Theory to Training Supervisors Through Behavorial Modeling," *Journal of Applied Psychology* 64 (1979): 239–46.

dinates before they can submit requests for a salary increase. Unfortunately, while such a top-down approach can ensure that a performance appraisal of some sort is conducted, it cannot guarantee that the job will be done properly. If all employees are trained in effective performance-appraisal procedures, they can more readily press managers for the type of interview they have learned to expect. In addition, organizations could establish some means by which an employee could indicate when he or she is not receiving an adequate performance appraisal. One approach might be an anonymous grievance system. Naturally, this method is not without its problems, because employees who receive poor performance ratings may use the system to get back at their managers. Nevertheless, the idea of creating demands for effective appraisals from employees by giving them some power to indicate dissatisfaction takes pressure off the hierarchical system, which has largely proven ineffective in enforcing a high-quality performance-appraisal process. If channels for bottom-up pressure are created, employees are less likely to blame the organization for inadequacies in performance appraisal.

CONCLUSION

Organizations will continue to require data about employee performance for personnel decisions, for protection against lawsuits, and for employee development. At the same time, employees will continue to want to know where they stand and will want help in career and performance development. These perspectives will always be in conflict, but better systems and more effective communication processes for managing the dilemmas inherent in performance appraisal are relatively well known. so are the methods and skills for setting goals for improving performance. It remains for managers to learn these skills and for organizations to be more effective in designing and introducing performance-appraisal systems and processes that will help managers learn how to evaluate in a nonevaluative manner.

19

The ecology of work groups
FRANK FRIEDLANDER

Imagine you have been called in as a consultant to the regional-headquarters organization for a large multi-installation firm that provides services to the public. The structure of the headquarters organization is portrayed in figure 19.1. You have been hired by the head of division A, Albert Agway, a senior vice-president and heir apparent to the director's position, with the concurrence of the head of division B, Bill Barney, also a vice-president. Agway describes the primary problem as intense conflict between department A1 and both departments B1 and B2. There is also a lesser conflict between departments B1 and B2. All three of these departments are highly interdependent, in that essential information and reports are exchanged several times among them before a project can be successfully completed. Their disagreements frequently flare up in public in front of customers, a situation that is both embarrassing and frustrating to Agway. He also mentions that Barney needs help in managing the conflict within his division B, managing it more participatively, and being more assertive with peers and superiors in the larger organization.

Interviews with members of several work groups in the organization reveal the following information: those in division B feel that Barney does not support them, that he acquiesces to most requests from elsewhere in the organization too easily, that he does not consult with them on matters in which they feel they have expertise, and that he is afraid of displeasing those outside his di-

vision, particularly the directors, and, to some extent, the head of department B1.

A straightforward organizational analysis at this point would consider the leadership style of Barney, the interdependencies between departments B1 and B2, and the conflict between departments B1/B2 and department A1. Change strategies could include modification of Barney's leadership style, bolstering his assertive stance with others in the organization, and helping in the management or reduction of the two sets of conflict. Psychological and structural interventions might be included.

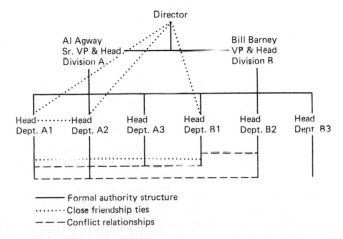

Figure 19.1 Organization chart for regional headquarters of large public service organization

But further analysis reveals larger issues in the system that are integrally connected to the identified problems. The director had a voice in appointing department heads in both divisions A and B (with the consent of Agway) and maintains close personal ties with the heads of departments A1, A2, and B2. The head of A1 had provided personal services and facilities for the director. The head of A2, the Education and Training Department, was the "personal ear" for the director, passing along information on any issue he thought relevant. Specifically, when Agway and A1 disagreed, the latter passed this information on to A2, who subtly convinced Barney to back down. The director was a golfing and drinking companion with both vice-presidents as well as the heads of departments A1 and A2. These informal and political ties are indicated by dotted lines on the organization chart in figure 19.1.

Clearly these ties undermined the formal structure of the organization. The personal relationships and support provided by the director to the head of department B1 undermined Barney's formal leadership authority and made it more difficult for him to deal with his subordinates. The subtle privileges accorded to B1 by Barney aggravated the task relationship between B1 and B2. Similarly, a visibly supportive relationship between the director and the head of department A1 unbalanced the power relationship between division B and department A1, undermining Barney's authority and responsibility, and creating havoc between A1 and B2. Finally, any interaction in which the head of department A2 was involved (providing guidance, education, training, or simply helping others clarify the issues) became shared knowledge with the director. This set of relationships clearly also undermined the formal authority structure, creating anxiety and frustration within the system.

Without looking beyond the boundaries of these divisions and people initially identified as "problems," one might well have settled on these "causes" and launched into working with division B, its manager, and its conflicts. Subsequently, one could have worked with division A1 and department B to help them manage their conflicts. This strategy would have failed, because the larger organizational system to which these work groups belonged was keeping the managers, the groups, and the intergroup conflict locked into their current patterns of interaction. We might temporarily resolve some of these issues, but they would soon revert to their earlier state. The system—its actors, relationships, and conflicts—was invested in the status-quo condition and resisted any effort to change. Furthermore, the organization's problems had no clear single cause or effect that could be identified. The numerous parts of the system (actors and work groups) simply colluded to maintain things as they were—and the system remained intact.

INTRODUCTION

This chapter attempts to shed light on work groups by exploring their interconnections with the organizational systems to which they belong. A work group is broadly considered to be a small set of people with a common overall goal, who are, to varying degrees, socially, structurally, and technically interdependent with each other and with the larger organization. This definition includes informal units, such as task forces and *ad hoc* or coordinating committees, as well as units within an organization's formal structure. The focus will be on the conditions affecting the boundaries that separate and connect work groups to relevant parts of the organization, that power and influence processes between groups and the organization, and that force inhibiting and facilitating change and learning in groups.

Managers tend to see work groups as distinct autonomous units connected to the rest of the organization only by the hierarchical chain of command. Academicians similarly conceive of groups as distinct entities unto themselves. The hope is that, by suggesting the myriad connections and forces linking groups within an organization, this chapter will encourage both managers and academicians to explore the problems and opportunities for bridging the spaces between groups rather than focusing only on the group within its boundaries. Viewing the organization as a system of highly interrelated work groups should help the manager to enhance its effectiveness, and the academician to understand its behavior, as an integrated whole. Toward this end, the chapter draws upon systems theory as a framework for understanding work groups. A set of general and more specific propositions have been formulated to summarize the discussions, and their implications for managerial thought and action are briefly stated.

Too often, our perspective on work groups, rooted in the fields of social psychology and group dynamics, sees them as virtually freestanding entities, devoid of an organizational setting or context. This perspective ignores the complex and crucial ties between the work group and the larger system. The error is reinforced by the fact that most academic research has focused on *non*organizational groups, and the tendency by organizational members and managers to define too sharply the boundaries surrounding work groups.

While work groups occupy a crucial position in organizational life (Cummings 1981), their position in the organizational-theory literature is less central. Relatively few studies exist on work groups in organizational settings. Most studies have been conducted under controlled laboratory conditions (Hoffman 1982), on isolated training groups, or on college students, rather than in business, government, or other natural settings where the organizational context would certainly have an impact. Extrapolating the results of nonorganizational groups to work-group processes (e.g., decision making) may be "fraught with danger and the conclusions should be accepted with utmost caution" (Hoffman 1982, 386).

Most organizational theorists pay lip service to the idea that the situational context profoundly influences behavior but focus their attention elsewhere. There are exceptions—the work of Barker (1968) on physical settings, Murray (1938) on environmental press, and Argyle, Furnham, and Graham (1981) on a taxonomy of situations—but these studies do not specifically relate to work groups. The recent efforts to examine sociotechnical systems and quality of work life in organizations (Cummings and Molloy 1977; Hackman 1977; Passmore and Sherwood 1978; Cummings and Srivasta 1977) certainly focus on work groups but do not dwell on the connections between the group and its setting. Almost all of the literature sees the group as a context for the behavior or welfare of the individual and focuses on the impact of group norms, socialization, and work design upon work attitudes, beliefs, or performance.

Yet the organizational context in which work groups are embedded is of great significance, both for understanding work groups and for making them more effective. A work group is simply a subsystem of the larger organizational system that it serves and upon which it depends for human, technological, and financial resources, for information and power, and eventually for its very existence.

THE WORK GROUP AS A SUBSYSTEM

A work group cannot be understood by merely examining and analyzing its components. Normally, to understand an entity, we might take it apart, explain the parts, and put the parts back together again. In "synthesis" (Ackoff 1974), we do just the opposite. Instead of regarding the work group as a whole to be taken apart, we see it as a component of the larger organization and extract an explanation of the group from an explanation of the organization. Thus, to understand the work group, we must view it as a subsystem embedded in a larger system. A work group may well have to operate somewhat inefficiently in order to maximize its contribution to the organization. If each component work group operates as efficiently as it can, the organization as a whole will probably operate inefficiently. If we get the organization behaving as well as it can, it may be that none of the individual work groups will work optimally on their own terms. As Ackoff points out, if the finest automo-

tive engineers were asked to select the very best transmission, the very best carburetor, the very best engine, and so on, and then to assemble these components, a naïve observer might expect the very best automobile. Most likely, however, we would not get any automobile at all, because the parts would be incompatible.

The performance of the whole organization is not simply the summation of the performance of the work groups or work functions. Thus efforts to diagnose, isolate, and improve a malfunctioning work group may well fail to produce a better-functioning organization. An important managerial function is to explore the relationships among work groups with a view toward improving the fit among groups.

Linear thinking often leads us to seek a single manageable, improvable cause for most organizational problems. We may identify a particular work group or function as the culprit, but seldom is the supposed cause of a problem *sufficient* in itself to cause that problem. By analogy, an acorn is necessary, but not alone sufficient, to produce an oak tree. Growth depends on other components such as climate, soil conditions, and a host of other environmental factors. Similarly, the causes of work-group effectiveness are in the organizational system, and it is impossible to disentangle them from happenings in the work group itself.

There are good reasons for our linear cause-and-effect thinking about work group problems. It allows us to believe that we have diagnosed the trouble spot and thus have found the beginning of a resolution, simplistic as it might be. Moreover, it enables us to escape blame by pointing toward evidence external to our own work group or function. And identifying the problem group may have the effect of uniting the remainder of the organization.

Frequently a problem is pervasive in the organization yet manifests itself within a particular work group or function. The blaming games that are then collectively played are overt methods of maintaining organizational homeostasis. Work-group problems are created by the organization, and organizational problems are created by component work groups.

According to a recently developed paradigm of family-systems theory (Minuchin 1974; Minuchin, Rosman, and Baker 1978), the "identified patient" (perhaps the disturbed child) participates with all other family members to maintain a dysfunctional family structure. Traditional individual therapy is effective until the identified patient returns to the family structure. Minuchin studied the total family system and devised methods for intervening that changed family structure and patterns. The identified patient was cured if the family structure was changed. One of the first goals of the therapy was to shift the problem from the identified patient to the system as a whole. Family members soon began to describe their family units in such organizational terms as having poorly differentiated system boundaries, enmeshed relationships, and rigid patterns that resisted change (Short 1982).

Translating from families to organizations, a dysfunctional work group is a symptom of an organizational dysfunction in which parties collude. The collusion may result in organized chaos, dysfunction, and blaming, but the appeal of stability, continuity, and predictability overrides these negative factors: "At least we know who we are, even though it is very frustrating." Work-group problems thus help maintain the organization just as the organization helps maintain work-group problems. Homeostasis is thus continued.

Because the internal organization of a work group is ordinarily well defined and continuously maintained, behaviors within the group are highly dependable and predictable. Even in work groups that appear highly chaotic, the chaos is well organized—that is, the same kind of chaos occurs regularly, dependably, and predictably. When certain things are done in certain ways, by certain people, at certain times, under certain circumstances, then certain types of behavior by others are likely to follow.

General Proposition. Many factors contribute to work-group and organizational ineffectiveness, but few clear, single causes can be pinpointed within the work group or the organization. Most causes are not identifiable as such, but are the result of multiple interactions throughout the organization. A dysfunctional work group participates with all other work groups to maintain a dysfunctional organizational system. Further, the dysfunctionality of a work group may increase the effectiveness of the organization.

> *Proposition 1.* To understand a work group, we must look to the larger organizational system of which it is a part.
>
> *Proposition 2.* To contribute to organizational system effectiveness, a work group may well have to suboptimize its own effectiveness.
>
> *Proposition 3.* Improving the effectiveness of a work group will not necessarily improve, and may decrease, the effectiveness of the organization.

Managerial Implications. Managers must look to the larger system of which they are a part to assess effectiveness, rather than appraise only the effectiveness of each work unit separately. They must look for causes of problems in the relationships among all components of the organization rather than in one or a few specific work units.

BOUNDARIES AND INTERFACES

The performance of the organization reflects the relationships among its work groups. McWhinney (1982) uses the term *coupling* to describe the development of a resonant exchange between subsystems in which the rhythms of one are related to those of the other. If the resonances of the systems are similar and if they are linked, they will entrain each other until they move synchronously and transfer energy efficiently. A pacemaker used to maintain the rhythmic pumping of the heart is an example of entraining in which the machine drives the heart into an appropriate rhythm. There are many examples of entraining in performances of musical groups. Entrainment does not imply that conflict, mismatch, and imbalance among work groups will not occur. Organizations and their component groups go through continual cycles of conflict, mismatch, and imbalance, which create opportunities for innovation, learning, and change.

Certain domains in the organization are especially relevant to the existence, development, and effectiveness of each work group. The group is by definition interdependent with these domains, whether they are specific people, roles, functions, or other work groups. To maximize the effectiveness of the organization, the relationships of such interdependent groups must ideally be resonant, that is, inputs to and outputs from other work units in the system. In the example with which this chapter began, the success of department A1's tasks was highly interdependent with those of departments B1 and B2. But a nonresonant relationship prevailed, in which the inputs from each department to the others were unsynchronized. The harmony and rhythm between these departments were discordant.

Organizations, like all living systems, tend to differentiate themselves into small units. The differentiation process adds specialized functions, roles, skills, and perspectives to the organization so that it may more effectively achieve its mission and cope with its differentiated environment. Differentiation makes the organization more complex and highlights the importance and difficulty of transactions across work-group boundaries. Complexity here means diversity, inconsistency, and lack of connectivity among work groups and their transactions with each other. Diversity is the amount and degree of difference among work groups; consistency refers to the degree of variation in the need for exchange among work groups; and connectivity is the degree to which information from one work group is relevant to other work groups (Von Glinow et al. 1983). In organizations with high diversity, low connectivity, and low consistency, boundary and interface issues become crucial.

The purpose of a boundary is to separate, contain, and define the work group or unit. Boundaries are lines or areas of demarcation that surround the work group and separate it from other subsystems in the organization. A boundary, of course, is not necessarily a physical line of demarcation, but rather a social fact (Durkheim 1949). A boundary is present when people are aware of its presence.

The interface that links groups or functions is composed of a sort of connective tissue or surface. These interfaces make possible the coordination and interaction of ideas, emotions, and products. Interfaces provide the means of communication and information flow across work-group boundaries. These transactions may include information sharing, suggestions and recommendations, problem identification and problem solving, negotiation, influence, and direction. The interface may be competitive or collaborative, conflictual or cooperative, controlling or participative, open or closed, trusting or distrusting, formal or informal. A work group's effectiveness and existence depend on the quality of its interface with relevant domains in the system.

Several conditions affect boundary transactions. Among these are boundary clarity and permeability, the degree of cohesion or adhesion between groups, the degree of match between groups in their functional identity, and the compatibility of the organization's and the work group's climates.

Clarity refers to the degree to which work groups are fully independent of each other, in appropriate contact with each other, or enmeshed with each other. Independent groups have no functional relationship, although there may be a potential need for greater contact. Such groups back away from contact for such reasons as competition or fear of being overwhelmed or overtaken. At the other extreme, enmeshed groups have lost the boundary necessary for contact. They essentially overlap each other, having lost their unique value and purpose. The boundary between completely independent groups is nonexistent; between overlapping groups, the boundary is diffuse and at times seems nonexistent. Appropriate contact between groups implies sufficient definition to separate them, yet sufficient expandability and contractability to adapt to needed change. Work groups that are enmeshed with each other tend to be more bonded with each other, to be more distant from other groups, and to have less contact with them. Two

enmeshed groups may isolate themselves from other groups; conversely, the distance of other groups may cause two groups to become enmeshed.

All these boundary characteristics have obvious effects upon working relationships both within and between groups. Work groups with insufficient definition and with diffuse boundaries tend to be overwhelmed, to lose their unique capabilities, and to be less cohesive. Groups with boundaries that are overly rigid and thick become fortresses unto themselves. Enmeshed groups alienate and are alienated by other work groups. Independent work groups have no boundary or means of contact with other work groups.

Permeability refers to the degree to which boundaries allow inputs to enter the work group and outputs to exit. Inputs and outputs include such factors as technological and economic information, support and confrontation, suggestions and recommendations, and values. Groups with highly porous boundaries not only allow these inputs to enter but reach out beyond their boundaries for new and relevant information, predictions, and trends that may affect them. Similarly such groups seem more prone to provide internal information to other work groups. Groups with nonporous boundaries frequently have "gatekeepers" guarding entranceways, hide information well, or make it relatively inaccessible to outside groups (or even to its own members). Work groups with highly porous boundaries generally create greater information flow to and from other work groups, which may mean more productive intergroup relations.

Group *cohesion* refers to the degree to which work-group members form a strong collective unit and are drawn inward to the centrality of the group. Cohesion is related to the willingness of members to commit energy and resources to the group. A group high in *adhesion*, on the other hand, tends to disperse its attention to other work groups (e.g., by attending their meetings), creating high rapport, comfort, and commitment with other groups.

Work groups need a strong sense of their own *functional identity*. A group knows what it is through its task purpose and task competence. A production group deals with production; a marketing committee considers marketing problems; a quality-circle task force is assigned to study quality work problems. Functional identity contributes to the sense of a "home base" and the security it provides.

Functional identity is closely related to the development of a local language tailored to the requirements of the group's work (March and Simon 1958; Lawrence and Lorsch 1967; Ritti and Gouldner 1969). Special technical languages permit groups to express large amounts of information with relatively few symbols (Randolph 1978; Cherry 1965; Allen 1977). Work groups similarly develop their own local social constructions of reality to help them define and interpret their social world (Berger and Luckman 1966; Van Maanen and Katz 1979). These shared beliefs provide rules by which group members can define and manage the unique and recurring problems of organizational life. But idiosyncratic language and coding schemes and local conceptual frameworks create problems in intergroup communication (Tushman 1982).

The larger organization affects the relationships among work groups by providing a *climate* that promotes cooperation, support, and innovation, or competition, nonsupport, and standardization. In a study of General Electric plants, Trist et al. (1977) found that failures of work teams were due primarily to negative external factors in the organizational context. Among the factors that would help teams and collaborative intergroup relationships were management support of more participation and a structure that represented a move away from strict hierarchical, narrowly defined job positions and control. The GE study recommended that work teams be designed to build collaboration, creativity, innovation, adaptability, autonomy, freedom, responsibility, self-regulation, learning, and the personal growth of workers. These qualities were met head-on in many established GE plants by authoritarian leadership, reinforced competition, win-lose situations, very close production controls, power struggles, one-person/one-job organization, and an apparent insensitivity to the changing work ethics of employees. In many cases the GE environment was inhospitable to the work-team concept.

Several conditions, then, affect boundary transactions between work groups. Many of these factors were important in the organizational example cited at the beginning of this chapter. The relationship between department A1 and division B ranged from independence (where interdependence was needed) to enmeshment (where clearer separation of functions was appropriate). Task functions were at times confused, with each party claiming it was responsible for the same functions. Cohesion was high with department A1 and moderately high in departments B1 and B2. Yet boundaries surrounding these departments were relatively nonpermeable, because neither departments B1 and B2 nor department A1 would allow suggestions, recommendations, or criticisms to enter through their boundaries. Finally, the climate and relationships of the higher levels permitted most of these conditions to occur and rarely took action to change them.

It is also useful to consider how groups vary in tightness of organization (boundedness) (Brown 1980; Kaplan 1982; Alderfer 1976, 1980). Brown (1980) describes loosely and tightly organized systems in terms of the extent to which group behavior is defined, constrained, and regulated by leadership (close vs. discretionary supervision), informal culture (norms, rituals, ideologies), formal structure (rules, procedures, roles), and technology (specification, mechanization, and routinization vs. looseness, creativity, and novelty).

The degree of boundedness may appropriately vary across work groups within a single organization depending on their tasks. Loosely organized systems are more effective in coping with turbulent environments (Lawrence and Lorsch 1967) or uncertain tasks (Galbraith 1977), and tightly organized systems are effective in stable environments and well-understood tasks (Lawrence and Lorsch 1967; Perrow 1970).

Thus, a work group may be overbounded or underbounded in terms of its tasks (Brown 1980). The degree of boundedness that is right for a group developing long-range strategy plans may be too loose for one that assembles automobiles, yet too tight for a group involved in research on a new missile design—a highly uncertain task.

Overbounded work groups may be too tightly constrained and regulated to accomplish their tasks. If leadership, informal cultures, formal structures, and technologies are too confining for effective operation (Brown 1980), the result may be apathetic resignation and distortion or suppression of information across boundaries between work groups. Differences between individuals within work groups are suppressed or smoothed over to avoid conflict, but at the expense of divergent information or alternatives. Activities are controlled by rules. Response to novel or uncertain situations is low, conservative, and not innovative. Boundaries are clearly defined and impermeable to novel inputs.

Underbounded work groups, on the other hand, lack sufficient constraint and regulation to accomplish their task. Human energy is diffused or dissipated by lack of direction and focus. Relevant information is unavailable because channels of responsibility for information flow are unclear. Differences between individuals within the work group result in escalation of conflict or withdrawal as a result of poor definition. Poorly defined and highly permeable external boundaries invite irrelevant and disruptive inputs and outputs (Brown 1980).

Thus, as organizations differentiate into departments and groups with specialized functions, a key consideration is the quality of the boundary separating each group from the remainder of the organization and the quality of the interface between work group and the organization. The effective coordination across work groups is a function of both boundary condition and the overall climate of the organization.

General Proposition. The more complex the organization, the more organizational effectiveness depends on the characteristics of work-group boundaries and the quality of interfaces. Complexity is described in terms of diversity (the amount and degree of differences among work groups), inconsistency (the degree of variation in the need for exchange among work groups), and connectivity (the degree to which information from one work group is relevant to other work groups).

> *Proposition 4.* The boundary interface between two or more work groups is affected by the clarity of the boundary (i.e., whether the groups are independent or enmeshed, or have appropriate contact surface with each other).
>
> *Proposition 5.* The boundary interface between two or more work groups is affected by the permeability of the boundary of each work group to specific other work groups.
>
> *Proposition 6.* The boundary interface between two or more work groups is affected by the degree of cohesion or adhesion within each group. Cohesive groups tend to draw energy from their members to their own group; adhesive groups tend to disperse energy to other work groups.
>
> *Proposition 7.* The boundary interface between two or more work groups is affected by each group's sense of its own task identity. Strong identities contribute to the security of members and their sense of "home base."
>
> *Proposition 8.* The boundary interface between two or more work groups is affected by the degree to which the organization's climate, structure, and values support cooperation and innovation or competition and standardization.

Managerial Implications. Management must be particularly aware of the relationships among work groups when they are very different or when there is significant variation in the need for exchange among them or in the relevance of one group's information to another. The relationships between two work groups results in greater effectiveness when the groups have an appropriate quality of contact with each other (i.e., not completely independent of each other and not confused as to identity and joint function). If the climate and values of the organization support and reflect cooperation and innovation, the relationship between any two work groups will result in greater cooperation and innovation.

POWER AND INFLUENCE

A work group's contribution to organizational effectiveness depends very much on the balance of power and influence between the group and the larger system. Power here means the work group's ability to influence the organization and to have its ideas and recommendations implemented by the organization. An earlier study (Friedlander and Schott 1981) showed the significance of the group's power and its strategy vis-à-vis top management. If a group has too little power or a poor strategy, the top-management group is more likely to disconfirm the group, question its credibility, change or co-opt its mission, disagree with its diagnosis, or procrastinate on action decisions. These reactions tend to inhibit or prevent the implementation of action steps recommended by the work group. What is needed is a sharing or even mutual enhancement of power between the work group and the top-management group.

A work group is likely to have more power and influence if its values and perceived task are congruent with those of the organization. If values are shared, the group's recommendations are likely to be more acceptable to the top-management group and to the organization. Similarly, if there is agreement on the group's assigned task, the work group is likely to be better attuned with the organization and to have greater power.

The more general issue of congruence between work groups and the structure and climate of the organization is discussed in the literature on autonomous work groups in sociotechnical experiments. Cummings (1981) notes that the larger organization has a major impact on whether autonomous work groups can be implemented effectively. Specifically, if the work group operates organically while the organization has a more mechanistic structure (Burns and Stalker 1961), both the internal dynamics of the group and its relationship with other organizational units will be affected. The experience of work teams at General Electric, as described earlier, is a good example.

The composition of the work group also influences the balance of power with the organization. The higher the position and status of its individual members, the more influence and power the group has with the rest of the organization, particularly top management. Group influence is also enhanced if its members have significant personal power and play important informal roles in the organization (Friedlander and Schott 1981). Individuals carry over into their work-group activity the status, power, and roles of their regular work lives. Thus work groups are a part of and draw upon the system of interlocking roles within the organization (Katz and Kahn 1966).

Finally, the work group's power and influence depend on the degree to which it integrates its activities and ideas with the organization, and in particular with the top-management group. Friedlander and Schott (1981) found that ideas and activities of a work group are more likely to be taken seriously if it has achieved good liaison with top management. Its ideas and activities are then empowered, resulting in their legitimization and implementation. Unless there has been a continued back-and-forth flow of ideas between the work group and top management, the group's recommendations may be received with skepticism. In one case, for example, work-group members agreed early in the group's life not to share any of the data they had collected until a formal presentation to management had been made. Despite an expressed interest in the findings, management was kept in the dark for a considerable time and had little chance to contribute to the work group's progress. When the group finally revealed its findings and recommendations in a formal presentation, management was highly uncomfortable and resistant to both the findings and the data-collection method.

Work groups that behave autonomously in this regard tend to produce more innovative solutions, while groups that emphasize liaison with top management tend to reproduce solutions more likely to be implemented. Groups with high overlap, participation, and involvement with the organization and highly permeable boundaries, particularly in regard to top management, are likely to produce ideas more congruent with those of the organization. Indeed, the output of such groups may reflect the very same malfunctional processes that gave rise to the problems currently facing the organization. On the other hand, autonomous work groups with relatively impermeable boundaries, permitting only limited and delayed interaction with top management, are likely to develop ideas that are less affected by the current norms, policies, and malfunctions of the organization. Such ideas are likely to be more incongruent with those of the organization and less acceptable to top management. A balance must be struck. Autonomy is necessary for innovation; collaboration is necessary for implementation. The effective work group must somehow maintain autonomy, yet create and develop personal, procedural, and structural linkages with top management and organization.

The issue of autonomy versus collaboration has much to do with the power struggles that occur between work groups and top management. In the Friedlander and Schott (1981) study, *ad hoc* task forces that kept top management in the dark as to their ideas and activities received little support from top management. Similarly, when top management dictated the results task groups were to discover, the task forces were either hostile or complacent. Little collaboration will occur if either party feels the other is attempting to grab power. Rather, it seems essential that each group work actively to increase the power of the other. Top management must provide active support, essential information, and adequate protection for the work group. The work group, in turn, should welcome top management's involvement and ideas and report continually on its progress. Thus mutual empowerment becomes the basis for collaboration. And respect for the integrity of each other's knowledge becomes the basis for granting autonomy.

General Proposition. A balance of power and influence between a group and the organization optimizes the effectiveness of the organizational system.

Proposition 9. The balance of power and influence is a function of the degree to which the work group and the organization have the same perception of the work group's task.

Proposition 10. The balance of power and influence is a function of the position and status of the work group's members in the organization.

Proposition 11. The balance of power and influence is a function of the degree to which the work group has developed ongoing liaison that integrates its activities and ideas with those of the organization, particularly with the top-management group.

Proposition 12. Work groups that do not maintain liaison and act autonomously from the organization tend to reproduce more innovative ideas and solutions, but ones that are less likely to be implemented by the organization. Work groups that maintain close liaison tend to produce more traditional ideas and solutions. These solutions reflect the status quo of the organization and its malfunctional processes but are more likely to be implemented.

Managerial Implications. Autonomy is necessary for innovation; collaboration is necessary for implementation. Maintaining autonomy yet creating and developing personal, procedural, and structural linkages with top management and the organization seems essential to effective work groups.

RESOURCE FLOW BETWEEN THE WORK GROUP AND THE ORGANIZATIONAL SYSTEM

A variety of environmental factors impinge upon the work group; conversely, factors within the work group influence its environment. The interaction of these factors reinforces the notion that the work group is an integral part of a larger system and not an autonomous unit.

Newcomers to the work group bring with them part of the larger organization's culture, or at least do not necessarily share the culture that has been developed within the work group. As aliens, newcomers tend to undergo an acculturation process, learning the norms of interaction within the group and forming new relations within it. If turnover is high, newcomers will always be a relatively large proportion of the work group, and fragmentation may be a problem. The more similar the work group's culture is to that of other work groups, the less the alien qualities and the less need for acculturation. If the newcomer has formal or informal authority within the group, the situation is more precarious. Newcomers may undercut the group's work if they do not understand its history or its idiosyncratic mode of operating; they may unknowingly take away some of the elements that have been crucial to its success. At the same time, of course, new members can bring vitality to the group— new ideas and perspectives and more relevant organizational connections. Louis (1981) suggests that many issues precipitated by newcomers reflect their unfamiliarity with the job itself as well as the local culture. Thus, insiders explain blunders, point out deviance, retell history, and answer naïve questions from newcomers, all of which have potential repercussions for the integrity and continuity of the group and its culture.

Turnover is a potential problem for work groups not only because new people enter but also because experienced people leave. Without some continuity of people a team may waste energy in constantly repeating itself, revising early decisions, or redefining its work. But because a team is only a small part of a larger system, its boundaries must be permeable (Kanter 1983).

A second important environmental factor is the advent of technological innovations developed elsewhere in the organization. These may be a major threat to the work group's current mode of operation and the associated security. New technologies and methods frequently result in revised work designs, call for new skills, and alter power equilibria among group members.

A third factor is a shortage of resources in the organization on which the work group is dependent. An actual or perceived shortage of manpower, funding, equipment, or information may prompt political maneuvering within the group or between the group and power sources in the organization. It can also result in competition among work groups for these resources.

General Proposition. A work group can be disrupted by the export and import of new people, technology, information, equipment, and funding.

> *Proposition 13.* To the extent that newcomers bring with them a cultural perspective different from that of the work group, efforts will be made by the group to acculturate them. If successful, this prevents fragmentation and disruption of the group but also prevents importation into the group of new vitality and perspectives.
>
> *Proposition 14.* To the extent that an imported technology differs from the work group's previous technology and calls for new skills, the group will resist and attempt either to fend off the introduction or to adapt it so that it resembles current technology and skills.
>
> *Proposition 15.* To the extent that resources such as people, technology, information, equipment, or funding are perceived to be in short supply, political maneuvering and competition within the group or between the group and the power sources in the organization will occur.

Managerial Implications. When new members join a work group, the process should be managed with two objectives: to reduce disruption by encouraging acculturation and to enhance the group by preserving the newcomer's perspectives and vitality. The group will be most effective if acculturation of the newcomer on some dimensions is balanced by "reverse acculturation" of the old-timers on other dimensions. Active managerial decisions will be required.

New technology calling for new skills is most likely to be implemented by the work group if it is at least partially created by the work group affected and resembles its current technology in some respects.

Perceived shortages of resources should be verified. Actual shortages should be dealt with as early as possible to avoid destructive political maneuvering and competition.

Integrative structures such as coordinating committees, *ad hoc* task groups, task forces, and cross-functional and interdepartmental committees are composed of representatives from several work groups and represent special kinds of linkages between the work group and the larger system. These special linkages are also present in the linking-pin concept of Likert (1967). To the extent that each member of the coordinating group also represents a constituency group, he or she may also be subject to political pressures from both sources. The coordinating group may well have to make decisions that affect the constituency groups, particularly through the allocation of scarce resources. The representative thereby becomes a crucial interface between the needs of the constituency and the coordinating group. Information flow, influence efforts, and political behaviors tend to characterize this interface. To the extent that members of the coordinating group are operating as individuals or as "representatives-at-large," there will be more cooperation and less political behavior.

> *General Proposition.* In groups that coordinate other work groups and are composed of members of at least some of these other groups, representation becomes an important issue.

>> *Proposition 16.* To the extent that an individual represents both a constituency group and the coordinating group, he or she will be subject to political pressures from both sources. But constituency groups will have greater influence.

>> *Proposition 17.* To the extent that a member of the coordinating group is operating as an independent individual or as a representative-at-large, there will be more cooperation and less political behavior. But constituency groups will have less influence.

So far we have focused on factors in the organizational system that impinge upon the work group. But work groups often have opportunities to influence the larger system of which they are a part. Dependent on the organization for crucial information, financial, and manpower resources, the group must make certain demands on the system in order to survive, be productive, and grow.

Two examples of work groups that were ineffective in dealing with the larger organization may be helpful. Both were groups of internal organizational system development and training consultants. In one case, the OD consultant group was unable to build the internal cohesion needed to deal with the power issues within its potential client system in a large organization designing and manufacturing aircraft and missile systems. Unable to develop close working relationships, each group member separately ventured forth into the organizational jungle, rarely meeting with enduring success. Each alone was powerless to deal with the external environment. In a second case, the internal consulting group in a large engineering and construction firm was cohesive, yet reluctant to develop a long-term strategy to create client-consultant relationships in its environment. It preferred instead to dwell on internal issues: the scheduling and equitable division of a basically dull work load; the lack of challenging consulting opportunities and the predominance of training duties; and the need for a more participative style of leadership. Much of the group's energy was directed inward. It made little effort to create the kind of client system in the organization that might empower it in relation to its environment. Creation of client-consultant relationships would have provided this group with greater choice in the kind of work it did and the way the work was scheduled.

In both cases an inappropriate internal structure and strategy prevented the work group from influencing the larger system of which it was a part. Neither work group made active, constructive efforts to develop an external environment in which it could contribute and grow. Neither was able to empower itself so as to thrive within the system it was expected to serve.

> *General Proposition.* Because it depends on the larger organizational system for crucial information, manpower, and funding, a work group must influence the organization in such a way that it can maintain its existence and growth.

>> *Proposition 18.* The lack of an appropriate internal structure and strategy prevents the work group from influencing the larger system of which it is a part, thus endangering the group's existence, production, and growth.

Managerial Implications. Because the work group is dependent upon the larger organizational system for its existence and growth, managers must consider ways of structuring the group so as to increase its influence within the organization. Similarly, the manager must develop and implement a work-group strategy to influence the organization.

CHANGE AND HOMEOSTASIS

A work group strives to maintain homeostasis (keeping its internal conditions stable in reference to a changing environment) and to maintain a state of quasi-stationary equilibrium (Lewin 1947a). It may encounter a variety of threats to this stability, for example, a declining need for the group or its output, a mass exodus of its personnel, a sudden loss of funding, or efforts elsewhere in the organization to change the group's basic way of operating or its norms, products, or internal power balance.

Work groups, like other systems, will generally go to great lengths to maintain current basic conditions despite frustration, confusion, chaos, high turnover, and poor performance. The same wish to maintain stability keeps people in unsatisfying careers or marriages and prevents families from moving out of economically depressed areas. It keeps organization from giving up counterproductive policies, outdated self-images and identities, and products whose sales are declining.

A work group, like any open system, adapts, learns, and changes by receiving feedback both from within its boundaries and from the larger organizational environment. The work group may respond to feedback by taking corrective action that treats the problem or disturbance as an error and adjusts itself accordingly (just as a thermostat automatically regulates the furnace to achieve the "correct" room temperature). This kind of corrective action to bring the group's operations, policies, and norms in line with previously set standard has been referred to as "single-loop learning" (Argyris and Schon 1978), and as "simple learning" (Friedlander 1983); it is said to occur in reactive systems (Von Glinow et al. 1983). On the other hand, systems that directly confront their strategies, goals, norms, or core identity are said to be self-reflexive (Von Glinow et al. 1983) and to engage in "reconstructive learning" (Friedlander 1983) or "double-loop learning" (Argyris and Schon 1978). Friedlander (1983) has constructed a model in which the reconstructive learning process begins with frustration, crisis, or imbalance, and proceeds through a series of phases, which include contact among parties with equal power but with very different perceptions, tension and conflict, self-confrontation, identity crisis, and reformulation. The same process holds for individual, group, and organizational learning. Clearly, this is a very different level and process from simple corrective learning.

Factors that prevent double-loop or reconstructive learning are the needs for system continuity, stability, and productivity. It may be useful to think of work groups as situated along a continuum of purpose that ranges from a production orientation at one extreme to an emphasis on exploration, learning, and change from the status quo at the other (Friedlander 1983). Von Glinow et al. (1983) make an analogous distinction between groups whose goals are to maintain the present state of affairs and those that have a developmental orientation requiring variable standards and frequent resetting of goals. It is difficult to integrate the two orientations within a single work group. Production calls for

stability and continuity; change calls for the innovation that comes from challenging stability and continuity.

Many kinds of feedback channels are found in work groups. These feedback patterns become established, are dependable, and bring a certain order and organization to the group. Similarly, feedback loops between the work group and its larger organizational system are generally highly organized and therefore highly dependable in their operation and occurrence. Nevertheless, it may sometimes be wise for the group or organizational system to seek out feedback on the efficacy of its current functioning or on future trends and plans that may affect it.

Feedback, as the term is used in cybernetics, is the return of small portions of the energy from a group's output to provide the group with information to control its output. The energy can be used "negatively" to reduce deviations (e.g., in quality or quantity) from some established level, or "positively" to amplify the deviations (McWhinney 1982). Negative feedback is rather automatic in its functioning, is corrective in nature, and keeps the work group's behavior and activities the same (at least within certain limits). Self-correcting adjustments are routinely made by work groups to preserve homeostasis. Positive feedback has the effect of either suggesting or actually making a change in the system and tends to upset homeostasis. "Positive" here does not mean good or better, nor does it have any moral connotation. "Positive" simply means that the information, if acted upon, would lead to change.

Negative feedback promotes homeostasis and, at an extreme, the "stuckness" that many work groups experience despite frustration and low effectiveness. By providing negative feedback, components of the larger organizational system keep each other in their current condition, even though change might be advantageous to all. Negative feedback can explain the capacity of a system to maintain constancy in the face of external perturbation (morphostasis). Developmental change (or morphogenesis) comes from positive feedback, or the amplification and reward of group behaviors and operations different from prior patterns.

> *General Proposition.* The forces toward homeostasis hinder major (double-loop) learning and change in work groups, but foster superficial (single-loop) learning and change.
>
> > *Proposition 19.* The need for continuity, stability, and productivity hinders learning and change in work groups.
> >
> > *Proposition 20.* Work groups are much more likely to make superficial changes that correct

errors in the process they use to reach their goals than they are to explore, confront, and make major changes in their goals, standards, or products.

Proposition 21. Reliable feedback loops from relevant parts of the organizational system are essential to a group's learning and change.

Managerial Implications. Because work groups must learn and change in order to be productive in a changing organization and a changing environment, managers must help them confront basic issues such as goals, products, and standards, and not merely correct errors so as to reach current goals. Feedback channels from relevant parts of the organization should be developed and nurtured to provide the necessary input.

The discussion thus far has emphasized the myriad of linkages between the work group and the system in which it is embedded. Beginning with Ackoff's proposition that the work group must be understood by understanding its organizational setting, we have considered boundaries and interface issues between the group and the organization.

The performance of the organization is affected by every work group within its boundaries. No one will have an independent effect on the organization. Rather, its impact will depend on what at least one other part of the organization is doing (Ackoff 1974).

A corollary of Ackoff's proposition is that change within a work group calls for change in the way it relates to the larger organizational system. Miller (1979, 218) states two relevant propositions concerning change: (1) "a change in the relatedness of a system to its environment requires internal changes within the system," and (2) "significant internal changes within a system cannot be sustained unless consistent changes occur in the relatedness of the system to its environment."

The first of these propositions indicates that a work group can change its relationship with other parts of the organization only by changing something about itself. In the case of the aircraft firm described earlier, no amount of effort to develop a client-consultant relationship with the organization would be successful unless the consulting group became more cohesive and developed closer, more supportive working relationships among members.

The second of Miller's propositions is equally profound: significant internal changes within a work group will not endure unless consistent changes occur in the relatedness of the work group to its larger organizational environment. In the case of the engineering and con-

struction firm, a cohesive internal consulting group had good working relationships among its members and capable leadership, yet refused to plan, strategize, and create a new set of relationships with its potential client system in the organization. Instead it dwelled inward in its deliberations, energy, and focus. Similarly, when change is occurring in a work group, components of the larger social system must become congruent with and thus support intended change in the work group. This is the "refreezing" process cited by Lewin (1947b).

Miller's second proposition has some important, if discouraging, implications for the training profession. There is ample evidence (Fleishman 1953) that training sessions conducted as an isolated event, away from the complex working relations that managers must explore and alter, result in only temporary changes. Participants revert to old behaviors soon after returning to the stability and continuity of their organizations. Even work groups that undergo training or team-building sessions as a unit tend to dissipate their learning soon after returning from such sessions (Friedlander 1968). The work group cannot maintain durable and significant change in its mode of operation, norms, and interaction patterns without concurrent and consistent change in its relationships with the rest of the organization. Team building itself generally results in greater cohesion and participation by group members, but not in higher work-group performance (Friedlander and Brown 1974), particularly when performance depends very much on the group's relations with units and people outside group boundaries. Similarly, we should not expect an individual to change behaviors or attitudes merely because he or she attends a human-relations workshop; concurrent changes in relations with others in the organization will also be necessary.

In summary, change is a mutually interactive systemic process. It tends to be most durable and of greatest benefit to the system when several adjacent organizational levels are concurrently involved in the process. Efforts to change a work group without a parallel exploration of change in its relatedness to the larger system will at best yield only temporary gains.

General Proposition. Learning and change in a work group call for change in the way it relates to its larger organizational system.

Proposition 22. A change in the relatedness of a group to the organization requires internal changes within the group.

Proposition 23. Significant internal changes within a group cannot be sustained unless consistent changes occur in the relatedness of the group to the organization.

Managerial Implications. The manager of a work group must realize that if changes are to occur in the way the work group and the organization relate to each other, some relevant quality or activity of the work group must be changed. Insisting on a changed response, receptivity, or support from the organization without a change in the work group itself will lead to failure. Similarly, success is unlikely if a manager tries to change some quality or activity of a work group without altering the relationship with the organization in a way that supports the internal change. At the more individual level, a manager who attempts to change the behavior of subordinates (e.g., by sending them to a human-relations training workshop) will find that they revert to old behaviors unless there is concurrent change in their relations with significant others (frequently the boss) in the organization.

REFERENCES

Ackoff, R. L. 1974. "The Second Industrial Revolution." Unpublished paper.

Alderfer, C. P. 1976. "Boundary Relations and Organizational Diagnosis." In *Humanizing Organizational Behavior*, ed. H. Meltzer and F. R. Wickert. Springfield, Ill.: Thomas.

————. 1980. "Consulting to Underbounded Systems." In *Advances in Experiential Social Process*, ed. C. P. Alderfer and C. L. Cooper, vol. 2. New York: Wiley.

Allen, T. J. 1977. *Managing the Flow of Technology*. Cambridge, Mass.: MIT Press.

Argyle, M., A. Furnham, and J. A. Graham. 1981. *Social Situations*. Cambridge, England: Cambridge University Press.

Argyris, C., and D. Schon. 1978. *Organizational Learning: A Theory of Action Perspective*. Reading, Mass.: Addison-Wesley.

Barker, R. G. 1968. *Ecological Psychology*. Stanford, Calif.: Stanford University Press.

Berger, P., and T. Luckman. 1966. *The Social Construction of Reality*. London: Penguin Books.

Brown, L. D. 1980. "Planned Change in Underorganized Systems." In *Systems Theory for Organization Development*, ed. T. G. Cummings, pp. 181–208. New York: Wiley.

Burns, T., and G. M. Stalker. 1961. *The Management of Innovation*. London: Tavistock.

Cherry, C. 1965. *On Human Communication*. Cambridge, Mass.: MIT Press.

Cummings, T. G. 1981. "Designing Effective Work Groups." In *Handbook of Organizational Design*. Vol. 1, *Adapting Organizations to Their Environments*, ed. P. C. Nystrom and W. H. Starbuck. New York: Oxford University Press.

Cummings, T., and E. S. Molloy. 1977. *Improving Productivity and the Quality of Work Life*. New York: Praeger.

Cummings, T., and S. Srivasta. 1977. *Management of Work*. Kent, Ohio: Comparative Administrative Research Institute, Kent State University.

Durkheim, E. *Division of Labor in Society*. 1949. Glencoe, Ill.: Free Press.

Fleishman, E. A. 1953. "Leadership Climate, Human Relations Training, and Supervisory Behavior." *Personnel Psychology* 6:205–22.

Friedlander, F. 1968. "A Comparative Study of Consulting Processes and Group Development." *Journal of Applied Behavioral Science* 4:377–99.

————. 1983. "Organizations and Individuals as Learning Systems." In *Functioning of the Executive Mind*, ed. S. Srivasta, pp. 192–220. San Francisco: Jossey-Bass.

Friedlander, F., and L. D. Brown. 1974. "Organization Development." *Annual Review of Psychology* 25:313–14.

Friedlander, F., and B. Schott. 1981. "The Use of Work Groups for Organizational Change." In *Groups at Work*, ed. C. Cooper and R. Payne, pp. 191–217. New York: Wiley.

Galbraith, J. 1977. *Organization Design*. Reading, Mass.: Addison-Wesley.

Hackman, J. R. 1977. "Work Design." In *Improving Life at Work*, ed. J. R. Hackman and J. L. Suttle. Santa Monica, Calif.: Goodyear.

Hoffman, L. R. 1982. "Improving the Problem-Solving Process in Managerial Groups." In *Improving Group Decision Making in Organizations*, ed. R. A. Guzzo. New York: Academic Press.

Kanter, R. M. 1983. *The Changemasters*. New York: Simon & Schuster.

Kaplan, R. E. 1982. "Intervention in a Loosely Organized System: An Encounter with Non-Being." *The Journal of Applied Behavioral Science* 18:415–32.

Katz, D., and R. Kahn. 1966. *The Social Psychology of Organizations*. New York: Wiley.

Lawrence, P., and J. Lorsch. 1967. *Organizations and Environment*. Cambridge, Mass.: Harvard University Press.

Lewin, K. 1947a. "Frontiers in Group Dynamics: Concept, Method, and Reality in Social Science, Social Equilibria, and Social Change." *Human Relations* 1:3–42.

————. 1947b. "Group Decision and Social Change." In *Readings in Social Psychology*, ed. E. E. Macoby, T. Newcomb, and E. Hartley, pp. 459–473. New York: Holt, Rinehart and Winston.

Likert, R. 1967. *The Human Organization*. New York: McGraw-Hill.

Louis, M. 1981. "The Emperor Has No Clothes: The Effect of Newcomers on Work Group Culture." Paper presented at Western Academy of Management Meetings, Monterey, Calif., April.

March, J., and H. Simon. 1958. *Organizations*. New York: Wiley.

McWhinney, W. 1982. "A Study Guide for Systems Praxis." Paper. 26 July.

Miller, J. C. 1979. "Open Systems Revisited: A Proposition

About Development and Change." In *Exploring Individual and Organizational Boundaries*, ed. W. G. Lawrence. New York: Wiley.

Minuchin, S. 1974. *Families and Family Therapy*. Cambridge, Mass.: Harvard University Press.

Minuchin, S., B. Rosman, and L. Baker. 1978. *Psychosomatic Families*. Cambridge, Mass.: Harvard University Press.

Murray, H. A. 1938. *Explorations in Personality*. New York: Oxford University Press.

Passmore, W., and J. Sherwood. 1978. *Sociotechnical Systems*. La Jolla, Calif.: University Associates.

Perrow, C. 1970. *Organizational Analysis: A Sociological View*. Belmont, Calif.: Wadsworth.

Randolph, W. 1978. "Organizational Technology and the Media and Purpose Dimensions of Organizational Communications." *Journal of Business Research* 6:337–59.

Ritti, R., and F. Gouldner. 1969. "Professional Pluralism in an Industrial Organization." *Management Science* 16:B-223–46.

Short, R. 1982. *Structural Family Therapy and Consultative Practice: A Paradigm Shift for O.D.* Spokane, Wash.: Whitworth College.

Trist, E., C. Dwyer, J. McCann, C. Pava, and R. Dreher. 1977. "Report to Corporate Employees on the General Electric Experience with Work Teams." Report. 20 June.

Tushman, M. L. 1982. *Readings in the Management of Innovation*. Marshfield, Mass.: Pitman.

Van Maanen, J., and R. Katz. "Cognitive Organization of Police Perceptions of Their Work Environment." *Sociology of Work and Occupations* 6:31–58.

Von Glinow, M. A., M. J. Driver, K. Brousseau, and J. B. Prince. "The Design of a Career Oriented Human Resource System." *Academy of Management Review* 8:23–45.

20

The design of work teams

J. RICHARD HACKMAN

In an essay written to commemorate the fiftieth anniversary of the well-known Hawthorne studies at Western Electric Corporation, Harold Leavitt (1975, 76) observed:

> Far and away the most powerful and beloved tool of applied behavioral scientists is the small face-to-face group. Since the Western Electric researches, behavioral scientists have been learning to understand, exploit and love groups. Groups attracted interest initially as devices for improving the implementation of decisions and to increase human commitment and motivation. They are now loved because they are also creative and innovative, they often make better quality decisions than individuals, and because they make organizational life more livable for people. One can't hire an applied behavioral scien tist into an organization who within ten minutes will not want to call a group meeting and talk things over.

Leavitt's paper, entitled "Suppose We Took Groups Seriously . . . ," raises the possibility that both people and organizations would be better off if groups, rather than individuals, were the basic building blocks in the design and management of organizations. Recent trends in organizational practice—such as the increasing use of quality circles, autonomous work groups, project teams, and management task forces—suggest that groups are indeed becoming a popular way to get things done in organizations.

While groups can yield the kinds of benefits Leavitt discusses, they also have a shady side, at least as they typically are designed and managed in contemporary organizations. They can, for example, waste the time and energy of members, rather than use them well. They can enforce norms of low rather than high productivity (Whyte 1955). They sometimes make notoriously bad decisions (Janis 1982). Patterns of destructive conflict can arise, both within and between groups (Alderfer 1977). And groups can exploit, stress, and frustrate their members—sometimes all at the same time (Hackman 1976).

Clearly, if Leavitt's vision is to be realized, we must expand what we know about how to design, manage, and consult to work groups in organizations. There is currently no well-tested and accepted body of research and theory to guide practitioners in using groups to do work, nor do we have a documented record of success in using behavioral-science techniques to help groups become more effective.

This chapter assesses what we do know about the design and management of work groups, provides a conceptual model for integrating and extending that knowledge, and offers some action guidelines for structuring, supporting, and managing groups in contemporary organizations.

This chapter was prepared as part of a research project on work team effectiveness supported by the Office of Naval Research (Organizational Effectiveness Research Program, Contract No. 00014-80-C-0555 to Yale University). The helpful comments and suggestions of Clay Alderfer, Susan Cohen, Russ Eisenstat, Connie Gersick, Judith Hackman, and Bill Kahn are gratefully acknowledged.

315

OVERVIEW

The chapter is organized in three major sections. We begin by assessing the findings from *descriptive* research on group behavior. Research in this tradition seeks to generate knowledge about what actually happens in groups and to develop generalizations about the associations among various features of the group and its context. To explore the implications of descriptive research for work-group effectiveness, we use an input-process-output framework. This framework posits that various input factors (such as features of the group, its task, and its work context) affect group-interaction processes (i.e., the interpersonal transactions that take place among members), which in turn affect the output of the group. Ideally, one should be able to discover how group interaction mediates between the way a group is set up and the results of its work—including its performance effectiveness. It turns out, however, that research in the descriptive tradition has produced neither a set of empirical generalizations sturdy enough to guide managerial practice nor interventions that reliably improve group performance.

As an alternative, we next present and discuss a *normative model* of group effectiveness. This model departs from the descriptive approach in two ways. First, the focus is on a single (albeit multidimensional) outcome: work-group effectiveness. Second, the model identifies potentially manipulable aspects of the group (and of its work context) that are particularly potent in promoting team effectiveness, thereby providing a basis for diag-nosing the strengths and weaknesses of groups as performing units. While based in part on findings from descriptive research, the normative model is essentially a theoretical statement in which existing knowledge is reconfigured to make it more useful in improving work-team effectiveness.

The final section of the chapter draws out the implications of the normative model and suggests the beginnings of an *action model* of group effectiveness. The focus here is on what one would actually do to create and maintain an effective work team. Beyond its use as a guide for designing, managing, and consulting to work teams, the action model also provides a means for testing and revising the normative model on which it is based (i.e., by determining the degree to which changes suggested by the normative model result in improvements in performance).

DESCRIPTIVE RESEARCH ON GROUP BEHAVIOR AND EFFECTIVENESS

There have been literally thousands of research studies of group behavior and performance. The great majority of them describe what takes place in various kinds of groups or map the empirical associations among variables that characterize a group, its performance context, and its products. These studies aim to develop and test

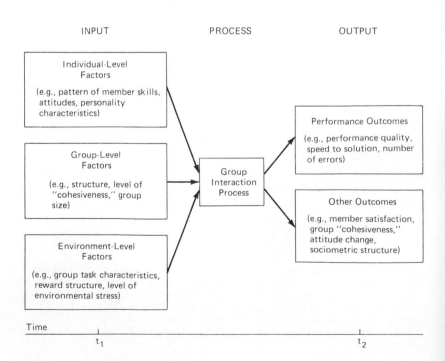

Figure 20.1   An input-process-output framework for analyzing group behavior and performance. (Adapted from J. E. McGrath, *Social Psychology: A Brief Introduction* [New York: Holt, Rinehart and Winston, 1964], by permission of the author.)

generalizations that chart what happens in groups reliably, validly, and relatively comprehensively.[1]

A general framework for organizing and systematizing this work has been developed by McGrath (e.g., 1964) and is depicted in figure 20.1. The framework classifies both input and output variables into three sets: those that describe individual group members, those that describe the group as a whole, and those that describe the environment in which the group operates. In principle, all relevant variables can be assessed at any two points in time (identified in the figure as t_1 and t_2), making it possible to trace changes in the state of the system over a specified time period.

A key assumption of the framework is that input states affect group outputs via the interaction that takes place among members. If, for example, a highly cohesive group (input at t_1) were to perform better on some task (output at t_2) than a group low in cohesiveness, it should be possible to explain the performance difference by comparing the interaction processes of the two groups. Perhaps members of the cohesive group talked more about their work and encouraged each other to work hard and quickly. Or perhaps they simply spent more time together and used part of that time for extra work on the task. Whatever the explanation for this (hypothetical) finding, it should be discernible in the group interaction.[2]

Most research and theory in the descriptive tradition shares McGrath's assumption that process mediates input-output relationships. This is not surprising: group interaction is readily apparent in all groups. It is interesting: we know some things about how to study it—and besides, *something* has to mediate between input and output states. Yet, as will be seen below, the input-process-output paradigm may have misdirected the search for useful knowledge about group effectiveness. Contrary to what one would hope, the key is not always under the lamppost, where the light is brightest.

Research on group behavior

Descriptive frameworks such as the one illustrated in figure 20.1 are helpful in organizing, summarizing, and integrating empirical research on group behavior. And a review of the links and categories in this framework reveals that we have learned quite a bit about group behavior over the last few decades. For example, we now have a reasonably good understanding of the *patterns of group process* that are typical of various kinds of groups. Several useful descriptive models of the group-development process have been based on these findings.[3] The *input-process* link in the framework also has received a good deal of research attention, with special emphasis on the effects of group composition variables (i.e., group size and the attributes of group members).[4] Research on *process-outcome* relationships has emphasized the impact of group interaction on the attitudes, beliefs, and behaviors of individual group members, and the ways that interaction shapes the outcomes of group decision making and problem solving.[5]

A great deal of research has been done on *input-output* relations in small groups. These studies have examined the effects of many different input variables on the subsequent behavior and attitudes of individual members, on changes in the state of the group as a social system, and on group performance outcomes. While input-output studies have not turned out to be as cumulative as group researchers had expected (see McGrath and Altman 1966), some important findings and insights have emerged.[6]

1. For an early (but still-useful) review and integration of literature on small-group behavior, see McGrath and Altman (1966). Current reviews are provided by Hare (1976), McGrath and Kravitz (1982), Davis and Hinsz (1982), and McGrath (1983). In addition, a book edited by Payne and Cooper (1981) provides substantive analyses of a number of different types of groups commonly used in organizations (e.g., policy-making groups, project groups, negotiating teams, and so on).

2. It is, of course, necessary to select an appropriate time interval and to focus on the most important aspects of interaction process if this kind of analysis is to be successful. These decisions often are far from straightforward.

3. Research describing group interaction and charting it over time stemmed primarily from the Bales (1950) method for coding group interaction. For a description of the current, multiple-level version of the Bales observational methodology, see Bales and Cohen (1979); other methods for describing group process are reviewed by Hare (1982, chaps. 1–4). Group-development models are reviewed by Hare (1976, chap. 4) and Tuckman (1965).

4. For an early but still-cogent review of findings on size-process relationships, see Thomas and Fink (1963). For the seminal work on group composition and member compatibility, see Schutz (1958). The relationship between member personality and behavior in groups is explored in detail by Bales (1970).

5. For an overview of group influences on individuals in organizations, see Hackman (1976). Literature on the way group interaction can result in "choice shifts" (i.e., choosing riskier or more conservative courses of action following group discussion) is reviewed by Myers and Lamm (1976). An overview of research on group decision processes is provided by Nagao, Vollrath, and Davis (1978). Janis (1982) provides a historical analysis of the effects of group interaction on policy decisions. Finally, a program of research showing how solutions gain credence and eventual acceptance as a function of what transpires in group discussions is summarized by Hoffman (1979b).

6. For example, Steiner (1972) has developed an informative set of models showing how the effect of group size on group productivity depends on the kind of task being performed. In the decision-making area, Davis and his colleagues (e.g., Davis 1973; Stasser and Davis 1981) have devised and tested sophisticated quantitative models that show how the prediscussion preferences of group members (in interaction with other variables) combine to determine both decision outcomes and members' postdiscussion preferences. McGrath (1983, chap. 9) reviews input factors that influence group performance on problem-solving and intellective tasks.

Two characteristics of input-output research on group behavior merit special note, as they have potentially important implications for the development of an action-oriented model of group task effectiveness. First, the relationships obtained appear to depend substantially on the properties of the group task being performed. Findings for one type of task often turn out not to hold for groups working on different kinds of tasks.[7] Second, while research reports typically discuss how group-interaction process may mediate input-output relationships, they usually do so inferentially—that is, by specifying what members may have done, or logically had to have done, to account for the results. Rarely has the mediating role of group process been assessed empirically. Moreover, few substantive findings have emerged that are useful as guides for creating and maintaining effective work teams (Hackman and Morris 1975).

How are we to understand these gaps in the group-performance literature? Has the high cost of conducting process studies dampened the interest of researchers in examining input-process-performance relationships? Or have the serious methodological problems that pervade this kind of research[8] so compromised its findings that one cannot be sure what has been found? While these possibilities are credible, the problem may run deeper, as will be seen below.

Implications for team effectiveness

If we had a robust set of generalizations that allowed us to predict, on the basis of prior assessments of input and process variables, how well a group would perform, then we should be able to translate these generalizations into prescriptions for the design and management of work teams. This is exactly what some scholars and practitioners mean by "applied social science": collecting the products of basic research and theory and using them as action guides in the world of practice. It is an inviting view of the relationship between scholarship and practice, and if I could have written this chapter in accord with that view I would have been tempted to do so.[9] It would have been a relatively straightforward task of summarizing what has been learned in research on group behavior and then using those summaries to generate guidelines for action.

Unfortunately, the research literature previously reviewed suggests that such an undertaking would not be very fruitful. For one thing, existing generalizations about group behavior are neither strong enough or stable enough to serve as guides for managerial practice. The generalizability of our findings appears to be quite low, and we do not have a good understanding of what is responsible for the seeming instability of our results across tasks and settings (Vidmar and Hackman 1971).

Moreover, when research has revealed statistically reliable associations between group effectiveness and various input or process variables, those associations have tended to be relatively weak or highly dependent on a particular task and situational context. A manager might think twice before making a significant group or organizational change in hopes of realizing a barely discernible improvement in team effectiveness.

Finally, some of the variables that have been shown to relate to group performance (e.g., certain aspects of group-interaction process or the cultural milieu within which the group operates) are not useful as points of intervention in designing and managing teams. In some cases, change of the variable is impractical (it would take a long time, for example, to modify the overall culture of an organization). In others, the focal variable itself is more a sign than a cause of performance problems. As will be seen, this is the case for certain aspects of group interaction process.

The bulk of this chapter is devoted to an alternative, explicitly action-oriented approach to analyzing the performance of work groups in organizations. Before proceeding, however, it may be worthwhile to look a little more closely at the reasons *why* the descriptive-empirical approach has not given rise to an applied social psychology of group effectiveness. We will give special attention to (1) the variables typically chosen for study in group effectiveness research, and (2) how group-interaction process typically is conceived and measured. In these discussions we will find some clues to guide the development of a normative model of team effectiveness.

THE CHOICE OF VARIABLES

A great deal of research on small groups has been conducted in the experimental laboratory. It is sometimes argued that laboratory research, because of its inherent artificiality, is not useful in understanding organizational phenomena. That argument is misplaced: when appropriately conceived and executed, laboratory research can generate powerful tests of conceptual propositions—including propositions about organizational phenomena (Weick 1965). The trick is to be sure that the phenomena

---

7. For an excellent typology of group tasks and a summary of what has been learned about group behavior and performance for each of them, see McGrath (1983).

8. For example, choosing the proper categories for coding interaction, devising appropriate analytic models for making sense of interaction patterns, and dealing with inconsistencies in the behavior of groups across tasks and settings (Hackman and Morris 1975, 56–61).

9. A good attempt to do this for group behavior, and one that acknowledges the limitations of such an approach, is provided by Hoffman (1979a).

of interest are actually created in the laboratory, and to make the right decisions about what variables to manipulate (or measure), what variables to control, and what variables to ignore (Runkel and McGrath 1972).

Laboratory studies of groups have tended to focus on personal and interpersonal variables and to hold constant or ignore contextual variables. Indeed, laboratory researchers learn quickly that one had *better* control variables such as the group task, experimenter-subject relationships, reward-system properties, and the demand characteristics of the setting where the research takes place. Not to do so is to invite these variables to overwhelm the more subtle intra- or interpersonal phenomena one is attempting to study.

The major contextual influence in the laboratory, then, is the *experimenter*: it is he or she who decides where the study will be conducted, recruits the subjects and forms them into groups, selects and assigns the group task, chooses what rewards will be available and administers them, provides groups with the information and resources they need to do their work, and establishes the basic norms of conduct for the research setting. In all, the experimenter serves as a powerful context for the group and (if expert in his or her role) makes sure that all groups are treated as nearly the same as possible.

Thus, in the interest of good experimental practice, some of the variables that may most powerfully affect what happens in groups are fixed at constant levels, *thereby making it impossible to learn about their effects.* By contrast, the approach to work-group effectiveness presented in this chapter gives special emphasis to the design of groups as performing units, and to their relations with their organizational contexts—an emphasis also seen in many state-of-the-art action projects involving work teams in organizations (e.g., Poza and Markus 1980).

THE ROLE OF GROUP PROCESS

Developing usable knowledge about group performance may require some changes in how we deal with group interaction process—in research (by going beyond descriptions of whatever interaction happens to develop naturally in work teams), in intervention (by reconsidering the viability of process as an intervention target), and in theory (by reconceptualizing the role of process in the causal chain that links input and output states). These three possibilities are explored below.

The descriptive emphasis. When social psychologists study group interaction, they typically focus on group processes that develop naturally, without direct process interventions. When competently done, these studies help us understand how groups function in the laboratory or field settings where the data were collected.

But what if the kinds of group processes typically observed were *dysfunctional* for group task effectiveness? Perhaps most groups operate in ways that minimize the frequency of anxiety-arousing episodes but, in the process, avoid difficult task problems. Or perhaps group members generally are not very adept at coordinating their efforts or at drawing out and using each other's task-relevant knowledge and skill.

If this were the case, descriptive studies would document the dysfunctionality of group interaction, scholars would conclude that group process serves mainly to impair group effectiveness, research attention would focus on understanding the nature and extent of "process losses" in task-oriented groups, and interventionists would try to help groups solve their process problems. And, in fact, this is approximately what has happened in social psychological research on group performance.

Consider, for example, Steiner's (1972) model of group process and productivity, which is probably the most widely accepted way of thinking about process-productivity relationships. Steiner posits that the actual productivity of a group is equal to its theoretical potential productivity (i.e., what would be achieved if all existing resources were optimally used) *minus* inevitable losses due to group process. No provision is made for any "process gains" that might result from the interaction among group members.

Few social psychological studies have addressed the possibility that groups might perform better if members worked together in ways that *differ* from typical interaction patterns. Argyris (1969) argues that this is a serious failure of social psychological theory. To develop knowledge useful in creating effective work teams, he suggests, it may be necessary to move beyond descriptive research to a more normative and action-oriented approach—attempting to create and test novel patterns of group interaction, ways members can work together that not only reduce process losses but also foster synergistic process gains.

Usefulness as a point of intervention. Although process interventions are not often employed in social psychological research on group performance, they are quite popular in consultative work with groups—for theoretical reasons certainly (see Cooper 1975), but also because process difficulties present themselves so vividly. It is easy to see wasted time and effort, dysfunctional conflict among members, and a variety of other process problems when observing a group that is having trouble with its work. And it may be very difficult for an interventionist to pass up the opportunity to provide consultative help with such problems.

A fairly extensive literature has developed on the effects of process interventions as a consultative tool.

These studies probe the effects of a wide variety of intervention techniques, including eclectic process consultation, systematic role negotiation, training in group-relations skills, and the use of structured procedures that minimize spontaneous group interaction.[10] Research findings on the efficacy of process interventions can be roughly summarized as follows:

1. Interventions that focus directly and primarily on the quality of relationships among members usually succeed in changing member attitudes, sometimes affect behavior in the group, but have no consistent effects on group performance effectiveness (for reviews, see Friedlander and Brown 1974; Kaplan 1979; and Woodman and Sherwood 1980). The same appears to be true for structured techniques aimed at improving group creativity.[11]

2. Interventions that structure group interaction to minimize opportunities for "process losses" do improve team effectiveness for certain kinds of groups and tasks (Green 1975; Stumpf, Zand, and Freedman 1979). Like the rules of parliamentary procedure, such interventions aim to (a) limit the amount of spontaneous interaction that can occur among members, and/or (b) structure the interaction that does take place so as to minimize the opportunity for dysfunctional group processes to develop. Indeed, in the Delphi technique (Dalkey 1967; Delbecq, Van de Ven, and Gustafson 1975), members communicate only through summaries of their inputs compiled by a coordinator, eliminating the possibility of *any* spontaneous member-to-member interaction.

In sum, research findings regarding process interventions suggest that structured techniques that minimize process losses (or reduce their effects) can be helpful. On the other hand, interventions that attempt to improve the quality of interpersonal relations among members or to promote synergistic "process gains" appear not to yield reliable improvements in group task effectiveness.

The role of process in the causal chain. The findings about process interventions raise some difficult questions about how group interaction relates to team effectiveness. Why do process interventions seem to help only when they constrain (or highly structure) interaction among members? Why do consultations that help members relate better to one another not result in more reliable or substantial improvements in performance? Why do groups plagued with conflict and dissension sometimes perform better than those with an abundance of warmth and mutual respect among members? What, indeed, *is* the role of group interaction process in transforming input states into performance outcomes?

One way of dealing with these questions is proposed in the normative model of group effectiveness to be described in the second part of this chapter. As background for that discussion, let us look briefly at two reasons why traditional conceptions of group process may have muddled understanding about its mediating role.

1. A basic premise of the input-process-output model is that input states affect performance outcomes exclusively through their intermediate effects on how members interact with one another. This model is so ingrained in our thinking about group behavior that it is hard to imagine alternatives. Yet there *are* some alternatives, as illustrated in parts B and C of figure 20.2.

Part A of the figure shows the traditional model. The alternative in part B suggests that *both* group process and performance effectiveness are consequences of the way a group is set up and managed. In this view, groups that are well designed and well supported have a better chance of achieving excellence in process and in performance than do groups with poor designs or unsupportive organizational contexts. The quality of group interaction would be correlated with group performance in this model—but would not determine it.

Another alternative is illustrated in part C of figure 20.2. Here again, input conditions affect both group process and performance, but these variables also have reciprocal effects on each other. This model suggests that group interaction *does* mediate the impact of input conditions, but also that performance outcomes influence group interaction. The latter proposition may seem an impossibility, because performance comes later in time than the interaction it is said to affect. However, the impossibility applies only to short-term, one-shot groups of the type run in experimental laboratories. Work

---

10. "Process consultation" is a general term used to describe interventions intended to help group members develop new, more task-effective ways of working together. In its most flexible form, the consultant and the group work together to diagnose the state of the group and to plan changes based on that diagnosis (Schein 1969). Four more focused approaches to team development are identified and discussed by Beer (1976): (1) goal-setting and problem-solving consultations, (2) assistance in improving interpersonal relationships among members, (3) role definition and negotiation, and (4) integrated consultative approaches, such as the managerial grid (e.g., Blake and Mouton 1969). Still other process interventions involve the introduction of highly structured procedures for doing the work of the group, such as the Nominal Group Technique (Delbecq, Van de Ven, and Gustafson 1975), and various creativity-enhancing procedures (for a compilation and review of these, see Stein 1975).

11. The best-researched of these techniques is brainstorming (Osborn 1957). For evidence on the efficacy of brainstorming, see Dunnette, Campbell, and Jaastad (1963) and the review by Stein (1975).

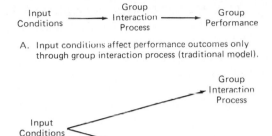

A. Input conditions affect performance outcomes only through group interaction process (traditional model).

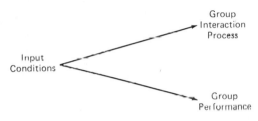

B. Input conditions affect both group process and group performance.

Group
Interaction
Process

Input
Conditions

Group
Performance

C. Input conditions affect both process and performance; there is also a reciprocal influence between process and performance.

Figure 20.2   Three ways of construing input-process-output relations in work teams

groups in organizations typically proceed through multiple performance episodes, even in getting a single piece of work done, providing many opportunities for group interaction to be affected by how well a group performs.[12]

Data are not currently available to determine whether these alternative perspectives are better representations of what happens in task-performing groups than the traditional view presented in figure 20.1. They do, however, prompt us to think about the determinants of group effectiveness in ways that we might otherwise overlook. They raise the possibility, for example, that group interaction may be as useful as an *indicator* of how a group is doing in its work (i.e., as diagnostic data) as it is as a point of intervention for improving group effectiveness. And the alternative models encourage us to search for "input" factors (such as how a group is designed and linked to the surrounding organization) that can foster *both* high-quality group process and effective task performance.

2. It may be that we have been looking at the wrong aspects of group process and examining them at the wrong level of analysis. When consultants or managers address the interaction process of a group, they usually focus on the interpersonal transactions that take place within the group: who is talking with whom (or not doing so), who is fighting with whom, who is pairing up with whom, and so on. Such interpersonal behaviors can tell a trained observer a great deal about social and emotional issues that are alive in the group, including issues driven by unconscious forces as well as those of which members are aware (see, for example, Colman and Bexton 1975).

If, however, we are interested in group effectiveness, it may be more appropriate to focus on those aspects of interaction that relate directly to a group's work on its task. It should be possible, for example, to assess whether a group is using the energy and talents of its members well (rather than wasting or misapplying them), and to determine whether the group interaction develops and expands (rather than diminishes) members' performance capabilities. Other ways group interaction contributes to task accomplishment also can be imagined and also are worthy of exploration. But whatever aspects of interaction are examined, it seems highly advisable to examine them at the *group* (rather than the interpersonal) level of analysis and to emphasize the *task* (rather than the social and emotional) significance of what happens.[13]

Conclusion. Group interaction provides the stage on which many dramas are played out, from political intrigues to romantic encounters. Our present focus on task effectiveness does not deny the multiple purposes served by group interaction, but it does direct our attention to two aspects of group process that are particularly useful in understanding and influencing group performance.

First, interaction process can serve as an *indicator* of how, and how well, a group is proceeding with work on its task—a window through which one can view the group as it does its work. One can assess, for example, the level of effort the group is applying to the task, the amount of knowledge and skill members are bringing to bear on it, and the task-appropriateness of the strategies they are using in carrying out the work. As will be seen later, such data turn out to be very useful in identifying the special strengths and weaknesses of a group as a performing unit, and in guiding interventions intended to help a group improve its performance.

Second, group interaction is a potential source of "group synergy." Synergy among members results in group outcomes that may be quite different from those

---

12. Reflection on one's own experience in groups that are failing ("through no fault of *ours!*") or that are succeeding beyond anyone's expectation ("we must be *charmed!*") will provide some nonscientific evidence for the existence of a performance to process causal link.

13. We must recognize, nonetheless, that among the influences on task-focused interaction are the social and emotional dynamics that occur among members.

that would be obtained by simply adding up the contributions of individual members. Synergistic contributions can be either positive (e.g., development of a creative way of working that transcends some of the limitations in a group's performance situation) or negative (e.g., a failure of coordination within the group so severe that *nobody* knows what he or she is supposed to be doing). Whatever their direction, synergistic effects have their roots in group-interaction process, and therefore attempts to alter their direction or potency necessarily will involve attention to how members relate to one another as they work together.

Summary

Descriptive research on group behavior has provided a good general understanding of what takes place in groups that perform tasks, and has generated a reasonable set of findings about the empirical associations among various input, process, and output variables. Research in the descriptive tradition has been less successful, however, in generating knowledge that can be used to design and manage work teams. In exploring the reasons for this failure, we have unearthed some leads that may be helpful in developing an alternative, more action-oriented approach to work-team effectiveness.

That approach will be laid out in the next section of this chapter. It gives special attention to the basic design of groups that do work and to their relationships with the organizational contexts in which they function. It moves group-interaction process from center stage to a supportive (but still important) role. Overall, the approach is normative rather than descriptive, emphasizing those factors that can be used to improve performance effectiveness, rather than focusing on descriptions of how groups actually behave in various circumstances.

A NORMATIVE MODEL OF GROUP EFFECTIVENESS

The model of work-group effectiveness described in this section is an attempt to bridge between *understanding* group behavior (the province of the descriptive approach just reviewed) and *doing something to improve it* (the topic of the final section of this chapter).[14] The intent of the normative model is to identify the factors that most powerfully enhance or depress the task effectiveness of

a group and to do so in a way that increases the possibility that constructive change can occur. This requires that the variables used in the model be powerful (i.e., they make nontrivial differences in how a group performs), potentially manipulable (i.e., it is feasible to change them in an organization), and accessible (i.e., people can understand them and use them). Moreover, they must be arranged sensibly: the model is not a naturalistic chronological description of what leads to what as a group goes about its work; yet if it is to be useful, it must be plausible.

That is a reasonably tall order, and if we are to have a chance of filling it, we must be very clear about both the kinds of groups to which the model applies and what we mean by "group effectiveness."

Scope of the model

DOMAIN

The normative model focuses exclusively on *work groups in organizations*. This means that the model applies only to (1) *real* groups (that is, intact social systems complete with boundaries and differentiated roles among members); (2) groups that have one or more *tasks* to perform, resulting in discernible and potentially measurable group products; and (3) groups that operate within an *organizational context*.

This turns out to be a fairly inclusive statement. The model would apply, for example, to a group of executives charged with deciding where to locate a new plant, a team of rank-and-file workers assembling a product, a group of students writing a case assigned by their instructor, a health-care team tending to the needs of a group of patients, and a group of economists analyzing the budgetary implications of a proposed new public policy.

Nonetheless, many sets of people commonly referred to as "groups" are excluded. Social groups are out (no task), as are reference groups (not an intact social system), coacting groups (i.e., people who may report to the same manager but who have their own, individual tasks to perform—no *group* task), and freestanding groups (no organizational context).

This statement of domain may seem relatively straightforward, but it often is difficult to determine what is a "real" group, a "group task," and an "organizational context." For a detailed and more formal discussion of these issues, see Hackman (1983).

GROUP EFFECTIVENESS DEFINED

In conducting experiments on group performance, researchers try to select tasks for which it is relatively easy to tell how well a group has performed: one can

---

14. The work of Cummings (e.g., 1978, 1981) on the design and management of work groups from a sociotechnical-systems perspective has much in common with what is presented here, although it comes from a rather different intellectual tradition. For an overview of that tradition, see Trist (1981).

count the number of right answers, or measure how long it takes the group to finish, or see if the group solved the problem correctly. For teams in organizations, effectiveness criteria are more complex. Most organizational tasks do not have clear right-or-wrong answers, for example, nor do they lend themselves to quantitative measures that validly indicate how well a group has done its work. Moreover, one needs to be concerned about more than raw productivity or decision quality when assessing groups in organizations. Unlike participants in laboratory experiments (who come in, do the task, and go home), members of work groups and committees usually continue to relate to one another long after the group task is completed; what happens in the work group can substantially affect their willingness (and their ability) to do so.

For these reasons, we use three criteria to assess team effectiveness. The first deals with the actual output of the group, the second with the state of the group as a performing unit, and the third with the impact of the group experience on individual members.

1. *The productive output of the work group should meet or exceed the performance standards of the people who receive and/or review the output.* If a group's output is not acceptable to its "clients" and/or to managers charged with evaluating its performance, then it cannot be considered effective. An effectiveness criterion that relies explicitly on assessments made by organization members or clients (rather than on "objective" indexes of performance) was chosen for two reasons. First, reliable and valid objective criteria are available for only a small proportion of work teams in organizations; to deal only with those teams would restrict radically the domain of the model. In addition, what *happens* to a group and its members usually depends far more on others' assessments of the group's output than on any objective performance index (even though such assessments may be based, in part, on whatever objective measures happen to be available).[15]

2. *The social processes used in carrying out the work should maintain or enhance the capability of members to work together on subsequent team tasks.* Some groups operate in such a way that the integrity of the group as a performing unit is destroyed; the group "burns itself up" in the process of performing the task. Even if the product

of such a group is acceptable, it would be difficult to argue that the group has been a fully effective performing unit.

3. *The group experience should, on balance, satisfy rather than frustrate the personal needs of group members.* If the primary effect of group membership is to keep individuals from doing what they want and need to do, or if members' predominant reactions to the group experience are disgust and disillusionment, then the costs of generating the group product, at least those borne by individual members, are probably too high.

The inclusion of social and personal criteria in a definition of effectiveness is a departure from tradition—as is the use of system-defined (rather than researcher-defined) assessments of a group's output. Yet the criteria themselves require neither extraordinary accomplishment nor exemplary social processes. All that is necessary is output judged acceptable by those who receive it, a team that winds up its work at least as healthy as when it started, and members who are at least as satisfied as they are frustrated by what has transpired. The challenge for researchers and practitioners is to develop ways of understanding, designing, and managing groups that help them meet or exceed these modest standards of team effectiveness.

The basic proposition

The normative model presented in the pages that follow rests on the validity of one key proposition. If this proposition is valid (and if its implications are appropriately developed), it should be possible to explain why some groups perform better than others, to assess the strengths and weaknesses of specific groups in organizations, and to determine what needs to be done to help a group become more effective.

Specifically, it is proposed that the overall effectiveness of work groups in organizations is a joint function of

- The level of *effort* group members collectively expend carrying out task work,
- The amount of *knowledge and skill* members bring to bear on the group task, and
- The appropriateness to the task of the *performance strategies* used by the group in its work.[16]

---

15. There are, however, occasions when it may not be sensible to rely on client assessments of a group's output. Consider, for example, a situation in which the legitimate clients of the group are seriously disturbed, ethnocentric, or competitive with the group. The very meaning of "good performance" under these circumstances is problematic.

16. For example, a group might decide to divide itself into two subgroups, each of which would do part of the overall task, with the final product to be assembled later. Or it might choose to free associate about task solutions in the first meeting, reflect for a week about the ideas that came up, and then meet to draft the product. Or it might decide to spend considerable time checking and rechecking for errors after learning that its client cares a great deal about product quality. All of these are choices about task performance strategy.

We will refer to effort, knowledge and skill, and performance strategies as *process criteria of effectiveness*. They are the hurdles a group must surmount to be effective. To assess the adequacy of a group's task processes, then, we might ask: Is the group working hard enough to get the task done well and on time? Do members have the expertise required to accomplish the task, and are they using their knowledge and skill efficiently? Has the group developed an approach to the work that is fully appropriate for the task being performed, and are they implementing that strategy well?

Answers to these questions provide diagnostic data about a group's strengths and weaknesses as a performing unit, and they should enable us to predict with some confidence a group's eventual performance effectiveness. But, as strongly implied by research on interventions that focus exclusively on improving group processes, direct attempts to *manipulate* a group's standing on the process criteria (e.g., by exhortation or instruction) are likely to fail.

A more promising approach is to design and manage a group so that task-effective group processes emerge naturally. Several features of the group and its context can potentially lead to improvements in a group's level of effort, its application of member knowledge and skill, and the appropriateness of its task performance strategies. In particular, we will examine the impact of the following three classes of variables on each of the process criteria:[17]

- The *design of the group* as a performing unit: the structure of the group task, the composition of the group, and group norms that regulate member behavior
- The *organizational context* of the group: the reward, education, and information systems that influence the group, and the material resources that are put at the group's disposal
- *Group synergy* resulting from members' interactions as they carry out the task[18]

Throughout, we will emphasize aspects of group design, context, and synergy that foster both high-quality task behavior and eventual team effectiveness. After completing this analysis, we will explore ways of assessing the standing of a group on the variables in the norma-

tive model, and speculate about the implications of the model for the creation and management of work teams in organizations.[19]

Conditions that support effort

Group members are most likely to work hard on their task if (1) the task itself is motivationally engaging, (2) the organizational reward system provides challenging performance objectives and reinforces their achievement, and (3) interaction among members minimizes "social loafing" and instead promotes a shared commitment among members to the team and its work. These factors are illustrated in figure 20.3 and discussed below.

DESIGN OF THE GROUP

We would expect a group to work especially hard on its tasks when the following conditions are met:

- The group task requires members to use a variety of relatively high-level skills.
- The group task is a whole and meaningful piece of work, with a visible outcome.
- The outcomes of the group's work on the task have significant consequences for other people (e.g., other organization members or external clients).
- The task provides group members with substantial autonomy for deciding about how they do the work—in effect, the group "owns" the task and is responsible for the work outcomes.
- Work on the task generates regular, trustworthy feedback about how well the group is performing.

If a group task meets these criteria, it is likely that members will experience their work as meaningful, they will feel collectively responsible for the products they create, and they will know, on a more or less continuous basis, how they are doing. And, extrapolating from Hackman and Oldham's (1980, chap. 4), model of individual task motivation, a group task with these properties should result in high built-in motivation for a group to try hard to do well (see, for example, Wall and Clegg 1981).

This emphasis on the group task runs counter to traditional wisdom about motivated work behavior. One often hears managers report that some group is "filled with lazy [or hard-working] people," or that group members "have a norm of not working very hard [or of always giving their best]." It is true that people have

---

17. For simplicity, feedback loops among classes of variables in the framework (e.g., how the organizational context may change in response to a team's level of effectiveness) are not shown or discussed here.

18. As applied to group behavior in this chapter, "synergy" refers to group-level phenomena that (1) emerge from the interaction among members, and (2) affect how well a group is able to deal with the demands and opportunities in its performance situation.

19. Some of the material that follows is adapted from Hackman and Oldham 1980, chaps. 7–8.

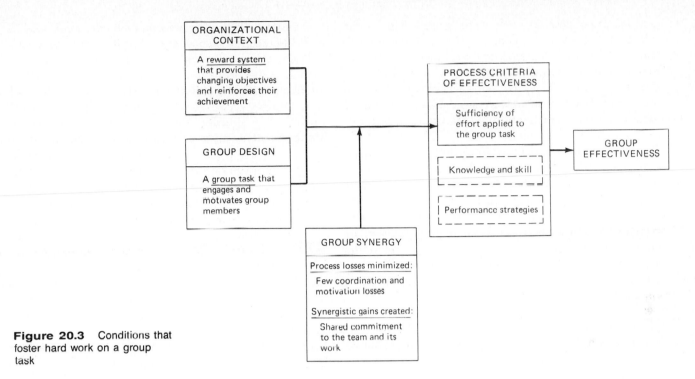

Figure 20.3 Conditions that foster hard work on a group task

different chronic energy levels, but there is not much one can do about that. And while norms do emerge in groups that encourage especially high or low effort, such norms usually develop as a *reaction* to how things are set up, as a means of coping with the group task and work situation.

Thus, if a group's work is routine and unchallenging, of dubious importance, and wholly preprogrammed with no opportunity for feedback, members are likely to develop antiproductivity norms. But if a group task is challenging, important to the organization or its clients, "owned" by the group, and consequential for group members, then a norm encouraging high effort on the task is likely to emerge. Improving the design of a group's work is usually a better way to foster high collective effort than directly addressing group norms about productivity.

ORGANIZATIONAL CONTEXT

A supportive organizational reward system can reinforce the motivational benefits of a well-designed team task, and a poorly structured reward system can undermine and erode those benefits. Reward systems that support high effort by work teams tend to have the following three features:

Challenging, specific performance objectives. There is a great deal of research evidence that goal-directed effort is greater when a group accepts moderately difficult performance objectives and receives feedback about its progress in attaining those objectives (Zander 1971, 1980). When the organization specifies a challenging performance target (e.g., a date by which the work must be done, the number of items to be produced, a quality level to be achieved), members often mobilize their efforts to achieve that target. Objectives, however, should supplement rather than replace task-based motivation. A group is unlikely to persist in working toward challenging objectives if its task is inherently frustrating and alienating.

Positive consequences for excellent performance. A reward system that recognizes and reinforces excellent group performance can complement and amplify the motivational incentives of a well-designed group task. People tend to engage in behaviors that are rewarded, and people in groups are no exception (Glaser and Klaus 1966). Which specific kinds of rewards will work best, of course, depends on what group members value. Sometimes simple recognition of excellence will suffice; in other cases, more tangible rewards will be required. But whatever the content of the consequences, their impact on team effort will be greater if members understand that they are contingent on performance—that is, that the group will receive them only if it earns them by performing well.

Rewards and objectives that focus on group, not individual, behavior. When rewards are given to individuals on the basis of managers' judgments about who has contributed most to a group product, dissension and conflict often develop within the group. This is the dilemma of the athletic coach, who must try to motivate the team as a whole while simultaneously cultivating and reinforcing individual performance. And it is a problem routinely faced by managers of work teams in organizations where the reward system has traditionally focused on the identification and recognition of excellent *individual* performers.

The destructive effects of rewarding individual contributions rather than team performance can be considerable. Therefore, if it is not feasible to provide performance-contingent rewards to the group as a unit, it may be better to base rewards on the performance of even larger groups (such as a department or division) or not to use contingent rewards at all, than to invite the divisiveness that can develop when members of a team are put into competition with one another for scarce and valued rewards (Lawler 1981).

GROUP SYNERGY

Group synergy can contribute to effective task behavior in two ways. First, group members can find innovative ways to avoid "process losses," and thereby minimize waste and misuse of members' time, energy, and talent. Second, members can interact synergistically to create *new* internal resources that can be used in their work—capabilities that did not exist before the group created them. Process losses and synergistic gains that affect how much effort a group applies to its task are discussed below.

Minimizing coordination and motivation losses. There are always some "overhead costs" to be paid when groups perform tasks. The need to coordinate member activities, for example, takes time and energy away from productive work, resulting in a level of actual productivity that is less than what theoretically would be possible with optimum use of member resources (Steiner 1972). In addition, group productivity often is compromised by what Steiner terms "motivation decrements" and what Latané (e.g., Latané, Williams, and Harkins 1979) has called "social loafing." As groups get larger, the amount of effort *each member* contributes to the group task decreases—perhaps because each individual feels less responsible for the outcome than would be the case in a smaller group or if one person were doing the task alone.

Some groups suffer much greater coordination and motivation losses than others. And group members can cultivate process skills that help them behave in ways that minimize such losses. But if the group is large or if the task is ill defined or alienating, it may be impossible for the group to avoid serious coordination and motivation losses.

Creating shared commitment to the team and its work. Some groups show great "spirit": everyone is committed to the team, proud of it, and willing to work hard to make it one of the best. When individuals value their membership in the group and find it rewarding to work collaboratively with their teammates, they may work considerably harder than they would otherwise. Managers often engage in group-building activities (such as encouraging members of an ongoing team to give the group a name, to decorate their work area, or to participate in an athletic league as a team) in the hope of increasing members' commitment to the group and their willingness to work especially hard on the group task.[20]

Commitment to a team sometimes can result in high effort on the group task even when objective performance conditions are highly unfavorable (e.g., a team that develops a "can do" attitude and comes to view each new adversity as yet another challenge to be met). It is questionable, however, whether such commitment is sustainable if performance conditions remain poor (e.g., a frustrating or alienating group task, or a reward system that does not recognize excellence).

Conditions that support knowledge and skill

A group is most likely to bring sufficient talent and expertise to bear on its task when (1) the group has an appropriate number of members with a good mix of skills, (2) the education system of the organization offers training or consultation as needed to supplement members' existing knowledge, and (3) group interaction avoids inappropriate "weighting" of members' contributions and instead fosters sharing of expertise and collective learning. These factors are illustrated in figure 20.4 and discussed below.

DESIGN OF THE GROUP

A group's composition is the most important condition affecting the amount of knowledge and skill members apply to their tasks. Well-composed groups have the following four characteristics:

Individual members have high task-relevant expertise. The most efficient way to make sure a group has the expertise it needs for its work is simply to assign talented individuals to it. This seemingly obvious principle, however, is not always straightforward in practice. Even when people with ample task-relevant knowledge and skill are available, they may be overlooked—for example, when groups are composed with only political

---

20. Such activities are not risk free. "Team spirit" can evolve into group ethnocentrism and can prompt dysfunctional competition and conflict *between* groups.

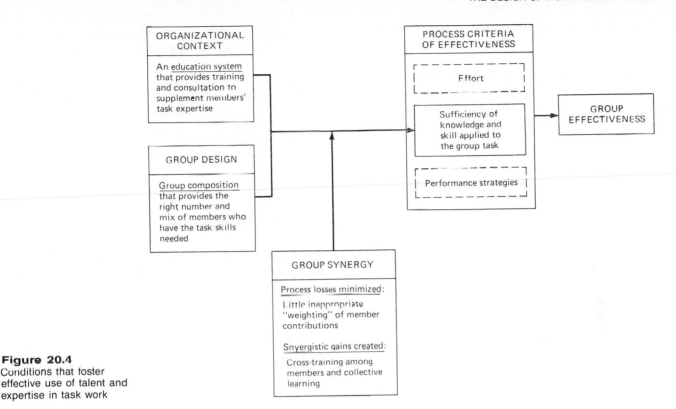

Figure 20.4
Conditions that foster
effective use of talent and
expertise in task work

considerations in mind. This can result in a team whose members cover all the right bases, but one that is not capable of carrying out well the work it was created to do.

The group is just large enough to do the work. If a task requires four sets of hands, then there should be four people in the group—but no more than that. The research literature offers abundant evidence documenting the dysfunctions that occur in large groups (see Steiner 1972, chap. 4 for a review) and establishing the advantages of groups that are slightly *smaller* than the task technically requires (Wicker et al. 1976). Yet large work groups (especially decision-making committees) are widely used in organizations. Often the decision to put additional people in a group allows managers to avoid difficult personnel choices or sensitive political issues (e.g., how to involve a department in the work of a task force on which it has no representatives), but the cost may be losses in the quality of the group product and the efficiency with which it is produced.

Members have interpersonal as well as task skills. If a group task is well designed (i.e., it provides the group considerable autonomy in managing a challenging piece of work), then at least moderate interpersonal skills are required to bring the *task* skills of members to bear on the group's work—especially if members are diverse (i.e., they come from different demographic groups, represent different organizational units, or have divergent personal

views on the matter at hand). Some individuals have little competence in working collaboratively with other people, especially if those people differ from themselves in important ways. Even one or two such individuals can significantly impede the ability of a group to bring members' expertise effectively to bear on the group task.

Membership is moderately diverse. Members of an excessively homogeneous group may get along well together but lack the resources needed to perform the task because the members essentially replicate one another. An excessively heterogeneous group, on the other hand, may have a rich complement of talent within the group but be unable to use that talent well because members are so diverse in values or perspective that they cannot work together effectively. The aspiration in composing a group is to strike just the right balance between homogeneity and heterogeneity: members should have a variety of talents and perspectives, yet be similar enough that they can understand and coordinate with one another.[21]

ORGANIZATIONAL CONTEXT
Sometimes a group has within its bounds all the knowledge and skill needed for optimum task performance.

---

21. A number of scholars have examined the impact of member *compatability* on task behavior and performance. See, for example, Belbin (1981); Hewett, O'Brien, and Hornik (1974); and Schutz (1958, 1961).

More commonly there are aspects of the work for which additional talent or expertise would be helpful. The educational system of the organization can play a useful role in helping the group obtain the outside expertise it needs for its work.

For this potential to be realized, two conditions must be met. First, relevant educational resources (which can include technical consultation as well as training) must exist somewhere in the organization. Second, some sort of "delivery system" must be in place to make those resources accessible to the group. This may not be a simple matter for rank-and-file teams in organizations where employees have never had the right to call on staff resources.

The particular kind of assistance required will, of course, depend on both the task requirements and the specific needs of the group. And the appropriate form of assistance will vary as well. Sometimes a one-shot technical consultation will suffice; sometimes a continuing consulting relationship will be needed; and sometimes a training program for group members will be more appropriate, to build the relevant expertise into the group itself. Whatever the content of the assistance and the vehicle used to provide it, the role of the educational system is the same: to help groups obtain the full complement of knowledge and skill required for excellent task performance.

GROUP SYNERGY

Minimizing inappropriate weighting of member contributions. The knowledge and skill of group members can be wasted if the group solicits and weights contributions in a way that is incongruent with members' expertise—as when the credence given a member's idea depends on such task-irrelevant considerations as his or her demographic attributes (e.g., gender, ethnicity, or age) or behavioral style (e.g., talkativeness or verbal dominance). This process loss has been well documented in the research literature (e.g., Johnson and Torcivia 1967; Thomas and Fink 1961; Torrance 1954). Groups often have trouble assessing which members have the special expertise needed for the task, and they appear to have even more difficulty explicitly acknowledging these differences and weighting members' contributions in accord with them. To the extent a group is able to minimize this problem, it will take better advantage of the expertise that was put in the group when it was composed.

Fostering collective learning. When members of a group interact in ways that help them learn from one another, they can increase the *total* pool of talent available for task work—a synergistic gain from group interaction. The practice of "cross-training," often encouraged in autonomous work groups in industry, is an example

of such behavior, as are more informal activities that involve the sharing of knowledge, expertise, and experience among members. A group that orients itself to collective learning and whose members share what is learned with each other should be far better able to exploit the educational resources of an organization than a group that takes a laissez-faire stance toward the development of its internal talent.

Conditions that support appropriate performance strategies

The likelihood that the group will employ a task-appropriate performance strategy increases when (1) group norms support explicit assessment of the performance situation and active consideration of alternative ways of proceeding with the work; (2) the information system of the organization provides members with the data they need to assess the situation and evaluate alternative strategies; and (3) group interaction results in little "slippage" when performance plans are executed and instead prompts creative new ideas about ways to proceed with the work. These factors are illustrated in figure 20.5 and discussed below.

DESIGN OF THE GROUP

Group members typically reach agreement on how they will go about performing their task relatively early in their time together. Indeed, for familiar tasks, members may not talk about their strategy at all, because it is obvious to everyone how the task should be done. Once a strategy is agreed to, whether implicitly or explicitly, members tend to behave in accord with it and enforce adherence to it (March and Simon 1958, chap. 6). Performance strategies thus become part of the fabric of the group, a "given" that is no more open to question than the task of the group or who is in the group.

The specific strategies that will be most appropriate for a given group depend both on the task to be done and on the imperatives and resources in the performance situation. No "one best strategy" can be specified in advance for most task-performing groups in organizations. It *is* possible, however, to build group norms that increase the likelihood that members will develop task-appropriate performance strategies and execute them well. Such norms have two properties, the first being a prerequisite for the second.[22]

---

22. Following Jackson (1965), norms are conceptualized as structural features of a group that summarize members' shared approval (or disapproval) of various behaviors. Norms simplify group influence processes because they make it possible for members to count on certain things being done and other things not being done. For more detailed discussion of how norms structure and channel behavior in a group, see Hackman (1976).

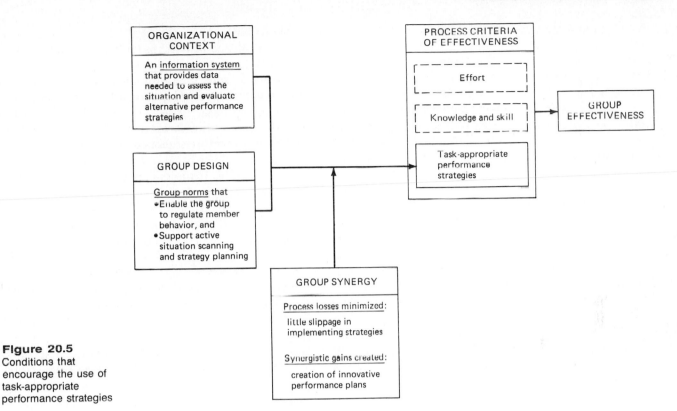

Figure 20.5
Conditions that
encourage the use of
task-appropriate
performance strategies

Group norms support self-regulation. Behavior in some groups is so chaotic and subject to individual whim as to approach anarchy. Such groups are unlikely to be able to execute *any* performance strategy in an orderly fashion, even one that has been specified in detail by management. Thus, a normative structure that enables a group to regulate member behavior is essential to the efficient execution of performance strategies. This requires that behavioral norms be sufficiently *crystallized* (i.e., members have consensus about them) and *intense* (i.e., compliance results in substantial approval or avoidance of substantial disapproval by other members) that individuals will wish to behave in accord with them (Jackson 1965).

Group norms support situation scanning and strategy planning. Groups that actively assess the demands and opportunities in the performance situation and that consider several alternative ways of proceeding with the work tend to develop more appropriate performance strategies than groups that do not (Hackman, Brousseau, and Weiss 1976; Maier 1963). Yet such activities tend not to take place spontaneously. Instead, it appears that the general disinclination of group members to "talk about process" extends even to discussions about how the work of the group will be carried out.[23]

For this reason, it is necessary somehow to prompt or encourage group members to engage in situation scanning and strategy planning activities. Group norms provide an efficient and powerful way to accomplish this. Such norms focus attention on opportunities and constraints that might otherwise be overlooked and make it difficult for members to fall into familiar or habitual patterns of behavior that may be inappropriate for the particular task at hand.[24]

Group norms governing performance processes can be established when a group is first formed or can be introduced during a hiatus in the work, when members are ready to reconsider how they operate as a team. Regardless of how and when they are developed, the norms that guide a group's performance processes are an important structural feature of the group— an aspect of group design that often has been overlooked by both scholars and managers interested in work-team effectiveness.

23. Spontaneous strategy planning does, of course, occur if a task is so novel that members are at a loss about how to proceed with it, and is generally more likely when the task is unfamiliar.

24. This analysis presumes that a team has at least some latitude for planning its own strategy. Usually this is the case. In some groups, however, behavior is so completely preprogrammed or closely supervised that members have essentially no strategy choices to make. For such groups, there is little need for a norm supporting scanning and planning, because those activities are someone else's responsibility. All that is needed is the orderly execution of the strategy that has been supplied. The implications of giving a team the authority to devise its own strategies (rather than reserving that authority for management) are explored later in this chapter.

ORGANIZATIONAL CONTEXT

The information system of an organization is critical to a group's ability to plan and execute a task-appropriate performance strategy. If a group cannot obtain clear information about its performance situation, or if it does not have access to data about the likely outcomes of alternative approaches to the task, it may develop a way of proceeding that seems reasonable to group members but that turns out, when executed, to be grossly inappropriate.

Clarity about the parameters of the performance situation. To develop a task-appropriate performance strategy, a group needs a relatively clear map of the performance situation. Of special importance is information about (1) task requirements and constraints that may limit strategic options, (2) the material resources available for use, and (3) the people who will receive, review, and/or use the group product, and the standards they are likely to employ in assessing its adequacy.

Access to data about likely consequences of alternative strategies. The information system also should make available to a group the data and analytic tools members need to compare and evaluate the probable consequences of alternative performance strategies. Consider, for example, a manufacturing team that is attempting to decide how to approach a complex assembly task. One possibility might be a cyclic strategy, in which all members build components for a period of time, then assemble final products (producing a relative flood of output), followed by another component-building period, and so on. How would this strategy compare to one in which some members build components continuously while others are dedicated to final assembly? To choose between these strategies, the group needs information about the timing of demand for their product, the availability of space for storing components and completed products, and the cost of obtaining and holding parts for use in batch-component production. It would be quite risky for a group to choose a strategy without data about such matters.

How much information a group needs depends in part on how much latitude it has to manage its own affairs. Groups that have the authority to invent their own strategies and manage their own performance processes will need relatively complete data on both the parameters of the performance situation and the likely consequences of alternative ways of proceeding. Groups with less authority for setting their own directions will have less need for such data.

Managers who control access to performance-relevant information must make sure that data needed by a team are realistically available to it. This is not always easy: the relevant data may not exist, they may be costly to obtain, or the manager may be unable to convince his or her colleagues that it is appropriate to share with the group politically or competitively sensitive information. In such circumstances, the group needs to know *that*—that it will have to make do with imperfect or incomplete data.[25] Care also must be taken not to flood the group with excess or irrelevant information, data that members must process but for which they have no present use. Some organizations minimize this risk by initially providing teams only with basic data about the parameters of the performance situation and a guide to other information available. The group has the responsibility for deciding what additional data it requires and for determining when and how to obtain it.

GROUP SYNERGY

Minimizing slippage in strategy implementation. Plans are never perfectly implemented—there is always a slip or two, something that wastes or misdirects the time and energy of group members, compromising even well-conceived plans. To the extent a group minimizes this process loss, the opportunities provided by norms that foster strategy planning and by a supportive information system can be well used. But if slippage is high, the group may fail to exploit even a highly favorable performance situation.[26]

Creating innovative strategic plans. On the positive side, groups can develop ways of interacting that occasionally result in truly original or insightful ways of proceeding with the work. For example, a group might find a way to exploit some resources that everyone else has overlooked; it might invent a way to get around a seemingly insurmountable performance obstacle; or it might come up with a novel way to generate ideas for solving a difficult problem. When group members get

---

25. Particularly unfortunate are occasions when a manager *deliberately* withholds performance-relevant information from a group, to make sure the group remains dependent on him or her. While this may preserve a manager's feelings of personal power, it can result in inappropriate performance strategies and needlessly poor team performance.

26. One particularly virulent form of this process loss bears special mention. Members of some groups collude with each other in a way that makes it impossible *ever* to implement performance plans. Such a group may have ample information about the performance situation and may develop a fully task-appropriate performance strategy. But once the plans are complete they are ignored. When members reconvene, they develop new plans and a new resolve, and the cycle repeats itself. The group acts as if a good strategy is all that is needed for team effectiveness, and its inevitable failures are always well-wrapped in new and better plans for the future. This kind of synergy often is driven by unconscious forces, it is not uncommon in groups that have high-pressure work environments, and it can be lethal to team effectiveness.

in the habit of thinking creatively about how they will do their work, interesting and useful ideas can emerge—ideas that did not exist before the group invented them.

Overview and summary

An overview of the normative model is presented in figure 20.6. It shows three major points of leverage for fostering group effectiveness: (1) the design of the group as a performing unit, (2) the supports provided by the organizational context in which the group operates, and (3) the synergistic outcomes of the interaction among group members. The contributions of each of these classes of variables are summarized next in brief.

DESIGN

The design of a group—task structure, group composition, and group norms—should promote effective task behavior and lessen the chances that members will encounter built-in obstacles to good performance. While a good group design cannot guarantee competent group behavior, it does create conditions that make it easier and more natural for task-effective behaviors to emerge and persist.

CONTEXT

The organizational context of a group—the reward, education, and information systems of the organization—should support and reinforce the design features. A supportive organizational context gives a group what it needs to exploit the potential of a good basic design (although it probably cannot compensate for a fundamentally flawed design). An unsupportive organizational context can easily undermine the positive features of even a well-designed team. Excellent group performance requires *both* a good design for the team and a supportive organizational context.

Figure 20.6 shows one important contextual feature not previously discussed—the *material resources* required to do the work. If a group lacks the tools, equipment, space, raw materials, money, or human resources it needs, its performance surely will suffer—even if it stands high on the process criteria of effectiveness. A talented, well-motivated production team, for example, will not perform well if the raw materials it needs to make its products are not available, or if production tools are unsatisfactory. Similarly, a committee formed to select a new agency manager cannot be successful if there are no qualified candidates available. And a group that provides human services to clients may have performance problems if members' work stations are so spread about

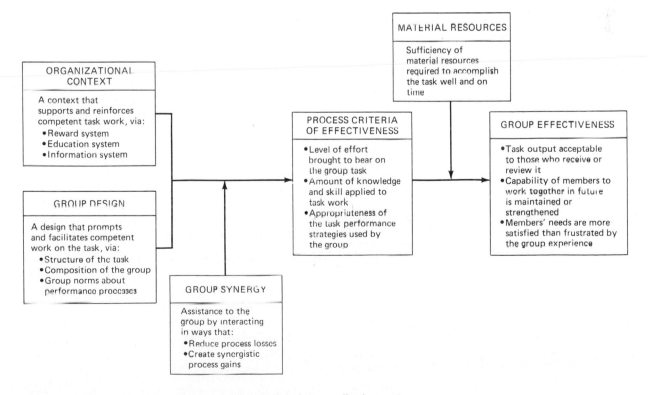

Figure 20.6 An overview of the normative model of group effectiveness

PERFORMANCE CONDITIONS
(Group Design and Organizational Context)

	Unfavorable	Favorable
GROUP SYNERGY Predominantly negative	Amplification of the impact of performance-depressing conditions	Failure by the group to exploit opportunities in the performance situation
Predominantly positive	Damping of the negative impact of performance conditions; perhaps transcending their effects for a limited period of time	Full exploitation of favorable performance conditions

Figure 20.7 Consequences for task behavior of the interaction between performance conditions and group synergy

that they cannot coordinate their activities, or if money is so scarce that needed support staff cannot be obtained.[27]

SYNERGY

Group synergy "tunes" the impact of design and contextual factors. Positive synergy—that is, when the synergistic gains from group interaction exceed group process losses—can help a group overcome the limitations of a poor performance situation (e.g., a badly designed group task or an unsupportive reward system). And if performance conditions are favorable, positive synergy can help a group exploit the opportunities those conditions provide. Negative synergy, when process losses exceed synergistic gains, has opposite effects. It can *amplify* the negative impact of a poor performance situation, and it can prevent a group from taking advantage of favorable circumstances. The relationship between performance conditions (i.e., the group design and the organizational context) and group synergy are illustrated in figure 20.7.[28]

---

27. The importance of mundane aspects of the performance situation such as these are increasingly being recognized as critical to effective work performance (see, for example, Peters and O'Connor 1980, and Peters, O'Connor, and Rudolf 1980). To overlook them is to jeopardize the effort expended to design a team well and provide it with appropriate contextual supports.

28. Although performance conditions and group synergy are placed on separate axes in the figure, they are not independent: positive synergy is more likely under favorable conditions, and negative synergy is more likely under unfavorable conditions. Thus performance *spirals* can develop. For example, good group performance can lead to management decisions that improve the group's performance situation, which promotes positive synergy, which results in even better performance, and so on. Equally plausible is a negative spiral, in which poor performance begets organizational "tightening up," resulting in negative synergy, and so on.

The normative model that has been discussed in this section specifies a number of factors that should be present if a group is to perform well. It does not say how the strengths and weaknesses of a group can be assessed, nor does it specify what managers can do to create an effective work group. We turn to these questions next.

TOWARD AN ACTION MODEL FOR IMPROVING GROUP EFFECTIVENESS

The normative model has helped us understand what *should* be present for a group to perform well. We now turn to some issues that arise in attempting to create those conditions. We will examine (1) the diagnosis of work teams, with special emphasis on assessing group task demands and the amount of authority groups have to manage their own affairs, (2) the creation and development of new work groups, and (3) requirements for the behavior of group managers.

Ultimately we need a *theory of action* that deals explicitly with implementing the prescriptions of the normative model (Argyris 1980, 1983). Such a theory would recognize the fact that many group phenomena are the product of multiple, interdependent factors, a kind of causation not well handled by traditional scholarly paradigms in social and organizational psychology. A theory of action would address the development of task-oriented groups over time and suggest ways to encourage self-reinforcing *spirals* of increasing effectiveness (and to avoid spirals of decreasing effectiveness). And it would give explicit attention to ways authority can be used to empower groups and support competent group behavior. While much remains to be learned, the following discussion should at least provide some leads worth pursuing in developing a true action model of group effectiveness.[29]

Diagnostic use of the normative model

If a normative model is to be useful in designing, managing, and consulting to work groups in organizations, it must be possible to assess the standing of work teams on the model-specified concept. For example, the model described above allows one to determine what aspects of a group's design, context, and process are strongest, and where improvement is most needed. Such an assess-

---

29. For a skeptical view of the value of pursuing this objective, see Goodman, Atkin, and Ravlin (1982).

ment can be made either informally (e.g., by a manager seeking a quick diagnosis of the assets and liabilities of a team) or more systematically (e.g., for research purposes or in preparing for a planned intervention).[30]

This kind of diagnosis can point to possible interventions for improving group effectiveness. One might discover, for example, that a given group is working hard on its task and using a fully appropriate performance strategy but that members frequently make substantive mistakes and errors of judgment in their work. One would then look carefully at the composition of the group, the educational and consultative resources available to it, and its method of assessing, weighting, and applying the knowledge and skills of its members.

Some additional information about a group and its work is required, however, to make sure that an intervention is appropriate. Specifically, one needs to know (1) what aspects of the group's design, context, and behavior are most *critical* to effectiveness for the specific work being done, and (2) who has the *authority* to make changes in those aspects of the performance situation. Without such information, one risks taking actions that miss the mark because they deal with the wrong things or the wrong people.

CRITICAL TASK DEMANDS

What is key to group effectiveness for one task can be totally irrelevant for another. Consider, for example, a team of park maintenance workers. Its performance will depend mostly on the effort members put into their work. No special knowledge and skill is required (the work is mainly raking and picking up debris), nor is there much room for team decision-making about performance strategy. The success of an advertising team developing an idea for a new campaign, on the other hand, may depend far more on performance strategy and on knowledge and skill than on effort. Different tasks have different critical demands and orient attention to different process criteria of effectiveness.[31]

Interventions should focus on the factors that most powerfully affect a group's standing on whatever process criteria are critical for the task being performed. So,

for the park workers, special attention should be given to the motivational properties of the group task, to the organizational reward system, and to group processes that affect member coordination and team spirit. For the advertising workers, on the other hand, attention should focus on those aspects of group design, context, and synergy that can improve a group's use of knowledge and skill and the appropriateness of its performance strategy.

All three process criteria are salient, at least to some degree, for most tasks done by groups in organizations. Yet one or two of them usually are *especially* important to team effectiveness in a particular case. By focusing on the design and contextual factors associated with these criteria, managers can improve the yield from the limited time they have to spend on team design and management.

It is not always simple, however, to analyze the critical demands of a group task and to trace their implications for team design and management. Thus, the present approach contrasts with the relatively casual and intuitive style of team management often practiced in contemporary organizations. The hope is that the extra thought and effort required will, in fact, result in groups that perform better than those designed and managed in traditional ways.

DISTRIBUTION OF AUTHORITY

The appropriate focus of an intervention also depends on how authority is distributed in the organization—specifically, who is responsible for managing what aspects of the performance situation. For example, who has responsibility for the routine monitoring and management of group performance processes? Who has responsibility for creating and fine-tuning the design of the group? Who has responsibility for structuring and managing the performance context?

The division of authority between the group and management varies from organization to organization, and from group to group within an organization. Three typical configurations are illustrated in figure 20.8. As will be seen, the targets of action intended to improve team effectiveness are quite different for the three configurations.

Manager-led work teams. These teams have responsibility only for the actual *execution* of their assigned work. Management is responsible for monitoring and managing performance processes (i.e., taking any action needed to change what is being done or how it is being done); for designing the group as a performing unit (i.e., structuring the group task, composing the group, and setting basic norms of acceptable behavior); and for structuring the organizational context in which the group

30. A strategy for assessing the standing of a group on these concepts using multiple methods is under development; for a preview of these methods, see Hackman (1982)

31. The idea of characterizing tasks in terms of their critical demands originated with Roby and Lanzetta (1958). Herold (1978) has developed a strategy for assessing task demands that has direct implications for interventions intended to improve group effectiveness. In brief, the approach involves separate measurement of the social complexity and the technical complexity of task requirements. Interventions, which are selected on the basis of the task analysis, help the group deal with the most challenging aspects of its work.

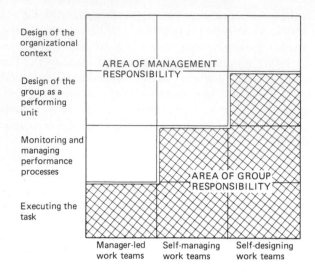

Figure 20.8   Authority of three illustrative types of work groups

functions (i.e., establishing supportive reward, education, and information systems).

Examples of manager-led groups include a military squad continuously provided with detailed instructions by the sergeant, and a crew of flight attendants whose duties have been choreographed in advance by planners and whose execution of these duties is monitored by an in-flight supervisor. How well a manager-led team performs depends much more on management than on decision making by the group itself.

Self-managing work groups. For these groups, management has responsibility for the organizational context and for the design of the group as a performing unit. Group members are responsible for monitoring and managing their own performance processes, as well as for actually executing the task. Examples include a faculty search committee, many "autonomous work teams" in industry, and a managerial task force charged with the design of a new compensation system. How well a self-managing group performs depends both on the quality of the team design and organizational context provided by management *and* on the competence of the group in managing and executing its work.

Self-designing work groups. For these groups, management has responsibility only for the team's organizational context. Group members are responsible for the design of their team (including structuring their task, deciding who will join or leave the group, and evolving their own norms to guide decision making about performance processes) as well as for the management and execution of work on the task.

Top-management groups and boards of directors usually are relatively self-designing in character (although the major portion of their performance context typically is external to the organization). Self-designing groups are found less frequently in the middle and lower regions of traditional organizations. Examples include a mature autonomous work team that has earned the right to revise its own design (e.g., to hire new members, to alter its task if necessary, and so on), and a labor-management "quality of work life committee" with a broad mandate to bring some people together to generate programs for improving organizational life. How well a self-designing group performs obviously depends much less on management than on the group itself.[32]

Summary. An organization that chooses to form manager-led work groups is essentially betting that a manager can run things more effectively than group members can. If it is believed that the group itself can do the job better, a self-designing group would be appropriate. And if *shared* control over the performance situation and performance processes seems optimal, a self-managing group would be chosen.

A manager or interventionist interested in improving team effectiveness should attend carefully to the way authority is allocated between a work group and its manager. To aim an intervention properly, one needs to know who has authority over what aspects of the performance situation. Moreover, it is important to assess how *appropriate* the distribution of authority is for the work to be done, and for the organizational culture within which the group exists. Sometimes the level of authority a group needs to do its work well will conflict with organizational norms or standard organizational practices. In such cases, implementing a good team design may involve negotiating a redistribution of authority within the organizational unit—something not to be undertaken lightly.

Guidelines for creating work teams

What are the implications of the normative model for creating effective teams? The quick answer, of course, is that teams should be set up so that they rank high on each of the variables in the model. But that is more easily said than done, and creating an effective team usually involves difficult choices among design alternatives.

Four stages in creating and developing work groups are discussed next. Within each stage, certain questions must be answered, one way or another, as a group is designed and built. The normative model provides some

---

32. There also are a few groups, largely in cooperative or worker-owned enterprises, whose members have responsibility for *all* aspects of the performance situation, including deciding their own purpose and establishing their own work context. Although rarely found in traditional industrial firms or public bureaucracies, such groups are good laboratories for learning about the problems and opportunities associated with very high levels of group autonomy.

possible answers to these questions, and we will refer to it frequently as we proceed. But the choice of the question format (rather than specifying fixed steps to be followed, for example) is deliberate. There are many ways to structure and manage a team, and one must actively think about and select among the available alternatives at each choice point. It is both inevitable and appropriate that these decisions will be guided as much by cultural, political, and technological realities as by any normative model of team effectiveness.

STAGE ONE: PREWORK

When a decision or task arises in an organization, managers often reflexively form a committee or create a task force to handle it. And the group sometimes turns out not to be a very good device for doing what needs to be done. A bit of thought *before* a group is created can decrease the likelihood that a team will be formed when it should not be, and improve the design of those teams that are created.

The objective in the prework phase is to establish the basic parameters of the performance situation: the nature of the work to be done, the feasibility of using a group to do it, and the appropriate partitioning of authority and responsibility between the group and its managers.

Question 1: What is the task? Sometimes nobody knows: not the group, and not the person who created the group. It is, of course, virtually impossible to design and support a group well if one does not know what it is supposed to accomplish. And, for group members, a vague and obscure task invites frustration and conflict. It is hard to excuse a manager who creates a group without a clear purpose. [33]

In some cases, the group is a deliberate sham. For example, it may have been formed simply to give angry people a setting in which to blow off steam. Or it may have been assigned a decision-making task to buy time while the *real* decision makers make their moves behind the scenes. Or it may have been created solely to provide a platform for a politically important manager to have his or her say. In other words, groups often serve organizational purposes other than getting work done. Such uses, of course, can lessen the credibility of future groups that *do* have important tasks to accomplish. In any event, we are concerned here only with groups created with the expectation that they will achieve excellent performance. And to design and manage these groups well requires that one be clear about what is to be accomplished.

Question 2: What are the critical task demands? What must the group do to accomplish its task well and on time? Does the task require great effort, complex knowledge or skills, careful attention to choices about performance strategy (as in a rapidly changing environment, for example)? The answers to these questions should have a significant bearing on the design of the group and the focus of managerial attention once it is under way.

Question 3: Will the group be manager-led, self-managing, or self-designing? Given the task and its demands, how much authority does the group need? Can that level of authority be provided, given the cultural and political realities of the organization? Are group members willing and able to operate on those terms? Might it make sense to start the group out with limited authority and increase it as members gain experience and skills in self-management? What are the implications of these decisions for the design of the team *manager's* role (see Walton and Schlesinger 1979).

Question 4: Overall, how advantageous is it to assign the work to a team? How feasible is it? What are the benefits of having a team perform the task? What are the risks and liabilities? Given that it typically takes more managerial skill to manage a team than to manage individuals working more or less on their own, are the advantages worth the costs?

Will it be possible to design and support the group well? What compromises will have to be made because of an inflexible technology, rigidities in personnel practices, an insufficiency of material resources, or other organizational factors that can get in the way of a good design? Are these compromises so numerous or serious that they will significantly interfere with the group's work?

When the compromises are substantial, or when a manager is unwilling to make the effort to create a good group design, it usually is better to find an alternative way to get the work done than to clutter up the organizational landscape with yet another unnecessary or poorly designed team.

STAGE TWO: CREATING PERFORMANCE CONDITIONS

The objective in this stage is to make sure that the group has an appropriate *design* and a supportive organizational *context*. These structures should make it easy for a group to do well, rather than require it to swim against the current. This may be difficult in organizations that traditionally have used individuals rather than teams as the basic unit for accomplishing work. The two questions posed next, therefore, sometimes will require crea-

---

33. This does not imply that one can always be clear about what needs to be done in an organization. It is perfectly reasonable, for example, to ask a group to "figure out what is going on in area X, and give me your views about it." *That* then becomes the group task, and the group can be structured and managed in a way that helps it do a good job of researching the question and preparing a report about what it learns.

tion of nontraditional organizational features—or the circumvention of existing structures and systems that are inappropriate for teams.

Question 5: How should the group be composed and the task structured? How can the task be designed to be as clear and as motivationally engaging as possible? What can be done to make the work more challenging and significant? Within the limits of the group's authority, how can task autonomy be increased? What feedback channels can be opened to provide members with regular and reliable knowledge of the results of their work?

How small can the group be and still have the human resources needed for effective performance? How diverse should the membership be? Do members have the interpersonal skills needed for collaborative work?

Question 6: What contextual supports and resources must be provided? What material resources (e.g., tools, equipment, money, or space) will members need in their work? Can these resources be secured? What organizational supports will help the group in its work? Will the reward, educational, and information systems provide the reinforcement, outside expertise, and data the group will need to perform well? Will the group have contact with people or groups in other parts of the organization (or external to it)? How will they influence the group? Do links with external parties need to be restructured?

STAGE THREE: FORMING AND BUILDING THE TEAM
Because long-lasting effects flow from events early in the life of a group, it is worth the trouble to help a work team get started on the right foot. Specific steps must be taken to create a group that can manage its own affairs competently.

Question 7: How can a team be helped to get off to a good start? What can be done, as members confront each other and their task for the first time, to increase the chance they will be able to work well together? Building a competent work team involves helping members (1) develop an appropriate *boundary* for their group, (2) come to terms with the *task* they will perform, and (3) begin to develop the *norms* that will guide behavior in the group.[34]

1. Forming boundaries. If group members are to work interdependently on the task, it must be clear who

is a member—and therefore shares responsibility for group outcomes—and who is not. Membership often is unclear in certain kinds of work groups, particularly temporary project and decision-making teams. And when there is ambiguity about group composition, members often become frustrated and performance can suffer. The group must be able to say, at some point, "This is us" and proceed from there. When that happens, the composition of the group, begun when members were assigned to the team, will have been completed.

2. Accepting and redefining the task. There may be some people in organizations who believe that the task assigned to a group is the one that the group actually performs. These people have not watched very closely what happens as a group goes to work: often *many* tasks are being performed, different ones by different members, and none of them the one the manager thought had been assigned. Misunderstandings about the task (whether between the group and the task giver, or among group members) can result in wasted effort or a product that misses the mark. It is better to identify and deal with such discrepancies when the group starts its work, rather than when the group product is submitted.

Task redefinition is a natural part of the group performance process (Hackman 1969). By acknowledging that and dealing with questions of task definition early in a group's life, confusion and idiosyncratic interpretations of what is required can be minimized. Consider, for example, tasks that have multiple and conflicting performance objectives (e.g., speed and perfection). The conflict between these objectives can be discussed by the team and its manager, and either resolved or accepted as a tension the group will need to manage. When all parties have come to an agreement about what the task is and what it requires, the process of task design, begun when the work was originally conceived, will have been completed.

3. Developing group norms and members roles. Although each member brings to a group certain assumptions about the kinds of behavior that will be appropriate, such matters are rarely discussed explicitly in the group. Instead, group norms and member roles develop gradually as individuals seek their own niches, and as the group as a whole struggles to find a comfortable way to operate. The process is a natural one, but the norms and roles that develop may be heavily influenced by forces of which members are unaware (e.g., a shared wish to suppress anxiety-arousing issues). Moreover, the norms that evolve may conflict with core-management values about appropriate and expected group behavior.

Groups are likely to function better if they give explicit attention, early in their lives, to the kinds of

---

34. There are numerous programs available to guide team-building activities (e.g., Bertcher and Maple 1977; Dyer 1977; Merry and Allerhand 1977; Rubin, Plovnick and Fry 1977). While 1977 clearly was a very good year for team builders, these guides (understandably) are based on the experience and conceptual frameworks of their authors; they are not designed to address systematically the three aspects of group life highlighted here.

behaviors that will be valued and the ways work on the group task will be managed. If members are expected to take responsibility for monitoring their performance situation and planning their performance strategies, they should be encouraged to explore the implications of that expectation and their willingness to accept it.

Norms evolve over the life-span of any group, and changes in norms and roles are the rule rather than the exception. By providing some assistance to the group early in its life, managers can help get this ongoing process off to a good start and help members come to grips with both the extent and the limits of their authority. As the group begins to move under its own power, the manager can pull back and the process of designing the group as a performing unit will have been completed.

STAGE FOUR: PROVIDING ONGOING ASSISTANCE

Once a group is functioning as a social system, it will control its own destiny to a considerable extent. Nevertheless, managers can assist the group by making it easy for members to renegotiate aspects of the performance situation that turn out to impede performance, by ensuring that members get the ongoing assistance they need to operate well as a team, and by helping the group learn from its experiences.

Question 8: How can opportunities be provided for the group to renegotiate its design and context? Some features of the initial design of a group and its context are sure to be flawed—and some groups simply accept those flaws as an unfortunate fact of organizational life. How can a group be encouraged to take initiatives to get unsatisfactory aspects of its performance situation improved? While it would be inappropriate for a manager to take unilateral action to change a group's design or context (that would undermine its responsibility for managing its own affairs), a manager can provide *occasions* for explicit review and renegotiation of the performance context. And when such discussions take place, he or she can help members become more skillful, and more comfortable, in taking initiatives to confront aspects of the performance situation (including the manager's own behavior) that are impeding group performance. As a group matures and demonstrates competence in its work, it may be appropriate to empower it even further, for example, by giving it greater authority for self-management, by arranging access to training activities that can help members improve their skills, and so on.

Question 9: What process assistance can be provided to promote positive group synergy? These activities are closest to traditional "process consultation," discussed earlier in this chapter. But they should emphasize aspects of group life that directly relate to its work on the *task*.

Indeed, it may be that one of the best ways to improve interpersonal relations in the group is to help members perform well on the task—a reversal of the traditional view that task performance depends on the quality of interpersonal relations.

Two aspects of group task behavior warrant special attention. First, efforts can be made to correct group-process losses and cultivate synergistic-process gains. Is the group suffering from poor coordination, inappropriate weighting of member talents, or flawed implementation of performance strategies? Are there unexploited opportunities to cultivate team spirit, to encourage members to learn from one another, or to develop uniquely appropriate performance strategies? The considerable literature on process consultation can provide ideas for useful activities and exercises, but some inventiveness by the manager or consultant also surely will be required to tailor what is done to the needs of specific groups.

In addition, the group can be helped to deal with developmental changes and transitions it encounters as it matures as a social unit. Although research and theory useful in guiding such activities in task-performing groups has just started to become available (e.g., Gersick 1983; Heinen and Jacobson 1976; Katz 1982), it is important that a manager be sensitive to the developmental issues a group will face as it moves through its life cycle, and that he or she be available to help the group manage them and learn from them.

Question 10: How can the group be helped to learn from its experiences? There are many opportunities for learning in a well-structured and well-managed group. How can these opportunities be exploited? Unfortunately, the press of task work often keeps members from acting on any impulse they may have to reflect together on their experience and learn from it. It is necessary, therefore, to set aside some times for reflection and learning—perhaps at a natural breakpoint in the task work, and certainly when a major phase of the effort has been completed. The manager of the group is in a good position to encourage members to take the time to learn from their experiences and to assist them in doing so.

SUMMARY

The stages of the action model sketched above are summarized in figure 20.9. Clearly, considerable managerial skill and no small measure of hard work are required to do a good job of creating and managing a task-performing team in an organization. A manager who wants a team task to be done well cannot simply call some people together, toss them a task, and hope for the best. That is the bad news.

The good news is that as managers learn how to design and manage groups well, and as members gain

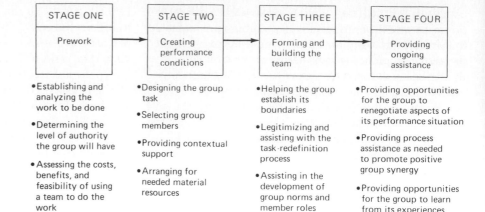

Figure 20.9 Stages of managerial work in creating an effective group

experience and skill in functioning effectively in teams, the plodding, deliberate, step-by-step process outlined above can become second nature, just "the way things are done" in an organization. When that stage is reached, the considerable investment required to learn how to use work teams well can pay substantial dividends—in work effectiveness and in the quality of the experiences of both managers and group members.

Implications for the management of teams

Because this chapter represents a departure from traditional thinking about group performance, it may be appropriate to conclude by briefly highlighting some of the broader management implications of what has been proposed.

ON LEADERSHIP

The research literature is rich with studies of leadership in groups (for reviews, see Hare 1976, chap. 13, and Stogdill 1974). Most of this research assesses what leaders do *within* groups or tests propositions about what leader traits and styles are most effective under what circumstances. Such questions are derivative in the approach taken here, because leaders are viewed as exercising influence primarily through the decisions they make about how to frame the group task, how to structure the group and its context, and how to help the group get started up well and headed in an appropriate direction.

Indeed, we have not even discussed whether an internal group leader should be named—let alone how he or she should behave. It often does make sense to have such a role, especially when substantial coordination among members is required, when there is lots of information to be processed (Maier 1967), or when it is advisable to have one person be the liaison with other groups or with higher management. Yet it is rarely a good idea to decide in advance about the leadership structure of a work group. If a group has been designed well and helped to begin exploring the group norms and member roles it wishes to have, questions of internal leadership should appear naturally. And while there invariably will be a good deal of stress and strain in the group as leadership issues are dealt with, when a resolution comes it will have the considerable advantage of being the group's own.

The manager's role, then, is to make sure a group confronts the leadership issue directly (even if members would prefer to deal with it implicitly or avoid it entirely), not to resolve it for the group. To do the latter is to short-circuit an important developmental task in the life of a team and to rob the group of a significant opportunity to organize and develop its own internal resources.

ON CREATING REDUNDANT CONDITIONS

There are many ways for a group to be effective in performing a task, and even more ways for it to be ineffective. Moreover, different task and organizational circumstances involve vastly different demands and opportunities. Thus it is impossible to specify in detail what specific behaviors managers should adopt to help groups perform effectively. There are simply too many ways a group can operate and still wind up with the same outcome.[35] Attempts to specify contingencies for managerial behavior do not help much, in that they usually result in prescriptions too complex for anyone to follow (Hackman 1984).

Thus, while many models of leadership call for the active manipulation of "causes" that are assumed to be

---

35. Systems theorists call this aspect of organized endeavor "equifinality" (Katz and Kahn 1978, 30). According to this principle, a social system can reach the same outcome from a variety of initial conditions and by a variety of methods.

tightly linked to "effects," our view of group behavior suggests that the key to effective group management may be to create redundant conditions that support good performance, leaving groups ample room to develop and enact their own ways of operating within those conditions.

A manager interested in encouraging a group to work hard, for example, would try to make the group task more motivationally engaging. *And* he or she would try to provide more (or more potent) positive consequences contingent on hard, effective work. *And* he or she would work with the group members to improve the efficiency of their internal processes and to build a positive team spirit. And if there were other steps that could be taken to create conditions supportive of high effort, these would be attempted as well.

Group performance does not have clean, unitary causes. To help a group improve its effectiveness involves doing whatever is possible to create multiple, redundant conditions that together may nudge the group toward more competent task behavior and, eventually, better performance.[36]

ON MANAGERIAL AUTHORITY

The approach taken in this chapter clearly favors the creation of conditions that empower groups, that increase their authority to manage their own work. While this does not imply a diminution of managerial authority, it does suggest that it be redirected.

One critical use of authority, already discussed at some length, is in creating organizational conditions that foster and support effective group behavior. Managers must not view design and contextual features as "givens" over which they have little control. Instead, influence

must be wielded upward and outward in the organization to make organizational structures and systems as supportive of team effectiveness as possible. If a manager does not have the authority to initiate discussions about making such changes, he or she should consider trying to get it, because it will be hard to be a good team manager without it.

Managerial authority also should be used to establish and enforce standards of group behavior and acceptable performance. When a manager defines a piece of work to be done, sets performance standards, and is clear about the bounds of acceptable group behavior, he or she is exercising managerial authority—and concurrently empowering the group that will do the work. To be vague about what is required and expected can be just as debilitating to a group as traditional, hands-on supervision. To enable groups to use their authority well, managers must not be afraid to exercise their own.

ON KNOWING SOME THINGS

The management behaviors implied by the model of team effectiveness explored in this chapter will seem unfamiliar and awkward to some managers, and may be hard for them to perform well. But any new endeavor can be difficult. Trying to make sense of a balance sheet, for example, or figuring out a good design for a production process can feel just as awkward and be just as hard for an unpracticed manager to do well. Yet for some reason we are far more willing to acknowledge the need for training and experience in these areas than we are in aspects of managerial work related to the effective use of human resources.

Managing work groups is every bit as tough as figuring out what to do about the numbers on a balance sheet. To manage teams well, one needs to know some things, have some skills, and have opportunities to practice. The sooner those requirements are acknowledged, the sooner we will be able to develop a cadre of managers who are expert in creating work teams, developing them, and harvesting the considerable contributions they have to make to organizational effectiveness.

---

36. We see here a key difference between descriptive and action models of behavior in organization. A descriptive model parcels up the world for conceptual clarity; in contrast, a good action model parcels up the world to increase the chances that something can be created or changed. Rather than seek to isolate unitary causes, an action model attempts to identify clusters of covarying factors that can serve as useful levers for change. For related views, see Hackman (1984), Mohr (1982), and Weick (1977).

REFERENCES

Alderfer, C. P. 1977. "Group and Intergroup Relations." In *Improving Life at Work*, ed. J. R. Hackman and J. L. Suttle. Santa Monica, Calif.: Goodyear.

Argyris, C. 1969. "The Incompleteness of Social Psychological Theory: Examples from Small Group, Cognitive Consistency, and Attribution Research." *American Psychologist* 24:893–908.

———. 1980. *The Inner Contradictions of Rigorous Research.* New York: Academic Press.

———. 1983. "Action Science and Intervention." *Journal of Applied Behavioral Science* 19:115–35.

Bales, R. F. 1950. *Interaction Process Analysis: A Method for the Study of Small Groups.* Cambridge, Mass.: Addison-Wesley.

———. 1970. *Personality and Interpersonal Behavior.* New York: Holt, Rinehart and Winston.

Bales, R. F., and S. P. Cohen. 1979. *SYMLOG: A System for the Multiple Level Observation of Groups.* New York: Free Press.

Beer, M. 1976. "The Technology of Organization Development." In *Handbook of Industrial and Organizational Psychology,* ed. M. D. Dunnette. Chicago: Rand McNally.

Belbin, R. M. 1981. *Management Teams: Why They Succeed or Fail.* London: Heinemann.

Bertcher, H. J., and F. F. Maple. 1977. *Creating Groups.* Beverly Hills, Calif.: Sage.

Blake, R. R., and J. S. Mouton. 1969. *Building a Dynamic Corporation Through Grid Organization Development.* Reading, Mass.: Addison-Wesley.

Colman, A. D., and W. H. Bexton. 1975. *Group Relations Reader.* Sausalito, Calif.: GREX.

Cooper, C. L., ed. 1975. *Theories of Group Processes.* London: Wiley.

Cummings, T. G. 1978. "Self-Regulating Work Groups: A Socio-Technical Synthesis." *Academy of Management Review* 2, no. 3 (July): 625–34.

———. 1981. "Designing Effective Work Groups." In *Handbook of Organizational Design,* ed. P. C. Nystrom and W. H. Starbuck, vol. 2. London: Oxford University Press.

Dalkey, N. C. 1967. *Delphi.* Santa Monica, Calif.: Rand.

Davis, J. H. 1973. "Group Decision and Social Interaction: A Theory of Social Decision Schemes." *Psychological Review* 80:97–125.

Davis, J. H., and V. B. Hinsz. 1982. "Current Research Problems in Group Performance and Group Dynamics." In *Group Decision Making,* ed. H. Brandstätter, J. H. Davis, and G. Stocker-Kreichgauer. London: Academic Press.

Delbecq, A. L., A. H. Van de Ven, and D. H. Gustafson. 1975. *Group Techniques for Program Planning.* Glenview, Ill.: Scott, Foresman.

Dunnette, M. D., J. Campbell, and K. Jaastad. 1963. "The Effect of Group Participation on Brainstorming Effectiveness for Two Industrial Samples." *Journal of Applied Psychology* 47:30–37.

Dyer, W. G. 1977. *Team Building: Issues and Alternatives.* Reading, Mass.: Addison-Wesley.

Friedlander, F., and L. D. Brown. 1974. "Organization Development." In *Annual Review of Psychology,* ed. M. R. Rosenzweig and L. W. Porter, vol. 25. Palo Alto, Calif.: Annual Reviews.

Gersick, C. J. G. 1983. "Life Cycles of *Ad Hoc* Groups." Technical report no. 3, Group Effectiveness Research Project, School of Organization and Management, Yale University.

Glaser, R., and D. J. Klaus. 1966. "A Reinforcement Analysis of Group Performance." *Psychological Monographs* 80, whole no. 621:1–23.

Goodman, P., R. Atkin, and E. Ravlin. 1982. "Some Observations on Specifying Models of Group Performance." Paper delivered at a symposium on Productive Work Teams and Groups, American Psychological Association Convention, Washington, D. C.

Green, T. B. 1975. "An Empirical Analysis of Nominal and Interacting Groups." *Academy of Management Journal* 18:63–73.

Hackman, J. R. 1969. "Toward Understanding the Role of Tasks in Behavioral Research." *Acta Psychologica* 31:97–128.

———. 1976. "Group Influences on Individuals." In *Handbook of Industrial and Organizational Psychology,* ed. M. D. Dunnette. Chicago: Rand McNally.

———. 1982. " A Set of Methods for Research on Work Teams." Technical report no. 1, Group Effectiveness Research Project, School of Organization and Management, Yale University.

———. 1983. "A Normative Model of Work Team Effectiveness." Technical report no. 2, Group Effectiveness Research Project, School of Organization and Management, Yale University.

———. 1984. "Psychological Contributions to Organizational Productivity: A Commentary." In *Productivity Research in the Behavioral and Social Sciences,* ed. A. P. Brief. New York: Praeger.

Hackman, J. R., K. R. Brousseau, and J. A. Weiss. 1976. "The Interaction of Task Design and Group Performance Strategies in Determining Group Effectiveness." *Organizational Behavior and Human Performance* 16:350–65.

Hackman, J. R., and C. G. Morris. 1975. "Group Tasks, Group Interaction Process, and Group Performance Effectiveness: A Review and Proposed Integration." In *Advances in Experimental Social Psychology,* ed. L. Berkowitz. New York: Academic Press.

Hackman, J. R., and G. R. Oldham. 1980. *Work Redesign.* Reading, Mass.: Addison-Wesley.

Hare, A. P. 1976. *Handbook of Small Group Research.* 2d ed. New York: Free Press.

———. 1982. *Creativity in Small Groups.* Beverly Hills, Calif.: Sage.

Heinen, J. S., and E. Jacobson. 1976. "A Model of Task Group Development in Complex Organizations and a Strategy of Implementation." *Academy of Management Review* 1:98–111.

Herold, D. M. 1978. "Improving the Performance Effectiveness of Groups Through a Task-Contingent Selection of Intervention Strategies." *Academy of Management Review* 3:315–25.

Hewett, T. T., G. E. O'Brien, and J. Hornik. 1974. "The Effects of Work Organization, Leadership Style, and Member Compatibility Upon the Productivity of Small Groups Working on a Manipulative Task." *Organizational Behavior and Human Performance* 11:283–301.

Hoffman, L. R. 1979a. "Applying Experimental Research on Group Problem Solving to Organizations." *Journal of Applied Behavioral Science* 15:375–91.

———, ed. 1979b. *The Group Problem Solving Process: Studies of a Valence Model.* New York: Praeger.

Jackson, J. 1965. "Structural Characteristics of Norms." In *Current Studies in Social Psychology,* ed. I. D. Steiner and M. Fishbein. New York: Holt, Rinehart and Winston.

Janis, I. L. 1982. *Groupthink.* 2d ed. Boston: Houghton Mifflin.

Johnson, H. H., and J. M. Torcivia. 1967. "Group and Individual Performance on a Single-Stage Task as a Function of Distribution of Individual Performance." *Journal of Personality and Social Psychology* 3:266-73.

Kaplan, R. E. 1979. "The Conspicuous Absence of Evidence that Process Consultation Enhances Task Performance." *Journal of Applied Behavioral Science* 15:346-60.

Katz, D., and R. L. Kahn. 1978. *The Social Psychology of Organizations.* 2d ed. New York: Wiley.

Katz, R. 1982. "The Effects of Group Longevity on Project Communication and Performance." *Administrative Science Quarterly* 27:81-104.

Latané B., K. Williams, and S. Harkins. 1979. "Many Hands Make Light the Work: The Causes and Consequences of Social Loafing." *Journal of Personality and Social Psychology* 37:822-32.

Lawler, E. E. 1981. *Pay and Organization Development.* Reading, Mass.: Addison-Wesley.

Leavitt, H. J. 1975. "Suppose We Took Groups Seriously . . ." In *Man and Work in Society,* ed. E. L. Cass and F. G. Zimmer. New York: Van Nostrand Reinhold.

Maier, N. R. F. 1963. *Problem Solving Discussions and Conferences: Leadership Methods and Skills.* New York: McGraw-Hill.

———. 1967. "Assets and Liabilities in Group Problem Solving: The Need for an Integrative Function." *Psychological Review* 74:239-49.

March, J. G., and H. A. Simon. 1958. *Organizations.* New York: Wiley.

McGrath, J. E. 1964. *Social Psychology: A Brief Introduction.* New York: Holt, Rinehart and Winston.

———. 1984. *Groups: Interaction and Performance.* Englewood Cliffs, N.J.: Prentice-Hall.

McGrath, J. E., and I. Altman. 1966. *Small Group Research: A Synthesis and Critique of the Field.* New York: Holt, Rinehart and Winston.

McGrath, J. E., and D. A. Kravitz. 1982. "Group Research." *Annual Review of Psychology* 33:195-230.

Merry, U., and M. E. Allerhand. 1977. *Developing Teams and Organizations.* Reading, Mass.: Addison-Wesley.

Mohr, L. B. 1982. *Explaining Organizational Behavior.* San Francisco: Jossey-Bass.

Myers, D. C., and H. Lamm. 1976. "The Group Polarization Phenomenon." *Psychological Bulletin* 83:602-27.

Nagao, D. H., D. A. Vollrath, and J. H. Davis. 1978. "Group Decision Making: Origins and Current Status." In *Dynamics of Group Decisions,* ed. H. Brandstätter, J. H. Davis, and H. C. Schuler. Beverly Hills, Calif.: Sage.

Osborn, A. F. 1957. *Applied Imagination.* Rev. ed. New York: Scribner's.

Payne, R., and C. L. Cooper, eds. 1981. *Groups at Work.* Chichester, England: Wiley.

Peters, T. H., and E. J. O'Connor. 1980. "Situational Constraints and Work Outcomes: The Influences of a Frequently Overlooked Construct." *Academy of Management Review* 5:391-97.

Peters, L. H., E. J. O'Connor, and C. J. Rudolf. 1980. "The Behavioral and Affective Consequences of Performance-Relevant Situational Variables." *Organizational Behavior and Human Performance* 25:79-96.

Poza, E. J., and M. L. Marcus. 1980. "Success Story: The Team Approach to Work Restructuring." *Organizational Dynamics* (Winter): 3-25.

Roby, T. B., and J. T. Lanzetta. 1958. "Considerations in the Analysis of Group Tasks." *Psychological Bulletin* 55:88-101.

Rubin, I. M., M. S. Plovnick, and R. E. Fry. 1977. *Task-Oriented Team Development.* New York: McGraw-Hill.

Runkel, P. J., and J. E. McGrath. 1972. *Research on Human Behavior.* New York: Holt, Rinehart and Winston.

Schein, E. H. 1969. *Process Consultation.* Reading, Mass.: Addison-Wesley.

Schutz, W. C. 1958. *FIRO: A Three-Dimensional Theory of Interpersonal Behavior.* New York: Holt, Rinehart and Winston.

———. 1961. "On Group Composition." *Journal of Abnormal and Social Psychology* 62:275-81.

Stasser, G., and J. H. Davis. 1981. "Group Decision Making and Social Influence: A Social Interaction Sequence Model." *Psychological Review* 88:523-51.

Stein, M. I. 1975. *Stimulating Creativity.* Vol. 2. New York: Academic Press.

Steiner, I. D. 1972. *Group Process and Productivity.* New York: Academic Press.

Stogdill, R. M. 1974. *Handbook of Leadership.* New York: Free Press.

Stumpf, S. A., D. E. Zand, and R. D. Freedman. 1979. "Designing Groups for Judgmental Decisions." *Academy of Management Review* 4:589-600.

Thomas, E. J., and C. F. Fink. 1961. "Models of Group Problem Solving." *Journal of Abnormal and Social Psychology* 63:53-63.

———. 1963. "Effects of Group Size." *Psychological Bulletin* 60:371-84.

Torrance, E. P. 1954. "Some Consequences of Power Differences on Decision Making in Permanent and Temporary Three-Man Groups." *Research Studies, State College of Washington* 22:130-40.

Trist, E. L. 1981. "The Evolution of Sociotechnical Systems as a Conceptual Framework and as an Action Research Program." In *Perspectives on Organization Design and Behavior,* ed. A. H. Van de Ven and W. F. Joyce. New York: Wiley.

Tuckman, B. W. 1965. "Developmental Sequence in Small Groups." *Psychological Bulletin* 63:384-99.

Vidmar, N., and J. R. Hackman. 1971. "Interlaboratory Generalizability of Small Group Research: An Experimental Study." *Journal of Social Psychology* 83:129-39.

Wall, T. D., and C. W. Clegg. 1981. "A Longitudinal Field Study of Group Work Design." *Journal of Occupational Behavior* 2:31-49.

Walton, R. E., and L. S. Schlesinger. 1979. "Do Supervisors Thrive in Participative Work Systems?" *Organizational Dynamics* (Winter): 24-38.

Weick, K. E. 1965. "Laboratory Experimentation with Organizations." In *Handbook of Organizations,* ed. J. G. March. Chicago: Rand McNally.

———. 1977. "Organization Design: Organizations as Self-

Designing Systems." *Organizational Dynamics* (Autumn): 31–46.

Whyte, W. F. 1955. *Money and Motivation: An Analysis of Incentives in Industry."* New York: Harper.

Wicker, A., S. L. Kirmeyer, L. Hanson, and D. Alexander. 1976. "Effects of Manning Levels on Subjective Experiences, Performance, and Verbal Interaction in Groups." *Organizational Behavior and Human Performance* 17:251–74.

Woodman, R. W., and J. J. Sherwood. 1980. "The Role of Team Development in Organizational Effectiveness: A Critical Review." *Psychological Bulletin* 88:166–86.

Zander, A. 1971. *Motives and Goals in Groups.* New York: Academic Press.

——. 1980. "The Origins and Consequences of Group Goals." In *Retrospections on Social Psychology*, ed. L. Festinger. New York: Oxford University Press.

21

Organization design

JAY R. GALBRAITH

The subject of organization design began to emerge in the late 1960s. During the 1970s it became a topic to be covered and occasionally an elective course in most schools of management. The phrase has appeared in book titles and, indeed, has become part of the language in the organizational field. Some confusion remains, however, as to how *design* differs from all those other nouns modified by *organizational*. Accordingly, the first section of this chapter defines the field of organization design; subsequent sections build on that foundation.

THE FIELD OF ORGANIZATION DESIGN

The concept of organization design emerged as a means of giving a *prescriptive* and *comprehensive* focus to knowledge about organizations. Those two attributes characterize the field today.

Organization design is prescriptive

Before the 1950s, most theories of management were prescriptive. At that time they were found to have little substance to prescribe. So management theorists turned

to the fields of psychology, sociology, economics, and political science to form a substantive theory of organizations. As this movement got under way, however, the theorists lost the prescriptive focus. Therefore, those of us who wanted to prescribe on the basis of substantive knowledge, distinguished ourselves by writing under the heading of organization design, not organization theory.

Thus, organization design is intended to produce knowledge useful for managers who must choose how to organize the efforts of large numbers of people. This focus has been criticized for being narrow and having the values of management (Pfeffer 1978). Such criticism misses the point. Organization design is aimed at helping the people who are charged with the stewardship of our institutions make organizing choices. The research of organization designers, then, includes the measurement of performance and the search for organizational characteristics associated with high performance.

Organization design is comprehensive

From the organization design perspective, the organization is more than just structure: it consists of processes that cut across structural lines, incentive systems, people development practices, and so on. Changing an organization requires changing all these factors. Changing only one factor limits the effect of a change or renders it useless.

The comprehensiveness of its approach distinguishes organization design from organization development (OD), organization behavior (OB), and organization theory (OT). The field of organization development also developed during the 1960s and was intended to be prescriptive and applied. However, it became narrowly focused on participative leadership, team building, and interpersonal-skill training. While these ideas were useful, they were not universally applicable and were often reversed if not accompanied by reinforcing changes in structure and rewards.

The theory of organizations soon became divided into organization behavior (OB) and organization theory (OT). OB was oriented to small-scale phenomena such as individual and small-group behavior, while OT focused on structure and environment. This micro/macro split makes it easier to teach courses, but is essentially artificial. Real problems are not either OB or OT problems—they are combinations. Organization designers want to be able to marshal all relevant knowledge needed to make organizing choices. So organization design attempts to be more comprehensive and prescriptive than other organizational interest areas.

Organization design is continuous

Organization designers have tried to view the design process as a continuous one. That is, rather than focus on reorganizations as events, we should see organizing as a continuous management task like scheduling, budgeting, and so on. As managers plan their tasks and strategies, they should plan their organizations. By viewing design as a process rather than an event, management buys the luxury of time. It can more easily make the transition from one structure to another (say from functional to divisional) by slowly phasing in business teams, profit-accounting systems, and strategic-planning processes. Structural moves can be coordinated with people moves, thereby avoiding disruptions.

Organizational design is high leveraged

Organizational choices have significant impact. Because their time is limited, high-level managers need to focus on the high-leveraged decisions, which include organizing choices. Determining who decides and what processes are used to decide will influence all subsequent decisions that are made. Thus, it is important that these organizing choices be made well.

Organization design is dual focused

The design of an organization involves two interrelated problems. The first is, What organization is needed to be successful in a given business? If a firm expands into Europe, how should it define its profit centers—as lines of business, countries, or some combination? By far the majority of organization design effort has addressed this type of question. A second issue arises when the firm's current organization is not appropriate for its future business. The problem of changing from today's organization to the appropriate future one has received a good deal of attention, but not from the organization design community. Organization designers have been weak on the power and political issues that form the crux of the transitional process. As a result, the change process is probably the highest-priority area for future work.

In summary, organization design focuses on prescribing to the managers who are responsible for the stewardship of our institutions. It attempts to be comprehensive in its prescriptions. That is, organization is not just structure, or training, or leadership, or compensation, but all of these things. Design should be a continuous and highly leveraged managerial activity, comprising the dual problems of how to organize and how to move to a new organization. The following discussion focuses first on the comprehensive nature of organization design, then examines the attempts to reduce the comprehensiveness to manageable proportions by looking at generic organizations and strategies. The next section reviews the economic performance of the generic types. Finally, the problems of managing change are considered.

COMPREHENSIVE DESIGN MODELS

The comprehensive focus of organization design developed partly as a reaction to various specialists who were selling solutions to management problems. Organizing was seen as more than just a choice of structure or methods of paying people. Instead, it was the simultaneous choice of structure, processes, rewards, training, and so on. A key concept that resulted from this view is the notion that all of the organizational components must "fit" together.

Leavitt (1965) was among the first to focus on the fit of various organizational policy areas. He portrays various groups vying for management's attention. Each group proclaims its specialty as a more powerful means of solving managment's problems. As shown in figure 21.1, some people focus on organizational structure as the means to improve performance, while others prescribe computers and mathematical models to allocate resources. Still another group recommends changing the human system to improve communications and interper-

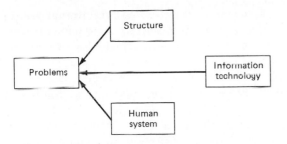

Figure 21.1 (Reprinted from H. Leavitt, "Applied Organizational Change in Industry," in *Handbook of Organizations,* ed. J. March [Chicago: Rand McNally, 1965], by permission.)

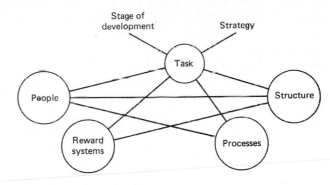

Figure 21.3 (Jay Galbraith, *Organization Design,* © 1977, Addison-Wesley, Reading, Massachusetts. Adapted figure. Reprinted with permission.)

sonal relationships. Leavitt's point is that none of these approaches is wrong, but each is only partially right. Each needs to be complemented by the others. That is, in order to divisionalize, the structuralists need a profit-accounting system by line of business and personnel practices to develop managers. The humanists need decentralized structures and cooperative bonus systems to accompany their prescriptions. Thus, any substantial change in structure, information technology, or the human system requires simultaneous and reinforcing changes in the other areas as well. Figure 21.2 illustrates the concept.

In subsequent work, the problem box of the diagram was replaced by task and sometimes strategy. The work of Lawrence and Lorsch (1967) initiated this contingency-theory approach, which argues that the choice of various organizational attributes (structure, rewards, leadership style) depends upon the task being performed. Further, they stated that an organization will not be effective unless all the attributes are consistent or in harmony among themselves and with the task. The components had to fit and function together.

Subsequent authors have elaborated upon and refined these ideas. Galbraith (1977) depicts the organization as consisting of structure, processes that cut across the structure (budgeting, planning, task forces), rewards, and people practice, such as training and selection, as

shown schematically in figure 21.3. All these elements must fit with each other and with the task to be performed, which, in turn, is influenced by management's choice of business strategy and the stage of development of the company or organizational entity.

Others authors have proposed additional models, which vary as to the elements making up the organization's attributes. Nadler and Tushman (1980) have cast their model in an open-systems framework. There has been a trend toward including softer elements of organizations, such as values, symbols, and shared beliefs (Peters 1978). These are captured in another model under the label of culture (Davis and Schwartz 1981). The most recent model to be proposed is the 7S concept attributed to the McKinsey organization (Waterman 1982). But in all cases, the idea is much the same: organization consists of many attributes to be chosen, and all the attributes must fit with one another and the organization's task or strategy.

CONTINGENCIES AND FIT

The next step is to specify what is meant by *fit.* How do all these organizational attributes interact? And how does one choose between alternative combinations of structure, people, and rewards? Because it is comprehensive, organization design is correspondingly more complex. Contingency theories were sought to provide some answers.

Jay Lorsch and his colleagues have done the most to generate contingencies around the organization's task. They base their work on the premise that as the task varies, so should the appropriate form of organization. Like others, they see the uncertainty, predictability, and understandability of the task as the key attributes upon which organization forms are contingent. They find that loose, informal structures and people with high toler-

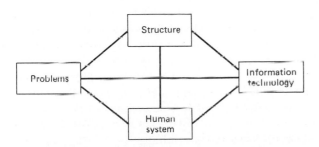

Figure 21.2 (Reprinted from Leavitt, *Handbook of Organizations,* by permission.)

ances for ambiguity fit well with tasks of high uncertainty. The opposites hold for more repetitive, predictable tasks. Another important task attribute is interdependence. When subtasks are tightly linked, they require more coordination than do independent, self-contained subtasks. This work is summarized in Lorsch's (1977) summary article.

A number of other authors have found that uncertainty and interdependence in one form or another are related to variation in organization forms. This work is summarized in the author's book *Organization Design* (Galbraith 1977), which sets forth the theoretical basis for the link between uncertainty and organization. The fundamental idea is that the more uncertain the task, the more information must be transmitted among the people who are performing it. Therefore, variations in organizational forms are variations in the capacity of organizations to process information. As organizations perform more uncertain tasks, they need either to increase their capacities to process information or to eliminate the need to process information by making subtasks more independent. Moreover, as tasks become more complex, it becomes more difficult to devise formal measures and rewards for performance. Therefore, organizations turn more to intrinsic sources of satisfaction and rely less on extrinsic.

A great deal more empirical validation of the comprehensive models is still needed. But the very comprehensiveness that increases the models' relevance, usefulness, and power to design organizations also makes them exceedingly difficult to test and validate. Lorsch's work has examined people, task, and structure by dichotomizing the measures in high and low categories. No one has yet tested the combinations and permutations of a 7S model. Designers must rely on the few tests that have been performed and the models' common-sense validity.

STRATEGY AND ORGANIZATION

One area that has received a good deal of attention is the match between strategy and organization. Most of this work consists of empirical tests of Chandler's ideas presented in *Strategy and Structure* (1960) and reviewed elsewhere (Galbraith and Nathanson 1978). Some recent work holds out considerable potential for understanding how different patterns of strategic change lead to different organization structures, management systems, and company cultures. In addition, some good relationships with economic performance have been demonstrated.

These new ideas rest on the concept that the organization has a center of gravity, driving force (Tregoe and Zimmerman 1980), or strategic anchor. This center of gravity arises from the firm's initial success in the industry in which it grew up. The concept can be used to shed light on the patterns of strategic change that have been followed by American enterprises.

A company's center of gravity depends on its original position in the industry supply chain. Figure 21.4 depicts the stages of supply in a manufacturing-industry chain. Six stages are shown here, but particular industries may have more or fewer stages. Service industries typically have fewer stages.

The chain begins with a raw-material-extraction stage, which supplies crude oil, iron ore, logs, or bauxite to the second stage of primary manufacturing. This is a variety-reducing stage, which produces a standardized output of petrochemicals, steel, paper pulp, or aluminum ingots. The third stage fabricates commodity products from this primary material. Fabricators produce polyethylene, cans, sheet steel, cardboard cartons, and semiconductor components. The next stage is the product producers, who add value through product development, patents, and proprietary products. Next is the marketing and distribution stage, in which the participants are the consumer-branded product manufacturers and various distributors. Finally, there are the retailers, who have direct contact with the ultimate consumer.

The vertical dotted line in the diagram marks a fundamental division of the industry into upstream and downstream halves. The upstream stages add value by reducing the variety of raw materials found on the earth's surface to a few standard commodities. The purpose is to produce flexible, predictable raw materials and intermediate products from which an interesting variety of downstream products are made. The downstream stages add value by producing a variety of products to meet varying customer needs. The downstream value is added through advertising, product positioning, marketing channels, and R & D. Thus, the upstream and downstream companies face very different business problems and tasks.

It is useful to distinguish between upstream and downstream companies because the factors for success, the lessons learned by managers, and the organizations used are fundamentally different. A successful, experienced manager is shaped in fundamentally different ways at different stages of the chain. The management processes are different, as are the dominant functions. In short, the company's culture depends on where it began in the industry chain.

Upstream managers must think in terms of stan-

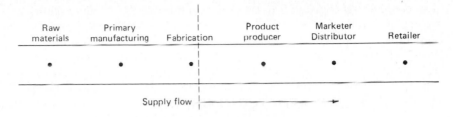

Figure 21.4 Industry value-added chain

dardization and efficiency. These are the producers of standardized commodity products. In contrast, downstream managers try to customize and tailor output to meet diverse customer needs. They segment markets and target individual users. The upstream company wants to standardize in order to reach as many end users as possible and build volume to lower costs. The downstream company wants to serve particular sets of end users. Thus, the upstreamers have a *divergent* view of the world to which their commodity is distributed. For example, the cover of the 1981 annual report of Intel (a fabricator of commodity semiconductors) is a listing of the ten thousand uses to which microprocessors have been put. The downstreamers have a *convergent* view of the world based on customer needs, and will select whatever commodity will best serve that need. In the electronics industry, there is always a conflict between those oriented toward upstream components and those oriented toward downstream systems, because of this contrast in perspectives.

The basis of competition also differs by stage. Commodities compete on price because the products are the same. Therefore, the successful upstreamer must be the low-cost producer. Their organizations are the lean and mean ones with a minimum of overheads. Low cost is also important for the downstreamer, but it is proprietary features that generate high margins. That feature may be a brand image (such as Maxwell House) or a patented technology, an endorsement (such as the American Dental Association's endorsement of Crest toothpaste), customer-service policy, and so on. Competition revolves around product features and product positioning rather than on price. This means that prices are set by marketing and product management. Products are moved by marketing pull. In contrast, the upstream company pushes its product through a strong sales force. Often, salespeople negotiate prices within limits set by top management.

The organizations are different as well. The upstream companies are functional and line-driven. They seek a minimum of staff, and even those staff that are used are in supporting roles. The downstream company with multiple products and multiple markets learns to manage diversity early. Profit centers emerge and

resources need to be allocated across products and markets. Larger staffs arise to assist top management in setting priorities among competing products and markets. Higher margins make the overhead tolerable.

Both upstream and downstream companies use research and development. The upstream company, however, invests in process development in order to lower costs. The downstream company invests primarily in product development in order to achieve a proprietary position.

The key managerial processes also vary. The upstream companies are driven by the capital budget and stress capital appropriations controls. The downstream companies also have a capital budget but are driven by the R & D budget (product producers) or the advertising budget (marketers). Further downstream it is working capital that becomes paramount. Managers learn to control the business by managing the turnover of inventory and accounts receivable. Thus, the upstream company is capital intensive, and technological know-how is critical. In more people-intensive, downstream companies, the critical skills have to do with human-resources management.

The dominant functions also vary with stages. The raw material processor is dominated by geologists, petroleum engineers, and traders. The supply-and-distribution function, which searches for the most economical end use, is powerful. The manufacturers of commodities are dominated by engineers who come up through manufacturing. Moving downstream, companies are dominated first by technologists in research and product development, then by marketing and merchandising. The line of succession to the CEO usually runs through the dominant power center.

In summary, upstream and downstream companies differ significantly in their organization structure, management processes, dominant functions, succession paths, management beliefs and values — in short, in the management way of life. Thus, companies in the same industry can be very different because each developed from a beginning at a particular stage of the industry. This beginning, and the initial successes, teaches management the lessons of that stage. The firm develops an integrated organization (structure, processes, rewards, and people) that is peculiar to that stage and forms the center of gravity.

STRATEGIC CHANGE

The first strategic change an organization makes is to integrate vertically within its industry. At a certain size, the organization can move backward to prior stages to guarantee sources of supply and secure bargaining leverage on vendors. It can also move forward to guarantee markets and volume for capital investments and become a customer to feed back data for new products. This initial strategic move does not change the center of gravity, because participation in the prior and subsequent stages is usually geared to the benefit of the center-of-gravity stage.

The paper industry provides a good illustration of the concepts of center of gravity and vertical integration. Figure 21.5 depicts five paper companies that operate from different centers of gravity. For the first, Weyerhaeuser, the center of gravity is at the land-and-timber stage of the industry. Weyerhaeuser seeks the highest-return use for a log. It makes pulp and paper rolls. It makes containers and milk cartons. But it is a timber company. If the returns are better in lumber than in pulp, Weyerhaeuser's pulp mills get fed with sawdust and chips.

International Paper, by contrast, is a primary manufacturer of paper. It also has timberland and con-tainer plants, and works on new products related to aseptic packaging. But, at least in the old days, if the pulp mills ran out of logs, the manager of the woodlands could be fired. IP's goal in the raw-material stage is to supply the manufacturing stage, not to seek the highest return for its timber. Similarly, while the fabricator company, Container Corporation, owns woodlands and pulp mills, they exist to supply the container-making operations. The product producer is Appleton, a maker of specialty paper products. For example, Appleton produces a paper with globules of ink embedded in it. The globules burst and form a letter or number when struck by an impact printer.

The last company is Procter & Gamble, a consumer-products firm. Like the others, it operates pulp mills and owns timberlands. But P & G is driven by the advertising or marketing function. Its CEOs are not drawn from the managers of its pulp mills or the woodlands. Rather, the path to success runs through brand management for Charmin or Pampers.

Each of these companies is in the paper industry and each operates at several stages in the supply chain. Yet each has its center of gravity at a different stage and, consequently, differs significantly from the others. The center of gravity establishes a base from which subsequent strategic changes are launched. As the industry matures, the company may feel a need to change its center of gravity if better returns can be obtained at another position in the chain. Alternatively, it may want to move to a new industry but use its same center of gravity. These options lead to different patterns of corporate development.

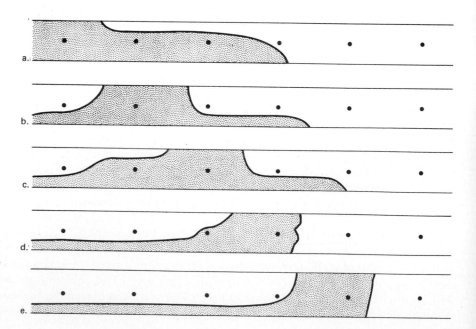

Figure 21.5 (a) Weyerhaeuser: raw materials; (b) International Paper (IP): primary manufacturer; (c) Container Corporation: fabricator; (d) Appleton: product producer; (e) Proctor & Gamble: consumer-products marketer

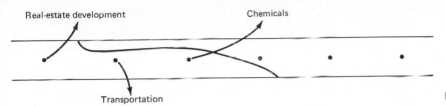

Real-estate development

Chemicals

Transportation

Figure 21.6 Alcoa

By-products diversification

One of the first diversification moves ordinarily made by a vertically integrated company is to sell by-products from several points along the industry chain, as shown schematically in figure 21.6. Such a company appears to be diversified in the sense that revenue is drawn from various industries. But while seeking additional sources of revenue and profit, the company is still psychologically committed to its center of gravity and its industry. Alcoa is such a firm. Even though it operates in several industries, its output varies directly with the aluminum cycle. It has not reduced its dependence on a single industry, as would be the case with real diversification. The company has changed neither its industry nor its center of gravity.

Related diversification

Another strategic change is to diversify into new industries that are related to the original business in the sense that they share the same center of gravity. Figure 21.7 depicts the related-diversification moves of Procter & Gamble. From its origins in the soap industry, P & G first integrated back into doing its own chemical processing (fatty acids) and seed crushing. Since then, to pursue new growth opportunities, it has been diversifying into paper, food, beverages, pharmaceuticals, coffee, and so on. But each move into a new industry is made at the company's center of gravity. The new businesses are all consumer products in which the key functions are ad-

vertising and brand management. The 3M company also follows a related diversification strategy, but one based on technology. Some seventy 3M divisions produce forty thousand different products, but 95 percent of the products are based on coating and bonding technologies. This company's center of gravity is as a product producer, and it adds value through R & D.

Linked diversification

A third type of diversification involves moving into new industries *and* operating at different centers of gravity in those new industries. The various businessess are linked in some way, however. Figure 21.8 illustrates this pattern of corporate development as pursued by Union Camp.

As a primary producer of paper products, Union Camp integrated backward to own woodlands. From there, it moved downstream within the wood-products industry by running sawmills and fabricating plants. Recently, it purchased a retail lumber business. This move is not vertical integration. Union Camp also moved into the chemical business by selling by-products from the pulping process. This business was successful and expanded, and recently Union Camp bid for a flavors and fragrances company—a product producer that adds value by creating flavors and fragrances primarily for consumer-products companies.

Thus, Union Camp is an upstream company that is acquiring downstream companies in industries to which it had already diversified from its upstream cen-

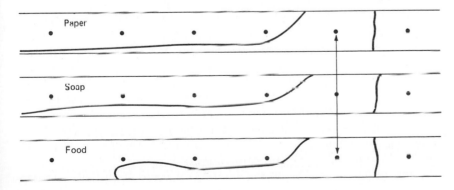

Paper

Soap

Food

Figure 21.7 Proctor & Gamble

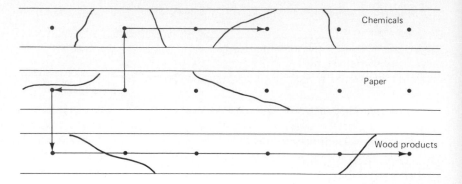

Figure 21.8   Union Camp

ter of gravity. But these new acquisitions are not operated as vertically integrated entities. They do not exist for the benefit of the center of gravity, but are stand-alone profit centers.

Unrelated diversification

A company may diversify into unrelated businesses, often at different centers of gravity. This sort of diversification almost always proceeds through acquisition, whereas related and linked companies will use some acquisitions but rely heavily on internal development. There is often very little relation among the industries into which the unrelated company diversifies. Textron and Teledyne have been the paradigms. These conglomerates operate in industrial equipment, aerospace, consumer products, insurance, and so on. Others have spread into retailing, services, and entertainment. The purpose is to insulate the company's earnings from the uncertainties of any one industry or from the business cycle.

Center of gravity change

Another possibility is for an organization to change its center of gravity within its industry. Recent articles describe the attempts of chemical companies to move downstream into proprietary products with higher margins. They want to get away from the overcapacity-undercapacity cycles of commodity businesses, with their low margins and high capital intensity. Similarly, some of the aerospace-systems integration houses are integrating backward into making electronic components—deemphasizing airplanes, for example, and putting more effort into the avionics, radars, weapons, and so on that go into airplanes. In either case, it means a shift in the company's center of gravity.

We have identified several patterns of strategic change in companies involving shifts in industry, center of gravity, or both. The principles of organization design suggest that certain kinds of organizations and measures of their economic performance are appropriate for certain kinds of strategic change.

STRATEGY, ORGANIZATION, AND PERFORMANCE

Studies of the *Fortune* 500 companies—most of them conducted by the Harvard Business School and reviewed by Galbraith and Nathanson (1978)—have suggested a close relationship between strategy and structure, as summarized in the following list:

Strategy	*Structure*
Single business	Functional
Vertical by-products	Functional with P & Ls
Related businesses	Divisional
Linked businesses	Mixed structures
Unrelated businesses	Holding company

Even in the 1980s one can still find companies that have remained in their original business (e.g., Wrigley Chewing Gum). These firms are run by centralized functional organizations. The next strategic type is the vertically integrated by-product seller. Despite some diversification, these companies remain committed to their industry and center of gravity. These companies, too, are functionally organized, but the sequential stages are often operated as profit-and-loss divisions, though they do not have the autonomy to run their own businesses. The companies usually are quite centralized and run by collegial management groups. These are almost all upstream companies.

The related businesses are companies that move into new industries at their center of gravity. Usually these are downstream companies. They adopt a decentralized profit-center structure, but the divisions are not completely decentralized. There are usually strong corporate staffs and some centralized marketing, manufacturing, and R & D. Several thousand people may be on the corporate payroll.

The clearest contrast to the related diversifier is the unrelated business company. These companies enter a variety of businesses at several centers of gravity, typically adopting a very decentralized holding-company organization. Their outstanding feature is the small corporate staff, perhaps fifty to two hundred people. Usually these are support staffs. All of the marketing, manufacturing, and R & D is decentralized to the divisions. Group executives have no staffs and are generally corporate oriented.

The linked companies fall between these extremes and are often transitory. The organizations they use are generally mixed forms that are not easily classified. Some divisions are autonomous, while others are managed out of corporate headquarters. Still others have strong group executives with group staffs. Some work has been done on classifying these structures (Allen 1978).

Virtually no work has been done on the changes in structure associated with shifts in the center of gravity. Likewise, there has been nothing done on comparisons for economic performance. But for the other categories and structures, some good data on relative economic performance are emerging.

The studies of economic performance have compared the various strategic patterns and the concept of fit between strategy and organization. Both sets of results have organization design implications. The economic studies use return on equity as the performance measure. Among the strategic categories listed previously, distinct performance differences are observed. The high performers are consistently the related diversifiers (Rumelt 1974, 1982; Galbraith and Nathanson 1978; Cassano and Nathanson 1982; Bettis 1981). There are several possible explanations of this performance difference. It may be that the related diversifiers are all downstream companies in businesses with high R & D and advertising expenditures. These businesses have higher margins and returns than other businesses. Thus, the critical factor may not be the strategy but the businesses the relateds happen to be in. If the unrelateds are good acquirers, however, why do they not enter the high-return businesses?

The other possible explanation has to do with organizational fit. The relateds learn a set of core skills and design an organization to perform at a particular center of gravity. When they diversify, they take on the task of learning a new business, but at the same center of gravity. Therefore, they get a diversified portfolio of businesses but each with a system of management and an organization that is understood by everyone. Thus, management is not spread too thin.

The unrelateds, however, must become familiar with new industries and must also learn how to operate at a different center of gravity. The latter change is the more difficult. One upstream company that diversified through acquisition into downstream companies consistently encountered control troubles. It instituted a capital-appropriation process for each investment of $50,000 but still had problems. The retail division opened a couple of stores with $40,000 leases, bypassing the capital-appropriation process. The company got blind sided because the stores required $40 million in working capital for inventory and receivables. The management systems did not fit the new downstream businesses.

Several authors have directly attributed low performance to a lack of organizational fit. The Lorsch and Allen (1973) study is typical. It examined the performance of four unrelated diversifiers and found that the low performers were more centralized and had larger corporate staffs. This study and others (e.g., Galbraith and Nathanson 1978) provide support for the hypotheses that fit and performance are related, but they do not establish the direction of causation. For example, it is not clear how one should interpret the finding that low-performing holding companies are too centralized; did centralization cause poor performance, or do poor performers become centralized in an effort to fix them? The evidence is confounded.

These problems have been overcome in some more recent work (Nathanson 1981; Cassano and Nathanson 1982). Using the companies in the Hay Associates data base, Nathanson measured diversity, economic performance, structure type, centralization, and location of staffs. His findings on diversification are consistent with work cited above. The measure of diversification was different, but the greater the diversity, the lower the performance of the company. Companies operating with no more than three technologies were the top performers. The lowest performers were those operating in seven different technologies. Within each diversity category, however, organization made a difference. The high-performing, single-business company was one that prematurely decentralized around profit centers. The previous finding that centralized unrelated companies were poor performers was also replicated. In all, the authors claim that the lack of fit between strategy and organization accounts for as much as 90 percent of the variance in performance.

Another recent study sheds some additional light on the organization-strategy fit. Even though highly diverse holding companies are outperformed by related businesses, there are some high-performing unrelateds (Rumelt 1974; Dundas and Richardson 1982). These companies have followed an intricate blend of acquisition strategy and organization. First of all, they do not manage their diverse businesses. They acquire, replace management, and then divest rather than fix a poor performing division. The poor performers buy diverse businesses and then try to manage the divisions when they run into problems. The businesses of the high performers, while unrelated, are still somewhat similar. That is, they are all manufacturing rather than services, entertainment, or high technology. The companies have only three or four major areas of business. The poor performers spread across as many as seven areas. Also, successful performers avoid having any subsidiary greater than 30 percent of revenues. They try to acquire companies that are number one or two in their industries. Turnaround situations are avoided unless the company can be purchased at a significant value. Unfriendly takeovers are usually avoided as well. In short, the companies are good acquirers and divestors.

The organization adopted by the high-performing unrelated companies is very decentralized around the divisions or businesses. The corporate office is small and has little operational involvement. The divisions are kept strictly independent for ease of measurement and divestment. No attempts to achieve synergy are made unless they are voluntary among the divisions. The key role is that of the group executive, who acts on behalf of the corporation in capital allocation for a homogeneous group of divisions. He or she understands the key success factors and acts as a one-person board of directors. It is the group executive who decides to replace management or divest the division. For this reason, group executives are chosen for their ability to be objective with the divisions. Because managers rarely divest a business with which they have been associated, the group executive will often be drawn from outside the divisions for which he or she will be responsible.

The systems also fit the strategy. Managers receive bonuses tied to return-on-investment measures. Group executives have less variable compensation and receive bonuses based on corporate profits. All businesses are measured on return on investment or net assets. The one area that is tightly controlled is cash. The cash-management systems are centralized and sophisticated, and the internal audit system is highly developed. In short, the management systems, staffing patterns, structure, and strategy of the successful unrelated business are a good fit. When there is good fit, there is high performance.

Overall, a good case is emerging for the importance of organization. It appears that organization makes a difference to the performance of the enterprise, with the critical variable being the fit between the firm's business strategy, its structure, its management systems, its rewards, and its staffing. There are still holes in the evidence for these assertions. A formal analysis of variance, for example, would require data on all possible combinations of business types and organizational variables. But no one in the real world would do anything as foolish as attempting to run unrelated businesses with a functional organization. The evidence we do have supports the case for organization design.

One additional piece of evidence has emerged from studies of economic performance, which found that the poorest performer of the strategic categories is the vertically integrated, by-product seller (Rumelt 1974). These companies are all upstream businesses focused on raw materials or primary manufacturing. They make up a good portion of "Smokestack America." These companies were most successful early in the century, and their value added is shifting to less-developed countries in the natural course of industrial development. The significant point here is their inability to change. Despite poor performance, they have continued to put money back into the same business.

The center-of-gravity concept provides an explanation of these companies' inertia. In the earlier period of their success, these companies put together an organization that fit their industry and stage. When the industry declined, downstream companies were better able to adapt than the upstream companies, which were functional organizations with few general managers. Their resource allocation was within a single business, not across multiple products. A significant part of their management skill was in the technological know-how. But technology does not transfer across industries at the primary manufacturing center of gravity. The knowledge of papermaking does not help very much in glassmaking. Yet both might be combined in a packaging company. Moreover, the capital intensity of these industries limits their potential for diversification. Usually it is necessary to choose one industry and invest capital there to be the low-cost producer. So there are a number of reasons why these companies have been notoriously poor diversifiers.

In addition, it appears to be very difficult to change centers of gravity, no matter where an organization is along the industry chain. A center-of-gravity shift requires a dismantling of the current power structure, rejection of parts of the old culture, and the establishment of all new management systems. The related diversification works for exactly the opposite reasons. A company can move into new businesses with minimal change to the power structure and accepted ways of doing things. Changes in the center of gravity are usually the result of new start-ups at a new center of gravity, rather than a shift in the center of the established firm.

The recent history of the oil companies illustrates the importance of a company's original center of gravity. During oil shortages and normal times with depletion allowances, these companies made their money at the wellhead. The upstream companies were integrated, and the function of retail outlets was to get rid of the oil that was pumped. Since OPEC's nationalization and the more recent oil gluts of the 1980s, however, companies have shifted their attention to downstream profitability. Now downstream operations must pay for themselves and make money. However, this change requires a power shift from the engineers, geologists, and supply and distribution people to marketing. In companies where top management is drawn from the upstream functions, the change has not occurred. The companies that are successful are those that began as downstream companies and established their center of gravity there. Amerada-Hess is an example. Once a delivery truck driver, Leon Hess knows the retail-distribution side of the business. The upstream companies have had great difficulty. Some have sold their downstream operations and tried to diversify into unrelated areas. Others have defined themselves as raw-material and energy companies and diversified into coal, uranium, and other mining and extractive industries. These diversifiers are having their problems in running multiple businesses. But those that have retained a raw-materials or energy focus will require no change in their center of gravity. They should be the better performers over the long run.

There are some exceptions that prove the rule. Some organizations have evolved from upstream commodity producers to downstream product producers and consumer-products firms. Formerly a flour miller, General Mills became a related diversified provider of products for the homemaker. Over a long period of time, they shifted downstream into consumer food products from their cake-mix-product beginnings. From there, they diversified into related areas after selling off the milling operations, the old core of the company. National Lead (NL) Industries is another example. Originally NL used a linked strategy to get into oil-drilling services. When demand for lead dropped, NL moved into lead-based paints, and from there into various drilling muds. During the 1970s, they used this entry point to expand the services provided to the drilling industry. Eventually, NL sold off its original lead business. Like General Mills, however, NL brought in new management and used acquisition and divestment to make the transition. So, even though vestiges of the old name remain, NL today is a substantially different company. Perhaps the Bell Sys-

tem will be the one to bootstrap itself into a new center of gravity.

The vast majority of our research has examined one kind of strategic change—diversification. The far more difficult change, a shift in center of gravity, has received far less attention. Center of gravity is difficult to measure, and is not a publicly reported statistic like the number of industries in which a company operates. Case studies will have to be used. But there is a need for more systematic knowledge about this kind of strategic change.

STAGEWISE DEVELOPMENT

The process of organization design is a dynamic one, yet most of our models and concepts are static. The concept of fit is like the static concept of equilibrium. Some of the limitations of a static model can be overcome by focusing on the stagewise process of the development of organizations and the management of transitions from one stage to another.

Virtually every phenomenon can be understood in terms of stages of growth. We talk about stages of economic development for countries and stages of cognitive development for children. Organizations are no different, as several researchers have recognized (e.g., Starbuck 1965; Galbraith and Nathanson 1978). All strategic changes do not follow the same pattern. In certain kinds of change, however, organizations typically pass through predictable stages. For example, as an export firm evolves into a multinational company, it passes through stages of using distributors, acquiring or building plants, starting country organizations in Europe, establishing European headquarters, and sometimes seeing regional businesses decline as products become global.

Another predictable process is the new venture start-up. Galbraith (1982) studied a number of high technology start-ups and found that all went through five identifiable stages, as shown in table 21.1. These ventures characteristically begin as small, homogeneous, innovating garage-shop organizations. At this stage a formal structure would inhibit progress. Later, significant capital is invested, and the transition is made to an operating organization. Now structure is necessary for progress. For each of these stages, there is a different task and hence a different fit between all the organizational elements.

Change to a new stage is often resisted by those in power at the existing stage. Deals and promises are made at one stage that will have to be reversed at a later one. If the organization knows the characteristic pattern of

Table 21.1

Stage \ Factor	I Proof of principal prototype	II Model shop	III Start-up volume production	IV Natural growth	V Strategic maneuvering
Task	Invent and make it	Make it well; test it	Make it and distribute it in volume	Make it profitable	Dominate a niche
People	Jacks-of-all-trades; risk takers	Jack and some special risk takers	Specialists; non-technical start-up types	Business people; planners	Planners and strategists
Reward	Equity; nonbureaucratic climate; make a mark	Nonbureaucratic climate; ground-floor advancement	Ground-floor advancement; career	Career; salary	Career; salary; bonus
Processes	Informal; face-to-face contact; personal control	Informal; personal contact; meetings	Formal; systems and procedures; budgets	Formal control; planning and budget information systems	Five-year plans; profit center; multi-dimensional plan
Structure	Informal; little need	Functions and hierarchy begin	Functional organization; division of labor; centralized	Functional with overlays; division of labor; decentralize	Matrix; profit center; decentralize
Leader	Quarterback	Player/coach	Coach	Manager	Strategist

Note: Adapted from Galbraith 1982.

evolution, it can more easily move on to each new stage in turn. The stagewise model gives useful previews of coming attractions. It can enable planners to buy the luxury of time and create smoother transitions.

The stagewise process has been described as consisting of stages of evolution, each followed by a revolution and then a new stage. The revolutions can be less painful if they are anticipated and planned for in advance. For example, almost all downstream companies start as single-product, functional organizations and later become multiproduct profit centers. This transition need not be revolutionary. As the number of products increases, cross-functional teams can be used to start the process of decentralization and the creation of general managers. Information systems can be established to support the teams. Product managers can be the next step. Teams led by product managers can create business plans used in the budgeting process. Next the assembly department and engineering can be reorganized around products as volume builds. In this manner, the organization can move step by step over three to five years into the profit-center form. When the organization is not planned, diversity eventually forces the rejection of the functional organization, and all those transitional steps have to be taken at once. New people must be brought in from the outside. Thus revolution is commonplace, but it does not have to be. Disruption can be minimized through organization design.

POWER AND POLITICS IN DESIGN

The organization design perspective has sometimes been criticized for taking too rational an approach to its subject (e.g., Pfeffer 1978). Some believe that power and politics are more crucial influences on organizational life, and that the key question is not what design is used, but who controls the organization. I would argue, however, that political factors dominate design only in certain special circumstances.

A valuable perspective on the importance of nonrational factors has emerged from research on European corporations (Franko 1974). Studies of strategy and structural relationships during the early 1960s showed that most large European firms, however diversified, were holding companies or functional organizations. After 1968, however, European firms began to show the same patterns as their American counterparts. The change seems to reflect the development of a competitive environment in Europe. Before 1968, tariff barriers protected local manufacturers, and prices were set by cartels and social elites. When tariff barriers fell with the establishment of the Common Market, governments began to enact and enforce antitrust laws. And, most important, American and Japanese firms began to enter the protected markets. European firms began to set business rather than country strategies. As a result, divisionalized structures began to emerge. The lesson is that, the more a market regulates a firm's activity, the more strategy and organization must move together. If the firm is a monopoly or a government-regulated entity, strategy and organization are less important.

Researchers who emphasize the importance of power and politics often cite data from firms that are not regulated by market forces—universities, hospitals, and government agencies, for example. These institutions may place less emphasis on being efficient than a profit-making firm would. The author's consulting experience with one government agency is illustrative. Three separate parts of this agency used satellites. The author suggested that these activities be consolidated into one group to capitalize on economies of scale and skilled personnel. The client agreed that this would be more efficient, but pointed out that NASA had the charter to operate satellites. If a satellite group were created, it might be lost to NASA. Political considerations of this sort are not unknown in profit-making enterprises, of course, but they are less likely to dominate rational market behavior than in the nonprofit sector.

Power and politics may play a crucial role during a period of strategic change, however. Resources, succession routes, and dominant functions are all up for grabs at such a time. For this reason, active management is important to ensure a smooth transition.

MANAGING TRANSITIONS

In the past, organizational changes were not singled out as a special management task. If a new product were introduced, a product manager would be assigned to oversee the process. If a new information system were established, a project manager would be responsible for seeing that nothing fell through the cracks. But new organizations were routinely established with no one to manage them except the CEO. Beckhard and Harris (1977) introduced the usual concept that a transition manager should project-manage the new organization.

Another issue in the design process is the involvement of all parties who will be affected by the change. Figure 21.9, which resembles the decision-making model of Vroom and Yetton (1973), represents the options available to management.

At the left end of the diagram, management is very active and other parties have very little involvement. As we move to the right, others become more involved by providing information and problem solving. The management makes the final choice. Farther to the right,

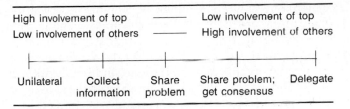

Figure 21.9 (Reprinted from *Leadership and Decision-Making* by Victor H. Vroom and Philip W. Yetton by permission of the University of Pittsburgh Press. © 1973 University of Pittsburgh Press.)

the others are highly involved and the top managers are not. Delegation is the extreme form on the right.

The criteria for choosing an appropriate position on this continuum are twofold. First, does the manager have the necessary knowledge and information to choose the organization that fits the business situation? Second, will the subordinates accept the unilateral decision as a determinant of their behavior? If the answers to these questions are affirmative, a unilateral decision is appropriate and saves everyone's time. If not, management needs to open up the decision process to the more active involvement of others. Management usually cannot make a unilateral decision in large organization changes, because such reorganizations strike at the charters and boundaries of people's work. Most people want to have a say about such changes.

If management does not involve people whose vested interests are affected, they may choose to resist or engage in what Pettigrew calls "power maintenance" (Pettigrew 1973). People throughout the organization have power by virtue of their control of resources. If they are denied access to the decision process, they may use their existing power base to maintain that power and thwart the change. They do so because that is the only means of influence available to them. One example of power-maintenance behavior is the withholding of information, a common result when management unilaterally introduces product management into a functional organization. Functional managers simply do not inform product managers, who do not know that they do not know. Being at crossroads of interfunctional information is supposed to be one of product managers' power bases. Without information, they are impotent, and the firm eventually finds itself saying, "We've tried product management, and it didn't work."

Total delegation is also an ineffective means of introducing change. In this case, the subordinate product managers run into the same power-maintenance phenomenon, but cannot have recourse to a higher authority. The product managers have been given two jobs: to manage the product, and to institutionalize a system of product management. The first is appropriately theirs, but the second is the job of top management.

Therefore, two mechanisms are needed to manage an organization design process. One is to formulate and design the organization, and the second is to legitimize or authorize the effort. There are several alternatives for these mechanisms. The first is usually performed by a task force, which ideally includes an individual from each constituency. The attempt is to recreate the organization in microcosm, so that no group feels compelled to adopt power-maintenance tactics. People can take their issues to the task force through their representative.

To minimize the likelihood of power maintenance, the task force must be neutral and legitimate. With appropriate representation, use of outsiders, and reporting relationships, an objective problem-solving group can be created. The other mechanism used to create legitimacy is top-level review, usually through a steering committee. By reviewing task-force work and by selecting good people to work on the task force, the steering committee vests the group with authority.

In this model, the top manager still chooses the organization form, but has had plenty of prior input. Political issues arise before a decision is made, instead of finding expression afterward in power-maintenance moves. The choice will still be difficult and implementation hard, but success is more likely.

In summary, managing a transition is a task equivalent to project management of a capital investment. A transition manager is needed. Moreover, the organization design decision process itself is in part a political decision. Representation of constituencies is a key to preventing resistance or power-maintenance moves by those whose vested interest is at stake. Appropriate design processes can help organizations resolve issues of this kind.

SUMMARY

In this brief chapter, the author has tried to define the topic of organization design and summarize the progress to date. Also, some new thoughts about organization and centers of gravity were presented. Some data on the relationships between the fit of strategy and organization and economic performance showed that organizing makes a difference. Finally, a couple of references to managing the design process were made. All of these points illustrate the progress that we have made in designing organizations.

REFERENCES

Allen, S. A. 1978. "Organizational Choices and General Management Influence Networks in Divisionalized Companies." *Academy of Management Journal* 21, no. 3 (September): 341–65.

Beckhard, R., and R. Harris. 1977. *Organizational Transitions.* Reading, Mass.: Addison-Wesley.

Bettis, R. A. 1981. "Performance Differences in Related and Unrelated Diversified Firms." *Strategic Management Journal* (October–December): 379–94.

Cassano, J., and D. Nathanson. 1982. "Organization, Diversity and Performance." *The Wharton Magazine* (Summer): 18–26.

Chandler, A. D. 1960. *Strategy and Structure.* Cambridge, Mass.: MIT Press.

Davis, S., and H. Schwartz. 1981. "Matching Corporate Culture and Business Strategy." *Organization Dynamics* (Summer): 30–48.

Dundas, K. M., and P. R. Richardson. 1982. "Implementing the Unrelated Product Strategy." *Strategic Management Journal* (October–December): 287–302.

Franko, L. 1974. "The Move Toward a Multidivisional Structure in European Organizations." *Administrative Science Quarterly* 19, no. 4 (June): 493–506.

Galbraith, J. 1977. *Organization Design.* Reading, Mass.: Addison-Wesley.

———. 1982. "The Stages of Growth." *Journal of Business Strategy* (Summer): 70–79.

Galbraith, J., and D. Nathanson. 1978. *Strategy Implementation.* St. Paul, Minn.: West.

Lawrence, P., and J. Lorsch. 1967. *Organization and Environment.* Boston: Division of Research, Harvard Business School.

Leavitt, H. 1965. "Applied Organizational Change in Industry." In *Handbook of Organizations,* ed. J. March. Chicago: Rand McNally.

Lorsch, J. 1977. "Organization Design: A Situational Perspective." *Organization Dynamics* (Autumn): 2–14.

Lorsch, J., and S. Allen. 1973. *Managing Diversity and Interdependence.* Boston: Division of Research, Harvard Business School.

Nadler, D., and M. Tushman. 1980. "A Model for Diagnosing Organizational Behavior." *Organizational Dynamics* (August).

Peters, T. 1978. "Symbols, Patterns and Settings." *Organization Dynamics* (Autumn): 2–23.

Pettigrew, A. 1973. *The Politics of Organizational Decision Making.* London: Tavistock.

Pfeffer, J. 1978. *Organization Design.* Arlington Heights, Ill.: AHM.

Rumelt, R. 1974. *Strategy, Structure and Economic Perfor-*

mance. Boston: Division of Research, Harvard Business School.

———. 1982. "Diversification Strategy and Profitability." *Strategic Management Journal* (October–December): 359–70.

Starbuck, W. "Organizational Growth and Development." In *Handbook of Organization,* ed. J. March. Chicago: Rand McNally.

Tregoe, B., and J. Zimmerman. 1980. *Top Management Strategy.* New York: Simon & Schuster.

Vroom, V., and P. W. Yetton. 1973. *Leadership and Decision-Making.* Pittsburgh: University of Pittsburgh Press.

Waterman, R. 1982. "The Seven Elements of Strategic Fit." *The Journal of Business Strategy* (Winter): 69–73.

22

The effective management of organizational change

DAVID A. NADLER

Consistently effective organizations are those that appropriately position themselves in their environment. They have determined what they need to do differently in order to take advantage of shifts in the markets, industries, technologies, or localities in which they operate. This repositioning may be forced by sudden or unexpected environmental shifts; it may be planned in anticipation of environmental moves; or it may be calculated to precipitate movement in the environment. The classic cases of failure (such as Penn Central, W. T. Grant, or Braniff) are organizations that were not able to reposition themselves in the face of environmental change.

Repositioning an organization involves modifying the way it functions or "does business." Strategies, formal structures, processes, cultures, operating styles, and people all may have to be changed. Thus a critical issue for organizations operating in dynamic and uncertain environments is the management of change.

In recent years, the management of change in organizations has become a more critical concern. Organizations face tremendous uncertainty and instability in the current environment. Technological change has been accelerating; deregulation has disrupted market patterns in traditionally stable industries such as communications, banking, and transportation; multinational competition is increasingly important; and a host of destabilizing

general macroeconomic and political forces are at work. In addition, organizations face challenges as a result of their own success: greater size, scope, and complexity also necessitate change.

Organizations have responded to these challenges with new business strategies, new ways of structuring the work, new technologies, the addition of new elements (through acquisition or merger), the casting off of elements (divestitures or splits), new cultures or operating styles, relocation to new settings, or the appointment of new management teams. All of these responses raise questions of change management. Experience has indicated that the effectiveness of any response depends as much on *how* the change is implemented as on *what* it is. The task of implementing new aspects or elements of organization is fundamentally a problem of change management.

This chapter presents an approach to change management based on both systematic research (Nadler 1981) and observation, over a number of years, of managers who have been responsible for implementing change. Because it is critical to have some view of how an organization functions before considering how to change it, the chapter begins with a brief outline of a model or approach for thinking about organizations. Next we present a way of thinking about changes and discuss some classic patterns of change management that have characterized large U.S.-based organizations. Then the issues in managing change are considered, as well as the techniques that effective change managers seem to employ. The chapter concludes by focusing on the specific case of managing change to uncertain future states. The objective is to provide a framework for thinking about change as well as a structure for planning effective management of significant organizational change.

A VIEW OF ORGANIZATIONS

There are many different ways of thinking about organizations and the patterns of behavior that occur within them. During the past three decades, there has emerged a view of organizations as complex open social systems (Katz and Kahn 1966), mechanisms that take input from the larger environment and subject it to various transformation processes, which result in output.

As systems, organizations are seen as composed of interdependent parts. Change in one element of the system will result in changes in other parts of the system. Similarly, organizations have the property of equilibrium: the system will generate energy to move toward a state of balance. Finally, as open systems, organizations need to maintain favorable transactions of input and output with the environment in order to survive.

While the systems perspective is useful, systems theory by itself may be too abstract a concept to be useful as a managerial tool. Thus, various organizational theorists have attempted to develop more pragmatic theories or models based on the system paradigm. The particular approach used here, known as "congruence model of organizational behavior" (Nadler and Tushman 1977, 1979, 1982), is based on the general systems model. In this framework, the major inputs to the system of organization behavior are the environment, which provides constraints, demands, and opportunities; the resources available to the organization; the history of the organi-

zation; and, perhaps the most crucial, the organization's strategy. Strategy is the set of key decisions about the match of the organization's resources to the opportunities, constraints, and demands in the environment within the context of history.

The output of the system is, in general, the effectiveness of the organization's performance in meeting the goals of strategy. Specifically, the output includes *organizational performance*, as well as *group performance* and *individual behavior and affect*; the latter two, of course, contribute to organizational performance.

The basic framework thus views the organization as a mechanism that takes inputs (strategy and resources in the context of history and environment) and transforms them into outputs (patterns of individual, group, and organizational behavior).

The major focus of organizational analysis is therefore the transformation process. The model conceives of the organization as composed of four major components: (1) the *task* of the organization—the work to be done and its critical characteristics; (2) the *individuals* who are to perform organizational tasks; (3) the *formal organizational arrangements*, including various structures, processes, and systems designed to motivate and help individuals in the performance of organizational tasks; and (4) *informal organizational arrangements*, which characterize how an organization actually functions. These patterns of communication, power, influence, values, and norms usually evolve without planning or explicit formulation.

A critical question is the degree of consistency, congruence, or "fit" among those four components. For example, are the demands of the organizational task consistent with the skills and abilities of the individuals available to perform it? Are the rewards that the work provides well-suited to the needs and desires of the individuals? All in all, six possible relationships among components need to be examined for congruence (see figure 22.1). The basic hypothesis of the model is that or-

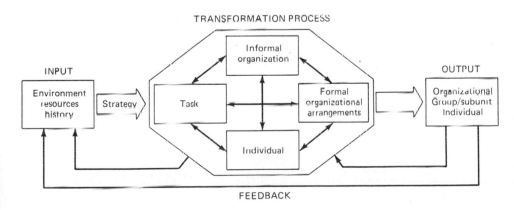

Figure 22.1 A congruence model of organizations. (Reprinted, by permission of the publisher, from "Managing Transitions to Uncertain Future States," by D. A. Nadler, *Organizational Dynamics,* Summer 1982, p. 38 © 1980 AMACOM, a division of American Management Associations, New York. All rights reserved.)

ganizations will be most effective when their major components are congruent with each other. Problems of effectiveness due to management and organizational factors will stem from poor fit, or lack of congruence, among organizational components.

This is a contingency approach to organizations. The model recognizes that individuals, tasks, strategies, and environments may differ greatly from organization to organization, and hence different patterns of organization and management will be appropriate. There is no one best organization design or style of management or method of working.

A CHANGE SCENARIO

The organization model provides us with a road map for thinking about how changes occur. A good example is the very dramatic changes that have occurred in the American Telephone & Telegraph Company (AT&T). (See Nadler 1982 for more detail on this case.)

For many years, the AT&T organization exemplified good fit. In response to the environment, the company developed an effective strategy of maintaining its monopoly through high-quality and low-cost universal phone service. Because this environment was relatively stable and manageable, AT&T could define a stable and predictable set of tasks to performance—"the end-to-end provision of universal telephone service." A highly formalized organizational structure and procedures fit this task well. Over time the company recruited, developed, and rewarded individuals who functioned well in this structured environment and could identify with the value of high-quality service, to the public. Finally, the infor-

mal organization, including the culture and leadership style, stressed high-quality service, adherence to rules and procedures, and compliance with the highly formal organizational structure. With an extremely high level of congruence, AT&T performed extremely well for many years.

What changed all this? As in most major organizational transitions, the impetus for change came from the outside. Starting in the late 1960s and through the 1970s, the regulatory environment posed increasingly serious challenges to the Bell monopoly. Concurrently, new and powerful competition arrived on the scene. Technological advances, such as satellite communications and private data-transmission networks, also challenged the Bell System's dominance in the communications market.

Over time AT&T began to modify its strategy to accept a redefinition of the monopoly and to become more market-driven, responsive, and, in some lines of business, competitively oriented. As the strategies of the organization changed, so did the nature of the task. Work became more unpredictable and faster paced, requiring greater coordination among the different units serving specific customer needs.

In recognition of this new set of strategic and work demands, AT&T began to reshape its formal organizational arrangements. Major reorganizations were undertaken in 1974, 1978, 1980, and again in 1982.

Events at AT&T fit the pattern of the classic change scenario shown in figure 22.2. A series of catalytic events in the environment lead to an adjustment in strategy that requires a redefinition of the nature of the organization's work. Key organizational arrangements are then modified to permit implementation of the strategy and performance of the new tasks. This sequence of events is typical of large, complex organizations.

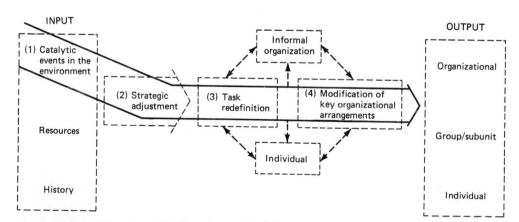

Figure 22.2 The classic "change" scenario. (Reprinted, by permission of the publisher, from "Managing Transitions to Uncertain Future States," by D. A. Nadler, *Organizational Dynamics,* Summer 1982, p. 40 © AMACOM, a division of American Management Associations, New York. All rights reserved.)

Several points about this change scenario are worth underlining. First, most change is brought about by events or forces outside the organization. As open systems, organizations try to adapt to significant environmental changes. While these changes may present new opportunities, they are more frequently seen as threats to the organization's existence or success.

Second, the pace of the sequence will depend on the situation. The first three steps shown in figure 22.2 could occur within a few months, but required ten years in the case of AT&T.

Third, the sequence is usually less linear than suggested by figure 22.2. In reality, change is very much tied up with the political life of the organization and, as such, is usually the result of various political processes: conflicts, bargains, agreements, and so on.

Finally, even if the organization successfully moves through these phases, it still faces several unresolved problems. The organizational arrangements will not have been fully adjusted for the new strategy and task, particularly the measures, rewards, and coordinating devices. In addition, the informal organization or culture may not fit well with the new task and organizational arrangements. And individuals may not fit the new task or organizational arrangements.

THE TASK OF IMPLEMENTING CHANGE

Implementing a change involves moving an organization to some desired future state. It is useful to think of changes in terms of transitions (figure 22.3). The effective management of change involves developing an understanding of the current state (A) and an image of a desired future state (B), and moving the organization from A through a transition period (C) to B (Beckhard and Harris 1977).

Major transitions usually occur in response to anticipation of organizational input (environmental or strategic shifts) or outputs (problems of performance). In terms of the congruence model, a change occurs when managers determine that the configuration of the components in the current state is not effective and the organization must be reshaped.

Organizational change is effectively managed when:

1. The organization is moved from the current state to the future state.
2. The functioning of the organization in the future state meets expectations, i.e., it works as planned.
3. The transition is accomplished without undue cost to the organization.
4. The transition is accomplished without undue cost to individual organizational members.

Of course, not every organizational change can be expected to meet these criteria, but they do represent an appropriate planning target. The question is how to manage the implementation process so as to maximize the chances that the change will be effective.

Problems of change

Effective change requires an understanding of both *what* the change should be and *how* it should be implemented. Clearly, managers must diagnose and understand organizational problems and causes before developing solutions. Otherwise problem solving becomes an expensive trial-and-error process.

We focus here on a second question—how the changes are implemented. Three types of problem seem to be encountered in some form whenever a significant organizational change is attempted. The first is *power*. Any organization is a political system made up of different individuals, groups, and coalitions competing for power (Tushman 1977; Salancik and Pfeffer 1977). Political behavior is thus a natural and expected feature of organizations, in both current and future states. In transition, however, these dynamics become even more intense as the old order is dismantled and a new order emerges. Any significant change poses the possibility of upsetting or modifying the balance of power among groups. The uncertainty associated with change creates ambiguity, which in turn tends to increase the probability of political activity (Thompson and Tuden 1959). In-

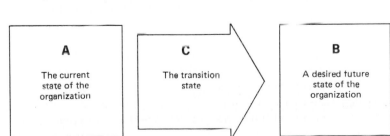

Figure 22.3 Organizational change as a transition state. (R. Beckhard and R. Harris, *Organizational Transitions* © 1977, Addison-Wesley, Reading, Massachusetts. Adapted material. Reprinted with permission.)

A The current state of the organization

C The transition state

B A desired future state of the organization

dividuals and groups may take action based on their perception of how the change will affect their power in the organization. They will be concerned about how the conflict of the transition period will affect the balance of power in the future state and will maintain or improve their own position. Individuals and groups may also engage in political action for ideological reasons: the change may be inconsistent with their shared values or image of the organization (Pettigrew 1972).

The second problem is individual *anxiety*. Change involves moving from something known toward something unknown. Individuals naturally wonder whether they will be needed in the future state, whether their skills will be valued, how they will cope with the new situation, and so on. These concerns are summarized in the question so frequently voiced during a major organizational change: What's going to happen to me? To the extent that this question cannot be fully answered (and frequently it cannot), individuals feel stress and anxiety. High levels of stress have some harmful behavioral effects, leading to difficulty in integrating information or hearing things, resistance to the changes, or, in the extreme, irrational and self-destructive acts. The resistance response is well documented (Watson 1969; Zaltman and Duncan 1977). Frequently, however, instead of actively resisting a change, people react in a variety of ways that objectively do not appear to be constructive for either the individual or the organization.

A third problem is that of organizational *control*. Change disrupts the normal course of events within an organization and undermines existing systems of management control. Change may make formal control systems irrelevant and/or inappropriate; thus it may be easy to lose control of the organization during a change. As goals, structures, and people shift, it becomes difficult to monitor performance and make corrections as in normal control processes.

A related problem is that most formal organizational arrangements are designed for stable states, not transition states. Managers focus on designing the most effective organizational arrangements for the future, and think of the change from A to B as simply a mechanical or procedural detail. They ignore the special needs of the transition state, which are ordinarily not well met by the steady state management systems and structures developed for A and B.

Implications for change management

The preceding discussion of problems in implementing change suggests some relatively straightforward implications for management. First, if a change may present

significant problems of power, it requires the management of the organization's political system to shape the political dynamics associated with the change, preferably before the actual implementation. Second, if change creates anxiety and the associated patterns of dysfunctional behavior, it is critical to motivate individuals through communications and rewards to react to the change in a constructive manner. Finally, if a change presents significant problems of control, it is important to pay attention to the management of the transition state.

SHAPING POLITICAL DYNAMICS

Most significant changes involve some modification of the political system, thus raising issues of power. As shown in table 22.1, steps can be taken in four specific action areas to *shape and manage the political dynamics* before and during the transition period.

First, it is important to *get the support of key power groups* within the organization in order to build a critical mass of favor of the change. The organization is a political system with competing groups, cliques, coalitions, and interests, each with its own views on any particular change. Change cannot succeed unless there is a critical mass of support. The first step in building the necessary support is identifying the power relationships as a basis for planning a political strategy. This step may involve identifying the key players in the organization or the individual and/or group stakeholders—those who have a positive, negative, or neutral stake in the change. In thinking about these relationships, it may be useful to draw a diagram or create a stakeholder or influence map. This map should show the relationships among the various stakeholders, who influences whom, and what the stakes are for each individual.

There are several possible approaches to building support. The first is participation, which has long been recognized as a tool for reducing resistance to change and gaining support. As individuals or groups become involved in the change, they tend to see it as their own rather than something imposed upon them. Participation may not be feasible or wise in all situations, however. In some cases, it merely increases the power of opposing groups to forestall the change. Thus, another approach may be bargaining with groups—winning support by providing some incentive. A third method is isolation. Some members of the organization may resist participation or bargaining and persist in attempting to undermine the change. Their impact on the organiza-

Table 22.1   Shaping political dynamics

Action	Purpose	Technique

Get support of key power groups	Build internal critical mass of support for change	Identify power relationships
		   Key players
		   Stakeholders
		   Influence relationships
		Use strategies for building support
		   Participation
		   Bargaining, deals
		   Isolation
		   Removal

Demonstrate leadership support of the change	Shape the power distribution and influence the patterns of behavior	Leaders model behavior to promote identification with them Articulate vision of future state Use reward system Provide support and resources Remove roadblocks Maintain momentum Send signals through informal organization

Use symbols	Create identification with the change and appearance of a critical mass of support	Communicate with:
		   Names and graphics
		   Language systems
		   Symbolic acts
		   Small signals

Build in stability	Reduce excess anxiety, defensive reactions, and conflicts	Allow time to prepare for change Send consistent messages Maintain points of stability Communicate what will not change

tion can be minimized by assigning them to a position outside the mainstream. In an extreme case, individuals who cannot be isolated or brought into constructive roles may have to be removed from the scene through transfer or firing. Clearly, one would prefer to rely entirely on the first two methods, participation and bargaining. But it would be naïve to assume that they will be successful in all cases.

Leader behavior can also have a powerful influence in support of change. Leaders can shape the power distribution and influence patterns in an organization and can create a sense of political momentum by sending out signals, providing support, and dispensing rewards.

Both through explicit statements and through their behavior, leaders provide a vision of the future state and a source of identification for different groups within the organization. Secondly, in addition, they can play a crucial role by rewarding key individuals and specific types of behavior. Leaders can provide support (or remove roadblocks) through political influence and needed resources and can use their public statements to maintain momentum. Finally, leaders can send important signals through the informal organization. During times of uncertainty and change, people throughout the organization tend to look to leaders for indications of appropriate behavior and the direction of movement in the organization. Often actions of little apparent conse-

quence, such as patterns of attendance at meetings or the words used in public statements, send potent signals. By careful attention to these subtly significant actions, leaders can greatly influence the perceptions of others.

The third action area involves the *use of symbols* associated with the change. Language, pictures, and symbolic acts can create a focus for identification and the appearance of a critical mass within the political system of the organization. Widely employed in public and social movements, symbols are equally useful in dealing with the political system within the organization. A variety of devices can be used, such as names and related graphics that clearly identify events, activities, or organizational units. Language is another type of symbol; it can communicate a different way of doing business. People who want to function effectively need to learn new terms of expression; by doing so, they create the perception of broad-scale support. And important signals can be sent through symbolic acts: a particular promotion, a firing, a moving of an office, or an open door.

Finally, managers can help implement change by *building in stability*. Too much uncertainty can create excess anxiety, defensive reactions, and political conflict. The organization must provide certain "anchors" to create a sense of stability during the transition. If organization members are prepared for the change by being given information in advance, they will be somewhat protected against uncertainty. Moreover, some stability can be preserved if managers are careful not to send inconsistent or conflicting messages to the organization during the period of change. It may also be important to maintain certain very visible aspects of the business, for example, by preserving certain units, organizational names, management processes, or staffing patterns, or by keeping people in the same physical locations. Finally, it may help to communicate specifically what will *not* be different—to assuage the fears that everything is changing or that the change will be much greater than what actually is planned.

MOTIVATING CONSTRUCTIVE BEHAVIOR

Most people are made anxious by the uncertainty associated with significant organizational change. They may react with withdrawal, panic, or active resistance. The task of management is somehow to relieve that anxiety and motivate constructive behavior. Four areas for man-

agement action are outlined in table 22.2 and discussed here.

First, managers can expose or create *dissatisfaction with the current state*. People may be psychologically attached to the current state, which is comfortable and known in comparison with the uncertainty associated with the change. They can be helped to see how unrealistic it is to assume that the current state has been completely good, is still good, and will always remain good. The goal is to "unfreeze" people from their inertia and create some willingness to explore the possibility of change. Their anxiety is based in part on fantasies that the future state will create problems, as well as fantasies about how wonderful the current state is.

A good approach to this problem is to supply organization members with specific information, for example, about the events in the environment that have created the need for change. In addition, it is useful to help people understand the economic and business consequences of *not* changing. It may be helpful to identify and emphasize discrepancies between what the situation is and what it should be. In critical cases, it may be necessary to paint a disaster scenario to show people what will

Table 22.2   Motivating constructive behavior

Action	Purpose	Technique
Surface or create dissatisfaction with the current state	Unfreeze from the present state; provide motivation to move away from the present situation	Present information on: Environmental impact Economic impact Goal discrepancies How change affects people Have organization members: Collect and present information
Obtain the appropriate levels of participation in planning and implementing change	Obtain the benefits of participation (motivation, better decisions, communication); control the costs of participation (time, control, conflict, ambiguity)	Create opportunities for participation Diagnosis Design Implementation planning Implementation evaluation Use a variety of participation methods Direct and indirect Information vs. input vs. decision making Broad vs. narrow scope Expertise vs. representation
Reward desired behavior in transition to future state	Shape behavior to support the future state	Give formal rewards Measures Pay Promotion Give informal rewards Recognition and praise Feedback Assignments
Provide time and opportunity to disengage from current state	Help people deal with their attachment and loss associated with change	Allow enough time Create opportunity to vent emotions Have farewell ceremonies

happen if the current state continued unchanged. For example, one manager remarked that if the division did not become successful within eighteen months, "they'll pull buses up to the door, close the plant, and cart away the workers and the machinery."

An alternative to management's presenting this kind of information may be to get organization members involved in collecting and presenting their own perceptions. The information may seem more believable if it comes from peers in the work force.

Here and in other action areas, it is important that managers overcommunicate. Above some threshold, anxiety impairs normal functioning; thus, people may be unable to hear and integrate messages when they first receive them. It may be necessary to communicate key messages two, three, four, and even five times through different media and methods.

Participation in planning and implementing change can also provide motivation. Employees' participation in the change process tends to capture people's excitement. It may result in better decisions because of employee input, and it may create more direct communications through personal involvement. On the other hand, participation also has some costs. It takes time, involves some concession of management control, and may create conflict and increase ambiguity. The question, then, is where, how, and when to build in participation. People may participate in the early diagnosis of problems, in the design or development of solutions, in implementation planning, or in the actual execution of the implementation. Different individuals or groups may participate at different times, depending upon their skills and expertise, the information they have, and their acceptance and ownership of the change. Participation can be direct and widespread, or indirect through representatives. Representatives may be chosen by position, level, or expertise. Some form of participation is usually desirable in view of the costs of no involvement at all.

Managers can also enhance motivation by *rewarding the desired behavior in both the future and the transition state*. People tend to do what they perceive they will be rewarded for. If their behavior seems likely to lead to rewards or outcomes they value, they will be motivated to perform as expected.

During change implementation, the old reward system frequently loses potency before new rewards are established. Sometimes the existing measurement system punishes people for doing things that are required to make the change successful. Management needs to pay special attention to the indicators of performance, to the dispensation of pay or other tangible rewards, and to promotion during the transition. In addition, informal rewards, such as recognition, praise, feedback, or the assignment of different roles should be used to support constructive behavior. And an appropriate reward system for the future state must be clearly reestablished.

Finally, managers can alleviate individual anxiety by *providing time and opportunity to disengage from the current state*. People feel a sense of loss associated with having to change, and predictably go through a process of "letting go" of the old structure. Management should allow the appropriate time for this essential "mourning" period, while giving people enough information and preparation to work through their detachment from the current state. Another technique may be to organize small group discussions in which people are encouraged to talk about their feelings concerning the organizational change. Some may object that such sessions are likely to promote resistance rather than facilitate change. But people will undoubtedly talk about these issues, either formally or informally. If management recognizes the concerns and encourages people to express their feelings, they may be better able to let go of them and move into constructive action. It may also be useful to create ceremony, ritual, or symbols, such as farewell or closing-day ceremonies, to help give people some psychological closure of the old organization.

MANAGING THE TRANSITION

Transitions are frequently characterized by high uncertainty and problems of control because the current state is being disassembled before the future state is fully operational. Managers need to devote as much care, resources, and skill to managing the transition as they would to any other major project. Four specific action areas are relevant (see table 22.3).

The first is to *develop and communicate a clear image of the future state*. It is difficult to manage toward something when people do not know what that something is. No one is sure what is appropriate, helpful, or constructive behavior. Without a clear direction, the organization develops "transition paralysis," and activity grinds to a halt. Managers can help in several specific ways. First, they can articulate a vision of the future state and develop as complete a design as possible. It may also be useful to draw up an impact statement describing the effect the change will have on different parts of the organization and on people. And it is important to maintain a stable vision and to avoid unnecessary or extreme modifications or conflicting views of that vision during the transition.

Finally, there is a need to communicate, repeatedly and through multiple channels—whether video, small-

Table 22.3 Management of transition

Action	Purpose	Technique

Develop and communicate a clear image of the future state	Provide direction for management of transition: reduce ambiguity	Develop as complete a design as possible
		Generate impact statements
		Communicate
		  Repeatedly
		  Multiple channels
		  Tell and sell
		Describe how things will operate
		Communicate clear, stable image or vision of the future

Use multiple and consistent leverage points	Recognize the systemic nature of changes, and reduce potential for creating new problems during transition	Use all four organizational components Anticipate poor fits Sequence changes appropriately
Use transition devices	Create organizational arrangements specifically to manage the transition state	Appoint a transition manager Provide transition resources Design specific transition devices (dual systems, backup) Develop a transition plan

Obtain feedback about the transition state; evaluate success	Determine the progress of the transition; reduce dependence on traditional feedback processes	Use formal methods
		  Interviews
		  Focus groups
		  Surveys and samples
		Use informal channels
		Use participation

group discussions, large-group meetings, or written memos. It is critical to think of this communication as both a telling and a selling activity. People need to be informed, but it is also important to convince them that the change is important. This may necessitate repeated explanations of the rationale for the change, the nature of the future state, and its advantages. The future state needs to be made real, visible, and concrete. Communications should include information on future decision-making and operating procedures. How this is communicated can help shape the vision of the future. For example, one company provided clear and memorable images of the specific types of customer service it was attempting to provide by showing television commercials both inside and outside its organization.

Managers should *use multiple and consistent leverage points for changing behavior*. During a transition, when certain aspects of the organization are being changed, problems may arise from a poor fit between the component elements of the organization. Managers need to use all of these levers for change, modifying the work, the individuals, the formal structure, and the informal arrangements as appropriate. It is also important to monitor and/or predict some of the poor fits that may occur when any of the organizational components are changed. Changes should be planned so as to minimize the mixed messages or the inconsistencies created among elements of the organization.

Certain *transition devices* may prove useful. Because the transition state is different from the current and future states, special organizational arrangements may be needed to manage it. These may include (1) the appointment of a transition manager; (2) the allocation of specific transition resources, including budget, time, and staff; (3) the use of specific transition structures, such as dual-management systems and backup support; and (4) the development of a transition plan. All of these devices can be helpful in bringing needed management attention to the transition itself.

Finally, managers should *build feedback and evaluation of the transition state*. The feedback devices managers normally use to collect information about how the organization is running often break down during a transition. This is particularly serious during a period of change, when anxiety may run high and people may be hesitant to deliver bad news. Therefore, it becomes critical to build in different channels to obtain feedback. Formal methods may include individual interviews, various types of focus-group data collection, surveys used globally or with select samples, or the gathering of feedback during a normal business meeting. Informal channels include senior managers meeting with individuals, having breakfast with groups, informal contacts, or field trips. Finally, feedback is more readily obtained when representatives of key groups participate directly in planning, monitoring, or implementing the change.

THE PROBLEM OF UNCERTAIN FUTURE STATES

The current state/transition state/future state paradigm is a useful means of conceptualizing change and structuring the problems of change. Many organizational changes, however, do not fall into this neat framework. Often, for example, a particular transition is just one of a long and continuous series of changes. The future state is not a stable state but merely a platform for the next transition.

Perhaps even more complex is the transition toward a highly uncertain future. This occurs when an organization moves into a new area of activity about which little is known or in which it will be subject to powerful forces beyond its control. In these cases, managers must plan changes involving movement toward uncertain or unknown future states.

Several special problems are associated with this type of transition. First, the power problem is greatly intensified, because the ambiguity of the unknown future state adds significantly to the uncertainty of the transition period. Because there are so many unknowns, political activity increases as individuals and groups try to position themselves to benefit from real, probable, or imagined events in the future. With an uncertain future state, the transition period is frequently extended—lengthening the time during which political activity is likely.

Second, the level of anxiety is greater. Managers are often unable to describe a specific future state and answer concretely the question, What's going to happen to me? The lack of a clear future state and a clear role for each individual makes it difficult for people to focus on the future and direct their energy at working toward the future. Instead, the free-floating anxiety is left to feed on itself.

Third, the problem of control becomes immensely more difficult if there is no clear future state toward which to manage. The whole concept of transition management seems at first glance to depend on the existence of a defined future.

Finally, situations with uncertain future states are by definition turbulent and potentially threatening to the organization. As a result, senior management is frequently preoccupied with environmental and strategic challenges with little time to attend to the human organization during the transition.

Clearly, then, the uncertain future state poses serious challenges to the basic concepts of implementation management. While it is not yet entirely clear how the problems can be solved, observation indicates several promising approaches for managing the uncertainty. As we become more experienced and collect more data, we should be able to test the validity of these suggested action steps. Figure 22.4 summarizes possible managerial actions related to each of the three problems described previously.

Shaping political dynamics

Several approaches may be useful in managing the political dynamics of transition toward an uncertain future. The first is stabilization through the formation of a small, cohesive planning group at the senior level of the organization to monitor movement toward the future on a regular basis. This group would be responsible for integrating information from different sources and responding to new environmental changes. It actually might be composed of the same people as the senior policy-making or decison-making group, but it would meet regularly with an agenda different from the normal—monitoring and guiding the transition. By staying informal, the group could develop a consensus and a set of relationships that would facilitate quick reactions and decisions when needed.

For such a process to work, the bases of reward in the organization might have to change. What is needed is a systemwide perspective in which each key manager thinks about what moves are best for the organization as a whole, not just for his or her piece of it. If this perspective is to prevail, both formal and informal rewards must be explicitly and significantly tied to performance as a team member rather than tied to one's performance in one's own individual domain.

Finally, leaders must be much more visible to the entire organization during this period. Given the increased levels of anxiety and political activity, the visible actions and words of organizational leaders demonstrating confidence and displaying consistency can

---

Shaping Political Dynamics

1. Create a senior planning group
2. Design special rewards for senior-management collaboration
3. Increase leader visibility

Motivating Constructive Behavior

4. Create a vision of the future
5. Prepare people for uncertainty
6. Define the future state as made up of transitions

Managing the Transition

7. Define a series of short, incremental transitions to alternative futures
8. Maintain tight linkage between planning and transition management
9. Create increased two-way communication flows

Figure 22.4 Implications for change management toward uncertain future states

help to reduce the possible perceptions of "drift" or lack of leadership that frequently occur and in turn lead to increased political maneuvering.

Motivating constructive behavior

While there is no concrete future state on which to focus, some picture of the future can be constructed and communicated. In this case, it is more likely to be a vision or a set of principles or guidelines for doing business than a concrete structure or set of organizational arrangements. It may simply be a statement of "what we will be and what we won't be," or a description of "why we are where we are, and where [in general terms] we're headed."

At the same time, it is important to prepare people to deal with the uncertainty. This may involve education or information that can help employees recognize the sources of the uncertainty and the necessity of living with that uncertainty for some time.

People may want to believe that the uncertainty and turbulence of the transition will someday cease and stability will be restored. In many cases, however, the tranquillity of the past will never return. (Frequently the past is only retrospectively perceived as tranquil—things were not really that stable.) Thus, individuals may have to be prepared to move to a future state that is made up of successive and continuous transition states.

Transition management

Transition management in an uncertain context must be refined into a series of shorter, smaller transitions toward a hypothesized future state or a set of alternative scenarios of the future. Thus, instead of one transition to a fixed future state, we might envision five transitions toward a set of different, possible, ultimate future states, with the first transition being concrete and feasible for all of the possible ultimate alternatives, the second being less concrete, the third even less so, and so on. Change is thus managed incrementally toward an evolving future.

During this process of incremental change management, those responsible for planning (including environmental analysis, strategic planning, and organizational planning) must work very closely with those who manage the transition. When uncertainty is high, the need to coordinate these two functions is critical, and information must move freely, in both directions, between them.

Finally, the management of these transitions requires greatly increased communication flows within the organization. Given the possible intensity and speed of activity, information must flow out to the organization regularly and effectively, and feedback data must be collected to monitor how people are perceiving and dealing with the change.

It is important that senior management balance the time and attention spent on strategy and implementation. The temptation is to focus entirely on strategic issues—to work on resolving the causes of the uncertainty. But the problems of power, anxiety, and control will persist even as senior management tries to find stability or determine directions. If these problems are ignored, the implementation process may become unmanageable. The key implication for managing transition to an uncertain future, then, is to balance the attention given to strategic and implementation concerns: they are concurrent, not sequential.

SUMMARY

The effect of implementation of organizational change is a critical task for managers. Change management requires an understanding of how organizations function as well as an appreciation of the peculiar dynamics of transitions. The view of change presented in this chapter is based on observation over a period of years, of how managers actually handle organizational transitions. Combining that empirical base with the insights of an organizational model, I have tried to provide concepts that can be helpful to managers in understanding and managing complex changes in demanding and uncertain times.

REFERENCES

Beckhard, R., and R. Harris. 1977. *Organizational Transitions.* Reading, Mass.: Addison-Wesley.

Katz, D., and R. L. Kahn. 1966. *The Social Psychology of Organizations.* New York: Wiley.

Nadler, D. A. 1981. "Managing Organizational Change: An Integrative Perspective." *Journal of Applied Behavioral Science* 17, no. 2:191–211.

———. 1982. "Managing Transitions to Uncertain Future States." *Organizational Dynamics* (Summer): 39–45.

Nadler, D. A., and M. L. Tushman. 1977. "A Diagnostic Model of Organizational Behavior." In *Perspectives on Behavior in Organizations,* ed. J. R. Hackman, E. E. Lawler, and L. W. Porter, pp. 35–47. New York: McGraw-Hill.

———. 1979. "A Congruence Model for Diagnosing Organizational Behavior." In *Organizational Psychology: A Book of Readings*, ed. D. Kolb, I. Rubin, and J. McIntyre. 3d ed. Englewood Cliffs, N.J.: Prentice-Hall.

———. 1982. "A Model for Diagnosing Organizational Behavior: Applying a Congruence Perspective." In *Managing Organizations*, ed. D. A. Nadler, M. L. Tushman, and N. G. Hatvany. Boston: Little, Brown.

Pettigrew, A. 1972. *The Politics of Organizational Decision-Making*. London: Tavistock.

Salancik, G. R., and J. Pfeffer. 1977. "Who Gets Power and How They Hold on to It: A Strategic-Contingency Model of Power." *Organizational Dynamics* (Winter): 3-21.

Thompson, J. D., and A. Tuden. 1959. "Strategies, Structures and Processes of Organizational Decision." In *Comparative Studies in Administration*, ed. J. D. Thompson et al., pp. 195-216. Pittsburgh: University of Pittsburgh Press.

Tushman, M. L. 1977. "A Political Approach to Organizations: A Review and Rationale." *Academy of Management Review* 2:206-16.

Watson, G. 1969. "Resistance to Change." In *The Planning of Change*, ed. W. G. Bennis, K. F. Benne, and R. Chin, pp. 449-93. New York: Holt, Rinehart and Winston.

Zaltman, G., and R. Duncan. 1977. *Strategies for Planned Change*. New York: Wiley.

23

The first-line supervisor: past, present, and future

LEONARD A. SCHLESINGER AND JANICE A. KLEIN

One of the major recent preoccupations of American management has been discovering the underlying reasons for our decline in productivity growth. As managers examined their foreign competition, they realized that American companies had fallen dramatically behind in the work application of computer-based technologies and that their supervisory systems and management styles had, in many instances, become outmoded. As an outgrowth of these findings, many organizations rushed to copy the Japanese style of participative management and, within capital constraints, increased investments in new technology. Many observers might argue that the changes occurring in the workplace today are not new and have had parallels in the past. Others might see the changes as mere technical or structural alterations in the work environment. However, there is clear evidence these changes will have major impacts on the nature of interpersonal relationships (especially supervisor-subordinate relations) within organizations.

One current stream of research focuses on the impact of new technologies on workers and their workplaces (Zuboff 1981; Shaiken 1980). Other researchers are attempting to evaluate the effect of new participative management techniques on both employee and employer goals (Goodman 1979; Witte 1980; Katz, Kochan, and Gobeille 1982). When reviewing this research, however,

one discovers that a critical element of the process is neglected, that is, the effect of such workplace transformations on the first-line supervisor. It has long been recognized that one of the keys to good employee-employer relations is the first-line supervisor. Yet as American industry moves to new technology and introduces worker participation programs, most senior managements have ignored the fact that the burdens of successful implementation will fall primarily on the first-line supervisor.

> The foreman, the top sergeant of the factory floor, is facing greater challenge—and probably greater frustration—than ever before. The foreman, management's first line of contact with labor, is caught up in a strange mix of declining powers but new-found importance. No longer master craftsman or shop room tyrant, the foreman is becoming a key figure in the new gospel of worker participation.
>
> But that is not all. Today's foreman is also inundated in increasingly complicated manufacturing technology, bewildering regulations and demands by number-crunching superiors in the front office for more detailed reporting on production data. (Feder 1981 sec. 3, p. 4)

This paper examines the new pressures on first-line supervisors. As a backdrop for that analysis, we first review the historical developments that led up to the formation of the Foreman's Association of America in 1941 and then compare that situation with today's supervisory environment. In this effort, several questions will be addressed.

- How has the first-line supervisor's role been perceived by workers, management, and society in general over time?
- How did the emergence of the Foreman's Association of America and the evolution of vacillating legislative rulings shape the supervisory role and affect the nature of the industrial relations system?

After presenting our historical findings we will outline our perspective on today's first-line supervisor. The major question to be addressed in this section is

- How will the introduction of computer-based technology and participative management or "quality of work life" (QWL) activities (as the major changes in today's workplace) affect first-line supervisors and their interaction with their subordinates?

We will show that the major issues facing first-line supervisors today are not dramatically different from those of the 1940s, although their actual day-to-day roles are undergoing dramatic changes.

The "forgotten man in the middle" was the subject of much research in the 1940s, apparently in response to the rise of the Foreman's Association of America (Gardner and Whyte 1945; Patten 1968; Wray 1949). The underlying reasons for the emergence of such foreman unions were found to be the loss of supervisory status, pay, and job security (American Management Association [AMA] 1945; Northrup 1945; U.S. National War Labor Board 1945; Larrowe 1961). Shortly after World War II, many of the supervisors' grievances appeared to be addressed by upper management. Extensive training programs were developed and administered to assist supervisors in carrying out their roles to help them regain their former status. Over the past two decades, however, the focus of most managerial research has shifted away from the first-line supervisor.

Current developments in computer-based technology and worker participation appear to be changing the role of the first-line supervisor. Both the day-to-day functions of supervisors and their relationships with the work force are being transformed in ways that have yet to be explored in detail. In addition to changes in supervisory status, the age-old issues of pay and job security are once again surfacing. Inflationary pressures, coupled with

contractual cost-of-living adjustments for union members, have contributed to wage-compression problems at the bottom of the management structure. The development of increasingly self-managing work teams is raising questions as to whether the supervisory role, as we have known it, is really needed. While the present legal structure in this country precludes a recurrence of a supervisory union,[1] current pressures on the first-line supervisor are likely to have significant effects on the successful implementation of new technology and QWL efforts. By attending to some of these underlying issues, managers and academics will be in a better position to predict and influence the response of first-line supervisors to changes being introduced in the workplace.

A HISTORICAL PERSPECTIVE

The word "foreman" is a very old one. As far as I know, it originated in trade guilds of Europe. In those days when the men wanted to talk to management there was always someone of mature judgment, probably a little older, a well-skilled man, who could talk a little on his feet. When the men got together, they referred to "John Anderson, fore" and he became the foreman; he was the man who came to the fore; therefore, he was a foreman. (U.S. House of Representatives 1944, 104)

Whatever the origins of the word *foreman*, the supervisor's role probably evolved from Adam Smith's division of labor. As jobs were divided into separate tasks, a need arose to coordinate the work. Initially, that role was performed by the owner of a factory. But as factories grew, one person could no longer possibly perform all required activities. Thus, the direction and coordination of the craftsmen was turned over to a leader or foreman. The foreman learned his new job through trial and error or by observing the owner's behavior. Because there were no formal work rules, the foreman had to devise ways to direct and control his fellow craftsmen. Of course wages were paid in return for production, but because of the inherent conflicts built into labor/management relationships, more was needed to keep an even, undisrupted production flow. Because the foreman was simply a working leader who had production responsi

---

1. This is not true in the public sector. Depending upon the particular inclination of individual state legislatures and administrative agencies, supervisors may or may not be protected under the public-sector collective-bargaining statutes (Hayford and Sinicropi 1976). If the organization of supervisors proves not to have a detrimental effect in the public sector, and the evolving issues in the private sector are not addressed, we may find renewed pressure to reform the National Labor Relations Act to bring supervisors back under the protection of the act.

bilities just as his workers did, he had to find a means of interaction with them.

As markets and production expanded, the management organization became a hierarchy. Increasingly, the foreman directed and coordinated workplace activities. He assumed almost total control over hiring and firing, the pace of work, and payment of workers. Many cite the growth of strikes and other forms of work-force resistance as a response to supervisory abuse of this absolute power (Edwards 1979; Miller 1981). Strikes, however, were not a constant event in all workplaces; thus there had to be some form of peaceful and positive interaction between the foreman and his subordinates. Despite the increased power and status differentials, the foreman found that the reciprocal arrangements developed in earlier times continued to fit well into these new structures. The foreman still found that favors could be traded for labor peace or increased production. He could get his subordinates to accept a technological change or deliver an increase in output simply by promising to hire a friend or relative.

These supervisory-subordinate arrangements worked quite well until the arrival of mass production. As Taylorism divided up craft jobs into simple individual tasks, the foreman's job was also deskilled. In outlining the fundamental principles of scientific management at the beginning of this century, Taylor (1947) described the concept of "functional foremanship," dividing the foreman's job into eight parts. In addition, with the birth of industrial trade unions and corporate welfare practices, company personnel departments emerged and assumed many of the foreman's reciprocal powers. For example, he no longer had the responsibility to hire and fire or to set wage rates (Miller 1981). In addition, the rise of production specialists and industrial engineers led to another layer of individuals who told the foreman and the work force how to perform their jobs, in what order, and how much. "The actual power to control work is thus vested in the line itself, rather than in the person or the foreman. Instead of control appearing to flow from boss to workers, control emerges from the much more impersonal 'technology' " (Edwards 1979, 120).

As these changes in the workplace grew, the work force obtained significant power and rewards by forming and expanding unions. Workers won the right to have formal grievance procedures and to question the actions of their supervisors, and they established their own representative, the steward, to represent them on an equal basis with the supervisor. As a result, while the foreman remained responsible for coordinating the flow of production, he was stripped of many of his managerial levers and status. And while he now had little to say in the formation of company rules and policies, he was ex-

pected to execute such decisions and enforce the procedures. As Wray (1949, 301) states,

> In short, the position of foreman has some of the characteristics of management positions but lacks other crucial ones. Such marginal positions are common in society, and there is reason to believe that they are especially difficult to occupy effectively and with peace of mind. With respect to management, the foreman's position is peripheral rather than in the middle. The poor fellow is in the middle, of course, in the sense that a person may be the middle one of three in a bed; he gets it from both sides!

The creation of the Foreman's Association of America

One night after a weekly bowling game in 1941, a small group of supervisors at the Ford Motor Company decided to form their own union. The organization was a grass-roots effort that mushroomed almost overnight.

> Our original idea was to form a group in just our division of the company for the protection of our rights. All of us were working foremen who had no idea that our movement would spread all through the Ford plants. Foremen whom we did not know personally, and had not heard of, would hear of it in other departments and divisions of Ford and voluntarily request membership. . . . Then, even more astonishing to us, we began getting inquiries from foremen in other large Detroit corporations. After inquiries, came demands for charters; something we did not have at the time. Moreover, we had more than 5,000 members before a single person was paid for his time and effort in handling the many details of membership activity. (Keys 1944, 251)

The rapid growth of the Foreman's Association of America (it had forty thousand members by 1946) indicated that there was indeed a restlessness among the supervisory ranks. Although foremen had been traditionally included in many craft unions (such as in the printing, maritime, construction, and railroad industries), most unions in mass production had specifically excluded foremen and supervisors from their jurisdiction for fear that management would take over control of the unions. Yet as industrial unions became more powerful and the supervisory ranks grew in size to manage the increasing number of production workers, these "middle men" discovered that they had some serious complaints and concerns in common with the work force. As the preamble to the constitution of the Foreman's Association of America (1942) stated, "The foreman has reason to feel that in the ceaseless struggle between ownership and wage labor the foreman will become a victim unless all foremen are organized to protect individuals and interests common and essential to the position of foremen in modern mass production." The increase in foreman unionization in the 1940s reflected several factors, as noted by a U.S. National War Labor Board (1945) panel investigating industrial disputes related to foremen and other supervisors.

1. Long-term changes in the responsibility and authority of foremen;
2. The uncertainty of the foremen concerning their terms of employment and their lack of participation in formulating those terms—in ever-sharpening contrast with the opposite trends in the case of the rank-and-file workers;
3. The lag in the adjustment of the compensation of foremen which occurred early in the war; and
4. The insecurity of the position of individual foremen resulting from the great temporary expansion in the number of foremen in many more plants as a result of the war.

In an American Management Association (AMA 1945, 5) publication, H. W. Anderson, vice-president of General Motors, provided a different perspective on foreman unionization.

1. Pressure on management organizations by rank-and-file unions to break its spirit and its authority;
2. The number of new supervisors to meet war emergency requirements who for the most part have been members of rank-and-file unions;
3. Uncertainty with respect to postwar future—security.

Fundamentally, foreman unionization reflected concerns about change in job status, pay, and job security. Today, these same issues once again threaten first-line supervisors.

Legislative status of first-line supervisors

In the early years of American labor legislation, the status and legal protection of the supervisor changed several times. In the 1934 amendments to the Railway Labor Act, "subordinate officials" were specifically included within the definition of the term *employee* as defined in the act. The Wagner Act of 1935 was silent as to the status of supervisors and foremen. It defined the term "employer" as "any person acting in the interest of an employer, directly or indirectly." The term "employee" was defined to include "any employee." Thus, there was much confusion as to whether supervisors were employees or employers under the Act. This question went

before the National Labor Relations Board on several occasions, with varying responses, until Congress finally resolved the issue in the Taft-Hartley Act of 1947, excluding supervisory employees from the act. This legislative seesaw made it difficult to resolve the foreman's ambiguous status vis-à-vis the rest of the organization.[2] To better understand the position of the supervisor in the early 1940s, it is useful to look at how the National Labor Relations Board and the courts viewed the role.

The NLRB's view of foremen (1935–1947)

It did not take long for the issue of the status of foremen to be raised before the National Labor Relations Board. Less than four months after the passage of the Wagner Act, the board was confronted with a case concerning the discharge of a foreman. By ordering the reinstatement of the foreman, they implicitly ruled that foremen were protected under the act and set the stage for a series of cases to follow. However, they did not explicitly consider whether foremen were employees and whether they could organize into a union for the purposes of collective bargaining. It was not until the formation of the Foreman's Association of America in 1941 that the latter issue was addressed directly.

In the first of a series of cases to decide whether supervisors were protected under the Wagner Act, the board found an organization of stationary engineers to be proper, but sided with the company in determining that assistant chief engineers were too high in the management hierarchy to be included in a bargaining unit (General Motors, 36 NLRB 439). This was the first step toward the board's decisive ruling in Union Collieries Coal Company that foremen were indeed employees and therefore entitled to protection under the Wagner Act. They cited the three specific exclusions in the act's definition of "employee" (agricultural laborers, domestics, and individuals employed by parent or spouse) and decided that because Congress did not explicitly exclude supervisory personnel, supervisors and foremen must be considered employees.

Gerald Reilly, a newly appointed board member, strongly objected to this majority ruling. In his dissent, Reilly formulated the basic position that he would hold in subsequent cases.

> In making this determination it is relevant for us to inquire into the status in the managerial hierarchy

---

2. It should also be noted that under the Fair Labor Standards Act of 1938, foremen and supervisors were considered to fall into the executive category and were exempted from the overtime provisions of the law.

of the personnel claiming to be an appropriate unit. It is likewise relevant for us to inquire as to the effect that their inclusion will have upon the exercise of the rights of self-organization and collective action of the production employees, and it is further relevant for us to inquire whether our determination in any particular case that supervisory employees constitute a unit appropriate for collective bargaining will so compromise the status of such employees as to result in disruption of the practice of collective bargaining rather than industrial peace. . . . To permit these foremen to renounce single-minded allegiance to management, to ally themselves in the same union with the production employees, and at the same time expect them to retain their places at the conference table in the capacity of management spokesmen will create a form of conflict of interest which the entire history of Anglo-American jurisprudence condemns. (Union Collieries Coal Co., 44 NLRB 165)

Executives of American industry were much concerned by the Union Collieries Coal Company decision, and by the board's ruling in Godchaux Sugars (45 NLRB 105), which stated that supervisors could not be denied the right to organize because they chose to be represented by an organization that was an affiliate of the same parent organization chosen by their subordinate employees. The Foreman's Association of America was multiplying in membership and regularly winning election victories. In response, Charles E. Wilson, president of General Motors, sent telegrams to four congressional committees requesting legislation prohibiting the organization of foremen into trade unions. This pressure from business led to the proposal of an amendment to the Selective Service Act prohibiting the organization of supervisory unions in firms supplying goods and services to the federal government. Although the bill did not pass, it stimulated the creation of a powerful management lobby against unionization, which had an opportunity to air its views before the Committee on Military Affairs. One of the classic (and representative) statements during these hearings was made by Wilson of General Motors.

To quote from an authority some 2,000 years old and generally accepted: "No man can serve two masters; for either he will hate the one and love the other; or else he will hold to the one and despise the other" (Matthew 6:24). A foreman could not function in such a position of dual allegiance—either he would be loyal to the union and be obligated to carry out its dictates or he would remain a part of management and carry out management policies. Any attempt on the part of any foreman to "ride both horses" would add to his own confusion and render him ineffective. (U.S. House of Representatives 1944, 66)

These hearings started the regulatory pendulum swinging in the opposite direction. In 1943, William Leiserson retired from the National Labor Relations Board, and President Roosevelt, succumbing to the political tide, replaced him with John M. Houston, a small businessman who owned a nonunion manufacturing plant. Houston and Gerald Reilly, the minority dissenter in the previous cases, now comprised a majority. In their first case together, Maryland Drydock (49 NLRB 733), the board reversed its position and found that units composed of supervisors did not constitute units appropriate to collective bargaining. In so doing, they clearly acknowledged the concerns of the foremen but felt that the foremen's interests lay predominantly with management and therefore they should not be considered employees.

We are not unmindful of the argument advanced by counsel for the union that the development of mass production industry has stripped foremen of much of the plenary authority and managerial discretion which was theirs in an earlier day. Nor are we unaware that the impetus toward foreman organization stems largely from a desire to reestablish the bargaining power of foremen commensurate with the growth of employee self-organization. Likewise, it may be conceded that the position of supervisors would be improved if the provisions of the Act were extended to facilitate collective bargaining by these groups. We are now persuaded that the benefits which supervisory employees might achieve through being certified as collective bargaining units would be outweighed, not only by the dangers inherent in the commingling of management and employee functions, but also in its possible restrictive effect upon the organizational freedom of rank and file employees. . . . To the extent that our decisions in the Union Collieries, Godchaux Sugars, and subsequent cases are inconsistent with this opinion, they are hereby overruled. (Maryland Drydock, 49 NLRB 733)

Chairman Millis, now in the minority, predicted that

Any attempt to frustrate a legitimate desire for self-organization and collective bargaining by such groups can only be harmful to the cause of good industrial relations and efficient production. Indeed denial of the right to bargain collectively under the Act is likely to cause foremen, "forgotten men," with their problems not threshed out, to suffer more in loyalty and to become more militant than would be the case if they were allowed to bargain under the Act. (Maryland Drydock, 49 NLRB 733)

Millis's prophecy, which was written on May 11, 1943, proved to be correct. From July 1, 1943, through November 1944, twenty strikes, involving 131,000 supervisors, were called, resulting in the loss of 699,156 man-days of work (61 NLRB 13).

These wartime strikes placed the board in a very difficult position. In 1944, it sought a middle ground in the Soss Manufacturing case (56 NLRB 348), ruling that supervisors were employees for purposes of section 8(1) and (3) of the act, but were not employees under section 8(5) and (9). Thus, supervisors were given the right to organize into trade unions without the fear of retaliation, but employers were not obligated to bargain with such unions. As a result, supervisors found themselves back in the middle without any clear identification.

Six months later the Soss Manufacturing decision came back to haunt the board. With a concern for the national interest of meeting war requirements, new board member Houston reversed his position on the issue and sided with Millis in the Packard Motor Company case (61 NLRB 4), arguing that employers must bargain with a foreman's union should one be certified.

The union won the election, which was ordered by the board, but Packard refused to bargain until ordered to do so by a federal court. Packard, in turn, filed suit, and it moved up to the Supreme Court (Packard Motor Car, 64 NLRB 1212, 157 F 2d 80, 330 U.S. 485, 490). In its decision, the Court affirmed the board's finding that supervisors were "employees" under the act and stated that it was the responsibility of Congress, not the Court, to create exceptions to the act. Thus this series of vacillating decisions had ended, but the success was short-lived.

Taft-Hartley Act and the Foreman's Association of America

While the Packard case was being forwarded through the judiciary, Congress was reviewing revisions to the Wagner Act. Less than three and one-half months after the Supreme Court had finally cleared the way for supervisory unions, Congress passed the Taft-Hartley Act of 1947, which excluded supervisors from the definition of "employees." Besides the exclusion from section 2(3), "the term 'employee' . . . shall not include any individual employed as a supervisor," Congress also added section 14(a):

> Nothing herein shall prohibit any individual employed as a supervisor from becoming or remaining a member of a labor organization, but no employer subject to this Act shall be compelled to deem individuals defined herein as supervisors as employees for the purpose of any law, either national or local relating to collective bargaining.

Table 23.1   Chronology of major legislative and judicial rulings

Date	Ruling
July 1935	Passage of National Labor Relations Act (Wagner Act)
August 1941	Formation of the Foreman's Association of America
September 1942	Union Collieries Coal Company (44 NLRB 165) supervisors considered as "employees"
October 1942	Godchaux Sugars, Inc. (45 NLRB 105)—right of supervisors to organize could not be denied because they selected a representative who was an affiliate of same parent union representing their subordinates
April 1943	Proposed amendment to the Selective Service Act prohibiting foreman unions in firms supplying goods and services to federal government
May 1943	Maryland Drydock Company (49 NLRB 733)—supervisors denied right to bargain collectively
May 1944	Soss Manufacturing Company (56 NLRB 348)—supervisors could form unions but employers were not required to bargain with them
March 1945	Packard Motor Car Company (61 NLRB 4)—employers required to bargain with foreman's union
March 1947	Packard Motor Car Company (330 U.S. 485, 490)—Supreme Court ruling affirmed supervisory right to bargain collectively
June 1947	Passage of Taft-Hartley Act

After the passage of the Taft-Hartley Act, the decline of the Foreman's Association of America was inevitable. From 1947 to 1952 the association made several attempts at influencing legislative reform but could not rally enough support for its cause. A major reason for its ultimate dissolution, apart from the specific language of the Taft-Hartley Act, was that many of the supervisors' bread-and-butter issues had been recognized and addressed by management.[3] Pay and job-security issues were addressed, and training programs were developed to help foremen regain some of their lost status. Yet, legally, supervisors were left back in the middle with the right to organize but with no guarantees that their employers would recognize them as a union if they should

---

3. It is interesting to note the possible parallel of these management adjustments to those pursued today by many organizations that are implementing comprehensive personnel policies in order to remain nonunion (Foulkes 1980).

decide to form one. In essence, the Taft-Hartley Act acknowledged that first-line supervisors had specific issues and concerns unique to their position, but held they were members of management, which should not have to be put in the position of bargaining with itself.

Table 23.1 summarizes the major legislative and judicial events described above.

Throughout the 1950s supervisory issues received a great deal of attention in organizations—primarily through the development of better selection procedures and training programs. Since then, explicit interest and attention has shifted away from the first-line supervisor. Recent management-oriented literature has focused on mechanisms to enhance industrial performance and competitiveness. Numerous cooperative arrangements have been proposed to improve labor-management relationships. Many writers, however, have lost sight of the fact that, while senior management and personnel managers can alter the formal rules or structures, the labor-management relationship rests fundamentally on the day-to-day informal interactions on the shop floor, shaped by the actions of the first-line supervisor. Thus it is important to explore how first-line supervisors have fared relative to changes in the industrial system, both economically and structurally.

TODAY'S FIRST-LINE SUPERVISOR: HISTORY REPEATS ITSELF

Today, first-line supervisors in industrial organizations confront the same issues that led to the formation of the Foreman's Association of America in 1941: job status, pay, and security. QWL activities and new computer-based technologies both appear to gnaw at supervisory status and job security. At the same time, inflation and increasing wage gains by blue-collar workers have been narrowing the pay differential between foremen and their subordinates.

Supervisory pay

At the end of World War II, wage controls were lifted and, in response to the wage grievances raised by the Foreman's Association of America, most employers adjusted supervisory salaries to a level about 15 percent above that of their subordinates. Since then, most major American corporations have maintained that differential; however, because most first-line supervisors are required to be in the plant at least forty-five minutes before

and after their shift, they spend about 19 percent more time on the job than their subordinates, without additional compensation (Zierden 1980). In addition, most first-line supervisors are paid under a salaried-management wage system in which an annual salary increase is based on performance. While this increase usually takes into account the prior year's increase in cost of living, supervisors do not receive any specific wage adjustment equivalent to the automatic annual, and often semiannual, increase granted to the rank-and-file workers. There is also no guarantee that supervisors will get an annual wage increase. If their performance is rated poorly, they may receive only a token salary increase or possibly none at all. These factors, coupled with the double-digit inflation of the 1970s, left first-line supervisors feeling that they had lost ground in their pay relative to the employees they supervised.

Job security

In response to the job-security issues raised by the Foreman's Association of America, many companies negotiated with their blue-collar unions contract clauses that protected supervisors' seniority should they desire to return to the bargaining unit. Their jobs as supervisors, however, were rarely protected by any formal seniority mechanisms. Many have argued that when large corporations attempt to reduce their work force, they are more reluctant to lay off supervisors than production workers. But since these practices have not been formally articulated as policy, first-line supervisors are often left with a feeling that their subordinates are more secure than they are.

An analysis of the 1977 Quality of Employment Survey indicated that first-line supervisors tend to feel more insecure than their subordinates in the face of a high probability of job loss (Sharp 1982). As shown in table 23.2, foremen, blue-collar workers, and leaders (workers assigned to assist the supervisors) report much the same level of satisfaction with job security on their current job

Table 23.2   Job security index (percent expressing security)

	Probability of job loss		
	Low	Medium	High
Supervisors	72%	58%	17%
Leaders	73%	59%	39%
Workers	69%	46%	26%

Note: Adapted from D. J. Sharp, "The Effect of Nonwork Factors on Perceived Job Security Among Blue Collar Workers," manuscript, Sloan School of Management, MIT, 1982, by permission.

when that job seems secure. As the probability of job loss increases, however, supervisors experience a greater sense of job insecurity, probably because they lack the seniority protection available to workers and leaders. Leaders show the smallest drop in the job-security index, presumably because they tend to be selected from the most senior groups of workers.

Status

Another response to the Foreman's Association of America was the development of extensive training programs to address the changing role and status of the first-line supervisor. These programs were designed to give supervisors a sense of importance as well as some new skills. Some would argue, however, that as long as the role remains unchanged and "in the middle," the first-line supervisor remains powerless (Kanter 1979).

Gouldner (1954b, p. 130) defined status as "a social position occupied by a person within a group . . . [which] exposes the occupant to certain culturally prescribed demands which define his rights and obligations." He notes that status is always in comparison with others and that the higher-status individual holds a power differential over the others. French and Raven (1959, 155–65) identified five bases of social power an individual may hold over others. All seem relevant in explaining first-line supervisors' ability to direct the activities of their subordinates and coordinate the production activity.

1. *Reward Power.* Historically, when supervisors controlled rates of pay and other conditions of employment, this was one of the key sources of formal power. Today, supervisory rewards have become more subtle and are often distributed on a more informal basis, i.e., praise for a job well done.
2. *Coercive Power.* Supervisors have always retained the authority to discipline their work force. In many respects, however, their power is limited by an increasing number of contractual and legal obligations and personnel and managerial review procedures.
3. *Legitimate Power.* This is the delegated power of the position provided to supervisors by the hierarchical structure. Many would argue that over the years this base of power has eroded, but in most organizations supervisors still retain the right to assign work and direct the work activities of their subordinates.
4. *Referent Power.* This power depends to a great extent on the individual supervisor; i.e., if a supervisor personifies a model with which a subordinate identifies, then the supervisor holds power over that individual. However, as long as the supervisor is viewed as the "man in the middle," referent power will be limited to those few subordinates who see the supervisor's position as a step up in the power hierarchy.
5. *Expert Power.* Historically, the most highly skilled craftsmen became the leaders or supervisors. They were respected and given authority because they knew more about the job than other workers did. Here again, many would argue that this power base has been severely eroded with the growth of technical and personnel support functions.[4]

Other views of supervisory status stem from the structure of formal organizations. Parsons distinguished two types of bureaucratic authority.

1. authority that rests on "incumbency of legally defined office," and
2. authority based on "the technical competence." (Gouldner 1954a, 23)

More recently, Witte (1980, 130) has argued that authority is based on two factors: "inducements available to person A (the superior) and the legitimacy of A in B's eyes."

To understand the status or power of the first-line supervisor, one must translate definitions into terms applicable to the factory floor. The interaction of first-line supervisors and their subordinates reveal two distinct sources of power.

1. Prestige or authority granted to supervisors by workers on the basis of their expertise or position.
2. Supervisors' ability to control reciprocal arrangements; or the trading of work for rewards.

Authority based on competence or legitimacy rests on workers' acknowledgement of supervisors' superior knowledge of the management policies, production schedules, and manufacturing processes or of their experience and training. This sort of deference is closely related to the concept of expert power defined by French and Raven (1959), "Where supervision is technically appropriate, it is dependent on the compliance of workers, a compliance which rests on the worker's acceptance of the authority of the foreman in principle (because he believes the foreman has the right to give orders) and on the worker's needs" (Westley 1981, 10).

Control over reciprocal arrangements—the other type of authority—is more associated with the power of the position than the individual. In French and Raven's

---

4. Adapted selection from *Group Dynamics: Research and Theory,* Third Edition, edited by Dorwin Cartwright and Alvin Zander Copyright 1953, 1960 by Harper & Row, Publishers, Inc. Copyright © 1968 by Dorwin Cartwright and Alvin Zander. Reprinted by permission of Harper & Row, Publishers, Inc.

(1959) terminology, this kind of authority would include legitimate as well as reward and coercive power. This is the power of hiring, firing, and otherwise disciplining subordinates, which some writers have cited in their description of the "abusive all-powerful foreman" (Edwards 1979; Miller 1981). But because continuous industrial strife is not the way of life in most workplaces, supervisors must be using some peaceful methods to fulfill their chief status obligation of keeping the production going (Gouldner 1954b, 213). Kotter's (1977, 128) description of a manager's ability to control employees states the problem succinctly.

> Trying to control others solely by directing them and on the basis of the power associated with one's position simply will not work—first, because managers are always dependent on some people over whom they have no formal authority, and second, because virtually no one in modern organizations will passively accept and completely obey a constant stream of orders from someone just because he or she is the "boss."

Supervisors' authority can be seen as an outgrowth of a "mutual dependency" built up between them and their workers. Emerson (1962) illustrated how these interactions could be viewed as reciprocal "power-dependent relationships." One actor may dominate the other, but to maintain an ongoing relationship, the power advantage of the dominant actor must be balanced with that of the other. As Emerson stated, "In general, it appears that an unbalanced relation is unstable for it encourages the use of power which in turn sets in motion processes which we will call (a) cost reduction and (b) balancing operations." (p. 34) This process is closely related to Homan's (1961) description of "distributive justice."

The concept of balance makes Emerson's theory particularly helpful in understanding the historical shift of power between first-line supervisors and workers. In the early days of industrial society, the foreman or supervisor was the dominant actor, with total control of hiring, firing, disciplining, wage rates, and most other decisions affecting a worker's employment. Abusive use of power was common (Edwards 1979; Miller 1981). As Emerson's theory predicts, such abuses drove workers to form coalitions (unions) to balance out the foreman's power. This development tipped the balance the other way, making workers the dominant actors. Seeking to regain their power, foremen formed their own union. Upper management then recognized that they had to enhance the status of the first line of management to regain a balanced relationship. In an environment regulated by the National Labor Relations Act, workplace rules, and union contracts, the reciprocity had to be informal. Foremen could no longer grant the big favors of hiring a friend, but they, as well as their workers, soon found other ways to make a job either enjoyable or miserable.

Supervisors, for example, can ignore violations of plant rules in return for labor peace. Night-shift supervisors are especially notorious for such behavior. As long as production quotas are met for the night, employees in many organizations are often free to do as they like. There are numerous other supervisory favors that have evolved over time, most of which do not require such blatant bending of the rules. If an employee has had a rough night and comes into work a little under the weather, his supervisor may ease up on work requirements for the day, expecting a little extra effort in a later production crunch. Similar arrangements can be traced throughout history:

- Bloch (1936, 205) refers to the reciprocal obligations between feudal lords and vassals. The lords provided protection and a livelihood for the vassals in return for their work and military service. When peasants entered the labor market in the early days of industrialization, they felt a loss of their personal ties with their landlords and viewed the supervisor as an "impersonal system of control" (Wilensky and Lebeaux 1958, 58).
- Gardner and Whyte (1945, 16) cite examples of foremen who helped subordinates carry out their jobs during peak demands or allowed time off for illnesses in the family. They recognized that a supervisor "gives help when it is needed; he asks help when he needs it. He builds up a system of reciprocal obligations which binds workers to him and binds him to them through strong ties of personal loyalty."
- Meyer and Rowan (1977, 358–59) describe a form of reciprocity in their "rituals of confidence and good faith":

> Participants not only commit themselves to supporting an oration's ceremonial facade but also commit themselves to making things work out backstage. The committed participants engage in informal coordination that, although often formally inappropriate, keeps technical activities running smoothly and avoids public embarrassments. In this sense the confidence and good faith generated by ceremonial action is in no way fraudulent. It may even be the most reasonable way to get participants to make their best efforts in situations that are made problematic by institutionalized myths that are at odds with immediate technical demands.

- High degrees of mutual dependence and reciprocity also exist between a police sergeant and his men. "He is dependent upon them to do their work smoothly, without causing untoward concern among the public or others in the department and they are dependent upon him for shielding them from the consequences of the mistakes they will, in good faith and bad, make" (Van Maanen, 1983). Manning (1977, 145) also notes that "these exchange networks channeling information, gifts, nonverbal affirmations, and written data between organizational segments constitute an important determinant of the internal morphology of the organization."

- Gouldner (1954a, 1734) notes that

> formal rules gave supervisors something with which they could "bargain" in order to secure *informal* cooperation from workers. The rules were the "chips" to which the company staked the supervisors and which they could use to play the game; they carved out a "right" which, should supervisors wish to, they could "stand upon." In effect, then, formal bureaucratic rules served as a control device not merely because they provided a legitimating framework for the *allocation* of punishments, but also because they established a punishment which could be *withheld*. By installing a rule, management provided itself with an instrument which was valuable even if it was not used; the rules were serviceable because they created something which could be *given up* as well as *given use*.

To the extent that these reciprocal arrangements are the bases for supervisory status, it is important to understand how, if at all, they are being transformed by changes occurring in American industrial organizations.

COMPUTER-BASED TECHNOLOGY

In many respects, the introduction of computer-based technology to the shop floor is likely to resemble the installation of new technologies in the past. In the early stages of introduction, the focus will be on the new technology; supervisors will have to maintain a close watch on the work force to insure that everything runs smoothly and that everyone looks productive when visitors or the senior management tour the organization (Gouldner 1954b). Over time, however, the new technology will transfer the control and monitoring of production flow and quality control from the supervisor to a computer program. In this way, these new systems will rob the supervisor of several sources for his reciprocal arrangements. In a number of recent contract discussions, unions have made specific demands concerning the utilization of computer-based technologies, because the worker can no longer negotiate with the supervisor for a rapid pace during the morning and a relaxed pace in the afternoon (Zuboff 1981).

The prestige of many of today's supervisors will also decline as the composition of the work force shifts toward children of the computer generation, who are more knowledgeable about the inner workings of the new electronic equipment. The supervisor's expert power will be threatened (French and Raven 1959; Kotter 1977). "One of the strongest causes of resistance to change is the fear of losing one's job or being required to learn new skills. This fear may be especially strong among supervisors, since much of their authority lies in their special knowledge of the system which may have been built up over many years" (Weir and Mills 1973, 63).

Managers must be concerned about the impact of the new computer-based technology on supervisors as well as workers, as suggested by Gouldner's (1954a, 69–70) classic description of the resistance of an older foreman to a new machine because it took away his "safety margin."

> The faster the machine went, the greater the wastage of board in event of a breakdown. If the machine was *not* working at its optimum speed when a breakdown occurred, then there was *less* wasted board. When that happened Johnson would *temporarily* increase the machine's speed and make up the wasted board. In this way no one would be the wiser; [the plant manager] would never know there had been a breakdown and Johnson would escape criticism. If, however, the machine worked at full speed continually, there was no way of making up wastage without calling it to management's attention. Partly for this reason, Johnson had resisted the effort to increase the board machine's speed, and the older foremen under him had shared his feelings.

QUALITY-OF-WORK-LIFE PROGRAMS

> The essential purpose of the introduction of a quality of work life program is to see to it that workers in fact are treated not as inferiors, as second-class citizens, but are given ample opportunity in a meaningful way to make significant contributions to the decision-making process in the plant. This is what it's all about. (Bluestone 1980, 26)

The recent trend toward a new industrial-relations system rests on the premise that labor and management can work together cooperatively to improve the quality of the work environment and increase overall industrial productivity. This movement is often viewed as an Americanization of Japan's family system, in which labor and management are considered equals. Attempting to narrow the gap between workers and management, companies have transferred many of the traditional duties of management to blue-collar employees. Groups of workers are being formed into "quality circles" or "productivity teams" to solve problems and implement solutions without the direction or presence of a supervisor. Self-directing work groups are setting their own production quotas, allocating overtime, and in some cases hiring, evaluating, and disciplining their own peers.

The role of shop management in these new settings is unclear. Several companies have experimented with eliminating the first-line supervisor. In a Philips Electric Company plant in Holland, for example, management found that the use of self-directing work groups made it possible to do without supervisors entirely in one section of the plant. Although the experiment was considered a success, it was not expanded to the rest of the facility because of fear of supervisory repercussions. One of the managers summed up the problem as follows: "Well, the fact is we would have a foremen's strike on our hands if we tried to expand the autonomous work groups. You know, unlike plants in the United States, our foremen are well organized. Lower management levels are extremely threatened by this sort of thing. After all, it makes them superfluous" (Shrank 1978, 221).

Clearly the introduction of participative-management approaches will have dramatic effects on the role of first-line management. Most likely, the role will be eliminated in only a very few circumstances, but supervisors must expect to make significant adjustments in the nature of their interactions with the work force.

Because supervisors bear primary responsibility for implementing QWL activities, they find themselves torn between established organizational norms and practices and the need to communicate and emulate new values of participation. Many companies are discovering that many old-guard supervisors cannot modify their supervisory style, and the process of "strategic replacements" has become commonplace (Gouldner 1954a). As a result, traditional communication channels and ties of loyalty to established personnel and systems are temporarily lost.

Like computer-based technology, participative management will modify both aspects of the first-line supervisor's power, prestige, and ability to control reciprocal arrangements. With the increased downward-communications efforts that characterize QWL activities, the first-line supervisor is no longer the "fountain of knowledge" concerning company policy or business conditions. In fact, as many companies attempt to narrow the information and communication gaps between the top and bottom levels of the hierarchy, senior executives are meeting directly with shop-floor workers, frequently with the unintended result of squeezing out the middle. First-line supervisors are often left out of this process (or allowed to sit in as innocent bystanders). Thus, they lose control of the flow of information between the shop floor and their superiors, which in effect lessens their power or status (Mechanic 1962).

The introduction of quality circles presents a similar dilemma for the first-line supervisor (Nosow 1981). After circle members have analyzed a problem and formulated a solution, they are typically expected to make a formal presentation of the recommendation to upper management for approval and funding. In the past, workers saw the first-line supervisor as the arbiter of requests or suggestions; upper management saw him as a critical link in the communication process. Now, although the supervisor must do much of the necessary background work for quality circle recommendations (to assure a smooth presentation and appropriate recognition of the workers' ideas), the glory tends to go to the workers. Again, supervisors' status may be deflated.

The more advanced QWL activities weaken the distinction between the roles of supervisors and workers. This movement has been prompted partly by the belief that the lack of status differentials has been a factor in the superior productivity of Japanese manufacturing systems. But a more significant force has been the development of successful utilization of self-directing work teams at plants such as the General Foods food operation in Topeka, Kansas. Many of these teams are being given the authority to hire, fire, and otherwise discipline fellow members of their work groups. In addition, many groups are setting their own production quotas and work schedules and determining who will or will not receive overtime. These new responsibilities have been carved out of the areas where first-line supervisors have traditionally controlled reciprocal arrangements.

Changing status alignment of the first-line supervisor

As in the 1940s, debate continues, both in the literature and in practice, as to whether first-line supervisors identify more with management or with workers. This is a critical question because a supervisor's alignment is likely to affect his referent power base (French and Raven 1959; Kotter 1977). If the introduction of computer-based technology and QWL programs shifts past allegiances, old ties will have to be dissolved and new ones formed. Testifying before the U.S. House of Representatives (1944, 105), C. C. Carlton, president of the Automobile Manufacturers Association, described the position of first line supervisors in most organizations.

> I always like to think of a foreman as the key of an arch. . . . A foreman stands between management, which is one side of the arch, and labor, which is the other side. There have always been two kinds of jobs since the beginning of man. One job was a work job, and the workers work at the work jobs; and, in my humble opinion, the authors of the Wagner Act intended to cover the worker who had a work job. The other type of job is the responsibility job, and I do not yet believe that the authors of the Wagner Act had any idea of organizing men who held responsibility jobs. A foreman is a supervisor. He is not a manager, but he is a part of management.

Various ideologies have attempted to explain this division between the workers and supervisors. Marxists would proclaim that the growth of technology divided the population into workers and capitalists, who needed to control the working class. Students of Weber would look to the growth of bureaucracies and cite the need to differentiate the work and thus the development of hierarchies. Others would use various historical events to explain the division of the employer from the employee.

Regardless of which framework is used, there is always a dividing line between the management and the rank and file—but often also a group of people who are caught in the middle. Such is the position of the first-line supervisor in today's organizational work settings.

Some would argue that the passage of the Taft-Hartley Act and the exclusion of supervisory protection under the National Labor Relations Act had an extremely positive effect on the role of foremen, by placing them clearly on the side of management. A "gradual but constant rise in the foreman's status in management" has been reported (Von Bleichen 1967, 474). But it is not clear that supervisors really found a niche in the organization that allows them to feel a part of management. In a 1944 study, Opinion Research Corporation found that 26 percent of the foremen they surveyed felt that they were "more like workers than management," and another 9 percent put themselves in an "in-between" position (AMA 1944, 8). Presumably the remaining 65 percent aligned themselves with management. But in a later study Halpern (1961, 76) found,

> Only 32 percent of the foremen in the study indicated complete identification with management; 50 per-

cent said they felt a part of management in some respects but not in others; 13 percent felt themselves in a special group—neither part of management nor part of the rank and file, and finally, 5 percent saw themselves as not very different from the rank and file.

If those who saw themselves as managers "in some respects but not in others" together with the "special group" are equivalent to the "in-between" supervisors of the earlier study, it would appear the foreman's perception of his management status had significantly declined. In a slightly different context, the Bureau of National Affairs (1971, 18) asked personnel and industrial-relations executives about their first-line supervisors' identification. Of the 226 companies surveyed, 44 percent felt that their supervisors identified mostly with management, 13 percent mostly with rank and file, and 43 percent about the same with both. Although it is technically impossible to compare the results of the three surveys, the findings do not indicate a trend toward higher status in management for supervisors. One might say that supervisors are still back where they started—walking the tightrope between management and workers.

The introduction of computer-based technology and QWL programs may ultimately have the effect of realigning first-line supervisors more with upper management. As duties are taken away from the first-line supervisor by the new technology or by worker participation, the void must be filled by new tasks (unless the role is to be totally eliminated). Many designers of these systems recommend that supervisors be given some of the tasks previously performed by middle managers, freeing top management to spend more time on strategic, long-run issues (Walton and Schlesinger 1979; Westley 1981; Schlesinger 1982). If that should occur, first-line supervisors will become more involved in administrative activities, which will remove them from the shop floor and minute-by-minute interaction with the work force. Supervisors will then be likely to view their new activities as traditionally managerial duties and to align themselves more with management. Inevitably, their status and interaction with their subordinates will also shift. How will this affect companies' abilities to realize the cooperative ideals of QWL programs?

CONCLUSION

The introduction of computer-based technology and QWL activities will bring significant changes in the role of first-line supervisors and their interaction with the work force, yet the major issues that influence supervi-

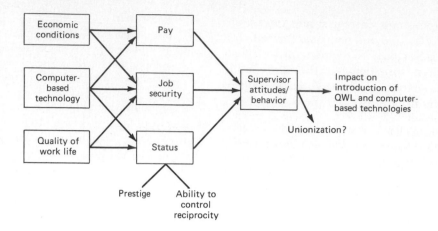

Notes:

I. *Economic conditions*

A. Inflationary pressures coupled with negotiated cost-of-living increases have created compression problems and reduced pay differentials between first-line supervisors and workers. This has created a feeling of inequity in the ranks of the first-line supervisors.

B. Recessionary conditions have contracted the rank-and-file work force, leading to a reduction in the number of first-line supervisors. Recent contract concessions in some industries have required reductions in the supervisory ranks in proportion to layoffs in the union-represented ranks.

II. *Computer-based technology (CBT)*

A. CBT replaces many of the first-line supervisory control functions of monitoring workers and determining the flow of production. Actual reductions in the number of first-line supervisors may not have occurred to date because of the complexity of the technology, which requires a different form of control and trouble shooting, but the perception of first-line supervisors is that their role will be reduced.

B. Replacement of workers with robotics will reduce the current need for first-line supervisors.

C. Reciprocal powers of assigning jobs and setting the work pace are being modified by CBT, which reduces supervisory status (ability to control reciprocity).

D. Often workers (especially younger ones) are more knowledgeable than their supervisors concerning CBT. The implementation of this technology will lead to a loss in supervisory status (prestige) due to the knowledge gap.

III. *Participation/quality of work life (QWL) activities*

A. With the introduction of QWL, many organizations are significantly altering the job of first-line supervisors. The role is often totally eliminated with the establishment of autonomous work groups. Thus, first-line supervisors may have concerns regarding their job security.

B. With increased open communications, first-line supervisors are often no longer more knowledgeable about business activities than their workers. Thus, the supervisory status (prestige) is reduced.

C. In participative work settings many workers are making decisions formerly made by first-line supervisors, such as assigning work, setting schedules, allocating overtime, etc. This reduces the supervisor's scope of reciprocal powers.

Figure 23.1 First-line supervisory pressures: a summary

sory satisfaction and effectiveness remain unchanged. As shown in figure 23.1, the combination of economic pressures, computer-based technology, and QWL activities is affecting the first-line supervisor's pay, job security, and status in ways quite similar to the threats to pay, security, and status that led to the formation of the Foreman's Association of America in the 1940s.

Without the support of supervisor unionization, little progress has been made on these issues over the past four decades. It remains to be seen whether we will utilize the opportunities provided by the coming role changes to address these issues creatively and with resolve.

REFERENCES

American Management Association. 1944. *Management and the Foreman.* AMA Production Series #154.

American Management Association. 1945. *Should Management Be Unionized?* AMA Personnel Series #90.

Bloch, M. 1936. "Feudalism: European." *The Encyclopedia of the Social Sciences.* Vol. 6:203–10.

Bluestone, I. 1980. *1980 General Motors QWL Executive Conference.* General Motors, Detroit.

Bureau of National Affairs. 1971. *Status of First Level Supervisors.* BNA Survey #95 (November).

Edwards, R. C. 1979. *Contested Terrain: The Transformation of the Work Place in the Twentieth Century.* New York: Basic Books.

Emerson, R. M. 1962. "Power-Dependence Relations." *American Sociological Review* 27:31–40.

Feder, B. J. 1981. "New Twists in the Foreman's World." *New York Times,* 17 May.

Foreman's Association of America. 1942. *Constitution of the Foreman's Association of America.*

Foulkes, F. K. 1980. *Personnel Policies in Large Nonunion Companies.* Englewood Cliffs, N.J.: Prentice-Hall.

French, J. R. P., and B. Raven. 1959. "The Bases of Social Power." In *Group Dynamics: Research and Theory,* ed. D. Cartwright and A. Zander, pp. 150–67. New York: Harper & Row.

Gardner, B. B., and W. F. Whyte. 1945. "The Man in the Middle: Position and Problems of the Foreman." *Applied Anthropology* 4, no. 2 (Spring).

Goodman, P. S. 1979. *Assessing Organizational Change: The Rushton Quality of Work Experiment.* New York: Wiley.

Gouldner, A. W. 1954a. *Patterns of Industrial Bureaucracy.* Glencoe, Ill.: Free Press.

———. 1954b. *Wildcat Strike.* Yellow Springs, Ohio: Antioch.

Halpern, R. S. 1961. "Employee Unionization and Foremen's Attitudes." *Administrative Science Quarterly* 6:73–88.

Hayford, S. L., and A. Sinicropi. 1976. "Bargaining Rights Status of Public Sector Supervisors." *Industrial Relations* 15 (February): 44–61.

Homans, G. C. 1961. *Social Behavior—Its Elementary Forms.* New York: Harcourt, Brace and World.

Kanter, R. M. 1979. "Power Failure in Management Circuits." *Harvard Business Review* (July-August): 65–75.

Katz, H. C., T. A. Kochan, and K. R. Gobeille. 1982. "Industrial Relations Performance and the Effects of Quality of Working Life Efforts: An Interplant Analysis." Manuscript, Sloan School of Management, MIT.

Keys, R. H. 1944. "Union Membership and Collective Bargaining by Foremen." *Mechanical Engineering* 66, no. 4 (April): 251–56.

Kotter, J. P. 1977. "Power, Dependence, and Effective Management." *Harvard Business Review* 55, no. 4 (July-August): 125–36.

Larrowe, C. P. 1961. "Meteor on the Industrial Relations Horizon: The Foreman's Association of America." *Labor History* 2, no. 3 (Fall): 259–94.

Manning, P. K. 1977. *Police Work: The Social Organization of Policing.* Cambridge, Mass.: MIT Press.

Mechanic, D. 1962. "Sources of Power of Lower Participants in Complex Organizations." *Administrative Science Quarterly* 7:349–364.

Meyer, J. W., and B. Rowan. 1977. "Institutional Organizations: Formal Structure as Myth and Ceremony." *American Journal of Sociology* 83, no. 2 (October): 279–303.

Miller, G. 1981. *It's a Living: Work in Modern Society.* New York: St. Martin's Press.

Moore, J. E. 1970. "The National Labor Relations Board and Supervisors." *Labor Law Journal* 21, no. 4 (April): 195–205.

Northrup, H. R. 1945. "The Foreman's Association of America." *Harvard Business Review* 23, no. 2 (Winter): 187–202.

Nosow, S. 1981. "The First Line Supervisor, The Linchpin in the Japanese Quality Control Circle." *Industrial Management* (January-February).

Patten, T. H. 1968. *The Foreman: Forgotten Man of Management.* American Management Association.

Schlesinger, L. 1982. *Quality of Work Life and the Supervisor.* New York: Praeger.

Shaiken, H. 1980. "Detroit Downsizes U.S. Jobs." *Nation* (11 October).

Sharp, D. J. 1982. "The Effect of Nonwork Factors on Perceived Job Security Among Blue Collar Workers." Manuscript, Sloan School of Management, MIT.

Shrank, R. 1978. *10,000 Working Days.* Cambridge, Mass.: MIT Press.

Taylor, F. 1947. *Scientific Management.* New York: Harper & Bros.

U.S. Congress. House. 1944. *Full Utilization of Manpower.* Hearings Before the Committee on Military Affairs. 78th Cong., 1st sess. HR 2239, HR 1742, and HR 922.

U.S. National War Labor Board. 1945. *Report and Findings of a Panel of the National War Labor Board in Certain Disputes Involving Supervisors.* Washington, D.C.: GPO.

Van Maanen, J. 1983. "The Boss: Supervision in the American Police Agency." In *Controlling the Police Organization,* ed. M. Punch. Cambridge, Mass.: MIT Press.

Von Bleichen, B. 1967. "Government, Labor, and the Foreman." In *The Foreman's Handbook,* ed. Carl Heyel. New York: McGraw-Hill.

Walton, R. E., and L. A. Schlesinger. 1979. "Do Supervisors Thrive in Participative Work Systems?" *Organizational Dynamics* 7, no. 3 (Winter): 25–38.

Weir, M., and S. Mills. 1973. "The Supervisor as a Change Catalyst." *Industrial Relations Journal* 4, no. 4 (Winter): 61–69.

Westley, W. A. 1981. *Quality of Working Life: The Role of the Supervisor.* Ottawa, Ontario: Minister of Labor, Government of Canada.

Wilensky, H. L., and C. N. Lebeaux. 1958. *Industrial Society and Social Welfare.* New York: Russell Sage Foundation.

Witte, J. F. 1980. *Democracy, Authority, and Alienation in*

Work: Workers' Participation in an American Corporation. Chicago: University of Chicago Press.

Wray, D. E. 1949. "Marginal Men of Industry: The Foremen." *American Journal of Sociology* 54:298–301.

Yale Law Journal 82. 1973. "New Standards for Domination and Support Under Section 8(a)(2)."

Zierden, W. 1980. "Needed: Top Management to the Role of the First Line Supervisor." *SAM Advanced Management Journal* 45, no. 3 (Summer): 18–25.

Zuboff, S. 1981. "Psychological and Organizational Implications of Computer-Mediated Work." Working paper #1224, Sloan School of Management, MIT.

24

Middle managers: their jobs and behavior
ROSEMARY STEWART

The term *middle manager* is ambiguous: where does "middle" start and end? In this handbook there is a practical limitation imposed by the chapters on supervisors and on general managers. The former poses no problem, as no one will want to call first-line supervisors "middle managers." In long hierarchies, particularly in production, there will be a level of junior management between the supervisors and the several levels of middle management. The cutoff between junior and middle may be clear in a particular organization but may be obscured when comparisons are made across organizations.

General managers must be excluded from this chapter even though in some organizations they may be responsible for the profitability of small divisions and sufficiently far down in the hierarchy to be called middle managers. However, it is right that general managers should be treated separately, as their jobs have distinctive characteristics, but much of the discussion here will also apply to them and to other managers.

In this chapter *middle manager* will be used broadly for all those below top management, other than general managers, who are responsible for the work of other managers. *Top management* will be considered to include the chief executive of the parent organization and, in large organizations of important subsidiaries, those reporting to him or her. A more precise definition of middle management is not necessary for the content of this chapter. The word *manager* will be used throughout; those who prefer *executive* can substitute it.

The purpose of this chapter is to describe the implications for practitioners of what research has shown about the nature of managerial jobs and how managers do them. These implications are relevant to human-resource managers, to any manager responsible for other managers, and to managers thinking about their own careers. A chapter about middle managers could discuss many other subjects: beliefs, attitudes, backgrounds, and careers, to mention only a few. One chapter cannot do justice to such a wide range, hence the limitation to jobs and behavior. And because these are the subjects I have been researching, teaching, and consulting on for many years, I can write about them most knowledgeably.

Recruitment, selection, job evaluation, appraisal, training and development, career planning, and management succession all require an understanding of the distinctive characteristics of individual jobs. Many of them require, too, a knowledge of what jobs can be grouped together for particular purposes. This means understanding the nature and implications of their similarities and differences. To increase this understanding is the main aim of this chapter.

USING MANAGERIAL BEHAVIOR TO UNDERSTAND MANAGERIAL WORK

The main advances in understanding the nature of managerial work have come from studying managerial behavior. The numbers included in the most important early studies were small: the pioneering study by Carlson (1951) of 9 Swedish company presidents; Sayles's (1964) interview and observational study of 75 junior and middle managers in one American company; Stewart's (1967) diary study of 160 middle and senior managers in different companies; and Mintzberg's (1973) observational study of 5 chief executives.

These studies gave some new perspectives upon managerial work. The extreme fragmentation of much of the working day was first noticed by Carlson, and it was confirmed in all the subsequent studies. The importance of personal contacts, face-to-face or on the telephone, was also highlighted. These were shown to take up the large majority of the time of the managers studied. Emerging from these and later studies was a picture of what managers do that differs from the traditional one, which stressed planning, organizing, motivating, and controlling. Carlson suggested the simile of a puppet with other people pulling the strings. This image of the chief executives whom he studied is too extreme, yet all the studies present a picture of managers who are less in command than traditional writings on management suggest. Managers, the studies showed, spend much of their time responding to people and events as they occur, switching their attention every few minutes from one person or problem to another; often very dependent upon the help of people in other departments; and trying to make the best of opportunities as they occur.

These are some of the generalizations about managerial work that can be made from the early studies of managerial behavior. However, there are limitations to generalizing from studies of particular managers, because doing so makes two assumptions that may be incorrect: (1) that other managerial jobs will have similar characteristics to those studied; (2) that the nature of a job can be equated with the behavior of the individual jobholder. Later studies have cast doubts on the truth of both these assumptions (Stewart 1967; Stewart, Smith, Blake, and Wingate 1980, and Stewart 1982.) Therefore, we need to consider what has been learned about differences in managerial jobs and in behavior.

THE DIVERSITY OF MIDDLE-MANAGEMENT JOBS

The most commonly used divisions between managerial jobs are by functions, such as production and marketing, and by level in the hierarchy: junior, middle, and top management. These two divisions make broad distinctions between the amount and nature of the manager's responsibility. This chapter will argue that

they are inadequate for many purposes of managing managerial resources. They can also be misleading, because they classify together jobs that differ in important respects and cut across these customary classifications.

A major need for any manager concerned with the selection, appraisal, training, and development of other managers, or for the individual manager making career decisions, is to know what dimensions to use in considering a job and in comparing it with others. One approach has been to produce a list of activities that a manager might, or would, have to carry out, such as "investigate complaints from customers"; next, the jobholder, or someone else, would be asked to rate how much the listed items apply to the job; then one would group jobs according to the relative importance of these different activities (cf. Hemphill 1960; Tornow and Pinto 1976). This method can highlight some of the differences between jobs, but it is laborious and relies on perceptions of the importance of different characteristics that are likely to vary for different jobholders. To be useful we need simpler, more easily recognized, categories for considering the differences between jobs and for grouping them together. We need, too, to know for what purposes we can generalize across broad categories of managers, even all middle managers, and for that we need to understand the difference within middle-management jobs.

One simple way of distinguishing between jobs came out of a study of the nature and difficulty of the relationships they require (Stewart 1976). This study showed that managerial jobs differ both in whom the manager has to work with and in the intrinsic difficulty of these relationships irrespective of the particular personalities. The contacts that a job may require are those with boss or bosses and other senior managers, subordinates, managers at the same level in the organization (peers), juniors in other departments, and people outside the organization. The research identified twelve contact types according to the amount of time spent with these different categories of people. These types are based on three main distinctions. The first is between the majority of managers who spend most of their time with other people and the small minority who have primarily backroom desk jobs requiring less than half their time with others. The latter includes some jobs in accounting and in research. The second is between the managers whose jobs require only contacts within the organization and those who have to spend some, or a large amount, of their time working with people outside it. The third is between jobs where the manager must enlist the cooperation of people in other departments compared with those that only need supervisory skills. Some jobs require mainly or wholly contacts within the straight-line hierarchy, though they may also involve external contacts. This is true, for example, of many branch managers and some other heads of separate units. In their internal contacts such jobs require good supervisory skills, but not the ability to influence peers. They contrast with the more political influencing skills required of most staff managers, of those working in many posts at head offices and in matrix organizations. In all these jobs the manager must be able to influence those over whom he or she has no authority.

It is easy to make broad distinctions between the categories of contacts that a job requires. Even such a simple question as Who does the manager in this job have to work with? can be helpful in thinking of the kind of relationship skills that the job demands. For selection, appraisal, and training one should go further and ask, Which are the most important contacts? and Whom does the manager *need* to influence or satisfy?

The need for particular contacts can be determined fairly easily. Jobs differ, for example, in the extent to which, and the reasons for which, the manager needs to spend time with subordinates. The subordinates may be competent and well motivated. They may indeed know much more about their work than their boss. The boss may meet them primarily to exchange information and to provide a sounding board for them to try out solutions to problems. The need for subordinate contact in such jobs is much less than where the subordinates are inexperienced and poorly qualified, or where their morale is low. In the same way, the need for contacts with peers, with external contacts, and with the boss can be determined (Stewart 1976).

Understanding the need for different contacts can help in trying to decide the suitability of candidates for a particular post. It can stimulate one to ask about their previous experience and the relationship skills they have displayed. In appraisals one can consider whether the subordinate is distributing his or her time and effort most effectively between different contacts. A marketing manager, for example, may spend too much time with her product managers and too little with the sales and production managers. A production manager may be spending nearly all his time with subordinates and almost none in peer contacts. What is the most effective distribution of time between different groups of people may vary at different periods in the job, but the current needs for particular contacts is something that the individual manager should be trying to assess and that his or her boss should consider during the appraisal interview.

Middle-management jobs differ in their need for different kinds of contacts. They also differ in the nature and difficulty of these relationships. Sayles's study (1964) can help us to understand the different kinds of

lateral relationships that exist. He observed engineering managers in a large chemical company and used them as an illustration of the nature and variety of these relationships. He distinguished seven kinds of lateral relationships, which he called work-flow, trading, service, advisory, auditing, stabilization, and innovation. A particular job can require a manager to be skillful at several of them. Sayles argued that managers had to recognize and learn to manage the diverse dependencies of their jobs and to distinguish between the influencing skills required in different kinds of relationships.

Stewart's 1976 study can help us to distinguish both the overall difficulty of a job and the difficulty of particular relationships. Sixteen diverse managerial jobs in industry, commerce, and transportation were studied using several diaries, observation, and interviews with the jobholders and their bosses. The jobs were found to differ widely both in the overall level of relationship difficulty and in the difficulty of particular kinds of relationships. An understanding of such differences is of most relevance for management education and training. Later work in particular companies has shown that managers in one organization who are at the same level, and even in the same function, can have jobs that differ in the nature and difficulty of their relationships. Such differences should be taken into account in selection, appraisals, in identifying training needs, and in career planning. Relationships with particular types of contacts are inherently more difficult in some kinds of middle-management jobs than in others. For example, managers who have to influence their peers to provide the services that they need will have a harder task if they have nothing to offer in exchange for good service than if they do. A job specification should describe both the relationships that are necessary in the job, those that are particularly important, and the factors that make it easy or difficult for the jobholder to get the necessary coooperation. An appraisal should also take these factors into account so that any training needs can be more precisely identified than a general statement about improving relationship skills.

The nature and the difficulty of relationships is one important and relatively easily identified way in which middle-management jobs can differ from each other. Such differences should be taken into account in considering the kinds of career experience that an individual needs and the kinds that different jobs can offer. A military practice of giving officers a period in a staff job is one that should be applied more often in other kinds of organization, because it provides experience in the exercise of influencing skills different from those required in many line-management jobs.

Traditional distinctions in the amount of responsibility focus on the size of the budget, the annual turnover, the number of staff, and other measures. Most of these can be expected to increase with one's level in the hierarchy, though there are some top jobs with only a few subordinates. However, there is one commonly neglected aspect of responsibility, that of exposure, which exists in some junior- and middle-management jobs and not in some top posts. An exposed job is one where the jobholder can make, and must run the risk of making, mistakes or a poor performance, either of which can be clearly identified as his or hers. Timing affects the degree of exposure: if the holder has time to try to retrieve a mistake or to improve on a bad month's sales figures the job is less immediately exposed than if the mistake of poor performance is immediately identifiable. In some jobs it is easy to retrieve mistakes; in others it may be difficult or impossible, such as an unguarded remark to a journalist that is published. The importance of the mistakes that can be made relative to the job responsibilities will also determine how exposed the job is. Probably the most important factor in exposure is whether the jobholder can in practice share responsibility for decisions so that he or she cannot be blamed. A general manager with profit responsibility is not able to do this, but other senior managers may be able to do so if many decisions are group ones. The existence and the amount of exposure in a job is an aspect of it that should be considered in selection, because some individuals will not be effective in an exposed job: they will either suffer too much stress or may play for safety. The previously mentioned study (1976) showed how exposure varied in the different jobs and suggested that the amount of exposure was most in danger of being underrated in some staff jobs.

One of the myths propounded in many management books, and even apparently believed by many top managers, is that top-management jobs are the only ones concerned with strategy. Middle management is seen as being responsible for implementation and perhaps occasionally also for tactics, but not for taking strategic decisions. This belief can be a costly error because it means that middle managers who are in jobs that require strategic thinking are not taught about or appraised on the quality of their strategic decisions—*strategic* meaning decisions about the nature of the work that should be done by the manager and his or her subordinates. The distinction between the middle-management jobs that require strategic thinking and those that do not is one of the most important and most neglected differences between them. It is a difference that is easy to distinguish if one asks whether the work for which the manager is responsible has a clearly defined and prescribed output. This is true, for example, of many production-management posts, particularly those that are part of a work flow process, like a melting-shop manager in a

steelworks. It is not true of many staff and service jobs. The kind of advice that is given and the types of services that are offered are often, in part at least, at the manager's discretion. This is true of departmental heads like personnel, management services, or market research, but it can be true too for the jobs of some of their immediate subordinates.

Decisions about the selection, appraisal, training, and career development of middle managers should take account of which jobs require strategic thinking. In selection it is important to decide what the organization wants: is it maintenance of the existing services and their smooth running, or is it their development? Some candidates would mainly think about the former when in the job while others would seek to change and improve their department's services. The need for strategic thinking is relevant to appraisals because the boss should, if necessary, be helping the subordinate to see that there are such strategic choices in the job, as well as appraising the suitability of the choices that are made. Training can help to illustrate the kinds of strategic choices that are likely to exist in different jobs. It can seek to encourage the attitude of mind that recognizes and appraises the strategic choices that have to be made. The distinction between jobs where the holder has an opportunity to change the nature of the department's output and those where it is fixed should also be considered in career development. It is another argument for the suggestion made earlier for a mixture of line and staff jobs in a manager's career to provide experience in the exercise of different kinds of analytical and interpersonal skills.

The word *choice* describes another way of thinking about differences in middle-management jobs (Stewart 1982). Choice in a job can be defined as the opportunities that it offers for one person to do different kinds of work and to do it in different ways from another person. The greater these opportunities the more "discretion" the job can be said to offer; but the word *choice* is preferable to *discretion* because the latter suggests something that is conferred, whereas choices are broader and take account of the fact that individuals will in practice exercise choice even if discretion has not been given.

The nature and the extent of the opportunities for choice is an important difference between middle-management jobs. Earlier we described other differences. Some of these also offer choices. Probably the most important choice in some middle-management jobs is to think strategically about what work the manager's department should be doing. Jobs that permit changes in the output for which the manager is responsible will also offer a choice in whether, and if so the extent to which, the manager thinks strategically.

Most middle-management jobs offer at least some choice in the time and attention given to different contacts. In many jobs there is a choice between the amount of time spent with subordinates compared with peers. In those jobs that require or permit contacts outside the organization there is usually a choice of emphasis between internal and external contacts. This may be so large that there can be a considerable difference in the work that jobholders choose to do. Members of a management team, or a manager and deputy or assistant, may be able to divide the work that has to be done in different ways, so that one is primarily the external person and the other(s) concentrate(s) upon internal management. The choice of the relative emphasis given to different contacts is an example of a more general choice of emphasis and of selection between different kinds of work. Middle-management jobs within the same organization, even within the same function, may offer considerable differences in the opportunities for these types of choice.

Membership in one or more management groups—more than one in many jobs in matrix organizations—can offer distinctive choices that do not exist in jobs that do not carry membership of such groups. There may be a choice between concentrating just on one's own responsibilities in the discussions or taking an interest in the wider activities of the group, particularly a group composed of one's boss and one's peers. As one manager put it, "I can delegate everything except my contribution to the management team." There may be a choice in whether the jobholder gets involved in the work of one or more other members of the group. There can be choices, too, in the roles that one plays in the group. Belbin (1981) in his account of eight different roles that can be played in a management team, suggested that although individuals have a preferred role they may be able to adopt another one. Whether a job is part of a management group(s) is one of the factors that ought to be considered in specifying the experience and abilities required for the post. It is relevant, too, in appraisals, because the superior should consider what contribution the manager is making to the group as well as how he or she is managing their own responsibilities. Jobs where group membership is an important component of the job can also be used for career development because they can help to prepare for team working, which in many companies is a top-management requirement.

A different kind of choice that exists in some jobs is the opportunity to become an expert beyond, or other than, that usually required of the jobholder. This may not be readily recognized as a potential characteristic of a job. In a recent study (Stewart 1982) this choice was found to exist in a surprisingly wide variety of jobs in certain types of companies: those with informal communications that cut across functions and levels. In such organizations individuals are freer to develop a distinctive expertise and it is more likely to be known and used. We found managers who exercised this choice in many staff jobs in marketing and in production and engineering. There can be advantages for an organization that allows sufficient flexibility in jobs for individuals to pursue their own interests to the extent of developing an expertise. One advantage is that this expertise can be useful both currently and sometimes as the seed corn for a new business. Another is that the individual will enjoy both acquiring the knowledge and the recognition that it may provide.

This account of some of the ways in which middle-management jobs in the same organization can differ from each other, apart from functional differences, points to the need to reconsider what similarities there are and to recognize what kind of differences exist. Once this is done one can apply this knowledge to selection for a particular job, to picking out the aspects of a job that should be discussed in an appraisal, to identifying the likely training needs for someone moving from a different kind of job, and to improving career development by providing experience in jobs that require a variety of abilities for success.

GENERALIZATIONS ABOUT MANAGERIAL WORK

Much has been learned about managerial work by studying managerial behavior, but in doing so the limitations to generalizing about it have now become clearer (Stewart 1967, 1976, 1982; Kotter 1982). This is true even if discussion is limited to middle managers. The variety of their jobs is one reason; another is that their behavior itself differs even among managers in similar jobs: they will do different kinds of work and do it in different ways. Some middle-management jobs offer a lot of scope for such individual choice.

A few generalizations about the nature of managerial work are still likely to be sufficiently applicable to be useful. There are broad statements, like Mintzberg's (1973) division of managerial work into three groups: interpersonal, informational, and decision-making. There are also more specific research findings, like the large amount of fragmentation of the working day. This fragmentation is true of most but not all managerial jobs; in most, too, there is an element of choice—as lecturers on the effective use of executive time are paid to point out.

The opportunities for choice of content and method that exist in managerial jobs is one of the useful generalizations. It has important implications for managing managerial resources. We should recast the ways in which we commonly think of jobs in order to take account of it. A new way of thinking about jobs will have repercussions upon our personnel practices. In our job descriptions we should say what kinds of choices are available, and in our job specifications, what the most important choices at the present time are. What the most appropriate choices for effectiveness in the job are may vary over time with changes in the situation. They will vary, too, with the qualifications, experience, and preferences of existing members of the role set. In assessing potential candidates for a post we should examine the preferences that they have displayed in previous jobs and ask ourselves what choices they are likely to make in the new one and whether these are what is wanted at the present time. For some jobs account needs to be taken of the choices that are currently being made by those with whom the jobholder will have to work closely so that theirs can be complemented or, if desirable, augmented.

BEHAVIOR OF MIDDLE MANAGERS

The behavior of middle managers is of vital concern to those at the top because much of the success of the organization rests upon what they do. This seems likely to remain true in large organizations despite earlier predictions that the computer will make most middle managers unnecessary. So far we have talked about managerial behavior in terms of the information that it can provide about jobs, but there are many other reasons for senior managers being interested in it. They may try to discover, for example, how head-office policies are being treated in practice; what aspects of the business are getting most attention and which are getting too little; what impression of the organization middle managers are giving to outsiders; what effects different remuneration packages have upon behavior; what impact middle managers are having upon their subordinates and whether they are developing them.

Top management seeks to determine or, if it is recognized that that aim may be unrealistic, to influence the behavior of middle managers. Foremost means are by recruitment, selection, induction, appraisal, training, and promotion policies. Then there are other organizational policies and procedures that seek to do so, including the ways in which managers are rewarded. Of

considerable importance, too, are the codes of behavior that top management seeks to promote both by its policies and by its example. The "climate" of the organization, which is another way of saying the codes of behavior that exist in practice, is an important influence upon what managers do and upon what they see they can do. Their perception of the choices that are available to them will be shaped by the climate. This is true both of the choices that top management would applaud and of those which, if they knew of them, they would seek to prevent being exercised.

One clear message for top management emerges from studies in many different areas: the need to recognize that middle managers will often exercise choices that top management does not expect and may not want. The most famous study of managerial behavior is still that of Dalton (1959), in which he showed how middle managers practiced deception to protect themselves from head office. Subsequent studies have confirmed the political character of much managerial activity. This fact is known by most managers, though there are still some, perhaps particularly those with a scientific training, who think that a good case is sufficient to gain acceptance or that a policy will necessarily get implemented. The latter belief is also a tempting one for human-resource managers!

Middle managers may or may not be committed to the organization, but even if they are they will still have their own individual and sectional interests. The choices that may be exercised by middle managers include political activity to further personal ambitions, particular group interests, and to circumvent control systems. Such political activity varies in its intensity in different organizations, but it is always likely to exist to some extent and, therefore, needs to be recognized as one of the characteristics of organizational life, particularly in large organizations.

Middle managers will differ in what they consider important, as Maccoby (1976) illuminatingly showed in his distinction between the gamesman, jungle fighter, craftsman, and companyman. This will affect what they do and how they relate to the organization. An understanding of what an individual considers most important will help in forecasting the choices that individuals are likely to make in their jobs.

SUMMARY AND IMPLICATIONS

The traditional ways of distinguishing between managerial jobs by level in the hierarchy and by function are not adequate for effective selection, appraisal, training, development, and career planning. There are other differences that cut across both level and function. An understanding of these can improve the management of managerial resources. The term *middle management*, although it is useful for some purposes, covers a much more heterogeneous group of jobs than is generally recognized. There are differences in the kind of contacts that the jobholder must make, in the need for them, and in the inherent difficulty of the relationships. These differences affect the kinds and amount of social skills that are required. Some jobs are more exposed than others; some are not exposed at all.

The nature and the amount of opportunities for choice is another important difference between middle-management jobs. It is evidenced by the fact that even individuals in similar jobs will, at the minimum, emphasize some aspects more than others, and in jobs offering greater choice may spend much of their time on different kinds of work. One simple illustration of this is the differences in the amount of time spent with subordinates, peers, and people outside the organization. The choice that exists in some middle-management jobs, particularly staff and service ones, is to think strategically about the nature of the output from the managers' unit. Strategic thinking is generally seen as a prerogative of top management, yet in any job where the output is not clearly defined there is scope, and a need, for such thinking. The extent of the choice that exists even within

middle-management jobs needs to be considered at all stages of managing managerial resources. It also needs to be understood by individual managers, who should be thinking about the best use of their own time.

It is easier to treat middle management as an entity, except for differences in the knowledge needed in each function, but that is to neglect other differences that are relevant for selection appraisal, training, career development, and management succession. The differences within middle-management jobs cited above need recognition at all stages to provide the managers that organizations need now and in the future. Some easily made distinctions have been suggested that managers can use to think more searchingly about how they and their subordinates do their jobs. They can also help human-resource managers to gain a better understanding of the types of job that exist within their own organization.

This chapter has concentrated primarily upon the behavior of middle managers as a way of understanding the nature of their jobs. It has shown their wide diversity. An interest in the behavior of middle managers is important to top management and to human-resource managers for other reasons as well. Whatever the reason, a useful generalization is the need to recognize that middle managers will often exercise more choice than they expect and will make some choices that they do not want. One reason for this is that political activity exists at the middle-management level, not just at the top.

REFERENCES

Belbin, R. M. 1981. *Management Teams: Why They Succeed or Fail.* London: Heinemann.

Carlson, S. 1951. *Executive Behaviour: A Study of the Work Load and the Working Methods of Managing Directors.* Stockholm: Strömbergs.

Dalton, M. 1959. *Men Who Manage: Fusions of Feeling and Theory in Administration.* New York: Wiley.

Hemphill, J. K. 1960. *Dimensions of Executive Positions.* Research monograph 98, Bureau of Business Research, Ohio State University.

Kotter, J. 1982. *The General Managers.* New York: Free Press.

Maccoby, M. 1976. *The Gamesman: The New Corporate Leaders.* New York: Simon & Schuster.

Mintzberg, H. 1973. *The Nature of Managerial Work.* New York: Harper & Row.

Sayles, L. R. 1964. *Managerial Behavior: Administration in Complex Organizations.* New York: McGraw-Hill.

Stewart, R. 1967. *Managers and Their Jobs: A Study of the Similarities and Differences in the Ways Managers Spend Their Time.* London: Macmillan.

——. 1976. *Contrasts in Management: A Study of the Different Types of Managers' Jobs: Their Demands and Choices.* Maidenhead, England: McGraw-Hill.

——. 1982. *Choices for the Manager: A Guide to Managerial Work and Behaviour.* Maidenhead, England: McGraw-Hill.

Stewart, R., P. Smith, J. Blake, and P. Wingate. 1980. *The District Administrator in the National Health Service.* London: King Edward's Hospital Fund for London, distributed by Pitman Medical.

Tornow, W., and P. Pinto. 1976. "The Development of Managerial Taxonomy: A System for Describing, Classifying and Evaluating Executive Positions." *Journal of Applied Psychology* 61:410–18.

25

General managers

JAY A. CONGER AND JOHN P. KOTTER

INTRODUCTION

General managers are often most effective when they behave in an apparently "unprofessional" manner. This chapter explores that paradox.

General managers—executives with some multifunctional responsibility for a business or businesses—find their ability to manage professionally severely constrained by people, time, and information. They overcome these handicaps primarily by using two processes: agenda setting and networking. Both techniques encourage and require behavior different from that associated with professional management.

Research has shown that certain personal and background traits seem to be related to effectiveness on the job. These findings have significant implications for the selection, development, and management of general managers.

MYTHS VERSUS REALITY

Popular mythology places the general manager

> . . . above the industrial din, away from the dirt, noise, and irrationality of people and products. He dresses well. His secretary is alert and helpful. His office is as clean, quiet, and subdued as that of any other

professional. He plans, organizes, and controls large enterprises in a calm, logical, dispassionate, and decisive manner. He surveys computer printouts, calculates profits and losses, sells and acquires subsidiaries, and imposes systems for monitoring and motivating employees, applying a general body of rules to each special circumstance. The symbols in which he thinks and works are those of finance, law, accounting, and psychology. Finessed and massaged into every new formulation, they yield wondrous abstractions.[1]

Only in recent years has this image of orderliness and rationality been challenged. Sune Carlson's (1951) pioneering study of company directors, for example, found that senior executives "scarcely had time to start on a new task or to sit down . . . before they were interrupted by a visitor or telephone call" (pp. 73–74). Similarly, Henry Mintzberg (1973) discovered that "the manager, particularly at senior levels . . . overburdened with work . . . is driven by brevity, fragmentation, and superficiality in his tasks. . . . And he can do little to increase his available time or significantly enhance his power to manage" (p. 173). John Kotter's (1982a) study of effective general managers (GMs) uncovered further obstacles.

---

1. See "The Profession of Management," *The New Republic*, 27 July, 1981.

Decision-making was often extremely difficult because of the great uncertainties involved, the diversity of issues, and the enormous quantity of potentially relevant information. At the same time, implementation was frequently problematic because of the large and diverse group of people involved and because the job typically supplied little control over those people . . . [2]

We no longer see the GM as a dispassionate, Olympian planner, but rather as a harried individual whose power is constrained by time, people, and inadequate information. For despite popular perceptions, GMs rely far less on a disciplined process of decision making and formal management than we might suspect. The nature of their jobs makes it impossible to spend the day in seclusion and reflection. Instead, they must be in constant interaction with others—not only peers and subordinates but hundreds and sometimes thousands of individuals outside their chain of command and even outside their organization (see Kotter 1982a; Mintzberg 1973; Harrell 1961).

The interactions themselves are typically short, spontaneous, and disjointed conversations, rich in information and covering a broad range of topics—many unrelated to the business or the organization. Seldom in these daily encounters does the GM make a major decision or directly order another person to do something. Instead, we see the GM asking question after question and reacting to others' initiatives. Much of his or her day is unplanned, filled with unexpected events, encounters, and interruptions. Even those with elaborately planned schedules find themselves continually drawn off onto topics not on their official agendas.

On the surface, this freewheeling behavior seems inconsistent with the professional manager's role. In fact, however, it represents an effective response to the demands and dependencies of the job. Good general managers rely very much on a system of informal agendas and relationship networks to meet the challenges of their job.

Common job demands

Despite differences in their specific responsibilities and the contexts in which they operate, all GMs face certain common, difficult job demands. These include (1) setting the basic goals, policies, and strategic objectives of the firm despite great uncertainty; (2) achieving a delicate balance in allocating scarce resources among a diverse and often competing set of functions and businesses; (3) keeping on top of a broad range of activities whose complexity makes it difficult to spot and solve problems; (4) getting the necessary information, cooperation, and support from bosses to do the job; (5) eliciting cooperation from corporate staff, other departments, and important external groups not under the GM's formal control; and (6) motivating, controlling, and coordinating a large and diverse group of subordinates. To put it more succinctly, two fundamental dilemmas confront GMs.

1. They must figure out what to do despite high uncertainty, great diversity, and an enormous quantity of potentially relevant information.
2. They must implement goals by relying on a large and diverse set of people over whom they may have little or no formal control.

These dilemmas in turn make it difficult for the GM to go about organizing, planning, staffing, and managing in a direct and formal way. As Tom Peters suggests, many of the more formal managerial tools are less effective under conditions of uncertainty and dependency on others. For instance, planning systems or organizational structures take time to implement, yet many situations demand more immediate action. Moreover, formal systems sometimes become so deeply embedded that they lose their ability to adapt to new contingencies and so outlive their effectiveness. Fletcher Byron, the chief executive officer of Koppers Co., once remarked, "Of all the things I have observed about corporations, the most disturbing has been a tendency toward overorganization, producing a rigidity that is intolerable in an era of rapidly accelerating change" (Peters 1978, 7).

Given these limitations, GMs require more flexible and informal tools to achieve their organizational goals—tools that enable them to manage uncertainty and a broad range of information while depending on a large number of people. Effective GMs use two such processes: agenda setting and networking.

Agenda setting

Because they are continually required to make decisions, GMs must have some formal plan or agenda to guide their choices. Otherwise short-term pressures almost always overwhelm longer-term responsibilities, leading to inconsistency in decision making. Yet unanticipated events or gaps in information may make it difficult to follow such plans, and formal planning systems may limit flexibility. As one executive explained the dilemma,

Table 25.1 The contents of a typical GM's agenda: Key issues

Time Frame	Financial	Business (product/market)	Organizational (people)
Long-run (5–20 years)	Usually contains only a vague notion of revenues or ROI desired in ten or twenty years.	Usually only a vague notion of what kind of business (products and markets) the GM wants to develop.	Usually vague; sometimes includes notion about the "type" of company the GM wants and the caliber of management that will be needed.
Medium-run (1–5 years)	Typically includes a fairly specific set of goals for sales and income and ROI for the next five years.	Typically includes some goals and plans for growing the business, such as: • see that three new products are introduced before 1981; • explore acquisition possibilities in the area of . . .	Usually includes a short list of items such as: • by 1982 will need a major reorganization; • before 1981, I need a replacement for Corey.
Short-run (0–12 months)	Typically includes a very detailed list of financial objectives for the quarter and the year in all financial areas; sales, expenses, income, ROI, etc.	Usually includes a set of general objectives and plans aimed at such things as: • the market share for various products; • the inventory levels of various lines.	Typically includes a list of items such as: • find a replacement for Smith soon; • get Jones to commit himself to a more aggressive set of five-year objectives.

Note: Reprinted with permission of The Free Press, a Division of Macmillan, Inc., from *The General Managers* by John P. Kotter, p. 62. Copyright © 1982 by The Free Press.

Formal planning . . . gets people to think about hypothetical choices and the consequences of those choices to the organization, and more importantly, to themselves. This can lead to conflict and political activity which can be very damaging to the company. Written plans can also . . . rigidify people's expectations. People make plans based on those expectations. Then if the world changes, and you have to change the plan, you run into great resistance. Don't misunderstand me now. I'm not suggesting that formal planning is bad or unnecessary. Quite the contrary, it's absolutely necessary. But it's not enough by itself. And you have got to be careful regarding what to include in the planning.[3]

If GMs are to accomplish their objectives, formal planning needs to be complemented by a flexible system of agenda setting.

Although effective GMs start their jobs with a knowledge of their business and some sense of what is needed, they rarely begin with a clear or comprehensive agenda. Instead, they spend the first six months to a year collecting information before beginning to build an agenda of specific, loosely connected objectives. Over time these agendas become more complete and connected so that ultimately they form a set of loosely connected goals and plans that address the GM's long-, medium-, and short-run responsibilities and a range of financial, product/market, and organizational issues (see table 25.1).

Both Kotter and Mintzberg observed that these plans are often not spelled out in formal documents. Mintzberg (1975, 51) reported, "The plans of the CEOs I studied seemed to exist only in their heads—as flexible but often specific intuitions." And while agendas were often consistent with formal plans, Kotter (1982b, 160–61) found three important differences.

- First, the formal plans tend to be written mostly in terms of detailed financial numbers. The GMs' agendas tend to be less detailed in financial objectives and more detailed in strategies and plans for the business or the organization.

- Second, formal plans usually focus entirely on the short and moderate run (3 months to 5 years), while GMs' agendas tend to focus on a broader time frame, which includes the immediate future (1 to 30 days) and the longer run (5 to 20 years).

- Finally, the formal plans tend to be more explicit, rigorous, and logical, especially regarding how various financial items fit together. GMs' agendas often contain lists of goals or plans that are not as explicitly connected.

Moreover, GMs do not rely primarily on formal planning meetings and documents for strategic information; rather they depend on a process of continuous questioning, day after day, in informal meetings and interactions to build or modify their agendas. By sampling as the opportunity arises, the GM can collect more timely, accurate, and pertinent information than would otherwise be possible. Peters (1979, 166) concurs: "The

---

3. Reprinted with permission of The Free Press, a Division of Macmillan, Inc., from *The General Managers* by John P. Kotter, pp. 76–77. Copyright © 1982 by The Free Press.

more views and visits in the top executive's schedule, and the more numerous interruptions and unscheduled encounters, the better informed he is likely to be." Mintzberg (1975, 52) provides additional support: "Managers seem to cherish 'soft' information, especially gossip, hearsay, and speculation. Why? The reason is its timeliness; today's gossip may be tomorrow's fact. The manager who is not accessible for the telephone call informing him that his biggest customer was seen golfing with his main competitor may read about a dramatic drop in sales in the next quarterly report. But then it's too late." And although the agenda-setting process seems contrary to conventional wisdom on management, studies by Quinn (1980), Stewart (1979), Aguilar (1967), McCaskey (1974), and others suggest that GMs commonly use such a process (see also Lindblom 1959, 79; March and Simon 1958; Barnard 1939; Mintzberg 1973).

While most effective GMs use some form of agenda setting, Kotter found that the better performers tended to develop agendas based on more explicit business strategies with longer time frames and covering a wider range of issues. They also looked for opportunities that would allow them to accomplish multiple goals at one time and that were consistent with their other plans. Projects that seemed important to others but failed to meet these criteria were either resisted or discarded. In addition, these GMs were generally more aggressive in getting information and more skillful in asking questions and in seeking out the bad news as well as the good (Kotter 1982b, 161).

Network building

The nature of the job also requires that GMs devote significant time and energy to developing a network of cooperative relationships. These represent a critical source of GMs' power; without them, it might well be impossible to accomplish their tasks. For networks are not only important in implementation but also represent a vital system of information processing, keeping the GM in touch with responsibilities and relationships more effectively than would be possible with any formal system, computer based or not. As Mintzberg (1975, 52) observed, "Every bit of evidence suggests that the manager identifies decision situations . . . not with the aggregated abstractions a MIS provides, but with specific tidbits of information."

These networks allow the GM to gather timely though initially fragmented pieces of information. When collected from a variety of sources and pieced together, these tidbits yield a fuller and richer set of insights into a decision than the GM could ever hope to achieve alone.

Richard Neustadt's (1960) study of U.S. presidents showed that their success rested on a similar process of information gathering.

> It is not information of a general sort that helps a president see personal stakes, not summaries, not surveys, not the bland amalgams. Rather . . . it is the odds and ends of tangible detail that pieced together in his mind illuminate the underside of issues put before him. To help himself, he must reach out as widely as he can for every scrap of fact, opinion, gossip, bearing on his interests and relationships as president. He must become his own director of his own central intelligence. (pp. 153–54)

The actual process of network building is generally most intense in the first few months of a GM's tenure. Thereafter the emphasis appears to shift toward using networks to implement and update agendas. The networks themselves become quite extensive and often include hundreds or thousands of individuals: subordinates, peers, superiors, superiors' superiors, subordinates' subordinates, and outsiders (see figure 25.1 for a typical GM's network).

Because of the diversity of these networks, relationships vary widely—some are stronger, some more personal than others. In general, however, the more dependent a GM feels on an individual or group of individuals, the stronger the relationship tends to be. Kotter (1982a) describes one typical executive's network.

> B. J. Sparksman . . . had a good working relationship with his four bosses and a close mentor-protege relationship with one of them. He had cordial-to-good relations with his peers, some of whom were friends and all of whom were aware of his track record and his mentorlike relationship to one of the three people who ran his organization. He also had a good working relationship with many of the subordinates of his peers (hundreds of people), based mostly on his reputation. B. J. had a close and strong working relationship with all but one of his main direct reports because they respected him, because he was the boss, and because he had promoted some of them into their current positions; those men also had strong cooperative relationships among themselves (they thought of themselves as a team). At least one of his direct reports looked to B. J. as a mentor and adviser, and was particularly close to him. B. J. also knew the vast majority of his subordinates' subordinates, if only by name, and had good relationships with them based on his reputation, the fact that he was the boss, and the fact that he tried to treat them fairly and with respect. Outside the firm, B. J. maintained fairly strong relationships with dozens of top people in firms that were important clients for his organization. He also had relationships with dozens of other important people in his local com-

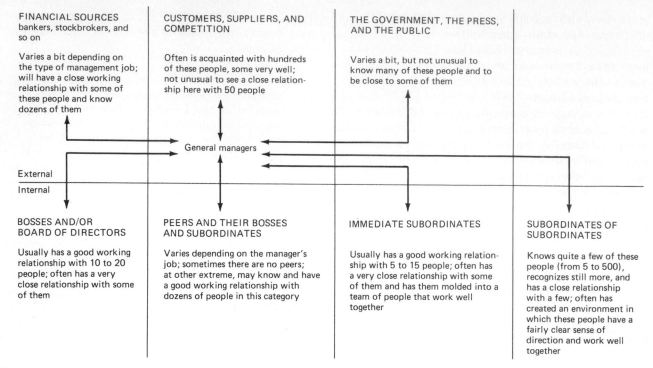

FINANCIAL SOURCES
bankers, stockbrokers, and so on

Varies a bit depending on the type of management job; will have a close working relationship with some of these people and know dozens of them

CUSTOMERS, SUPPLIERS, AND COMPETITION

Often is acquainted with hundreds of these people, some very well; not unusual to see a close relationship here with 50 people

THE GOVERNMENT, THE PRESS, AND THE PUBLIC

Varies a bit, but not unusual to know many of these people and to be close to some of them

General managers

External

Internal

BOSSES AND/OR BOARD OF DIRECTORS

Usually has a good working relationship with 10 to 20 people; often has a very close relationship with some of them

PEERS AND THEIR BOSSES AND SUBORDINATES

Varies depending on the manager's job; sometimes there are no peers; at other extreme, may know and have a good working relationship with dozens of people in this category

IMMEDIATE SUBORDINATES

Usually has a good working relationship with 5 to 15 people; often has a very close relationship with some of them and has them molded into a team of people that work well together

SUBORDINATES OF SUBORDINATES

Knows quite a few of these people (from 5 to 500), recognizes still more, and has a close relationship with a few; often has created an environment in which these people have a fairly clear sense of direction and work well together

Figure 25.1 A typical GM's network. (Reprinted with permission of The Free Press, a Division of Macmillan, Inc., from *The General Managers* by John P. Kotter, p. 68. Copyright © 1982 by The Free Press.)

munity, which he had acquired through his participation on civic projects, on charity boards, and similar activities.[4]

Research by Pettigrew (1973), Peters (1978), Pfeffer (1981), and Kotter (1977, 1982a) has shown that GMs use a wide range of influence tactics to build such networks. For instance, GMs can try to make others feel legitimately obligated to them by doing favors or by stressing formal relationships. Or they can encourage individuals to identify with them by role modeling or by taking an appealing stand or action. They may carefully nurture perceptions of their professional reputation, or try to make others feel dependent on them for resources, status, career advancement, or other support.

In addition to developing relationships with existing personnel, they can strengthen and alter their networks by moving, hiring, or firing subordinates. In a similar way, they can change suppliers or bankers, lobby to get different people into peer positions, and even reorganize the board of directors to ensure resources and support. Furthermore, they can attempt to shape relationships among the various parts of their networks by employing formal management tools—plenary

processes, organizational structure, control and reward systems, and so on—and informal methods to create appropriate environments or cultures that support their agendas and encourage cooperation.

If fewer people were involved and more time were available, it might well be possible to build a network without resorting to such indirect or manipulative approaches. But given the reality of limited authority and high dependence on others, GMs have found a very useful approach. Most effective GMs appear to use this process, although Kotter found that the better performers tended to use networking more aggressively and skillfully. For example, they used a wider variety of methods with greater skill and created networks with many more talented people in them. In addition they built strong ties to and among their subordinates. Their less able counterparts tended to use fewer network-building methods, employed them less aggressively, and thereby created weaker networks (Kotter 1982b, 163).

Getting networks to implement agendas

After developing an agenda and network, effective GMs turn their attention toward using their relationships to implement the organization's goals. In doing so, they call upon practically their entire network for help—not just subordinates or superiors. In their own actions, GMs aim

---

4. Reprinted with permission of The Free Press, a Division of Macmillan, Inc., from *The General Managers* by John P. Kotter, pp. 67–68. Copyright © 1982 by The Free Press.

to satisfy multiple goals while avoiding activities that would seriously disturb their important relationships.

The more effective GMs limit their interventions once their networks have been set in motion, giving those capable the authority to carry out the agenda's objectives. As Jack Gabarro (1979, 4) points out, "The greater the size or complexity of an organization, the more difficult it is for managers to exercise direct influence. . . . Generally speaking, the higher a manager rises in an organization or the greater the scope of responsibilities the more dependent he or she becomes—of necessity—on key subordinates for the success of the organization's performance." Thus GMs achieve much of their impact in a very indirect way, becoming directly involved only when they feel something on the agenda will not be accomplished otherwise.

Kotter found that the better-performing GMs mobilized more people to get more things done and did so by using a wider range of influence tactics. They asked, encouraged, cajoled, praised, rewarded, demanded, manipulated, and motivated others with great skill in face-to-face interactions. They also relied more heavily on indirect influence than did less-able managers, who tended to use a narrower range of influence techniques and to apply them with less finesse (Kotter 1982b, 166).

Why it all works

Given traditional notions about executive work, we might expect GMs to approach their agenda-setting task in a formally structured and analytical manner and to rely on the hierarchy for building relationships (e.g., through official authority and selection of subordinates). And in executing and updating agendas, we might expect GMs to depend primarily on their direct subordinates and to deal with them in a straightforward manner, controlling and evaluating their efforts.

Instead, we find more informal and subtle processes at play. The responsibilities and activities of the typical GM are subject to so much uncertainty that more formal procedures are often ineffective. Similarly, because so many diverse relationships are associated with the job, representing a bond of dependence rather than a source of power, GMs cannot rely on their authority to be effective. Instead, they must skillfully use agendas and networks to accomplish their goals. The very behavior that seems superficially "unprofessional"—informal interactions, impromptu questioning, unplanned interruptions, and so on—permits the flexibility and timeliness needed to manage the job's uncertainty and dependence.

Kotter's (1982b, 158–59) study identifies ten patterns of daily behavior that seem surprisingly unmanagerial.

But when viewed in the light of the requirements of agenda setting and networking, these behaviors begin to make sense.

1. *Most GMs spend 70 percent or more of their time with others, and most of that time is spent in short, disjointed conversations. A typical conversation might cover ten unrelated topics in five minutes.* Working through networks inevitably means spending time with other people. Short, disjointed conversations allow the GM to cover quickly the range of important issues.

2. *The people with whom the GM spends time include many in addition to their direct subordinates and their bosses. GMs regularly go around the formal chain of command and see people who may appear to be unimportant outsiders.* Because their networks tend to include everyone on whom they depend, GMs cast their nets wide.

3. *GMs' discussions are not limited to planning, business strategy, and other "top management concerns," but cover a wide range of topics,* because their agendas tend to include items related to all the long-, medium-, and short-term responsibilities associated with their jobs.

4. *In their conversations, GMs typically ask a great many questions—perhaps hundreds in a half hour.* This is because agenda setting requires the GM to collect information on a continuous basis from network members.

5. *During these conversations, GMs rarely seem to make significant decisions.* Rather, working with unwritten agendas, GMs often make invisible decisions within their own minds.

6. *GM conversations often include a considerable amount of joking and talking about issues unrelated to work,* which can help to build and maintain relationships with network members.

7. *Even in GM conversations that focus on business matters, the substantive issue may be relatively unimportant to the organization.* Maintaining relationships requires the GM to deal with issues that other people care about, regardless of their intrinsic importance.

8. *In these encounters, GMs seldom give orders in the traditional sense.* For a GM who works primarily through a network rather than the hierarchy, a direct order is only one possible method of getting another person to do something, and often may not be feasible.

9. *GMs often try to influence other people by asking, cajoling, persuading, or intimidating.* The GM tries to elicit help from network members through a variety of indirect means.

10. *In allocating their time, GMs often react to others' initiatives, so that their day is largely unplanned. Even those with elaborately detailed schedules often end*

up spending a great deal of time on topics not on their official agendas. The ability to respond flexibly to opportunities as they arise may be the key to the efficiency of the networking/agenda-setting approach.

Of all these patterns observed in the GM's daily behavior, perhaps the most difficult to understand is the lack of planning. Executives do not map out their days in advance but react to situations as they arise; this seemingly unmanagerial behavior may be the most important and efficient of all. Consider the following example: On his way to a meeting, a GM bumped into a staff member who reported to him. In a two-minute conversation, he was able to (1) ask two questions and receive the information he needed; (2) reinforce their good relationship by sincerely complimenting the staff member on something she had done; and (3) get her to agree to do something the GM needed done.

Throughout the encounter, the GM's behavior was guided by an internalized agenda that prompted him to ask important questions and request an important action. His relationship with this member of his network allowed him to get the cooperation he needed to do all this very quickly. Planning the encounter in advance, perhaps by setting up a meeting, would have required far more time, and if the manager had not already developed a good relationship with the staff member, such a meeting might have been ineffective. So, paradoxically, the efficiency and effectiveness of the encounter is due precisely to its informal and reactive nature.

In summary, general managers' agendas allow them to react in a highly efficient way to opportunities in the flow of events around them while remaining true to some broader and more explicit framework. GMs' networks permit short, efficient conversations that might otherwise be impossible. Together, the agendas and networks help GMs to deal effectively with very demanding jobs in fewer than sixty hours per week.

Networking and agenda setting in different kinds of managerial jobs

Agenda setting and network building are more important in some GM jobs than others. In addition, job differences determine the focus and time frame of agendas, the size and character of the network, and the GM's control over it. To understand these differences, we need to consider both the type of job involved and the context in which the job is found.

Before World War I, there was essentially only one type of corporate GM: the chief executive officer (CEO) in a functionally organized firm who reported to a board of directors. Even up to World War II, perhaps 95 percent or more of GM jobs were of this type. In the last forty years, however, as corporations have become larger, more diverse, and more complex, many new kinds of GM jobs have been invented to fit these new structures. Today, at least seven types can be distinguished: the functional CEO, the multidivisional CEO, the group GM, the autonomous divisional GM, the semiautonomous divisional GM, the product/market GM, and the operations GM. The operations GM, the functional CEO, and the autonomous divisional GM are probably the most common types, and the group GM and the multidivisional CEO are perhaps the rarest (accounting for only 1 percent of the total) (Juers 1979). Other types also exist, but they are rare or only now emerging.

Figure 25.2 describes the seven forms and highlights differences in responsibilities and relationships. It also shows differences in job demands among six types of GM jobs in one corporation. As one moves down the hierarchy in large companies, the GM job tends to become less demanding in terms of long-run issues and more demanding in terms of short-run concerns and lateral relations. Job demands also may be related to an organization's size, age, performance, product/market diversity, and culture. For example, in larger businesses, GMs tend to have bigger jobs simply because of the sheer volume of demands and activities. Their responsibilities are more complex, causing decision making to be more difficult. Because job-related relationships tend to be more numerous in large organizations, it can be much harder to accomplish tasks through others. And the monitoring of daily operations is more difficult because GMs can seldom get as much detailed information for decision making as would be available in a smaller organization.

The age of the firm and the maturity of its products and markets also create differences in job demands. In a business that has been around for some time and has a mature marketplace, standard routines have been developed for collecting information and making decisions; as a result, the overall level of uncertainty is lower. The human environment may also be different in long-established mature contexts. The work force is often older and may hold more rigid beliefs about responsibilities and relationships within the firm. These factors will obviously affect the quality of the implementation and relationship demands on the GM.

Performance level is a third major variable that creates differences among GM jobs. When a business is performing well, Kotter (1982a) found GMs do not have to think hard about new directions or new ways of allocating resources. Poor performance, on the other hand, requires more demanding decisions in both areas. In addition, speed is typically more important when perfor-

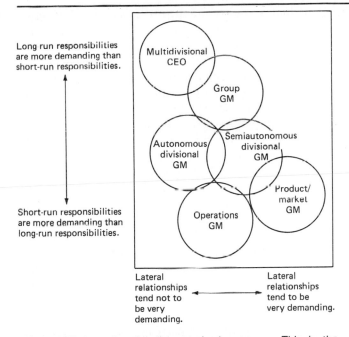

Long run responsibilities are more demanding than short-run responsibilities.

Short-run responsibilities are more demanding than long-run responsibilities.

Lateral relationships tend not to be very demanding.

Lateral relationships tend to be very demanding.

3. Group GM: This type of GM job reports to a general manager and has GMs reporting to him or her. A typical group GM, for example, might report to a multidivisional CEO and have six or seven division GMs reporting to him or her. This job also tends to have fewer long-run responsibilities than a CEO and fewer important external lateral relations (e.g., to bankers).

4. Autonomous divisional GM: This type of GM is in many ways like the traditional job (no. 1), except that it reports to a GM, not a chairman or a board of directors. Like the group GM, it tends to have fewer long-run responsibilities than a CEO, more short-run responsibilities, and fewer corporate external lateral relations. Often the key responsibility in this job is for profit.

5. Semiautonomous divisional GM: This GM job is like the last, except that it has fewer downward but more internal lateral relations (to corporate staff), it reports more closely upward, and it tends to have slightly fewer responsibilities overall. For example, a typical semiautonomous divisional GM might report to a group GM (who has several other divisions with related products/services/markets) and have to rely to some degree on corporate (or group-level) personnel, legal, accounting, public-relations, and financial staff.

6. Product/market GM: This type of general manager tends to have even fewer types of subordinates and more lateral relations. Typically, for example, most marketing people will report to this job, but the GM will be responsible for coordinating the manufacturing and engineering people associated with his business (or businesses). This job also has still fewer long-run responsibilities.

7. Operations GM: This final type of common GM job tends to have the least overall long run and the most short-run responsibility. It tends to have mostly manufacturing or sales/service personnel reporting to it and to have some lateral relations (which, unlike the product/market GM, it does not have to coordinate closely). A typical operations GM might be the manager of a plant or a group of plants who is only partially responsible for a calculated profit, and who has some personnel, accounting, and other staff reporting to him.

1. CEO in a functionally organized company: This is the traditional GM job, which reports to a board of directors (or chairman) and has functional managers reporting to it.

2. Corporate CEO in a multidivisional company: The most obvious difference between this and the first type is that general managers, in addition to some staff functional managers, report to this position. Furthermore, the multidivisional CEO usually has fewer short-run responsibilities.

Figure 25.2 Differences in job demands among six types of GM jobs in one corporation (Diagram reprinted, descriptions adapted, with permission of The Free Press, a Division of Macmillan, Inc., from *The General Managers* by John P. Kotter, pp 23–26. Copyright © 1982 by The Free Press.)

mance is unsatisfactory. A turnaround situation, for instance, often requires rapid decisions and actions if the organization is to be saved. Performance also seems to affect the quality of relationships. A GM may be able to effect a turnaround, for example, only by working through others, yet in such a situation, the GM often inherits subordinates of limited performance potential.

WHAT WE KNOW ABOUT THE KINDS OF PEOPLE WHO DO WELL AS GENERAL MANAGERS

Research has shown some similarities among individuals who perform well in GM jobs. Certain personal and background characteristics seem to give the GM an ability and inclination to deal with the difficult decision-making and implementation issues of the job. Recognizing these traits may help companies in selecting and developing future GMs.

Common characteristics

Recent studies suggest that more than a dozen personal traits are shared by many GMs (see Campbell et al. 1970; Harrell 1961; Schein 1980; McClelland 1975; Kotter 1982a, 1982b). Most relate to elements of the basic personality: needs or motives, cognitive orientation, temperament, and interpersonal orientation. Common themes center on extroversion, power, achievement, ambition, emotional stability, optimism, intelligence, analytical ability, personable style, intuition, and an ability to relate easily to a wide range of business specialists. Other common traits relate to information and relationships that are accumulated and developed in adulthood. (Figure 25.3 lists the shared traits identified in Kotter's 1982 study.)

Why these particular traits? Both interpersonal and intellectual skills are essential for success because the GM's job is a never-ending series of dilemmas and challenges. A strong analytical mind and above-average intelligence are necessary simply to tackle the complex issues of the job and to build effective agendas. Simi-

BASIC PERSONALITY

Needs/Motives
- Like power
- Like achievement
- Ambitious

Temperament
- Emotionally stable and even
- Optimistic

Cognitive orientation
- Above-average intelligence (but not brilliant)
- Moderately strong analytically
- Strong intuitively

Interpersonal orientation
- Personable, and good at developing relationships with people
- Unusual set of interests that allows them to relate easily to a broad set of business specialists

ACCUMULATED INFORMATION AND RELATIONSHIPS

Information
- Very knowledgeable about their businesses
- Very knowledgeable about their organizations

Relationships
- Have cooperative relationships with a very large number of people in their organization
- Have cooperative relationships with many people in their industry also

Figure 25.3 Shared personal characteristics of general managers (Adapted with permission of The Free Press, a Division of Macmillan, Inc., from *The General Managers* by John P. Kotter, p. 36. Copyright © 1982 by The Free Press.)

larly, optimism and emotional stability are critical in confronting the often anxiety-provoking and severely challenging situations that confront the GM. An extensive knowledge of the business and organization is imperative for effective managerial decision making—helping to guide the GM through the enormous quantities of potentially relevant but complex information. A personable style, skill in developing relationships, and an ability to relate to a diverse group of business specialists are important in cultivating and maintaining the GM's network of relationships. Finally, ambitious people who enjoy having power are more likely than others to be attracted to the GM job, despite its pressures and demands, and to be motivated to use their abilities on the job.

A limited body of research suggests that many general managers grow up in similar environments and share some common educational and career experiences (Harrell 1961; Campbell et al. 1970; Kotter 1982a). Harrell (1961, 99) found that GMs have great drive and dominance derived in part from their relations with their parents; that they are in the top 10 percent of the population in terms of intellectual ability; that they are more likely to have a great breadth of interests than great depth; and that they appear to be better adjusted emotionally than most people.

Of the sample of GMs studied by Kotter (figure 25.4), most had upwardly mobile parents and reported a close relationship with at least one parent. At least one

parent had a college education in almost every case, matched their interests and values. Once settled in, they though only two of fifteen fathers had a graduate degree. All GMs had at least an undergraduate education, and most had been school leaders at some time. The more successful performers were more likely to have fathers who had been managers. These GMs also appeared to have been very close to one of their parents, often had two or more siblings, and more often had a graduate degree (Kotter 1982a).

On entering their careers, Kotter's GMs generally settled quickly into an industry and company that stayed. On the average, these GMs had spent 90 percent of their careers in the same industry and 81 percent with their present employer. These statistics run counter to popular notions about executive mobility, yet studies by *Fortune*, Kron/Ferry International, the Conference Board, Arthur Young, and others[5] all support the view that top-level managers spend most of their careers with one employer.

The GM's fidelity to a particular industry and company has several possible explanations. First, the detailed

---

5. See *Fortune* (May 1976): 176–77; *Management Review* (July 1979): 15–20; "The Chief Executive and His Job," *Studies in Personnel Policy* (1969) no. 214; Arthur Young, the accounting firm, *The Chief Executive: Background and Attitude Profiles*, a report (1980); George Farris, "Executive Cohesiveness and Financial Performance of the *Fortune* 500," paper delivered at the 1979 Management Meeting, Atlanta, Ga., 1979; and "How the Chief Executives Get to the Top," *Chief Executive* (December 1980).

CHILDHOOD FAMILY ENVIRONMENT
- Upwardly mobile parents
- Both original parents at home while growing up
- Close relationship with one or both parents
- At least one parent with two- or four-year college education
- Fathers associated with business and/or working as managers in nonbusiness setting
- Brothers and sisters (no only children)

EDUCATIONAL EXPERIENCES
- An undergraduate or graduate (master's) education
- Business-related degree
- Student leaders in high school, college, or both

EARLY CAREER EXPERIENCES
- Joined (or started) a firm (or industry) that closely fit personal interests and values
- Spent the vast majority of career time in that one industry
- Spent the vast majority of career time with current employer
- Rose through one function (or two at the most)
- Rapidly promoted
- Promoted into first general-management job early in career (between the ages of thirty-four and forty)

Figure 25.4 General managers: shared background characteristics. (Reprinted with permission of The Free Press, a Division of Macmillan, Inc., from *The General Managers* by John P. Kotter, p. 45. Copyright © 1982 by the Free Press.)

knowledge of an industry and organization is not easily transferred, and it would be difficult to develop new knowledge and relationships quickly in another industry. Moreover, GMs who have learned how much success depends on commitment and loyalty may have little inclination to change employers. Finally, they may simply be doing well and feeling generally happy, and therefore have little reason to leave.

Once in an organization, many GMs quickly develop what could be called "success syndromes." They perform well on an initial assignment and are promoted to a more challenging one. This reinforces their self-esteem and motivation, which in turn leads to greater power and opportunities. Over time, more challenging assignments stretch them and build their skills, while simultaneously expanding their network of important relationships and increasing their knowledge. These gains further reinforce their performance on the job and again lead to more promotions—over and over again. Kotter (1982a, 48) found that the better performers were particularly likely to develop such success syndromes. They were also more likely to join companies that fit them well in the first place, and to find strong mentors in those companies.

Differences do appear

Some differences are apparent in the backgrounds of GMs. Younger and older executives clearly differ along several dimensions, although surprisingly few corporations acknowledge these variations. Today's younger GMs tend to come from homes with better educated parents, fathers with more professional and top-management careers, and more diverse religious backgrounds. They are also less likely to have served in the armed forces and more likely to have working spouses. To a large extent, these differences result from the broad economic and social changes of the last thirty years.

There are also many job-related differences. Different sets of job demands seem to be associated with different types of people. When job responsibilities are more demanding and decision making more difficult, effective GMs are more likely to be strong in characteristics such as optimism, intelligence, analytical and intuitive skills, achievement orientation, and knowledge of the business and organization. When implementation is a particular challenge, GMs tend to have more personable styles, more even temperaments, greater abilities to relate to diverse business specialists, a stronger liking of power, skills at developing relationships, and more extensive organizational and industrial relationships (Kotter 1982a, 53).

IMPLICATIONS

Corporate selection and development

SELECTING GMS: INSIDERS VERSUS OUTSIDERS
Current research implies that "insiders" are more likely to be successful as GMs. There are clear risks in choosing outsiders. While an outsider may be talented and may have an impressive track record, he or she will only rarely have the detailed knowledge of the business and organization, or the solid, extensive network of relationships that are necessary to succeed. This is not to say that firms should never hire outside executives, but rather that the choice of an outsider is most likely to be appropriate if

- The relevant relations and knowledge can be developed quickly, say in six months (a typical example would be for a small division in a relatively mature industry); or
- The key relationships and knowledge can be transferred across companies (because, for example, it is a mature industry, all businesses are pretty much alike, and the key relationships are external, to customers or suppliers); or
- The organization is simply desperate and must take a risk (as in a turnaround situation); or
- Things are changing so fast that relevant knowledge and relationships quickly become obsolete.

SELECTING GMS: GETTING AN APPROPRIATE FIT
No matter how talented or previously successful, a GM candidate whose characteristics do not fit the specific demands of the job will have great difficulty performing well. As one GM explained,

> If a person doesn't fit the job, then he must constantly expend extra energy to get things done right. He has to fight the natural flow, so to speak. If the job is a particularly demanding one, even the strongest, best motivated person may not have enough extra energy, and will eventually fail. Such a failure can hurt many people. If the job is not done adequately, all that depends on it can be hurt. And unless the individual really understands that he was in the wrong job in the first place, the blow to his self-esteem can be very damaging.[6]

Ensuring an appropriate job fit may mean designing jobs to match the characteristics of available candidates. It may be necessary to break large divisions down

---

6. Reprinted with permission of The Free Press, a Division of Macmillan, Inc., from *The General Managers* by John P. Kotter, p. 138. Copyright © 1982 by The Free Press.

into two or more parts to make jobs more manageable, divesting operations, or limit diversification so that the GM's job can be handled by one individual.

DEVELOPING GMS

Research by Campbell, Dunnette, Lawler, and Weick (1970, 224–25), Kotter (1982a, 135–36), and others indicates that it may be difficult to develop a large enough pool of insiders from which to select general managers. Effective GMs are constantly growing in knowledge, relationships, and skills. The best performers have typically not been moved too often or put into positions that are changing too rapidly to allow them to learn or perform well. Nor were they left to stagnate in jobs with few growth opportunities. It is imperative, then, that GM candidates not be moved too quickly or too slowly—a difficult process to control. It is all too easy for decision makers to allow short-run business pressures to push them into reassigning GMs without careful consideration of their careers and personal growth.

Training programs after graduate school can play some role in developing GMs. But many currently popular seminars may do more harm than good. Some "time management" programs, for example, urge executives to defend their daily schedules against interruptions, thus barring the use of the flexible system of agenda setting and networking, which we have seen as so effective. Executive courses at universities can be especially helpful in broadening the tunnel vision that sometimes afflicts those who have spent their entire career in one company. In-house programs can also be of benefit, especially those that aim to help participants

- Learn important information that is specifically relevant to the firm and its business and that they are not likely to learn on the job;
- Develop good relationships with others that will be helpful to them in their jobs in the future, relationships that they are not likely to develop by themselves as part of their normal routines; and
- Think more systematically about themselves and their own careers, so that they can manage their own development better and work themselves into positions that really fit their capabilities.

MANAGING GMS

Appropriate selection and development are necessary but not enough to ensure effective GM performance. GMs also need to be managed properly. Poor management can often stunt performance and destroy a success syndrome.

Effective management begins with helping GMs get up to speed, perhaps assisting them with agenda setting and network building. Because considerable time is required to collect information, select an appropriate agenda, and establish relationships, the GM's superiors should limit their demands on him or her during the first three to six months.

Formal planning and performance appraisals can do much to help, or hinder, a GM's performance. An effective planning system should aid the GM in creating a more workable agenda and a strong network to implement it. It should encourage the GM to think strategically, to take into account both the short and the long run, and not to ignore any key functional issues. It should also be useful in network building, giving the GM leeway and options. Unfortunately many systems impose rigid quantitative requirements on the GM, requiring only limited strategic thinking in agenda setting and often creating conflict within the network.

Like an effective planning system, a good performance appraisal should help the GM focus on the entire job. Unfortunately many such systems highlight and reward only short-run or quantifiable performance, and by creating conflicts among people, they make network building among subordinates difficult.

A further complication is that, with a track record of win after win, some successful GMs develop an "I can do anything" attitude. Up to a point, of course, self-confidence enhances their ability to succeed; beyond that point, it becomes foolhardy. Not recognizing just how specialized their skills, knowledge, and relationships really are, overconfident GMs may feel they can manage anything. This problem generally affects only the successful, because those who have experienced a few failures learn that they have limitations. Educational institutions can help keep ambition within bounds by encouraging students and managers to assess themselves realistically. By their assignments and daily interactions, superiors can also mitigate (or magnify) the problem.

CONCLUSION

Effective GMs are a rare and valuable resource. Their selection, development, and management can make the difference between mediocre and excellent performance for the organization. If we adhere too tightly to traditional models of "professional" behavior, we may fail to train or allow for behavior that actually meets the demands of the job, for there is a method in the seeming madness of an effective GM's day. Organizations should strive to develop in its younger managers the agenda and network-building skills they need to cope with the uncertainty, complexity, and dependency of their jobs.

REFERENCES

Aguilar, F. 1967. *Scanning the Business Environment.* New York: Macmillan.

Barnard, C. 1939. *The Functions of the Executive.* Cambridge, Mass.: Harvard University Press.

Campbell, J. P., M. D. Dunnette, E. E. Lawler III, and K. Weick, Jr. 1970. *Managerial Behavior, Performance and Effectiveness.* Englewood Cliffs, N.J.: Prentice-Hall.

Carlson, S. 1951. *Executive Behavior: A Study of the Work Load and the Working Methods of Managing Directors.* Stockholm: Strombergs.

Gabarro, J. 1979. "Socialization at the Top: How CEOs and Their Subordinates Evolve Interpersonal Contacts." *Organizational Dynamics* 7, no. 3 (Winter): 2–23.

Harrell, T. W. 1961. *Manager's Performance and Personality.* Dallas: Southwest.

Juers, A. F. 1979. "The Group Executive." *Management Review* (March).

Kotter, J. P. 1977. "Power, Dependence, and Effective Management." *Harvard Business Review* 55, no. 4 (July/August): 156–67.

———. 1982a. *The General Managers.* New York: Free Press.

———. 1982b. "What Effective General Managers Really Do." *Harvard Business Review* (November/December).

Lindblom, C. 1959. "The Science of 'Muddling Through.'" *Public Administration Review* 19:79–88.

March, J., and H. Simon. 1958. *Organizations.* New York: Wiley.

McCaskey, M. 1974. "A Contingency Approach to Planning: Planning with Goals and Planning Without Goals." *Academy of Management Journal* (June).

McClelland, D. C. 1975. *Power: The Inner Experience.* New York: Irvington.

Mintzberg, H. 1973. *The Nature of Managerial Work.* New York: Harper & Row.

———. 1975. "The Manager's Job: Folklore and Fact." *Harvard Business Review* 53, no. 4 (July/August): 49–61.

Neustadt, R. 1960. *Presidential Power.* New York: Wiley.

Peters, T. 1978. "Symbols, Patterns, and Settings: An Optimistic Case for Getting Things Done." *Organizational Dynamics* 7, no. 2 (Autumn).

———. 1979. "Leadership: Sad Facts and Silver Linings." *Harvard Business Review* 57, no. 6 (November/December): 169–72.

Pettigrew, A. M. 1973. *The Politics of Organizational Decision Making.* London: Tavistock.

Quinn, J. B. 1980. *Strategies for Change: Logical Incrementalism.* Homewood, Ill.: Irwin.

Stewart, R. 1979. "Managerial Agendas: Reactive or Proactive." *Organizational Dynamics* 8, no. 2 (Autumn): 34–47.

ADDITIONAL READINGS

Kotter, J. P. 1977/78. "Power, Success, and Organizational Effectiveness." *Organizational Dynamics* (Winter).

———. 1979. *Power in Management.* New York: AMACOM.

Pfeffer, J. 1981. "Management as Symbolic Action." In *Research in Organizational Behavior,* vol. 3, ed. L. L. Cummings and B. M. Shaw. Greenwich, Conn.: Jai Press.

———. 1981. *Power in Organizations.* Marshfield, Mass.: Pitman.

Pfeffer, J., and J. Salancik. 1977. "Who Gets Power and How They Hold On to It." *Organizational Dynamics* 5 (Winter): 3–21.

Schein, E. H. 1980. *Organizational Psychology.* 3d ed. Englewood Cliffs, N.J.: Prentice-Hall.

Shetty, Y. K., and N. S. Perry, Jr. 1977. "Are Top Executives Transferable Across Companies?" *Business Horizons* (June).

Skinner, W., and E. Sasser. 1977. "Managers with Impact: Versatile and Inconsistent." *Harvard Business Review* 55, no. 6 (November/December): 140–48.

Stewart, R. 1967. *Managers and Their Job.* New York: Macmillan.

———. 1976. "To Understand the Manager's Job: Consider Demands, Constraints, Choices." *Organizational Dynamics* (Spring).

———. 1976. *Contrast in Management.* New York: McGraw-Hill.

26

The generation of practical theory: schools as political organizations

SAMUEL B. BACHARACH AND STEPHEN M. MITCHELL

Many studies of organizational behavior implicitly assume that certain basic, typological forms are common to all organizations. This assumption is most apparent in the field of comparative organizational analysis where, despite repeated calls to attend to the unique characteristics of specific organizational forms (e.g., Clegg and Dunkerly 1980; Pinder and Moore 1979), the principles of relationships between sets of structures and component processes are often haphazardly generalized from one type of organization to another. Inevitably, the specifics of the empirical referents are lost and the emergent theoretical generalizations come to the forefront, preventing the identification of precise variables and situations relevant in a given type of organization. Because specificity has been sacrificed, the body of theory that has developed is difficult to apply to the practical concerns of organizational design, development, and management.

The study of school districts as organizations is one of the more dramatic illustrations of this tendency. The first section of this paper reviews the basic elements of a comparative structural analysis and demonstrates how these elements both inform and limit the study of school districts as organizations. Alternative approaches to the study of schools as organizations are noted, and a political organizational framework for the study of schools

is proposed. The second section discusses the requirements of a political analysis of schools as organizations, which include identifying the key actors, specifying the linkages between these actors, and delineating the types of strategies and tactics used to create and maintain consensus. The final section explores the implications of a political perspective for educational practitioners, particularly those involved in organizational design.

THE LIMITS OF GENERALIZATION

Organizational theory tended to develop general, overarching theories that are assumed to be applicable to all organizations. Ordinarily, little effort is made to examine how these theories will unfold empirically in daily organizational life. We would argue that this tendency toward theoretical generalization can prevent a thorough understanding of schools as organizations.

Structuralist analysis

The limits of generalization are most apparent if we consider the type of analysis undertaken by the compara-

405

tive structuralists (e.g., Blau and Schoenherr 1971; Hage and Aiken 1970; Pugh et al. 1968). This research perspective dominated the late 1960s and 1970s and remains the context within which most comparative research is conducted. In essence, the structuralist approach has accepted a causal model of organizational life composed of four crude elements: (1) external constraints, (2) structure, (3) process, and (4) output. External constraints have been seen primarily as the environment and the technological factors that affect the internal structures and processes of the organization. Internal structures have often been discussed in terms of the morphology of the organization, for example, size, differentiation, span of control, role specialization (Hall 1982; Aldrich 1979; Bacharach 1978). Structures, in this context, are viewed as independent of the action they may encompass. That is, structures are objectified, reified aggregate characteristics of organizations. Processes are the actual tasks carried out by actors in pursuit of their work activity. Because they involve the behavior of specific actors or groups of actors in pursuit of functional goals, organizational processes are more difficult to reify than structures. Processes tend to include a cognitive component; thus they are more subjective and should not be studied on an aggregate level. Output is seen as an indicator of organizational performance or achievement.

If external constraints and internal structures and processes are connected, it seems likely that specific structural configurations and patterns of processes will emerge under particular environmental and/or technological conditions (Perrow 1967; Aldrich 1979; McKelvey 1982). For example, it is maintained that under positive economic conditions, organizations can afford to expand, and therefore will be larger and more differentiated. Likewise, it is suggested that routine technologies will be associated with a high degree of differentiation and role specialization, and nonroutine technologies, with low levels of differentiation and role specialization. Parallel assumptions govern the relationships between external constraints and the internal processes of organizational life. For example, in a turbulent environment, work processes may involve a higher level of role ambiguity and role conflict than in a stable environment. Likewise, we would expect a higher level of role ambiguity and role conflict when the constraining technology is nonroutine. Output variables are viewed as contingent upon the interactions among the three previous sets of variables. An effective organization is one in which structures, processes, and external constraints are appropriately matched.

This general orientation may be broadly described as "contingency analysis." That is, output is contingent on the direct and interactive effects of different sets of variables. Output depends on (1) the direct effect of external constraints, (2) the direct effect of process variables, (3) the direct effect of structural variables, (4) the interaction of external constraints and processes, (5) the interaction of external constraints and structures, (6) upon the interaction of structures and processes, and (7) the three-way interaction effect of external constraints, structure, and process.

Researchers of the last fifteen years have differed in their emphasis on those various relationships. But the structuralist perspective invariably employs the organization as the unit of analysis. Those who adopt such an orientation may be accused of reifying and anthropomorphizing organizations (Bacharach 1978). That is, structuralists treat organizations as organic entities that are part of the natural world and subject to their own principles of operation (Wolin 1969); in addition, they may fall into the trap of dealing with organizations as actors, as evidenced by the use of such terms as *organizational control, organizational power,* and *organizational communication* (Weick 1979). An analysis of the organization as a whole assumes that it is a rational system of interdependent units functionally held together by a common goal. When aggregate data are used as the basis of empirical analysis, the appearance of a harmonious whole is reinforced. Such a perspective assumes a uniform effect of structure and process across the organization, combining scores to create one measure of each variable for the total organization.

While this approach may help us recognize the generic typological forms that are common to all organizations, practitioners find it extremely limited. Indeed, those who live in organizations, more than those who study them, are constantly aware of the idiosyncrasies inherent in organizational life—that is, the nonpatterned behavior of groups and actors within the organization. For the most part, organizational behavior as a discipline has ignored those types of behavior. In our pursuit of the common patterns, we have ignored cognition, volition, and self-interest

The clearest example of this oversight may be the contingent model's inability to recognize the effect of strategic decision making. If the environment is to influence specific structures and internal processes, key actors in the organization must cognitively interpret the environment, voluntarily choose among strategic alternatives, and implement changes based on their notion of how to serve the organization's interests (or their own). Organizations do not adapt; individuals adjust. The common patterns that we call external constraints, structures, and processes limit alternatives and/or enhance uncertainty, but they tell us little or nothing about the deductive logic used in the decision-implementation process. To a large degree, the analysis of organizations has assumed many strategic actors. We do not see organizations as emergent phenomena dependent on the conscious calculations of actors, but rather as *sui generis* entities governed by abstract self-fulfilling macro principles. Recent work on the ecology of organizations and organizational demography is only the latest manifestation of this tendency (Hannan and Freeman 1977; McKelvey 1982; Aldrich 1979). Such an approach has considerable merit, scientific and aesthetic appeal; but for the practitioner concerned with the redesign of an organization, this tendency to ignore the strategic actor results in a gap between theory and practice.

The structural analysis of schools

Educational organizations provide a good example of the difficulty of applying organizational theory to the specific concerns of practitioners. As discussed earlier, structuralist analysis adopts a causal model of organizational life that emphasizes the determinants of organizational output. For educational practitioners, the most obvious output relates to the educational attainment of the students. The goals of primary and secondary education have included such objectives as minimizing dropout rates, increasing the percentage of students who continue their education beyond high school, and obtaining high achievement scores, particularly in reading and math. A structural analysis of schools would select a specific set of outputs and then examine the effect of environment, structure, and process on these outputs.

Bidwell and Kasarda (1975) exemplify this approach, and a brief consideration of their work will highlight some of the limitations of a structuralist analysis of schools as organizations. They measure scholastic achievement—and hence judge the effectiveness of schools—primarily in terms of students' reading and mathematical ability. While such items have the distinct advantage of being susceptible to relatively objective measures, they tend to be embedded in a narrow conceptualization of school districts. Specifically, we cannot equate the goals of elementary schools with the goals of high schools. While sixth-grade reading and math achievement-test scores may be appropriate measures of effectiveness for elementary schools, it can be argued that students' reading and math scores should be viewed as an independent variable when examining secondary-school effectiveness. There is apparently much truth in the traditional high school teacher's view that once students have begun their secondary education, it is too late to teach them reading and arithmetic. To focus on reading and math scores, which essentially measure the success of the elementary schools, is to miss the primary mission of the secondary schools, that is, to socialize students toward appropriate career plans. Students with reading problems and "math anxiety" in high school are reduced to remedial education, and the high school's effectiveness consists primarily of preventing them from dropping out.

Two points are worth noting. First, even when we can agree on the organization's primary goals, measures may not be easy to identify. Output and its measures are problematic. Second, even if possible measures of goal achievement can be found, one cannot assume that they are applicable to the entire organization. Treating the organization as a whole conceals important differences within the system. While we have been using output as an example, the same argument applies to structure and process. Thus, while it is possible to construct aggregate measures of structure and process for the entire school district, these measures would conceal the very substantial differences that exist between structure and process on the secondary and the elementary level (e.g., Bacharach, in press).

The failure to take account of the variations in structure, process, and output among schools within a district severely limits the practical application of the results produced by structural analysis. Critics of this perspective have also noted the tendency to overlook the internal dynamics of schools and the various tensions that exist within the organization (e.g., Silverman 1971). This tendency also detracts from the practical utility of the structural approach.

One of the primary sources of tension within school districts is the need for educational administrators to satisfy goals related to administrative efficiency as well as educational attainment. Administrators are expected to decrease employee turnover, initiate innovation, minimize costs in relation to output, tap state and federal funds, and so on. On the surface, these seem to be goals that everyone would accept as valid. But suppose some measure of educational attainment in a school or district decreases dramatically. For example, searching for a way to raise reading scores, and drawing on the results of a structural analysis (e.g., Bidwell and Kasarda 1975), one might propose hiring more teachers or better qualified teachers. Either of these solutions, however, would raise the costs to the district and therefore conflict with the goals of administrative efficiency.

This admittedly oversimplified example illustrates the kind of conflicts that may confront practitioners as they try to balance their roles as educators with their roles as administrators. If an analysis of schools as organizations is to be of any value to practitioners, it must be able to take account of these conflicts. To do so requires that the researcher be able to focus on the use that is made of output data (or other information) in order to reveal the internal dynamics present in the system (Sproull and Zubrow 1981).

Conflicts between educational and administrative goals arise as a school district translates its official public goal of providing education into specific operative goals—a decision to emphasize math and reading as opposed to arts and athletics, for example, or to hire additional teachers to improve reading scores. "Where operative goals provide the specific content of official goals they reflect choices among competing values" (Perrow 1974, 216). Thus, operative goals are open to conflicting interests, and the educational administrator must be prepared to play a political role. For better or worse, school districts are composed of at least four identifiable spheres of interest: the community, the school board, the administration, and the teachers (Bacharach and Mitchell 1981b). Each group brings its own set of values to bear on every issue, so that an operative goal cannot be determined without creating and maintaining consensus among these groups. How consensus is achieved thus becomes of critical importance to the analysis of schools as organizations (Bacharach and Mitchell 1981b). Unfortunately, many researchers (e.g., Bidwell and Kasarda 1975) treat the goals of education organizations as if they were reified and had achieved a level of objective consensuality. As Hannan and Freeman (1977) point out, this engineering approach to effectiveness is common to much of the organizational literature. It may be appropriate to assume general agreement on such educational goals as math and reading scores. But insofar as these measures of effectiveness are moderated by such factors as administrative goals, the diversity of the district, and the activity of the teacher's union, the assumption of consensuality becomes precarious.

To summarize, school districts as organizations have at least three characteristics that are not adequately handled by researchers who adopt a structuralist approach. First, although there is general agreement that schools exist to provide education, measures of goal achievement are more difficult to specify. In particular, a structuralist analysis fails to account for the distinct differences between secondary and elementary schools in output, structure, and process. Second, a structuralist analysis cannot reveal the internal dynamics of school systems striving for two often-conflicting goals: educational attainment and administrative efficiency. Third, efforts to resolve these conflicting goals are exacerbated by the presence of multiple interest groups, each of which may bring a different set of values to bear on any issue. A structuralist analysis cannot capture the political process that lies behind the creation and maintenance of consensus in schools. Because of these limitations, the results of a structuralist analysis of schools are of dubious value to the educational practitioner.

Alternative perspectives

Although we have focused on the shortcomings of structural analysis, other theoretical approaches that share the same unstated assumptions have the same limitations when applied to the study of schools. In particular, the assumption that organizations are harmonious, unified entities seriously limits the applicability of organizational theory to schools as organizations. Yet this assumption pervades the organizational literature. Despite discussions of differentiation, the fact is that most of organizational theory assumes a norm of consensus and treats conflict or chaos as something that must be explained. This is probably one reason why educational practitioners lament the inapplicability of theory to their practical concerns (Cunningham, Hack, and Nystrand 1977; Immegart and Boyd 1979; Boyan 1981).

Recognizing the limitations of such assumptions, some have tried to develop alternative perspectives to the study of organizations. One of the leading alternatives—the loosely coupled systems approach elaborated by Weick (1976)—emerged from an examination of schools. In contrast to structuralists, the proponents of the loosely coupled system take the individual, not the organization, as the unit of analysis. Coupling a student is a means of explaining how individuals come to be organized. Although this argument would, on the surface, appear to be similar to our concern with the creation and maintenance of consensus, in fact research into the loosely coupled has focused on showing that differences exist, rather than that similarities are problematic (e.g., Davis et al. 1977). Thus, despite their theoretical differences, the proponents of loosely coupled systems seem to be heavily influenced by the same assumptions of unity that limit the structuralists. Yet "where the structuralists err in failing to consider the internal dynamics of organizations, the adherents of the loosely coupled systems approach fail to consider the structural constraints that impinge on the individual's cognitions and actions" (Bacharach 1981, 21–22). Further, the loosely coupled system is often taken as a metaphor and applied to organizations as a whole, without showing how the individual properties on which the theory is founded can be validly applied to the organization. Finally, while the concept of loosely coupled systems was elaborated by focusing on schools, the specifics of this empirical referent have been largely forgotten as attention shifts to theoretical generalizations. The end result is the creation of an approach as limited as that which it was developed to critique.

If internal dynamics are obscured when the organization is taken as the unit of analysis, and if focusing on the individual prevents one from recognizing the forces of cohesion, how can we best study schools as organizations? We favor an approach that uses the group as the unit of analysis. From such a perspective, objective structures are considered as constraints on individual group action within an organization. By focusing on the group as the primary unit of analysis, however, we are sensitized to the differences in cognition and action that occur across groups within an organization—something not possible within the strict confines of a structuralist approach. This approach recognizes individuals but considers their membership in groups as the critical point for explaining their behavior in the organization.

In this context educational organizations are seen as political systems composed of structurally interdependent interest groups and coalitions perpetually engaged in bargaining. Educational organizations must therefore be viewed as systematic political entities. The systemic component results from the rational interdependence of groups created by the organization's structure. The political component results from the differential interests and goals of the various groups. The cognitive element so important to the loosely coupled system perspective is also recognized here in the tactical action of the parties.

Although the idea of considering schools as political organizations may be new to organizational theorists, the basic elements of a political perspective have been part of research in educational administration for some time. In fact, despite efforts to depoliticize the administration of schools, a political perspective began to take shape in the 1930s as researchers examined the function and composition of school boards (Counts 1937). Other roles were occasionally examined as they related to the school board (e.g., the superintendent in Gross et al. 1958). Interest-group politics in public education proliferated during the 1960s. Nearly all those concerned with public schools realized they had become embattled political entities, attempting to mediate the conflicting demands of parents, teachers, minorities, teachers' unions, state departments of education, state legislatures, faculties of state teachers' colleges, state and federal courts, and the federal educational bureaucracy. It became obvious that schools had to contend with competing imperatives—one of governance in community settings, one of administration, and one of educational attainment.

No unified approach to the political study of schools has emerged; rather, researchers have employed a variety of models and focused on different kinds of school-district personnel. A brief review of some of these studies will illustrate this point, while suggesting ways to overcome the weakness of past research.

Ziegler and Jennings (1974) tried to determine whether the principle of representative democracy guided the governing process of local school districts. Whereas earlier research had focused on the composition of school boards, they looked at the interactions between the school board, the superintendent, and the public, exploring not only who governs the school district but how it is governed. The main drawback of their study is that it equates board, superintendent, and community relationships with the entire governing process. Moreover, rather than participant observation, they relied upon interviews as the sources of data, thus presenting perceptions of political participation, board responsiveness, and sources of consensus and conflict. Investigating the perceptions of consensus and conflict provides few insights into how consensus is maintained and how conflicts are resolved.

Wirt and Kirst (1975) also looked at school districts from a political perspective, noting that

> Educational administration is "political" in two senses. . . . First, educational administration is the object of activity from political influences outside the school walls. These external forces may be community groups, state and federal governments, or private forces, such as professionals or foundations.
>
> Second, educational administration is the subject of political activity, that is, its practitioners can—by their mobilization of resources, skill of leadership, and knowledge of the social territory   shape policy and behaviors within the school system.

Having recognized the interacting, interdependent elements of the school district, Wirt and Kirst proposed adopting a systems framework as their model. On the surface, a systems model would appear to provide several advantages for the study of school districts as political organizations. First, such a framework clearly delineates how schools respond to the demands in their environment. Second, the emphasis on dynamics encourages the researcher to examine the structural and process components of the relationship between the school district and its environment. Third, the systems model presents the school district as a dynamic political entity constantly interacting with various other entities. This notion of interdependence is particularly important when considering the school district as a governmental unit embedded in a larger system of government. Finally, a systems framework is broader in scope than previous models that concentrated solely on formal structure, role delineation, or community impact. While Wirt and Kirst adopt a systems framework, however, they fail to integrate their dynamic model with a dynamic connective concept. They identify key participants in governance and administration, but do not explore how their activities confer authority or influence on them, or how these activities affect what actually gets done in school districts.

More recently, Smith, Prunty, and Dwyer (1981) have introduced the concept of the "longitudinal nested system," which emphasizes the interactions of a number of discernable systems with their environment. Because they were concerned with following a trail of results through time and space, however, Smith and his associates failed to distinguish the processes by which causes in one system became results in another.

Perhaps the most thoroughly developed analysis of schools as complex political organizations is that of Corwin (1965). By identifying key actors and their interactions, developing a differentiated view of the organizational environment, and emphasizing the notion of bargaining and adaptive strategies, Corwin has taken an important preliminary step toward developing a comprehensive political model of the school system and its environment.

Although educational researchers have employed elements of a political perspective, few, if any, have attempted a full analysis of schools as political organizations (Bacharach 1981). Research has tended to focus on specific roles or linkages between roles, in many instances artificially separating internal organizational elements from external environmental concerns. Emphasizing practice, those in educational administration have tended to rely on detailed empirical descriptions of educational systems rather than to develop broad theories of organizations. Much use has been made of case studies and other intensive research techniques, which tend to reveal the more idiosyncratic and dynamic aspects of school systems, with little effort devoted to comparative analyses. It is this tendency that leads to the adoption of elements of a political perspective and to a failure to develop general theories of educational administration. Compounding the problem is the division of educational researchers into a number of subfields, which makes it increasingly difficult to speak of a field of educational administration.

Thus, neither organizational theorists nor educational researchers have achieved the ideal of a practical theory. Organizational theorists' fondness for developing general models limits applicability of their work to the study of schools as organizations. At the same time, an overemphasis on idiosyncratic aspects of schools also works against the generation of knowledge useful to both scholars and practitioners. What is needed is a middle ground that recognizes the unique properties of schools as organizations and develops general theories based on these properties. Only then can we construct a realistic image of schools as organizations that has direct implications for the development and refinement of theory, research, and practice. It is our contention that a fully developed political perspective offers the best foundation for such practical theory (Bacharach and Mitchell 1981a).

SCHOOLS AS POLITICAL ORGANIZATIONS

We must now elaborate on what we mean by a political perspective and how it applies to schools.

The elements of a political perspective

Educational organizations are best understood as political systems, both internally and in their external relationships. Constant tactical power struggles occur at all levels of the organization as actors try to obtain control over real or symbolic resources. These struggles may be between the superintendent and the school board, the school board and the state, or principals and teachers. The important point is that the dynamics of power struggles over resources are integral to any organizational analysis.

Members of educational organizations are political actors with their own needs, objectives, and strategies to achieve those objectives. While there may be some consensus regarding the normative goals of educational organizations (e.g., education itself), the various actors will differ in the weight given to different subgoals and the strategies to pursue them.

The decision-making process is the primary arena of political conflict. Each subgroup can be expected to approach a decision with the objective of furthering its specific interests rather than a general organizational objective. If its self-interest does not seem to be at stake, a group may decide not to become involved in a specific decision. For others, however, the decision-making process becomes the arena in which to attempt to ensure that the decision outcome reflects their self-interests.

Subgroups also differ in their views of who has the formal power (authority), who has the informal power (influence), and who should have the power to make organizational decisions. A group's efforts to have its point of view reflected in the decision outcome centers in large part on questions of authority and influence—for representation is granted only to viewpoints that others agree should have some influence on a decision. The extent to which parties agree about who should have authority and influence over various decisions is constrained by the structure of educational organizations, their work processes, and the different goals of groups.

Given the importance of the decision-making process and groups' efforts to have their views reflected in decision outcomes, the level of conflict and ultimately educational quality depend on how closely the various parties agree as to where power lies in the decision-making process.

The ability of a single individual or group to have its interests represented in the decision-making process is often limited. As a consequence, coalitions of actors emerge, identify collective objectives, and devise strategies to achieve those objectives. For example, a coalition of teachers (i.e., the union) often has substantially more power than individual teachers or groups of teachers. Should the teachers' union elicit the support of the PTA, an even more influential coalition could result.

The formation of coalition is constrained by organizational structures, ideologies, and environment. For example, the types of coalitions that emerge and the strategies they follow will depend greatly on whether the school district is small or large and highly bureaucratic, whether the community is liberal or conservative, and whether the district population is well educated or poorly educated.

Any school district probably includes a number of different coalitions, either actually or potentially. The dominant coalition is the one that controls the authority structure and resources of the organization at a given point in time; their actions and orientations can be described in terms of their logic of action (that is, a rationale that, from the observer's perspective, seems to give their actions meaning and coherence).

A dominant coalition may remain in place for a long time, either through astute political maneuvering or because it is never seriously challenged, but no coalition is sacrosanct. A dialectical relationship exists between the organizational structures, ideologies, and environment and the emergence and aspirations of coalitions. Coalitions emerge in reaction to structures, ideologies, and environment and in turn reformulate and institutionalize structures, work processes, and ideologies, which engender, over time, a reaction from emergent coalitions. The rotation of coalitions on school boards illustrates this process. The point is that educational organizations must be seen as political entities that shape and are shaped by their environment.

The dialectic interplay between political actors and organizational structures occurs over time and within a specific context. Thus educational organizations are best understood from a historical perspective that recognizes the specificity and structure of the institutional system of which they are a part (Bacharach 1981).

Three fundamental questions

The output of schools depends very much on the interests and cognitive orientations of the component interest groups. If we are to understand the operation of educational organizations as political entities, it is necessary to answer three fundamental questions: (1) What are the component interest groups in the school system? (2) What are the primary linkages between these interest groups? and (3) What is the basic "logic of action" embedded in each interest group?

COMPONENT INTEREST GROUPS: SCHOOLS AS MULTISYSTEMS

As already noted in connection with the work of Smith and others (e.g., Bacharach and Mitchell 1981b), a school district is a multisystem—a system of parts each one of which is "a miniature social system in itself" (Smith, Prunty, and Dwyer 1981). Figure 26.1 provides examples of these systems, with an indication (not an exclusive listing) of some potential subgroups in the individual systems. This breakdown should provide a sense of the coalitions and interest groups that may attempt to participate in a decison.

Two significant points should be made here. First, each of the systems is identified by function and is relatively autonomous. Each has rights and responsibilities, methods of decision making, and constraints upon its actions. The community of citizens oversees a public institution; the school board makes policies in accordance with the demands of the citizens; the administration manages in accordance with the policies; and the teachers perform the hands-on operations in accordance with management's decisions. Obviously, such identifications are extremely indefinite because it is difficult to find the boundaries and because the linkages are so complex that a change in one segment requires adjustments with others (Oettinger and Marks 1974). But system identifications do indicate the legitimate bases for participation in decision making. Each system participates on the basis of what is ordinarily a legal definition of its function. In times of conflict, each group may not only argue the "rightness" of its specific position, but define the issue in terms of its own function. Thus, if a decision to eliminate an administrative position in an affirmative-action program may be viewed by the community as a serious threat to minority protections, it may be described as a budgetary necessity by the school board. In discussions of class size, one finds administrators mentioning finance and child-population statistics while teachers speak of pedagogical technique.

A second important point concerns participation. Not all groups may choose to participate in a given decision. For example, in a choice between purchasing new school buses and increasing the use of currently owned buses by staggering students' arrival and leaving times, citizens may be concerned with such factors as the general traffic patterns in the community, cost, students' being out of school until mid-morning, and students' arriving home after dark. While sensitive to the concerns of the community, the school board may be very strongly committed to the staggered schedule, having already determined that its costs would be significantly lower than those associated with the purchase of new buses. School administrators may be concerned about possible congestion around the buildings and the disruption of classes as students arrive and depart. Teachers may be entirely uninterested and may not attempt to participate. In any given decisions, only a specific subset of actors is likely to participate actively. Identifying those actors is a matter of delineating the operative influence network in the district (Bacharach, Lawler, and Mitchell 1984).

PRIMARY LINKAGES BETWEEN GROUPS: AUTHORITY AND INFLUENCE

Authority means final decision-making power. In school districts, teachers have the authority to assign learning activities to children; principals have the authority to assign children to classes; superintendents have the author-

ity to assign teachers to schools; school boards have the authority to select superintendents; and the community has the authority to elect school board members. In short, each position in a district is vested with authority over specific issues by virtue of its place in the organizational structure. In addition, as shown by the solid lines in figure 26.1, the systems in the district are arranged hierarchically in terms of authority (Smith, Prunty, and Dwyer 1981). Each system constrains the authority of the lower systems. Thus, the authority structure represents a fundamental linkage between actors in the school system. It is within this structure that the goals of the school system are pursued.

Figure 26.2 is a graphic representation of the relationship between the four systems in a school district as they are generally assumed to operate. The school board, as elected representatives of the community, perpetuates the normative framework underlying district policy. That is, the board and its members set the tone for the dominant educational ideology. (Over the last ten years the shift from progressive education to an emphasis on basic skills has been most dramatically reflected in the ideological composition of school boards.)

The role of translating the normative expectations of school boards into executable tasks for teachers and

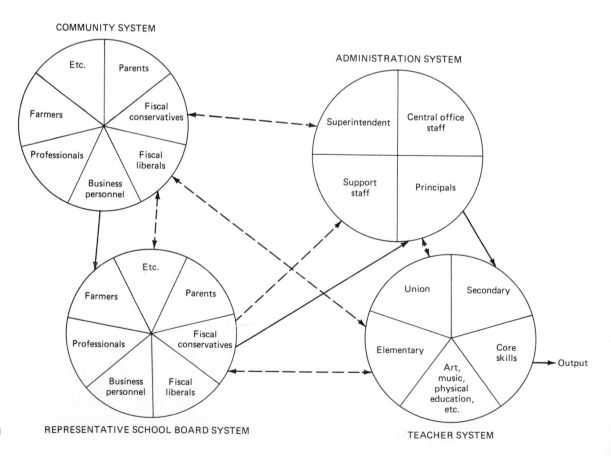

Figure 26.1   REPRESENTATIVE SCHOOL BOARD SYSTEM

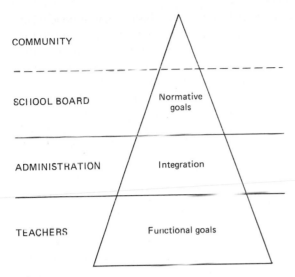

Figure 26.2 Type 1—The normatively integrated school district

lower-echelon administrators falls generally to the superintendent and the principals. They are expected not only to supervise their subordinates, but to translate ideology into specific policy. Teachers are primarily concerned with the basic tasks of education. Thus, the type 1 normatively integrated school district assumes a specified ideology on the part of the school board, the ability of the administrators to translate normative expectations into functional goals, and a teaching corps whose own professional orientation is congruent with the normative goals of the board.

Three points need to be made regarding the notion of a normatively integrated school district. First, the authority structure on which it rests requires that each actor recognize the legitimacy of the decision-making power of other actors. Authority can be exercised only if the individual, superiors, and subordinates all acknowledge the power of the individual to make the decision. One common point of conflict within school districts is disagreement as to who has authority over an issue. For example, as noted earlier, in discussions of class size, administrators tend to bring up financial and child-population statistics, while teachers speak of pedagogical technique. Each group defines the issue in terms of its own function. The conflict here is not only about the number of children in a room, but also about the authority of the superintendent to make that decision. Teachers challenge on the basis of their pedagogical expertise, and the superintendents defend on the basis of their systemwide financial responsibilities. Such challenges pose a direct threat to the apparent stability of a normatively integrated school district.

Challenges to authority are most likely to arise when

there is a lack of consensus on goals. Whereas challenges to authority represent a disagreement regarding organizational *form*, lack of consensus on goals relates to organizational *content* (Bacharach and Lawler 1980). As we will see, the two need not go together; therefore, the conceptual distinction is important to keep in mind. Disagreement over goals may occur at either the normative level (what assumptions underlie the basic direction of district policy?) or the functional level (how is an agreed-upon policy to be implemented?).

Lack of consensus on normative goals is much more disruptive to school-district operations than disagreement about functional goals. It is not surprising, then, that districts tend to transform potentially normative disagreements into functional disagreements. Thus, community members may agree that the school board has the authority to make policy, but they might oust board members for taking a position contrary to community desire. The superintendent has the authority to administer the district, but he or she will be fired if administrative decisions are not in keeping with policy goals. Teachers have authority to teach, but they will be disciplined if their methods are not in accordance with administrative procedures. The stability of the basic authority structure is used to present an image of consensus over normative goals. As Meyer and Rowan (1978) note, there is a logic of confidence operating that helps to avoid the disruption of normative disagreement. For this reason, it is generally assumed that all districts are normatively integrated. Further, when challenges to normative integration do arise, they are couched within the framework of a normatively integrated school district.

We have argued that challenges to normative integration occur when an actor or group either questions someone's authority or disagrees with the district's normative or functional goals. Such challenges will usually focus on a specific issue and represent an effort to have the actor's self-interest reflected in decisions regarding that issue. Given the relative resiliency of the authority structure, these interests are ordinarily expressed through the exercise of influence.

Influence functions less formally than authority and is less obvious. The sources of influence reside in individuals and the groups they represent. A single citizen may exert little influence, but one who speaks for the business community is in a strong position to influence a decision. All members of the school board are equal in authority, but the financial expert is more influential in financial decisions. An effort by the superintendent to control the agenda of a school-board meeting and thus to control the flow of information is an attempt to ensure that the administrative voice is the most influential. While the teacher system, at the low end of the

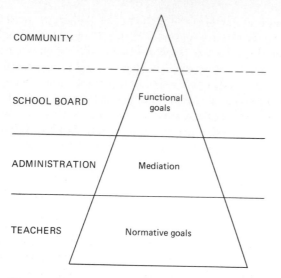

Figure 26.3 Type 3—Normatively inverse school district

hierarchy, has less authority than the other systems, teachers can influence decisions because they control the classroom technology, share the goals of other professional educators, and are represented by a formal group, that is, the teachers' union. Thus, while only a few individuals have authority over an issue, a virtually limitless number can exercise influence. The broken lines of figure 26.1 indicate the influence network; they show every system influencing and being influenced by every other system.

Identifying which lines of influence actually operate in a district is an important task for research conducted from a political perspective. Although the specific

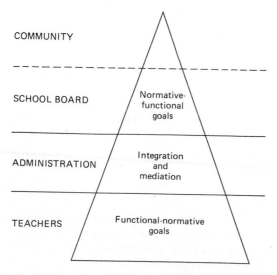

Figure 26.4 Type 2—Politically discrete school district

form of the influence network will vary from district to district, the general impact of influence on the roles played by various actors is limited. At one extreme is the type 3 normatively inverse district pictured in figure 26.3. In such a district, it is the teachers' normative orientations that are most visible, and the administrators become mediators rather than translators of school board policy. School boards seldom become concerned with functional issues and teachers with normative positions except in times of crisis. Generally, most school districts occupy a middle ground between normative integration and normative inversion. This position, a type 2 politically discrete district, is shown in figure 26.4. In such districts, school boards have both a normative and a functional orientation, as do teachers. Administrators, therefore, must both translate policy and mediate. Clearly, the mix is neither proportionally even nor consistent over time. Thus, the primary orientation of most school boards is normative, while their secondary orientation is functional; the daily demands of the job make the teachers' primary orientation functional and their secondary orientation normative. Which functions are emphasized, and therefore what type of school district approximates, will depend on what issues arise and how the various actors orient themselves toward those issues.

"LOGIC OF ACTION" EMBEDDED IN EACH INTEREST GROUP: STRATEGIES AND TACTICS

Challenges to normative integration and efforts to exert influence within the normative framework revolve around specific issues. The issues may be imposed upon the district by its environment, as in the case of federally mandated programs or state budget rules, or may arise from routine operations. The source is less crucial than the various actors' perceptions of the issue and their reactions to it. From a political perspective, it is the dynamics of the decision process surrounding specific issues that energize the system. Tracking actors' perceptions and reactions—their decisions to participate or not to participate, their efforts to have their interests reflected in the decision outcome—is at the core of a political analysis of schools as organizations.

A political analysis assumes, then, that individual actors will view each issue that arises in terms of their own self-interests. For example, in making up the school budget, principals of small schools on the outskirts of the district want their concerns to carry the same weight as those of principals from larger, more centrally located schools. Farmers, whose own financial security rests in land and equipment, may vie with teachers, administrators, and other community members about the importance of a pension plan. The important question is how each actor attempts to ensure that his or her interests are represented.

Actors choose their strategies and tactics in light of their perceptions of the district and the other actors' positions in the district. The notion of a "logic of action" presumes that the strategies and tactics selected represent a rational outcome, given the actors' perception of the situation. It follows that strategies and tactics will be determined, in part, by the history and structure of the school district.

Two broad classes of strategies and tactics may be identified. The first involves an individual actor's use of some expertise, authority, or work-related behaviors. Members of the community may attempt to exert influence as taxpayers or parents. They may threaten to mobilize, expressing public protest at school-board meetings or in letters to the editor of the local paper. School-board members may threaten to vote against an issue or may use their positions to obtain or disseminate information on a specific issue. Administrators rely on their expertise as a basis of influence but are not averse to skillful manipulation of information as a form of influence (Bacharach and Mitchell 1981b). Teachers also rely on their expertise as a basis of influence, falling back to the threatened withdrawal of services (e.g., job action or strike) only under crisis conditions. The point is that in choosing strategies and tactics, the actor is most likely to focus first on those that are immediately available, namely those involving individual action. If an actor believes that individual action will be sufficient to influence the decision outcome, then the search for viable strategy and tactics need go no further.

For many actors, however, individual influence is extremely limited. In a coalition, the range and scope of activities that can be brought to bear is much greater. Thus, the individual may consider forming a coalition with other actors and/or interest groups. The actor can then benefit from the expertise and authority of the coalition partner as well as his or her own. For example, by joining together with the school board, teachers would bring both classroom expertise and the use of the board's vote to bear on an issue. A coalition with the community, potentially threatening mobilization of the citizenry, would be equally effective in blocking administrative action. Were this to occur for an extended period and involve issues related to normative goals, the district would approach the type 3 paradigm of normative inversion.

In evaluating potential coalition partners, an actor usually looks for someone whose self-interest favors the same decision outcome desired by the actor, or someone who is either neutral or undecided on the issue. In the latter case, an attempt may be made to persuade the potential partner of the merits of the actor's position. Alternatively, the actor may try to establish a trade-off, possibly promising to assist the partner in the future in return for help in the present (Bacharach and Lawler 1980). For example, teachers may try to persuade members of the PTA to support their position, while school-board members may trade votes on issues.

Although coalitions often form around specific issues, they do not always dissolve when the issue is resolved. When a powerful coalition remains in place over time, it may effectively control school-district policy. The district becomes what they say it is. For example, in one school district we observed (Bacharach and Mitchell 1981b), the superintendent and a majority faction of the school board constituted the dominant coalition. Although they were challenged by other groups, such as the teachers and the minority faction of the school board, no single group or coalition of groups had sufficient influence to replace them as the dominant coalition. With the superintendent's control over his administration and the majority faction's control over school-board votes, the coalition could ensure that the district was run as it saw fit. The strategies and tactics employed (such as superintendent's control over information and the majority faction's ties to the community elite) were consistent with their perceptions of their official roles and responsibilities. Similarly, those who challenged the dominant coalition also followed a consistent set of rules or exceptions. Thus, there was an underlying logic in what often appeared to be a chaotic state of affairs. The ultimate aim of a political analysis is to uncover this logic.

Identifying the logic underlying activity can also help clarify important points of change in a school district. From a political perspective, the most important change centers on alteration of the dominant coalition or authority structure. For example, in one district we observed (Bacharach and Mitchell 1981b), a taxpayers' group concerned about rising school costs was able to mobilize sufficient community support to gain a majority of seats on the school board. This coalition then ousted the superintendent from office, changed the content and definition of other administrative roles, and began to review the district curriculum with an eye to adopting a more fundamental or back-to-basics approach to education. Shocked by some of these actions, teachers, parent groups, and members of the community elite formed a rival coalition and, after intensive campaigning, were able to replace the taxpayers' group as the majority faction of the school board. This new coalition then proceeded to implement a series of its own changes in school-district policy. A political perspective provides a means of analyzing these changes, which would be ignored by a structural analysis and would seem totally chaotic in a descriptive analysis.

A political perspective, in short, allows the observers to develop a realistic image of school districts as organizations—an image that can capture the logic underlying the apparent chaos of school-district activity and highlight areas in which significant change is likely to occur. As such, it is a perspective that holds promise for both researchers and practitioners.

THE GENERATION OF PRACTICAL THEORY

We need theories of organization that are general enough to be of interest to organizational theorists, yet specific enough to be of use to practitioners. To illustrate the value of such "practical theory," we have focused on the study of school districts as organizations. We saw that the dominant perspectives in organizational theory are too general to capture the specific dynamics of school districts, while the approaches that have been used in educational research are too specific to allow for useful generalization. To overcome these limitations, we advocate the use of political analysis for the study of schools as organizations. Political approaches to the study of organizations have received increasing attention in recent years (Bacharach and Lawler 1980; Pfeffer 1981), and the application of a political perspective to a specific type of organization promises to help refine the theoretical framework of these approaches. It also offers a viable theory of schools as organizations for use by educational researchers, something that has been lacking in the past (Cunningham, Hack, and Nystrand 1977; Immegart and Boyd 1979; Boyan 1981).

A political analysis of schools as organizations would also have direct implications for educational practitioners. From a political perspective, educational administrators play a critical role mediating between the various systems in the district in an effort to integrate diverse perspectives and achieve the consensus necessary to ensure the functioning of district operations. As we have seen, the structure of the organization has a direct effect on the political dynamics of a district. If we consider organizational design (i.e., the development of organizational structure) as a matter of strategic choice (Child 1969), then a political analysis of schools as organizations should be able to suggest design alternatives that would assist in the achievement of consensus.

The structure of the school district affects consensus by specifying what authority each actor has, what information each actor has assess to, and what work-related activities each actor may engage in. A strategic organizational design would aim to provide actors with only that authority, information, and activity necessary

to achieve consensus. Too little might cause unrest as actors seek out more information or authority, while too much might create conflict between actors who feel their "rights" are being infringed upon by others. The proper design will vary from district to district, but several possibilities can be outlined.

First, consider the community. As public institutions, schools are ultimately responsible to the community. Yet the community as a whole is often apathetic; consensus is most threatened when community groups mobilize around an issue (Bacharach and Mitchell 1981b). Thus, the critical question is What structures can forestall such mobilization? A district might consider establishing a public-relations position, whose responsibility would be to disseminate information and to keep tabs on community sentiment. To assess where mobilization is most likely to occur, this official might also keep track of voting in the various segments of the district. Alternatively, administrators could be required to address community groups to maintain contact between the public and the school. Another possibility is involving the community in district decision making through the formation of community advisory groups for specific issues. The attempt here would be to defuse criticism by providing a forum for its expression. The feasibility of this strategy, or of any strategy for dealing with the community, will depend very much on the diversity of the community (Bacharach and Mitchell 1981b). The more diverse the community, the greater care must be taken in handling community affairs. A homogeneous community may require relatively little attention.

The school board is the legitimate authority in terms of school-district policy. The primary challenges to consensus arise when the board is split into factions or when it tries to extend its authority beyond district policy. One of the primary design decisions bearing on the factionalization problem is the question of whether to use a system of committees or to rely on the board as a whole. A committee system may defuse criticism by allowing board members to become involved in specific areas of expertise. On the other hand, this level of involvement may result in extended, in-depth questioning that would slow board activity. In that case, it may be better if the board functions as a whole. Often, the development of factors centers on access to information. Board members may be allowed to solicit information on their own from any school personnel; alternatively, they may receive information from all administrators, or information may be channeled through the superintendent. Which of these structures is appropriate will depend upon the district's particular circumstances. In general, the most successful structures are ones in which the board accepts the role equivalent to that of a board of directors

(Bacharach, Lawler, and Mitchell 1984). Questions regarding involvement in nonpolicy issues and access to information then become less important.

Before the school board can act like a board of directors, however, the administration itself must be in order. Threats to consensus may arise in the administration because of insufficient breadth of expertise or a lack of unity in the administration (Bacharach and Mitchell 1981b). If the administration is to act as mediator or integrator, it must have the expertise needed to relate to all the other parties in the district on their own level. More important, it must be able to answer any challenges posed by others. Two kinds of structure may be employed to handle this problem. In the first, usually feasible only in smaller school districts, every administrator is a generalist with knowledge of several different areas. In larger districts, the use of specialized administrators is the more common alternative.

Expertise within the administration will do no good, however, if the administration itself cannot act as a unit. While conflict within the administration may occur on several levels, the relationship between the principals and the central office is particularly troublesome (Bacharach, Lawler, and Mitchell 1984). Principals expect to have a high degree of autonomy in running their buildings, an expectation that often conflicts with the centralization imposed by central office administrators. One possible solution is to establish a principals' committee to address areas of conflict. Alternatively, principals could be rotated through the schools to establish loyalty to the district rather than a specific school. Both alternatives attempt to develop a sense of unity within the administration.

The potential conflict between the principals and central office is particularly apparent in labor relations. The ability of principals to establish rapport with their staffs helps to create and maintain consensus, at least on the school level. Inconsistency in the handling of labor relations across schools, however, threatens consensus at the district level, where teachers are represented by a union. At least two structural arrangements might help avoid this problem. One possibility is to establish a centralized office to handle all labor-relations matters. Again, this sort of specialization is most feasible in larger districts. In smaller districts, the superintendent may fill this role. In either case, an effort should be made to educate the principals as to what they can and cannot do under the contract. A second structural arrangement would be the establishment of labor-management committees on the school and/or district level. These committees would address specific issues of concern to teachers not covered under the union contract, reducing the likelihood of threats to consensus.

Obviously, these are not the only implications for organizational design that can be drawn from a political analysis of schools as organizations. Nor is the practical utility of political analysis limited to recommendations for organizational design. Our intention was merely to demonstrate the potential for practical application. This potential, combined with the theoretical value of a political analysis for organizational theorists and educational researchers, has convinced us that viewing schools as political organizations is an important first step toward the generation of a practical theory of schools as organizations.

REFERENCES

Aldrich, H. E. 1979. *Organization and Environments.* Englewood Cliffs, N.J.: Prentice-Hall.

Bacharach, S. B. 1978. "Morphologie et processus: Une critique de la recherche organisationnelle contemporaine" (Morphology and process: A critique of contemporary organizational research). *Sociologie du travail (Sociology of work)* 20:153–73.

Bacharach, S. B., ed. 1981. *Organizational Behavior in Schools and School Districts.* New York: Praeger.

Bacharach, S. B., S. C. Bauer, and S. C. Conley. 1986. "Organizational Analysis of Stress." *Work and Occupations* 13, no. 1:7–32.

Bacharach, S. B., and E. J. Lawler. 1980. *Power and Politics in Organizations.* San Francisco: Jossey-Bass.

Bacharach, S. B., E. J. Lawler, and S. M. Mitchell. 1984. *Organizational Process and Labor Relations.* New York: Praeger.

Bacharach, S. B., and S. M. Mitchell. 1981a. "Toward a Dialogue in the Middle Range." *Educational Administration Quarterly* 17:1–14.

———. 1981b. "Critical Variables in the Formation and Maintenance of Consensus in School Districts." *Educational Administration Quarterly* 17:74–97.

Bidwell, C. E., and J. D. Kasarda. 1975. "School District Organization and Student Achievement." *American Sociological Review* 40:55–70.

Blau, P., and R. Schoenherr. 1971. *The Structure of Organizations.* New York: Basic Books.

Boyan, N. 1981. "Follow the Leader: Commentary on Research in Educational Administration." *Educational Researcher* 21:6–13.

Child, J. 1969. *The Business Enterprise in Modern Industrial Society.* London: Macmillan, Collier Books.

Clegg, S., and D. Dunkerly. 1980. *Organization, Class and Control.* London: Routledge & Kegan Paul.

Corwin, R. G. 1965. *A Sociology of Education.* New York: Appleton-Century-Crofts.

Counts, G. 1937. *The Social Composition of School Boards.* Chicago: University of Chicago Press.

Cunningham, L., W. Hack, and R. Nystrand, eds. 1977. *Educational Administration: The Developing Decades.* Berkeley, Calif.: McCutchan.

Davis, M., et al., eds. 1977. *The Structure of Educational Systems.* Stanford, Calif.: Stanford Center for Research and Development.

Gross, N., C. Ward, S. Mason, and A. W. McEachern. 1958. *Explorations in Role Analysis: Studies in School Superintendency Roles.* New York: Wiley.

Hage, J., and M. Aiken. 1970. *Social Change in Complex Organizations.* New York: Random House.

Hall, R. H. 1982. *Organizations: Structure and Process.* Englewood Cliffs, N.J.: Prentice-Hall.

Hannan, M. T., and J. H. Freeman. 1977. "The Population Ecology of Organizations." *American Journal of Sociology* 82:926–64.

Immegart, G., and W. Boyd, eds. 1979. *Problem Finding in Educational Administration: Trends in Research and Theory.* Lexington, Mass.: Heath.

McKelvey, B. 1982. *Organizational Systematics.* Berkeley, Calif.: University of California Press.

Meyer, J. W., and B. Rowan. 1978. "The Structure of Educational Organizations." In *Environments and Organizations,* ed. M. W. Meyer and Associates. San Francisco: Jossey-Bass.

Oettinger, A., and S. Marks. 1974. "Educational Technology: New Myths and Old Realities." In *Human Service Organi-* zations, ed. Y. Hasenfeld and R. A. English. Ann Arbor, Mich.: University of Michigan Press.

Perrow, C. 1967. "A Framework for the Comparative Analysis of Organizations." *American Sociological Review* 32:194–208.

———. 1974. "The Analysis of Goals in Complex Organizations." In *Human Service Organizations,* ed. Y. Hasenfeld and R. A. English. Ann Arbor, Mich.: Univeristy of Michigan Press.

Pfeffer, J. 1981. *Power in Organizations.* Marshfield, Mass.: Pitman.

Pinder, C., and L. Moore. 1979. "The Resurrection of Taxonomy to Aid in the Development of Middle Range Theories of Organizational Behavior." *Administrative Science Quarterly* 24:99–118.

Pugh, D., D. Hickson, C. Hinings, and C. Turner. 1968. "Dimensions of Organizational Structure." *Administrative Science Quarterly* 13:65–105.

Silverman, D. 1971. *The Theory of Organizations: A Sociological Framework.* New York: Basic Books.

Smith, L. M., J. J. Prunty, and D. C. Dwyer. 1981. "A Longitudinal Nested Systems Model of Innovation and Change in Schooling." In *Organizational Behavior in Schools and School Districts,* ed. S. B. Bacharach. New York: Praeger.

Sproull, L., and D. Zubrow, "Performance Information in School Systems: Perspectives from Organizational Theory." *Educational Administration Quarterly* 17:61–79.

Weick, K. 1976. "Educational Organizations as Loosely Coupled Systems." *Administrative Science Quarterly* 21:1–19.

———. 1979. *The Social Psychology of Organizing.* Reading, Mass.: Addison-Wesley.

Wirt, F., and M. Kirst. 1975. *The Political Web of American Schools.* Boston: Little, Brown.

Wolin, S. 1969. "A Critique of Organizational Theories." In *A Sociological Reader on Complex Organizations,* ed. A. Etzioni, 133–49. New York: Holt, Rinehart and Winston.

Ziegler, H., and M. Jennings. 1974. *Governing American Schools.* North Scituate, Mass.: Duxbury Press.

27

Health-care organization
DUNCAN NEUHAUSER AND EDWARD EIGNER

INTRODUCTION

Health-care services account for a large and growing proportion of the gross national product of the United States: 10.5 percent in 1983, up from 5.3 percent in 1960. Hospitals account for 40 percent of these expenditures, employ most of the health-care managers, and have been the subject of most of the literature on health-care management.[1]

The seemingly inexorable rise in health- and medical-care costs has prompted increasing public concern that these expenditures be controlled and efficiently allocated. More attention has been devoted to the systematic study of the administration of institutions devoted to health. Included in these efforts is an attempt to place the study of health-care organizations, medical sociology, and health economics within the general body of social science theory.

Although health care has similarities to various other fields in many particulars, it also presents a unique distinguishing combination of features. This chapter offers a brief history and descriptive anatomy of the health-care field, some theoretical physiology or system explanations, and a discussion of major managerial and organizational problems, that is, its pathology.

THE HEALTH-CARE FIELD DESCRIBED

Historical evolution

In 1873 there were only about 175 hospitals in the United States. The introduction of ether anesthesia in 1848, aseptic surgery in the 1870s and 1880s, and laboratory medicine and Roentgen's X rays at the turn of the century created the technological base that made the hospital a medical necessity. By 1915 there were over 5,000 hospitals in this country.[2] The first half of the twentieth century saw the achievement of substantial control of infectious disease. The work began with Koch and Pasteur in the 1880s; gradually the evidence of an infectious rather than a miasmatic cause of contagious disease was accepted; and after World War II the widespread availability of penicillin to the civilian population completed the process. Effective drugs for the control of psychosis and tuberculosis[3] appeared in the 1950s, nearly eliminating tuberculosis hospitals and reducing the number of people in mental hospitals.

1. U.S. Department of Health and Human Services, Public Health Service, *Health United States 1982* (Washington, D.C.: 1982).

2. Duncan Neuhauser, *Coming of Age. Fifty Years of the American College of Hospital Administrators and the Profession It Serves* (Chicago: American College of Hospital Administrators, 1984); Paul Starr, *The Social Transformation of American Medicine* (New York: Basic Books, 1982); Paul Lawrence and Davis Dyer, *Renewing American Industry* (New York: Free Press, 1983) chap 4.

3. Harry F. Dowling, *Fighting Infection* (Cambridge, Mass.: Harvard University Press, 1977).

Before infections were controlled, hospitals were built in the pavilion style, with long corridors between patient wards. By the 1930s infection was sufficiently controllable that urban hospitals could be built vertically, with efficiency rather than infection control as the guiding architectural principle. The managerial specialty of hospital administration traces its origins to the founding of the American College of Hospital Administrators in 1933 and the establishment of the first successful graduate degree program in hospital administration in 1934, at the University of Chicago.[4]

The first nursing schools in the United States based on Florence Nightingale's principles were established in 1873. Nurses were then largely managers of unskilled workers, concerned primarily with cleanliness, strict order, and food preparation. With the steady rise of technology in medicine came a division of labor and a growth in hospital size, so that today there are well over three hundred specialized and professionalized occupations in health care.[5] In contrast to the experience of industry, technological advances in medicine have generally led to higher costs, not higher productivity, as measured by person-hours required for each patient admission or day of care.

Before 1900, hospital trustees were often directly involved in decisions on which patients to admit, based on the criterion of the deserving poor.[6] Many hospitals had no administrator, and the tasks such an officer would have performed were shared among the trustees (chairman and treasurer), the nursing matron, and the chief physician, who spent most of his time in private practice.

With the advent of the technology that made the hospital essential at the turn of the century, physicians became more influential.[7] Medical condition, as defined by the physician, became the criterion for admission. The work of nurses was to a large degree defined by the doctor's orders, as written in the patient's chart.

The Pure Food and Drug laws of 1906 gave the monopoly power of the prescription pad to doctors, started the demise of the patent nostrum trade, and defined the economic environment of the pharmacy and the pharmaceutical manufacturing industry.[8]

Hospital administration was little affected by the scientific management ideas of Frederick Taylor. Far more important was the industrial standardization

Table 27.1 The number of Americans with health insurance coverage

Year	Number of people
1940	11,962,000
1950	76,639,000
1960	122,500,000
1965	138,671,000
1970	158,847,000
1979	183,238,000

Source: *Source Book of Health Insurance Data 1980–1981* (Washington, D.C.: Health Insurance Institute, 1982), 13.

movement—a movement rarely referred to in the management textbooks. Standards of excellence were to be defined as the basis of comparison and as goals to which to aspire. The Flexner report on medical education in 1910 urged that other medical schools either work toward meeting the standard set by the Johns Hopkins Medical School or close down.[9] The last substandard medical school was closed before 1940. There was a similar movement to standardize hospital-based nursing education. In 1918 the American College of Surgeons started its hospital-standardization program, which directly evolved into the present Joint Commission on the Accreditation of Hospitals. One important result of this effort is the organizational similarity of the country's thousands of hospitals and the capacity of health workers, including doctors and nurses, to adapt easily to the work in new places.

Although most of the health-care system was in place by 1920, the critical component of health insurance, including Blue Cross and Blue Shield, had its impetus in the depression and explosive growth after World War II (see table 27.1). Health insurance was both a response to and a driving force behind the rapid rise in health-care costs. The nature of health insurance, requiring a definable benefit with a predictable limit of payout, led to a greater flow of funds to hospitals, thus further increasing their influence.

A recent turning point was the establishment of Medicare (for the elderly) and Medicaid (for the poor) in 1966. The result was an even more rapid growth of medical-care costs. Since the 1950s massive R & D funding through the federal government's National Institutes of Health has spurred technological development. The federal response to rising costs in the 1970s was regulation, health planning, requirement of certificates of need, rate review, and other administrative regulations.

The industry response was organizational diversification. By 1978, for the first time, the number of patients

4. Neuhauser, *Coming of Age.* (Chicago: Plenum Press, 1984).

5. Florence Wilson and Duncan Neuhauser, *Health Services in the United States,* 2d ed. (Cambridge, Mass.: Ballinger, 1982).

6. Davis Rosner, *A Once Charitable Enterprise* (Cambridge, England: Cambridge University Press, 1982).

7. Charles Perrow, in *The Hospital in Modern Society,* ed. Eliot Freedson (Glencoe, Ill.: Free Press, 1963).

8. James Harvey Young, *The Toadstool Millionaires and the Medical Messiahs* (Princeton, N.J.: Princeton University Press, 1961; 1967)

9. Abraham Flexner, *Medical Education in the United States and Canada* (New York: Carnegie Foundation for the Advancement of Teaching, 1910).

in nursing homes exceeded the number of patients in hospitals. The introduction of effective drugs in the mid-fifties had reduced the size of the large state mental hospitals. Community mental-health centers, neighborhood health centers, larger medical-group practices, health-maintenance organizations (HMOs), and regulatory agencies created a very complex external environment for the hospital manager. Many hospitals adopted a "corporate structure" with a president concerned with external affairs and an executive vice-president to manage the internal affairs of the hospital.

In response to this complex external environment, along with a growing sophistication of hospital management (finance, industrial engineering, computerized information systems, marketing), many single hospitals joined together into larger groups, such as the for-profit Hospital Corporation of America (340 hospitals). The formerly decentralized Sisters of Mercy Health Corporation (20 hospitals) developed a strong corporate headquarters to manage its system of hospitals. The Fairview Community Hospitals in Minneapolis, using the concept of the bank holding company, joined together 6 hospitals.[10] Integration has been both vertical and horizontal.

According to the American Hospital Association, 1,924 hospitals are now organized into 256 multihospital systems. Of these systems 104 are related to the Roman Catholic Church, 21 to other churches, 104 are other nonprofit organizations, and 27 are for-profit investor owned.[11]

Hospitals' movement toward integration has been less rapid than that of manufacturing industries such as automobiles. One reason is the preponderance of government and nonprofit hospitals, which cannot be captured through stock ownership. If a publicly owned industrial corporation is poorly managed, it can be taken over; not so the voluntary hospital.

One reason for the growth of the multihospital systems is their access to capital. By and large they can obtain lower bond ratings than nonprofit hospitals. As many states have moved away from a regulatory approach to cost control, the limiting factor on growth becomes access to low-cost capital.

At the macro level

EXPENDITURES

In 1979, 40.3 percent of the health-care dollar went to hospitals, 18.9 percent to physician services, 6.4 percent

to dentists, and 2.2 percent to other professional sources; 7.8 percent went to drugs and medical supplies, 2 percent to eyeglasses and appliances, 8.4 percent to nursing-home care, 2.2 percent for other personal health services, 4.2 percent to the costs of prepayment and insurance companies and governmental administration, 3.0 percent to government public-health activities, 2.2 percent to research, and 2.5 percent to construction.[12]

The predominant large health-care organizations are hospitals, nursing homes,[13] third-party insurance payers,[14] government agencies, and drug manufacturers.[15] Predominant small organizations are the professional office practice and pharmacies.

SOURCES OF PAYMENTS

In 1979 patients paid directly out of pocket for 31.8 percent of personal health-care expenditures (primarily for professional services, drugs, and eyeglasses). Private health insurance paid 26.7 percent (primarily for hospital care, nursing homes, and physicians' services). Philanthropy paid 1.3 percent, primarily to hospitals. The federal government paid 28.3 percent (primarily for hospital and nursing-home care through Medicare, 15.6 percent, and Medicaid, 6.2 percent). State and local government paid 12 percent (5.3 percent of Medicaid), primarily for hospitals and nursing homes (see table 27.2)

HOSPITALS

Hospitals are owned by federal, state, and local government, by nonprofit corporations, including religious organizations, and by for-profit corporations. In terms of patient care, there are three major classifications of hospitals: psychiatric, long-term care, and short-term general and other special hospitals.

Of the 6,988 hospitals existing in the United States in 1980, 361 were federally owned (24 psychiatric, 337 general). Among the nonfederal hospitals, 527 were psychiatric (94 nonprofit, 146 for-profit, 287 state and local government). There were 177 long-term general, nonpsychiatric hospitals and 5,923 short-term general and nonpsychiatric special hospitals. Of these short-term hospitals, 3,350 were nonprofit, 727 were for profit, and 1,846 were owned by state and local government.

The two major types of hospitals are the large state-owned psychiatric hospitals and the acute general voluntary hospitals. They differ substantially in average dura

10. *Directory of Multihospital Systems* (Chicago: American Hospital Association, 1983).

11. *Multihospital Systems*, 85–86.

12. Wilson and Neuhauser, *Health United States 1982.*

13. Bruce C. Vladeck, *Unloving Care* (New York: Basic Books, 1980).

14. *Source Book of Health Insurance* (Washington, D.C.: Health Insurance Institute, yearly).

15. Milton Silverman and Philip R. Lee, *Pills, Profits and Politics* (Berkeley, Calif.: University of California Press, 1974); Cotton M. Lindsay, *The Pharmaceutical Industry* (New York: Wiley, 1978).

Table 27.2 Personal health-care expenditures by selected third-party payers and type of expenditure, 1979

Source of payment	Total	Hospital care	Physicians' services	Dentists' services	Other professional services	Drugs and medical sundries	Eyeglasses and appliances	Nursing home care	Other health services
				Amount (in millions)					
Total	188,551	85,342	40,599	13,607	4,687	16,975	4,353	17,807	5,180
Direct payments	59,973	6,905	14,813	9,938	2,832	14,216	3,789	7,481	—
Third-party payments									
Private health insurance	50,286	29,803	15,138	3,130	604	1,339	155	117	—
Philanthropy and industrial in-plant	2,407	942	24	—	52	—	—	107	1,283
Government									
Federal									
Medicare	29,328	21,651	6,407	—	552	—	249	373	97
Medicaid	11,770	4,347	1,203	243	249	665	—	4,775	287
Other	12,213	8,888	389	54	47	39	82	313	2,399
State and local									
Medicaid	9,913	3,662	1,015	205	210	560	—	4,021	241
Other	12,660	9,144	1,611	36	143	155	77	621	874

Source: Robert Gibson, "National Health Care Expenditures 1979," *Health Care Financing Review* 2 (Summer 1980), 16–22. Also in Wilson and Neuhauser, *Health Services* (see no. 5).

tion of patient stay and technological complexity of care. Prolonged patient stays in psychiatric hospitals have allowed a more elaborated patient subculture to develop. Goffman describes this as a total organization.[16] This can also develop in general hospital wards, but to a lesser degree.[17]

Just as hospitals are under diverse ownership, health insurance is provided by the federal government (Medicare), federal and state governments (Medicaid), by private nonprofit organizations (Blue Cross-Blue Shield), and by private for-profit insurance companies. These third parties exist for two reasons: (1) to make predictable, through the pooling of risk, the unpredictable and high costs of care, particularly hospital care; and (2) to provide for medical care for those who cannot pay for it. The societal commitment to provide medical care to all, regardless of ability to pay, is also an important distinguishing feature of medical care. It is a major reason why government pays for 40.2 percent of personal health care.

With the introduction of Medicare (acute care for people over age 65) and Medicaid (care for the indigent, including the elderly in nursing homes), the government's

financing role has changed dramatically. In 1965, before those programs had begun, government paid for 21.9 percent of personal medical care. This money mostly went to pay the operating budgets of hospitals owned and operated by the government. Control here is exercised through the budget process. Because Medicare and Medicaid called for payment of nongovernment organizations, government regulations and controls were required to channel this money appropriately. The growth of all forms of health-insurance coverage, particularly after World War II, permitted and indeed promoted an increase in medical care costs; to control this increase, regulation intensified substantially in the 1970s.

THE THEORY OF HOSPITAL OWNERSHIP

The mix of hospital ownership in the United States reflects a combination of the societal commitment to medical care for all, the technological need for the hospital, cultural attitudes, and the existence of social class differences. Countries with minimal class-income variation (Sweden, Finland, Iceland) and/or a political philosophy that assumes a classless society and a state economy (the USSR, Eastern Europe) do not officially have this variation. In these countries hospitals are owned by the state. Within such systems, however, there may be special government hospitals or hospital units set aside for elite groups, as in the USSR. The American philosophical distaste for government ownership is con-

16. Erving Goffman, *Asylums* (Garden City, New York: Doubleday, 1961); William Caudill, *The Psychiatric Hospital as a Small Society* (Cambridge, Mass.: Harvard University Press, 1958).

17. Rose Laub Coser, *Life in the Ward* (East Lansing, Mich.: Michigan State University Press, 1962).

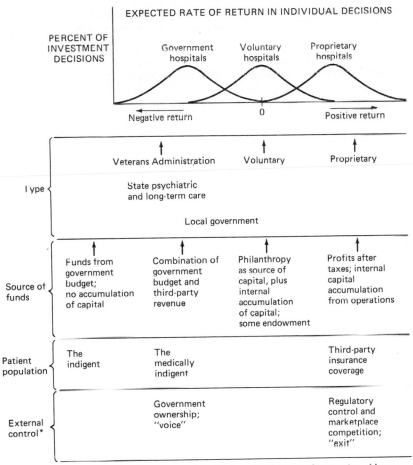

EXPECTED RATE OF RETURN IN INDIVIDUAL DECISIONS

Figure 27.1 The theory of hospital ownership and investment behavior

*See Albert O. Hirschman, *Exit, Voice, and Loyalty* (Cambridge, Mass.: Harvard University Press, 1970).

sistent with a comparatively small government-owned medical-care sector in this country.

The *nonprofit hospital* is a concept derived from the traditions of the Roman Catholic Church and other religious organizations and the nonchurch, nonprofit organizations originally evolving from Henry VIII's dissolution of British monasteries in the 1500s and their replacement by private philanthropy voluntarily given. Richard Titmus gives the best description of voluntarism in health in his book about the donation of blood.[18] Another example is the free work given by hospital volunteers. Such unpaid activities do not exist in Sweden, reflecting a different cultural tradition.

The idea of hospitals run for profit is an anathema in many countries of this world, but not in France, Spain, Italy, some South American countries, or the Philippines, where private hospitals are sought by those who can afford them. In the United States, for-profit hospitals saw their greatest growth at the turn of this century, predominantly in the South and West, where there was little private philanthropy and rapid population growth.[19] Proprietary hospitals tended to be small, initially started by doctors for their own practices; in the last ten years many have been combined into a few international investor-owned, for-profit, multihospital corporations. By far the largest of these is the Hospital Corporation of America, whose revenue and assets both exceeded $1 billion by 1982, when revenues were $2.5 billion.

Investor-owned hospitals have several distinguishing features. They are able to respond rapidly to changes in demand.[20] They have better access to capital because they can offer investors convertible bonds.[21] They face

18. Richard Titmus, *The Gift Relationship* (New York: Pantheon, 1971); David B. Johnson, *Blood Policy: Issues and Alternatives* (Washington, D.C.: American Enterprise Institute for Public Policy Research, 1976).

19. Bruce Steinwald and Duncan Neuhauser, "The Role of the Proprietary Hospital," *Journal of Law and Contemporary Problems* 35, no. 4 (Autumn 1970): 817–38.

20. Steinwald and Neuhauser, "Proprietary Hospital," 817–38.

21. Richard B. Siegrist, "Wall Street and the For-Profit Hospital Management Companies," in *The New Health Care for Profit*, ed. Bradford Gray (Washington, D.C.: National Academy Press, 1983).

varying degrees of distaste on the part of professionals.[22] For any given type of patient, they are more costly to third-party payers.[23]

Shortell hypothesizes that decision making is also different. He proposes that decisions are more "computational" and "judgmental" rather than "compromise and inspirational" because organizational preferences and cause-effect relationships are more certain.[24]

Another way of looking at the differences among government, voluntary, and proprietary hospitals in decision making has to do with expected return on investment, as shown schematically in figure 27.1. The proprietaries make investment decisions expecting a positive rate of return. Growth and replacement is through internal capital accumulation. At the other extreme are the state psychiatric and long-term-care Veterans Administration hospitals, which are funded by government budgets with separable appropriations for capital (new buildings and equipment). Cost control is achieved through budget constraints. These institutions do not make investment decisions on the basis of positive expected rate of return from patient or third-party payments, but rather on the basis of decisions by politicians.

The Veterans Administration hospitals cannot accept Medicare or Medicaid reimbursement. The tendency has been for patients eligible for such reimbursement in state psychiatric hospitals to be transferred to nursing homes, which are largely proprietary in ownership.

In the course of this century, the voluntary hospitals have been moving to the right of the diagram shown in figure 27.1. At the turn of the century, trustees were expected to pay for most of the deficit through charitable contributions; capital accumulation was through philanthropy. With the growth in costs, the voluntaries have sought government funding and are accumulating capital from revenues.[25] Many local government hospitals, often rural, are practically indistinguishable from voluntaries in their behavior. They may receive local government budgetary support for capital and to pay for deficits.

The traditional large city hospitals like Cook County in Chicago, Bellevue in New York, and Los Angeles General Hospital were created to serve the urban poor. They were initially supported entirely by local government budgets, but since 1966 a substantial share of their income has come from Medicare and Medicaid rather than from local government tax revenues.

At the micro level

At the center of health care is the dyadic relationship between a sick person and a healer—a relationship that exists in all cultures—and specifically, in the developed world, between a patient and a physician.

THE SICK ROLE
One of the central contributions of medical sociology is the definition of the role characteristics of the patient.[26] The healthy person becomes aware of disease, becomes worried, possibly in pain; the patient plays a dependent, almost childlike submissive role, particularly in a hospital, where many of the adult decisions are removed from the patient (what to wear and eat, personal privacy) and turned over to the physician and the nurses and other workers allied with the physician. The patient is expected to make an effort to recover; patient dependency can turn to irritation as the recovery process occurs, along with a return to independence.[27]

IGNORANCE AND KNOWLEDGE AND PROFESSIONALISM
The role of the physician includes the assumption of expertise about illness obtained through years of education. The converse of the physician's knowledge is the patient's lack of knowledge (ignorance) about the cause of the symptoms and the tasks required to diagnose the disease and provide treatment.[28]

With knowledge of medical care goes the cluster of role characteristics associated with professionalism: a body of scientific knowledge, acquired by formal edu-

22. Arnold Relman, "The New Medical Industrial Complex," *New England Journal of Medicine* 303 (Oct. 23, 1980): 963–70.

23. Robert V. Pattison and Hallie M. Katz, "Investor-Owned and Not-for-Profit Hospitals: A Comparison Based on California Data," *New England Journal of Medicine* 309, no. 6 (August 11, 1983): 347–53.

24. Stephen Shortell, "Physician Involvement in Hospital Decision Making," in *The New Health Care for Profit*, Gray, 73–102.

25. Rosemary Stevens, " 'A Poor Sort of Memory' ": Voluntary Hospitals and Government before the Depression," *Milbank Memorial Fund Quarterly* 60, no. 4 (Fall 1982): 551–84; Rosner, *Once Charitable Enterprise*.

26. Stanley King, "Social Psychological Factors in Illness," in *Handbook of Medical Sociology*, ed. Howard E. Freeman, Sol Levine, and Leo G. Reder. (Englewood Cliffs, N.J.: Prentice-Hall, 1963), 99–121.

27. The classic articles on the sick role by Talcott Parsons, David Mechanic, and Edward Suchman can be found in E. Gartley Jaco, ed., *Patients, Physicians, and Illness*, 2d ed. (New York: Free Press, 1972); for a current review of this area see David Mechanic, ed., *Handbook of Health, Health Care and the Health Professions* (New York: Free Press, 1983), sect. 5, "Health, Illness, Social Adaptation: Psychosocial and Behavioral Issues," chaps. 25–29.

28. William C. Richardson and D. Neuhauser, "First Question in Health Planning: Does the Public Know What it Wants or Not?" *Modern Hospitals* (May 1968): 115–17.

cation; public recognition of this knowledge through academic degree, professional licensure, titles (Dr.), legally defined special activities (the prescription pad, the surgical knife, the injection); high social status; special clothing (the white coat); a presumed altruistic commitment to caring for people; organizational independence (private practice); and authority.[29]

Professionalism is often viewed as inconsistent with the ideal marketplace, in which the buyer (patient) and seller (doctor) are presumed to be equally knowledgeable. Professionalism is in the English tradition derived from the role of the gentleman, inconsistent with the marketplace and consistent with voluntary organizations.[30] This preference for voluntary hospitals probably explains why the proportion of proprietary hospitals fell from 32 percent of the total in 1923 to 10 percent in 1980. When the proprietaries' advantage of rapid response is neutralized, professional (and public) preference has led to their transformation into voluntary organizations. Existing investor-owned hospital corporations tend to make their presence known on Wall Street, but not at the local hospital level, where the corporate ownership is downplayed.

Today the prototype profession is medicine, and this professional role has been part of the model aspired to by the other occupational groups in medicine, including nurses, clinical psychologists, social workers, dieticians, laboratory technicians, and many others.[31]

THE PLACEBO EFFECT AND MEDICINE'S EXACTING STANDARD OF EFFICACY

Perhaps the one feature that most distinguishes medical care from other marketplace exchanges is the placebo effect. The patients' and physicians' belief that a treatment will work, makes it work.[32] A possible physiological explanation is that the otherwise inert treatment may trigger endorphin excretion, which in turn is related to pain control.[33] This placebo effect is well documented and is used as the control in drug experiments with human subjects. It usually elicits a significant beneficial response over a wide range of conditions. In 1955 Beecher estimated that the placebo could account for about one-third of the benefit of medical care.[34] This helps explain why the healing role is a cultural universal and why chiropractics, faith healing, Christian Science, and other "nonscientific" providers of care continue to exist. The placebo response may have developed as an evolutionary survival characteristic in humans. This hypothesis is, however, empirically untestable. The benefit from medical treatment independent of the placebo effect is very difficult to measure accurately in human beings. The randomized double-blind clinical trial is the standard for evaluation, but it is difficult to carry out because of cost and ethical considerations.[35] Randomization requires that patients voluntarily accept assignment to either an experimental or a control group. In double-blind trials, neither the patient nor the treating and examining physician knows whether the patient is in the control or experimental group. Such studies are usually limited to drugs and injectables.

The difficulty of conducting randomized clinical trials explains the persistence in medicine of treatment techniques of doubtful efficacy beyond the placebo effect.[36] With respect to welfare economics it implies a clear benefit accruing to the ignorant patient and the enthusiastic doctor. The market for personal medical services is perhaps the only one where the buyer can gain from ignorance of the product or service purchased.

Whereas the marketplace and profitability provide the agreed-upon test of performance industry, medicine has a different standard. Does the treatment provided improve the quantity and quality of the patient's life above and beyond the effect achieved by a placebo? This is a very exacting standard of performance, and only a fraction of medical care has met this test. However, the Food and Drug Administration requires such evidence before a new drug can be sold. Other, often expensive, therapeutic measures have not met this test, including a variety of cancer treatments, electronic fetal monitoring of deliveries, and intensive-care units.[37]

29. Ernest Greenwood, "Attributes of a Profession," in *Man, Work, and Society* ed. Sigmund Nosow and William Form (New York: Basic Books, 1962).

30. W. J. Reader, *Professional Men* (London: Weidenfeld and Nicholson, 1966); other professions tend to be associated with voluntary and government organizations, lawyers and law courts, the clergy, army officers, and all with universities.

31. Amitai Etzioni, *The Semi-Professions and Their Organizations* (New York: Free Press, 1969).

32. Jerome D. Frank, *Persuasion and Healing*, rev. ed. (Baltimore: Johns Hopkins University Press, 1973).

33. Robert Kanigal, "The Placebo Effect," *Johns Hopkins Magazine* 34, no. 4 (August 1983): xii–xvi.

34. Henry K. Beecher, "The Powerful Placebo," *Journal of the American Medical Association* 159 (1955): 1602–6.

35. U.S. Congress, Office of Technology Assessment, *The Impact of Randomized Clinical Trials on Health Policy and Medical Practice: Background Paper*, OTA BP H-22 (Washington, D.C.: August 1983).

36. A. L. Cochrane, *Effectiveness and Efficiency—Random Reflections on Health Services* (Abington, England: Nuffield Provincial Hospitals Trust, 1971).

37. John Bunker, B. Barnes, and F. Mosteller, *Costs, Risks and Benefits of Surgery* (New York: Oxford University Press, 1977); Ivan Illich, *Medical Nemesis* (New York: Pantheon, 1976); U.S. Congress, Office of Technology Assessment, Series of publications on medical technology assessment, Washington, D.C.: GPO 1978–1983.

Because the standard is so exacting and so infrequently applied, the causal links between medical-care inputs and outcome are often unclear. There is an ongoing debate as to whether, at the margin, more medical care will reduce mortality.[38] This characteristically low visibility of consequences in health care has a variety of organizational effects, including monopoly concentration, routinization, cyclical behavior, unclear objectives, usurpation of organizational control, and rigidity.[39]

Under such circumstances, tasks can be carried out on the basis of tradition rather than efficacy, provider preference rather than patient preference, economic benefit to the provider, or provider politics. For example, hospital admission rates per one thousand population are about 40 percent lower for members of health-maintenance organizations than for others. The HMO plan must survive on the fixed yearly payments by enrollees. Outside such plans, doctors and hospitals are typically paid on a fee-for-service basis. The HMO is rewarded for not admitting, while elsewhere the reward system favors admission.

Such differences occur in large part because there is no clear means-ends relationship for much of medical care.

UNCERTAINTY AND HEALTH INSURANCE

Kenneth Arrow says that one of the key characteristics of the micro economics of medical care is the uncertainty of need for services and of outcome.[40] The patient usually cannot predict what procedures will be called for, nor can the physician.

Because of the uncertainty of need and the small probability of large expense, insurance coverage is appropriate. The *ideal insurable event* has several defining characteristics. The event must be statistically independent. Accidental disease fits this criterion better than a plaguelike infectious disease or wartime civilian injuries. The event must be unambiguously definable. Surgery fits this criterion better than the need for psychotherapy. The event should be large enough and rare enough (but not too rare) that coverage is affordable and the proportion of premiums going to administrative costs is minimized. Each individual event should be uncontrollable and un-

predictable, but in aggregate they should be predictable by the insurer.[41]

Medical care only partly fits this model of the ideal insurable event. The disparity between ideal and reality creates some of the major dislocations and problems of medical care and helps explain medical-care-system dynamics.

The problem called "moral hazard" arises when the insured can influence the occurrence of the insured-against event. The classic example is the bankrupt store owner who burns his building to get the insurance. In medical care moral hazard takes a different form. Some patients seek more medical care than others, and some physicians urge more medical care on their patients than others.[42] For many patient conditions several different treatments are possible. For breast cancer, limited and radical surgery with and without chemotherapy, with and without radiation therapy, are all possible treatments, and different physicians will choose different combinations. Although the differences in benefit resulting from these alternatives are very unclear, the cost differences are large and unambiguous.

The number of age-adjusted total days of care per one thousand people per year for prepaid group-practice HMOs is 20–40 percent lower than for fee-for-service care.[43] That difference has clear economic implications for purchasers of care.

Different approaches have been proposed for coping with this moral hazard created by health-insurance coverage where means-ends relationships are unclear. The possibilities include health-planning regulation, price competition,[44] large deductibles,[45] second surgical opinion before admission certification, different budgetary incentives for hospitals, and reeducating physicians to practice cost-effective medicine.

The insurance model must be modified to fit the needs of the poor who cannot pay for the premiums. Two such modifications are Medicare for the elderly and Medicaid for the poor, which goes primarily to families sup-

38. Jack Hadley, *More Medical Care, Better Health?* (Washington, D.C.: Urban Institute Press, 1982); Victor R. Fuchs, *Who Shall Live?* (New York: Basic Books, 1974).

39. Selwyn Becker and Gerald Gordon, "An Entrepreneurial Theory of Formal Organizations," *Administrative Science Quarterly* 11, no. 3 (December 1966); Selwyn Becker and D. Neuhauser, *The Efficient Organization* (New York: Elsevier Science, 1975).

40. Kenneth J. Arrow, "The Welfare Economics of Medical Care," *American Economic Review* 53 (1963), 941.

41. Wilson and Neuhauser, *Health United States 1982*, chap. 5.

42. John Wennberg and A. Gittelsohn, "Small Area Variation in Health Care Delivery," *Science* 182:1102–7; John Wennberg, John Bunker, and Benjamin Barnes, "The Need for Assessing the Outcome of Common Medical Practices," *Annual Review of Public Health 1980* 1:277–95 (Palo Alto, Calif.: Annual Reviews, 1980).

43. Harold S. Luft, "How Do Health Maintenance Organizations Achieve their Savings?" *New England Journal of Medicine* 298 (1978): 1336–43; Harold S. Luft, *Health Maintenance Organizations* (New York: Wiley, 1981), 90.

44. Alain C. Enthoven, *Health Plan* (Reading, Mass.: Addison-Wesley, 1980).

45. Martin Feldstein, "A New Approach to National Health Insurance," in *Hospital Costs and Health Insurance* (Cambridge, Mass.: Harvard University Press, 1981).

ported by Aid to Families with Dependent Children (AFDC) and the elderly in nursing homes.

The basic cell of the medical-care organism is the dyadic relationship between the dependent, unknowing, worried, unique patient and the physician, whom society has vested with a role of authority and high prestige. The potential but unpredictable high costs of care, combined with a social acceptance of the necessity of providing medical care to all, and the American distrust of the government, have led to our mix of public and private insurers and providers. Because there is often no clear relationship between medical care and health result, there is substantial variation in the use of medical care, which is substantially independent of medical need.

THE COORDINATION OF SPECIALIZED WORKERS IN THE CARE OF UNIQUE PATIENTS: THE CENTRAL MICRO PROBLEM

The central health-care organizational problem, particularly in hospitals, is the coordination of highly specialized workers around the care of numerous unique individual patients with often unpredictable needs for medical care inputs, within urgent time constraints.

Although universities have many highly specialized faculty, the problems of coordination are usually minimal. Although airframe manufacturers have specialized workers and must closely coordinate their efforts, their time horizon spreads over several years for the development of a new airplane. A supermarket has customers with urgent unique needs, but they fill their shopping baskets themselves, and specialized workers are not required to advise them on what to buy. In Joan Woodward's organizational typology, unit production (vs. large batch or process) best fits the hospital but hardly does it justice.[46]

For each patient in a hospital the doctor in charge calls forth, usually in a specific temporal order, a series of activities, diagnostic tests, therapeutic interventions and, after recuperation, discharge. Although the mix of activities required is often unpredictable, the activities themselves are well defined or programmed.

A patient with angina (heart pain) may undergo angiography to see if the blood vessels of the heart are blocked in such a way as to be surgically correctable. If

so, coronary-artery-bypass surgery may be appropriate. On admission, the angiography is certain but the surgery is not. Both this test and surgery are in part highly routinized activities. This type of surgery involves thousands of specific, often-repeated tasks on the part of a team of workers (three surgeons, an anesthesiologist, and four nurses in the operating room would be typical). In 90 percent of such cases these tasks will be routine, and only one patient in a hundred dies within thirty days of the operation.

This division of labor is reflected in the growth of specialized departments within hospitals (dietary, laboratory, X ray, surgery, intensive-care units). Because over 60 percent of the hospital's costs are fixed, it is economically important to maintain a high utilization of this service capacity, exacerbating the problem of coordination.

A single physician is responsible for each patient and has the final say in what is done for him or her. Resident physicians may work under that physician's direction, often with wide latitude in decision making, and other experts may be brought in as consultants, including the radiologist and pathologist. In this way the physician organization around each patient follows the classical management principles of unity of command and delegation of authority, but not responsibility, line authority, and staff consultation. In American hospitals the attending physician is typically only on the in-patient unit for a few hours a day. In his or her absence the patient's chart is a central coordinating mechanism for defining relevant tasks and recording information for the three nursing shifts, which cover the floor twenty-four hours a day, seven days a week.

The problems of coordination arise not only between specialized workers and departments, but between the daily shifts of nursing and other personnel. The tasks that must be performed in patient care are unpredictable, often urgent, and clustered in nearly unique combination for each patient. This high level of complexity is probably unique in organizational history. (A possible exception to this is the launching of a space vehicle. However, here there is a long preparation period before the shot and only one shot at a time.) Such complexity can and does result in errors of omission and commission on the part of hospital workers. These errors are observed with exasperation by patients, result in the problem of malpractice, and cannot be completely eliminated in this imperfect world.

Rarely will two patients require the same set of activities.[47] The proliferation of tests and procedures and

46. Joan Woodward, *Industrial Organization: Theory and Practice* (London, Oxford University Press, 1965).

47. Jeffrey E. Harris, "The Internal Organization of Hospitals: Some Economic Implications," *The Bell Journal of Economics*, 467–82.

the growing number applied to each patient have made problems of coordination increasingly difficult. The development of new tasks has led to a greater division of labor, so that more and more different types of workers are drawn into the care of each patient. *Professional dominance* is a term used to define the control that physicians have in defining the activities of a large number of allied health personnel.[48]

Nursing is a profession in a state of flux.[49] Nursing, in the person of the floor supervisor, usually has been responsible for the ongoing management of nurses, aides, orderlies, and clerical personnel working on that floor, and for the coordination of other workers based elsewhere but coming to the floor to do special tasks (blood drawing, inhalation therapy, social work, occupational or physical therapy, physician consultants, etc.). Some nurses have moved away from this managerial role, turning it over to nonnurse unit managers.

Licensed practical nurses (LPNs) and other non-degree, nonprofessional substitutes have been used as a lower-cost alternative to registered nurses (RNs). Large hospitals, however, have found it perhaps more efficient (and therefore less expensive) to employ a greater number of RNs, who can effectively handle common problems a nonprofessional is not prepared to address. Some hospitals employ only RNs. Another approach to the problem of coordination on the patient floor has been the development of the unit manager.[50]

With the division of labor and growing technological specialization, some aspects of general nursing activities have been assumed by technical specialists (IV teams, clinical pharmacists, risk managers). Nursing remains as the profession with twenty-four-hour contact with the in-patient, who is otherwise seen by a parade of technical specialists.

The role relationship between physician and nurse, mediated through the order page of the patient chart, was fixed at the turn of the century and seems to match the stereotypical authoritarian relationship between husband and wife in the Victorian era. It is far removed from management ideas of participation, colleagueship, collective decision making, and career mobility.

The complexity of patient-care coordination has enough potential for failure that it probably requires a high degree of *goal congruence* on the part of the specialized workers involved. The goal congruence around concern for excellent patient care is seen as consistent with professionalism and the voluntary philosophy. Instilling goal congruence is a major implicit part of education for the health professions.

Although much writing on the organization of medical care relates to status, career, and money rewards, which promote or fail to promote high quality of care, health-care workers' desire for excellence is probably motivated primarily by their face-to-face personal contact with another human being (the patient) who needs help. This personal concern must be balanced by objectivity and disinterest, of course. A painful injection is given to a child who cries, with the understanding that the disease avoided thereby is far worse than the momentary pain inflicted.

RESPONSE AT THE ORGANIZATION LEVEL

The organization of the hospital can be seen as a response to the core relationship of patient-physician-nurse. It is useful to divide the hospital into two organizational components: the administrative hierarchy and the collegially organized medical staff. The administrative component is hierarchical, departmentalized, and staffed by full-time salaried employees. The medical staff is typically more loosely organized in the United States. Medical (physician) staff members spend most of their time outside the hospital in their office practices, earning a living by fee-for-service payment.

Hospitals are largely fixed-cost operations with revenues dependent on the number of patients cared for. For this reason the central concern of administration is to keep the beds filled with patients whose bills are paid. Because only physicians can admit a patient, their good will must be maintained and cultivated. Their exclusive authority to admit and to order tasks and to cut with the surgical knife assures them far more organizational independence. This has led some health economists to describe hospitals as doctors' cooperatives, giving them free access to capital as embodied in the hospital. The nonprofit organization of the hospital can allow the physicians to extract any monopoly profits for themselves.[51]

48. Eliot Freidson, *Professional Dominance* (New York: Atherton Press, 1970). Wilson and Neuhauser, *Health United States 1982*, 95–6.

49. Philip Kalish and Beatrice Kalish, *The Advance of American Nursing* (Boston: Little, Brown, 1978).

50. Fred Munson, "What Kind of Unit Management?" in *SUM: An Organizational Approach to Improved Patient Care*, ed. R. Jellinek et al. (W. K. Kellog Foundation, February 1971), 31–56. Reprinted in Anthony Kovner and Duncan Neuhauser, *Health Services Management: Readings and Commentary*, 2d ed. (Ann Arbor, Mich.: Health Administration Press, 1983), chap. 11.

51. Mark Pauly and M. Redisch, "The Not-for-Profit Hospital as a Physician's Cooperative," *American Economic Review* 63, no. 1 (March 1973): 87–100.

Departmentalization and technology

In some industries new technology can have wide-ranging effects, requiring the entire organization to readjust.

Hospitals' organizational structure is such that many new technologies are readily absorbed into the existing organization. EEG machines, cobalt therapy, CT scanners, and heart surgery are easily accepted. A new sub-department is created, a new physician specialist is recruited, and space is found. Typically new technology is well reimbursed by third-party payers; moreover it attracts patients and adds prestige. Nonreimbursible cost, such as research in a teaching hospital, is simply shifted to those who pay out of pocket or to those whose third-party insurance covers cost. If anything, technological advance is too rapid. Careful studies of efficacy often lag behind the widespread adoption of new technique.[52]

A theory of nonprofit hospital growth

About 80 percent of a hospital's costs are fixed in the short run (say in a one-year period). Therefore, for a given hospital size, as measured by the number of in-patient beds, and for a given complexity, as measured by the scope of services provided, there are large economies to be achieved by keeping occupancy rates high. For a given level of complexity, there are long-run economies of scale as measured by the number of beds. The major concern of the hospital manager is to keep the beds filled with patients whose bills are paid.

Figure 27.2 shows schematically the interplay of size and cost. The cost curve labeled C_{x_1} shows that, for a hospital of complexity level 1, cost per patient-day declines as the hospital gets larger. At the same time, revenues rise. Point A shows the break-even number of patient-days for complexity level 1. If the number of patient-days increases (e.g., to B), the hospital's revenue exceeds its costs. Because insurance reimbursements are based on cost and there is no effective price competition, the hospital has little reason to use this surplus to reduce price. (Because the hospital is nonprofit, the surplus is not taken as profit.) It can be used in one of three ways: (1) to pay for free care, which would lower the revenue line R; (2) to increase the hospital's size; or (3) to increase the scope of services. If scope of services (complexity) is increased, the cost curve shifts to the right, to C_{x_2}, and the patient census must increase to reach the new break-

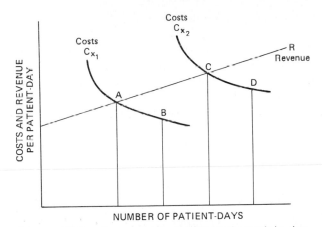

Figure 27.2   Theory of voluntary hospital growth in size and complexity (hospital average daily census = hospital occupancy rate × number of hospital beds; number of patient-days per year = average daily census × 365)

even point C for this complexity level. If more beds are added and more patients found, then the census can move to D, thus potentially starting the process all over again.

The revenue curve rises with increasing hospital size because, on the average, more services are provided and paid for in larger hospitals. Because physicians, who have the exclusive power to admit patients, are attracted by more services, this growth process is fueled. It eventually stops because there is a limit to the number of patients who can be brought to the hospital. This limit is set in part by patient travel time and the existence of other competing hospitals. In the 1970s certificate-of-need regulations were established to limit this growth, and more recently the limits have been set by the hospital's borrowing capacity. Thus, voluntary hospital growth may systematically increase rather than reduce costs. Berry has shown that the growing hospital adds services in a predictable way from "basic" to "community" to "quality-enhancing" services.[53]

In the past hospitals have usually been single institutions whose size was limited by patient transportation costs. Beyond one thousand beds the management problems begin to be overwhelming, and the hospital is likely to be managed in subunits (pediatrics, psychiatry, etc.), which may function as decentralized smaller hospitals within the larger hospital. Only recently have hospitals moved to consider the development of multi-institution systems using excess revenue to create or purchase other hospitals elsewhere. Increasingly hospitals are trying to protect their patient-referral networks by creating freestanding ambulatory health centers, doctors' offices, emergency-care centers, and even smaller satellite hospi-

52. U.S. Congress, Office of Technology Assessment, Series of publications on medical technology assessment (Washington, D.C.: GPO), 1978-1980.

53. Ralph Berry, "On Grouping Hospitals for Economic Analysis," Inquiry 10, no. 4 (1973): 5-12.

tals, which are intended to assure the flow of patients to the central hospital.[54]

The managerial role in the hospital is that of a "broker of interests." Given the high level of fixed costs, the manager's key objective is to keep the beds filled with patients whose bills will be paid. Because only physicians can admit a patient, the medical staff becomes the most critical constituency. In nonprofit organizations, the trustees may take a more relaxed view of their role than would be the case if their investment were at stake. Because profitability is replaced by the harder-to-measure goals of high quality of care (and perhaps teaching and research) within a budget constraint, it is hard for trustees to measure performance. Basil Georgopoulos points out that the greatest conflict in a hospital is within the medical staff, in part because they are in competition with one another for patients.[55] Thus the administrator does not confront the medical staff as a body united in its interests.

Add to this the concerns of the myriad of other professional groups, external organizations (insurers, rate-setting commissions, regulatory agencies, competing hospitals, ambulatory-care services, nursing homes, government), the patients, their families, and the immediate community. One result of the competition among those diverse forces is the high turnover of hospital administrators. It is easier for the trustees to dismiss the administrator than the medical staff.

ORGANIZATION AND ENVIRONMENT

If the 1970s was the era of regulation in health care, the 1980s may be an era of competition. Payment mechanisms are shifting away from a cost basis to capitation and a fixed payment per type of patient (Diagnostic Related Groups). Employees are increasingly being offered options of health-insurance benefit packages at different price levels (different payroll deductions). Some 30 percent of general hospitals are now part of multi-institution systems, and this proportion is expected to increase. Marketing is a concept new to the health field (outside pharmaceuticals), but is being avidly adopted. New capital formation through bond issues is compelling a concern for a positive cash flow. We appear to be moving away from an aspiration of the 1960s that the rich and poor would all have access to the same health-care system.

At one level these changes seem momentous, but at another level much remains the same: the sick role, the uncertainty of the occurrence of illness, the resultant need for insurance, the extensive division of labor that must be organized around each patient in a hospital, the singular legal status of the physician, and the nonprofit nature of most health-care organizations. The basic organizational response also persists.

54. Jeff Goldsmith, *Can Hospitals Survive?* (Homewood, Ill.: Dow Jones-Irwin, 1981).

55. Basil Georgopoulos and Floyd Mann, *The Community General Hospital* (New York: Macmillan, 1962).